T0211234

Lecture Notes in Computer Science 10039

Commenced Publication in 1973
Founding and Former Series Editors:
Gerhard Goos, Juris Hartmanis, and Jan van Leeuwen

Editorial Board

David Hutchison
Lancaster University, Lancaster, UK
Takeo Kanade
Carnegie Mellon University, Pittsburgh, PA, USA
Josef Kittler
University of Surrey, Guildford, UK
Jon M. Kleinberg
Cornell University, Ithaca, NY, USA
Friedemann Mattern
ETH Zurich, Zurich, Switzerland
John C. Mitchell
Stanford University, Stanford, CA, USA
Moni Naor
Weizmann Institute of Science, Rehovot, Israel
C. Pandu Rangan
Indian Institute of Technology, Madras, India
Bernhard Steffen
TU Dortmund University, Dortmund, Germany
Demetri Terzopoulos
University of California, Los Angeles, CA, USA
Doug Tygar
University of California, Berkeley, CA, USA
Gerhard Weikum
Max Planck Institute for Informatics, Saarbrücken, Germany

Xingming Sun · Alex Liu
Han-Chieh Chao · Elisa Bertino (Eds.)

Cloud Computing and Security

Second International Conference, ICCCS 2016
Nanjing, China, July 29–31, 2016
Revised Selected Papers, Part I

 Springer

Editors
Xingming Sun
University of Information Science and
  Technology
Nanjing
China

Alex Liu
Michigan State University
East Lansing, MI
USA

Han-Chieh Chao
National Dong Hwa University
Shoufeng
Taiwan

Elisa Bertino
Purdue University
West Lafayette, IN
USA

ISSN 0302-9743   ISSN 1611-3349   (electronic)
Lecture Notes in Computer Science
ISBN 978-3-319-48670-3   ISBN 978-3-319-48671-0   (eBook)
DOI 10.1007/978-3-319-48671-0

Library of Congress Control Number: 2016955502

LNCS Sublibrary: SL3 – Information Systems and Applications, incl. Internet/Web, and HCI

Printed on acid-free paper

This Springer imprint is published by Springer Nature
The registered company is Springer International Publishing AG
The registered company address is: Gewerbestrasse 11, 6330 Cham, Switzerland

Preface

This volume contains the papers presented at ICCCS 2016: the Second International Conference on Cloud Computing and Security held during July 29–31, 2016, in Nanjing, China. The conference was hosted by the College of Computer and Software at the Nanjing University of Information Science and Technology, who provided the wonderful facilities and material support. We made use of the excellent EasyChair submission and reviewing software.

The aim of this conference is to provide an international forum for the latest results from research, development, and applications in the field of cloud computing and information security. This year we received more than 270 submissions from 15 countries and regions, including USA, UK, France, Australia, Ireland, South Korea, South Africa, India, Iraq, Kazakhstan, Indonesia, Vietnam, Ghana, China, and Taiwan. Each submission was allocated to three Program Committee (PC) members and each paper received on average of three reviews. The committee decided to accept 97 papers.

The program also included ten distinguished talks: "A Bacteria-Inspired Solution for 5G Mobile Communication" by Prof. Han-Chieh Chao, National Dong Hwa University, Taiwan; "Flow-Net Accountable Logging and Applications" by Dr. Yang Xiao, University of Alabama, USA; "Security and Privacy in Cloud Computing: Challenges and Opportunities" by Prof. Yang Xiang, Deakin University, Australia; "Internet of Vehicles: When Cloud Computing Meets Intelligent Transport Systems" by Prof. Yan Zhang, Simula Research Laboratory and University of Oslo, Norway; "Children's Privacy Protection Engine for Smart Anthropomorphic Toys" by Prof. Patrick C. K. Hung, University of Ontario Institute of Technology (UOIT), Canada; "Bioinformatics and Cloud Computing" by Dr. Zemin Ning, Wellcome Trust Sanger Institute, UK; "Towards Smart and Secure Connected Health" by Dr. Honggang Wang, University of Massachusetts Dartmouth, USA; "Semantic Searchover Encrypted Cloud Data" by Dr. Zhangjie Fu, Nanjing University of Information Science and Technology, China; "Coverless Information Hiding Method Based on the Text Big Data" by Dr. Xianyi Chen, Nanjing University of Information Science and Technology, China.

We would like to extend our sincere thanks to all authors who submitted papers to ICCCS 2016, and all PC members. It was a truly great experience to work with such talented and hard-working researchers. We also appreciate the external reviewers for assisting the PC members in their particular areas of expertise. Finally, we would like to thank all attendees for their active participation and the organizing team who nicely managed this conference. We look forward to seeing you again at next year's ICCCS.

July 2016

Xingming Sun
Alex Liu
Han-Chieh Chao
Elisa Bertino

Organization

General Chairs

Xingming Sun   Nanjing University of Information Science and
         Technology, China
Alex Liu   Michigan State University, USA
Han-Chieh Chao   National Dong Hwa University, Taiwan
Elisa Bertino   University of Purdue, USA

Technical Program Committee Chairs

Chin-Feng Lai   National Chung Cheng University, Taiwan
Yang Xiao   University of Alabama, USA
Yun Q. Shi   New Jersey Institute of Technology, USA
Jian Shen   Nanjing University of Information Science and
         Technology, China

Technical Program Committee

Saeed Arif   University of Algeria, Algeria
Zhifeng Bao   Royal Melbourne Institute of Technology University,
         Australia
Hanhua Chen   Huazhong University of Science and Technology, China
Jie Chen   East China Normal University, China
Xiaofeng Chen   Xidian University, China
Ilyong Chung   Chosun University, South Korea
Jintai Ding   University of Cincinnati, USA
Zhangjie Fu   Nanjing University of Information Science and
         Technology, China
Jinguang Han   Nanjing University of Finance and Economics, China
Mohammad Mehedi   King Saud University, Saudi Arabia
   Hassan
Debiao He   Wuhan University, China
Wien Hong   Nanfang College of Sun Yat-Sen University, China
Qiong Huang   South China Agricultural University, China
Xinyi Huang   Fujian Normal University, China
Yongfeng Huang   Tsinghua University, China
Zhiqiu Huang   Nanjing University of Aeronautics and Astronautics, China
Patrick C.K. Hung   University of Ontario Institute of Technology, Canada
Hai Jin   Huazhong University of Science and Technology, China
Sam Tak Wu Kwong   City University of Hong Kong, SAR China

Mingwu Zhang   Hubei University of Technology, China
Wei Zhang   Nanjing University of Posts and Telecommunications,
                        China
Xinpeng Zhang   University of Science and Technology of China, China
Yan Zhang   Simula Research Laboratory, Norway
Yao Zhao   Beijing Jiaotong University, China

Organizing Committee Chairs

Chih-Hsien Hsia   Chinese Culture University, Taiwan
Yingtao Jiang   University of Nevada at Las Vegas, USA
Eric Wong   University of Texas at Dallas, USA
Zhangjie Fu   Nanjing University of Information Science
                        and Technology, China

Organizing Committee

Xianyi Chen   Nanjing University of Information Science
                        and Technology, China
Zhiguo Qu   Nanjing University of Information Science
                        and Technology, China
Zhaoqing Pan   Nanjing University of Information Science
                        and Technology, China
Yan Kong   Nanjing University of Information Science
                        and Technology, China
Zhili Zhou   Nanjing University of Information Science
                        and Technology, China
Baowei Wang   Nanjing University of Information Science
                        and Technology, China
Zhihua Xia   Nanjing University of Information Science
                        and Technology, China

Contents – Part I

Information Hiding

Cloud Computing

Cloud Security

Contents – Part II

Multimedia Applications

Multimedia Security and Forensics

Information Hiding

A Blind Image Watermarking Algorithm in the Combine Domain

Qingtang Su[(✉)]

School of Information Science and Engineering,
Ludong University, Yantai 264025, People's Republic of China
acsqtwhy@163.com

Abstract. This paper presents a novel blind digital image watermarking algorithm in the combine domains to resolve the protecting copyright problem. For embedding watermark, the generation principle and distribution features of direct current (DC) coefficient are utilized to directly modify the pixel values in the spatial domain, then 4 different sub-watermarks are embedded into different areas of the host image for four times, respectively. When extracting watermark, the sub-watermark is extracted with blind manner according to DC coefficients of watermarked image and the key-based quantization step, and then the statistical rule and "first to select, second to combine" are proposed to form the final watermark. Hence, the proposed algorithm not only has the simple and quick performance of the spatial domain but also has the high robustness feature of DCT domain. Many experiments have proved the proposed watermarking algorithm has good invisibility of watermark and strong robustness for many added attacks, e.g., JPEG compression, cropping, adding noise, etc. Comparison results also have shown the preponderances of the proposed algorithm.

Keywords: Information security · Digital watermarking · Combine domain · DC

1 Introduction

As an important technique, watermarking technique was proposed to prevent copyright infringement, which is intended to embed useful information in digital data without obvious perceptual alterations and can extract the embedded information for many purposes, i.e., content authentication, integrity verification and copyright protection [1–4]. However, how to protect the copyright of color image in blind detection is one of the research hotspots.

For the type of the processing domain of digital images, the image watermarking process can be performed on two different domains, i.e., frequency domain [5–8] and spatial domain [9–12]. Among them, the former can exploit signal features and human visual properties to obtain strong robustness and invisibility, but the image transformation forward and its inverse transformations are usually needed in the processing [6–8, 13–15], which may result to the higher computational complexity. For example, the two-level discrete cosine transform (DCT) was performed independently on each block of the image and inverse two-level DCT was used to the modified DCT coefficients of each embedded block to rebuild the watermarked image when embedding

X. Sun et al. (Eds.): ICCCS 2016, Part I, LNCS 10039, pp. 3–17, 2016.
DOI: 10.1007/978-3-319-48671-0_1

the watermark in [15]. Moreover, the two-level DCT was also performed independently for each block of the watermarked image when extracting the watermark in [15]. For the latter, the main feature is to embed the watermark into the host image by modifying part of selected pixel values in the host image. Hence, the watermarking techniques in spatial domain are simpler than those in frequency domain. In [10], a new digital watermarking technique for protecting the copyright of digital color images was proposed. In which, 4 similar watermarks were directly combined after extracting the sub-watermarks, then the final watermark was selected from 4 similar watermarks according to correlation coefficient (CC), that is, the original watermark was required. Thus, Nasir's method [10] was a non-blind watermarking scheme. Seriously, the true state of extracted sub-watermark was not reflected by its final watermark since using the method that "first to combine sub-watermark to 4 whole watermarks, then select the optimum final watermark from the whole watermarks". Thus, how to achieve the blind extracting and stronger robustness is an important issue in the current research on watermarking techniques.

Motivated by these discussions, by combining these advantages of the frequency domain and spatial domain, a blind watermarking algorithm for color image is proposed to extract embedded watermark in the spatial domain based on the statistical rule and the method that "first to select the optimum sub-watermark from 4 sub-watermarks, then combine the optimum sub-watermarks to the final watermark", i.e., "first to select, second to combine", which is different from the algorithm [10]. Experimental results show that the proposed algorithm not only can resolve the non-blind extraction problem existed in [10], but also can embed and extract watermark in the spatial domain instead of the DCT domain used in [15].

The rest of this paper is organized as follows. Section 2 introduces the technique of modifying DC coefficients in the spatial domain. Section 3 gives the procedures of the watermark embedding and extraction. The experimental results prove the performance of the proposed algorithm in Sect. 4. Finally, Sect. 5 concludes this paper.

2 The Technique of Modifying DC Coefficients in Spatial Domain

2.1 The Important Feature of DC Coefficient

Discrete cosine transform (DCT) is a type of data transform way, and its transform function is the cosine function. An image can be transformed from the spatial domain to the DCT domain by 2-D DCT, which can also be restored from DCT domain to the spatial domain via 2-D inverse DCT.

The 2-D DCT of one image I with size of $P \times Q$ is given as follows:

$$C(h,v) = \alpha_h \alpha_v \sum_{m=0}^{P-1} \sum_{n=0}^{Q-1} I(m,n) \cos\frac{\pi(2m+1)h}{2P} \cos\frac{\pi(2n+1)v}{2Q} \tag{1}$$

where P, Q represents the width and height size of I (m, n), $0 \leq m \leq P - 1$, $0 \leq n \leq Q - 1$, (m, n) denotes the pixel position in image I, while h and v are the horizontal and vertical frequencies, $0 \leq h \leq P - 1, 0 \leq v \leq Q - 1$, and $C(h, v)$ represents the DCT coefficient of image I.

$$\alpha_h = \left\{ \begin{array}{l} \sqrt{1/P}, h = 0 \\ \sqrt{2/P}, 1 \leq h < P - 1 \end{array} \right., \quad \alpha_v = \left\{ \begin{array}{l} \sqrt{1/Q}, v = 0 \\ \sqrt{2/Q}, 1 \leq v < Q - 1 \end{array} \right. \tag{2}$$

DCT coefficients of an image include two kinds of coefficients, i.e. one direct current (DC) coefficient and some alternating current (AC) coefficients with different frequencies. From Eq. (1), DC coefficient can be obtained by

$$DC = C(0,0) = \frac{1}{\sqrt{PQ}} \sum_{m=0}^{P-1} \sum_{n=0}^{Q-1} I(m,n) \tag{3}$$

As can be seen from Eq. (3), DC coefficient has an important feature, that is, which can be directly obtained in the spatial domain instead of the DCT domain.

2.2 Modifying DC Coefficients in the Spatial Domain

When DC coefficient of the image block has been changed in the DCT domain, the value of each pixel in the spatial domain will be changed after inverse DCT, that is, the modified quantity of each pixel of the image block is decided by the changed quantity of DC coefficient. Now, the key problem is how to determine the modified quantity of each pixel in the spatial domain according to the changed quantity of DC coefficient in DCT domain [14, 15].

According to DCT principle, the inverse DCT of the image I with size of $P \times Q$ is described as follows.

$$I(m,n) = \sum_{h=0}^{P-1} \sum_{v=0}^{Q-1} \alpha_h \alpha_v C(h,v) \cos \frac{\pi(2m+1)h}{2P} \cos \frac{\pi(2n+1)v}{2Q} \tag{4}$$

The inverse DCT in Eq. (4) can be rewritten by

$$I(m,n) = \frac{1}{\sqrt{PQ}} DC + AC(m,n) \tag{5}$$

where $AC(m,n)$ is image matrix which includes all AC coefficients.

Suppose the host image is represented by

$$I(m,n) = I_{i,j}(m,n), 0 \leq i < \frac{P}{b}, 0 \leq j < \frac{Q}{b}, 0 \leq m, n < b \tag{6}$$

where P, Q refers to the width and height size of $I(m,n)$ respectively, the host image is partitioned into many $i \times j$ non-overlapping blocks with $b \times b$ pixels, and (i,j) represents the block position of each block in the host image indexes, while (m,n) is the pixel position in each block.

When embedding watermark W into DC coefficient of the (i,j)-th block, the modified quantity of DC coefficient is denoted as $\Delta M_{i,j}$. According to Eq. (3), the traditional process of embedding the watermark into DC coefficient of the (i,j)-th non-overlapping $b \times b$ block is given by

$$DC'_{i,j} = DC_{i,j} + \Delta M_{i,j} \tag{7}$$

where $DC_{i,j}$ is DC coefficient of the (i,j)-th block, $DC'_{i,j}$ is the modified DC coefficient with increment $\Delta M_{i,j}$.

According to Eq. (5), the recovered image block $I'_{i,j}(m,n)$ can be described as follows.

$$I'_{i,j}(m,n) = \frac{1}{b}DC'_{i,j} + AC_{i,j}(m,n) \tag{8}$$

Using Eqs. (6), (7) and (8) can be rewritten as

$$
\begin{aligned}
I'_{i,j}(m,n) &= \frac{1}{b}DC'_{i,j} + AC_{i,j}(m,n) \\
&= \frac{1}{b}DC_{i,j}\Delta M_{i,j}) + AC_{i,j}(m,n) \\
&= \frac{1}{b}\Delta M_{i,j}\frac{1}{b}DC_{i,j} + AC_{i,j}(m,n) \\
&= \frac{1}{b}\Delta M_{i,j} + I_{i,j}(m,n) \\
&= PM_{i,j} + I_{i,j}(m,n)
\end{aligned}
\tag{9}
$$

where $PM_{i,j}$ denotes the modified quantity of each pixel in the spatial domain, and it is defined by

$$PM_{i,j} = \frac{1}{b}\Delta M_{i,j} \tag{10}$$

As can be seen from Eq. (9), the procedure of modifying DC coefficients to embed watermark in the DCT domain will be directly carried out in the spatial domain instead of DCT domain.

3   The Proposed Watermarking Scheme

A novel digital image blind watermarking algorithm is proposed by integrating spatial domain with frequency domain in this work. First, the binary digital watermark is partitioned to 4 sub-watermarks, and the blue component of the color host image is also partitioned to 16 sub-images. When embedding the watermark, the distribution features and quantization table of DC coefficients are utilized and the pixel values are directly modified in the spatial domain, which means DC coefficients in DCT domain are modified indirectly. All of the 4 sub-watermarks can be repeatedly embedded into the 16 sub-images for four times based on the security key Key1, which can effectively improve the security and robustness of watermark. Moreover, the key-based quantization step will be utilized to extract the watermark with blind manner.

3.1 Watermark Pre-processing

In order to decrease the possibility of whole watermark be attacked, the 32×32 original watermark is divided into 4 sub-watermarks W_i with size 32×8, $W_i = (0,1)$ $1 \leq i \leq 4$). Meanwhile, the key-based Hash pseudo-random permutation algorithm is utilized to permute the sub-watermarks with different keys K_i ($1 \leq i \leq 4$). It should be noted that the MD5-based encryption method is adopted to the specific Hash function in the proposed algorithm, which is difficult for the third party to completely detect the right watermark without the right private keys and which enhancing the security of this proposed algorithm [16]. The permuting process of the original watermark W is demonstrated in Fig. 1.

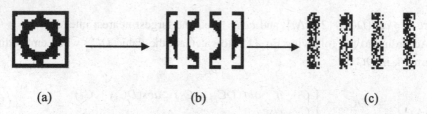

(a)   (b)   (c)

Fig. 1. The permuting process of original watermark: (a) Original watermark, (b) Sub-watermark blocks and (c) Permuted sub-watermark blocks

3.2 Watermark Embedding Scheme

It is well known that human eyes are insensitive to the change of the blue component. Hence, the permuted watermark is embedded into the blue component of the host image in this paper. Firstly, the blue component of the host image is firstly divided into many sub-images and each host sub-image is further divided into sub-blocks with 8×8 pixels, and DC coefficient of each sub-block is calculated. Then, the modified quantity of DC coefficient is decided according to the watermark information and DC coefficient of the present sub-block. Finally, one watermark bit is embedded into one pixel block by modifying the pixel value via Eq. (9). The detailed steps of embedding watermark are given as follows.

Step1. Obtaining DC coefficients in the spatial domain.

In order to improve the robustness of watermarking, the 512×512 blue component of the original host image I is divided into 16 sub-images I_j ($1 \leq j \leq 16$) with size 128×128 pixels based on the security key Key1, and each sub-image is divided into 256 embedding-blocks with 8×8 pixels. Thus, the whole host image can be divided into 4096 embedding-blocks. And then, their DC coefficients are further calculated according to Eq. (3).

Step2. Establishing the modified DC coefficient.

DC coefficient quantization directly influences the embedding strength of watermark. In this paper, the quantization step Δ based on key Key2 is used to decide the modifying magnitudes T_1 and T_2, as described in the following Eqs. (11) and (12).

$$T_1 = \begin{cases} 0.5 \times \Delta, & \textit{if } w = 1 \\ -0.5 \times \Delta, & \textit{if } w = 0 \end{cases} \tag{11}$$

$$T_2 = \begin{cases} -1.5 \times \Delta, & \textit{if } w = 1 \\ 1.5 \times \Delta, & \textit{if } w = 0 \end{cases} \tag{12}$$

The possible quantization results C_1 and C_2 can be computed by the modifying magnitudes T_1 and T_2 as shown in Eqs. (13) and (14).

$$C_1 = 2k\Delta + T_1 \tag{13}$$

$$C_2 = 2k\Delta + T_2 \tag{14}$$

where $k = ceil(DC_{i,j}/(2 \times \Delta))$, and $ceil(.)$ gets the largest nearest integer.

According to the following Eq. (15) to calculate the value $DC'_{i,j}$ when embedding watermark in $DC_{i,j}$.

$$DC'_{i,j} = \begin{cases} C_2 & \textit{if } \ abs(DC_{i,j} - C_2) < abs(DC_{i,j} - C_1) \\ C_1 & \textit{else} \end{cases} \tag{15}$$

where $abs(.)$ denotes the absolute value, and $DC'_{i,j}$ is the quantified DC coefficient.

Step 3. Calculating the modified quantity of each DC coefficient.

The modified quantity $\Delta M_{i,j}$ of each DC coefficient can be calculated by Eq. (16).

$$\Delta M_{i,j} = DC'_{i,j} - DC_{i,j} \tag{16}$$

Step 4. Embedding watermark.

By using Eqs. (9) and (10), the pixel value can be modified in the spatial domain instead of DCT domain by $\Delta M_{i,j}$, that is, one binary watermark bit is embedded into one embedding-block. In this procedure, the modified quantity is between 0 and 2.5, which will enhance the invisibility of watermark.

By repeating the procedures of Steps 3 and 4, the sub-watermark W_i ($1 \le i \le 4$) can be embedded into 16 different positions according to the order number in Fig. 2. Thus, each sub-watermark is embedded into the host image for four times.

3.3 Watermark Extraction Scheme

When extracting the watermark, the quantization step is used to directly extract watermark from DC coefficients without the original carrier data and watermark

W_2	W_1	W_2	W_1
W_4	W_3	W_4	W_3
W_1	W_2	W_1	W_2
W_3	W_4	W_3	W_4

Fig. 2. The embedded positions of sub-watermarks.

nformation. Firstly, 4 sub-watermarks of each sub-image are extracted. Then, the optimum sub-watermark is obtained by the statistics-based optimum. Finally, these optimum sub-watermarks are combined to attain the whole watermark.

Step1. Obtaining DC coefficients in the spatial domain.

The watermarked image is processed by using the similar operation of Step 1 in Sect. 3.2, and DC coefficient $DC'_{i,j}$ of each embedded block is obtained by Eq. (3).

Step2. Extracting the sub-watermarks.

According to Eq. (17), the quantization step Δ, which based on key Key2, is employed to get the embedded watermark bit $W'_{i,j}$ from $DC'_{i,j}$, until all sub-watermarks are extracted.

$$W'_{i,j} = mod(ceil(DC'_{i,j}/\Delta), 2) \tag{17}$$

where $W'_{i,j}$ represents the extracted sub-watermark from the (i,j)-th embedding block, and mod(.) is modulo operation.

Step 3. Getting the optimum sub-watermark.

Because each sub-watermark is repeatedly embedded for four times, 4 similar or identical watermarks of the same sub-watermark $W'_{i,j}$ can be extraction. Hence, the optimum sub-watermark $W^*(m, n)$ $(1 \leq m \leq 32, 1 \leq n \leq 8)$ of each sub-watermark $W'_{i,j}$ can be statistically *computed* by Eq. (18).

$$W^*(m,n) = \begin{cases} 1, & if \quad sum(W'_{i,j}(m,n)) \geq 2 \\ 0, & if \quad sum(W'_{i,j}(m,n)) < 2 \end{cases} \tag{18}$$

where $W'_{i,j}(m,n)$ is the watermark bit in the coordinate (m,n) of sub-watermark $W'_{i,j}$, sum(.) is sum function.

Step 4. Obtaining the final watermark.

By using the secret key K_i $(1 \leq i \leq 4)$, Hash inverse permutation is performed on the 4 optimum sub-watermarks, respectively. Then, these permuted sub-watermarks are connected to get the whole extracted watermark image W'.

In summary, the proposed algorithm firstly selects the optimum sub-watermark of each part via the statistic feature of the extracted 4 sub-watermarks, and then combines the selected optimum sub-watermarks to form the final watermark. Hence, this proposed algorithm, i.e. "first to select the optimum sub-watermark from 4 sub-watermarks, then combine the optimum sub-watermarks to the final watermark", not only extract the optimum watermark to improve the watermark robustness, but also can obtain the result of blind detection.

4   Experimental Results and Discussion

In this paper, the binary image of size 32 × 32, as shown in Fig. 1(a), is used as original watermark, and all 24-bit color images of size 512 × 512 in the image database CVG-UGR are taken as original carrier images [17]. For limitation space of the paper, only three 24-bits color images, which are shown in Fig. 3, are taken as examples. In order to not just only keep the embedded watermark's invisibility, but also to enhance its robustness, the quantization step is set to 20 in this experiment.

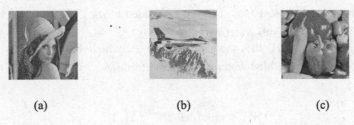

(a)   (b)   (c)

Fig. 3. The host images: (a) Lena, (b) Avion and (c) Peppers

The peak signal-to-noise ratio (PSNR) in Eq. (19) is employed to evaluate the degree of similarity between the original image I and the distorted one I'.

$$PSNR = (\sum_{j=1}^{3} PSNR_j)/3 \qquad (19)$$

where $PSNR_j$, $j \in \{1, 2, 3\}$, denotes PSNR value of their R, G and B component, respectively,

$$PSNR_j = 10 \lg \frac{M \times N \times \max\{[I(x,y,j)]^2\}}{\sum\limits_{x=1}^{M} \sum\limits_{y=1}^{N} [I(x,y,j) - I'(x,y,j)]^2} \qquad (20)$$

where $I(x, y, j)$ stands for the pixel value of the row x column y in layer j of the host image I, $I'(x, y, j)$ stands for the pixel value of the row x column y in layer j of the distorted image I', and M, N refers to the numbers of row and column of the host images, respectively.

Meanwhile, Wang et al. [18] proposed a new method to evaluate the degree of similarity between the host image I and the distorted one I', i.e., structural similarity index measurement (SSIM), which further considered the quality perception of the human visual system, and which is defined as:

$$SSIM(I,I') = l(I,I')c(I,I')s(I,I') \tag{21}$$

where

$$\begin{cases} l(I,I') = (2\mu_I\mu_{I'} + C_1) \big/ (\mu_I^2 + \mu_{I'}^2 + C_1) \\ c(I,I') = (2\sigma_I\sigma_{I'} + C_2) \big/ (\sigma_I^2 + \sigma_{I'}^2 + C_2) \\ s(I,I') = (\sigma_{II'} + C_3) \big/ (\sigma_I\sigma_{I'} + C_3) \end{cases} \tag{22}$$

The first term $l(I,I')$ of Eq. (22) denotes the luminance comparison function that calculates the closeness degree of mean luminances ($\mu_I, \mu_{I'}$) between the original image I and the distorted one I'. The second term $c(I,I')$ of Eq. (22) denotes the contrast comparison function that calculates the closeness degree of contrasts between the original image I and the distorted one I'. The contrast is measured by the standard deviation σ_I and $\sigma_{I'}$. The third term $s(I,I')$ Of Eq. (22) is the structure comparison function that calculates the correlation coefficient between the original image I and the distorted one I'. Noting that $\sigma_{II'}$ is the covariance between I and I'. The non-negative value of the SSIM is between 0 and 1. The value of 0 means no correlation between images, while 1 means that $I = I'$. The positive constants C_1, C_2 and C_3 are adopted to prevent the denominator is null.

In addition, the Normalized Croos-correlation (NC) between the original watermark W and the extracted watermark W' is used to evaluate the robustness of watermark, which is shown as follows.

$$NC = \frac{\sum\limits_{x=1}^{P} \sum\limits_{y=1}^{Q} (W(x,y) \times W'(x,y))}{\sqrt{\sum\limits_{x=1}^{P} \sum\limits_{y=1}^{Q} [W(x,y)]^2} \sqrt{\sum\limits_{x=1}^{P} \sum\limits_{y=1}^{Q} [W'(x,y)]^2}} \tag{23}$$

where P and Q shows the width and height of the original watermark image, (x, y) represents the watermark position (x, y) in watermark image.

4.1 Testing the Watermark Invisibility

In general, if the value of PSNR is more than 35 dB or SSIM is near to 1, then the watermarked image is very like to the original image, which means the watermarking algorithm has good invisibility of watermark. If the value of NC is near to 1, then the extracted watermark is very like to the original watermark, which shows the watermarking algorithm has good robustness of watermark.

Table 1 shows the experimental results of watermark invisibility among the proposed algorithm, algorithm [10] and algorithm [15]. It can be seen from Table 1, the whole embedded watermarks can be completely extracted from the watermarked images without any attacks (all NC values are 1), and the proposed algorithm has better

Table 1. The invisibility comparison results between the different algorithms without any attacks

Image	PSNR(dB)			SSIM			NC		
	Proposed	[10]	[15]	Proposed	[10]	[15]	Proposed	[10]	[15]
Lena	49.9906	38.6647	43.1546	0.9893	0.9804	0.9817	1.0000	1.0000	1.0000
Avion	49.9064	38.8254	45.7889	0.9863	0.9872	0.9847	1.0000	1.0000	1.0000
Peppers	50.1008	45.5216	48.0982	0.9817	0.9808	0.9847	1.0000	1.0000	1.0000

invisibility (their PSNR values are more than 45 dB and SSIM values are bigger than other algorithms). This is because the modified quantity of each pixel is fixed value 5 in [10]; while in the proposed algorithm, the modified quantity of each pixel ranges from 0 to 2.5 according to the watermark bit and DC coefficient. Less modified amplitude will get a better invisibility and obtain bigger PSNR or SSIM values. Hence, the proposed algorithm can obtain higher watermark invisibility than other algorithms.

4.2 Testing the Watermark Robustness

In practice, the watermarked image will be subjected to a variety of distortions before reaching the detector. Watermarks designed to survive legitimate and everyday usage of image, e.g., JPEG compression, noise, filtering, are referred to as robust watermark. To verify the watermark robustness of the proposed algorithm, all watermarked images are attacked by common image processing operations and geometrical distortions (such as rotation, crop operation etc.). At the same time, the proposed algorithm is compared with algorithms [10, 15], and NC is used as the measure parameter.

Lossy compression techniques are commonly employed to encode color image with efficient storage and communication. The watermark robustness towards the attack of lossy compression is important to be evaluated. In this simulation, JPEG compression is employed to attack the watermarked image. It is shown in Table 2 that the embedded watermarks can be detected in all attacked images when compression factor is 70 by the proposed algorithm and algorithm [15], which because the NC value is more than 0.75. On the contrary, the original watermark can be extracted only when the compression factor reaches 85 by Nasir's algorithm in [10]. Hence, the proposed algorithm has strong resistance to JPEG compression attacks.

Table 2. The comparison of extracted watermark by different algorithms after JPEG compression attacks

JPEG compression factor	Lena			Avion			Peppers		
	Proposed	[10]	[15]	Proposed	[10]	[15]	Proposed	[10]	[15]
30	0.6677	0.5230	0.6410	0.6809	0.5691	0.6427	0.6651	0.5069	0.6580
60	0.7560	0.5829	0.7470	0.7509	0.5530	0.7369	0.7908	0.5645	0.7499
90	0.9938	0.8986	0.9877	0.9888	0.8641	0.9719	0.9976	0.8894	0.9411

The watermarked image is easily and inevitably attacked by adding noise in the image transmission. Hence, adding noise is a classical attack and can affect the embedded watermark. Table 3 shows the experimental results of the extracted watermarks from the images attacked by adding Salt & Pepper noise with different noise intensities. It can be seen from it that the watermark still can be extracted normally when the noise intensity is 0.012 in the proposed algorithm and algorithm [15], but the watermarks can hardly be extracted when noise intensity is below 0.008 with algorithm [10]. Relatively, the proposed algorithm has stronger robustness (NC value is bigger than 0.75) to resist noise adding attack than other algorithms [10, 15].

Table 3. The comparison of extracted watermark by different algorithms after Salt & Pepper noise attacks

Salt & pepper noise	Lena			Avion			Peppers		
	Proposed	[10]	[15]	Proposed	[10]	[15]	Proposed	[10]	[15]
0.002	1.0000	0.9124	0.9812	0.9957	0.9286	0.9788	1.0000	0.9585	0.9817
0.008	0.9108	0.7212	0.8878	0.9431	0.7719	0.9200	0.9509	0.8212	0.9280
0.012	0.8768	0.6636	0.8599	0.8677	0.6613	0.8449	0.9089	0.7373	0.8907

Filtering is one of the classical attacks. Since the embedded watermark can be removed by the filter with different sizes, Table 4 gives the experimental results of extracted watermarks from the watermarked images attacked by median filtering with different sizes.

Table 4. The comparison of extracted watermark by different algorithms after median-filter attacks

Median filtering	Lena			Avion			Peppers		
	Proposed	[10]	[15]	Proposed	[10]	[15]	Proposed	[10]	[15]
2 × 2	0.9503	0.8318	0.9219	0.9571	0.8548	0.9488	0.9509	0.8018	0.9462
4 × 4	0.9217	0.7673	0.9029	0.9529	0.8249	0.9311	0.9409	0.7696	0.9312
6 × 6	0.9002	0.7350	0.8804	0.9477	0.8203	0.9249	0.9112	0.7281	0.8999

In addition, Table 5 shows the experimental results of the extracted watermarks from the watermarked images distorted by Butterworth low-pass filtering with cut-off frequency 50 Hz and different fuzzy radii N, which illustrates that the watermark can be extracted in the whole test range. Relatively, the algorithm in this paper has stronger robustness to resist median-filtering attack and filtering attack than other algorithms [10, 15].

In the image processing, the image rotation is one of the geometric operation, which will lead to the change of image size and image pixel values. Hence, the

Table 5. The comparison of extracted watermark by different algorithms after Butterworth low-pass filtering attacks

Butterworth low-pass filtering	Lena			Avion			Peppers		
	Proposed	[10]	[15]	Proposed	[10]	[15]	Proposed	[10]	[15]
(1,50)	0.9677	0.8157	0.9531	0.9734	0.8687	0.9647	0.9908	0.8433	0.9816
(3,50)	0.9808	0.8848	0.9799	0.9566	0.8456	0.9447	0.9897	0.8756	0.9831
(5,50)	0.9804	0.8641	0.9701	0.9406	0.8203	0.9355	0.9905	0.8802	0.9800

Table 6. The comparison of extracted watermark by different methods after rotation attacks

Rotation	Lena			Avion			Peppers		
	Proposed	[10]	[15]	Proposed	[10]	[15]	Preposed	[10]	[15]
−1	0.7189	0.5392	0.7008	0.7949	0.6060	0.7810	0.7851	0.5922	0.7834
−0.75	0.7834	0.5991	0.7639	0.8710	0.6705	0.8649	0.7903	0.6014	0.7856
0.75	0.7719	0.6106	0.7687	0.8249	0.6452	0.8091	0.7765	0.6060	0.7718
1	0.7235	0.5438	0.7008	0.7788	0.6106	0.7619	0.7535	0.5876	0.7511

embedded watermark will be affected by rotation operation. Table 6 gives the experimental result of the extracted watermarks from the watermarked images attacked by different rotations, and illustrates the robustness of the proposed algorithm is better to other algorithms [10, 15]. However, three methods have lower robustness when increasing the rotation angle, which will be further researched in future.

Obviously, the cropping attack can cut part of image pixel, which directly decides the quality of the extracted watermark. Figure 4 is the experimental results of the extracted watermarks from the watermarked Lena images attacked by cropping with different sizes in different positions, in which Fig. 4(a) is the cropped watermarked images, Fig. 4(b), (c) and (d) show the extracted watermarks and NC values by algorithm [10], algorithm [15] and the presented one, respectively. By comparison, it is found the presented algorithm has strong robustness to resist cropping attack because of each sub-watermark is embedded for four times in different positions of the original host image.

It can be seen from the above comparison results that the presented algorithm has stronger robustness than those of [10] under common image processing operation and genetic attacks. The main feature in the presented algorithm is based on the idea "first to select the optimum sub-watermark from 4 sub-watermarks, then combine the sub-watermarks to the final watermark", which is different with [10], i.e., "first to combine sub-watermark to 4 whole watermarks, then select the optimum final watermark from the whole watermarks".

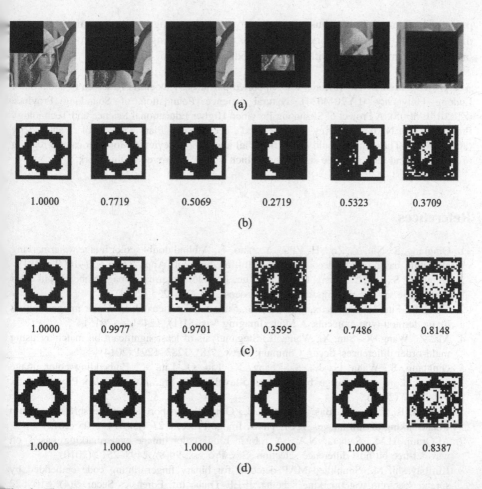

(a)

| 1.0000 | 0.7719 | 0.5069 | 0.2719 | 0.5323 | 0.3709 |

(b)

| 1.0000 | 0.9977 | 0.9701 | 0.3595 | 0.7486 | 0.8148 |

(c)

| 1.0000 | 1.0000 | 1.0000 | 0.5000 | 1.0000 | 0.8387 |

(d)

Fig. 4. The comparison of extracted watermark by different algorithms after cropping attacks: (a) Cropped watermarked image, (b) Extracted watermark from (a) by algorithm [10] (*NC*), (c) Extracted watermark from (a) by algorithm [15] (*NC*), and (d) Extracted watermark from (a) by the presented algorithm (*NC*)

5 Conclusion

In this paper, we have presented a blind watermarking based on DC coefficients in combine domain which combines the spatial domain and the DCT domain. When embedding watermark, the principle of DC coefficient modification in DCT domain is used to repeatedly embed watermark in the spatial domain for four times, which can improve the invisibility and robustness of watermark. Then, the sub-watermark is extracted by the extraction rules without the original data in this algorithm. Moreover, the statistical rule and the idea of "first to select the optimum sub-watermark from 4 sub-watermarks, then combine the optimum sub-watermarks to the final watermark" are presented to combine the sub-watermarks. Many experimental data have proved the presented scheme is very robust against many common image operations and geometric distortions. In the further work, the dual color watermarking that using color image as original watermark image will be researched.

Acknowledgements. The research was supported partially by Doctoral Research Foundation of Ludong University (LY2014034), Natural Science Foundation of Shandong Province (ZR2014FM005), A Project of Shandong Province Higher Educational Science and Technology Program (J14LN20), and Key Science and Technology Plan Project of Yantai City (2016ZH057). The authors would like to thank all anonymous reviewers for their careful reading of this paper and their valuable suggestions which greatly improved of this work.

References

1. Qingtang, S., Niu, Y., Zou, H., Zhao, Y., Yao, T.: A blind double color image watermarking algorithm based on QR decomposition. Multimedia Tools Appl. **72**(1), 987–1009 (2014)
2. Qingtang, S., Niu, Y., Wang, G., Jia, S., Yue, J.: Color watermark image embedded in color host image via QR decomposition. Sig. Process. **94**, 219–235 (2014)
3. Chen, B., Shu, H., Coatrieux, G., Chen, G., Sun, X., Coatrieux, J.-L.: Color image analysis by quaternion-type moments. J. Math. Imaging Vis. **51**(1), 124–144 (2015)
4. Xia, Z., Wang, X., Sun, X., Wang, B.: Steganalysis of least significant bit matching using multi-order differences. Secur. Commun. Netw. **7**(8), 1283–1291 (2014)
5. Qingtang, S., Wang, G., Jia, S., Zhang, X., Liu, Q., Liu, X.: Embedding color image watermark in color image based on two-level DCT. Sig. Image Video Process. **9**(5), 991–1007 (2015)
6. Mathon, B., Cayre, F., Bas, P., Macq, B.: Optimal transport for secure spread-spectrum watermarking of still images. IEEE Trans. Image Process. **23**(4), 1694–1705 (2014)
7. Al-Otum, H.M., Samara, N.A.: A robust blind color image watermarking based on wavelet-tree bit host difference selection. Sig. Process. **90**(8), 2498–2512 (2010)
8. Kuribayashi, M.: Simplified MAP detector for binary fingerprinting code embedded by spread spectrum watermarking scheme. IEEE Trans. Inf. Forensics Secur. **9**(4), 610–622 (2014)
9. Jun, L., Lizhi, L.: An improved watermarking detect algorithm for color image in spatial domain. In: Proceedings of International Seminar on Future BioMedical Information Engineering, FBIE 2008, pp. 95–99. IEEE (2008)
10. Nasir, I., Weng, Y., Jiang, J., Ipson, S.: Multiple spatial watermarking technique in color images. Sig. Image Video Process. **4**(2), 145–154 (2010)
11. Chan, C.-K., Cheng, L.-M.: Hiding data in images by simple LSB substitution. Pattern Recogn. **37**(3), 469–474 (2004)
12. Zhong, Q.-C., Zhu, Q.-X., Zhang, P.-L.: A spatial domain color watermarking scheme based on chaos. In: Proceedings of International Conference on Apperceiving Computing and Intelligence Analysis, ICACIA 2008, pp. 137–142. IEEE (2008)
13. Sun, J., Lan, S.: Geometrical attack robust spatial digital watermarking based on improved SIFT. In: Proceedings of Asia-Pacific Conference on Innovative Computing & Communication, 2010 International Conference on and Information Technology & Ocean Engineering, CICC-ITOE 2010, pp. 98–101. IEEE (2010)
14. Huang, J., Shi, Y.Q., Shi, Y.: Embedding image watermarks in DC components. IEEE Trans. Circ. Syst. Video Technol. **10**(6), 974–979 (2000)

15. Zeng, G., Qiu, Z.: Image watermarking based on DC component in DCT. In: Proceedings of International Symposium on Intelligent Information Technology Application Workshops, IITAW 2008, pp. 573–576. IEEE (2008)
16. Rivest, R.: The MD5 message digest algorithm. Internet RFC 1321, April 1992
17. University of Granada, Computer Vision Group. CVG-UGR Image Database. http://decsai. ugr.es/cvg/dbimagenes/c512.php. Accessed 22 Oct 2012
18. Wang, Z., Bovik, A.C., Sheikh, H.R., Simoncelli, E.P.: Image quality assessment: from error visibility to structural similarity. IEEE Trans. Image Process. **13**(4), 600–612 (2004)

Reversible Contrast Enhancement

Zhenxing Qian[1(✉)], Xinpeng Zhang[1], Weiming Zhang[2],
and Yimin Wang[3]

[1] School of Communication and Information Engineering,
Shanghai University, Shanghai 200444, China
zxqian@shu.edu.cn
[2] School of Information Science and Technology,
University of Science and Technology of China, Hefei 230026, China
[3] School of Computer Science and Engineering,
Shanghai University, Shanghai 200444, China

Abstract. This paper proposes a novel idea of reversible contrast enhancement (RCE) for digital images. Different from the traditional methods, we aim to embed the reversible feature into image contrast enhancement, making sure that the processed image can be losslessly turned back to the original. The original image is enhanced by histogram shrink and contrast stretching. Meanwhile, side information is generated and then embedded into the contrast enhanced image. On the other end, we extract side information from the processed image and reconstruct the original content without any error. Experimental results show that good contrast and good quality can be achieved in the RCE processed image.

Keywords: Reversible image processing · Reversible contrast enhancement · Reversible data hiding · Steganography

1 Introduction

Traditional image processing achieves a specified image by modifying the pixel values, e.g., image enhancement, denoising and restoration. Meanwhile, different assessment algorithms are developed to evaluate the processing capability, like the human visual effect, the minimal square errors, and so on. In the past few decades, a huge amount of methods have been proposed to promote the research field [1].

Nowadays, more and more images are used in social networks like Facebook, Twitter, Flickr, and so on. With many processing tools, people can prettify their contents before image uploading or storage. In this situation, one problem emerges. If one hopes to possess both the original and the processed images, he/she has to save two copies, which requires more storage overhead. To resolve this problem, we propose a novel idea of reversible image processing (RIP). As shown in Fig. 1, the processing method guarantees that the processed image can be reversibly processed to the original without any errors. Hence, the image owner only needs to save one copy of the image. To the best of our knowledge, few image processing works have been done in the field of RIP. One work might be semantic image compression [2]. An image is compressed to a visible one with smaller size, and the original can be decompressed with lossy or lossless quality. This work can be viewed as a generalized RIP.

© Springer International Publishing AG 2016
X. Sun et al. (Eds.): ICCCS 2016, Part I, LNCS 10039, pp. 18–27, 2016.
DOI: 10.1007/978-3-319-48671-0_2

Fig. 1. Reversible image processing

The proposed idea of RIP is inspired by the works [3, 4]. Purpose of steganography works is to embed additional message into digital images [8, 9]. Alternatively, we change the aim from steganography to reversible image processing. In this paper, we provide a method of reversible contrast enhancement (RCE). To this end, we propose an algorithm based on state-of-the-art contrast enhancement method in [5] to indicate that RCE with good processing results can be achieved by combing image processing with data hiding [6]. We also believe that the proposed work would be of some help to the development of image processing, and more works like reversible image denoising and reversible image restoration can be developed in the future.

Framework of the proposed RCE method is shown in Fig. 2. We first enhance the original image by histogram shrink and global image enhancement, and then embed the generated side information into the processed image. On the recovery end, we extract side information from processed image and reconstruct the original content without any error. Experimental results show that the processed image with good contrast and quality can be achieved using the proposed method.

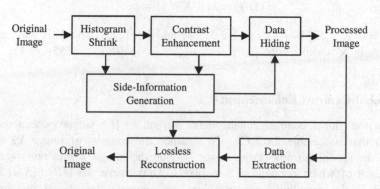

Fig. 2. Framework of reversible image processing

2   Proposed Method

2.1   Histogram Shrink

Given a digital image $\mathbf{X} = \{X(i,j) \mid X(i,j) \in [0, 255], i = 1, 2, \ldots, M, j = 1, 2, \ldots, N\}$ with $M \times N$ pixels, we first calculate its histogram as $\mathbf{h}_X = \{h_X(k) \mid k = 0, 1, \ldots, 255\}$, where $h_X(k) \in [0, \mathbb{Z}^+]$ is the number of occurrences of the gray-level k in $\mathbf{X}$. Let $A = \{a_1, a_2, \ldots, a_K\}$ be the set of all possible gray-levels in $\mathbf{X}$, where $a_1 < a_2 < \ldots < a_k$, and K is the number of existing gray-levels.

We further choose a threshold T satisfying $1 \leq T \leq 128$. Let $S = 255-K$. If $S < T$, find $T-S$ gray-levels from $\mathcal{A}$. Initially we let $\mathcal{A}' = \mathcal{A}$ and $\mathcal{B} = \{\}$. Find the gray-level $a_i(i \in [1, K])$ that satisfies $h(a_i) = \min\{h_X(a_k)|a_k \in A'\}$, and remove a_i from A'. If $a_i > 1$, $h(a_i-1) \neq 0$ and $a_i-1 \notin B$, we add a_i to B, $i.e.$, $B = B + \{a_i\}$. Repeat the operation until there are $T-S$ elements in B. Assuming $B = \{b_1, b_2, \ldots, b_{T-S}\}$, we modify the original image to construct a new image $\mathbf{X}'$ by

$$X'(i,j) = \begin{cases} X(i,j) - 1, & \text{if } X(i,j) \in B \\ X(i,j), & \text{otherwise} \end{cases} \tag{1}$$

where $i = 1, 2, \ldots, M$, $j = 1, 2, \ldots, N$. Meanwhile, generate a binary map $\mathbf{M}$ to record the modification by

$$M(i,j) = \begin{cases} 1, & \text{if } X(i,j) \in B \\ 0, & \text{otherwise} \end{cases} \tag{2}$$

If $S \geq T$, the binary map is not required and $\mathbf{X}' = \mathbf{X}$.

Thus, there are $J = max(255-K, T)$ zeros in the histogram $\mathbf{h}_{X'}$. Denote the gray-levels that does not exist in $\mathbf{X}'$ as a set $Z = \{z_i|z_i \in [0, 255], i = 0, 1, \ldots, J-1\}$. Let $\{p_0, p_1, \ldots, p_{255-J-1}\}$ be the set of all gray-levels that exist in $\mathbf{X}'$, where $p_0 < p_1 < \ldots < p_{255-J-1}$. Next, we construct a new image $\mathbf{Y}$ by

$$Y(i,j) = k, \text{if } X'(i,j) = p_k \tag{3}$$

where $k = 0, 1, \ldots, 255-J-1$, $i = 1, 2, \ldots, M$ and $j = 1, 2, \ldots, N$. This way, existing gray-levels in $\mathbf{X}'$ shrinks from $\{p_0, p_1, \ldots, p_{255-J-1}\}$ to $\{0, 1, \ldots, 255-J-1\}$.

2.2   Global Contrast Enhancement

Based on the global contrast enhancement method in [5], we propose a modified algorithm that is suitable for **RCE**. To enhance the contrast of image $\mathbf{Y}$, we first calculate the spatial entropy of the image. Divide the image $\mathbf{Y}$ into non-overlapped blocks, each of which contains $m \times n$ pixels. Thus, there are $[M/m]\cdot[N/n]$ blocks, where $[\cdot]$ is the rounding operator. Next we generate the spatial histogram of gray-levels in each block by

$$\mathbf{H} = \{H_k(i,j) \mid k = 0, 1, \ldots, 255 - J - 1\}$$

where $H_k(i,j)$ is the number of occurrence of the gray-level k in the (i,j)-th block, $i = 1, 2, \ldots, [M/m]$ and $j = 1, 2, \ldots, [N/n]$. The size of each block can be identified by

$$m = \left[((255 - J)/(M/N))^{1/2}\right]$$

$$n = \left[((255 - J) \cdot (M/N))^{1/2}\right]$$

With the spatial histogram, the entropy measure for each level k is computed by

$$E(k) = \sum_{i=1}^{[M/m]} \sum_{j=1}^{[N/n]} H_k(i,j)log_2 H_k(i,j) \tag{4}$$

where $k = 0, 1, \ldots, 255-J-1$. Accordingly, the importance of each gray-level with respect to the other gray-levels is calculated using

$$f(k) = E(k)/\sum_{l=0, k \neq l}^{255-J-1} E(l) \tag{5}$$

The measure $f(k)$ is further normalized using

$$f(k) \leftarrow f(k)/\sum_{l=0}^{255-J-1} f(l) \tag{6}$$

Then, we find J gray-levels $\{k_1, k_2, \ldots, k_J\}$ $(k_1 < k_2 < \ldots < k_J)$ corresponding to J minimal $f(k)$ values. Accordingly, we construct a contrast-enhanced image $\mathbf{Z}$ by

$$Z(i,j) = \begin{cases} Y(i,j) + J, & \text{if } Y(i,j) > k_J \\ Y(i,j) + t - 1, & \text{if } Y(i,j) = k_t \\ Y(i,j) + t, & \text{if } k_t < Y(i,j) < k_{t+1} \\ Y(i,j), & \text{otherwise} \end{cases} \tag{7}$$

where $t = 1, 2, \ldots, J-1$, $i = 1, 2, \ldots, M$ and $j = 1, 2, \ldots, N$. After contrast enhancement, all existing gray-levels in $\mathbf{Z}$ is shifted to the range of $[0, 255]$, and the gray-levels $\{k_1, k_2, \ldots, k_J\}$ are modified to $\{k_1, k_2 + 1, \ldots, k_i + i - 1, \ldots, k_J + J - 1\}$.

2.3   Data Hiding

During the procedure of contrast enhance, we have to record the side information including the set of gray-levels $\mathbf{Z} = \{z_i | z_i \in [0, 255], i = 0, 1, \ldots, J-1\}$ and the binary map $\mathbf{M}$. We record J gray-levels in $\mathbf{Z}$ using $8 \cdot (J + 1)$ bits containing an 8-bit header representing the number J. Meanwhile, we compress the binary map $\mathbf{M}$ to m_a bits using the *arithmetic encoding* algorithm. Next, the $8(J + 1) + m_a$ bits are embedded into the contrast-enhanced image $\mathbf{Z}$.

To accommodate the encoded bits, we select L gray-levels from $\{k_1, k_2 + 1, \ldots, k_i + i - 1, \ldots, k_J + J - 1\}$ that have the largest values of $f(i) (i = k_1, k_2, \ldots, k_J)$, such that

$$\sum_{l=K_J+j-L}^{K_J+j-1} h_z(l) \geq 8L + 8(J+1) + m_a \tag{8}$$

where h_z is the histogram of image $\mathbf{Z}$ excluding eight pixels. Denote the selected gray-levels as $\{s_1, s_2, \ldots, s_L\}$ $(s_1 < s_2 < \ldots < s_L)$.

We hide the value s_L into the least significant bits (LSB) of the excluded eight pixels by bit replacement. Meanwhile, the values of $\{s_1, s_2, \ldots, s_{L-1}\}$ and LSBs of the excluded pixels are recorded. This way, we have $8L + 8(J + 1) + m_a$ bits to be embedded into **Z**. A marked image **W** can be generated by data hiding,

$$W(i,j) = \begin{cases} Z(i,j) + b_k, & \text{if } Z(i,j) \in S \\ Z(i,j), & \text{otherwise} \end{cases} \tag{9}$$

where $S = \{s_1, s_2, \ldots, s_L\}$, b_k is the k-th bit (0 or 1) to be hidden, $k = 1, 2, \ldots, 8L + 8(J+1) + m_a$, $i = 1, 2, \ldots, M$ and $j = 1, 2, \ldots, N$.

2.4   Image Recovery

With the marked contrast-enhanced image **W**, the original image **X** can be losslessly recovered. We first extract the LSBs from the excluded eight pixels and recover the value s_L. With this value, part of the hidden bits can be extracted from **W** by

$$b_k = \begin{cases} 1, \text{ if } Z(i,j) = s_L + 1 \\ 0, \text{ if } Z(i,j) = s_L \end{cases} \tag{10}$$

where $k = 1, 2, \ldots, h_Z(s_L) + h_Z(s_L + 1)$.

From these bits, we can recover the values of $\{s_1, s_2, \ldots, s_{L-1}\}$. Accordingly, the other hidden bits can be extracted by

$$b_k = \begin{cases} 1, \text{if } Z(i,j) = g + 1 \\ 0, \text{if } Z(i,j) = g \end{cases}, g \in \{s_1, \ldots, s_{L-1}\} \tag{11}$$

where $k \in [h_Z(s_L) + h_Z(s_L + 1) + 1, 8L + 8(J + 1) + m_a]$.

Meanwhile, we remove the hidden bits from **W** to reconstruct the image **Z** by

$$Z(i,j) = \begin{cases} W(i,j) - 1, & \text{if } W(i,j) \in S' \\ W(i,j), & \text{otherwise} \end{cases} \tag{12}$$

where $S' = \{s_1 + 1, s_2 + 1, \ldots, s_L + 1\}$.

According to the values of $\{k_1, k_2 + 1, \ldots, k_i + i - 1, \ldots, k_J + J - 1\}$, we shrink the histogram of image **Z** by

$$Y(i,j) = \begin{cases} Z(i,j) - J, & \text{if } Z(i,j) > k_J + J - 1 \\ Z(i,j) - t + 1, & \text{if } Z(i,j) = k_t + t - 1 \\ Z(i,j) + t, & \text{if } k_t + t - 1 < Z(i,j) < k_{t+1} + t \\ Z(i,j), & \text{otherwise} \end{cases} \tag{13}$$

where $t \in [1, J-1]$, $i = 1, 2, \ldots, M$ and $j = 1, 2, \ldots, N$. Thus, the existing gray-levels in **Y** belongs to $\{0, 1, \ldots, 255 - J - 1\}$.

From the extracted bits, we can identify the set $Z = \{z_i | z_i \in [0, 255], i = 0, 1, \ldots, J - 1\}$. Accordingly, the supplementary set $\{p_0, p_1, \ldots, p_{255-J-1}\}$ can be identified, where $p_0 < p_1 < \ldots < p_{255-J-1}$. Thus, the image **X**′ can be reconstructed by

$$X'(i,j) = p_k, \text{ if } Y(i,j) = k \tag{14}$$

where $k = 0, 1, \ldots, 255-J-1, i = 1, 2, \ldots, M$ and $j = 1, 2, \ldots, N$.

Also, compressed bits of the binary map **M** can also be separated from the extracted bits. Using the *arithmetic decoding* algorithm, the original map **M** can be reconstructed. Subsequently, we recover the original image **X** using

$$X(i,j) = \begin{cases} X'(i,j)+1, & \text{if } M(i,j) = 1 \\ X'(i,j), & \text{if } M(i,j) = 0 \end{cases} \tag{15}$$

where $i = 1, 2, \ldots, M$ and $j = 1, 2, \ldots, Nn$.

3 Experimental Results

To evaluate the proposed method, we implemented the reversible algorithm in many images. Two examples are shown in Figs. 3 and 4. In these experiments, we use the parameter T = 50. Figures 3(a) and 4(a) are the original images containing 512×512

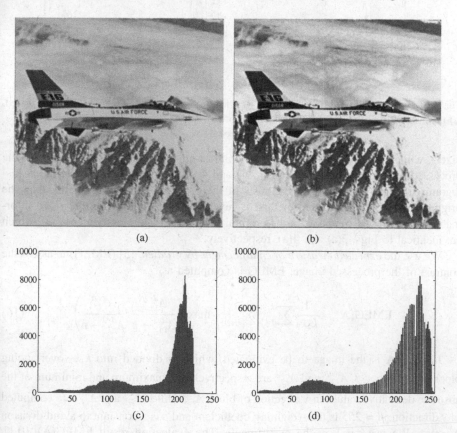

Fig. 3. Reversible contrast enhancement for airplane, (a) is the original image, (b) the processed, (c) the histogram of (a), and (d) the histogram of (b).

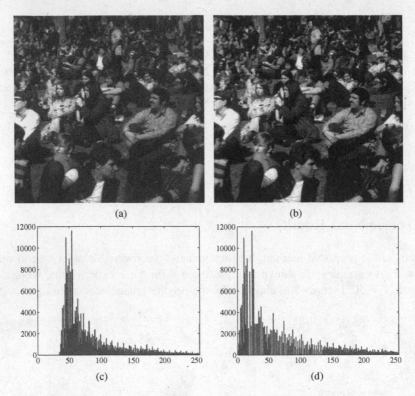

Fig. 4. Reversible contrast enhancement for crowd, (a) is the original image, (b) the processed, (c) the histogram of (a), and (d) the histogram of (b).

pixels, while Figs. 3(b) and 4(b) are the contrast-enhanced image. Histograms of the processed images are shown in Figs. 3(d) and 4(d). Compared with the original histograms in Figs. 3(c) and 4(c), contrasts of the processed images are better than the original images. The proposed method is reversible. After extracting the sided information from Figs. 3(b) and 4(b), the original image can be losslessly recovered, which are identical to Figs. 3(a) and 4(a), respectively.

We use the *expected measure of enhancement by gradient* [5] (EMEG) to assess the contrast of the processed image. EMEG is computed as

$$\text{EMEG}(\mathbf{A}) = \frac{1}{k_1 k_2} \sum_{i=1}^{k_1} \sum_{j=1}^{k_2} \frac{1}{\beta} \max \left(\frac{A_{i,j}^{dx,h}}{A_{i,j}^{dx,l} + \varepsilon}, \frac{A_{i,j}^{dy,h}}{A_{i,j}^{dy,l} + \varepsilon} \right) \tag{16}$$

In (16), $\mathbf{A}$ is the image to be evaluated, which is divided into $k_1 k_2$ overlapping blocks of size 8×8. $A_{i,j}^{dx,h}$ and $A_{i,j}^{dx,l}$ are respectively the maximum and minimum of the absolute derivative values in x direction of block $A_{i,j}$, while $A_{i,j}^{dy,h}$ and $A_{i,j}^{dy,l}$ are computed in y direction. $\beta = 255$ is the weighting coefficient and ε is a constant to avoid division by zero. We use $\varepsilon = 1$ in the experiments. The evaluation result $\text{EMEG}(\mathbf{A}) \in [0,1]$.

Table 1. I contrast and quality of the enhanced images using EMEG, SSIM and PSNR

		Original	Imadjust	Histeq	Adapthisteq	SECE	Proposed
Lena	EMEG	0.087	0.126	0.149	0.173	0.118	0.118
	SSIM	—	0.91	0.87	0.78	0.95	0.95
	PSNR	—	21.9	19.1	18.9	23.4	24.0
Baboon	EMEG	0.206	0.314	0.434	0.387	0.275	0.270
	SSIM	—	0.92	0.81	0.75	0.96	0.96
	PSNR	—	19.6	17.6	17.1	21.9	23.5
Barbara	EMEG	0.121	0.156	0.197	0.208	0.149	0.150
	SSIM	—	0.93	0.91	0.81	0.96	0.96
	PSNR	—	24.3	20.8	17.1	25.8	26.1
Crowd	EMEG	0.121	0.142	0.204	0.196	0.155	0.155
	SSIM	—	0.78	12.9	0.80	0.80	0.82
	PSNR	—	18.6	12.9	18.7	19.8	21.0
Pepper	EMEG	0.104	0.130	0.157	0.190	0.126	0.126
	SSIM	—	0.97	0.91	0.80	0.98	0.98
	PSNR	—	21.2	20.7	18.8	22.3	23.3
Sailboat	EMEG	0.142	0.181	0.194	0.246	0.171	0.173
	SSIM		0.94	0.91	0.79	0.98	0.97
	PSNR		23.1	24.5	17.9	24.7	24.1

Images with higher contrast have larger EMEG values. Meanwhile, we use SSIM [7] and PSNR to measure the quality of processed image. SSIM indicates the structure similarity between the processed image and the original image, and PSNR represents the modification of the processing. The larger values of SSIM and PSNR are, the better qualities of the processed images have.

The proposed **RCE** method is compared with the traditional contrast enhancement methods, including *imadjust*, *histeq*, *adapthisteq* algorithms in Matlab system, and *SECE* in [5]. We use the parameter $T = 30$. Experimental results are shown in Table 1. Both contrast and quality of the proposed method are close to *SECE*, meaning that the **RCE** processed image preserves good contrast and good quality. Though the contrast of *imadjust*, *histeq* and *adapthisteq* are larger than the proposed method, quality of the processed method is better. Most importantly, the proposed method is reversible, *i.e.*, the original image can be recovered.

We also evaluate the impact when using different values of parameter T. The results are shown in Fig. 5, in which the parameter T ranges from 30 to 90. EMEG values in Fig. 5(a) show that the contrast increases when we use larger T. Contrarily, SSIM values in Fig. 5(b) show that larger T could result in the lower quality. This indicates that effect of **RCE** can be controlled by T.

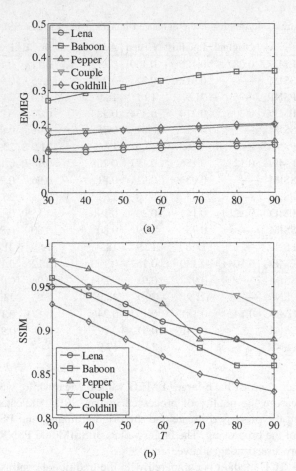

Fig. 5. Contrast and quality corresponding different parameters, (a) shows the EMEG measurement and (b) the SSIM

4   Conclusions

In this paper, we propose a novel idea of reversible image processing, which is different from the traditional image processing. We provide an example of reversible contrast enhancement to show that RIP can be achieved by combining data hiding with image processing. We enhance the original image by histogram shrink and contrast stretching. Meanwhile, some side information is generated and hidden into the contrast-enhanced image. With the processed image, we can losslessly recover the original image. Experimental results show that the proposed method provides good contrast and quality for the contrast-enhanced image. We believe that RIP would be a new research topic for image processing. Other reversible methods for denoising and restoration can also be investigated in the future.

Acknowledgement. This work was supported by the Natural Science Foundation of China (Grant 61572308 and Grant U1536108, Grant 61572452 and Grant 61402279), Shanghai Rising-Star Program under Grant 14QA1401900, Shanghai Natural Science Foundation under Grant 14ZR1415900, and 2015 Shanghai University Filmology Summit Research Grant

References

1. Gonzalez, R.C., Woods, R.: Digital Image Processing. Pearson Education, Upper Saddle River (2002)
2. Zhang, X., Zhang, W.: Semantic image compression based on data hiding. IET Image Proc. **9**(1), 54–61 (2014)
3. Wu, H.-T., Dugelay, J.-L., Shi, Y.-Q.: Reversible image data hiding with contrast enhancement. IEEE Sig. Process. Lett. **22**(1), 81–85 (2015)
4. Gao, G., Shi, Y.-Q.: Reversible data hiding using controlled contrast enhancement and integer wavelet transform. IEEE Sig. Process. Lett. **22**(11), 2078–2082 (2015)
5. Celik, T.: Spatial entropy-based global and local image contrast enhancement. IEEE Trans. Image Process. **23**(12), 5298–5308 (2014)
6. Fridrich, J.: Steganography in Digital Media: Principles, Algorithms, and Applications. Cambridge University Press, Cambridge (2009)
7. Wang, Z., et al.: Image quality assessment: from error visibility to structural similarity. IEEE Trans. Image Process. **13**(4), 600–612 (2004)
8. Chen, B., Shu, H., Coatrieux, G., Chen, G., Sun, X., Coatrieux, J.-L.: Color image analysis by quaternion-type moments. J. Math. Imaging Vis. **51**(1), 124–144 (2015)
9. Xia, Z., Wang, X., Sun, X., Wang, B.: Steganalysis of least significant bit matching using multi-order differences. Secur. Commun. Netw. **7**(8), 1283–1291 (2014)

On Improving Homomorphic Encryption-Based Reversible Data Hiding

Xiaotian Wu[1(✉)], Zhuoqian Liang[1,2], Bing Chen[3], and Tong Liu[4]

[1] Department of Computer Science, Jinan University, Guangzhou, China
wxiaotian@mail.sysu.edu.cn
[2] Management School, Jinan University, Guangzhou, China
[3] School of Data and Computer Science, Sun Yat-sen University, Guangzhou, China
[4] Department of Electronic Science, Huizhou University, Huizhou, China

Abstract. Reversible data hiding for encrypted images with improved performance is introduced in this paper. Each unit in the original image is separated into three components, and each component is encrypted by Paillier homomorphic encryption. Additional bits can be concealed into the encrypted image by manipulating the encrypted signals. Finally, the original image is obtained without error when the direct decryption is applied. The embedded bits are perfectly extracted as well. Optimal visual quality and improved embedding rate are obtained by the proposed approach, since the value of the directly decrypted unit is the same as the original one. Experimental results and comparisons are demonstrated to illustrate the effectiveness and advantages of the proposed method.

Keywords: Reversible data hiding · Homomorphic encryption · Visual quality · Perfect reconstruction · Embedding rate

1 Introduction

In recent years, signal processing in encrypted domain has attracted considerable research interest. Encryption is a well known effective and popular means for providing confidentiality for images. The image content owner can transform the meaningful content to incomprehensible one with the help of encryption. But in some scenarios, a content owner does not trust the processing service provider, and does not want the service provider to access the content. The content owner may encrypt the image before transmission. The service provider would embed some additional messages within the encrypted image for other purposes such like image notation, authentication, analysis [1,11] and transmission [9].

To achieve the above-mentioned purpose, reversible data hiding in encrypted images in introduced. In Ref. [7], one additional bit is concealed into an AES encrypted image block. By analyzing the local standard deviation of the marked encrypted image, bits can be extracted and the original image can be reconstructed. Zhang [13] introduced a reversible data hiding approach in encrypted images, where the data hiding is performed on the encrypted image block by flipping the corresponding 3 least significant bits (LSBs). Hong et al. [3] improved

© Springer International Publishing AG 2016
X. Sun et al. (Eds.): ICCCS 2016, Part I, LNCS 10039, pp. 28–38, 2016.
DOI: 10.1007/978-3-319-48671-0_3

Zhangs method [13] by adopting a better metric for measuring the block smoothness. Further, Zhang [14] introduced a separable method, where some encrypted data are firstly compressed, and space for data embedding is emptied out. A receiver having the data hiding key can extract the embedded data with any error, while a receiver having the encryption key can decrypt received data to obtain a directly decrypted image similar to the original one. If both the data hiding and encryption keys are obtained, the receiver can retrieve the embedded data and recover the original image. An error-free data extraction is guaranteed in this approach. For providing improved rate-distortion performance, an efficient method using low-density parity-check codes and side information is presented in Ref. [15]. For the purpose of obtaining a reconstructed image without errors, Ma et al. [5] proposed a reserving room before encryption based method, where the reserved room is used to accommodate the additional bits prior to image encryption. Zhang et al. [12] introduced a reversibility improved approach. By shifting the histogram of estimating errors of some pixels, room for data hiding can be emptied out before image encryption. By using histogram modification and n-nary data hiding, Qian et al. [8] introduced a separable reversible data hiding method for encrypted images.

More recently, homomorphic encryption is adopted for reversible data hiding in encrypted images. With the additive homomorphic property of Paillier encryption [6], Chen et al. [2] firstly proposed a homomorphic encryption based reversible data hiding approach. In their method, the receiver can sets the public key and private key. The image owner encrypts the image by the public key according to Paillier encrytion. The data hider is possible to embed additional message into the encryted image by using the public key. The receiver uses the private key for decryption, and finally retrieves the original image and embedded message. Since shared key is utilized, a secure channel among all involved identities is no longer required. Shiu et al. [10] improved Chen et al.'s method [2] by adopting the concept of difference expansion into homomorphic encryption. Li et al. [4] introduced another method by using modular additive homomorphism and difference histogram shifting.

In total, homomorphic encryption based reversible data hiding exhibits the capability of achieving high embedding rate and improved visual performance, while comparing to non-homomorphic encryption based methods.

In this paper, we further improve the performance of reversible data hiding in homomorphic encrypted images by the proposed method. Contributions of the proposed method can be formulated as follows.

- Perfect reconstruction of directly decrypted image. Once the marked encrypted image is decrypted, the original image is achieved simultaneously, since the directly decrypted image is the original one.
- Improved embedding capacity. The maximal embedding rate can be improved to be 1 bit per pixel (bpp).
- Real reversibility. Data extraction and image recovery are free of any error.
- Homomorphic data embedding. Data embedding procedure is directly performed in the homomorphic encryption domain.

– No overflow. In Chen et al.'s method [2], each pixel is divided into two parts: an even integer and a bit, where the summation of them is equal to the pixel value. The bit is encrypted and modified later for data embedding. However, the embedding is possible to cause overflow problem. But in the proposed method, it can be solved.

The remaining part of this paper is organized as follows. The proposed method is elaborated in Sect. 2. Experimental results and discussions are given in Sect. 3. Finally, Sect. 4 draws some conclusions.

2   The Proposed Method

2.1   Framework of the Proposed Method

The proposed method consists of four phases: key generation phase, image encryption phase, data embedding phase and data extraction and image recovery phase. Three identities are active in this method, they are image content owner $\mathcal{O}$, data hider $\mathcal{H}$ and the valid receiver $\mathcal{R}$. The framework of the proposed method is illustrated in Fig. 1.

In key generation phase, the receiver $\mathcal{R}$ sets his/her public key and private key according to Pailiier encryption. In image encryption phase, the image content owner $\mathcal{O}$ adopts the public key to encryption the image by Paillier algorithm, and sends the encrypted image to the data hider $\mathcal{H}$. In the data embedding phase, the data hider $\mathcal{H}$ encrypts the message by the public key, and embeds

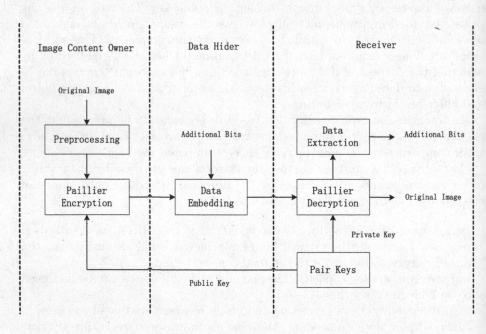

Fig. 1. Framework of the proposed method.

he encrypted message into the encrypted image to form the marked encrypted image. In data extraction and image recovery phase, the receiver $\mathcal{R}$ can simultaneously decrypt the marked encrypted image and extract the embedded bits. The directly decrypted image is the original image, and the message is obtained by decrypting the extracted bits.

2.2 Key Generation Phase

In Key generation phase, the receiver $\mathcal{R}$ generates the public key and private key used in Paillier encryption. First, $\mathcal{R}$ selects two large primes, denoted as p and q, and computes $N = pq$. Then, $\mathcal{R}$ computes $\lambda = lcm(p - 1, q - 1)$, and selects $g \in \mathbb{Z}_{N^2}^*$ with $gcd(L(g^\lambda mod N^2), N) = 1$ where $L(x) = \frac{x-1}{N}$ and $\mathbb{Z}_{N^2}^* = 1, 2, \cdots, N^2 - 1$. Finally, $\mathcal{R}$ sets (N, g) as a public key pk and sets (p, q, λ) as a private key sk.

2.3 Image Encryption Phase

In image encryption phase, the image content owner $\mathcal{O}$ utilizes the public key pk to encrypt the image I. Let p_i be a unit in the image, p_i can be represented by the sum of three integers, as denoted as $p_i = t_i + a_{0i} + a_{1i}$. The construction of the three integers is formulated by the following three steps. First, x_i is obtained by $x_i = 2\lfloor p_i/2 \rfloor$. Second, an integer r_i is randomly selected from $\{0, 1, 2, \cdots, x_i\}$. Finally, a_{0i} and a_{1i} are set to be r_i, and t_i is set to be $p_i - 2r_i$.

For the next step, the image I is encrypted unit by unit according to the Paillier algorithm. That is,

$$\begin{aligned} E(p_i) &= E(t_i + a_{0i} + a_{1i}) \\ &= E(t_i)E(a_{0i})E(a_{1i}). \end{aligned} \tag{1}$$

When all the units are encrypted, the encrypted units comprise the encrypted image EI.

On the other hand, the data hider $\mathcal{H}$ uses the public key pk to encrypt a message m by Paillier encryption. Denote the encrypted message as $E(m)$.

2.4 Data Embedding Phase

In data embedding phase, the data hider $\mathcal{H}$ embeds the encrypted message $E(m)$ into the encrypted image EI bit by bit. Each bit is embedded into each encrypted unit of EI. An encrypted unit in EI can be represented by $(E(t_i), E(a_{0i}), E(a_{1i}))$. The to-be-embedded bit b is concealed into $E(a_{0i})$ and $E(a_{1i})$, and the marked $E(a'_{0i})$ and $E(a'_{1i})$ are generated. Specifically, the embedding procedure is formulated by

$$E(a'_{0i}) = \begin{cases} E(a_{0i} - a_{1i} - 1), \text{if } b = 0, \\ E(a_{0i} + a_{1i} + 1), \text{if } b = 1, \end{cases} \tag{2}$$

and

$$E(a'_{1i}) = \begin{cases} E(a_{0i} + a_{1i} + 1), \text{if } b = 0, \\ E(a_{0i} - a_{1i} - 1), \text{if } b = 1. \end{cases} \tag{3}$$

According to the additive homomorphic property of Paillier encryption, we have

$$E(a_{0i} - a_{1i} - 1) = E(a_{0i})E(a_{1i})^{-1}E(1)^{-1},$$
$$E(a_{0i} + a_{1i} + 1) = E(a_{0i})E(a_{1i})E(1). \tag{4}$$

That is, the embedding procedure can be implemented by operating the corresponding encrypted signals, as represented by

$$E(a'_{0i}) = \begin{cases} E(a_{0i})E(a_{1i})^{-1}E(1)^{-1}, \text{if } b = 0, \\ E(a_{0i})E(a_{1i})E(1), \text{if } b = 1, \end{cases} \tag{5}$$

and

$$E(a'_{1i}) = \begin{cases} E(a_{0i})E(a_{1i})E(1), \text{if } b = 0, \\ E(a_{0i})E(a_{1i})^{-1}E(1)^{-1}, \text{if } b = 1. \end{cases} \tag{6}$$

Since $a_{0i} = a_{1i}$, the result of $E(a_{0i})E(a_{1i})^{-1}$ is 1. Equations (5) and (6) are reduced to

$$E(a'_{0i}) = \begin{cases} E(1)^{-1}, \text{if } b = 0, \\ E(a_{0i})E(a_{1i})E(1), \text{if } b = 1, \end{cases} \tag{7}$$

and

$$E(a'_{1i}) = \begin{cases} E(a_{0i})E(a_{1i})E(1), \text{if } b = 0, \\ E(1)^{-1}, \text{if } b = 1. \end{cases} \tag{8}$$

Totally, when one bit is embedded, the corresponding marked encrypted unit is generated, as denoted as $(E(t_i), E(a'_{0i}), E(a'_{1i}))$. When all the bits are embedded, an marked encrypted image MEI is formed.

2.5   Data Extraction and Image Recovery Phase

In data extraction and image recovery phase, the receiver $\mathcal{R}$ uses the private key sk to decrypt the marked encrypted image MEI, and obtains a directly decrypted image DI. The decryption is conducted unit by unit. Each decrypted unit is denoted as (t_i, a'_{0i}, a'_{1i}). The value of the directly decrypted unit p'_i is calculated by $p'_i = t_i + a'_{0i} + a'_{1i}$.

In this paper, the direct decrypted image DI is the original image I. For each directly decrypted unit (t_i, a'_{0i}, a'_{1i}), when the embedded bit is 0, we have

$$a'_{0i} = a_{0i} - a_{1i} - 1$$

and

$$a'_{1i} = a_{0i} + a_{1i} + 1$$

according to Eqs. (2) and (3). Since $a_{0i} = a_{1i}$, we get

$$a'_{0i} + a'_{1i} = a_{0i} + a_{1i}. \tag{9}$$

When the embedded bit is 1, we have

$$a'_{0i} = a_{0i} + a_{1i} + 1$$

and

$$a'_{1i} = a_{0i} - a_{1i} - 1.$$

according to Eqs. (2) and (3). Since $a_{0i} = a_{1i}$, we get

$$a'_{0i} + a'_{1i} = a_{0i} + a_{1i}. \tag{10}$$

No matter the embedded bit is 0 or 1, we have

$$a'_{0i} + a'_{1i} = a_{0i} + a_{1i}. \tag{11}$$

Therefore, we have

$$
\begin{aligned}
p'_i &= t_i + a'_{0i} + a'_{1i} \\
&= t_i + a_{0i} + a_{1i} \\
&= p_i
\end{aligned} \tag{12}
$$

As a result, the direct decrypted image DI is the original image I.

In the next step, the embedded bits are extracted from the decrypted units. The extraction procedure is formulated by

$$b = \begin{cases} 0, \text{if } a'_{0i} < a'_{1i}, \\ 1, \text{if } a'_{0i} > a'_{1i}, \end{cases} \tag{13}$$

where b is the corresponding bit extracted from the decrypted unit (t_i, a'_{0i}, a'_{1i}). When all the bits are extracted, an encrypted message $E(m)$ is obtained. The receiver $\mathcal{R}$ decrypts $E(m)$ by the private key, and gets the original message m. An example of the proposed method is given below.

Example 1. Let the original pixel be $p_i = 134$ and let the to-be-embedded bit be $b = 0$. In image encryption phase, $x_i = 2\lfloor p_i/2 \rfloor = 2\lfloor 134/2 \rfloor = 67$ is computed. Suppose that $r_i = 5$ is randomly selected from $\{0, 1, \cdots, 67\}$. Then, $a_{0i} = r_i = 5$, $a_{1i} = r_i = 5$ and $t_i = p_i - a_{0i} - a_{1i} = 124$. And p_i is represented by $p_i = t_i = t_i - a_{0i} - a_{1i} = 124 + 5 + 5$. When p_i is encrypted, we obtain $E(124)E(5)E(5)$. In data embedding phase, when $b = 0$, we obtain the corresponding marked $E(a'_{0i}) = E(-1)$ and $E(a'_{1i}) = E(11)$. The marked encrypted pixel is computed as $E(p'_i) = E(124)E(-1)E(11)$. In data extraction and image recovery phase, the directly decrypted pixel is $p'_i = 124 + (-1) + 11 = 134$, which is the original pixel as well. The extracted bit is $b = 0$ since $-1 < 11$.

3   Experimental Results and Discussions

3.1   Performance Evaluation

For reversible data hiding methods in encrypted images, embedding rate, the visual quality of directly decrypted image and the visual quality of recovered image after data extraction are utilized to measure the performance. The embedding rate can be calculated by

$$\text{Embedding rate} = \frac{\text{Total embedded bits}}{\text{Total pixels of the image}}. \tag{14}$$

The embedding rate (bit per pixel, bpp) is expected to be as large as possible so that more information can be concealed. Peak signal-to-noise ratio (PSNR) is adopted to evaluate the visual quality, as computed by

$$PSNR = 10\log_{10}\frac{255^2}{\frac{1}{MN}\sum_{i=1}^{M}\sum_{j=1}^{N}(O_{i,j}-M_{i,j})^2} \tag{15}$$

where $O_{i,j}$ and $M_{i,j}$ are original pixel value and modified pixel value, respectively.

(a)   (b)

(c)   (d)

Fig. 2. Four test images used in the experiments. (a) Lena, (b) Baboon, (c) Airplane, and (d) Pepper.

3.2   Experiments of the Proposed Method

Four test images, consist of 512×512 pixels, illustrated in Fig. 2 are adopted for the experiments. Paillier encryption is used to encrypt the four images. In the experiments, $512 \times 512 = 262144$ bits are embedded into each encrypted images. The corresponding embedding rate is 1. The directly decrypted images are demonstrated in Fig. 3, all the directly decrypted images are lossless recovered. Table 1 summarizes these four experiments.

3.3   Performance Comparisons

Visual quality of the directly decrypted image and embedding rate are two major issues of reversible data hiding in encrypted images. Herein, PSNR of directly decrypted images and embedding rate comparison among the proposed method and related approaches [2, 3, 10, 12–14] is illustrated in Fig. 4. For the proposed method, at most each encrypted pixel can be embedded with one bit. The maximal embedding rate can reach at 1. Due to the fact that the directly decrypted

(a)   (b)

(c)   (d)

Fig. 3. Four directly decrypted images with perfect reconstruction by the proposed method. (a) Decrypted Lena, (b) Decrypted Baboon, (c) Decrypted Airplane, and (d) Decrypted Pepper.

Table 1. Visual quality (PSNR) of the directly decrypted image, embedded bits and embedding rate (bpp) of the experiments.

Test image	PSNR (dB)	Embedded bits	Embedding rate (bpp)
Lena	$+\infty$	262144	1
Baboon	$+\infty$	262144	1
Airplane	$+\infty$	262144	1
Pepper	$+\infty$	262144	1

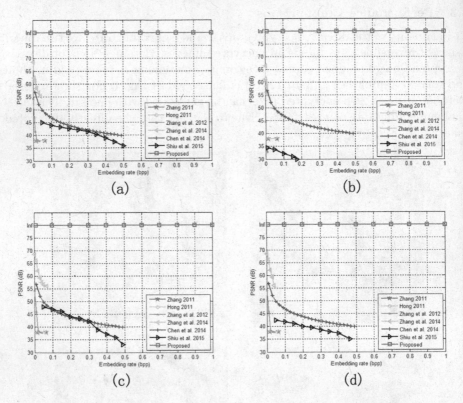

Fig. 4. PSNR of directly decrypted images and embedding rate comparison. (a) Lena, (b) Baboon, (c) Airplane, and (d) Pepper.

pixel value is the same as the original pixel value, no matter which embedding rate is utilized, the associated PSNR of the directly image is $+\infty$ dB. However, all the mentioned methods [2,3,10,12–14] affect the directly decrypted pixel value due to the embedding procedure, they cannot obtain the optimal visual quality of the directly decrypted image. By observing the comparison, the proposed method provides improved performance on visual quality and embedding rate.

Table 2. Feature comparison.

Method	Real reversibility	Public key encryption	Data expansion
Ours	Yes	Yes	Yes
Zhang [13]	No	No	No
Hong et al. [3]	No	No	No
Zhang [14]	No	No	No
Zhang et al. [12]	No	No	No
Chen et al. [2]	Yes	Yes	Yes
Shiu et al. [10]	Yes	Yes	Yes

3.4 Feature Comparison

Feature comparison among the proposed method and related methods is provided in Table 2. For the proposed method, public key encryption is adopted for the image encryption. It allows multiple image content providers and data hiders if they know about the receiver's public key. It further enriches the application scenarios. The real reversibility is guaranteed by the proposed method, since both the embedded bits and original image can be obtained without any error. However, due to the fact that Paillier encryption is used in the proposed method, the size of encrypted image is expanded.

4 Conclusions

In this paper, reversible data hiding for encrypted images with prefect reconstruction of directly decrypted image is presented. Each unit in the original image is divided into three parts, and they are encrypted by Paillier homomorphic encryption. Additional information can be embedded into the encrypted image by manipulating the encrypted signals. The original image can be obtained without any error when the direct decryption is applied. And the embedded bits are perfectly extracted as well. Optimal visual quality and improved embedding rate is obtained by the proposed method, since the value of the directly decrypted pixel is the same as the original pixel.

Acknowledgment. This work was partially supported by China Postdoctoral Science Foundation (Grant No. 2014M552269 and Grant No. 2015T80933), the National Nature Science Foundation of China under Grant Nos. 61401174 and 61602211 and PhD Research Startup Foundation of Huizhou University under Grant No. 156020023.

References

1. Chen, B., Shu, H., Coatrieux, G., Chen, G., Sun, X., Coatrieux, J.L.: Color image analysis by quaternion-type moments. J. Math. Imaging Vis. **51**(1), 124–144 (2015)
2. Chen, Y.C., Shiu, C.W., Horng, G.: Encrypted signal-based reversible data hiding with public key cryptosystem. J. Vis. Commun. Image Represent. **25**(5), 1164–1170 (2014)
3. Hong, W., Chen, T.S., Wu, H.Y.: An improved reversible data hiding in encrypted images using side match. IEEE Sig. Process. Lett. **19**(4), 199–202 (2012)
4. Li, M., Xiao, D., Zhang, Y., Nan, H.: Reversible data hiding in encrypted images using cross division and additive homomorphism. Sig. Process. Image Commun. **39**, 234–248 (2015)
5. Ma, K., Zhang, W., Zhao, X., Yu, N., Li, F.: Reversible data hiding in encrypted images by reserving room before encryption. IEEE Trans. Inf. Forensics Secur. **8**(3), 553–562 (2013)
6. Paillier, P.: Public-key cryptosystems based on composite degree residuosity classes. In: Stern, J. (ed.) EUROCRYPT 1999. LNCS, vol. 1592, pp. 223–238. Springer, Heidelberg (1999). doi:10.1007/3-540-48910-X_16
7. Puech, W., Chaumont, M., Strauss, O.: A reversible data hiding method for encrypted images. In: Proceedings of Electronic Imaging, p. 68191E. International Society for Optics and Photonics (2008)
8. Qian, Z., Han, X., Zhang, X.: Separable reversible data hiding in encrypted images by n-nary histogram modification. In: Proceedings of 3rd International Conference on Multimedia Technology, pp. 869–876. Atlantis Press (2013)
9. Shen, J., Tan, H., Wang, J., Wang, J., Lee, S.: A novel routing protocol providing good transmission reliability in underwater sensor networks. J. Internet Technol. **16**(1), 171–178 (2015)
10. Shiu, C.W., Chen, Y.C., Hong, W.: Encrypted image-based reversible data hiding with public key cryptography from difference expansion. Sig. Process. Image Commun. **39**, 226–233 (2015)
11. Xia, Z., Wang, X., Sun, X., Wang, B.: Steganalysis of least significant bit matching using multi-order differences. Secur. Commun. Netw. **7**(8), 1283–1291 (2014)
12. Zhang, W., Ma, K., Yu, N.: Reversibility improved data hiding in encrypted images. Sig. Process. **94**, 118–127 (2014)
13. Zhang, X.: Reversible data hiding in encrypted image. IEEE Sig. Process. Lett. **18**(4), 255–258 (2011)
14. Zhang, X.: Separable reversible data hiding in encrypted image. IEEE Trans. Inf. Forensics Secur. **7**(2), 826–832 (2012)
15. Zhang, X., Qian, Z., Feng, G., Ren, Y.: Efficient reversible data hiding in encrypted images. J. Vis. Commun. Image Represent. **25**(2), 322–328 (2014)

Coverless Information Hiding Method Based on Multi-keywords

Zhili Zhou[1(✉)], Yan Mu[1], Ningsheng Zhao[1], Q.M. Jonathan Wu[2],
and Ching-Nung Yang[3]

[1] School of Computer and Software and Jiangsu Engineering Center
of Network Monitoring, Nanjing University of Information Science
and Technology, Nanjing 210044, China
{zhou_zhili,muyan_my,zhao_ning_sheng}@163.com
[2] Department of Electrical and Computer Engineering,
University of Windsor, Windsor, ON, Canada
[3] Department of Computer Science and Information Engineering,
National Dong Hwa University, Shoufeng, Hualien, Taiwan

Abstract. As a new information hiding method, coverless information hiding has become a hot issue in the field of information security. The existing coverless information hiding method has realized that one Chinese character can be hidden in one natural text. However, the problem of the method is that the hiding capacity is too small. To address this problem, a novel method named coverless information hiding method based on multi-keywords is proposed in this paper. The main idea of the method is that the number of keywords will be hidden in the text where keywords have been hidden. Experimental results show that the proposed method can improve the capacity of information hiding in text.

Keywords: Coverless information hiding · Natural text · Hiding capacity · Multi-keywords

1 Introduction

In recent years, because of the significance on the privacy, copyright and others, information hiding is used as a protective measure which has attracted more attention. As a result, more people have devoted themselves to the research field of information security. The purpose of information hiding is to embed the secret message into the cover. It is difficult for illegal users to intercept the secret message through the cover [1]. The method of Information hiding can be divided into different types according to the kinds of covers, such as information hiding based on text, information hiding based on image, and so on [2]. During the past two decades, the traditional information hiding methods based on the text mainly change the letter-spacing to embed secret message. Latter, Maxemchuk, Brassil, Low and etc. [3–9] have proposed some methods to change the line-spacing, letter-spacing, character height and character width to realize embedding secret message. The typical image steganography methods include LSB matching [10–12, 17], histogram-based methods [13], quantization table [14], and so on.

© Springer International Publishing AG 2016
X. Sun et al. (Eds.): ICCCS 2016, Part I, LNCS 10039, pp. 39–47, 2016.
DOI: 10.1007/978-3-319-48671-0_4

Due to above methods, we can find that the existing information hiding methods have a common ground that these traditional methods modify the designated cover [15]. The modification traces caused by these methods will be left in the cover which can be detected by steganalysis tools [20]. Coverless information hiding [15, 18] is used to address the problem, because it can hide the secret message in the cover without any modification.

Coverless information hiding is a new concept which was first proposed to resist steganalysis tools. As we know, any natural texts contain a large number of Chinese keywords. These Chinese keywords may already contain the message needed to be hidden with a certain probability [15]. The existing method can hide one Chinese character in each text. However, the problem in this method is that the hiding capacity is small. It is urgent to address the problem of the capacity.

This paper proposes a new method, called coverless information hiding method based on multi-keywords [16, 19] to address the problem. The method can hide multiple Chinese keywords in each text. This method hides both secret message and the number of keywords in the same text simultaneously. Receiver will extract the number of keywords and the secret message from the texts they have received.

This paper is organized as follows. Section 2 summarizes the prepared work which is related to the method. Our proposed method is discussed in Sect. 3. Section 4 explains the experimental data and presents the results of our experimental research. Finally, Sect. 5 concludes the paper with brief words.

2   Prepared Work

There are three parts of prepared work, including the construction of text database, the construction of inverted index structure, and the design of scheme to select location tags.

2.1   Construction of Text Database

Natural texts are mainly collected by the following ways: fetching the news from the normal news web sites; downloading short articles from the writing platform; collecting the various novels from free website and ancient literature. Through these ways, a large-scale text database whose size is 5.6G has been constructed, and the size of each text in this database is about 1 KB. At the same time, the text database can be expanded constantly.

2.2   Construction of Inverted Index Structure by Text Indexing

An inverted index structure is needed to be constructed to reduce the huge cost of search time when we search for the texts which have the keywords exhaustively. And the index structure is constructed by using the Chinese mathematical expression [21, 22]. We divide the Chinese keyword into various components by using the Chinese mathematical expression when we index the text database. We adopt the first appearance of the components, and select the Chinese keyword behind these components as useful

Index structure

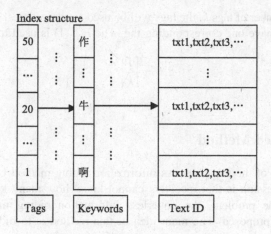

| Tags | Keywords | Text ID |

Fig. 1. The design of index structure

message. Figure 1 shows the index structure. The index files can be updated timely when we have new natural texts to expand the large-scale text database.

2.3 The Design of Scheme to Select Location Tags

We adopt to use the Chinese character component as the location tags. So that the text s in the large-scale text database are statistically analyzed. According to the analysis of statistical results, 50 components are selected from all Chinese character components as the location label of the secret message. Figure 2 shows the Chinese keyword coverage of each component.

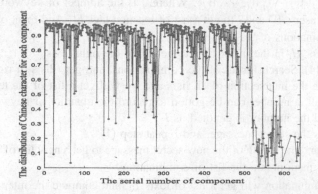

Fig. 2. The distribution of keywords for each component

A scheme is designed to get different tags from the 50 tags by the user's identity. Users can use their ID to get their unique tags. When the length of secret message l is longer than the number of tags k, the tags will be used around s times. This ensures that one keyword will have one corresponding tag. The Eq. (1) is used to calculate s.

$$s = \left\lceil \frac{l}{k} \right\rceil \tag{1}$$

3   The Proposed Method

The main problem of the the coverless information hiding method based on Chinese mathematical expression is that receivers cannot know how many keywords in each texts. To solve the problem, the coverless information hiding method based on multi-keywords is proposed. The main idea of this method is to hide the number of keywords in the same text by the same manner. Consequently, the receiver knows the number of keywords in each text, and the secret message can be extracted exactly from the texts.

3.1   The Process of Information Hiding

There is difference between the coverless information hiding method based on Chinese mathematical expression [18] and our method that our method includes two hiding operations. The first one is hiding the keywords in the text, and the second is hiding the number of the keywords.

By using the user's ID and the secret message I_1, the process of information hiding is shown as follows:

(1)   The secret message I_1 would be segmented into several keywords, denoted as $I_1 = \{W_1, W_2, \cdots, W_i, \cdots, W_l\}$. Where, l is the number of keywords of I_1.

(2)   Use the user's ID and l to get a list of location tags L_i^1. And then, obtain the list of combinations of "tag + keyword", denoted as $H_i = L_i^1 + W_i$.

(3)   Search for H_i in the index files to get all of the right texts.

(4)   Repeat (4). Search for all of the combinations, and get l lists of right texts.

(5)   Compute the intersection of all lists and we will get a list of the texts T_1.

(6)   Above all, a number can be gotten to record the quantity of keywords in each text, and the number is denoted as I_2.

(7)   Let I_2 as the secret message, and repeat step (1).

(8)   Use ID and the length of the new secret message to get a new list of location tags L_j^2. And then, obtain the list of combinations.

(9)   Each combination will get a list of texts T_2, and compute the intersection of T_2 and T_1 to get a new list of texts T_3.

(10) Select a text randomly from each list, and send texts to receiver.

Figure 3 illustrates the process of several Chinese keywords hiding upon the method.

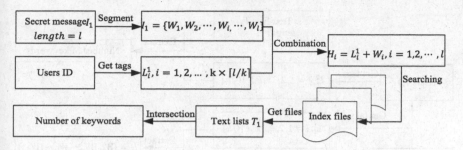

Fig. 3. The process of secret message hiding

The number of keywords will be hidden in the same text. Figure 4 shows the process of the number of keywords hiding.

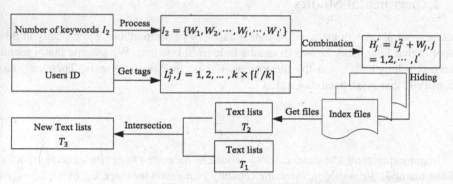

Fig. 4. The process of the number of keywords hiding

3.2 The Process of Information Extraction

By using the texts and user's ID, the secret message can be extracted from texts. The process of the secret message extraction is described as follows:

(1) Use user's ID and the number of texts to get the location tags L_j^2.
(2) By using L_j^2 and the texts T_i, the message I_2 which represents the number of keywords in each text will be extracted.
(3) Based on the number of keywords, we can know that how many keywords in each text, and the length of the secret message l.
(4) The same to step (1), take ID and l to get a list of location tags L_i^1.
(5) Use L_i^1, the number of keywords in each text and the texts, to extract the secret message I_1 from these texts.

Figure 5 shows the process of information extraction.

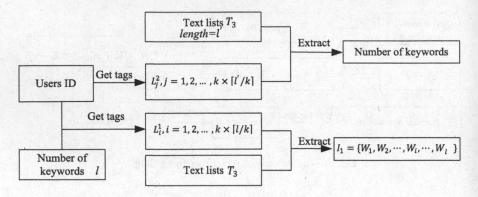

Fig. 5. The process of information extraction

4 Experimental Studies

In this section, we will measure the hiding capacity of our method. The capacity in this paper is that how many keywords can be hidden in one text. We assume that a secret message's length is l, and the message would be hidden in m texts. Therefore, the capacity C can be defined as Eq. (2).

$$C = \frac{l}{m} \tag{2}$$

In our experiment, the mean capacity would be measured to get the general capacity of our method. We would measure the capacity of n secret message C_i ($i = 1, 2, \cdots, n$) and take the average of the capacity C_i. The average of C_i named $\bar{C}$ can be calculated by Eq. (3).

$$\bar{C} = \frac{1}{n} \sum_{i=1}^{n} C_i \tag{3}$$

In our experiment, our method is compared with the coverless information hiding method based on Chinese mathematical expression, denoted as CME-CIHM [18]. The experiment employs the dataset from the Sogou Labs [23]. The experimental results are composed of the capacity of each secret message and the mean capacity of the coverless information hiding method. The capacity of each secret message can be computed by using the Eq. (2). Figure 6 shows the capacity of each secret message. We find that the maximum capacity is 1.77, and the minimum capacity is 1.29. The capacity of each secret message is greater than 1. The mean capacity is 1.57. That implies that our method can enhance the capacity to some extent. Consequently, our proposed method is effective in improving the hiding capacity.

According to the results of experiment, the mean capacity would be calculated by the Eq. (3), and the consequence of the mean capacity is shown in Table 1.

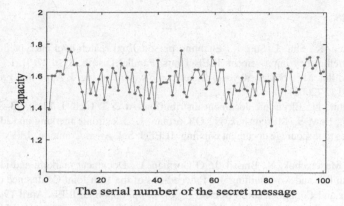

Fig. 6. The capacity of each secret message

Table 1. Experimental results

Methods	Mean capacity
CME-CIHM [18]	1
Our method	1.57

5 Conclusion

In this paper, we propose a new method to improve the capacity of the coverless information hiding. In order to prove the validity of our method, 100 texts are selected from the Sogou Labs as the secret message to measure the capacity of the method. According the results, the capacity of coverless information hiding is improved to a certain extent. However, the improvement of the method is limited. The main reason is the underutilization of the text when we indexed the text database. Moreover, our method hide the number in Chinese text. However, there are few numbers in one text. As a consequence, the success rate of the method is low. Future work will focus on how to create a mapping relationship to map the number into Chinese keywords, and improve the utilization of text in building index files.

Acknowledgments. This work was supported in part by the National Natural Science Foundation of China under Grant 61602253, Grant U1536206, Grant 61232016, Grant U1405254, Grant 61373133, Grant 61502242, and Grant 61572258, in part by the Jiangsu Basic Research Programs-Natural Science Foundation under Grant BK20150925,BK20151530 in part by the Priority Academic Program Development of Jiangsu Higher Education Institutions (PAPD) fund, in part by the Collaborative Innovation Center of Atmospheric Environment and Equipment Technology (CICAEET) fund, and in part by College Students Practice Innovation Training Program under Grant 201610300022, China.

References

1. Fu, Z., Ren, K., Shu, J., Sun, X.: Enabling personalized search over encrypted outsourced data with efficiency improvement. IEEE Trans. Parallel Distrib. Syst. **27**(9), 1 (2015)
2. Cox, I., Miller, M.: The first 50 years of electronic watermarking. J. Appl. Sig. Process. **2002** (2), 126–132 (2002)
3. Maxemchuk, N.: Electronic document distribution. At & T Tech. J. **73**(5), 73–80 (1994)
4. Brassil, J., Low, S., Maxemchuk, N., O'Gorman, L.: Electronic marking and identification techniques to discourage document copying. IEEE J. Sel. Areas Commun. **13**(8), 1495–1504 (1995)
5. Low, S., Maxemchuk, N., Brassil, J., O'Gorman, L.: Document marking and identification using both line and word shifting. In: Proceedings of the 14th Joint Conference of the IEEE Computer and Communications Societies, vol. 2, pp. 853–853. IEEE, April 1995
6. Brassil, J., Low, S., Maxemchuk, N., O'Gorman, L.: Electronic marking and identification techniques to discourage document copying. IEEE J. Sel. Areas Commun. **13**(8), 1495–1504 (1995)
7. Low, S., Maxemchuk, N., Lapone, A.: Document identification for copyright protection using centroid detection. IEEE Trans. Commun. **46**(3), 372–383 (1998)
8. Low, S., Maxemchuk, N.: Performance comparison of two text marking methods. IEEE J. Sel. Areas Commun. **16**(4), 561–572 (1998)
9. Brassil, J., Low, S., Maxemchuk, N.: Copyright protection for the electronic distribution of text documents. Proc. IEEE **87**(7), 1181–1196 (1999)
10. Xia, Z., Wang, X., Sun, X., Wang, B.: Steganalysis of least significant bit matching using multi-order differences. Secur. Commun. Netw. **7**(8), 1283–1291 (2014)
11. Mielikainen, J.: LSB matching revisited. IEEE Sig. Process. Lett. **13**(5), 285–287 (2006)
12. Xia, Z., Wang, X., Sun, X., Liu, Q., Xiong, N.: Steganalysis of LSB matching using differences between nonadjacent pixels. Multimedia Tools Appl. **75**(4), 1–16 (2014)
13. Li, Z., Chen, X., Pan, X., Zheng, X.: Lossless data hiding scheme based on adjacent pixel difference. In: International Conference Computer Engineering and Technology, vol. 1, pp. 588–592. IEEE Computer Society, January 2009
14. Li, X., Wang, J.: A steganographic method based upon JPEG and particle swarm optimization algorithm. Inf. Sci. Int. J. **177**(15), 3099–3109 (2007)
15. Zhou, Z., Sun, H., Harit, R., Chen, X., Sun, X.: Coverless image steganography without embedding. In: Huang, Z., et al. (eds.) ICCCS 2015. LNCS, vol. 9483, pp. 123–132. Springer, Heidelberg (2015). doi:10.1007/978-3-319-27051-7_11
16. Fu, Z., Sun, X., Liu, Q., Zhou, L., Shu, J.: Achieving efficient cloud search services: multi-keyword ranked search over encrypted cloud data supporting parallel computing. IEICE Trans. Commun. **E98.B**(1), 190–200 (2015)
17. Shahrokh, H., Mosayeb, N.: A novel LSB based quantum watermarking. Int. J. Theor. Phys. **55**(10), 1–14 (2016)
18. Chen, X., Sun, H., Tobe, Y., Zhou, Z., Sun, X.: Coverless information hiding method based on the chinese mathematical expression. In: Huang, Z., et al. (eds.) ICCCS 2015. LNCS, vol. 9483, pp. 133–143. Springer, Heidelberg (2015). doi:10.1007/978-3-319-27051-7_12
19. Xia, Z., Wang, X., Sun, X., Wang, Q.: A secure and dynamic multi-keyword ranked search scheme over encrypted cloud data. IEEE Trans. Parallel Distrib. Syst. **27**(2), 340–352 (2015)
20. Duric, Z., Jacobs, M., Jajodia, S.: Information hiding: steganography and steganalysis. Handb. Stat. **24**, 171–187 (2005)

21. Sun, X., Chen, H., Yang, L., Tang, Y.: Mathematical representation of a Chinese character and its applications. Int. J. Pattern Recognit. Artif. Intell. **16**(6), 735–748 (2011)
22. Liu, Y., Sun, X., Cox, I.J., Wang, H.: Natural language information hiding based on Chinese mathematical expression. Int. J. Netw. Secur. **8**(1), 10–15 (2009)
23. Sogou Labs. http://download.labs.sogou.com/

Reversible Data Hiding with Low Bit-Rate Growth in H.264/AVC Compressed Video by Adaptive Hybrid Coding

Tian-Qi Wang[✉], Hong-Xia Wang, and Yue Li

School of Information Science and Technology,
Southwest Jiaotong University, Chengdu 611756, China
tianqiwang@my.swjtu.edu.cn, hxwang@swjtu.edu.cn

Abstract. For the reversible data hiding algorithm in compressed-domain videos, secret data embedding process usually lead to a large bit-rate growth of video stream, thus the imperceptibility and security will be decreased. In order to solve this problem, a reversible data hiding algorithm with low bit-rate growth in H.264/AVC compressed video by adaptive hybrid coding is proposed in this paper. In the proposed scheme, the hybrid coding algorithm has been adaptively applied on different trailing coefficients, which makes the algorithm have a considerable embedding capacity and a low bit-rate growth. Compared with the existing reversible data hiding algorithm for video, the proposed scheme has a lower bit-rate growth with the same hiding capacity.

Keywords: Reversible data hiding · Compressed video · H.264/AVC · Adaptive hybrid coding · Bit-rate

1 Introduction

Data hiding is a kind of technique, which the secret data are embedded in the various communication signals, and it is widely applied in domains such as covert communication, media annotation and integrity authentication [1], etc. Video, as a carrier of data hiding technique, is a kind of multimedia which contains large amount of data, and nowadays H.264/Advanced Video Coding (H.264/AVC) as a compression coding standard of video at domestic and overseas has been widely used. In the video domain, data hiding technique can be roughly categorized as watermarking, steganography, error recovery (resilient), and general data embedding [2]. But in most of data hiding technique, the operation of embedding will destroy the video quality permanently [3]. Due to the requirements of application in some special fields, such as medical imaging, military video and forensic, etc., it is sometimes desired that the embedded video can be losslessly restored to the original video after extracting the hidden data [4].

Reversible data hiding is proposed for the first time by Ref. [5]. After that, there are a lot of literature, such as Refs. [6–9], proposed the related algorithms and applications. In the existing algorithms, histogram compression and histogram shifting is relatively advanced reversible data hiding scheme. Ref. [10] give full consideration to the intra-prediction mode, so that the phenomenon of distortion drift is avoided when we

© Springer International Publishing AG 2016
X. Sun et al. (Eds.): ICCCS 2016, Part I, LNCS 10039, pp. 48–62, 2016.
DOI: 10.1007/978-3-319-48671-0_5

hiding data into video, and the video quality of the embedded video is improved. In Ref. [11], the Motion Vector (MV) of current Macro Block (MB) is reversibly embedded into the neighboring MB as an important data, so that the video error resilience is realized. In Ref. [12], the histogram shifting algorithm is combined with BCH syndrome code, thereby improving the robustness of the proposed scheme. Due to the large amount of data in the I-frame and a large number of secret data can be hided, the process of data hiding in Ref. [10–12] is implemented in I-frame, but the process of data hiding in Ref. [13, 14] is implemented in P-frame, and the reversible data hiding in the encrypted domain is implemented in Ref. [13, 14] by using the code table of entropy coding.

Although the reversible video data hiding algorithms of the above literature have a large embedding capacity and a better embedded video quality, the bit-rate growth of the embedded video is big. In order to solve this problem, a reversible data hiding algorithm with low bit-rate growth in compressed-domain videos via adaptive hybrid coding is proposed. The proposed scheme has a considerable embedding capacity and a low bit-rate growth. In view of the distorted successive effect of I-frame, we do the hiding process in P-frame. In this paper, the entropy coding – Context-based Adaptive Variable Length Coding (CAVLC) of H.264/AVC is fully considered, and the secret data is embedded in trailing coefficients of P-frame. Meanwhile, the adaptive hybrid coding is proposed by combining the histogram shifting algorithm and matrix coding, and it can effectively reduce the bit-rate growth of embedded video.

The rest of the paper is organized as follows. In Sect. 2, we explain the location and the process of the embedding in more detail. In Sect. 3, we present the experimental results and analysis with different parameters, and compared the proposed scheme with Refs. [3, 13] in various performance. Finally, the conclusion and directions of future work are drawn in Sect. 4.

2 Reversible Data Hiding Scheme for H.264/AVC Video

A reversible video data hiding scheme based on H.264/AVC is proposed in this paper. The proposed scheme includes three parts. They are data embedding, data extraction and video recovery.

2.1 Embedding Location

In the view of video coding, the secret data is embedded in the residual coefficients of P-frame after the transform, quantization and Zig-zag scan. As for application, the location of embedding, as shown in Fig. 1, is after the entropy decoding of the original video sequence and before the inverse process of Zig-zag scan. The first reason for this is that the modifications of residual coefficients in I-frame may lead to distortion drift, and the modifications will have an effect on surplus P-frame and B-frame in Group of Pictures (GOP). The second reason is that the adoption of P-frame is more often than I-frame in video sequence GOP. The last reason is that we need to avoid the great changing of the original video to increase the bit-rate growth of embedded video.

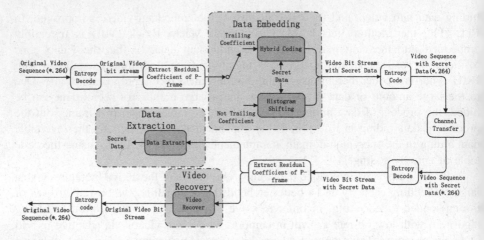

Fig. 1. The framework of proposed scheme

Therefore, the process of embedding is after the entropy decoding and before the inverse process of Zig-zag scan to avoid getting into the reconstruction loop. The location of secret data extraction and video recovery are shown in Fig. 1.

2.2   Data Embedding

In the H.264/AVC, there are two kinds of entropy encoding, CAVLC and Context-based Adaptive Binary Arithmetic Coder (CABAC), the proposed scheme in this paper is based on the CAVLC. CAVLC is used to code the Quantized Discrete Cosine Transform Coefficients (QDCTC) of residual. Each CAVLC codeword can be expressed as the following format [14]:

$$\{Coeff\_token, Sign\_of\_TrailingOnes, Level\_codeword, Total\_zeros, Run\_before\} \quad (1)$$

The *Sign_of_Trailingones* (bit sign of trailing coefficients), *Total_zeros* (total number of zero coefficients) and *Run_before* (the number of continuous zero coefficients of run coding) should remain unchanged. The secret data embedding can be accomplished by modifying the codeword of *Coeff_token* and *Level_codeword*. The *Coeff_token* is CAVLC codeword of *Trailingones* (trailing coefficients) and *Total-Coeffs* (the number of NQDCTC (Non-zero QDCTC)). The *Level_codeword* is CAVLC codeword of *Level* (the NQDCTC excluding trailing coefficients) in current 4 × 4 block. Each *Level_codeword* can be expressed as the following format [14]:

$$Level\ codeword = [level\_prefix], [level\_suffix] \quad (2)$$

The *level_prefix* is prefixed codeword and the *level_suffix* is suffixed codeword. The *suffixLength* is the bit length of level_prefix. When *suffixLength* == 0, *Level* is the last *Level* coefficients of the current 4 × 4 block. In order to distinguish that the first trailing coefficient whether be changed or not by data embedding, we need to do some modification of this last *Level*. Therefore, in the proposed scheme, some different embedded algorithms are adopted adaptively in different value of *suffixLength*. We use the histogram shifting algorithm to embed the secret data when *suffixLength* $\neq 0$. When *suffixLength* $== 0$, the hybrid coding algorithm is used to embed data in the trailing coefficients.

In data-hider, the secret data W is shown as the following format:

$$W = \{w_l | l = 1, 2, \cdots, M, w_l \in \{0, 1\}\} \tag{3}$$

The *NQDCTC* of 4×4 block of luma MB in P-frame is shown as the following format:

$$\{f_{i,j}(k) | i, j \in \{0, 1, 2, 3\}; k < TotalCoeffs; TotalCoeffs \in \{0, 1, 2, \cdots, 15\}\} \tag{4}$$

The modified coefficients $f_{i,j}(k)$ is expressed as $\overline{f_{i,j}}(k)$. The $f_{i,j}(k)|_{k=t}$ are the trailing coefficients after $zig - zag$ scan. The $f_{i,j}(k)|_{k=z}$ is the last *Level*. Now, we will particularly explain the proposed algorithm under two cases of *suffixLength* $\neq 0$ and *suffixLength* $== 0$, respectively.

(1) Case 1: *suffixLength* $\neq 0$

The *suffixLength* $\neq 0$ means $k \in \{0, 1, 2, \cdots, z - 1\}$ in $f_{i,j}(k)$, the histogram shifting algorithm with peak $|N| = 1$ is used to embed the secret data W.

When $|f_{i,j}(k)| > |N|$, the modified coefficients $\overline{f_{i,j}}(k)$ is shown as the following format:

$$\overline{f_{i,j}}(k) = \begin{cases} f_{i,j}(k) + 1, & f_{i,j}(k) > 0 \\ f_{i,j}(k) - 1, & f_{i,j}(k) < 0 \end{cases}, \quad k \in \{0, 1, 2, \cdots, z - 1\}, |N| = 1 \tag{5}$$

When $|f_{i,j}(k)| = |N|$, use the following format:

$$\overline{f_{i,j}}(k) = \begin{cases} f_{i,j}(k) + 1, & f_{i,j}(k) > 0 \text{ and } w_l == 1 \\ f_{i,j}(k) - 1, & f_{i,j}(k) < 0 \text{ and } w_l == 1 \\ f_{i,j}(k), & w_l == 0 \end{cases}, \quad k \in \{0, 1, 2, \cdots, z - 1\}, |N| = 1 \tag{6}$$

(2) Case 2: *suffixLength* $== 0$

The *suffixLength* $== 0$ means $k == z$ in $f_{i,j}(k)$, and the $f_{i,j}(z)$ is the last *Level* in current 4×4 block. In order to reduce the bit-rate growth of data embedding, the hybrid coding algorithm is used to embed the secret data into the trailing coefficients in the proposed scheme. According to the different value of *TrailingOnes*, $f_{i,j}(z)$ is modified in different way.

The value range of *TrailingOnes* is *TrailingOnes* $\in \{0, 1, 2, 3\}$. If we embed the secret data by format (6), the *TrailingOnes* will be changed and the bits number of *Coeff_token* will substantial increase according to the Table 1. So we need to reduce

Table 1. Experimental results of the proposed scheme with different video sequences (Akiyo, Hall, Carphone, News, Foreman, Bridge-Close, Coastguard, Table and Mobile)

Video name	QP	Standard PSNR (dB)	Bit-rate (kbts/s)	Embedding capacity (bits)	Bit-rate growth (%)	PSNR_dif (dB)	PSNR_var_5k (dB)	BR_var_5k (%)	MC_0.01 (bits)
Akiyo	24	41.66	187.7472	3551	0.7005	0.14	0.2	0.9864	5069
	28	38.93	130.1616	1124	0.3374	0.05	0.24	1.501	3331
	32	36.07	91.0416	284	0.1213	0.02	0.31	2.1349	2342
Hall	24	40.4	261.972	11027	1.7425	0.69	0.31	0.7901	6328
	28	38	179.472	5992	1.3653	0.42	0.35	1.1393	4389
	32	35.22	123.9936	2920	0.9871	0.2	0.35	1.6903	2958
Carphone	24	40.65	286.5408	16309	2.2481	0.62	0.19	0.6892	7255
	28	37.96	183.8952	6524	1.4239	0.31	0.24	1.0912	4582
	32	35.32	119.508	2193	0.7933	0.12	0.28	1.8086	2765
News	24	40.42	299.3496	12198	1.6644	0.49	0.2	0.6822	7329
	28	37.5	208.0464	5944	1.1767	0.28	0.23	0.9898	5052
	32	34.49	143.9424	2524	0.7336	0.13	0.25	1.4533	3440
Foreman	24	39.55	356.1216	19884	2.567	0.78	0.2	0.6455	7746
	28	36.96	232.1112	9264	1.8715	0.45	0.24	1.0101	4950
	32	34.35	152.1672	4167	1.2555	0.22	0.26	1.5064	3319
Bridge-Close	24	38.34	427.4592	38542	2.7646	0.73	0.09	0.3587	13941
	28	35.4	235.0704	14563	1.8816	0.29	0.1	0.646	7739
	32	32.72	130.2912	3547	0.8971	0.1	0.13	1.2645	3954
Coastguard	24	37.58	617.8584	82669	4.7786	1.19	0.07	0.289	17300
	28	34.48	358.608	32713	3.3376	0.48	0.07	0.5101	9801
	32	31.67	190.9344	9514	1.8729	0.19	0.1	0.9843	5080
Table	24	37.63	723.0312	81207	4.1167	1.76	0.11	0.2535	19726
	28	34.67	424.4016	37229	3.3104	1.04	0.14	0.4446	11246
	32	32.13	238.6536	16093	2.5523	0.62	0.19	0.793	6305
Mobile	24	37.31	1092.0216	117392	3.6659	1.62	0.07	0.1561	32023
	28	33.88	682.0992	45627	2.2969	0.67	0.07	0.2517	19865
	32	30.62	417.8928	13990	1.14	0.21	0.08	0.4074	12272

the time spent on modifications of trailing coefficients while ensure the scheme to have a considerable embedding capacity. In order to solve this problem, the hybrid coding algorithm is proposed in this paper.

The hybrid coding algorithm is proposed by combining the histogram shifting algorithm and matrix coding. The essence of hybrid coding is that, we judge whether the bit is modified or not by utilize the histogram shifting algorithm, so that we only need $\{b_0, b_1, \cdots, b_i\}$ of bit stream s to embed the data and the rest bit stream $\{b_{t+1}, \cdots, b_n\}$ of s can be used to embed the next data. In this way, the inherent advantage of matrix coding is retained, the occupied resources of data embedding are saved and embedding capacity is increased by using the histogram shifting algorithm.

The process of 4 bits data embedding is explained as following. The *num* is used to count the number of trailing coefficients $f_{i,j}(t)$, the pseudocode of data embedding is shown as following:

$$(w_l, w_{l+1}, w_{l+2}, w_{l+3})_B \rightarrow (m_l)_D$$

$num = 0$

while the 4 bits data embedding is unfinished

{

    if $f_{i,j}(k)|k == t$,   *current coefficient is trailing ones*

    {

        if $num == m_l$

$$\overline{f_{i,j}}(t) = \begin{cases} f_{i,j}(t) + 1 & ,f_{i,j}(t) == +1 \\ f_{i,j}(t) - 1 & ,f_{i,j}(t) == -1 \end{cases} \tag{7}$$

        else

            $num + +$

    }

    read the next $f_{i,j}(k)$

}

In order to extract the secret data in data extracting side, the $f_{i,j}(z)$ in the case of $TrailingOnes \neq 3$ need to be modified by using histogram shifting with peak $|N| = 2$, the format is shown as following:

$$\overline{f_{i,j}}(z) = \begin{cases} f_{i,j}(z) + 1, & f_{i,j}(z) \geq |N| \\ f_{i,j}(z) - 1, & f_{i,j}(z) \leq -|N| \end{cases}, \quad |N| = 2 \tag{8}$$

2.3 Data Extraction and Video Recovery

For data extracting side, secret data need to be extracted from the embedded video, and the video need to be recovered, this is the inverse process of data embedding. In the following, we will describe how to extract the secret data under two cases of *suffixLength* $\neq 0$ and *suffixLength* $== 0$, respectively.

(1) *suffixLength* $\neq 0$

For data extracting side, when $\overline{f_{i,j}}(k) != 0$, the secret data W can be extracted by the following equation:

$$w_l = \begin{cases} 0, & |\overline{f_{i,j}}(k)| == |N| \\ 1, & |\overline{f_{i,j}}(k)| == |N| + 1 \end{cases}, \quad k \in \{0, 1, 2, \cdots, z-1\}, |N| = 1 \tag{9}$$

and $\overline{f_{i,j}}(k)$ can be recovered to $f_{i,j}(k)$ by the following format:

$$f_{i,j}(k) = \begin{cases} \overline{f_{i,j}}(k) - 1, & \overline{f_{i,j}}(k) > |N| \\ \overline{f_{i,j}}(k) + 1, & \overline{f_{i,j}}(k) < -|N| \\ \overline{f_{i,j}}(k), & |\overline{f_{i,j}}(k)| == |N| \end{cases}, \ k \in \{0,1,2,\cdots,z-1\}, |N| = 1 \quad (10)$$

(2) *suffixLength* $== 0$

According to the different data embedding, the data extraction and video recovery have corresponding algorithm. At first, the number of trailing coefficients before embedding *Original_TrailingOnes* need to be extracted by using the following format:

$$Original\_TrailingOnes = \begin{cases} TotalCoeffs - 1 - k, & |\overline{f_{i,j}}(k)| > |N| \\ 3, & |\overline{f_{i,j}}(k)| \le |N| \ and \ TotalCoeffs - k == 3, \{|N| = 2\} \\ undetermined, |\overline{f_{i,j}}(k)| \le |N| \ and \ TotalCoeffs - k < 3 \end{cases} \quad (11)$$

In the format, the input sequence of current coefficients is inverted order, the first input is $k = TotalCoeffs - 1$, if the output is *"undetermined"* the next one is $k = k - 1$ and so on. After we get *Original_TrailingOnes*, the current coefficients can be recovered to the original one by using the following equation:

$$f_{i,j}(k) = \begin{cases} \overline{f_{i,j}}(k) - 1, & \overline{f_{i,j}}(k) > 0 \\ \overline{f_{i,j}}(k) + 1, & \overline{f_{i,j}}(k) < 0 \end{cases} \quad \begin{cases} k = TotalCoeffs - 1 - Original\_TrailingOnes \\ and \ Original\_TrailingOnes \ne 3 \end{cases} \quad (12)$$

Then the number of continuous $|\overline{f_{i,j}}(k)| == 1, \{k \ge TotalCoeffs - Original\_TrailingOnes\}$ is recorded in *num*, Then the 4 bits secret data can be extracted and the coefficients can be recovered by using the procedure as following pseudocode:

> $num = 0$
> *while the 4 bits data extraction is unfinished*
> {
> $\quad$ *if* $|\overline{f_{i,j}}(k)| == 1$
> $\quad$ $num++$
> $\quad$ *else*
> $\quad$ {   (13)
> $\quad\quad (num)_D \to (w_i, w_{i+1}, w_{i+2}, w_{i+3})_B$
> $\quad\quad f_{i,j}(k) = \begin{cases} \overline{f_{i,j}}(k) - 1, \overline{f_{i,j}}(k) == 2 \\ \overline{f_{i,j}}(k) + 1, \overline{f_{i,j}}(k) == -2 \end{cases}$
> $\quad$ }
> $\quad$ *read the next* $\overline{f_{i,j}}(k), k \ge TotalCoeffs - Original\_TrailingOnes$
> }

3   Experimental Results and Analysis

The proposed scheme has been implemented in the H.264/AVC JM-8.6 reference software. Nine well-known standard video sequences (i.e., Akiyo, Hall, Carphone, News, Foreman, Bridge-Close, Coastguard, Table and Mobile) in Quarter Common Intermediate Format (QCIF) format (176 × 144) at the frame rate of 30 frames/s are used for this simulation. The first 100 frames in each video sequence are used in the experiments. The GOP structure is "IPPPP: one I-frame followed by four P-frames [Quantization Parameter (QP): 24, 28, 32]" [13].

3.1   Experimental Results and Performance Analysis

The experimental results of the proposed scheme with different video sequences are shown as the following Table 1. When the embedding capacity is 5 kbits, the *PSNR_var_5k* is the decrease of PSNR between embedded video and original video, and the *BR_var_5k* is bit-rate growth of embedded video. The *MC_0.01* is the MC (maximum capacity) of embedding when the bit-rate growth is 1 %.

3.1.1   Embedding Capacity

We can see that there is a great difference of the MC between different video sequences in Table 1. For video sequence "Mobile", the MC is 117392 bits when $QP == 24$, but for video "Akiyo", the MC is only 284 bits when $QP == 32$, there are hundreds of times between them. By observed, we found that the MC is relate to the complexity of video content and the QP of coding process. As we can see from the changing trends in the Table 1, the MC tends to increase with increasing in bit-rate of the original video, and for a certain video the MC tends to decrease with increasing in QP. Generally, for a certain video, the smaller the QP, the larger the quantized coefficients, and the more the NQDCTC, therefore the bit-rate of video will increase with decreasing in QP. From the perspective of algorithm, the secret data is embedded into the quantized coefficients which the absolute value $|NQDCTC| == 1$, with the bit-rate of video sequence increasing, growing number of quantized coefficients conforms with the condition of embedding, thereby the more secret data can be embedded.

3.1.2   Bit-Rate Variety

For video sequences, if the memory spaces, which is occupied by embedded video or original video, have a huge difference, it is easy to arouse suspicion and expose the fact that the embedded video have secret data. Therefore the bit-rate growth of embedded video need to be as small as possible, it is an important performance for data hiding. The bit-rate growth is shown as the following equation:

$$BR\_var = \frac{BR\_em - BR\_orig}{BR\_orig} \times 100\% \qquad (14)$$

The *BR_em* is the bit-rate of the embedded video, and *BR_orig* is the bit-rate of the original video. The bit-rate growth *BR_var* of the proposed scheme for different video sequences are shown in Table 1, but because the embedding capacity of each video is different, the *BR_var* is different too. In order to have a reasonable comparison, we introduce a new performance index about bit-rate growth. The new performance index is an bit-rate growth when embedding capacity is a constant value *C*, in this paper, we set *C* = 5000. The new performance index *BR_var_5k* is equal to:

$$BR\_var\_5k = \frac{5000}{MC} \times BR\_var \tag{15}$$

Furthermore, we introduce *MC_0.01* to observe the situation of bit-rate growth intuitively. The *MC_0.01* is the maximum capacity of scheme when *BR_var* == 1%, and is equal to:

$$MC\_0.01 = \frac{MC}{BR\_var} \tag{16}$$

BR_var_5k and *MC_0.01* express the bit-rate growth of data hiding in different aspects. As shown in Table 1, along with the increasing of bit-rate of the original video, the *MC_0.01* tends to increase and the *BR_var_5k* tends to decrease. In other words, generally, the larger the bit-rate of the original video, the smaller the bit-rate growth of embedded video, when we embed same amount of secret data. In the same way, the larger the bit-rate of the original video, the larger the maximum capacity generally, with the same variation of *BR_var* of embedded video. Analyzed from the perspective of theory, the larger the bit-rate, the more the number of quantized coefficients, and the number of trailing coefficients will increase. As shown in 2.2.2, the secret data can be embedded into the trailing coefficients with slightly modification, so that the bit-rate has a high utilization, the proposed scheme increase the *MC_0.01* and decrease the *BR_var_5k*.

3.1.3 Video Quality

The embedded video quality is another important influence factor of the imperceptibility of reversible video data hiding, the big visual differences of embedded video and original video is unacceptable. To investigate the embedded video quality, an original frame from some videos are given in Fig. 2, and their corresponding embedded results and the differences between original and embedded frame are shown in Figs. 3 and 4.

In this paper, we select Peak Signal to Noise Ratio (PSNR) to evaluate the video quality. The PSNR is small means that there is a huge difference between the contradistinctive videos. Inversely, the PSNR is big means that the difference between the contradistinctive videos is small.

In Table 1, we list the PSNR about original videos and embedded videos. Since H.264/AVC is a lossy compression, in order to better illustrate the data hiding on the video quality, we should test the visual quality of an original video stream. The "Standard PSNR" is the PSNR between original video stream (YUV) and standard video stream (YUV) after encoding and decoding process. In order to test the visual quality of embedded video stream, we calculate "Embedded PSNR" which is the PSNR between original video stream (YUV) and embedded video stream (YUV) after

Fig. 2. Original video frames

Fig. 3. Embedded video frames

encoding and decoding process. The *PSNR_dif* in Table 1 is the different value between "Standard PSNR" and "Embedded PSNR". Due to the difference of video capacity for different video sequences, the *PSNR_dif* has no comparability. So we introduce *PSNR_dif_5k* which means the *PSNR_dif* when embedding capacity is a constant value C, and we set $C = 5000$. From Table 1, we can see that the variation of *PSNR_dif_5k* is not very consistent, but in generally, the tendency of *PSNR_dif_5k* is

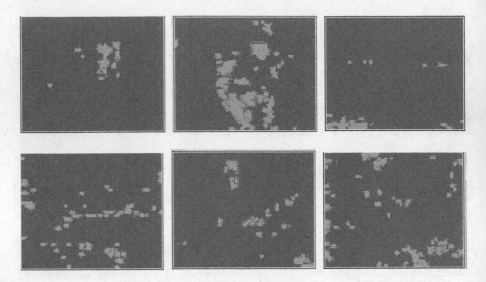

Fig. 4. The differences of original video and embedded video

reduce along with the increasing of bit-rate of video. The reason of this tendency is as same as the variation of bit-rate growth, taken together, the bigger the proportion of embedded secret data by using hybrid coding, the better the performance of reversible data hiding.

3.2   Performance Comparison

From the embedding location and manner, we find that the Refs. [3, 13] is similar with this paper in recent years. In order to explain the performance of the proposed scheme concretely, we compare the performance of Refs. [3, 13] and the proposed scheme in same parameters. The results of the comparison is shown as the following:

In Table 2, we list the MC, *PSNR_dif_5k*, *BR_var_5k* and *MC_0.01* of three schemes for different videos, due to the absence of Ref. [3] in some videos, the information about "Table" and "Mobile" is not shown in Table 2. Now we will analyze the performance from three aspects, bit-rate growth, maximum capacity and video quality. From Table 2, we can see that when video sequence is "Hall" and $QP = 24$, the *BR_var_5k* of the proposed scheme is 0.84 times of Ref. [13], and *MC_0.01* is 1.19 times of Ref. [13]. And when $QP = 32$, the *BR_var_5k* of the proposed scheme is 0.65 times of Ref. [13], and *MC_0.01* is 1.54 times of Ref. [13]. From the "Average Performance", we can see that, when $QP = 24$ the *BR_var_5k* of the proposed scheme is less than Ref. [13] 15.26 %, and *MC_0.01* is more than Ref. [13] 11.77 %. When $QP = 32$ the *BR_var_5k* of the proposed scheme is less than Ref. [13] 34.53 %, and *MC_0.01* is more than Ref. [13] 50.13 %. In order to compare the performance of bit-rate growth intuitively, we draw the Fig. 5 as follows:

Table 2. Performances comparison between the proposed scheme and Refs. [3, 13]. (a): Maximum Capacity (bits). (b): PSNR_var_5k (dB). (c): BR_var_5k (%). (d): MC_0.01 (bits).

Sequence		[13]	[3]	Proposed	[13]	[3]	Proposed	[13]	[3]	Proposed
QP		24			28			32		
Bit-rate (kbts/s)		261.972			179.472			123.9936		
Hall	(a)	12316	11255	11027	5437	4928	5992	2302	2098	2920
	(b)	0.22	0.21	0.31	0.27	0.26	0.35	0.3	0.29	0.35
	(c)	0.9378	0.964	0.7901	1.5634	1.6437	1.1393	2.6064	2.693	1.6903
	(d)	5332	5187	6328	3198	3042	4389	1918	1857	2958
Bit-rate (kbts/s)		286.5408			183.8952			119.508		
Carphone	(a)	18792	16468	16309	6036	5194	6524	1537	1339	2193
	(b)	0.18	0.18	0.19	0.2	0.19	0.24	0.26	0.26	0.28
	(c)	0.8567	0.8775	0.6892	1.5739	1.6461	1.0912	2.7001	2.8006	1.8086
	(d)	5836	5698	7255	3177	3037	4582	1852	1785	2765
Bit-rate (kbts/s)		299.3496			208.0464			143.9424		
News	(a)	11668	10559	12198	5139	4597	5944	1893	1686	2524
	(b)	0.22	0.21	0.2	0.23	0.23	0.23	0.26	0.27	0.25
	(c)	0.8785	0.8902	0.6822	1.3913	1.4466	0.9898	2.3244	2.3428	1.4533
	(d)	5692	5616	7329	3594	3456	5052	2151	2134	3440
Bit-rate (kbts/s)		356.1216			232.1112			152.1672		
Foreman	(a)	20505	18681	19884	5259	4689	9264	1245	1070	4167
	(b)	0.12	0.12	0.2	0.15	0.15	0.24	0.2	0.23	0.26
	(c)	0.6852	0.7039	0.6455	1.3311	1.3862	1.0101	2.4096	2.4766	1.5064
	(d)	7297	7103	7746	3756	3607	4950	2075	2019	3319
Bit-rate (kbts/s)		723.0312			424.4016			238.6536		
Table	(a)	96062		81207	40451		37229	16122		16093
	(b)	0.11		0.11	0.14		0.14	0.19		0.19
	(c)	0.2649		0.2535	0.5018		0.4446	0.9676		0.793
	(d)	18872		19726	9963		11246	5167		6305
Bit-rate (kbts/s)		1092.0216			682.0992			417.8928		
Mobile	(a)	140786		117392	49701		45627	12116		13990
	(b)	0.08		0.07	0.09		0.07	0.09		0.08
	(c)	0.173		0.1561	0.3229		0.2517	0.69		0.4074
	(d)	28909		32023	15483		19865	7525		12272
Bit-rate (kbts/s)		503.1728			318.3376			199.3596		
Average performance	(a)	50021.5		43002.8	18670.5		18430	5869.2		6981.2
	(b)	0.16		0.18	0.18		0.21	0.22		0.23
	(c)	0.6327		0.5361	1.1141		0.8211	1.9497		1.2765
	(d)	11989.7		13401.2	6528.5		8347.1	3448		5176.5

In Fig. 5 we show the bar chart of three schemes in *BR_var_5k* and *MC_0.01*, due to the absence of Ref. [3] in some videos, the information about "Table" and "Mobile" is not shown in Fig. 5. Obviously, from Fig. 5 we can see that the proposed scheme has a huge advantage than the other schemes in bit-rate growth. The bigger the QP, the more the advantages of the proposed scheme in bit-rate growth. The main reason is that, the secret data is embedded into trailing coefficients directly by using the scheme

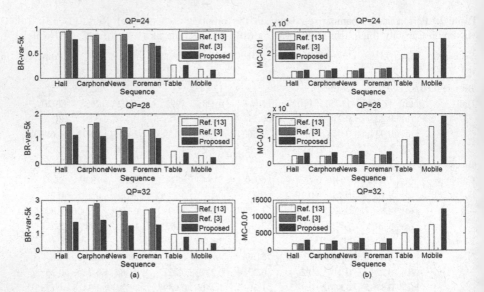

Fig. 5. The comparison of Refs. [3, 13] and the proposed scheme in bit-rate growth (a) *BR_var_5k* (b) *MC_0.01*

of Refs. [3, 13]. But in this paper, the secret data is embedded by using adaptive hybrid coding. By utilizing the characteristic of histogram shifting algorithm and matrix coding, adaptive hybrid coding compensate for the disadvantage of this two algorithms. The histogram shifting algorithm has a huge MC, but the modification of coefficients is big and the bit-rate growth is too large. The matrix coding can embed secret data with a tiny modification of coefficients, but the maximum capacity is small. In this paper, the adaptive hybrid coding is proposed by combining the histogram shifting algorithm and matrix coding, and it can provide a considerable embedding capacity and reduce the bit-rate growth of embedded video effectively. In histogram shifting algorithm, in order to embed the secret data reversibly, the original coefficients which are greater than peak value need to be modified. But this modification will do nothing for embedding capacity, and it will reduce the video quality. In consideration of this problem we embed the secret into the trailing coefficients by using histogram shifting with peak $|N| = 1$. In this way, we need not to modify the coefficients except the trailing ones, and we can avoid the unnecessary modifications. Therefore the more the trailing ones, the better the advantage of the proposed scheme in bit-rate growth.

For the maximum capacity and video quality, the MC and *PSNR_dif_5k* are be considered in this paper. In order to compare the performance of MC and video quality intuitively, we draw the Fig. 6 as the following:

From the manifestation of MC in Fig. 6(a), we can see that the MC of the proposed scheme is greater than Refs. [3, 13] when $QP = 28$ or $QP = 32$. The data obtained by calculating the information in Table 2 shows that the MC of the proposed scheme is 1.69 times of Ref. [13] when $QP = 32$. The *PSNR_dif_5k* in Fig. 6(b) shows that the embedded video quality of the proposed scheme is slightly below other schemes. When $QP = 28$, the *PSNR_dif_5k* of the proposed scheme is 1.28 times of Ref. [3].

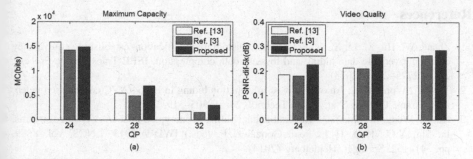

Fig. 6. The comparison of Refs. [3, 13] and this paper in MC and video quality (the data is the average of "Hall", "Carphone", "News" and "Foreman")

Theory analysis that the coefficients of MB have been eliminated by considered the characteristic of Direct Current (DC) or Alternating Current (AC) coefficients to embed data in Refs. [3, 13]. In the proposed scheme, the secret data is embedded into all AC coefficients, so the maximum capacity of the proposed scheme is better than Refs. [3, 13], but the embedded video quality is not.

4 Conclusions

Along with the development of data hiding technique and the continuously improve of the requirements in various fields, the reversible video data hiding becomes more and more important. In this paper, a reversible data hiding algorithm with low bit-rate growth in compressed-domain videos via adaptive hybrid coding is proposed. The proposed scheme has a considerable embedding capacity and a low bit-rate growth by adaptively applied the hybrid coding algorithm on different trailing coefficients in entropy coding. Compared with the existing reversible data hiding algorithm in video, the proposed scheme has a lower bit-rate growth when embed the same amount of secret data into the video. The lower bit-rate growth improve the imperceptibility of data hiding, and reduce the possibility of exposure of secret data.

Certainly, the reversible video data hiding algorithm with low bit-rate growth will get more and more attention, and this technique is in the initial stage of development, so there are many places need to be ameliorated and perfected. In the future, considerably more effort is needed to improve the performance of bit-rate growth in reversible video data hiding algorithm.

Acknowledgments. This work is supported by the National Natural Science Foundation of China (U1536110).

References

1. Zhang, W., Hu, X., Li, X., et al.: Recursive histogram modification: establishing equivalency between reversible data hiding and lossless data compression. IEEE Trans. Image Process. **22**(7), 2775–2785 (2013)
2. Tew, Y., Wong, K.S.: An overview of information hiding in H.264/AVC compressed video. IEEE Trans. Circuits Syst. Video Technol. **24**(2), 305–319 (2014)
3. Xu, D., Wang, R., Shi, Y.Q.: Reversible data hiding in encrypted H.264/AVC video streams. In: Shi, Y.Q., Kim, H.-J., Pérez-González, F. (eds.) IWDW 2013. LNCS, vol. 8389, pp. 141–152. Springer, Heidelberg (2014)
4. Liu, Y., Hu, M., Ma, X., et al.: A new robust data hiding method for H.264/AVC without intra-frame distortion drift. Neurocomputing **151**, 1076–1085 (2015)
5. Barton, J.M.: Method and apparatus for embedding authentication information within digital data: US. US 6047374 A[P] (2000)
6. Tian, J.: Reversible data embedding using a difference expansion. IEEE Trans. Circuits Syst. Video Technol. **13**(8), 890–896 (2003)
7. Ni, Z., Shi, Y.Q., Ansari, N., et al.: Reversible data hiding. IEEE Trans. Circuits Syst. Video Technol. **16**(3), 354–362 (2006)
8. Hu, Y., Lee, H.K., Li, J.: DE-based reversible data hiding with improved overflow location map. IEEE Trans. Circuits Syst. Video Technol. **19**(2), 250–260 (2009)
9. Zeng, X., Chen, Z., Xiong, Z.: Issues and solution on distortion drift in reversible video data hiding. Multimed. Tools Appl. **52**(2–3), 465–484 (2011)
10. Liu, Y.X., Li, Z., Ma, X.: Reversible data hiding scheme based on H.264/AVC without distortion drift. J. Softw. **7**(5), 1059–1065 (2012)
11. Li, R., Wang, R., Li, R., et al.: Video error resilience scheme using reversible data hiding technique for intra-frame in H.264/AVC. In: Proceedings of International Conference on Multimedia Technology, vol. 84, pp. 462–469 (2013)
12. Liu, Y., Ju, L., Hu, M., et al.: A robust reversible data hiding scheme for H.264 without distortion drift. Neurocomputing **151**, 1053–1062 (2015)
13. Xu, D., Wang, R.: Efficient reversible data hiding in encrypted H.264/AVC videos. J. Electron. Imaging **23**(5), 053022 (2014)
14. Xu, D., Wang, R., Shi, Y.Q.: Data hiding in encrypted H.264/AVC video streams by codeword substitution. IEEE Trans. Inf. Forensics Secur. **9**(4), 596–606 (2014)
15. H.264/AVC Reference Software JM8.6. http://iphome.hhi.de/suehring/tml/download/

An Information Hiding Algorithm for HEVC Based on Differences of Intra Prediction Modes

Qi Sheng, Rangding Wang$^{(\boxtimes)}$, Anshan Pei, and Bin Wang

College of Information Science and Engineering,
Ningbo University, Ningbo 315211, China
wangrangding@nbu.edu.cn

Abstract. Concerning the problem that the existing HEVC video data hiding algorithms have great influence on the video quality, a novel algorithm based on differences of intra prediction modes was proposed. During the process of 4×4 luminance prediction coding, we establish a mapping relationship between secret bits and differences of two consecutive intra predictions with directions and embed secret bits by modulating the prediction modes according to Lagrange rate distortion model. For two consecutive non-directional prediction modes, i.e. planar mode or DC mode, we embed the secret bits by modifying the prediction modes directly in order to increase the embedding capacity. The extraction of secret bits only requires decoding the intra prediction modes from the bit stream. The experimental results show that the average decrease of peak signal to noise ratio (PSNR) value was about 0.05 dB. Increment of bitrate was bounded to 1.1 %. The structural similarity (SSIM) values are all about 0.95. The experimental results indicate that the proposed algorithm has little impact on the video quality and also has considerable capacity.

Keywords: Information hiding · HEVC · Differences of prediction modes · Rate distortion

1 Introduction

With the rapid development of internet, advancement of information technology and popularization of digital multimedia, the multimedia flies are copied and tampered seriously so that the information security is attracting more and more attention [1]. Information hiding technology is developed quickly as the effective means of secret communication, multimedia integrity and authenticity authentication and copyright protection. Digital video information hiding is an important part of multimedia information hiding technology as its characteristics of large amount of data and high efficiency [2], which is usually stored and transmitted in compressed form.

HEVC is the latest video coding standard which is developed by the Joint Collaborative Team on Video Coding (JCT-VC). The main objective is to improve the coding efficiency which makes 50 % bitrate reduction under the premise of same video quality compared with H.264/AVC [3]. It will play an important role in the application of high resolution video. So the research on information hiding algorithm for HEVC has high practical significance and theoretical value.

© Springer International Publishing AG 2016
X. Sun et al. (Eds.): ICCCS 2016, Part I, LNCS 10039, pp. 63–74, 2016.
DOI: 10.1007/978-3-319-48671-0_6

Currently, most of the existing video information hiding algorithm are based on H.264/AVC. It can be divided into the flowing four categories according to the embedding locations: prediction mode, DCT coefficients, bit stream and motion vectors. The earliest information hiding based on prediction mode was presented in [4] which embedded secret information according to the mapping relationship between prediction modes and secret bits. But the method is not universal applicable because of the mapping relationship is established based on statistical results of multiple video testing sequences. Secret bits could embed not only in I frame but also in P frame and B frame by modulating their encoding modes in [5]. After that, an optimized processing for the macro block is carried out to improve the coding efficiency. The secret information is embedded by modulating the prediction modes of 4 × 4 luminance blocks which are selected by values of the reference pixels in [6]. Matrix coding is used in [7], it embedded 2 secret bits in 3 intra prediction modes and only one of them need to modified which reduced the distortion. Three secret bits were embedded in 7 modes by introduction of embedding matrix in [8]. Although the algorithm can efficiently avoid the fast grow of bit rate, the embedding capacity is not high.

However, the data hiding algorithm for HEVC is still in its infancy. Literature [9] presented a hiding algorithm based on prediction modes which uses LBP (Local Binary Patterns) screening high complexity texture as the embedding area and modifies the prediction modes according to the parity of the secret information. But the lossy compression technology of video lead to the difference in pixel at decoder compared with original pixel which caused the extraction of secret information error. Intra prediction modes of 4 × 4 luminance blocks are mapped to the angle values in [10] and secret bits were embedded according to the mapping relationship between the angle differences and secret information. However, the algorithm has a greater impact on the quality of the video and the capacity is insufficient because of the modulation range is too large. An information hiding algorithm for HEVC based on DCT/DST coefficients are proposed in [11]. It has the advantage in intra-frame error propagation-free and improving the visual effect of video.

From the analysis above, the video information hiding algorithm for HEVC has plenty of room for improvement. The paper proposed an information hiding algorithm based on differences of prediction modes. It embedded 2 secret bits or 3 secret bits in the difference of two continuous prediction directions of intra luminance 4 × 4 block. For two consecutive non-directional prediction modes, i.e. planar mode or DC mode, we embed the secret bits by modifying them directly in order to increase the embedding capacity.

The rest of this paper is organized as follows. Section 2 introduces the process of intra prediction coding in HEVC. Section 3 describes the proposed data hiding algorithm based on difference of predictions modes. Experimental results are presented in Sect. 4 and we draw the conclusion of the paper in Sect. 5.

2   Intra-picture Prediction in HEVC

Although the video coding layer of HEVC employs the same hybrid structure used in all video compression standards since H.261 [12], it also makes improvement and innovation in some techniques, such as coding tree units (CTU) and coding tree block (CTB) structure and Intra-picture Prediction [13] which improved the coding efficiency of high-definition video.

2.1   Prediction Mode of 4 × 4 Luminance Block

The intra prediction coding is one of the core technologies in video coding process and the main method to improve the video compression efficiency. There is a strong spatial correlation between the adjacent pixels in a picture for video signal. Therefore, intra prediction coding technology was introduced to H.265/HEVC. It removed the spatial correlation of video and achieved the compression effect by predicting the neighboring pixels using the coded pixels in a video frame. Then, the prediction residual is used as the input of the following coding process.

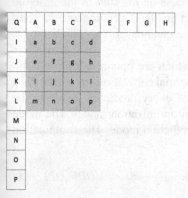

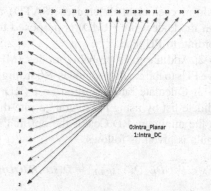

Fig. 1. 4 × 4 intra prediction model of HEVC

Fig. 2. 35 prediction modes for HEVC

4 × 4 intra prediction model of H.265/HEVC is shown in Fig. 1. Where the 16 pixels labeled from a to p are predicted by using the boundary pixels of the left and upper blocks which are already coded labeled from A to Q. We can see from the graph that it increases the lower left boundary pixels as the reference pixels compared with H.264/AVC, which makes the prediction direction greatly increased and improve the accuracy of prediction. This is because H.264/AVC uses fixed size macro block for coding and the lower left boundary pixels are not allowed to reference. While the H.265/HEVC uses coding tree units (CTU) and coding tree block (CTB) structure which make this region available for reference.

Intra prediction of H.265/HEVC adopts the same technology as H.264/AVC, but increases the number of the prediction mode. HEVC provides as many as 35 intra prediction modes which make intra prediction more accurate and reduce the spatial redundancy, as shown in Fig. 2. Compared to the eight prediction directions of H.264/AVC, HEVC adopts a total of 33 prediction directions, denoted as Intra_ Angular[k], where k is a mode number from 2 to 34. In the range of 2–17, the samples located in the left column. In the range of 18–34, the samples located at the left column are projected as samples located in the above row. HEVC also supports two alternative prediction modes-Intra_planar (0) and Intra_DC (1) which same modes were also used in H.264/AVC. While Intra_planar prediction uses an average value of two linear predictions using four corner reference samples to prevent discontinuities along the block boundaries and an average value of reference samples for prediction were used in Intra_DC prediction. It is better to adapts the different texture and different content in the video which make prediction more accurate.

2.2 Selection of Optimal Intra Prediction Mode

The selection of optimal intra prediction mode from 35 modes can divided into three steps [14].

Step 1: Calculate the cost of 35 prediction modes base on the sum of the absolute transform coefficient differences (SATD) and sort in the ascending order. Then rough mode decision (RMD) is proposed to choose candidates form all 35 modes according to PU size.

Step 2: Add the most probably modes (MPMs), which are obtained from left and above PUs to the candidate modes according to the spatial correlation among the PUs.

Step 3: Calculate rate distortion cost (RD Cost) of every prediction mode in the candidate list by using the Lagrange rate-distortion optimization model. The mode with the minimum RD Cost is the optimal intra prediction mode. The computation formula is given as follows:

$$J(s, c, IMODE/QP, \lambda_{MODE}) = D(s, c, IMODE/QP) + \lambda_{MODE} \cdot R(s, c, IMODE/QP) \quad (1)$$

where s represents original block and c represents reconstructed block. QP is quantization parameter and λ_{MODE} is Lagrange multiplier. R is bit-rate and D is distortion degree.

3 Information Hiding Algorithm

3.1 The Principle of Information Hiding

The paper proposed an information hiding algorithm based on differences of prediction modes. It embedded 2 secret bits or 3 secret bits in the difference of two continuous prediction directions of intra luminance 4 × 4 block and embedded 2 secret bits in two continuous Intra_planar mode or Intra_DC mode. The experimental result indicates that the proposed algorithm has little impact on the video quality.

HEVC supports as many as 33 prediction directions labeled from 2 to 34. We establish a mapping relationship between secret bits and the difference of two consecutive prediction directions, and embed the secret bits by modulating the prediction mode. Three or two secret bits can embedded in the difference by modulating the first one of them. The modulation of prediction mode can reduce the video quality. And it is reduced seriously if the modified mode has large difference with the optimal mode. We can reduce the distortion by using the nearing mode to replace the optimal mode considering the correlation ship of prediction modes. In order to explore the relationship between the hidden capacity and the embedded distortion, the difference interval of two consecutive modes is refined as Tables 1 and 2 which represent the relationship between secret bits and the differences. Table 1 is the representative of embedding 2 secret bits and Table 2 is the representative of embedding 3 secret bits. Take example for embedding 2 secret bits. Assuming that the two prediction directions are M_1 and M_2 and the two secret bits are S_1 and S_2. Firstly, calculate the absolute value of the difference which marked $D = |M_1 - M_2|$, $D \in [0, 32]$. Secondly, convert the two secret bits to decimal which is marked $N = 2 \times S_1 + S_2$. And then get the remainder from $D \bmod 4$. If $N = D \bmod 4$, do not modify anyone of them. If $D \bmod 4 \neq N$, modify M_1 to M_1' in the range of [2, 34] to ensure $D' = |M_1' - M_2'|$ and $D' \bmod 4 = N$. In order to avoid the great effect on the video quality caused by the modulation of prediction mode, we select the most suitable prediction mode according to the Lagrange rate-distortion optimization model.

Table 1. The mapping relationship between difference of prediction mode and 2 secret bits

D	Secret bits
0, 4, 8, 12, 16, 20, 24, 28, 32	00
1, 5, 9, 13, 17, 21, 25, 29	01
2, 6, 10, 14, 18, 22, 26, 30	10
3, 7, 11, 15, 19, 23, 27, 31	11

Table 2. The mapping relationship between difference of prediction mode and 3 secret bits

D	Secret bits
0, 8, 16, 24, 32	000
1, 9, 17, 25	001
2, 10, 18, 26	010
3, 11, 19, 27	011
4, 12, 20, 28	100
5, 13, 21, 29	101
6, 14, 22, 30	110
7, 15, 23, 31	111

To elaborate the principle of the embedding clearly, we give an example to illustrate the rules. For the two consecutive 4 × 4 intra luminance blocks, the optimal prediction modes are extracted. Assuming the two intra prediction modes are $M_1 = 5$,

$M_2 = 16$, two secret bits are $S_1 = 1$, $S_2 = 0$. Firstly, calculate the absolute value of the difference $D = 11$. Secondly, convert the two secret bits to decimal $N = 2$. Then $D \bmod 4 = 3 \neq 2$, so we need to modify M_1 to make $D' \bmod 4 = 2$. That is to say, we should select the most suitable mode in 2, 6, 10, 14, 18, 22, 26, 30, 34 which has the minimum RD cost. Assuming that is 6, so $M_1' = 6$.

Considering the synchronization and capacity of secret bits at decoder, we modify the mode 0 (Intra_planar) and mode 1 (Intra_DC) based on the secret information because this two modes is independent of direction. Figure 3 (a) presents the probability distribution of the sub-optimal prediction mode when the optimal mode is 0 and Fig. 3 (b) presents the probability distribution of the sub-optimal prediction mode when the optimal mode is 1. We can see from the figures that the sub-optimal mode would be mode 1 or mode 0 with a high probability when the optimal mode is mode 0 or mode 1. So there is little impact on the video quality if the prediction mode modify from 0 to 1 or from 1 into 0. If the secret bit is 0, then the prediction mode is modified to 0. If the secret bit is 1, then the prediction mode is modified to 1. There is no modification if one of prediction mode in two 4×4 luminance blocks is 0 or 1 and the other one is in the range of [2, 34].

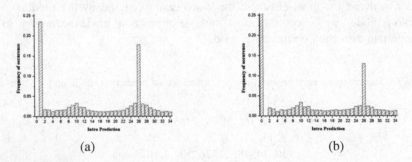

(a)   (b)

Fig. 3. The distribution of sub-optimal prediction when optimal prediction mode is determined

3.2 Data Embedding Procedure

In the proposed method, we embed the secret bits according to the mapping relationship between the differences of two consecutive prediction directions and modulation 2 kinds of non-directional modes in the coding process. The hiding algorithm is described as follows:

  Step 1: In the process of prediction coding, extract the optimal prediction modes from two consecutive 4×4 luminance blocks.
  Step 2: If the two consecutive prediction modes are all in range of [2, 34], calculate the absolute value difference of two prediction directions. Then modify the first prediction mode according to Table 1 if we want to embed 2 secret bits. The embedding of 3 secret bits is according to Table 2. If the two consecutive prediction modes are 0 or 1, modify them directly according to the secret bits. There is no modification if one of prediction modes is 0 or 1 and the other is in the range of [2, 34].

Step 3: Compare the Lagrange cost with other encoding modes after modulation of modes. If the cost of the 4 × 4 blocks is less than other encoding modes, save the embedded information. Otherwise, embed the current bits next time without saving the embedded bits.

Step 4: Repeat the above steps until all the secret bits have been embedded.

3.3 Data Detection Procedure

Data extraction procedure is convenient and simple. What is needed is only to decode I frame. The steps are performed as following:

Step 1: Determine whether the block coding mode of current block is 4 × 4 type. If the current block coding mode is other coding mode, go to Step 3. If the block coding mode is 4 × 4 type, decode the prediction modes of two consecutive 4 × 4 luminance blocks including current block.

Step 2: If two prediction modes are within [2, 34], calculate the absolute value of the difference marked D. Divided D by 4 or 8 so that we can get the remainder. Two or three secret bits can be obtained by converting the remainder to binary. If the two prediction modes are 0 or 1, extract the secret bits directly. Otherwise, do not extract secret bits and go to Step 3.

Step 3: Repeat the two steps for the 4 × 4 blocks until extracting all the secret information have been extracted.

4   Experimental Results and Discussions

The proposed algorithm has been simulated in the HM-12.0 model of the HEVC reference software. Four different resolutions (416 × 240, 832 × 460, 1280 × 720, 1920 × 1080) of the test sequences were used in the experiment. The main reference software coding configuration parameters are shown in Table 3, and the remaining parameters are set to the default configuration.

Table 3. Configuration parameters of the HM 12.0

Parameters	Configuration
Frames to be encoded	96
Frame rate	30 fps
Intra period	16
GOPSize	8
RDOQTS	1
QP	26

4.1 Subjective Video Quality Analysis

Figure 4 shows the second frame of two reconstructed video (Basketballpass, BQMall) before and after embedded secret information. As shown in the picture, the proposed information hiding algorithm will not have any noticeable impact on perceptual video quality.

(a) Original video frame

(b) The video frame after embedding secret bits

Fig. 4. Comparison of the visual quality

4.2 Objective Video Quality Analysis

PSNR and bitrate are used to evaluate the proposed algorithm Fig. 5 shows the change curve of PSNR with bitrate in different QP (QP = 22, 24, 26, 28, 30, 32) when embed 2 secret bits. Structural Similarity [15] (SSIM) and Video Quality Metric (VQM) are also introduce to evaluate the video quality. The value of SSIM is in the range of [0, 1], the value of SSIM is closer to 1 and the value of VQM is closer to 0 indicates that the higher similarity. As can be seen from Fig. 5 and Table 4, the value of PSNR and bitrate are slightly decreased after embedding the secret information. The values of SSIM are all above 0.94 and some test sequence can reach 0.98. The value of VQM altered little.

The embedding secret bits caused the video quality degradation, but there is a little influence on the video. In addition to replace the optimal prediction mode, the deviation made by the prediction of contiguous blocks which made intra-frame distortion is a more important factor to the volatility of the PSNR and bitrate. From the results we can see that the recoding can control the distortion drift effectively. The algorithm of embedding two secret bits is better than embedding three secret bits and method in [10] because of the modulation range is too large. And algorithm of embedding three secret

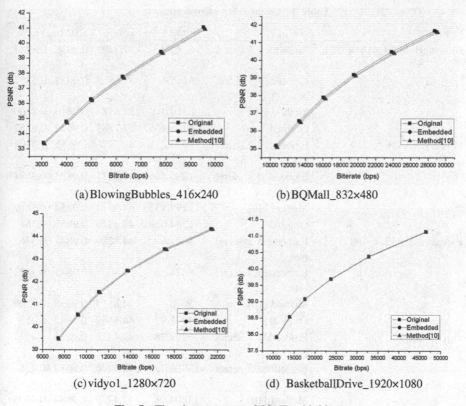

(a) BlowingBubbles_416×240

(b) BQMall_832×480

(c) vidyo1_1280×720

(d) BasketballDrive_1920×1080

Fig. 5. The change curve of PSNR with bitrate

bits is close to the method in [10]. Due to the recoding, the number of 4×4 luminance blocks in embedding 2 bits is more than embedding 3 bits that make a larger capacity.

4.3 Embedding Capacity Analysis

Embedding capacity is also an important indicator of an information hiding algorithm. Figure 6 shows the comparison of capacity between the proposed algorithm and the method in [10] when QP = 26. From which we can draw some conclusions as follows:

(1) For the same content video test sequence (Flowervase_416 × 240, Flowervase_832 × 480), the different resolution of video test sequence leads to the different embedding capacity.
(2) For the same resolution video test sequence (BlowingBubbles_416 × 240, Flowervase_416 × 240), the different content of the video test sequence leads to the different embedding capacity.
(3) The proposed algorithm of embedding two secret bits has larger capacity than the algorithm of embedding three secret bits and method in [10].

Table 4. Comparison of performance

Sequence		Bitrate	PSNR	SSIM	VQM
BlowingBubbles_416 × 240	Embedded 2 secret bits	6280.2	37.7492	0.9638	0.8234
	Embedded 3 secret bits	6285.4	37.6813	0.9632	0.8357
	Method [10]	6310.4	37.6784	0.9610	0.8200
	Original	6246.4667	37.7883	0.9642	0.8357
Flowervase_416 × 240	Embedded 2 secret bits	1293.2	44.3976	0.9855	0.3708
	Embedded 3 secret bits	1296.4667	44.3671	0.9853	0.3691
	Method [10]	1299.1333	44.3574	0.9854	0.3657
	Original	1284.6667	44.4343	0.9857	0.361
Flowervase_832 × 480	Embedded 2 secret bits	5023.6	44.8289	0.9842	0.3462
	Embedded 3 secret bits	5024.16	44.803	0.9841	0.3522
	Method [10]	5030	44.8114	0.9838	0.3509
	Original	4971.92	44.8649	0.9842	0.353
vidyo1_1280 × 720	Embedded 2 secret bits	13799.28	42.4828	0.9685	0.4547
	Embedded 3 secret bits	13820.72	42.4706	0.9684	0.458
	Method [10]	13804.08	42.4779	0.9684	0.4608
	Original	13705.2	42.4937	0.9685	0.4585
BasketballDrive_1920 × 1080	Embedded 2 secret bits	23705.4	39.6901	0.9431	0.5430
	Embedded 3 secret bits	23793.6667	39.6867	0.9430	0.5432
	Method [10]	23791.3333	39.6849	0.9430	0.5433
	Original	23688.6667	39.697	0.9431	0.5429

Not only the better quality of the proposed algorithm, but also the larger capacity. The main reason is that search range of prediction modes is slightly larger than that of embedding 3 secret bits and method in literature [10] and recoding make the number of 4 × 4 luminance blocks less.

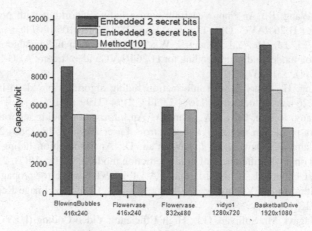

Fig. 6. Comparison of capacity

5 Conclusion

In this paper, a new information hiding algorithm for HEVC based on prediction mode has been proposed. A mapping relationship between secret bits and two consecutive intra prediction modes has been established and we embedded the secret bits by modulating the prediction mode according to Lagrange rate distortion model. Experiment shows that the algorithm has a good perceptual quality which the PSNR decreased within 0.05 db and the increment of bitrate was bounded to 1.1 %. Moreover, the value of SSIM and VOM altered little compared to the original video sequences. The proposed method can satisfy the imperceptibility, rate stability and requirement of capacity.

Acknowledgements. This work was supported by the National Natural Science Foundation of China (Grant No. 61300055, 61672302), Zhejiang Natural Science Foundation (Grant No. LZ15F020002), Ningbo University Fund (Grant No. XKXL1405, XKXL1503) and K.C. Wong Magna Fund in Ningbo University.

References

1. Cox, I.J., Miller, M.L., Bloom, J.A.: Digital Watermarking. Morgan Kaufmann Publishers, San Francisco (2002)
2. Bi, H.: A New Generation of Video Coding Standard-H.264/AVC. The People's Posts and Telecommunications Press, Peiking (2005)
3. Han, G.J., Ohm, J.R., Han, W.J., et al.: Overview of the high efficiency video coding (HEVC) standard. IEEE Trans. Circuits Syst. Video Technol. **22**(12), 1649–1668 (2012)
4. Yang, H., Zhang, C., Yuting, S.: An information hiding algorithm based on H.264/AVC. J. Electron. **36**(4), 690–694 (2008)
5. Wang, R., Zhu, H., Dawen, X.: An information hiding algorithm for H.264/AVC based on encoding mode. Opto-Electron. Eng. **37**(5), 144–150 (2010)

6. Dawen, X., Wang, R.: An improved information hiding algorithm with prediction mode modulation for H.264/AVC. Opto-Electron. Eng. **28**(11), 99–105 (2011)
7. Yang, G.B., Li, J.J., He, Y.L., Kang, Z.W.: An information hiding algorithm based on intra-prediction modes and matrix coding for H.264/AVC video stream. AEU-Int. J. Electron. Commun. **65**(4), 331–337 (2011)
8. Yin, Q., Wang, H., Zhao, Y.: An information hiding algorithm based on intra-prediction modes for H.264. J. Optoelectron. Laser **23**(11), 2194–2199 (2012)
9. Wang, J., Wang, R., Xu, D., Li, W., Yan, D.: An information hiding algorithm for HEVC based on intra prediction modes. J. Optoelectron. Laser **25**(8), 1578–1585 (2014)
10. Wang, J., Wang, R., Dawen, X., Li, W., Yan, D.: An information hiding algorithm for HEVC based on angle differences of intra prediction mode. J. Softw. **10**(2), 213–221 (2015)
11. Chang, P.C., Chung, K.L., Chen, J.J., et al.: A DCT/DST-based error propagation-free data hiding algorithm for HEVC intra-coded frames. J. Vis. Commun. Image Represent. **25**(2), 239–253 (2013)
12. Sze, V., Budagavi, M., Sullivan, G.J.: High Efficiency Video Coding (HEVC): Algorithms and Architectures. Springer, Switzerland (2014)
13. Wan, S., Yang, F.: A New Generation of High Efficient Video Coding Standard-H.265/HEVC: Principle and Implementation. Pubishing House of Electronics Industry, Peking (2014)
14. Li, W., Wang, R., Wang, J., Xu, D., Li, Q.: A fast intra coding algorithm with low complexity for HEVC. J. Optoelectron. Laser **26**(3), 597–604 (2015)
15. Wang, Z., Bovik, A.C., Sheikh, H.R., Simoncelli, E.P.: Image quality assessment: from error visibility to structural similarity. IEEE Trans. Image Process. **13**(4), 600–612 (2004)

Improvement of Universal Steganalysis Based on SPAM and Feature Optimization

Lei Min[1], LiuXiao Ming[2($\boxtimes$)], Yang Xue[3], Yang Yu[1],
and Wang Mian[1]

[1] Information Security Center, Beijing University of Posts
and Telecommunications, Beijing, China
[2] National Computer Network Emergency Response Technical Team,
Coordination Center of China, Beijing, China
liuxm@cert.org.cn
[3] Electronic Information Engineering Institute,
North China University of Technology, Beijing, China

Abstract. The tendency for high-dimension of universal steganalysis characteristics toward intensifying, and lead to the rapid rise in complexity of algorithm in time and space domain. So maintain the level of detection rates, and reduce the dimension of features at the same time, have significance in research of steganalysis. This paper determines the optimal dimension of feature vectors by principal component analysis; using the concept of Fisher linear discriminant, with the degree of "aggregations within class" and "discreteness between classes" to evaluate the ability of each dimension features to distinguish natural and hidden carrier, and then select the optimal subset. The analysis directs at the mainstream universal steganalysis model–SPAM model, and the simulation results show that optimal subset has a good detection and low computational complexity.

Keywords: Universal steganalysis · SPAM · Fisher score · Statute of the dimension

1 Introduction

With the rapid development of multimedia technology and computer networks, digital image information hiding technologies are widely used in the fields of information security. Steganalysis is one of important branches of information hiding technologies. And it is a technology to analyze the intercepted signals and determine whether the signals contained secret messages [1]. Steganalysis can be divided into two categories: special steganalysis and universal steganalysis. Special steganalysis is designed to certain algorithms and certain steganalysis tools specifically. While universal steganalysis is used to analyze one or more kinds of steganalysis algorithms which is increasingly valued [2].

In consideration of the diversity of current steganography techniques, universal steganalysis has more adaptability significantly. So it has attracted more attention. As one of the most typical steganalysis scheme, SPAM model [3] has received widely

© Springer International Publishing AG 2016
X. Sun et al. (Eds.): ICCCS 2016, Part I, LNCS 10039, pp. 75–83, 2016.
DOI: 10.1007/978-3-319-48671-0_7

recognized and extensive concern of the academia, which works by adding a low-amplitude independent stego signal to the intercepted signals. Yu [4] provide an optimization method to Adaptive Pixel Pair Matching (APPM) which is proposed by Hong and Chen [5]. Steganalysis algorithm proposed by Hou is based on a two-layer difference model matrix and makes a use of two-order Markov chain. This scheme extracts features from two-layer difference matrix and classify the original image and stego image using the SVM classification. Wang et al. [6] proposed the Subtractive pixel joint distribution (SPJD) based on SPAM, and the image segmentation algorithm was added to improved performance of the algorithm. Thus each segmented subimage can obtain a steganalysis result and the detection accuracy can be improved significantly. Kodovsky et al. [7] steganalyze YASS using several recently proposed general purpose steganalysis feature sets and demonstrate experimentally that twelve different settings of YASS can be reliably detected even for small embedding rates and in small images. This paper combining SPAM characteristics with the 548-dimensional features which derived from DCT domain quantization coefficient mix a 1234-dimensional eigenvectors, to implement universal steganalysis on transform domain. Zhang et al. [8] proposed new feature vectors which are extracted from the spatial image and from the grayscale-inverted image based on parallel subtractive pixels other than the SPAM feature vectors only. The feature matrices become symmetrical and the dimensionality of matrices are reduced by half because of the addition of parallel subtractive pixels. They also used a new type of adjacent matrix, about 3/4 of the feature vectors' dimensionality is decreased. The research achievements at the improvement of steganalysis based on SPAM and feature optimization are summarized above, from which we can find the analysis and optimization in SPAM is of great value in practice.

With the development of steganography, steganalysis algorithms with high-performance are constantly emerging. But the higher feature dimension, the longer classifier training time and the lower detection efficiency etc., are common problems on the algorithms currently. In most cases, the features have some correlation to each other in the high-dimension feature set which was extracted from steganalysis algorithm. It can be explained as some of these features are redundant and the detection performance has some overlap. Features for universal steganalysis tend to become high-dimensional and increase time and space complexity remarkably and it is necessary to reduce the dimension of the features without reducing the detection rate of steganalysis, which means a great deal to the practicability and feasibility of the algorithm. Choosing characteristics with good divisibility and reducing the dimensionality of the feature space, is of great significance.

Figure 1 shows the block diagram of this research program. Research in this paper determines the optimal dimension of the feature vectors by principal component analysis firstly. The concept of Fisher linear discriminant is in use. And then the proposed algorithm distinguishes natural covers and stego-covers to obtain the optimal subsets and to make a classification. Analysis of the paper based on SPAM scheme which is the foundation of common detection frameworks. A performance analysis of the proposed scheme shows that proposed scheme on universal steganalysis has higher detection sensitivity and lower computational complexity.

The rest of the paper is organized as follows. Section 2 briefly describes the SPAM model and characteristic optimization algorithm. Section 3 makes the detailed

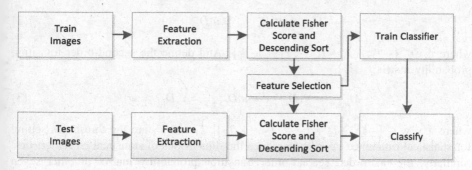

Fig. 1. Steganalysis process with feature selection

introduction to the SPAM algorithm optimization based on Fisher. The experimental setup and results are given in Sect. 4. The paper is concluded in Sect. 5.

2 Research Foundation

2.1 SPAM Model Profile

Reference [3] raised the subtractive pixel adjacency matrix (SPAM) feature to test LSB matching algorithm. As one of the best steganalysis method currently, this article improved algorithm performance on the basis of SPAM. By reduce the feature dimension, the universal steganalysis performance of SPAM characteristics can be improved. This chapter will describe the characteristics of SPAM briefly.

For a given image which size is W × H, make its pixel matrix to be I, and then the calculation steps of SPAM characteristics for this image are as follows (where $\rightarrow$ represents horizontal direction left-to-right, $\leftarrow$ represents horizontal direction right-to-left, $\downarrow$ represents vertical top-to-bottom, $\uparrow$ represents vertical bottom-to-top, $\searrow$ represents diagonally left-to-right, $\nwarrow$ represents diagonal right-to-left, $\swarrow$ represents minor diagonal right-to-left, and $\nearrow$ represents minor diagonal left-to-right).

First, calculate the difference matrix between adjacent pixels along the eight directions. Take the horizontal direction for an example to explain, the other direction using the same rules. Define the horizontal direction (from left to right) difference matrix to:

$$D_{i,j}^{\rightarrow} = I_{i,j} - I_{i+1,j} \tag{1}$$

where i = 1, …, W, j = 1, …, H. The other seven directions difference matrix are recorded respectively as $D_{i,j}^{\leftarrow}, D_{i,j}^{\downarrow}, D_{i,j}^{\uparrow}, D_{i,j}^{\searrow}, D_{i,j}^{\nwarrow}, D_{i,j}^{\swarrow}, D_{i,j}^{\nearrow}$.

Then, extracted the Markov characteristics based on difference matrix $D_{i,j}^{\rightarrow}$, and define the first-order transition probability matrix:

$$M_{u,v}^{\rightarrow} = P(D_{i,j+1}^{\rightarrow} = u | D_{i,j}^{\rightarrow} = v) \tag{2}$$

where $u, v \in \{-T_1, -T_1 + 1, \cdots, T_1 - 1, T_1\}$. And define the second-order transition probability matrix:

$$M_{u,v,w}^{\rightarrow} = P(D_{i,j+2}^{\rightarrow} = u | D_{i,j+1}^{\rightarrow} = v, D_{i,j}^{\rightarrow} = w) \tag{3}$$

where $u, v, w \in \{-T_2, -T_2 + 1, \cdots, T_2 - 1, T_2\}$. T_1 and T_2 are the thresholds setting for statistical difference in order to reduce the dimensions of statistical characteristics. Similarly, the first-order, second-order transition probability matrix of other seven directions can be defined.

Finally, the transition probability matrix is converted to a one-dimensional vector, and calculate the average of the four results in horizontal and vertical direction. The result matrix is converted to a one-dimensional vector, too.

$$F_{1,\cdots,k} = \frac{1}{4}\left(M^{\rightarrow} + M^{\leftarrow} + M^{\downarrow} + M^{\uparrow}\right) \tag{4}$$

$$F_{k+1,\cdots,2k} = \frac{1}{4}\left(M^{\searrow} + M^{\nwarrow} + M^{\swarrow} + M^{\nearrow}\right) \tag{5}$$

Calculate the corresponding order SPAM characteristics from first-order and second-order transition probability matrix respectively. For first-order SPAM characteristics, $k = (2T_1 + 1)^2$; for second-order SPAM characteristics, $k = (2T_2 + 1)^3$.

We can get the conclusion from reference [3] that compared with using first-order features, using second-order SPAM features can get a higher detection rate. So the features optimization study is mainly for the second-order SPAM features.

2.2   Feature Selection Algorithm

Among the universal steganalysis algorithms, the characteristic dimension number is larger. There may be features that are not relevant or there may be mutual dependencies between features. It can easily lead to the following consequences: the more number of features, the longer time will be used for analysis features and training model; the more number of features, it is likely to cause "dimensions of disaster" [9]. Meanwhile, the model is also more complex, and has serious impact on the detection efficiency. Optimization of characteristics can eliminate the irrelevant features or the redundant features to reduce the number of features, improve model accuracy and reducing the running time.

Fisher Linear Discriminant (FLD) is a common dimension reduction technique. The basic principle of FLD is that the high dimensional samples was projected onto the optimal discriminant vector space in order to achieve the effect that extract classified information and compressed feature space dimension. It makes sure that the distance within classes should be as small as possible, the distance between classes should be as large as possible after projection, which means features have the best separability in space domain.

In the process of steganalysis, we need to consider characteristics optimization of both natural image samples and steganography image samples. In the case of FLD, the dimensionality of the feature space is compressed, and the separable of characteristics are fully considered. So it's adequate to use FLD to optimize the characteristics. On this basis, we use the basic idea of FLD to analyze the characteristics, and optimize SPAM model by find the optimal feature subset of SPAM.

3 Optimization of SPAM Algorithm Based on Fisher Score

This paper select FLD as the foundation to reduce the number of dimensions, with "aggregations within class" and "discreteness between classes" evaluation the ability of various dimension characteristics to distinguish natural carriers and carrier of steganography, and then select the optimal subset.

3.1 Feature Selection Based on Fisher Score

Fisher criterion [10] is one of the most effective methods of feature selection. The main idea of it is that the feature with strong ability for classification was showed that the distance within class should be as small as possible, the distance between classes should be as large as possible. The Fisher score of single character was took as guidelines. Sorting the features according Fisher score, and electing characteristics with strong performance on recognition properties, so as to achieve the purpose of dimensionality, and get better performance. Fisher score of the feature is larger, classification capacity of the feature is better.

Considering the training sample $X = (C_1, S_1), (C_2, S_2), \cdots, (C_m, S_m), C_i, S_i \in R^k$, $i = 1, 2, \cdots, m$, where m is the sample size and k is the dimension of the feature vector; C_i indicates the natural image features, S_i indicates the steganography feature. The samples set of natural image features in the set X is recorded as X_1, and the number recorded as N_1; The samples set of steganography images features is recorded as X_2, and the number recorded as N_2. The Fisher score was defined as:

$$F = S_b/S_w \tag{6}$$

where S_b is the dispersion for classes, describing the distance between two samples; S_w is the dispersion within classes, describing the distance between similar samples. Its definition is as follows:

$$S_b = (\overline{m_1} - \overline{m_2})^2 \tag{7}$$

$$S_w = \frac{1}{N_1} \sum_{X \in X_1} (X - \overline{m_1})^2 + \frac{1}{N_2} \sum_{X \in X_2} (X - \overline{m_2})^2 = \delta_1^2 + \delta_2^2 \tag{8}$$

where $\overline{m_1}$ is the mean for natural images features sample, $\overline{m_2}$ is the mean for steganography images features sample. Of which $\overline{m_1} = \frac{1}{N_1} \sum_{X \in X_1} X$, $\overline{m_2} = \frac{1}{N_2} \sum_{X \in X_2} X$;

δ_1^2 and δ_2^2 are the variances for natural images features sample and steganography images features sample respectively. So the Fisher score of the r-th feature can be expressed as:

$$F_r = \frac{S_{b,r}}{S_{w,r}} = \frac{(\overline{m_{1,r}} - \overline{m_{2,r}})^2}{\delta_{1,r}^2 + \delta_{2,r}^2} \tag{9}$$

where $\overline{m_{1,r}}$ and $\overline{m_{2,r}}$ is the mean of the r-th character property for natural images features sample and steganography images features sample respectively.

3.2   Characteristics Analysis Before and After Optimization

In consideration of that the SPAM characteristics values of image have a large difference, in order to solve the phenomenon of "large number eating smaller numbers" which is may appear for the range of different features were too different, and don't ignore each feature's contribution to the Fisher score, after the extraction of image features, we normalized the characteristics of SPAM.

Performance Analysis of Fisher Score. In order to illustrate the classification performance of Fisher Score, selected characteristics with the highest and the lowest Fisher score, by drawing histograms to analyze the performance of features.

Selected 2700 natural images and 2700 steganography images randomly, and extracted SPAM features. Calculate the Fisher score of each dimension characteristics, and sorted them in descending order. Drew the natural features and the steganography features with highest Fisher score and lowest Fisher score respectively. The simulation results are shown in Fig. 2.

In Fig. 2, (a) and (b) express the histogram which corresponds to the greatest Fisher score of natural feature and steganography feature; (c) and (d) express the histogram which corresponds to minimum Fisher score of natural feature and steganography feature. It can be seen that (a) and (b) have made a big difference, when the difference of (c) and (d) is very small. We know that the histogram is the approximation of probability density function for natural and steganography carrier. The farther two distributions away from, the better detection performance of corresponding features. Therefore, it could be explained that the bigger Fisher score of a feature, classification capacity of character is stronger.

4   Experimental Setup and Results

4.1   Data Preprocessing

Since there are large differences among the SPAM features that extracted from different steganography images, in order to reduce the effects of different steganography algorithms, and get more accurate Fisher score value, experiment take the method that calculate the Fisher scores respectively and then calculate their average. The specific steps of research are: extracted the SPAM features from the natural images and the

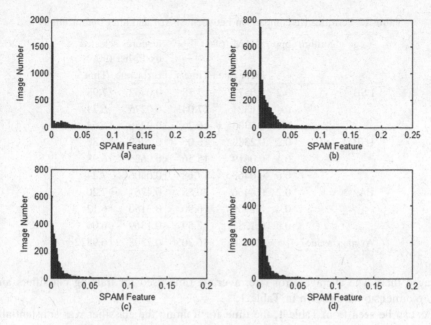

Fig. 2. Characteristic histogram of different Fisher values

steganography images, and calculated Fisher score between them respectively; calculated the average of multiple sets of results, then sorted the average from largest to smallest. According to the sorted Fisher score, arrange the original SPAM feature and get the new feature set.

Experimental computer is configured to use Intel(R) Core(TM) CPU (2.30 GHz), 6.00 GBRAM, and simulation using MATLAB R2012a. The LSB [11], LSBM (LSB Matching) [12] and EA (Edge Adaptive) [13] algorithms were used to simulate the universal steganalysis algorithm which proposed in this paper, in which the EA algorithm is adaptive steganography. Experiments using the BossBase-1.01 database [14], which consists of 10000 grayscale images in PGM with fixed size 512×512 and without JPEG compression. Images content involving a range of natural landscapes, people, architecture etc. LSB, LSBM and EA algorithms are used with payloads 0.2 bits per pixel (bpp), 0.4 bpp and 0.6 bpp to created steganography images. Selected 300 images from different steganography image library randomly, blend images with a total of $3 \times 3 \times 300 = 2700$ steganography images used for training. Selected 2700 images from remaining steganography image library randomly used for testing.

4.2 Simulation Testing and Analysis of Results

To test the performance of optimized algorithms, using the algorithm of this paper and SPAM (calculate second-order Markov transition probability matrix, T = 3) to test the LSB, LSBM and EA algorithm under the same conditions. For the two feature sets (this paper and SPAM), the experiment has been conducted 10 times. All the results are

Table 1. Performance comparison between SPAM and after optimization

Stego algorithm	bpp	SPAM (686)		Features selected by Fisher (300)	
		Error rate	Time/s	Error rate	Time/s
LSB	0.2	0.0577	17.38	0.0462	7.98
	0.4	0.0321	17.04	0.0275	6.74
	0.6	0.0303	16.26	0.0256	6.64
LSBM	0.2	0.2383	16.06	0.2269	7.88
	0.4	0.0619	15.56	0.0625	6.98
	0.6	0.0463	17.68	0.0406	7.24
EA	0.2	0.4466	20.88	0.4761	7.20
	0.4	0.2909	16.90	0.3150	6.12
	0.6	0.1281	12.59	0.1369	6.06
Average value		0.1480	16.7056	0.1508	6.9822

averaged then. The average error rate, average time used for training classifiers and feature dimension are shown in Table 1.

As can be seen from Table 1, the time for training the classifier was substantially reducing after optimized the features of SPAM, so the detection efficiency of algorithm has been greatly improved. At the same time, the error detection rate remained unchanged generally.

5 Conclusion

This article does an exploratory study about optimization analysis for one of the best universal steganalysis methods–SPAM model. By calculating the Fisher score of characters, reduced the feature dimension. Experimental results show that, compared with the SPAM, the algorithm of this paper keep the detection rate basically unchanged, and improving the detection speed greatly at the same time, enhanced the practicability of SPAM. Compared with SPMA, the proposed algorithm reduces the detection time by 58.20 % while the error detection ratio of the algorithm is just increased by 1.89 %. So the algorithm optimized based on SPAM has good practicability and feasibility obviously.

Since the paper only considered the greedy algorithm when optimized the SPAM features, the effects of feature direction on results was ignored. Therefore, in the further work, we consider combine the concept of PCA and FLD to improve the performance of steganalysis algorithms. PCA looking at all samples (vector set) as a whole, and trying to find an optimal linear mapping projection in case of mean square error is minimum. Using the reduced-dimension idea of PCA, simply walk through different feature combinations of feature set, and combine the classification performance of Fisher score to find the optimal feature subset.

Acknowledgment. This work was supported by the National Key Technology Support Program (2015BAH08F02). Open Foundation of Jiangsu Engineering Center of Network Monitoring (Nanjing University of Information Science and Technology) (Grant No. KJR1509) the PAPD fund and CICAEET fund.

References

1. Huang, W., Zhao, X.F., Feng, D.G., Sheng, R.N.: JPEG steganalysis based on feature fusion by principal component analysis. J. Softw. **23**(7), 1869–1879 (2012). (in Chinese)
2. Fridrich, J., Goljan, M.: Practical steganalysis of digital images-state of the art. In: SPIE on Security and Watermarking of Multimedia Contents, USA, pp. 1–13 (2001)
3. Pevný, T., Bas, P., Fridrich, J.: Steganalysis by subtractive pixel adjacency matrix. IEEE Trans. Inf. Forensic Secur. **5**(2), 215–224 (2010)
4. Yu, H.: Image Steganalysis. Beijing Jiaotong University, Beijing (2015)
5. Hong, W., Chen, T.S.: A novel data embedding method using adaptive pixel pair matching. IEEE Trans. Inf. Forensics Secur. **7**(1), 176–184 (2012)
6. Wang, R., Xu, M.K., Ping, X.J., Zhang, T.: Steganalysis of spatial images based on segmentation. Acta Automatica Sinica **40**(12), 2936–2943 (2014). (in Chinese)
7. Kodovsky, J., Pevný, T., Fridrich, J.: Modern steganalysis can detect YASS. In: Proceedings of SPIE on Electronic Imaging, Media Forensics and Security, San Jose, USA, pp. 02-01–02-11. SPIE (2010)
8. Zhang, H., Ping, X.J., Xu, M., Wang, R.: Steganalysis by subtractive pixel adjacency matrix and dimensionality reduction. Sci. China Inf. Sci. **57**(4), 1–7 (2014)
9. Bhasin, V., Bedi, P., Singhal, A.: Feature selection for steganalysis based on modified stochastic diffusion search using Fisher score. In: International Conference on Advances in Computing, Communications and Informatics (ICACCI), pp. 2323–2330 (2014)
10. Zhang, X.-Q., Gu, C.-H.: A method to extract network intrusion detection feature. J. South China Univ. Technol. (Nat. Sci. Ed.) **38**(1), 81–86 (2010)
11. van Schyndel, R.G., Tirkel, A.Z., Osborne, C.F.: A digital watermark. In: The IEEE International Conference on Image Processing, Austin, Texas, USA, vol. 2, pp. 86–90 (1994)
12. Sharp, T.: An implementation of key-based digital signal steganography. In: Moskowitz, I.S. (ed.) IH 2001. LNCS, vol. 2137, pp. 13–26. Springer, Heidelberg (2001)
13. Luo, W., Huang, F., Huang, J.: Edge adaptive image steganography based on LSB matching revisited. IEEE Trans. Inf. Forensics Secur. **5**(2), 201–214 (2010)
14. Filler, T., Pevný, T., Bas, P.: BOSS (Break Our Steganography System) [EB/OL] (2014). http://agents.fel.cvut.cz/stegodata/BossBase-1.01-cover.tar.bz2
15. Kodovsky, J., Fridrich, J., Holub, V.: Ensemble classifiers for steganalysis of digital media. IEEE Trans. Inf. Forensics Secur. **7**(2), 432–444 (2012)

Optimizing Feature for JPEG Steganalysis via Gabor Filter and Co-occurrences Matrices

Bing Cao[1], Guorui Feng[1(✉)], and Zhaoxia Yin[1,2]

[1] School of Communication and Information Engineering,
Shanghai University, Shanghai, China
fgr2082@aliyun.com
[2] Key Laboratory of Intelligent Computing and Signal Processing,
Ministry of Education, Anhui University, Hefei 200444, China

Abstract. For modern steganography algorithms, there are many distortion functions designed for JPEG images which are difficult to be detected for the steganalyst. Until now, the most successful detection of this kind steganography named GFR (Gabor Filter Residual) is currently achieved with detectors for training on cover and stego sets. These features extract the image texture information from different scales and orientations, and the image statistical characteristics can be captured more effectively. In this paper, we describe a novel feature set for steganalysis of JPEG images. The features are composed of two parts. All of them are obtained based on GFR in the spatial domain. Its first part is to extract the histograms features, and the other part is co-occurrence matrices features. Due to its high dimensionality, we make the best of the label to reduce these features. Compared with state-of-the-arts methods, the most advantage of this proposed steganalysis features is its lower detection error while meeting the advanced steganographic algorithms.

Keywords: Steganalysis · Gabor filter · Spatial domain · Histograms · Co-occurrence

1 Introduction

Steganagraphy is a process of embedding secret information in a digital medium (usually in the digital image) and not found in vision. On the contrary, steganalysis aims to detect whether a digital medium has been distorted or a secret message is embedded in medium. Image steganography includes spatial-domain and transform-domain methods. The former directly alters the spatial pixel values to achieve steganography, and the latter usually uses JPEG image as the cover, and secret information can be embedded by changing the DCT coefficients slightly. In this paper we only discuss JPEG image as the digital medium. Up to now, there are numerous steganography algorithms for the JPEG domain, such as nsF5 [1], UED (Uniform Embedding Distortion) [2], JUNIWARD (JPEG Universal Wavelet Relative Distortion) [3, 5]. Steganalysis which can detect those steganography algorithms from complicating image texture and edge region has attracted more and more attentions.

X. Sun et al. (Eds.): ICCCS 2016, Part I, LNCS 10039, pp. 84–93, 2016.
DOI: 10.1007/978-3-319-48671-0_8

Steganalysis consists of two steps: feature extraction and classification. As for JPEG image feature extraction in reference [7], the authors build a high-dimensional feature set named CFstar feature set of 7850-dims by utilizing elements of co-occurrence matrices. Later, Li et al. calculate the co-occurrence matrices of DCT coefficients to design 15700-dims features [10]. Furthermore, as a popular trend [6], JPEG rich model contains much more sub-models which catch more differences between cover and stego images, and increase the Cartesian calibration form the CC-JRM [3, 4, 6] feature set of 22510-dims. Compared with above-mentioned features, DCTR (Discrete Cosine Transform Residual) feature has been proposed in [8] recently where it convolutes to the spatial domain of the original image with 64 DCT base models sized 8 × 8, and gets 64 new planes. DCT residuals are used to build the final feature as the histograms. Advantages of DCTR include low complexity computing, low dimensionality (8000-dims) and better detection accuracy. Even so, detection accuracy still remains to be improved. The state-of-the-art method proposed in [9], where the features (17000-dims) are extracted from different scales and more orientations to capture the embedding changes using 2D Gabor filter [12]. Its result is better in which steganography algorithms utilize the wavelet decomposition coefficients in one scale and three different orientations to define distortion, such as JUNIWARD steganography. However, with those steganography algorithms (such as J-UNIWARD) due to its distortion function design. It is desired to improve the performance furthermore.

In this article, we put forward a new view for feature extraction methods, and its detection accuracy is better than most of existing methods. The feature set is composed of two kinds of enhanced feature based on the optimal model, the first kind through reducing the 17000-dims histogram features extracted from different scales and more orientations to capture the embedding changes using 2D Gabor filter. Another kind technique is to reduce the co-occurrence matrices from new planes which sampling the 2D Gabor filter planes according to specific element positions. Since our approach requires fast machine learning, we use the FLD ensemble classifier [14] (its low computational complexity and ability to efficiently work with high dimensional features and large training data sets). This paper starts in the next section with a summary of basic concepts and notational conventions, we introduce the supervised feature extraction methods, and explain the essential principal of proposed methods in Sects. 2 and 3 introduces the realization process. In Sect. 4, we explain the detection accuracy of the proposed feature set and contrasted with the other steganalysis features. The paper is concluded in Sect. 5.

2 Prepare Work of Feature Extraction

The proposed steganalysis method includes three parts: filtering by 2D Gabor filters with different scales and orientations, then, the histogram features are extracted from all the filtered images and forming new planes by sampling 2D Gabor filters images according to specific positions [11], after extracting the co-occurrence matrices from the new planes with intra-block and inter-block pairing modes. Finally, choosing the enhanced feature based on the optimal model.

2.1 Extracting the Histogram Features

With regard to a given JPEG grayscale image $\mathbf{X}$ with the size of $M \times N$, the first step is decompressed to the spatial domain called decompressed image, then, doing filter operation. The 2-D Gabor filters is defined as a set of 2-D Gabor function with difference parameters. 2D Gabor filtering means the fact that the decompressed JPEG image is convoluted with a 2-D Gabor function to produce a Gabor feature image. The formula is expressed as follows:

$$u(x,y) = \sum_{\xi} \sum_{\eta} I(\xi,\eta) f(x - \xi, y - \eta) \tag{1}$$

where $x, y \in \Phi$, Φ is the set of the images. $I(x, y)$ denotes the decompressed JPEG image. $g(x, y)$ denotes the 2-D Gabor function. In this paper, $f(x, y)$ is represented as:

$$f_{\lambda,\theta,\varphi}(x,y) = e^{-((x'^2 + \gamma^2 y'^2)/2\sigma^2)} \cos(2\pi \frac{x'}{\lambda} + \varphi) \tag{2}$$

where $x' = x \cos\theta + y \sin\theta, y' = x \sin\theta + y \cos\theta, \sigma = 0.56\lambda$, and σ represents the scale parameter. By setting different parameters σ, we obtain different spatial resolution in Eq. (2). Due to 2D Gabor filters with different parameters own symmetrical characteristic, merging the filters with symmetrical direction and same scale, the final feature will be decreased and the feature will be better.

After the process that the decompressed JPEG image is convolved using each 2D Gabor filter, the histogram features are extracted from the filtered image by under equation:

$$h_{a,b}^{k,t}(x) = \frac{1}{\left| U_{a,b}^{k,t} \right|} \sum_{u \in U_{a,b}^{k,t}} [Q_T(|u|/q) = x] \tag{3}$$

where Q_T is a quantizer with integer centroids $\{0, 1, ..., T\}$, q is the quantization step, and [P] is the Iverson bracket equal to 0 when the statement P is false and 1 when P is true [9]. In addition, the histogram features extracted from the filtered sub-images also can be merged to reduce the feature dimensionality. For each filtered image, all histogram features can be merged to one histogram feature with $25 \times (T + 1)$ dimensions. Furthermore, in Ref. [9], with all the 136 2D Gabor filters, the total histogram feature is $136 \times 25 \times (T + 1)$ dimension.

2.2 Extracting the Co-occurrence Features

This section includes two steps: forming new planes by sampling the filtered image which filtered by 64 2D Gabor filters according to specific positions, and extracting the co-occurrence matrices from the new planes with intra-block pairing modes.

In this section, we just select 64 2D Gabor filters. After decompressing JPEG image X with the size of M × N and filtering image with 64 2D Gabor filters, then we obtain 64 convolution planes corresponding to 64 basis patterns, sized (M − 7) × (N − 7). In next step, we cut the last row and column of every plane to get a cropped plane sized (M − 8) × (N − 8) for the convenience of computing, where M − 8 and N − 8 are both divisible by 8. In Fig. 1, the $U^{(k,l)}$ means the filtered image that JPEG image convolved with (k + 1)-th 2D Gabor filters. Finally new planes $R^{(k,l)}$ indicated to $U^{(a,b)}$ can be obtained, where every $R^{(a,b)}$ is computed from all of $U^{(k,l)}$. Then, the final feature sets will be extracted from every $R^{(a,b)}$, but if we implement the extraction of co-occurrence matrices to all of planes $R^{(a,b)}$, the dimensions will be very high and the performance is not satisfied [11]. To solve this problem, through a large number of experiments, 15 planes of the new planes $R^{(a,b)}$ are selected to extract co-occurrence matrices features. There are $R^{(1,1)}$ $R^{(2,2)}$ $R^{(3,3)}$ $R^{(4,4)}$ $R^{(5,5)}$ $R^{(6,6)}$ $R^{(7,7)}$ $R^{(8,8)}$ and in order to better results, combinations the planes $R^{(1,0)}R^{(0,1)}$, $R^{(3,0)}R^{(0,3)}$, $R^{(5,0)}R^{(0,5)}$, $R^{(7,0)}R^{(0,7)}$, $R^{(7,2)}R^{(2,7)}$, $R^{(7,4)}R^{(4,7)}$, $R^{(7,6)}R^{(6,7)}$ respectively. Before extracting co-occurrence feature sets for steganalysis, only a part of region of the 8 × 8 DCT block are used because most of the high frequency AC coefficients in the lower right corner are zeros. It will be different in the proposed scheme where we use the whole coefficients in the 8 × 8 block, but the pairing modes will greatly increase at the same time, for the reason of suppressing the dimension, only a portion pairing modes will be used in this article.

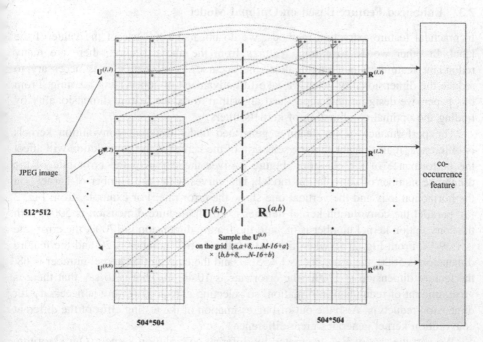

Fig. 1. The process of sampling from $U^{(k,l)}$ into $R^{(a,b)}$

For the feature extraction in steganalysis, the quantization for the image filtering coefficients can make the feature more sensitive to embedding changes at spatial discontinuities in the image. Therefore, the image filtering coefficients are quantized to improve the detection accuracy in the proposed feature extraction method. Based on a large number of experiments, we set q = 3. For each new plane, let $G_{xy}^{(i,j)}$ represent the (x, y)th coefficient in the (i, j)th 8×8 block, $[x, y] \in \{1,...,8\} \times \{1,...,8\}$, i = 1,..., (M − 8)/8, j = 1,..., (N − 8)/8. Our feature set will be built as co-occurrence matrices $C_{xy}(dx, dy)$ for all of the coefficient pairs modes [i, j] and $[x \pm dx, y \pm dy]$. And $C_{xy}(dx, dy) = \{c_{\alpha,\beta}\}_{(\alpha,\beta)=-T}^{T}$ is a matrix of $(T + 1)^2$–dimensionality.

$$c_{\alpha,\beta} = \frac{1}{\sum} \sum_{i,j} \left\{ \left\langle X_{x,y}^{(i,j)} = \alpha \right\rangle, \left\langle X_{x \pm dx, y \pm dy}^{(i,j)} = \beta \right\rangle \right\} \quad (4)$$

where $\sum$ is the normalization constant to ensure that $\sum_{i,j} c_{\alpha,\beta} = 1$. The truncation operator $\langle \cdot \rangle$ is defined as:

$$\langle x \rangle_T = \begin{cases} x & \text{if } x \in [0, T] \\ T & \text{otherwise} \end{cases} \quad (5)$$

In our experience, we set T = 2.

2.3   Enhanced Feature Based on Optimal Model

In practical feature extraction methods, we do not make full use of the value of the label. In other words, to extract features from the above section, there are many redundant features which might affect the accuracy of classifier, it is necessary to reduce the dimensionality when we take full advantage of supervising learning. From this paper, we design a new supervised algorithm to reduce feature dimensionality by finding the optimal combination of kernels filters.

The performance of the features generated under different convolution kernels is difference. It also means that the selection of the kernel of the convolution will affect the performance of the classifier. Figure 2 gives the curve of the error rate of the difference number of convolution model. The curves with "the number of kernel" on the horizontal axis and the vertical one show the error rata. For example, from Fig. 2 (a), parallel the convolution kernel number is 20, the feature dimension is 5000, with the convolution kernel number is 68, and the feature dimension is 17000, the error rate is 1.39 %. From Fig. 2(b), when the convolution kernel number is 20 and the feature dimension is 5000, the error rate is 11.55 %, and the convolution kernel number is 68, the feature dimension is 17000, the error rate is 10.46 %. That is to say that there is great amount of redundant information, so selecting enhanced feature is necessary for dimension reduction. Also the out-of-bag estimation of the testing error of the different convolution kernel generates great difference.

We sort the size of E_{oob} generated by different convolution kernels. Our algorithm is presented in Algorithm 1.

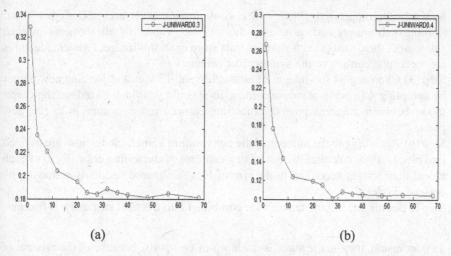

Fig. 2. The curve of the error rate of different convolution model number with J-UNIWARD feature (a) payload is 0.3 bpac and (b) payload is 0.4 bpac

---

Algorithm 1 Optimal model

Input : Extracted features

1: Sort the size of Eoob generated by all convolution kernels, each piece named F_i

2: set i =1 , dim= D, d =0, lump =L

3: while d ≤ dim

4: $F_{next} \leftarrow [\, F_{current}, F\,(\, findNext\,()\,)\,]$

5: if $E_{oob}(F_{next}) \prec E_{oob}(F_{current})$ then

　$E^*{}_{oob} \leftarrow E_{oob}(F_{next})$

　$F_{current} \leftarrow F_{next}$

　i←i+1

　End

6: $F_{next} \leftarrow F_{current}$

7: d ← i × lump

8: end while

---

3 Proposed Method of Supervised Feature Extraction

In this section, the proposed feature extraction method based on histograms and co-occurrence is described in details. Figure 3 shows the diagram of the proposed method of supervised feature extraction and we will describe the procedures in details as follows:

Step (1) The first step for JPEG image is decompressed to the spatial domain but not quantizing the pixel values to {0,1..., 255} in case to avoid any loss of information.

Step (2) Decompressed JPEG image convolutions with each 2D Gabor filter, forming sub-images and quantizing the absolute values of all elements in each sub-image, then, histogram features extract from each sub-image. Extracted features are merged according to the symmetrical orientations.

Step (3) Choosing 64 sub-images of all the 136 sub-images and forming new planes by sampling 64 choice planes according to specific positions to reduce the correlation between adjacent points, extracting co-occurrence feature from the new planes.

Step (4) According to the number of the convolution kernel, the features are divided into blocks, then, calculate the out-of-bag estimate of the testing error (E_{oob}) of each block, then sorting according to the size of E_{oob}. Enhanced feature is extracting by optimal model.

Step (5) In the end, all the features are combined into the final steganalysis features.

In conclusion, the final features is made up of two parts, because of the process of extracting feature by optimal model, the histogram feature set cuts to 5000-dims feature, and the co-occurrence feature is 7020-dims. Then by merging all these feature vectors we can get a 12020-dims high-dimensional feature set for JPEG steganalysis.

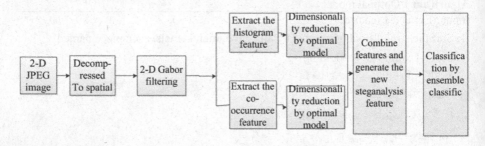

Fig. 3. The diagram of the proposed method of supervised feature extraction

4   Experimental Results

In this section, the proposed supervised feature extraction method will be used to detect two steganographic algorithms: J-UNIWARD [3] and UED [15]. The proposed features are evaluated according to the detection performance for adaptive JPEG feature extraction methods such as DCTR [6] and GFR [9]. A total of 10000 JPEG grayscale images of the BOSSbase 1.01 including the same size of 512×512 and quality factor 75 are used as the original covers [14]. We use the FLD ensemble classifier as the measurement for the detection performance.

Figure 4(a) indicates that we test the proposed steganalysis scheme against JUNIWARD with the different payloads, in some situations, the detection error rate is better than GRF while the dimension is not too high, and the optimal number of sub-classifier is also difference. While the same as in Fig. 4(b) with proposed steganalysis scheme against UED [15].

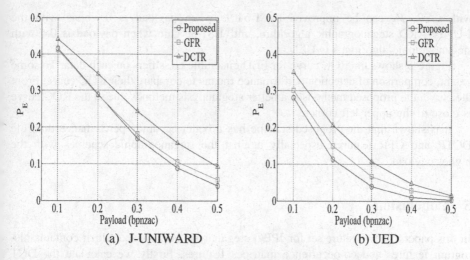

Fig. 4. The detection error of the proposed method of supervised feature extraction

With the same conditions, we perform GFR of 17000-dims features, DCTR of 8000-dims and the proposed scheme of 12020-dims on two steganographic algorithms: JUNIWARD of different bpac payloads shown in Fig. 4(a) and JC_UED of different bpac payloads shown in Fig. 4(b). As shown, the detection accuracy P_E of proposed scheme is always better for all cases than DCTR and GFR. For example, compared

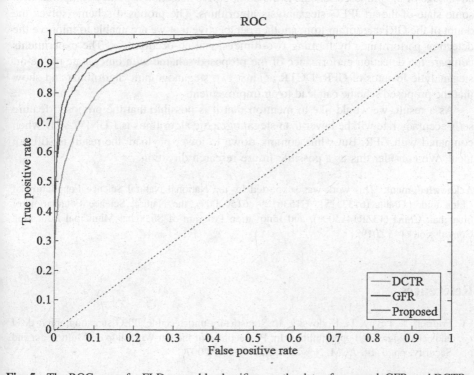

Fig. 5. The ROC curve for FLD ensemble classifiers on the data of proposed, GFR, and DCTR.

with GFR, P_E can be improved by 1.64 % when payload is 0.4 bpac with the J-UNIWARD steganographic algorithm, and 1.81 % gain when payload is 0.4 with steganographic algorithms is UED.

Figure 5 shows the ROC curve for FLD ensemble classifiers on each data. To some extent, comparison of detection performance means to compare their ROC curve. From the curve, the proposed methods is a better steganalysis methods due to the ROC curve is close to the upper left corner.

It is shown that the proposed scheme has a better accuracy performance than the DCTR and GFR features, especially against the steganographic schemes with the higher payload.

5   Conclusion

In this paper, a new feature set for JPEG steganalysis is proposed which contains histogram features and co-occurrence matrices features. Firstly we calculate the DCT coefficients by Gabor Filter which is same to the first part of GFR, and we have described 2-D Gabor Filter in Sect. 2, then we put forward a new idea to reduce the feature. Second, we just select 64 filter bases to subsample the DCT coefficients on 15 different grids corresponding to different specific positions in an 8×8 block to get 15 new planes $\mathbf{R}^{(a,b)}$, and extract the co-occurrence matrices for each of the planes $\mathbf{R}^{(a,b)}$ as the co-occurrence feature vectors. Finally, merging the two features form the finally feature vectors. The advantage of the proposed scheme is the competitive detection accuracy compared with some state-of-the-art JPEG steganalysis algorithms. The proposed scheme solves the doubt of the GRF algorithm from another perspective that we are unable to improve the detection performance by forming two-dimensional co-occurrences. The experiments compare the detection performance of the proposed scheme with other state-of-the-art steganalytic features of GFR, DCTR against two steganographic algorithms and show that the proposed scheme can lead to an improvement.

As a result, we would like to mention that it is possible that the proposed feature set's accuracy rate will be lower than steganographic algorithms is J-UNIWARD when compared with GFR. But while coming down to lower payload, the result is still not ideal. We consider this as a possible future research direction.

Acknowledgment. This work was supported by the National Natural Science Foundation of China under Grants (61373151, U1536109, 61502009), the Natural Science Foundation of Shanghai, China (13ZR1415000), and Innovation Program of Shanghai Municipal Education Commission (14YZ019).

References

1. Fridrich, J., Pevný, T., Kodovský, J.: Statistically undetectable JPEG steganography: dead ends challenges, and opportunities. In: Proceedings of the 9th Workshop on Multimedia and Security, pp. 3–14. ACM, New York, September 2007

2. Guo, L.J., Ni, J.Q., Shi, Y.Q.: An efficient JPEG steganographic scheme using uniform embedding. In: Proceedings of the 7th IEEE International Workshop on Information Forensics and Security, pp. 169–174. IEEE, December 2012
3. Holub, V., Fridrich, J.: Digital image steganography using universal distortion. In: Proceedings of the first ACM Workshop on Information Hiding and Multimedia Security, pp. 59–68. ACM, New York, June 2013
4. Fridrich, J., Kodovsky, J.: Rich models for steganalysis of digital images. IEEE Trans. Inf. Forensics Secur. 7(3), 868–882 (2012)
5. Holub, V., Fridrich, J., Denemark, T.: Universal distortion function for steganography in an arbitrary domain. EURASIP J. Inf. Secur. 2014(1), 1–13 (2014)
6. Kodovsky, J., Fridrich, J.: Steganalysis of JPEG images using rich models. In: Proceedings of International Society for Optics and Photonics, SPIE Electronic Imaging, pp. 83030A–83030A-13, January 2012
7. Kodovsky, J., Fridrich, J.: Steganalysis in high dimensions: fusing classifiers built on random subspaces. In: Proceedings the 3rd SPIE Workshop on Media Watermarking, Security, and Forensics, SPIE Electronic Imaging, pp. 78800L–78800L-13, January 2011
8. Holub, V., Fridrich, J.: Low complexity features for JPEG steganalysis using undecimated DCT. IEEE Trans. Inf. Forensics Secur. 10(2), 219–228 (2014)
9. Song, X.F., Liu, F.L., Yang, C.F., Luo, X.Y., Zhang, Y.: Steganalysis of adaptive JPEG steganography using 2D Gabor filters. In: Proceedings of the 3rd ACM Workshop on Information Hiding and Multimedia Security, pp. 15–23. ACM, New York, June 2015
10. Li, F., Zhang, X., Chen, B., Feng, G.: JPEG steganalysis with high-dimensional features and Bayesian ensemble classifier. IEEE Signal Process. Lett. 20(3), 233–236 (2013)
11. Wang, C., Feng, G.R.: Calibration-based features for JPEG steganalysis using multi-level filter. In: Proceedings of International Conference on Signal Processing, Communications and Computing, pp. 1–4. IEEE, September 2015
12. Daugman, J.G.: Uncertainty relation for resolution in space, spatial frequency, and orientation optimized by two-dimensional visual cortical filters. J. Opt. Soc. Am. A 2(7), 1160–1169 (1985)
13. Bas, P., Filler, T., Pevný, T.: "Break Our Steganographic System": the ins and outs of organizing BOSS. In: Filler, T., Pevný, T., Craver, S., Ker, A. (eds.) IH 2011. LNCS, vol. 6958, pp. 59–70. Springer, Heidelberg (2011)
14. Kodovsky, J., Fridrich, J., Holub, V.: Ensemble classifiers for steganalysis of digital media. IEEE Trans. Inf. Forensics Secur. 7(2), 432–444 (2012)
15. Guo, L.J., Ni, J.Q., Shi, Y.Q.: Uniform embedding for efficient JPEG steganography. IEEE Trans. Inf. Forensics Secur. 9(5), 814–825 (2014)

Improved Separable Reversible Data Hiding in Encrypted Image Based on Neighborhood Prediction

Shu Yan, Fan Chen[✉], and Hongjie He

Sichuan Key Lab of Signal and Information Processing,
Southwest Jiaotong University, Chengdu, Sichuan, China
{yan_shu,mrchenfan,hehojie}@126.com

Abstract. Recently, separable reversible data hiding in encrypted image attracts more and more attention. Data extraction and image decryption are separable in the separable reversible data hiding method in encrypted image, which makes it possible for cloud server to extract the additional data without knowing the original content. In this paper, we focus on the user side and introduced two improved methods based on neighborhood prediction to obtain the good quality decrypted image without data hiding key. Our experiment results prove both the two methods achieve good performance on decrypted image.

Keywords: Data hiding · Reversible data hiding · Encrypted image · Neighborhood prediction

1 Introduction

Reversible data hiding is a technique that embeds additional data into original image, the embedded data can be extracted and the covered image can be recovered to the original one. Recently, many reversible data hiding methods have been proposed and can be divided into four categories: compression based [1, 2], difference expansion (DE) [3, 4], histogram shifting (HS) based [5, 6] and prediction-error based [7, 8].

For privacy protection, an image owner may encrypt the original image before transmission or storage (as in body area networks [9] and cloud storage) since he does not want the service provider know the original image content. For the service provider who do not know the original image, they would embed some additional data in an encrypted image for other application such as image notation or authentication. In recent years, some methods on reversible data hiding in encrypted image (RDH-EI) have been proposed. In 2011, Zhang proposed a joint RDH-EI method [10], an original image is encrypted by XOR operation, and additional data is embedded in the 3LSBs of parts of the encrypted image to generate a marked encrypted image. At data extraction and image recovery phases, a marked encrypted image was firstly decrypted by the encryption key. And then, according to the data hiding key, the additional data was extracted and the original image was recovered by utilizing the spatial correlation in natural image. In Zhang's method [10], the embedding rate is low and error bits exist in extracted data. To improve Zhang's method, some joint RDH-EI methods [11–13] have

© Springer International Publishing AG 2016
X. Sun et al. (Eds.): ICCCS 2016, Part I, LNCS 10039, pp. 94–103, 2016.
DOI: 10.1007/978-3-319-48671-0_9

been proposed. For those joint methods, data extraction and image recovery are performed jointly, and the reported joint RDH-EI methods are not capable of obtaining error-free extracted bits when high payload embedding is adopted.

In application scenario, it is unreasonable to know both the encryption key and the data hiding key for image owner or data hider. For example, in cloud storage, image owner only has encryption key and cloud service provider only has data hiding key. For data hider, he needs to extract the additional data without image decryption. And for the image owner, he hopes to conveniently download an encrypted image and obtain the decrypted image according to his encryption key. For this aim, another type named separable method has been proved. In the separable method, data extraction and image decryption is separable. Roughly, five types of separable method have been proposed: [14, 15] compress the encrypted image to create spare space for data hiding. [16, 17] encrypt original image by pseudo-randomly realigning pixels of the original image. And data hiding is achieved by histogram shifting. [18, 19] achieved high embedding rate by reserving room before encryption. And [20] is a universal method which can be used completely in the encrypted domain, like image signal, video signal and text signal.

In [21], Wu proposed separable method based on prediction-error. In Wu's separable RDH-EI method, if receiver only have data hiding key, he can extract additional data without any error. If receiver only have encryption key, a decrypted image similar with the original one can obtained. If receiver have both key, data extraction and image recovery can be down. Wu's separable method realized separable in data extraction and image decryption. The separable method also provides improved reversibility and good visual quality of recovered image for high payload embedding [21]. In Wu's separable method, though the PSNR of recover image is high, the performance of decrypted image is not good. As in cloud storage, users possibly only have encryption key, so he can only get a decrypted image. As a result, how to improve quality of the decrypted image is of great significant. To achieve this aim, two improved methods based on neighborhood prediction of Wu's separable method are designed to obtain a good quality decrypted image.

The rest of this paper is organized as follows. Wu's separable method is described in Sect. 2. Section 3 introduced the two improved methods. The experimental results and discussions are presented in Sects. 4 and 5 gives conclusions and future work.

2 Wu's Algorithm

In [21], Wu proposed a separable algorithm for reversible data hiding in encrypted image. For explicitly indicating the condition of a recovery image obtaining, the extension diagram of Wu's separable RDH-EI method is given in Fig. 1, where "Image decryption" is added. It can be seen from Fig. 1 that the decrypted image is obtained by one secret key (encryption key) and the reconstructed image is obtained by two secret keys (encryption key and data hiding key).

In this algorithm, content owner uses encryption key to encrypt original image, then send it to data hider. Data hider use data hiding key to embed additional data into the encrypted image. At the receiver side, according to the data hiding key, the embedded

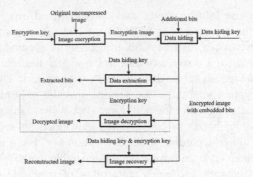

Fig. 1. Extension diagram of Wu's separable RDH-EI method

data can be extracted without any error. And if the receiver has encryption key, he can obtain a vision similar with the original image. If the receiver has both keys, he can extract additional data and recovery the original image. Wu's separable algorithm consists of four phases: image encryption, data hiding, data extraction and image recovery.

(1) Image encryption: According to encryption key, content owner generates a pseudo random bit stream K_{XOR}. Using K_{XOR}, content owner encrypts the uncompressed original image I_O by bitwise exclusive-or operation and obtains encrypted image I_E.

(2) Data hiding: According to data hiding key, data hider first pseudo-randomly chooses two sets of locations of the encryption image. Denote the two sets as Γ_{Qual} and Γ_{Forb}, respectively. Additional bits are going to be embedded in pixels on locations in set Γ_{Qual}, while pixels on locations belong to set Γ_{Forb} remain unchanged. The relationship of locations in Γ_{Qual} and Γ_{Forb} are given in Fig. 2. In Fig. 2, location of pixel B $\in \Gamma_{Qual}$, locations of pixels t_1, t_2, t_3, $t_4 \in \Gamma_{Forb}$. Denote additional bits as $S(1), S(2), \ldots, S(L)$, here L is the total number of additional bits. From encrypted image I_E, select L pixels on the positions belong to set Γ_{Qual}, denote them as $B(1), B(2), \ldots, B(L)$. Additional data are embedded into the tth ($t \geq 7$) bit of the selected pixels by

$$B'(d) = B(d) - b \times 2^{(t-1)} + S(d) \times 2^{(t-1)}, \quad 1 \leq d \leq L \qquad (1)$$

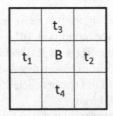

Fig. 2. The position relationship of B and B's four neighboring pixels

$$b = \left\lfloor \frac{B(d)}{2^{(t-1)}} \right\rfloor \mod 2 \tag{2}$$

Where $B'(d)$ is marked encrypted pixel. When all L bits are embedded, a marked encrypted image is generated. Denote the marked encrypted image as I_E'.

(3) Data extraction: Using data hiding key, receiver can extract the additional bits from the marked encrypted image I_E' by

$$S(d) = \left\lfloor \frac{B'(d)}{2^{(t-1)}} \right\rfloor \mod 2, \quad 1 \leq d \leq L \tag{3}$$

Here $B'(1), B'(2), \ldots, B'(L)$ is the marked encrypted pixels.

(4) Image decryption: If the receiver only has encryption key, he can use the encryption key to decrypt marked encrypted image I_E' and obtain a directly decrypted image. Denote the directly decrypted image as I_{DIR}. Then a median filter is used on image I_{DIR}, and a decrypted image I_{DEC} similar to the original vision is generated.

(5) Image recovery: If the receiver has two secret keys (encryption key and data hiding key), he can first extract the additional data from marked encrypted image I_E', as data extraction phase mentioned. Then the receiver uses the encryption key to decrypt the marked encrypted image, and gets directly decrypted image I_{DIR}. Then according to the data hiding key, receiver can find out the position of marked pixels. According to pixels on the positions belong to Γ_{Forb}, original image can be recovered. Denote the recovered image as I_{REC}.

We find that in Wu's image decryption phase, noise appears in directly decrypted image I_{DIR}. Although Wu used a median filter on the directly decrypted image, edge blur effect exists and the PSNR of decrypted image is not high, especially for the texture-rich image like Baboon. That is, in Wu's separable RDH-EI method, though using encryption key can obtain a decrypted vision similar to the original image, the quality of decrypted image cannot satisfy user. If the quality of decrypted image can be improved, the user can obtain content from decrypted image without knowing data hiding key, which has no impact on using. By this way, not only the difficulty of the secret key management can be reduced, but also makes Wu's separable RDH-EI method applies on more application scenarios. Therefore, this work focuses on improving the quality of the decrypted image by improving the image decryption method based on neighborhood prediction.

3 Improved Algorithm

To obtain high quality decrypted image, we have two improved methods at image decryption phase (as the dashed frame in Fig. 1 shows). Inspired by [22–24], pixels containing secret bit have features different form unchanged pixels, so utilizing the spatial correlation of natural image, both of our two improved methods are based on neighborhood prediction. In our two improved methods, image encryption phase, data encryption phase, data extraction phase and image recovery phase are the same as those in Wu's method. In our first method, we predict the marked pixel (pixel containing additional data) by calculating the difference between to-be-predict pixel and its eight neighboring pixels. Then median filtering operation is applied on marked pixel. In our second method, for each pixel in directly decrypted image I_{DIR}, we first flip its tth ($t \geq 7$) bit and obtain a flipped pixel. Then comparing the fluctuation of the flipped pixel and that of un-flipped pixel, regard the pixel whose fluctuation is smaller as the original one.

3.1   The First Method

In the first method, according to neighbor pixels, we can first predict whether the to-be-predict pixel is a marked pixel. If the to-be-predict pixel is a marked pixel, use its eight neighboring pixels to estimate to-be-predict pixel. Otherwise, the to-be-predict pixel remains unchanged.

At image decryption phase, first use data hiding key to generate a directly decrypted image I_{DIR}. Let (i,j) be the pixel position, and denote the gray value of pixel to be estimated as $I_{DIR}(i,j)$. Calculate the difference between $I_{DIR}(i,j)$ and its eight neighbors by

$$DE = \left| I_{DIR}(i,j) - \frac{1}{8} \sum_{u=i-1}^{i+1} \sum_{v=j-1}^{j+1} I_{DIR}(u,v) \right| \tag{4}$$

Here DE is the difference of $I_{DIR}(i,j)$ and its eight neighbors. Compare DE with a predefined threshold β, then calculate the estimate value of $I_{DIR}(i,j)$ by

$$I_{DEC}(i,j) = \begin{cases} [\text{med}(I_{DIR}(u,v))], u \in [i-1,i+1], v \in [j-1,j+1] \text{ and when } u = i, v \neq j, & \text{if } DE \geq \beta \\ I_{DIR}(i,j), & \text{if } DE < \beta \end{cases}$$

$$\tag{5}$$

Here I_{DEC} is the decrypted image.

3.2   The Second Method

In Wu's method, comparing directly decrypted image I_{DIR} with original image I_O, only marked pixels may have change. Exactly, it is the tth ($t \geq 7$) bit of the pixels belong to set Γ_{Qual} flipped that leads to the noise. In our second method, we first flip the tth ($t \geq 7$) bit of pixel in directly decrypted image I_{DIR}, then calculate the fluctuation of the flipped pixel and un-flipped pixel, respectively. We regard the pixel whose fluctuation is smaller as the original pixel.

In directly decrypted image I_{DIR}, for the pixel $I_{DIR}(i,j)$, flip its tth bit, and the flipped pixel $\overline{I_{DIR}(i,j)}$ is obtained. Then calculate the fluctuation of $I_{DIR}(i,j)$ and $\overline{I_{DIR}(i,j)}$ by

$$f = \left| I_{DIR}(i,j) - \frac{I_{DIR}(i-1,j) + I_{DIR}(i,j-1) + I_{DIR}(i,j+1) + I_{DIR}(i+1,j)}{4} \right| \quad (6)$$

$$\bar{f} = \left| \overline{I_{DIR}(i,j)} - \frac{I_{DIR}(i-1,j) + I_{DIR}(i,j-1) + I_{DIR}(i,j+1) + I_{DIR}(i+1,j)}{4} \right| \quad (7)$$

here f is the fluctuation of $I_{DIR}(i,j)$, $\bar{f}$ is the fluctuation of $\overline{I_{DIR}(i,j)}$. Comparing f with $\bar{f}$, regard the pixel whose fluctuation is smaller as the estimate value.

$$I_{DEC}(i,j) = \begin{cases} I_{DIR}(i,j), & \text{if } f \leq \bar{f} \\ \overline{I_{DIR}(i,j)}, & \text{if } \bar{f} \leq f \end{cases} \quad (8)$$

Here $I_{DEC}(i,j)$ is the estimate value of $I_{DIR}(i,j)$, I_{DEC} represents the decrypted image.

4 Experimental Results

The test image is Lena and Baboon, as shown in Fig. 3. Both of the test images contain 512×512 pixels. To analyze the performance of the two improved methods, we test the decrypted image of Lena and Baboon, using the first method and the second method, respectively. For each method and each test image, 5 groups parameters (embedding bit plane t and total embedding bits L) are tested: $\{t = 7, L = 4096\}$, $\{t = 7, L = 16384\}$, $\{t = 8, L = 4096\}$, $\{t = 8, L = 16384\}$, $\{t = 8, L = 40960\}$. For each group, we test 100 times (100 different data hiding keys).

(a) Lena   (b) Baboon

Fig. 3. Test image Lena and Baboon

The PSNR of decrypted image of Lena and Baboon using the first method is shown in Fig. 4. Figure 4(a) shows the PSNR of image Lena. Figure 4(b) shows the PSNR of image Baboon. Figure 4 demonstrates that our first method effectively improves the PSNR of decrypted image. And when embedding rare keeps unchanged, embed additional bits into the 8th bit plane can achieve a better performance than embedding in the 7th bit plane.

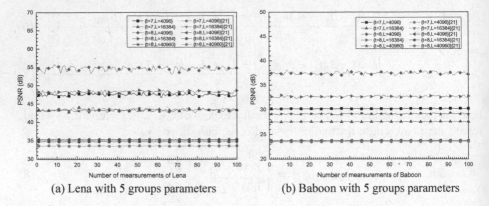

(a) Lena with 5 groups parameters   (b) Baboon with 5 groups parameters

Fig. 4. PSNR of Lena and Baboon with the first method

The average PSNR and variance of image Lena and Baboon of method one using 5 groups parameters are given in Fig. 5. Figure 5(a) shows the average PSNR of Lena and Baboon. The minimum average PSNR of Lena is larger than 40 dB, when using the first method. Figure 5(b) gives the variance of Lena and Baboon. All the variance is less than 0.4, so the stability of the first method is good, especially in texture-rich image.

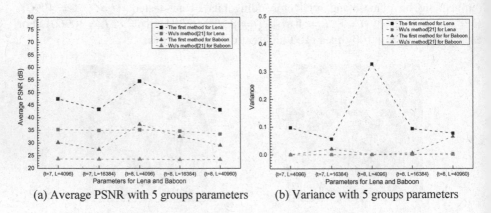

(a) Average PSNR with 5 groups parameters   (b) Variance with 5 groups parameters

Fig. 5. Average PSNR and variance of Lena and Baboon with the first method

The PSNR of image Lena and Baboon using the second method is shown in Fig. 6. In Fig. 6(a), some points disappear when the parameter is $\{t = 8, L = 4096\}$, this is because the PSNR is ∞ dB at these points. Figure 6 demonstrates that our second method also greatly improved the PSNR of decrypted image. And when embedding rate keeps unchanged, embed additional bits into the 8th bit plane can achieve a better performance than embedding in the 7th bit plane.

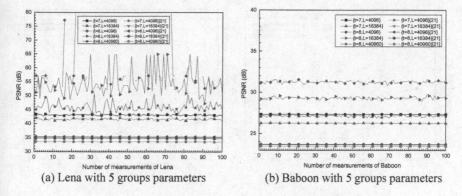

(a) Lena with 5 groups parameters   (b) Baboon with 5 groups parameters

Fig. 6. PSNR of Lena and Baboon with the second method

The average PSNR and variance of image Lena and Baboon of method two using 5 groups parameters are given in Fig. 7. Figure 7(a) shows the average PSNR of Lena and Baboon. The minimum average PSNR of Lena is larger than 40 dB, when using method one. Figure 7(b) gives the variance of Lena and Baboon. And the second method is stable in texture-rich image. Figures 4, 5, 6 and 7 prove that our two improved methods both efficiently improved the PSNR of decrypted image a lot. And the PSNR is higher when cover image is smoother.

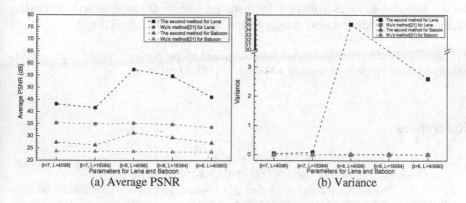

(a) Average PSNR   (b) Variance

Fig. 7. Average PSNR and variance of Lena and Baboon with the second method

Figure 8 gives the average PSNR and variance of Lena and Baboon with the first method, the second method and Wu's method, respectively. Figure 8 demonstrates that the first method is more stable than the second method. When additional data is embedded in the 7th bit plane, the first method performs better. But in some situations, use the second method can generate perfect image, for example, when 4096 bits are embedded into the 8th bit plane in Lena, the maximum PSNR of decrypted image is ∞ dB. The experiment results demonstrate the two improved methods in image decryption phase perform well and largely improved the PSNR of decrypted image.

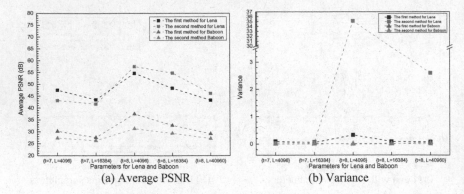

(a) Average PSNR   (b) Variance

Fig. 8. Average PSNR and variance of Lena and Baboon with two proposed methods

5   Conclusion and Expectation

We introduced two schemes of separable reversible data hiding in encrypted image based on neighborhood prediction. The two schemes efficiently improved the performance of decrypted image when receiver only has encryption key, the PSNR of decrypted image is much higher than that of Wu's method, which makes it possible for Wu's separable RDH-EI method applying on application scenario that user only use one secret key (encryption key) to obtain high visual quality of decrypted image. There are still some issues for us to discuss, for instance, whether the prediction of data hiding location brings hidden security danger to the steganography algorithm.

Acknowledgements. The research has been supported by the National Natural Science Foundation of China, People's Republic of China (61373180, 61461047).

References

1. Fridrich, J., Goljan, M., Du, R.: Lossless data embedding–new paradigm in digital watermarking. Sig. Process. **2002**(2), 185–196 (2002)
2. Celik, M., Sharma, G., Tekalp, A., Saber, E.: Lossless generalized–LSB data embedding. IEEE Trans. Image Process. **14**(2), 253–266 (2005)
3. Tian, J.: Reversible data embedding using a difference expansion. IEEE Trans. Circ. Syst. Video Technol. **13**(8), 890–896 (2003)
4. Thodi, D., Rodríguez, J.: Expansion embedding techniques for reversible watermarking. IEEE Trans. Image Process. **16**(3), 721–730 (2007)
5. Ni, Z., Shi, Y., Ansari, N.: Reversible data hiding. IEEE Trans. Circ. Syst. Video Technol. **16**(3), 354–362 (2006)
6. Tai, W., Yeh, V., Chang, C.: reversible data hiding based on histogram modification of pixel differences. IEEE Trans. Circ. Syst. Video Technol. **19**(6), 906–910 (2009)
7. Luo, L., Chen, Z., Chen, M., Zheng, X., Xiong, Z.: reversible image watermarking using interpolation technique. IEEE Trans. Inf. Forensics Secur. **5**(1), 187–193 (2010)

8. Li, X., Yang, B., Zeng, T.: Efficient reversible watermarking based on adaptive prediction-error expansion and pixel selection. IEEE Trans. Image Process. **20**(12), 3524–3533 (2011)

9. Shen, J., Moh, S., Chung, I.: enhanced secure sensor association and key management in wireless body area networks. J. Commun. Netw. **17**(5), 453–462 (2015)

10. Zhang, X.: Reversible data hiding in encrypted image. IEEE Sig. Process. Lett. **18**(4), 255–258 (2011)

11. Hong, W., Chen, T., Wu, H.: An improved reversible data hiding in encrypted images using side match. IEEE Sig. Process. Lett. **19**(4), 199–202 (2012)

12. Liao, X., Shu, C.: Reversible data hiding in encrypted images based on absolute mean difference of neighboring pixels. J. Vis. Commun. Image Represent. **28**, 21–27 (2015)

13. Qian, C., Zhang, X.: Effective reversible data hiding in encrypted image with privacy protection for image content. J. Vis. Commun. Image Represent. **31**, 154–164 (2015)

14. Zhang, X.: Separable reversible data hiding in encrypted image. IEEE Trans. Inf. Forensics Secur. **7**(2), 826–832 (2012)

15. Zhang, X., Qian, Z., Feng, G., Ren, Y.: Efficient reversible data hiding in encrypted images. J. Vis. Commun. Image Represent. **25**(2), 322–328 (2014)

16. Qian, Z., Han, X., Zhang, X.: Separable reversible data hiding in encrypted images by n-nary histogram modification. In: Proceedings of ICMT, pp. 869–876. Atlantis Press (2013)

17. Jose, R., Abraham, G.: A separable reversible data hiding in encrypted images with improved performance. In: Proceedings of ICMiCR, pp. 1–5. Atlantis Press (2013)

18. Ma, K., Zhang, W., Zhao, X., Yu, N., Li, F.: Reversible data hiding in encrypted images by reserving room before encryption. IEEE Trans. Inf. Forensics Secur. **8**(3), 553–562 (2013)

19. Zhang, W., Ma, K., Yu, N.: Reversibility improved data hiding in encrypted images. Sig. Process. **94**, 118–127 (2014)

20. Karim, M., Wong, K.: Universal data embedding in encrypted domain. Sig. Process. **94**, 174–182 (2014)

21. Wu, X., Sun, W.: High-capacity reversible data hiding in encrypted images by prediction error. Sig. Process. **104**, 387–400 (2014)

22. Li, J., Li, X., Yang, B., Sun, X.: Segmentation-based image copy-move forgery detection scheme. IEEE Trans. Inf. Forensics Secur. **10**(3), 507–518 (2015)

23. Xia, Z., Wang, X., Sun, X., Liu, Q., Xiong, N.: Steganalysis of LSB matching using differences between nonadjacent pixels. Multimedia Tools Appl. **75**(4), 1947–1962 (2016)

24. Xia, Z., Wang, X., Sun, X., Wang, B.: Steganalysis of least significant bit matching using multi-order differences. Secur. Commun. Netw. **7**(8), 1283–1291 (2014)

Fragile Watermarking with Self-recovery Capability via Absolute Moment Block Truncation Coding

Ping Ji[1,2], Chuan Qin[1,2(✉)], and Zhenjun Tang[1]

[1] Guangxi Key Lab of Multi-source Information Mining and Security,
Guangxi Normal University, Guilin 541004, China
{chuckping, tangzj230}@163.com, qin@usst.edu.cn
[2] School of Optical-Electrical and Computer Engineering,
University of Shanghai for Science and Technology, Shanghai 200093, China

Abstract. In this paper, we propose a fragile image watermarking scheme based on Absolute Moment Block Truncation Coding (AMBTC) and self-embedding. According to the constructed binary map and two reconstruction levels, each non-overlapping block in original image can be compressed with the AMBTC algorithm. Then, after scrambling, the compression codes are extended through a random matrix, which can introduce more redundancy into the reference bits to be embedded for content recovery. Also, the relationship between each image block and each reference bit is built so that the recoverable area for tampered image can be increased. Experimental results demonstrate the effectiveness of the proposed scheme.

Keywords: Fragile watermarking · AMBTC · Tampering detection · Content recovery

1 Introduction

Nowadays, the transmission of multimedia data has been increasingly widely. At the same time, the problem is that digital images can be much more easily tampered by image processing tools than before. Image integrity protection has attracted more attention regardless of academics and corporation. To this purpose, many researchers has deeply study the solution to the problem of the image authentication. [1–4].

In general, hash function, such as MD5, can be utilized to identify the integrity of data. Nonetheless, if we directly transplant the technique of hash function into the image authentication, there are some disadvantages: firstly, in consequence of the much larger volume of digital image data than a short text message, this will require a high computational cost. Secondly, the judgment result is only true or false so that it is unable to conduct tamper location accurately and content recovery. Last but not least, even a bit change of original data with conventional hash function influences the outcome of the decision and cause a misjudgment, however, the reserved changes on visual sense for digital images should be permitted. Hence, fragile image watermarking has been presented to resolve these drawbacks of traditional hash function in image

© Springer International Publishing AG 2016
X. Sun et al. (Eds.): ICCCS 2016, Part I, LNCS 10039, pp. 104–113, 2016.
DOI: 10.1007/978-3-319-48671-0_10

integrity authentication [5]. Through embedding the watermark into original image at the sender, image authentication can be realized at the receiver by the extracted watermark information. In practical terms, since malicious tampering operations damage image contents, some embedded watermark, and the relationships between them, tampering detection can be achieved. Moreover, some intact embedded watermark can be utilized to conduct further content recovery. Because the embedded watermark is usually jointed with original image itself for mostly schemes, this type of schemes is also known as self-embedding fragile watermarking scheme [6].

Chang *et al.* presented a watermarking method for ownership detection and tampering detection of digital images [1]. This scheme has adaptive embedding capacity. Although the accuracy of the tamper detection is very high, the tampered images cannot be recovered. Lin *et al.* proposed a hierarchical watermarking scheme for both tamper detection and content recovery [7]. A 3-level stage detection of tampered blocks based on parity check bits is applied in this method. Average intensity is also used to recover the tampered image. Due to only recover with the small tampered areas effectively, it cannot restore images with higher tampering rate very well. Lee and Lin proposed a dual watermark scheme for image tamper detection and recovery [8]. This scheme provided the second opportunity for content recovery, if the recovery information was beyond repair at the first time. Even if the image was destroyed about higher tampering rate, the recovery vision quality of the recovered image can be still recognized. In [9], Zhang *et al.* proposed a novel self-embedding watermarking scheme. Reference bits were generated from the principal content with a reference sharing mechanism in this method. By applying this scheme, original image can be retrieved when the tampering rate was not too high. As a consequence, the lower the tampering rate is, the better the quality of restored results will be.

In this paper, we propose a novel self-embedding fragile watermark scheme based on Absolute Moment Block Truncation Coding (AMBTC) sharing. In our scheme, the reference bits for content recovery are derived from the AMBTC algorithm applied on the original image. In order to obtain satisfactory quality of watermarked image, watermark bits are embedded into 2 least significant bits (LSB). The reference sharing mechanism is employed to recover tampered image. Redundancy is introduced to expand the two parts of bits generated from AMBTC algorithm. Even if tampering rate is extensive, the watermark bits derived from the reserved regions can supply the wealthy information to recover the main content of the original image. That is to say, the quality of recovered image can be acceptable.

2   Preliminaries

As a lossy image compression technique, Block Truncation Coding or AMBTC [10] has an advantage of fewer calculation and efficient. BTC algorithm calculates the mean and the standard deviation for each block in original image. Suppose original image is divided into non-overlapping $m \times m$ blocks. The mean value b_{avg} and the standard deviation b_{std} of each block can be computed through Eqs. (1 and 2):

$$b_{avg} = \frac{1}{m^2} \sum_{i=1}^{m^2} p_i, \tag{1}$$

$$b_{std} = \left\{ \frac{1}{m^2} \sum_{i=1}^{m^2} p_i^2 - b_{avg}^2 \right\}^{1/2}, \tag{2}$$

where p_i is denoted as the gray value of each pixel in the block.

Both values are sent with a binary map which contains zeros in those pixels where $p_i < b_{avg}$ and ones otherwise. The binary map is as shown in Fig. 1. The block is recovered with its binary map and two levels that can be computed with b_{avg} and b_{std}, as shown in Eqs. (3) and (4).

$$h = b_{avg} + b_{std} \sqrt{\frac{m^2 - q}{q}} \quad \text{for } p_i \geq b_{avg}, \tag{3}$$

$$l = b_{avg} - b_{std} \sqrt{\frac{q}{m^2 - q}} \quad \text{for } p_i < b_{avg}, \tag{4}$$

where q is the number of ones for each block in binary map. Both h and l are presented by 8 bits.

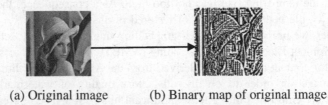

(a) Original image   (b) Binary map of original image

Fig. 1. Generation of binary map ($m = 4$)

However, the self-embedding fragile watermark is more focused on the quality of the recovered image. So, in order to make the quality of the quality of recovered image higher, an algorithm called Absolute Moment Block Truncation Coding or AMBTC [11] which is superior to BTC is utilized in proposed scheme. AMBTC is also a lossy compression scheme, which can be applied in block-wise embedding watermark. Let an original image divided into non-overlapped $m \times m$ blocks. In compression stage, a binary map can be obtained in the same way like BTC. At the receiver, The block is also recovered with its binary map and two levels as shown in Eqs. (5) and (6). For each block, h is the average of those pixels which are greater than b_{avg} and l is the average of those pixels which are lower than b_{avg}. This advantage makes the quality of recovered image reach as high as possible.

$$h = \frac{1}{q}\sum_{i=1}^{q} p_i \quad \text{for } p_i \ge b_{avg}, \tag{5}$$

$$l = \frac{1}{m^2 - q}\sum_{i=1}^{m^2 - q} p_i \quad \text{for } p_i < b_{avg}, \tag{6}$$

where q is the number of ones for each block in binary map. As applying AMBTC, the compression and recovery results are shown in Fig. 2.

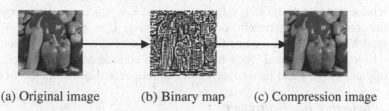

(a) Original image   (b) Binary map   (c) Compression image

Fig. 2. Compression and recovery results from applying AMBTC ($m = 8$)

As all mentioned above, when the value of m increases, the compression rate C also increases, which is determined with binary map, high level and low level; on the contrary, the quality of decoded image (PSNR and SSIM [12]) for BTC and AMBTC, which are denoted as R_1 and R_2, decrease. Relationship among m, C, R_1 and R_2 is as shown in Table 1. What we can find in Table 1 is that R_1 are all less than R_2. AMBTC can be more suitable for our watermarking scheme.

Table 1. Relationship among m, C, R_1 and R_2

Image	m	C	R_1		R_2	
			PSNR (dB)	SSIM	PSNR (dB)	SSIM
Lena 512 × 512	2	8/5	38.38	0.999	39.92	0.999
	4	4/1	32.70	0.989	33.19	0.990
	8	32/5	29.52	0.958	29.90	0.963
	16	128/17	26.80	0.900	27.18	0.901

3 Proposed Scheme

In the proposed scheme, the 6 most significant bits (MSB) of all pixels in the original image keep unchanged and 2 LSB of those are replaced with the watermark bits including the reference bits and hash bits. The reference bits are derived from binary map and two levels of AMBTC compressed version for the 6 MSB and size of $m \times m$ blocks, where m can be equal to 4, and the hash bits are determined by the 6 MSB and the reference bits together. On the authentication side, the receiver can detect tampered regions according to hash bits, and the tampered regions can be recovered through the reference bits from other reserved regions in the whole image.

3.1 Watermark Embedding Procedure

(1) *Compression Bits Generation Based on AMBTC*

First, the 2 LSB layers of the original image $\mathbf{I}$ with size of $N_1 \times N_2$ are set as zero to obtain the initialized image $\mathbf{I'}$. Denote the total number of pixels in the image as N ($N = N_1 \times N_2$). Then, the image $\mathbf{I'}$ is divided into a series of non-overlapping blocks sized $m \times m$, and through AMBTC algorithm, the binary pattern and the two reconstruction levels (denoted as l_n and h_n, $n = 1, 2, ..., N/16$) for each block can be obtained, where n is the block number. Since 2 LSB of all pixels are removed to shorten the range of gray value from [0, 255] to [0, 63], thus, both l_n and h_n can be represented by 6 bits, i.e., $l_{n,5}, l_{n,4}, ..., l_{n,0}$ and $h_{n,5}, h_{n,4}, ..., h_{n,0}$, respectively. Denote the combined binary pattern for the whole image $\mathbf{I'}$ as $\mathbf{B}$ sized $N_1 \times N_2$. Collect the total N bits of $\mathbf{B}$ and the bits for all $N/16$ pairs of l_n and h_n and denote them as $\mathbf{U}$, which consists of total $7 \cdot N/4$ bits. $\mathbf{U}$ can be considered as the compression bits of original image $\mathbf{I}$ and be interleaved to generate reference bits in the next stage.

(2) *Reference Bits Generation*

Through the secret key, we permute and divide $\mathbf{U}$ into f subsets with equal size K: $\mathbf{U} = \{\mathbf{U}^{(1)}, \mathbf{U}^{(2)}, ..., \mathbf{U}^{(f)}\}$, where $f = (N + 12 \cdot N/m^2)/K$ and K is a positive integer. Then, through the interleaving operation, we can extend these f subsets of $\mathbf{U}$ to generate reference bits. Detailedly, for each subset $\mathbf{U}^{(j)}$ of binary patterns, its K bits, i.e., $u_1^{(j)}, u_2^{(j)}, ..., u_K^{(j)}$, are extended into K' reference-bits, i.e., $r_1^{(j)}, r_2^{(j)}, ..., r_{K'}^{(j)}$, see Eq. (7).

$$\begin{bmatrix} r_1^{(j)} \\ r_2^{(j)} \\ \vdots \\ r_{K'}^{(j)} \end{bmatrix} = \mathbf{H}^{(j)} \cdot \begin{bmatrix} u_1^{(j)} \\ u_2^{(j)} \\ \vdots \\ u_K^{(j)} \end{bmatrix}, \quad j = 1, 2, ..., f, \tag{7}$$

where $\mathbf{H}^{(1)}, \mathbf{H}^{(2)}, ..., \mathbf{H}^{(j)}$ are the f pseudo-random binary matrices sized $K' \times K$ generated according to the secret key. The arithmetic operation in Eq. (7) is modulo-2. After the operation in Eq. (7), each bit in the subset $\mathbf{U}^{(j)}$ is shared by all the reference bits $r_1^{(j)}, r_2^{(j)}, ..., r_{K'}^{(j)}$, and each reference bit is also related with all the compression bits $u_1^{(j)}, u_2^{(j)}, ..., u_K^{(j)}$ in $\mathbf{U}^{(j)}$.

In the design of our scheme, 2 LSB layers of the image, i.e., $2 \cdot N$ bits in total, are utilized to accommodate watermark bits including authentication bits for tampering detection and reference bits for content recovery, and the accuracy of tampering detection is set as 8×8 block. Thus, for the 128 bits in the 2 LSB layers of each 8×8 block, 16 bits and 112 bits are allocated to accommodate authentication bits and reference bits, respectively. As a result, among the $2 \cdot N$ bits in 2 LSB layers of the whole image, besides the $16 \cdot N/64$ authentication bits, there are totally $2N - 16 \times N/64 = 7 \cdot N/4$ reference bits. Therefore, the value of K' in Eq. (7) must satisfy the relationship: $f \cdots K' = \lambda \cdot 7N/4 = 7N/4$, where $\lambda = K'/K$ denotes the extension rate between reference bits and the AMBTC compression bits. Here, $\lambda = 1$ and $K' = K$.

After the above operation, $7 \cdot N/4$ reference bits generated from the compression bits of the AMBTC-based binary patterns and reconstruction levels can be acquired and then concatenated to form a set $\mathbf{R}$.

(3) Reference/Hash Bits Embedding

After reference-bits generation, the image $\mathbf{I}'$ is divided into the $N/64$ non-overlapping blocks sized 8×8, i.e., $\mathbf{W}^{(1)}$, $\mathbf{W}^{(2)}$, ..., $\mathbf{W}^{(N/64)}$. Then, the $7 \cdot N/4$ reference bits in set $\mathbf{R}$ are permuted with the secret key and also divided into $N/64$ groups with equal size, i.e., $\mathbf{R}^{(1)}$, $\mathbf{R}^{(2)}$, ..., $\mathbf{R}^{(N/64)}$. Therefore, each subset $\mathbf{R}^{(n)}$ contains 112 bits ($n = 1, 2, ...,$ $N/64$). Note that each subset $\mathbf{R}^{(n)}$ corresponds to each 8×8 block $\mathbf{W}^{(n)}$ during embedding procedure.

For each block $\mathbf{W}^{(n)}$ in $\mathbf{I}'$, the 384 bits of its 6 MSB and its corresponding 112 reference bits are fed into a hash function to produce 16 authentication bits, i.e., $\mathbf{A}^{(n)}$. The hash function is a one-way function as well as any change on the input information leads to the completely different output information. Then, the 112 reference bits, i.e., $\mathbf{R}^{(n)}$, and the 16 authentication bits, i.e., $\mathbf{A}^{(n)}$, are permuted again according to the secret key and then are embedded into the 2 LSB of the 8×8 block $\mathbf{W}^{(n)}$. After finishing the above processing for all the blocks $\mathbf{W}^{(1)}$, $\mathbf{W}^{(2)}$, ..., $\mathbf{W}^{(N/64)}$, the watermarked image $\mathbf{I}_w$ can be acquired.

In the procedure of watermark embedding, the 6 MSB layers of original image $\mathbf{I}$ are kept unchanged and the 2 LSB layers are replaced with the random watermark bits. Therefore, the theoretical PSNR value of watermarked image $\mathbf{I}_w$ is:

$$E_D = \frac{1}{16} \cdot \sum_{\xi=0}^{3} \sum_{\eta=0}^{3} (\xi - \eta)^2 = 2.5 \,. \tag{8}$$

$$\text{PSNR} \approx 10 \cdot \log_{10}(255^2/E_D) = 44.15 \text{ dB} \,, \tag{9}$$

3.2 Content Recovery Procedure

The content of watermarked image may be altered by an adversary. The tampered blocks can be detected according to the extracted hash bits, and then be recovered by using the extracted reference bits from other reserved blocks.

(1) Tamper Detection

The received, suspicious image $\mathbf{I}_w^*$ is divided into $N/64$ non-overlapping blocks sized 8×8. For each 8×8 block, the 128 watermark bits extracted from the 2 LSB layers are separated into two parts, i.e., 112 reference bits and 16 authentication bits, using the same secret key on the sender side. If the extracted 16 authentication bits differ from the hash for the 384 bits of the 6 MSB layers and the 112 extracted reference bits, the block is judged as tampered, which means some contents in this block are altered. Otherwise, the block is judged as intact. Obviously, a block without being tampered must not be judged as tampered, and the error probability that a tampered block is judged as intact is 2^{-16}, which is negligibly low. As a result, all tampered blocks in $\mathbf{I}_w^*$ can be correctly detected on the receiver side.

(2) *Compression Bits Restoration and Tampered Content Restoration*

First, the 2 LSB layers of all pixels in I_w^* are set to 0, and all N/m^2 blocks sized $m \times m$ in I^{w*} are encoded with the AMBTC algorithm proposed in Subsect. 3.1. The obtained bits of binary patterns and reconstruction levels are concatenated to form the set U^*. Then, the set U^* is permuted and divided into f subsets with the equal sizes K: $U* = \{U^{(1)*}, U^{(2)*}, \ldots, U^{(f)*}\}$. Once the image I_w^* is tampered, some bits in U^* are incorrect and different with those in U generated from I'. Due to tampering, the f subsets $U^{(1)*}$, $U^{(2)*}$, $\ldots$, $U^{(f)*}$ contain some incorrect bits that should be restored. Thus, the K bits in each subset $U^{(f)*}$ can be classified into two groups: $U^{(j)*} = \{U_D^{(j)}, U_C^{(j)}\}$ where and $U_D^{(j)}$ consists of the n_j incorrect bits obtained from the detected, tampered regions, $U_C^{(j)}$ consists the $(K - n_j)$ correct bits obtained from the intact regions, and $0 \le n_j \le K$. Next, we should restore the n_j bits of $U_D^{(j)}$ for each $U^{(j)*}$. (Here, $j = 1, 2, \ldots, f$).

On the sender side, the K bits in each subset $U^{(j)}$ are extended into the K' reference bits by Eq. (8) and are embedded into 2 LSB layers of I after permutation. Therefore, for each subset $U^{(j)*}$, its corresponding K' extended reference bits can be extracted from the 2 LSB layers of I_w^* with the same secret key. However, some of these K' reference bits that come from the tampered regions may be incorrect and cannot be utilized to restore the compression bits of binary patterns and reconstruction levels. Hence, we suppose that, among the K' extracted reference bits corresponding to $U^{(j)*}$, the K_j'' bits are extracted from the intact regions $(K_j'' \le K')$, which can be utilized to restore the n_j incorrect compression bits of $U_D^{(j)}$. Denote these K_j'' correct reference bits as the column vector $R_C^{(j)}$. Thus, Eq. (7) can be re-written as: $R_C^{(j)} = H^{(j|E)} \cdot U^{(j)*}$ $(j = 1, 2, \ldots, f)$, where the subset $U^{(j)*}$ consisting of K bits is arranged as a $K \times 1$ column vector, and $H^{(j|E)}$ is a $K_j'' \times K$ matrix with the K_j'' rows retrieved from the K' rows of $H^{(j)}$ corresponding to the K_j'' correct reference bits $R_C^{(j)}$. Note that the f random binary matrices, i.e., $H^{(1)}, H^{(2)}, \ldots, H^{(f)}$, sized $K' \times K$ can be exactly obtained with the same secret key on the sender side. As mentioned above, the K_i bits of $U^{(j)*}$ include the n_j incorrect bits denoted as the column vector $U_D^{(j)}$ and the $(K - n_j)$ correct bits denoted as the column vector $U_C^{(j)}$. Hence, Eq. (10) can be acquired:

$$R_C^{(j)} - H^{(j|E,C)} \cdot U_C^{(j)} = H^{(j|E,D)} \cdot U_D^{(j)}, \quad j = 1, 2, \ldots, f_i, \qquad (10)$$

where $H^{(j|E, C)}$ and $H^{(j|E, D)}$ are the two matrices sized $K_j'' \times (K - n_j)$ and $K_j'' \times K$, and their columns are retrieved from the K columns of $H^{(j|E)}$ corresponding to the bits of $U_C^{(j)}$ and $U_D^{(j)}$, respectively. Obviously, all items in Eq. (10) are known except the n_j bits of $U_D^{(j)}$. In order to restore the n_j incorrect bits of $U_D^{(j)}$ within each subset $U^{(j)*}$ for the compression bits, we need to solve the n_j unknowns in Eq. (10). Both $R_C^{(j)}$ and $U_C^{(j)}$ from intact regions can contribute to the restoration for the n_j incorrect compression bits $U_D^{(j)}$ from tampered regions.

After the above operations, for the tampered blocks, compression bits solved in Eq. (10) can be rearranged with the secret key, and for the reserved blocks, 6 MSBs are kept unchanged. After all tampered blocks are processed by AMBTC decoding, the recovered image can be acquired.

4 Experimental Results and Comparisons

A lot of images were utilized to show the effectiveness and superiority of our scheme. Four test images sized 512×512 are used, i.e., Lake, Milk, Lena and Plane. The watermarked images and their corresponding tampered versions are shown in Figs. 3 and 4. The tampering rates for the four images are 9.03 %, 23.63 %, 30.76 % and 31.64 %, respectively. Tampering detection results are shown in Fig. 5. We can observe that tampered blocks can be judged accurately. After tampering detection, the recovered bits can be derived to recover the tampered content of received image, see Fig. 6. The comparative experiments for recovery performance among our scheme, scheme [7, 8, 12] were conducted. The recovered images for four forged images in Fig. 4 are listed Fig. 6. PSNR and SSIM values of recovered images for the four schemes are shown in Table 2. In conclusion, the recovery results of the proposed scheme are satisfactory. With the increase of tampering rate, the quality of recovered image is superior to that of three schemes in [7, 8, 12]. We can find obviously from Table 2 that when tampered rates are higher, the recovered images of [7, 8] and [12] have a bit lower, meanwhile the visual quality of ours is better.

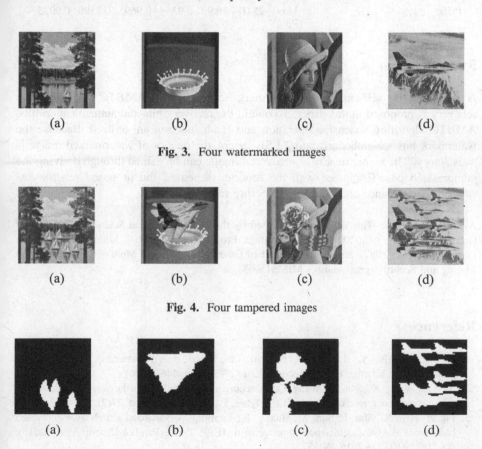

(a)   (b)   (c)   (d)

Fig. 3. Four watermarked images

(a)   (b)   (c)   (d)

Fig. 4. Four tampered images

(a)   (b)   (c)   (d)

Fig. 5. Tampered detection results

(a) [41.67, 0.9966]   (b) [40.99, 0.9923]   (c) [35.41, 0.9915]   (d) [36.98, 0.9925]

Fig. 6. Recovered results of the proposed scheme

Table 2. PSNR and SSIM Comparisons among Our Scheme with [7, 8, 12]

Image	Tampering rate α	PSNR of recovered image (dB)				SSIM of recovered image			
		[7]	[8]	[12]	Ours	[7]	[8]	[12]	Ours
Lake	9.03 %	34.66	37.17	35.50	41.67	0.9933	0.9896	0.9788	0.9966
Milk	23.63 %	32.79	36.70	31.00	40.99	0.9799	0.9767	0.9257	0.9923
Lena	30.76 %	28.08	32.11	26.23	35.41	0.9384	0.9712	0.8572	0.9915
Plane	31.64 %	27.81	31.60	25.07	36.98	0.9364	0.9693	0.8590	0.9925

5   Conclusion

A novel fragile self-embedding watermark scheme using AMBTC for tampering recovery is proposed in this paper. To obtain the recovery bits and authentication bits, AMBTC algorithm, extension operation and Hash function are utilized. Because the watermark bits are embedded into 2 LSB layers, the quality of watermarked image is satisfactory. The higher quality of recovered image can be gained through deriving the compression bits. Compared with the reported schemes, the proposed scheme has superior performance under higher tampering rate.

Acknowledgments. This work was supported by the National Natural Science Foundation of China (61303203, 61562007), the Innovation Program of Shanghai Municipal Education Commission (14YZ087), and Research Fund of Guangxi Key Lab of Multi-source Information Mining and Security (grant number MIMS15-03).

References

1. Chang, C., Hu, Y., Lu, T.: A watermarking-based image ownership and tampering authentication scheme. Pattern Recogn. Lett. **27**(5), 439–446 (2006)
2. Xia, Z., Wang, X., Sun, X., Wang, Q.: A secure and dynamic multi-keyword ranked search scheme over encrypted cloud data. IEEE Trans. Parallel Distrib. Syst. **27**(2), 340–352 (2015)
3. Fu, Z., Ren, K., Shu, J., Sun, X., Huang, F.: Enabling personalized search over encrypted outsourced data with efficiency improvement. IEEE Trans. Parallel Distrib. Syst. (2015). doi:10.1109/TPDS.2015.2506573

4. Fu, Z., Sun, X., Liu, Q., Zhou, L., Shu, J.: achieving efficient cloud search services: multi-keyword ranked search over encrypted cloud data supporting parallel computing. IEICE Trans. Commun. **E98-B**(1), 190–200 (2015)

5. Xia, Z., Wang, X., Sun, X., Wang, B.: Steganalysis of least significant bit matching using multi-order differences. Secur. Commun. Netw. **7**(8), 1283–1291 (2014)

6. Xia, Z., Wang, X., Sun, X., Liu, Q., Xiong, N.: Steganalysis of LSB matching using differences between nonadjacent pixels. Multimedia Tools Appl. **75**(4), 1947–1962 (2016)

7. Lin, P., Hsieh, C., Huang, P.: A hierarchical digital watermarking method for image tamper detection and recovery. Pattern Recogn. **38**(12), 2519–2529 (2005)

8. Lee, T., Lin, S.: Dual watermark for image tamper detection and recovery. Pattern Recogn. **41**(11), 3497–3506 (2008)

9. Zhang, X., Wang, S., Qian, Z., Feng, G.: Reference sharing mechanism for watermark self-embedding. IEEE Trans. Image Process. **20**(2), 485–495 (2011)

10. Tsou, C., Hu, Y., Chang, C.: Efficient optimal pixel grouping schemes for AMBTC. Imaging Sci. J. **56**(4), 217–231 (2008)

11. Wang, Z., Bovik, A., Sheikh, H., Simoncelli, E.: Image quality assessment: from error visibility to structural similarity. IEEE Trans. Image Process. **13**(4), 600–612 (2004)

12. Yang, C., Shen, J.: Recover the tampered image based on VQ indexing. Sig. Process. **90**, 331–343 (2010)

Schur Decomposition Based Robust Watermarking Algorithm in Contourlet Domain

Junxiang Wang[1,2(✉)] and Ying Liu[1]

[1] School of Mechanical and Electronic Engineering,
Jingdezhen Ceramic Institute, Jiangxi 333403, China
{wjx851113851113,ly6930892}@163.com
[2] School of Computer and Software, Nanjing University of Information Science
and Technology, Jiangsu 210000, China

Abstract. Most of the existing watermarking schemes utilized SVD decomposition to embed watermark, which lead to a high computational complexity and incidental the false positive detection problem. Therefore, this paper provides a robust copyright protection scheme based on a simple decomposition scheme (schur decomposition) and Quantization Index Modulation (QIM) in Contourlet domain. In addition, some stable features are acquired by using schur decomposition in the Contourlet domain. Consequently, the watermark is embedded into those stable features with QIM method. Experimental results show that the proposed scheme has some superiorities in terms of robustness and imperceptibility, which could against most common attacks such as JPEG compression, filtering, cropping, noise adding and so on.

Keywords: Robust watermarking · Schur decomposition · Contourlet transform · Quantization Index Modulation

1 Introduction

With the development of network and multimedia techniques, data transmission and edition become more simple, which leads to the fact that some persons could simply publish their works through the Internet and maybe results in some serious copyright issues. In addition, malicious attackers may forge digital products to achieve their worse purpose. Therefore, how to achieve copyright protection and ensure information security has become an open issue. Robust watermarking and steganography [1–3] offered effective solution for copyright protection and steganalysis [13, 14] on multimedia.

During the past decades, many digital watermarking techniques, especially for SVD-based and QR-based ones [4–8, 11], have been proposed. For instance, Ali and Ahm [5] proposed an optimized watermarking technique using the self-adaptive DE in DWT-SVD transform domain to obtain high robustness with better imperceptibility. In [6], a blind speech watermarking scheme embedded secret data in AC coefficients of DWT with quantization of the Eigen-value and achieved a better trade-off between robustness, capacity, and imperceptibility. Agoyi et al. [7] proposed a robust algorithm

© Springer International Publishing AG 2016
X. Sun et al. (Eds.): ICCCS 2016, Part I, LNCS 10039, pp. 114–124, 2016.
DOI: 10.1007/978-3-319-48671-0_11

based on Chirp Z-transform and Singular Value Decomposition (SVD). Since Chirp-z has the ability of detecting the fundamental frequency and analyzing frequency spectrum with a high resolution, a desired balance between imperceptible and robustness was achieved. In [8], another kind robust algorithm based on chaotic system and QR factorization was proposed to protect copyright of digital images. In the scheme, blocks were firstly selected by using pseudorandom circular chain (PCC) generated with logistic mapping and then the watermark is embedded into the first column of Q matrix. Similarly, paper [9] still offered a robust scheme by using QR decomposition based on cover image. The method is implemented in DWT and has low computational complexity. Su et al. [4] extended QR decomposition to color image and designed a novel blind watermarking scheme, which embedded messages in the first low of R matrix and achieved a high robustness. Since the absolute values of those elements in the first row of R matrix are probably greater than those in other rows, the robustness maybe more improved.

In the paper, a new robust watermarking scheme based on Contourlet transform (CT) and Schur decomposition is developed. In order to increase robustness, the stable coefficients are acquired by using Schur decomposition and the Contourlet transform domain. Then watermark is embedded into those evaluated coefficients by using QIM method. Experimental results show that the proposed method is more robust than other typical ones and meanwhile achieves lower computational complexity due to employment of CT.

The rest paper is organized as follows. Sections 2 and 3 describe related works and the embedding and extraction process, respectively. Section 4 provides some experimental results. A conclusion is finally described in Sect. 5.

2   Related Works

2.1   Schur Decomposition

Schur decomposition is a significant matrix decomposition method [12] in the aspect of image processing and mentioned as follows.

Theorem 1 (Schur lemma). For a given hypothesis matrix $A_{n \times n} \in C^{n*n}$, exist a unitary matrix $U_{m \times n} \in C^{m*n}$ and an upper triangular matrix $T_{m \times m} \in C^{n*n}$, which meets the following formulate and called Schur factorization.

$$A_{n \times n} = U_{n \times m} \times T_{m \times m} \times U_{m \times n}^{H} \tag{1}$$

where notation $U_{m \times n}^{H}$ means the transposition of $U_{m \times n}$.

Compared with QR and SVD decompositions, Schur decomposition owns some characteristics as follows.

(1) Any real matrix A could be uniquely represented as the sum of a symmetric matrix B and an anti-symmetric matrix C, i.e.

$$A = B + C \tag{2}$$

where $B = \frac{1}{2} \times (A + A')$, $C = \frac{1}{2} \times (A - A')$.

(2) For above mentioned symmetric matrix B, exist an orthogonal matrix Q and diagonal matrix T follows Eq. 1 and is expressed as follows.

$$B_{n \times n} = Q_{n \times m} \times T_{m \times m} \times Q^H_{m \times n} \tag{3}$$

where T could be denoted as $T = diag(\lambda_1, \ldots \ldots, \lambda_n)$ and its element λ_i, $i \in [1, n]$ means an eigen value of B.

(3) It is clear that some perturbations should be loaded into the cover media to hide secret data. According to [13], it is found that the perturbation σ, which originally should be loaded on the cover matrix A and denoted as σA, could be transformed to be the change of decomposed T, denoted as $\sigma \lambda$, and meets the inequality.

$$\|\sigma \lambda\|_2 \leq \|\sigma B\|_2 \leq \|\sigma A + (\sigma A)'\|_2 = \|\sigma A\|_2 \tag{4}$$

where σB represents the perturbation to the symmetric matrix B, $\|\|_2$ denote the 2-norm of a matrix. The inequality denotes the perturbation σ originally loaded on the matrix A could be reduced by performed it on T, which could improve the robustness when we perform data hiding on T by using Schur decomposition.

2.2   Quantization Index Modulation (QIM)

As a novel data embedding method, QIM is proposed by Chen and Wornell and achieves effective balance between embedding capacity, imperceptibility and robustness. The method is briefly mentioned as follows.

For each pixel x and one bit watermark $w \in \{0, 1\}$, two quantification functions, denoted as $Q_i(i = 0, 1)$ are designed as follows.

$$Q_i(x) = Q_i(x - d_i) + d_i \tag{5}$$

where $Q_i(x) = q\lfloor x/q \rfloor$, and $\lfloor \bullet \rfloor$ is the floor function. In addition, q is the quantization step, $d_0 = -q/4$, $d_1 = q/4$. d_0 and d_1 are used for embedding one bit secret data "0" or "1" respectively. The notations 'O' and 'X' as shown Fig. 1 denote different quantizes, i.e. Q_0 and Q_1, respectively and QIM based embedding process is described as follows and shown in Fig. 1.

$$x' = \begin{cases} Q_0(x) & w = 0 \\ Q_1(x) & w = 1 \end{cases} \tag{6}$$

During extraction process, the watermark can be extracted from the marked image by using the following formula.

$$w = \arg \min \|x' - Q_i(x')\|_2 \quad i \in \{0, 1\} \tag{7}$$

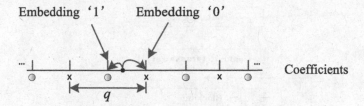

Fig. 1. The watermark embedding method

3 Embedding and Extraction Process

3.1 Embedding Process

The embedding process is illustrated in Fig. 2, and mentioned as follows.

(1) Perform Contourlet Transform on the host image and acquire corresponding coefficients. Then, those low frequency coefficients are chosen to embed watermark.
(2) Divide those low frequency matrix coefficients into non- overlapping blocks of size $M \times N$.
(3) Select each block and perform DCT on it. Then apply Schur decomposition on those DCT coefficients by using Eq. 1, and thus obtain the upper triangular matrix T.
(4) Quantify the first coefficient DC in T and perform data hiding process with QIM as follows. Then marked T' is generated.

$$DC' = \begin{cases} q \times \lfloor (DC + q/4)/q \rfloor - q/4 & w = 0 \\ q \times \lfloor (DC - q/4)/q \rfloor + q/4 & w = 1 \end{cases} \tag{8}$$

(5) Predefine a threshold $Thold$, and calculate $d = DC' - DC$. If $d > Thold$, it means the distance between DC' and DC is sufficient and the robustness is strong. Thus, the block will be selected to embed the watermark by (8). Otherwise, no watermark is embedded in the block. Meanwhile, build a bitmap to record whether the block is utilized.
(6) Based on T', Inverse Schur factorization, IDCT, inverse Contourlet transform and so on are perform in the reverse order as above steps to reconstruct the marked image.

3.2 Extraction Process

The extracting process is illustrated in Fig. 3 and briefly mentioned as follows.

(1) Perform identical Contourlet transform, DCT and Schur factorization as embedding process to acquire T'.
(2) Extract the bitmap to distinguish whether one block hides a bit w or not.
(3) Perform watermark extraction process by using Eq. 7.
(4) Undergo all the blocks and then the watermark could be completely extracted.

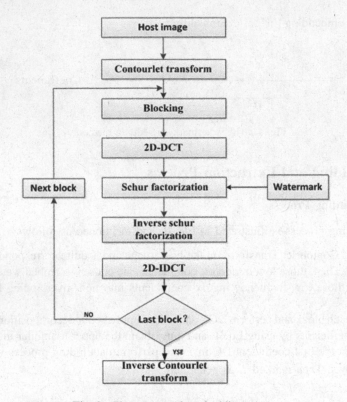

Fig. 2. The watermark embedding process

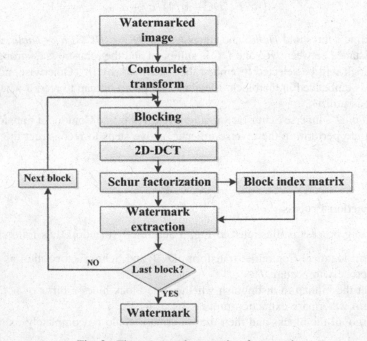

Fig. 3. The watermark extracting framework

4 Experimental Results

Some experiments have been implemented to testify the performance of our scheme. In the paper, four standard test images, i.e. "Man", "Clock", "Airplane" and "Boat", are chosen from USC-SIPI image database of 512×512 and shown in Fig. 4. The watermark is a 32×32 binary image as shown in Fig. 5. In addition, the step size q used in QIM method is set to be 450. The threshold to control the embedding strength is 75. The host image is divided into 4×4 sized blocks. To evaluate the performance of robust watermarking system, i.e. robustness and imperceptibility, some parameters are introduced, i.e. NC, PSNR and SSIM, where NC is employed to measure robustness and calculated by Eq. 9. Imperceptible can be estimated by both peak signal-to-noise ratio (PSNR) and structural similarity (SSIM), which are calculated by Eqs. 10 and 12 respectively.

$$NC(W, W') = \frac{\sum\limits_{i=0}^{X-1}\sum\limits_{j=0}^{Y-1} W(i,j)W'(i,j)}{\sqrt{\sum\limits_{i=0}^{X-1}\sum\limits_{j=0}^{Y-1} W^2(i,j)}\sqrt{\sum\limits_{i=0}^{X-1}\sum\limits_{j=0}^{Y-1} W'^2(i,j)}} \qquad (9)$$

Fig. 4. Four test images

(a) Original image   (b) The watermark

Fig. 5. (a) Original image (b) the watermark

where $W(i,j)$ and $W'(i,j)$ represent the pixel values of the original watermark and the extracted one, respectively. X and Y are the height and width of the original watermark, respectively.

$$PSNR = 10 \lg \frac{255^2}{MSE} \tag{10}$$

where MSE is the mean-square error between the original image and the attacked image, and it is computed by

$$MSE = \frac{1}{M \times N} \sum_{i=0}^{M-1} \sum_{j=0}^{N-1} (F(x,y) - F'(x,y))^2 \tag{11}$$

where $F(x,y)$ and $F'(x,y)$ are the gray level intensity value of the original image and attacked watermarked one at (x,y) respectively. In addition, M and N are image dimensions.

$$SSIM(H,H') = l(H,H') \times c(H,H') \times s(H,H') \tag{12}$$

where $l(H,H') = \frac{2*\mu_H*\mu_{H'}+C_1}{\mu_H^2+\mu_{H'}^2+C_1}$, $c(H,H') = \frac{2*\delta_H*\delta_{H'}+C_2}{\delta_H^2+\delta_{H'}^2+C_2}$ and $s(H,H') = \frac{\delta_{H,H'}+C_3}{\delta_H*\delta_{H'}+C_3}$. $C1$, $C2$ and $C3$ are positive real numbers, μ_H and $\mu_{H'}$ are the mean values of H and H', respectively. δ_H and $\delta_{H'}$ are the standard variances of H and H', respectively. $\delta_{H,H'}$ means the covariance between H and H'.

To test the robustness and imperceptibility of proposed scheme, several typical attacks are performed, such as cropping (Cr) including 1/4 corner-cropping (Ccr) and side-cropping (Scr), Scaling (Scl), median filtering (Md) with window size 3×3, low-pass filtering (Lp) with window size 3×3, meaning filtering (Mf) with window size 3×3, gaussian filter (Gf) with window size 3×3, gaussian noise (Gn), salt and pepper noise (Ps) and speckle noise (Spn).

4.1 Imperceptibility Analysis

For the test image Lena, the marked version and extracted watermark are shown in Fig. 6. The image quality can be measured by parameters PSNR and SSIM. The results for different images are listed in Table 1. It is observed that, for all the test images, SSIM values are no smaller than 0.9852, which means our proposed scheme could achieve high imperceptibility. In addition, PSNRs are also more than 40. Based on previous experience, when PSNR is more than 35, the degradation caused by watermark embedding could not be perceptible. Therefore, it is verified that our scheme could achieve better imperceptibility.

(a) Watermarked image   (b) Extracted watermark

Fig. 6. (a) Watermarked image (b) extracted watermark

4.2 Robustness Analysis

To evaluate the robustness of proposed algorithm, some simulation results are performed. The simulation results for six attack operations i.e. Ccr, Scr, Ps, Lp, Gn and Scl on standard "Lena" image are described in Fig. 7. Table 2 lists the comparison results between our scheme and other typical ones, i.e. SVD and DCT based scheme proposed by Liu et al. [10] in 2009, QR decomposition based algorithm proposed by Song et al. [8] in 2010, and chaotic system based method provided by Naderahmadian and Hosseini-Khayat [9] in 2011. It is observed that our scheme could achieve larger NC, which demonstrates the superiority of that proposed approach in terms of robustness.

Table 1. PSNR and SSIM for four test images

Image name	SSIM	PSNR
Man	0.9924	40.82
Clock	0.9852	40.61
Airplane	0.9862	40.68
Boat	0.9945	40.45

Fig. 7. The watermarked image and *NC* under above-mentioned six attacks

Table 2. Results of a comparison between different schemes based on robustness

Attacks	Liu	Naderahmadian	Song	Proposed
No attack	1.0000	1.0000	1.0000	1.0000
Md (3 × 3)	0.8728	0.8982	0.5626	0.9985
Mf (3 × 3)	0.9622	0.8917	0.5558	0.9993
Scl (1/2)	0.8809	0.8053	0.7497	0.8654
Gn	0.5100	0.5163	0.6758	0.9867
Ps	0.5150	0.6237	0.9656	0.9978
1/4Scr	0.9048	0.9048	0.9283	0.9015
Ccr	0.8963	0.8963	0.8955	0.9088

5   Conclusion

A novel Schur decomposition and Contourlet transform (CT) based robust water-marking algorithm is proposed in this paper. The method has three advantages. (1) Schur decomposition is simple version of SVD decomposition and thus requires fewer computations. (2) Two continuous transforms, i.e. DCT and CT, make the energy more centralized into DC and low frequency coefficients, which leads to better robustness when watermark is embedded in them. (3) QIM technique will further improve the robustness of our scheme. Experimental results verified its effectiveness.

Acknowledgement. This work is supported by the National Science Foundation of China (61402209, 61563022), Invention Patent Industrialization Demonstration Project of Jiangxi Province (20143BBM26113), Youth Science Fund Major Projects of Jiangxi Province (20161ACB21009), Guild of technological innovation of science and technology projects in Jiangxi Province (20161BBE53004). A Project Funded by the Priority Academic Program Development of Jiangsu Higher Education Institutions and Jiangsu Collaborative Innovation Center on Atmospheric Environment and Equipment Technology.

References

1. Cox, I.J., Kilian, J., Leighton, F.T., Shamoon, T.: Secure spread spectrum watermarking for multimedia. IEEE Trans. Image Process. **6**(12), 1673–1687 (1997)
2. Hartung, F., Kutter, M.: Multimedia watermarking techniques. Proc. IEEE **87**(7), 1079–1107 (1999)
3. Lei, B.Y., Soon, I.Y., Li, Z.: Blind and robust audio watermarking scheme based on SVD-DCT. Sig. Process. **91**(8), 1973–1984 (2011)
4. Su, Q., Niu, Y.G., Wang, G., Jia, S.L., Yue, J.: Color image blind watermarking scheme based on QR decomposition. Sig. Process. **94**, 219–235 (2014)
5. Ali, M., Ahn, C.W.: An optimized watermarking technique based on self-adaptive DE in DWT-SVD transform domain. Sig. Process. **94**, 545–556 (2014)
6. Nematollahi, M.A., Al-Haddad, S.A.R., Zarafshan, F.: Blind digital speech watermarking based on eigen-value quantization in DWT. Comput. Inf. Sci. **27**, 58–67 (2015)

7. Agoyi, M., Çelebi, E., Anbarjafari, G.: A watermarking algorithm based on chirp z-transform, discrete wavelet transform, and singular value decomposition. SIViP **9**(3), 735–745 (2015)
8. Song, W., Hou, J.J., Li, Z.H., Huang, L.: Chaotic system and QR factorization based robust digital image watermarking algorithm. J. Cent. South Univ. Technol. **9**(1), 116–124 (2011)
9. Naderahmadian, Y., Hosseini-Khayat, S.: Fast watermarking based on QR decomposition in wavelet domain. In: 6th International Conference on Intelligent Information Hiding and Multimedia Signal Processing (IIH-MSP 2010), vol. 39, pp. 127–130, October 2010
10. Liu, F., Han, K., Wang, C.Z.: A novel blind watermark algorithm based on SVD and DCT. In: IEEE International Conference on Intelligent Computing and Intelligent Systems, vol. 12, pp. 283–286, November 2009
11. Lai, C.C., Tsai, C.C.: Digital image watermarking using discrete wavelet transform and singular value decomposition. IEEE Trans. Instrum. Meas. **59**(11), 3060–3063 (2010)
12. Joel, N.: Franklin: Matrix theory. Dover Publications, New York (2000)
13. Xia, Z.H., Wang, X.H., Sun, X.M., Wang, B.W.: Steganalysis of least significant bit matching using multi-order differences. Secur. Commun. Netw. **7**(8), 1283–1291 (2014)
14. Xia, Z.H., Wang, X.H., Sun, X.M., Liu, Q.S., Xiong, N.X.: Steganalysis of LSB matching using differences between nonadjacent pixels. Multimedia Tools Appl. **75**(4), 1947–1962 (2016)

Improved Uniform Embedding for Efficient JPEG Steganography

Yuanfeng Pan, Jiangqun Ni[(⊠)], and Wenkang Su

School of Electronics and Information Technology,
Sun Yat-sen University, Guangzhou 510006, China
issjqni@mail.sysu.edu.cn

Abstract. With the wide application of the minimal distortion embedding framework, a well-designed distortion function is of vital importance. In this paper, we propose an improved distortion function for the generalized uniform embedding strategy, called improved UERD (IUERD). Although the UERD has made great success, there still exists room for improvement in designing the distortion function. As a result, the mutual correlations among DCT blocks are utilized more efficiently in the proposed distortion function, which leads to less statistical detectability. The effectiveness of the proposed IUERD is verified with the state-of-the-art steganalyzer - JRM on the BOSSbase database. Compared with prior arts, the proposed scheme gains favorable performance in terms of secure embedding capacity against steganalysis.

Keywords: JPEG steganography · JPEG steganalysis · Distortion function · Uniform embedding

1 Introduction

Steganography and steganalysis are a pair of modern technologies that have been developed swiftly over the past years. Steganography attempts to hide secret messages within a communication channel generally referred as a cover source. On the other hand, steganalysis aims at detecting the presence of hidden messages. The conflicting between these two objectives is a diving force for the rapid development of the both sides.

As the most widely used format for image transmission and storage, JPEG steganography becomes the domain of extensive research. In the literature, the message is generally embedded in the images by slightly modifying some individual elements of cover, e.g., the LSBs [1–3] of quantized DCT coefficients. Nowadays, the most common and effective approach for JPEG steganography is minimizing a heuristically-defined embedding distortion for the empirical cover images. The development of JPEG steganography benefits a lot from the applications of channel coding, e.g., Hamming code for F5 [4], modified matrix coding for MME [6] and BCH code for BCHopt [7], etc. In 2011, Filler *et al.* developed a breakthrough coding framework by utilizing the syndrome-trellis codes (STCs), which is able to minimize an additive distortion function while embedding a near-maximal payload [5].

Over the past few years, the emerging JPEG steganographic schemes all focused on the design of the distortion function. In [9], the distortion functions for spatial (S-UNI),

© Springer International Publishing AG 2016
X. Sun et al. (Eds.): ICCCS 2016, Part I, LNCS 10039, pp. 125–133, 2016.
DOI: 10.1007/978-3-319-48671-0_12

JPEG (J-UNI) and side-informed JPEG (SI-UNI) domain are all derived from the wavelet domain. Unlike the conventional JPEG steganographic schemes which only embed the secret message into non-zero AC coefficients, J-UNI uses all DCT coefficients (DCs, zero and non-zero ACs) as possible cover elements, and achieves so far the best security performance. However, the computational complexity of attaining distortion from the wavelet domain may be the major problem in implementation. In [8], by following the concept in spirit of "spread spectrum communication", the authors proposed the UED distortion for JPEG steganography, i.e., "spreading" the embedding modifications uniformly to quantized DCT coefficients of all possible magnitudes. In this way, less statistical detectability can be achieved, owing to the reduction of the average changes of the first- and second-order statistics of DCT coefficients as a whole. Later, they further developed UERD in [10] by taking into account the relative change of the statistical image model, which needs to be proportional to the "coefficient of variation", and can be regarded as the generalized uniform embedding. Compared with the original UED, the UERD achieves considerable performance improvement in terms of secure embedding capacity.

In this paper, we propose a new distortion function for the generalized uniform embedding strategy. Notice that the UERD would not work quite well in the intersections between smooth and texture regions of images, the proposed distortion function, i.e., IUERD, tries to improve the UERD by taking into account of the mutual correlations among DCT blocks and utilizing them more efficiently. The proposed IUERD outperforms its predecessor – UERD by a clear margin, and rivals the current state-of-the-art J-UNIWARD with much reduced computational complexity.

The rest of this paper is organized as follows. In Sect. 2, the generalized uniform embedding strategy and its distortion function (UERD) are briefly reviewed. The proposed distortion function IUERD is presented in Sect. 3, which is followed by the experimental results and analysis. Finally the conclusion remarks are drawn in Sect. 5.

2 Uniform Embedding Strategy

Currently, the most secure approach to steganography is the minimal distortion embedding framework, which includes a well defined distortion function and a practical coding scheme to minimize the distortion. With the introduction of syndrome-trellis codes (STCs), which can embed near the rate-distortion bound, the only task left to the steganographers is the design of the distortion function. By following the concept in the spirit of "spread spectrum communication", Guo et al. [8] proposed a distortion function known as uniform embedding distortion (UED). Subsequently, they further refine the uniform embedding strategy from the perspective of statistical image models, which can be regarded as generalized uniform embedding with the corresponding distortion function called uniform embedding revisited distortion (UERD). In the rest of this section, we will shortly review the generalized uniform embedding strategy.

2.1 Generalized Uniform Embedding Strategy

Nowadays, the best image steganalyzer is constructed through feature based ste- ganalysis and machine learning. Generally, the feature sets for JPEG steganalysis utilize natural image model in terms of first- and second-order statistics of quantized DCT coefficients. Therefore, it makes sense to exploit the properties of statistical image model to design the distortion function which is resilient to the attack of steganalyzer.

As mentioned in [10], the generalized uniform embedding strategy refines UED by considering the relative changes of statistical image model, aiming to make the embedding modifications to be proportional to the coefficient of variation (*CV*) [11]. For instance, let $\mu(x)$ and $\sigma(x)$ denote the mean value and the standard deviation of the histogram of DCT coefficients $p(x)$ over 10,000 JPEG images with QF = 75 from Bossbase [12], respectively. The coefficient of variation $CV(x)$ is defined as the ratio of the standard deviation to the mean:

$$CV(x) = \frac{\sigma(x)}{\mu(x)} \tag{1}$$

As is shown in Fig. 1, $CV(x)$ increases with the magnitude of coefficients (i.e., $|x|$), which implies that $p(x)$ tends to deviate heavily when the $|x|$ increase. Hence, the statistical impact in first-order statistics could be minimized if the relative change of each x is proportional to its *CV*, and the similar effects can also be observed with other higher-order statistics. Therefore, the main idea of the generalized uniform embedding strategy is to control the relative change of each bin to be proportional to the $CV(x)$, which leads to a better security performance than UED.

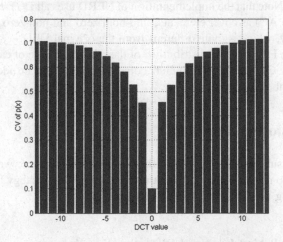

Fig. 1. *CV* of $p(x)$ over 10,000 JPEG images

2.2   Distortion Function of UERD

As mentioned above, the general method to implement the generalized uniform embedding strategy is to increase the selection probability for those coefficients with larger CV of the statistical model, while decrease the ones with smaller CV. Based on the implement method, the corresponding distortion function UERD is constructed as follows.

Let x_{ij} be a coefficient in position (i, j) of a 8×8 DCT block in position (m, n), and q_{ij} be the corresponding quantization step of x_{ij}, the energy of the mn^{th} block is computed by:

$$D_{mn} = \sum_{k=0}^{7} \sum_{l=0}^{7} |x_{kl}| \cdot q_{kl} \tag{2}$$

We then have the distortion function ρ_{ij} for x_{ij}:

$$\rho_{ij} = \begin{cases} \dfrac{0.5^*(q_{(i+1)j} + q_{i(j+1)})}{D_{mn} + 0.25^* \sum\limits_{d \in \hat{D}} d}, & if \ (i,j) \bmod 8 = (0,0) \\[4mm] \dfrac{q_{ij}}{D_{mn} + 0.25^* \sum\limits_{d \in \hat{D}} d}, & otherwise \end{cases} \tag{3}$$

where $\hat{D} = \{D_{(m-1)(n-1)}, D_{(m-1)n}, D_{(m-1)(n+1)}, D_{m(n-1)}, D_{m(n+1)}, D_{(m+1)(n-1)}, D_{(m+1)n}, D_{(m+1)(n+1)}\}$. When the considered block is located in the image boundary, then the nonexistent blocks are obtained by block padding. In addition, considering the difference of statistical characteristics between DC and AC coefficients, the distortions for the DC coefficients are defined as the mean of their neighborhood AC coefficients in the same DCT block. Note that the implementation of UERD uses all DCT coefficients (DC, zero and non-zero AC) as cover elements, and both zero and non-zero AC coefficients are treated equally, which is quite different from the original UED.

As is shown in Fig. 2(a), the distribution of the relative change of each bin is almost proportional to its CV (see Fig. 2), which coincides with the main idea of the generalized uniform embedding strategy.

3   A New Distortion Function

Although UERD substantially improved the security performance, we find there still exists possibility to refine the generalized uniform embedding strategy by exploring the correlations among neighboring DCT blocks more efficiently.

3.1   Motivation Behind Improved Distortion Function

Let's look back to (2) for more detail, where the denominator of the distortion function is a weighted sum of the energies of the block and its adjacent blocks. The distortion function constructed in this way may not work well for some regions in the image.

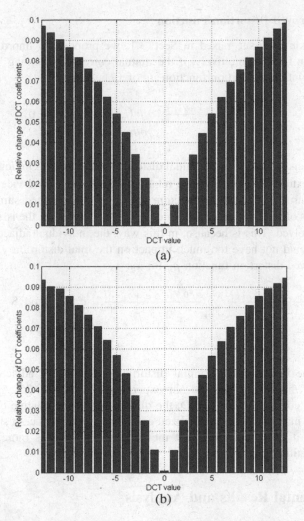

Fig. 2. (a) and (b) are the relative change of the DCT coefficients with UERD and the proposed IUERD at 0.2 bpnzac, respectively

Specifically, if we compute the distortion value ρ_{ij} for x_{ij} in the mn^{th} block, and the block energy D_{mn} is small enough, i.e., in smooth region. For the case when one or two adjacent blocks of the mn^{th} block have relatively high energy, which is likely to be widespread at the boundary alone smooth and texture regions in images, the obtained distortion value ρ_{ij} is small due to the large denominator. The small ρ_{ij} leads to large modification probability for x_{ij}, which contradicts to the convention that the pixels in smooth region should be less modified. As a result, the application of UERD in the intersections between smooth and texture regions is not appropriate, and would inevitably results in a loss of security performance.

3.2   The Improved Distortion Function

In order to tackle the issue raised in Sect. 3.1, we propose an improved distortion function base on UERD. Intuitively, if the mutual correlations among blocks are not taken into account, the distortion function $\hat{\rho}_{ij}$ of x_{ij} becomes:

$$\rho_{ij} = \begin{cases} \frac{0.5^*(q_{(i+1)j} + q_{i(j+1)})}{D_{mn}}, & \text{if } (i,j) \text{ mod } 8 = (0,0) \\ \frac{q_{ij}}{D_{mn}}, & \text{otherwise} \end{cases} \quad (4)$$

For convenience, we call $\hat{\rho}_{ij}$ the initial distortion value for x_{ij}. Obviously, the initial distortions in texture DCT blocks have relatively small value, and vice versa. Therefore, if we construct the distortion function for x_{ij} by the weighted sum of the initial distortion values of x_{ij} and its inter-block neighboring coefficients, the issue in Sect. 3.1 could be well solved. This is because, in this way, the individual adjacent block with large energy would not have too much impact on the final distortion value. We then have the improved distortion function ρ_{ij} for x_{ij}:

$$\rho_{ij} = \begin{cases} \frac{0.5^*(q_{(i+1)j} + q_{i(j+1)})}{D_{mn}} + \sum_{d \in \hat{D}} \frac{w_d^* 0.5^*(q_{(i+1)j} + q_{i(j+1)})}{d}, & \text{if } (i,j) \text{ mod } 8 = (0,0) \\ \frac{q_{ij}}{D_{mn}} + \sum_{d \in \hat{D}} \frac{w_d^* q_{ij}}{d}, & \text{otherwise} \end{cases} \quad (5)$$

where w_d is the weight for the initial distortion value of the adjacent inter-block coefficients and the default value in our experiments is set to 0.25. As is shown in Fig. 2(b), when compared with UERD, the distribution of the relative change of each bin has a closer match with the generalized embedding strategy, i.e., it should be more proportional to its *CV*, indicating that the proposed IUERD is more preferable in practical applications.

4   Experimental Results and Analysis

In this section, experimental results and analysis are presented to demonstrate the feasibility and effectiveness of the proposed IUERD steganographic scheme, which include the comparisons with some recently proposed schemes, such as Guo et al.'s UERD and Holub et al.'s J-UNIWARD. In our experiments, we concentrate on the comparison of the distortion functions for the involved schemes. Therefore, all tested schemes are simulated at their corresponding payload-distortion bounds.

4.1   Experiment Setup

Cover Source and Feature. All experiments are carried out on the image database BOSSbase 1.01 [12] containing 10,000 grayscale 512 × 512 images. The images are the JPEG compressed using quality factors 75 and 95. Thus, we have two image databases each with 10,000 grayscale cover images of different texture characteristics in format of JPEG, which serve as the cover for JEPG embedding. In our experiments, the relative payloads are set 0.05, 0.1, 0.2, 0.3, 0.4 bpnzac (bits per non-zero AC DCT coefficient) for all tested schemes. In the experiment, all tested schemes will be steganalyzed using the state-of-the-art feature set JRM [13] with dimension 22,510.

Machine Learning. The ensemble classifier with Fisher linear discriminant as the base learner in [14] is employed in our experiments as is used in [13]. For the covers and their corresponding stego images with different steganographic schemes, relative payloads and QFs, the features for the involved steganalysis tool are firstly extracted.

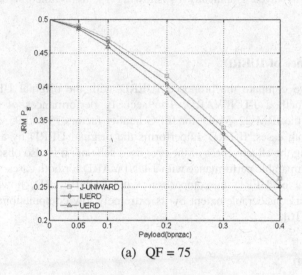

(a) QF = 75

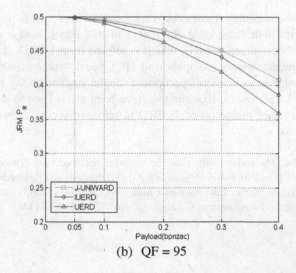

(b) QF = 95

Fig. 3. Detection errors as a function of relative payload for J-UNIWARD, IUERD and UERD on BOSSbase with JRM-22, 510D and ensemble classifier for (a) QF = 75 and (b) QF = 95.

Typically, half of the cover and the stego features will be used as the training set for the ensemble classifier, and the remaining half will be used as test set to evaluate the trained classifier. In this paper, we use the ensemble's "testing_error" to represent the P_E which quantified the security performance.

$$P_E = \min_{P_{FA}} \frac{P_{FA} + P_{MD}(P_{FA})}{2}$$

where P_{FA} is the false alarm rate and P_{MD} is the missed detection rate. The performance is evaluated using the mean value of P_E over ten random tests. And, the security performance is displayed graphically by showing P_E as a function of the relative payload.

4.2   Performance of IUERD

In this paper, we compare the proposed IUERD with the original UERD and the state-of-the-art method J-UNIWARD. The security performances of the involved schemes against the JRM-22, 510D, for JPEG quality factors 75 and 95, are illustrated in Fig. 3. For both cases, IUERD outperforms the original UERD by a considerable margin, indicating the effectiveness of the proposed scheme. It is also observed that our IURED has a comparable performance with J-UNIWARD for both cases. Note that, the performance loss of UERD in comparison with J-UNIWARD, however, can be compensated to a considerable extent by its extremely low computational complexity as described in [10].

5   Conclusion

Minimal distortion embedding framework is a successful approach to implement JPEG steganography with high embedding efficiency. In this paper, a new efficient JPEG steganographic scheme called IUERD, which is refined from UERD, is presented. By exploring the correlation among neighboring DCT blocks more efficiently, the proposed IUERD is shown to be more appropriate for the steganography in images with different texture characteristics. Experiments have been carried out to demonstrate the superior performance of the proposed IUERD in terms of secure embedding payload against steganalysis.

Acknowledgements. The authors appreciate the supports received from National Natural Science Foundation of China (No. 61379156 and 60970145), the National Research Foundation for the Doctoral Program of Higher Education of China (No. 20120171110037) and the Key Program of Natural Science Foundation of Guangdong (No. S2012020011114).

References

1. Xia, Z., Wang, X., Sun, X., Wang, B.: Steganalysis of least significant bit matching using multi-order differences. Secur. Commun. Netw. **7**(8), 1283–1291 (2014)
2. Li, J., Li, X., Yang, B., Sun, X.: Segmentation-based image copy-move forgery detection scheme. IEEE Trans. Inf. Forensics Secur. **10**(3), 507–518 (2015)
3. Xia, Z., Wang, X., Sun, X., Liu, Q., Xiong, N.: Steganalysis of LSB matching using differences between nonadjacent pixels. Multimedia Tools Appl. **75**(4), 1947–1962 (2016)
4. Westfeld, A.: F5 – a steganographic algorithm. In: Proceedings of the 4th Information Hiding Conference, vol. 2137, pp. 289–302 (2011). http://wwwrn.inf.tu-dresden.de/_westfeld/f5.html
5. Filler, T., Judas, J., Fridrich, J.: Minimizing additive distortion in steganography using syndrome-trellis codes. IEEE Trans. Inf. Forensics Secur. **6**(3), 920–935 (2011)
6. Kim, Y.H., Duric, Z., Richards, D.: Modified matrix encoding technique for minimal distortion steganography. In: Camenisch, J.L., Collberg, C.S., Johnson, N.F., Sallee, P. (eds.) IH 2006. LNCS, vol. 4437, pp. 314–327. Springer, Heidelberg (2007)
7. Sachnev, V., Kim, H.J., Zhang, R.: Less detectable JPEG steganography method based on heuristic optimization and BCH syndrome coding. In: Proceedings of the 11th ACM Workshop on Multimedia and Security, pp. 131–140 (2009)
8. Guo, L., Ni, J., Shi, Y.Q.: Uniform embedding for efficient JPEG steganography. IEEE Trans. Inf. Forensics Secur. **9**(5), 814–825 (2014)
9. Holub, V., Fridrich, J., Denemark, T.: Universal distortion function for steganography in an arbitrary domain. EURASIP J. Inf. Secur. **2014**, 1–13 (2014)
10. Guo, L., Ni, J., Su, W., Tang, C., Shi, Y.Q.: Using statistical image model for JPEG steganography: uniform embedding revisited. IEEE Trans. Inf. Forensics Secur. **10**(12), 2669–2680 (2015)
11. Freedman, D.A.: Statistical Models: Theory and Practice. Cambridge University Press, Cambridge (2009)
12. Bas, P., Filler, T., Pevný, T.: Break our steganographic system: the ins and outs of organizing BOSS. In: Proceedings of the 13th International Workshop on Information Hiding, pp. 59–70 (2011). http://www.agents.cz/boss/
13. Kodovský, J., Fridrich, J.: Steganalysis of JPEG images using rich models. In: Proceedings of SPIE, vol. 8303, p. 83030A, February 2012
14. Kodovský, J., Fridrich, J., Holub, V.: Ensemble classifiers for steganalysis of digital media. IEEE Trans. Inf. Forensics Secur. **7**(2), 432–444 (2012)

A Tunable Bound of the Embedding Level for Reversible Data Hiding with Contrast Enhancement

Haishan Chen[1,2], Wien Hong[2], Jiangqun Ni[1], and Junying Yuan[2(✉)]

[1] School of Electronics and Information Engineering, Sun Yat-sen University, Guangzhou, China
chenhsh3@mail3.sysu.edu.cn, issjqni@mail.sysu.edu.cn
[2] Nanfang College of Sun Yat-sen University, Guangzhou, China
wienhong@gmail.com, cihisa@outlook.com

Abstract. Recently, histogram modification based reversible data hiding (RDH) techniques are exploited to enhance the image contrast. To avoid overflow and underflow, the cover image has to be pre-processed by pre-shifting a number of the histogram bins at the lower and upper ends. When the payload size becomes large, a larger number of histogram bins has to be pre-shifted, and thus the image contrast may be over enhanced. As a result, human eye perceivable image degradation may appear in the over-sharpened image. To avoid image over-sharping, the just noticeable difference measurement is exploited to estimate the maximum number of pre-shiftable histogram bins. In addition, a tunable parameter is designed to balance between the visual degradation and the embedding capacity. The experimental result shows that the proposed work is effective in estimating the bound of embedding level.

Keywords: Contrast enhancement · Image over-sharping · Reversible data hiding · Embedding level · Just noticeable difference

1 Introduction

Reversible data hiding (RDH) is a technique to embed data bits into a cover media (image, voice or document) in a reversible way. In other words, the embedded data bits and the cover media can be completely recovered. Among the various cover medias, image is the mostly widely studied cover signal due the high embedding capacity and its broad applicability. In the last decade, RDH techniques have been extensively studied, many algorithms have been designed and applied into secrecy sensitive fields, e.g. image authentication [1,2], image watermarking [3–5], and medical image processing [6–8], etc.

Existing RDH methods can roughly be classified into three categories, the compression appending framework [9], the difference expanding (DE) techniques [3,10,11] and the histogram shifting (HS) schemes [4–6,12–17]. The DE technique and the HS technique embed data bits into cover images via histogram modification, including histogram expansion and histogram shifting. The first histogram

© Springer International Publishing AG 2016
X. Sun et al. (Eds.): ICCCS 2016, Part I, LNCS 10039, pp. 134–144, 2016.
DOI: 10.1007/978-3-319-48671-0_13

modification based method is proposed by Ni et al. [12]. In this method, the peak bin of the grayscale histogram is expanded to embed data bits. Since each pixel is modified by one, this method performs well in preserving the image fidelity with a limited embedding capacity (EC). To improve EC, Tian [10] proposed the first DE-based RDH methods, which embeds one data bit into a selected pixel pair. Since the EC is increased together with improved image fidelity, the DE-based histogram modification technique has been widely developed.

The aforementioned RDH methods usually focus on improving the embedding capacity and/or preserving the image fidelity, but seldom consider improving the image quality. Recently, Wu et al. [18] proposed a novel HS-based RDH method with contrast enhancement. In their method, a number of bin pairs (usually the peak bins) are selected for expansion. For each pair of bins, the smaller bin is expanded to the left-side, and the bigger bin is expanded to the right side. As a result, the histogram is spread into a broader range and thus the image contrast is enhanced. Let L be the number of to-be-expanded bin-pairs (namely the embedding level). L should be set to large enough so as to provide a larger embedding capacity. To avoid overflow and underflow caused by histogram expansion and shifting, the cover image has to be pre-processed. Specifically, the histogram bins in the ranges of $[0, L - 1]$ and $[256 - L, 255]$ are pre-shifted to $[L, 2L - 1]$ and $[256 - 2L, 255 - L]$, respectively.

Compared to conventional RDH methods, Wu et al.'s work [18] improves the image contrast while providing a consider amount of payload. Their work is later extended into medical image to increase the image contrast of region of interest [19]. However, when the embedding level L gets too large, the image contrast may get over-sharpened due to image pre-processing via histogram pre-shifting. To alleviate the issue of image over-sharping, Gao and Shi [20] proposes to control the degree of image contrast. In Gao et al.'s work, the level of image contrast is restrained by an experimentally derived threshold of relative contrast error (RCE), and L is determined according to the RCE threshold before data embedment. Even though the visual degradation is alleviated, the issue of over-sharping still exists.

This paper aims at providing a technique to avoid image over-sharping in RDH with contrast enhancement by devising a bound of the embedding level. Specifically, the just noticeable distortion (JND) [21,22] measurement in the human visual system (HVS) is exploited into the process of image pre-processing. And the maximum allowed embedding level L is derived adaptively according to the JND threshold. In addition, a tunable parameter based on the JND measurement is employed to balance between the visual image quality and the embedding capacity. Experimental results on typical images illustrates the effectiveness of the proposed work.

The rest of this paper is organized as below. Section 2 briefs the related concept of RDH with contrast enhancement and JND. The proposed work is illustrated in Sect. 3. The effectiveness of the proposed work is evaluated in Sect. 4. And the conclusion is drawn in Sect. 5.

2   Related Works

In this section, the Just Noticeable Distortion Measurement and the idea of RDH with contrast enhancement are briefed.

2.1   RDH Methods with Contrast Enhancement

The RDH method with contrast enhancement generally takes three steps to perform data embedment, namely image pre-processing, contrast enhancement via HS-based data embedment and further data embedment. The first step aims at pre-processing the cover image by pre-shifting the grayscale histogram, and thus rooms can be preserved for histogram expansion or histogram shifting. To make the pre-shifting process revertible, a local map is employed to register the pre-shifted pixels. Let $x \in [0, 255]$ be the pixel value of a cover image $\mathbf{I}_C$, $h(x)$ be the grayscale histogram, (h_a, h_b) denote the selected to-be-expanded bin pair, where $h_a < h_b$, $m \in \{0, 1\}$ be a to-be-embedded data bit. The second step is to perform L iterations of HS-based data embedment using the equation

$$
x' = \begin{cases}
x - 1, & x < h_a \\
x - m, & x = h_a \\
x, & h_a < x < h_b \\
x + m, & x = h_b \\
x + 1, & x > h_b,
\end{cases} \tag{1}
$$

where x' is the modified pixel value. In the final step, the embedding capacity can be further extended using other RDH techniques, e.g. integer transform [20].

2.2   The Just Noticeable Distortion Measurement

According to HVS, human eyes behave differently to pixel changes in different image regions. Generally speaking, human eyes are more sensitive to changes in flat regions but less sensitive to changes in complex regions. Therefore, the JND measure is employed to describe the level of local contrast when perceivable changes can be obtained.

In fact, the JND measure has been employed in DE-based RDH methods [11, 23] to reduce the visual image distortion. In these two methods, the JND at a pixel in cover image $\mathbf{I}_C$ is estimated before data embedment. Let (i, j) be the location of a pixel, and $x = I_C(i, j)$ denote the pixel value. The JND estimation begins by edge prediction. An edge, where the pixel $I_C(i, j)$ is located, has to be estimated from a local neighboring causal window Ω_{ij} using the equation

$$
E(i, j) = \begin{cases}
1, & \text{if } \mathrm{var}(\Omega_{ij}) > T_e \\
0, & \text{if } \mathrm{var}(\Omega_{ij}) \leq T_e,
\end{cases} \tag{2}
$$

where 1 and 0 of $E(i, j)$ represent an edge and non-edge area, respectively, and T_e is a predefined threshold.

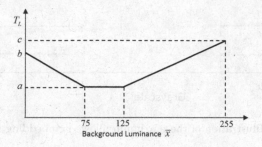

Fig. 1. Visibility threshold against background luminance [21].

Then, the JND value at location (i, j) can be calculated according to the visibility threshold $T_L(i, j)$ and the activity threshold $T_A(i, j)$, as specified by

$$J(i, j) = T_L(i, j) + \lambda \frac{T_A(i, j)}{T_L(i, j)}, \tag{3}$$

where $\lambda = 0.5$ [21]. The visibility threshold $T_L(i, j)$ can be approximately determined by the background luminance $\bar{x}$ as illustrated in Fig. 1 [21], where $\bar{x}$ is the averaged value of the pixels in the neighboring causal window. The three parameters, a, b and c in Fig. 1, are set to $a = 10, b = 20$ and $c = 24$ for non-edge pixels, and $a = 8, b = 18$ and $c = 22$ for edge pixels. The activity threshold $T_A(i, j)$ is defined as the maximum pixel difference value in the neighboring causal window.

3 The Proposed Work

In this section, the JND measurement is exploited to determine the maximum embedding level L without generating human eye perceivable distortions for RDH methods with contrast enhancement. In addition, a tunable parameter $\beta \in [0, 1]$ is designed to balance between the visual image quality and the embedding capacity.

3.1 The Maximum L Under the Constraint of JND

According to HVS, JND indicates that no human visible distortion can be perceived if the pixel value is changed within the range of $-J(i, j)$ to $J(i, j)$. Therefore, the JND measurement can be exploited to determine the maximum allowed L in RDH methods with contrast enhancement. Let $\mathbf{S}$ be the pre-shifted pixel set. To avoid image over-sharping, which is induced in by histogram pre-shifting in RDH with contrast enhancement, the maximum allowed variation $V_{\max}$ for a single pixel of the pre-shifted pixels can be determined by the minimum JND value of the pixels in $\mathbf{S}$, as specified by

$$V_{\max} = \min(\lfloor J(i, j) \rfloor), \text{ for } I_C(i, j) \in \mathbf{S}, \tag{4}$$

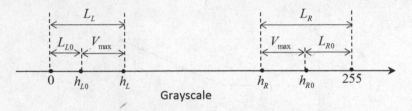

Fig. 2. Illustration of the maximum allowed embedding level.

$(i\text{-}2,j\text{-}2)$	$(i\text{-}2,j\text{-}1)$	$(i\text{-}2,j)$	$(i\text{-}2,j\text{+}1)$	$(i\text{-}2,j\text{+}2)$
$(i\text{-}1,j\text{-}2)$	$(i\text{-}1,j\text{-}1)$	$(i\text{-}1,j)$	$(i,j\text{+}1)$	$(i,j\text{+}2)$
$(i,j\text{-}2)$	$(i,j\text{-}1)$	(i,j)	$(i,j\text{+}1)$	$(i,j\text{+}2)$
$(i\text{+}1,j\text{-}2)$	$(i\text{+}1,j\text{-}1)$	$(i\text{+}1,j)$	$(i\text{+}1,j\text{+}1)$	$(i\text{+}2,j\text{+}2)$
$(i\text{+}2,j\text{-}2)$	$(i\text{+}2,j\text{-}1)$	$(i\text{+}2,j)$	$(i\text{+}2,j\text{+}1)$	$(i\text{+}2,j\text{+}2)$

Fig. 3. The window Ω_{ij} for JND estimation in the proposed work.

where $\lfloor \cdot \rfloor$ denotes the flooring operation. The JND value $J(i,j)$ is derived using Eq. 3, where the neighboring window Ω_{ij} is illustrated in Fig. 3.

Given the grayscale histogram $h(x)$, Fig. 2 illustrates the determination of the maximum allowed L without causing perceivable image distortion. In Fig. 2, $h(x) = 0$ for $x \in [0, h_{L0}]$ and $x \in [h_{R0}, 255]$, which indicates that the pixel values of cover image $\mathbf{I_C}$ falls in the scope of (h_{L0}, h_{R0}). Since $V_{\max}$ denotes the maximum allowed pixel variation without human eye perceivable degradation, the maximum L can be derived using the equation

$$L_{\max}^0 = \min(L_L, L_R), \tag{5}$$

where $L_L = L_{L0} + V_{\max}$ and $L_R = L_{R0} + V_{\max}$, and $L_{L0} = h_{L0} + 1, L_{R0} = 256 - h_{R0}$. When $L \leq L_{\max}^0$, the maximum pixel value variation is less than $V_{\max}$, and thus no human eye perceivable image degradation would be produced. Therefore, the applicable L should not overpass $L_{\max}^0$ under the constraint of JND.

3.2   Balancing Between Visual Distortion and Embedding Capacity

For simplicity, the image pre-processing with $L \geq L_{\max}$ and $L < L_{\max}$ are named as visible histogram pre-shifting and invisible histogram pre-shifting, respectively. For invisible histogram pre-shifting, the embedding level L tends to be small and thus the embedding capacity is generally not high. To balance between image degradation and the embedding capacity, a tunable parameter, $\beta \in [0, 1]$, is introduced. Let N be the cardinality of pre-processed pixel set **S**. The tunable parameter β is defined by the ratio of visible pre-shifting operations N_{vi} to N, as specified by

$$\beta = \frac{N_{vi}}{N}. \tag{6}$$

When $\beta = 0$, the maximum allowed L equals to the $L_{\max}^0$ in Eq. 5. When $\beta = 1$, the pre-shifting operation for all the pixels in **S** would be visible to human eyes. For $0 < \beta < 1$, the accurate value of L with respect to β can be computed using the equation

$$L_{\max}(\beta) = \arg\max_L \left(N_{vi} \leq \beta * \left(\sum_0^{L-1} h(x) + \sum_{256-L}^{255} h(x) \right) \right). \tag{7}$$

According to Eq. 7, the embedding capacity get improved as the increment of β, but at the cost of reduced visual image quality.

3.3   Histogram Pre-shifting

Let $L_{T0} = \min(L_{L0}, L_{R0})$, which presents the minimum of L_{L0} and L_{R0}, as illustrated in Fig. 2. The histogram pre-shifting process for $L \leq L_{\max}^0$ can be determined as follows. When $L \leq L_{T0}$, no image pre-processing is required since $h(x) = 0$ for $x \in [0, h_{L0}]$ and $x \in [h_{R0}, 255]$. When $L \in (L_{T0}, L_{\max}^0]$, the cover image can be pre-processed via histogram pre-shifting using the equation

$$x' = \begin{cases} x + max(0, L - L_{L0}), \ h_{L0} < x < L \\ x, \qquad\qquad\qquad\quad L \leq x \leq 255 - L \\ x - \max(0, L - L_{R0}), \ 255 - L < x < h_{R0}, \end{cases} \tag{8}$$

where x' denotes the pre-processed pixel value. To make the histogram pre-shifting process reversible, a location map is used to register the pre-shifted pixels.

Since L_{L0} and L_{R0} are determined adaptively according to the content of cover images, the proposed histogram pre-shifting technique can reduce the range of pixel change. Therefore, during histogram pre-shifting, the proposed histogram pre-shifting technique tends to produce less image distortion compared to that in Wu et al.'s work in [18].

3.4   Data Embedment, Extraction and Image Recovery

Let **I** be the pre-processed cover image using Eq. 8, and **PS** be the to-be-embedded data bit sequence. Note that, **PS** is composed of the secret message and the compressed location map. Given $L \leq L_{\max}$, the data bit sequence **PS** can be embedded into **I** by expanding the selected two peak bins h_a and h_b, as specified by Eq. 1. The process of histogram expansion and histogram shifting repeats for $L-1$ times. To make the data embedment procedure revertible, some side information should also be embedded into the L-th pair of peak bins. To be specific, the side information includes:

- h_{L0} and h_{R0}, $2 * 8$ bits,
- L, 5 bits,
- the length of the compressed location map, 18 bits,
- the first $L - 1$ pairs of peak bins h_a and h_b, $(L - 1) * 8$ bits,
- the LSBs of a preserved region, 16 bits.

The values of the last pair of expanded peak bins is recorded into the LSBs of a preserved region.

To extract the message bits and recovery the image, the last pair of expanded peak bins h_a and h_b is firstly picked out from the LSBs of the preserved region. Then side information is extracted according to h_a and h_b by inverting Eq. 1. The secret message and the compressed location map are then extracted using side information by inverting Eq. 1. Note that the image recovery process is performed along with data extraction. By far, the pre-processed image $\mathbf{I}$ is recovered. Finally, the cover image $\mathbf{I_C}$ is recovered using the decompressed location map by inverting Eq. 8, and thus the procedure of data extraction and image recovery completes.

4   Experiments

In the experiments, eight typical images, including six typical images obtained from the SIPI-USC [24] (Figs. 4(a)–(f)) and two medical images (Figs. 4(g)–(h)) obtained from http://www3.americanradiology.com/pls/web1/wwimggal. vmg, are used for performance evaluation. The embedding performance is evaluated using the peak-signal-to-noise (PSNR) and relative contrast error (RCE) [25] by comparing to that of Wu et al.'s work [18]. RCE indicates the degree of contrast enhancement, and its value is restricted to the range $[0, 1]$. When RCE

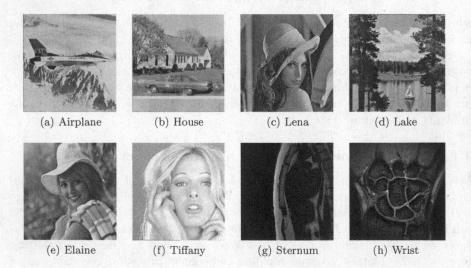

(a) Airplane   (b) House   (c) Lena   (d) Lake

(e) Elaine   (f) Tiffany   (g) Sternum   (h) Wrist

Fig. 4. The eight test images.

is greater than 0.5, the image contrast is enhanced, and the bigger RCE is, the better the image contrast is enhanced. The predefined threshold T_e in Eq. 2 is set to 200 in all the experiments.

By varying the tunable parameter β, the maximum embedding level L, namely $L_{max}(\beta)$, the related payload (the embedding rate), the RCE value and the PSNR results are derived and illustrated in Table 1. Note that, as the increment of β, $L_{max}(\beta)$ get bigger, the embedding capacity and the RCE get improved. However, the improvement of RCE may produce human eye perceivable distortion, as illustrated in Fig. 5. When $\beta = 0.0$, no visible degradation is found, as illustrated in Figs. 5(a), (d) and (g). However, when $\beta = 0.4, 0.2$ and

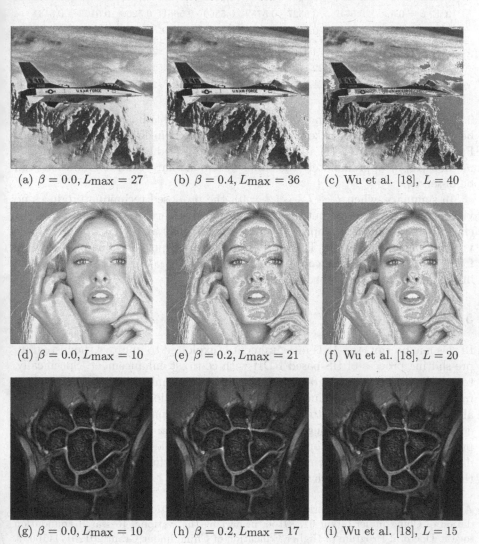

(a) $\beta = 0.0, L_{max} = 27$ (b) $\beta = 0.4, L_{max} = 36$ (c) Wu et al. [18], $L = 40$

(d) $\beta = 0.0, L_{max} = 10$ (e) $\beta = 0.2, L_{max} = 21$ (f) Wu et al. [18], $L = 20$

(g) $\beta = 0.0, L_{max} = 10$ (h) $\beta = 0.2, L_{max} = 17$ (i) Wu et al. [18], $L = 15$

Fig. 5. Visual quality comparison. (a)–(c) Airplane, (d)–(f) Tiffany and (g)–(i) Wrist.

Table 1. L_{max} and the related embedding capacity for the eight test images.

	Airplane	House	Lena	Lake	Elaine	Tiffany	Sternum	Wrist
$L_{max}, \beta = 0.0$	27	19	19	13	10	10	10	10
$L_{max}, \beta = 0.4$	36	25	28	19	21	21	18	18
$L_{max}, \beta = 1.0$	39	31	31	25	23	25	22	22
Payload, $\beta = 0.0$	0.8987	0.4798	0.3178	0.2667	0.1591	0.3556	0.8350	0.4402
Payload, $\beta = 0.0$	1.1862	0.5796	0.4501	0.3681	0.3314	0.8387	1.0754	0.7367
Payload, $\beta = 0.0$	1.3299	0.6781	0.4909	0.4621	0.3593	0.9615	1.1811	0.8727
RCE, $\beta = 0.0$	0.5578	0.5407	0.5530	0.5271	0.5320	0.5162	0.5050	0.5060
RCE, $\beta = 0.4$	0.5719	0.5527	0.5752	0.5360	0.5661	0.5260	0.5102	0.5131
RCE, $\beta = 1.0$	0.5750	0.5613	0.5818	0.5483	0.5709	0.5285	0.5147	0.5191
PSNR, $\beta = 0.0$	21.46	24.47	24.74	29.78	28.98	29.68	27.76	27.86
PSNR, $\beta = 0.4$	19.09	22.74	22.10	27.80	22.96	22.44	22.91	22.77
PSNR, $\beta = 1.0$	18.19	21.12	21.39	25.40	22.37	20.58	20.59	21.09

0.4 for Airplane, Tiffany and Wrist, respectively, visible image degradation can be observed from the marked images, as illustrated in Figs. 5(b), (e) and (h). Furthermore, Figs. 5(c), (f) and (i) presents the marked images using Wu et al.'s method [18] at approximately the same L, and similar visual degradations can be observed.

In summary, when $L \leq L_{max}(\beta = 0)$, the proposed technique produces no visible image degradation but with limited embedding capacity. When $\beta > 0$, the embedding capacity get improved obviously, but may at the cost of observable visible image degradation. Therefore, by selecting a proper value of β ranging from 0 to 1, the RDH with contrast enhancement can balance between the visual image quality and the embedding capacity.

5   Conclusion

In this manuscript, the JND measurement is exploited to improve the histogram pre-shifting process of HS-based RDH with contrast enhancement. Specifically, to avoid visible image degradation, the maximum embedding level is derived from the smallest JND value of the pre-shifted locations. Furthermore, a tunable parameter is devised to balance between the visual image quality and the embedding capacity. Although the proposed histogram pre-shifting technique is proved to be effective, the optimal value of the tunable parameter is still image dependent and needs experimental verification. And thus this problem is one of the authors' future research topics.

Acknowledgment. This work is supported in part by National Natural Science Foundation of China under Grant 61379156, in part by the National Research Foundation for the Doctoral Program of Higher Education of China under Grant 20120171110037, and in part by the Key Program of Natural Science Foundation of Guangdong under Grant S2012020011114.

References

1. Hsu, C.S., Tu, S.F.: Probability-based tampering detection scheme for digital images. Opt. Commun. **283**(9), 1737–1743 (2010)
2. Yang, H., Kot, A.C.: Binary image authentication with tampering localization by embedding cryptographic signature and Block Identifier. IEEE Signal Process. Lett. **13**(12), 741–744 (2010)
3. Thodi, D.M., Rodriguez, J.J.: Expansion embedding techniques for reversible watermarking. IEEE Trans. Image Process. **16**(3), 721–730 (2007)
4. Sachnev, V., Kim, H.J., Nam, J., Suresh, S., Shi, Y.-Q.: Reversible watermarking algorithm using sorting and prediction. IEEE Trans. Circuits Syst. Video Technol. **19**(7), 989–999 (2009)
5. Li, X., Yang, B., Zeng, T.: Efficient reversible watermarking based on adaptive prediction-error expansion and pixel selection. IEEE Trans. Image Process. **20**(12), 3524–3533 (2011)
6. Wu, H.-T., Huang, J.: Reversible image watermarking on prediction error by efficient histogram modification. Signal Process. **92**(12), 3000–3009 (2012)
7. Coatrieux, G., Le Guillou, C., Cauvin, J.M., Roux, C.: Reversible watermarking for knowledge digest embedding and reliability control in medical images. IEEE Trans. Inf. Technol. Biomed. **13**(2), 158–165 (2009)
8. Battisti, F., Carli, M., Neri, A.: Secure annotation for medical images based on reversible watermarking in the integer Fibonacci-Haar transform domain. In: Proceedings of SPIE EI, Image Processing: Algorithms and Systems IX, vol. 7870, pp. 78700G–78700G-10 (2011)
9. Fridrich, J., Goljan, M., Du, R.: Lossless data embedding for all image formats. In: Proceedings SPIE, vol. 4675, pp. 572–583 (2002)
10. Tian, J.: Reversible data embedding using a difference expansion. IEEE Trans. Circuits Syst. Video Technol. **13**(8), 890–896 (2003)
11. Hong, W., Chen, T.-S., Wu, M.-C.: An improved human visual system based reversible data hiding method using adaptive histogram modification. Opt. Commun. **291**, 87–97 (2013)
12. Ni, Z., Shi, Y.-Q., Ansari, N., Su, W.: Reversible data hiding. IEEE Trans. Circuits Syst. Video Technol. **16**(3), 354–362 (2006)
13. Hong, W., Chen, T.-S.: A local variance-controlled reversible data hiding method using prediction and histogram-shifting. J. Syst. Softw. **83**(12), 2653–2663 (2010)
14. Li, X., Zhang, W., Gui, X., Yang, B.: A novel reversible data hiding scheme based on two-dimensional difference-histogram modification. IEEE Trans. Inf. Forensics Secur. **8**(7), 1091–1100 (2013)
15. Ou, B., Li, X., Zhao, Y., Ni, R., Shi, Y.-Q.: Pairwise prediction-error expansion for efficient reversible data hiding. IEEE Trans. Image Process. **22**(12), 5010–5021 (2013)
16. Li, X., Zhang, W., Gui, X., Yang, B.: Efficient reversible data hiding based on multiple histograms modification. IEEE Trans. Inf. Forensics Secur. **10**(9), 2016–2027 (2015)
17. Hong, W., Chen, T.S., Chen, J.: Reversible data hiding using Delaunay triangulation and selective embedment. Inf. Sci. **308**, 140–154 (2015)
18. Wu, H.-T., Dugelay, J.L., Shi, Y.-Q.: Reversible image data hiding with contrast enhancement. IEEE Signal Process. Lett. **22**(1), 81–85 (2015)
19. Wu, H.-T., Huang, J., Shi, Y.-Q.: Reversible data hiding method with contrast enhancement for medical images. J. Vis. Commun. Image Represent. **31**, 146–153 (2015)

20. Gao, G., Shi, Y.-Q.: Reversible data hiding using controlled contrast enhancement and integer wavelet transform. IEEE Signal Process. Lett. **22**(11), 2078–2082 (2015)
21. Lin, W., Dong, L., Xue, P.: Visual distortion gauge based on discrimination of noticeable contrast changes. IEEE Trans. Circuits Syst. Video Technol. **15**, 900–909 (2005)
22. Lubin, J.: A visual discrimination model for imaging system design and evaluation. Vis. Models Target Detect. Recogn. **2**, 245–357 (1995)
23. Jung, S.W., Ko, S.J.: A new histogram modification based reversible data hiding algorithm considering the human visual system. IEEE Signal Process. Lett. **18**(2), 95–98 (2011)
24. The USC-SIPI Image Database. http://sipi.usc.edu/database
25. Gao, M.-Z., Wu, Z.-G., Wang, L.: Comprehensive evaluation for HE based contrast enhancement techniques. Adv. Intell. Syst. Appl. **2**, 331–338 (2013)

Coverless Text Information Hiding Method Based on the Word Rank Map

Jianjun Zhang[1,2(✉)], Jun Shen[2], Lucai Wang[2], and Haijun Lin[2]

[1] College of Computer Science and Electronic Engineering,
Hunan University, Changsha 410080, China
jianjun998@163.com
[2] College of Engineering and Design,
Hunan Normal University, Changsha 410081, China
842166947@qq.com, wlucai9776@vip.sina.com,
linhaijun801028@126.com

Abstract. Text information hiding has attracted the attention of many scholars and made a lot of achievements. However, for the text information hiding methods such as text format-based, generation method-based, text image-based and so on, there is a major flaw that cannot resist steganography detection. Based on the rank map of the words, a novel method of coverless text information hiding is presented. Firstly, stego-vectors are directly generated from the secret message by using the rank map. Then, some normal texts, stego-texts including the generated sgeto-vectors, will be searched form the text big data. Finally, the secret information can be sent to the receiver without any modification of the stego-texts. The proposed algorithm has a higher theoretical significance and practice value because it is robust for almost all current steganalysis methods.

Keywords: Coverless text information hiding · The rank map · The text big data · Steganography

1 Introduction

Information hiding is a research field of techniques that hide secret data imperceptibly into a cover medium for protection of intellectual property rights or secret communication [1]. Because the text is frequently used in people's daily lives, the text information hiding has attracted many researchers' interest, and has many results. The text information hiding can be classified into four categories: text information hiding based on text format, based on text images, and natural language information hiding based on generating method and based on embedding method.

Text format-based information hiding method is introduced since 1994, when Maxemchuk, Brassil, and Low, et al. proposed information hiding method by changing the line spacing, word spacing, character height, character width and other characteristics, and tested these hiding methods with the Postscript document. Later, many scholars improved these methods [2–9]. [10] adjusted the statistic feature of space of words or characters in a group unit to embed information. According to the theory of

X. Sun et al. (Eds.): ICCCS 2016, Part I, LNCS 10039, pp. 145–155, 2016.
DOI: 10.1007/978-3-319-48671-0_14

Chinese mathematical expressions, [11] split a Chinese character into parts, used parts interconnected diagram graph matching, and concluded the similarity of texts to hide information. The secret information can be hid by inserting or deleting the line feeds and the invisible characters (such as spaces, tabs, special spaces) at the end of a sentence, the end of a line, the end of a paragraph, and the end of a text file [12–15]. These invisible-based methods have some characteristics such as considerable capacity of embedding, and good invisibility, but cannot resist the steganography detection based on statistical analysis, therefore, the security is not high [16].

There are many kinds of information hiding method based text format, and the hiding capacity is large, but most of them cannot resist reformatting attacks, OCR attacks, and steganography detection based on statistical analysis [17–20]. If the document is generated without format after extracting the text content, the embedded information, hidden in the text format, will no longer exist.

A text can be seen as a binary image, and has some special properties compared with the grayscale and color images, so the **text image-based information hiding method** takes advantage of these properties to hide information. For example, [21, 22] modified the parity of the number of black and white pixels in the block to embed information, and [23] embedded information by modifying the proportion of black and white pixels in the block. [24] modified the connected components of the borders to embedded in binary. [25] proposed an embedded method based on pixel-flipping. [26] embed the hiding information in the original DWT domain of a text by combining the DCT domain with the DWT domain. A major flaw of the information hiding method based on the text image is completely unable to resist reformatting and OCR attacks. If the characters in the stego-text are reformatted, the hiding information will disappear completely.

There are two other methods commonly used in text information hiding. One is the **Nature language Information hiding method based on text generation**, also known as natural language information hiding based on generating method, automatically generate nature text-like to contain secret information by using natural language processing techniques. The method can fool the computer statistical analysis, but is relatively easy to be identified by people [27]. The other is the information hiding method based on changing text content, also known as **embedding method-based natural language information hiding**, modifies the text with different granularity to hide information while remaining the semantics of the local and global text unchanged [28, 29]. This method has more robust and better concealment than text format-based information hiding, but the hiding algorithm is very difficult, and there are some deviations and distortions in the statistic and linguistics because of the limitation of the natural language processing [30].

From the above we can see that the text information hiding has attracted the attention of many scholars and made a lot of achievements, but there are still some problems such as weak ability in anti-statistical analysis, bad text rationality and so on. Furthermore, theoretically as long as the carrier is modified, the secret message will certainly be detected. As long as the secret information exists in the cover, it can hardly escape from steganalysis. Thus, the existing steganography technology is facing a huge security challenge, and its development has encountered a bottleneck [31].

The proposed method is based on the rank map computed by statistically analyzing the text big data, converts the hiding information, computes the rank tab, and retrieves the text big data to get the stego-text including the converted words. Finally, the stego-text can be sent to the receiver without any modification. Because the method does not modify the stego-text, it is robust for all current steganalysis methods, and the proposed algorithm has a higher theoretical significance and applied value.

2 Coverless Information Hiding

Coverless information hiding is a new challenging research field. In fact, "coverless" is not to say that there is no carrier, but compared with the conventional information hiding, coverless information hiding requires no other carries [31]. The idea of coverless information hiding has a profound historical heritage, and the ancient acrostic poem is a classic example. An acrostic is a poem or other form of writing in which the first letter, syllable or word of each line, paragraph or other recurring feature in the text spells out a word or a message. Charles Lutwidge Dodgson (27 January 1832–14 January 1898), better known by his pen name Lewis Carroll, was an English writer, mathematician, logician, Anglican deacon, and photographer. His most famous writings are *Alice's Adventures in Wonderland*. Lewis Carroll wrote a unique double acrostic for Gertrude Chataway, the most important child-friend in the life of the author. It was Gertrude who inspired his great nonsense mock-epic *The Hunting of the Snark* (1876), and the book is dedicated to her, and opens with the poem that uses her name as a double acrostic. That acrostic poem is shown in Fig. 1.

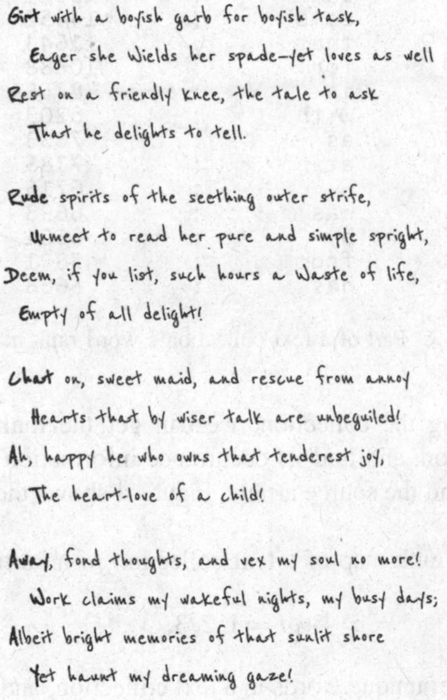

Girt with a boyish garb for boyish task,
    Eager she wields her spade—yet loves as well
Rest on a friendly knee, the tale to ask
    That he delights to tell.

Rude spirits of the seething outer strife,
    Unmeet to read her pure and simple spright,
Deem, if you list, such hours a waste of life,
    Empty of all delight!

Chat on, sweet maid, and rescue from annoy
Hearts that by wiser talk are unbeguiled!
Ah, happy he who owns that tenderest joy,
    The heart-love of a child!

Away, fond thoughts, and vex my soul no more!
Work claims my wakeful nights, my busy days;
Albeit bright memories of that sunlit shore
    Yet haunt my dreaming gaze!

Fig. 1. The acrostic written by Charles Lutwidge.

3 Proposed Method

3.1 Preprocessing

Let us suppose we have get a text database and let there be U unique words in the collection (the vocabulary). For each word in the collection, we compute the frequency of its occurrence-how many times word occurs in the collection. Then we rank the words in descending by their frequency (Most frequent word has rank 1, next frequent word has rank 2...).

Figure 2 shows the result of ranking that defined as the **word rank map** of the text collection. Form the rank map, we find that the total number of words in the collection (not number of unique words) is 1282023, the number of unique words is 33268, and the most frequent word is the word "the". At the same time, we can get the word rank map of every article in the collection. Figure 3 shows the rank map of an article, named as "1 dead, 1 injured in small plane crash in Texas", in which there are 178 words, and 120 unique words.

Rank	Words	:	Frequency
1	the	:	85042
2	of	:	35709
3	to	:	35441
4	in	:	31856
5	and	:	31335
6	a	:	26815
7	on	:	15521
8	said	:	14452
9	that	:	11644
10	for	:	10688
11	is	:	8758
12	with	:	8203
13	as	:	7633
14	at	:	7185
15	-	:	6716
16	was	:	6698
17	by	:	6661
18	from	:	5851
19	has	:	5688

Fig. 2. Part of a text collection's word rank map.

By statistic analyzing the collection, we can get the rank map for every word appearing in the collection, and find its occurrence information in the collection, such as, frequency, ranking and the source article. Figure 4 shows the rank map of the word "said".

We define the word rank map of a text collection or an article as

$$W = \{w_i | i = 1, 2, 3, \ldots, U\}. \tag{1}$$

Where U is the number of unique words in a text collection, and i is the rank of w_i. For the example in the Fig. 2, we can get $W = \{\text{the}, \text{of}, \text{to}, \text{in}, \text{and}, \text{a}, \text{on}, \text{said}, \ldots\}$.

Rank		Words		Rrequency	
1	:	the	:	12	:
2	:	in	:	7	:
3	:	of	:	6	:
4	:	to	:	5	:
5	:	local	:	4	:
6	:	plane	:	4	:
7	:	reported	:	3	:
8	:	said	:	3	:
9	:	at	:	3	:
10	:	small	:	2	:
11	:	Texas	:	2	:
12	:	crashed	:	2	:
13	:	Sunday	:	2	:
14	:	hangar	:	2	:
15	:	a	:	2	:
16	:	was	:	2	:
17	:	when	:	2	:
18	:	been	:	2	:
19	:	pilot	:	2	:
20	:	emergency	:	2	:
21	:	rushed	:	2	:
22	:	one	:	2	:
23	:	person	:	2	:
24	:	another	:	2	:
25	:	injuring	:	1	:
26	:	and	:	1	:
27	:	media	:	1	:
28	:	crash	:	1	:
29	:	Dozens	:	1	:

Fig. 3. Part of an article's word rank map.

Word:said

Rank	Frequency	Source Document
1	4	Strong magnitude 7 quake strikes eastern Russi
2	6	Death toll from Haiyan in Philippines rises to
2	9	Suspect of killing 8 Mexican official capture
2	3	Air Force fighter jet crashes in W india
2	4	India protests US arrest of diploma
2	6	Death toll from Haiyan in Philippines rises to
2	11	17 killed as typhoon hits Japan's coas
2	6	Gunmen shoot dead town mayor at Philippine air
2	8	Japanese carriers adhere to China's air zone
2	8	More than 3,100 pregnant women in Colombia hav
3	6	NASA finds clues to possible water flows on Ma
3	15	Amtrak to resume scheduled service after deadl
3	9	Russian airline rules out technical fault, pil
3	10	Jack Ma applauded for new global visio
3	7	Talks with ROK to 'set example
3	11	21 killed in Kabul suicide attack
3	6	China drives off US destroyer intruding into X
3	9	Indonesia arrests 12 linked to Jakarta attack,
3	12	Frantic rescue for 5 kids trapped in US cras
3	4	Kidnapped Taiwanese released in Philippine
3	22	Cousin admitted fatally stabbing mom, 4 kids
3	4	Venezuela expels 3 US consular officials
3	5	Kremlin asks US to explain accusations on Puti
3	9	Arrest made in San Francisco Chinese consulate
3	6	18 dead, scores trapped as Pakistan factory co
3	11	Gunman kills himself, 1 other at Reno hospita
3	4	Kidnapped Taiwanese released in Philippines
3	9	Arrest made in San Francisco Chinese consulate
4	5	China expects Korean Peninsula nuclear issue t
4	8	Canadian whale-watching boat sinks, killing at
4	7	Putin blames internal reason for economic slow
4	18	90%-plus US firms make profits in China Repor

Fig. 4. Part of the "said" word rank map.

For every word w_i appearing in the text collection, we define its rank map as

$$RW_i = \{rw_{ij} | i, = 1, 2, 3, \ldots, U; \ j = 1, 2, 3, \ldots Z\} \qquad (2)$$

where rw_{ij} is the rank of the word w_i in an article according to its occurrence, and Z is the number of the articles w_i appearing. For the example as shown in the Fig. 4, we find that $RW_8 = \{4, 6, 9, 3, 4, 6, 11, 6, 8, 8, 7, 15, 9, 10, 7, 11, 6, 9, 12, \ldots\}$ for the word "said" and 8 is its rank of occurrence in the text database as shown in the Fig. 2.

3.2   Information Hiding

For the coverless text information hiding based on a text collection, firstly, we segment the secret information into some individual words. By analyzing the rank map of the collection and ones of every word appearing in it, we convert these words into some top words in the rank map of the collection by using the transformation protocol. Then, we design the rank tag for converted words by using the rank locating protocol and get the words that contain the secret information and their rank tag. Finally, we search these words' rank maps to find some articles containing the secret information, and achieve the information hiding with zero modification. Let m be a word, and suppose the secret Information is $M = m_1, m_2, m_3, \ldots, m_n$ where m_i is an individual word, and n is the number of words in the secret message. The conversion and ranking process of its secret information is shown as Fig. 5. The details is introduced as the following.

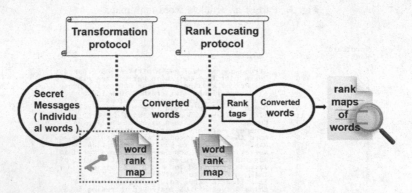

Fig. 5.   Secret information conversion and ranking location process

(1) Words Conversion. In order to enhance the security of data, we do not deal directly with the secret information, but convert the individual words in M into some frequent words by using the conversion protocol agreed upon beforehand by the communicating parties. The conversion protocol can be designed as follow: $m_i' = f_w(m_i, T), i = 1, 2, 3, \ldots, n$; Where $f_w(m_i, \cdot)$ is the word mapping function and $\bullet$ is the private key, such as the T of the above formula, and the n is the number of the words in M. T can be generated by running the synchronization function between communication parties, and changed every day. The word mapping function is used to convert the secret message to a subset consisting of top T words in W that is defined as the formula (1) in the section 'Preprocessing'. Suppose T is 50, so the set of $\{m_i' | i = 1, 2, 3, \ldots, n\}$ is a subset of the word set consisting of top 50 words in W. In order to strengthen the randomness, we can design a set of transformation functions according to the communication of an agreement beforehand, and use different transformation function

every communication, so as to map the individual words in M to different subsets of the set of frequent words, and improve data security. We can get the converted secret message $M' = m'_1 m'_2 \ldots m'_n$ by applying the conversion function with the secret message M. Here, M' is obviously a subset of W defined in the section of 'Preprocessing'.

(2) Getting the Rank Tag. In order to get the rank tag for the secret message M', the procedure is introduced as follows:

Step 1. For every word of top T words in W, compute its rank map in the text collection. For example, Suppose a word is the word "an", whose rank is 26 shown in Fig. 3, its rank map is {7, 21, 21, 4, 4, 8, 8, 3, 9, 4, 5, ...}. We can get a set of rank map for top T words in W, and let it be RW_i where $i = 1, 2, 3, \ldots, T$. RW_i is defined as the formula (2) in section 'preprocessing'.

Step 2. Get the intersection of $RW_i (i = 1, 2, 3, \ldots, T)$, and let it be IR. So $IR = \bigcap_{i=1}^{T} RW_i$. Because these words are top T words in W, so the intersection is not null, and the values of elements in IR are integers, the common ranks of top T words in W.

Step 3. For the secret message M', choose a rank number from the intersection IR, by implementing the rank location protocol agreed upon by communication parties. Let the chose rank of M' be r'. The rank location protocol can be designed as follows: $r' = f_r(IR)$, Where $f_r(IR)$ is the integer generation function, and the generated integer is in IR. This function can be designed as a synchronization function between communication parties.

(3) Searching the Stego-Text. For every m'_i, we retrieve the its rank map by the chose rank r' and achieve a stego-text from the text collection, and the rank of m'_i is r' in the rank map of the stego-text. So, we get a stego-text set. Here, these stego-text is a normal text set that contains the converted secret message, and they can be sent to the receiver.

3.3   Information Extraction

In traditional text information hiding, the stego-text is abnormal for the receiver, but it is normal for others, so the receiver can extract hidden information by analyzing these abnormalities. However, in the coverless information hiding, the stego-text is actually an open and normal text, and the receiver can't extract the secret information by finding the abnormal place [31]. Suppose the stego-text is S, so the S is a set of normal texts. The number of elements in S is the number of words in secret message. Let T be the private key for the receiver, then the process of extraction is showed as Fig. 6. The details can be introduced as follows.

(1) Get the Rank Map. After received the stego-texts, the receiver computers the frequency of words' occurrence, and rank the words in descending by their frequency. Then, the receiver can get the rank map as shown in Fig. 3.

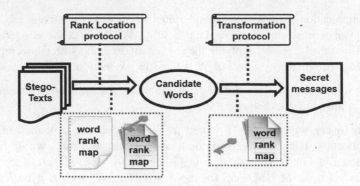

Fig. 6. Secret message extracting process

(2) Get the Rank Tab. Because the text collection is open for all users, so the receiver can get the set W defined in section of 'preprocessing', and get a subset of W with the private key T. The elements of this subset are the top T words in W. Then, for every word in the subset, the receiver can get its rank map set $RW_i(i = 1, 2, 3, \ldots, T.)$, where RW_i is defined as the formula (2) in section 'preprocessing'. So, the receiver can get the intersection $IR = \bigcap_{i=1}^{T} RW_i$, and the rank tab by implementing the function $f_r(IR)$, and let it be R_r. R_r is obviously equal to the rank tab r' computed by the sender

(3) Get the Candidate Words. The receiver can find the candidate words by retrieving the rank maps of the stego-texts by the key R_r, and get the candidate word m'. Because the sequence of the receiving stego-textes is the sequence of the individual words in secret message, the receiver can get the candidate words $M' = m'_1 m'_2 \ldots m'_n$ converted from the secret message by the sender.

(4) Get the Secret Message. After get the candidate words, the receiver can get the individual words in secret message by using $f_w^{-1}(m'_i, \cdot)$ with the private key T, and then get the secret message $M = m_1, m_2, m_3, \ldots, m_n$.

4   Example Verification

In order to clearly explain the above coverless text information hiding process, we illustrate it by a simple example. For example, let the secret information M be only one word "information". For more than one word in the secret message, the operation procedure is same. Here, we suppose the private key is the digit 50, and the text collection is the set of 3571 normal texts collected from the Internet. The operating procedure of the information hiding is introduced as follows:

Firstly, the sender computes the rank map of the text collection and ones of every article in it, as shown in Figs. 3 and 4. Because the private key is 50, the sender can get the top 50 words set $W_{top50} = \{w_i | i = 1, 2, 3, \ldots, 50\}$, where w_i is the word in the rank map of the collection, and i is its rank. The W_{top50} is:

{the, of, to, in, and, a, on, said, that, for, is, with, as, at, $-$, was,

by, from, has, he, it, us, will, have, china, an, be, are, its, his, were,

not, which, this, after, but, goverment, people, been, president,

also, new, chinese, two, their, who, we, more, had, minister}.

Sender computes the converted message M' by implementing the transformation protocol with the private key, and let M' is the word "us".

Secondly, sender computes the rank map for every word in W_{top50} as shown in Fig. 4, and the rank map matrix $RW = \{rw_{ij} | i, = 1, 2, 3, \ldots, 50; j = 1, 2, 3, \ldots Z\}$, where rw_{ij} is the rank of the word w_i in an article according to its occurrence, and Z is the number of the articles w_i appearing. The rank map matrix is shown as follow:

$$
\begin{pmatrix}
1, 2, 2, 19, 1, & \cdots & 1, 1, 1, 1, 2 \\
\vdots & \ddots & \vdots \\
142, 214, 63, 175, 35 & \cdots & 12, 124, 5, 8, 79
\end{pmatrix}
$$

It is worth mentioning here that, because the number of the articles appearing is not equal for every word in W_{top50}, the number of elements in each row is not same, and the number of the columns is 50. The sender compute the rank intersection of rows in the matrix, and get the intersection is:

$$IR = \{11\ 13\ 14\ 15\ 16\ 17\ 18\ 19\ 20\ 22\ 23\ 24\ 26\ 31\ 35\ 37\ 42\}$$

Obviously, there are 17 elements in the intersection, and for every element in it, there must be some articles, in which the rank of the word is it for every word in W_{top50}.

Thirdly, the sender compute the rank tab for M' by implementing the rank location protocol. For example, let us suppose the rank location function is simply a function mapping the date when transmitting message to the sequence number of elements in the rank intersection IR. Then, if the sequence number is 2, the sender can get the rank tab is 13.

Finally, the sender retrieves the rank map of the word "us" that is converted from the secret message "information", and find an articles named as "G20 urges US to act quickly to avoid default" in the text collection, in which the rank of the word "us" is 13. Then, the sender sends the article to the receiver.

Because the text collection is open for all users, the information extraction process is the inverse process of the information hiding process, and we will not repeat them now. However, it is worth mentioning that, in order to improve the anti-detection performance, there are two works must be done: one is to change periodically the private key to ensure that the converted words are different subsets of the words with top ranks; the second is to establish a large text database (text big data) to make sure that the rank tab has more choices.

5 Conclusions

For the text information hiding methods commonly used, the secret information is embedded in the stego-text which is abnormal for the receiver, but is normal for others. Because the stego-text is modified, the receiver can extract the secret information by analyzing these abnormalities as the result of sender's modification. Therefore, it can hardly escape from steganalysis. We firstly proposed the concept of word rank map, and designed a coverless text information hiding method by taking advantage of the word rank map in this paper. The proposed method only requires normal texts without any modification to hide information, so the receiver does not need analyzing the unusual places to abstract hidden information. Therefore, the proposed method can resist all kinds of existing steganalysis methods.

Acknowledgments. This work is supported by Open Fund of Demonstration Base of Internet Application Innovative Open Platform of Department of Education (KJRP1402), Hunan Province Science And Technology Plan Project Fund (2012GK3120), Scientific Research Fund of Hunan Province Education Department (13CY003, 14B106), Changsha City Science and Technology Plan Program (K1501013-11), and Hunan Normal University University-Industry Cooperation Fund.

References

1. Liu, T.Y., Tsai, W.H.: A new steganographic method for data hiding in microsoft word documents by a change tracking technique. IEEE Trans. Inf. Forensics Secur. **2**(1), 24–30 (2007)
2. Maxemchuk, N.F., Liu, T.Y., Tsai, W.H.: Electronic document distribution. AT&T Tech. J. **73**(5), 73–80 (1994)
3. Low, S.H., Maxemchuk, N.F., Brassil, J.T.: Document marking and identification using both line and word shifting. In: Proceedings of Infocom 1995, vol. 2007, pp. 853–860. IEEE (1995)
4. Brassil, J.T., Low, S.H., Maxemchuk, N.F.: Electronic marking and identification techniques to discourage document copying. IEEE J. Sel. Areas Commun. **13**(8), 1495–1504 (1995)
5. Low, S.H., Maxemchuk, N.F., Lapone, A.M.: Document identification for copyright protection using centroid detection. IEEE Trans. Commun. **46**(3), 372–383 (1998)
6. Low, S.H., Maxemchuk, N.F.: Performance comparison of two text marking methods. IEEE J. Sel. Areas Commun. **16**(4), 561–572 (1998)
7. Brassil, J.T., Low, S.H., Maxemchuk, N.F.: Copyright protection for the electronic distribution of text documents. In: Proceedings of the IEEE, vol. 87, pp. 1181–1196 (1999)
8. Huang, D., Yan, H.: Inter word distance changes represented by sine waves for watermarking text images. IEEE Trans. Circ. Syst. **11**(12), 1237–1245 (2001)
9. Adnan, M.A., Osama, M.A.: Watermarking electronic text documents containing justified paragraphs and irregular line spacing. In: Proceedings of the SPIE, pp. 685–695 (2004)
10. Kim, Y.W., Moon, K.A., Oh I.S.: A text watermarking algorithm based on word classification and inter word space statistics. In: Proceedings of Seventh International Conference on Document Analysis and Recognition, pp. 775–779 (2003)
11. Xie, L., Huang, H., Qin, J.: A text similarity detection algorithm based on components interconnected graph. In: Proceedings of 2015 China Information Hiding and Multimedia Security Workshop (CIHW2015), pp. 251–260 (2015)

12. Por, L.Y., Ang, T.F., Delina, B.: WhiteSteg: a new Scheme in information hiding using text steganography. WSEAS Trans. Comput. **7**(6), 735–745 (2008)

13. Lee, I.S., Tsai, W.H.: Secret communication through web pages using special space codes in HTML files. Int. J. Appl. Sci. Eng. **6**(2), 141–149 (2008)

14. Bender, W., Gruhl, D., Morimoto, N.: Techniques for data hiding. IBM Syst. J. **35**(34), 313–336 (1996)

15. Takizawa, O., Makino, K., Matsumoto, T., Nakagawa, H., Murase, I.: Method of hiding information in agglutinative language documents using adjustment to new line positions. In: Khosla, R., Howlett, R.J., Jain, L.C. (eds.) KES 2005. LNCS (LNAI), vol. 3683, pp. 1039–1048. Springer, Heidelberg (2005)

16. Koluguri, A., Gouse, S., Reddy, P.B.: Text steganography methods and its tools. Int. J. Adv. Sci. Tech. Res. **2**(4), 888–902 (2014)

17. Goyal, L., Raman, M., Diwan, P.: A robust method for integrity protection of digital data in text document watermarking. Int. J. Sci. Res. Dev. **1**(6), 14–18 (2014)

18. Sui, X.G., Luo, H.: A steganalysis method based on the distribution of space characters. In: Proceedings of IEEE International Conference on Communications, Circuits and Systems, vol. 1, pp. 54–56. IEEE (2006)

19. Luo, G., Sun, X., Liu, Y.: A text hiding information detection algorithm based on noise detecting. J. Hunan Univ. (Nat. Sci.) **32**(6), 181–184 (2005)

20. Kwon, H., Kim, Y., Lee, S.: A tool for the detection of hidden data in microsoft compound document file format. In: Proceedings of International Conference on Information Science and Security (ICISS), pp. 141–146 (2008)

21. Wu, M., Tang, E., Liu, B.: Data hiding in digital binary image. In: Proceedings of IEEE International Conference on Multimedia and Expo, pp. 393–396 (2000)

22. Wu, M., Liu, B.: Data hiding in binary images for authentication and annotation. IEEE Trans. Multimedia **6**(4), 528–538 (2004)

23. Zhao, J., Koch, E.: Embedding robust labels into images for copyright protection. In: Proceedings of the International Congress on Intellectual Property Rights for Specialized Information, Knowledge and New Technologies, pp. 242–251 (1995)

24. Mei, Q., Wong, E.K., Memon, N.: Data hiding in binary text documents. In: Proceedings of International Society for Optics and Photonics, pp. 369–375 (2001)

25. Qi, W., Li, X., Yang, B., Cheng, D.: Document watermarking scheme for information tracking. J. Commun. **29**(10), 183–190 (2008)

26. Wang, H., Li, R.: A binary text digital watermarking algorithm. J. Syst. Simul. **16**(3), 521–524 (2004)

27. Bo, S., Hu, Z., Wu, L., Zhou, H.: Steganography of Telecommunication Information. National Defense University, Beijing (2005)

28. Nematollahi, M.A., Al-Haddad, S.A.R.: An overview of digital speech watermarking. Int. J. Speech Technol. **16**(4), 471–488 (2013)

29. Mali, M.L., Patil, N.N., Patil, J.B.: Implementation of text watermarking technique using natural language. In: Proceedings of IEEE International Conference on Communication Systems and Network Technologies, 482–486 (2013)

30. Meng, P., Huang, L., Chen, Z., Yang, W., Yang, M.: Analysis and detection of translation based steganography. Acta Electronica Sinica 38(8), 1748–1852 (2012)

31. Chen, X., Sun, H., Tobe, Y., Zhou, Z., Sun, X.: Coverless information hiding method based on the chinese mathematical expression. In: Aixiang, Z., et al. (eds.) ICCCS 2015. LNCS, vol. 9483, pp. 133–143. Springer, Heidelberg (2015). doi:10.1007/978-3-319-27051-7_12

A Phishing Webpage Detecting Algorithm Using Webpage Noise and N-Gram

Qiong Deng, Huajun Huang[✉], Liangmin Pan, Shuang Pang,
and Jiaohua Qin

College of Computer and Information Engineering,
Central South University of Forestry and Technology, Changsha 410004, China
hhj0906@163.com

Abstract. Although anti-phishing solutions were highly publicized, phishing attack has been still an important serious problem. In this paper, a novel phishing webpage detecting algorithm using the webpage noise and n-gram was proposed. Firstly, the phishing webpage detecting algorithm extracts the webpage noise from suspicious websites, and then expresses it as a feature vector by using n-gram. Lastly, the similarity of feature vector between the protected website and suspicious is calculated. Experimental results on detecting phishing sites samples data show that: this algorithm is more effective, accurate and quick than existing algorithms to detect whether a site is a phishing website.

Keywords: Phishing · Anti-phishing · Web noise · N-gram

1 Introduction

Phishing, a term coined in 1996, is a form of online identity theft [1, 2]. Phishing was originally used to describe theft of AOL passwords and corresponding accounts. A phishing attack today typically employs generalized "lures". For example, a phisher disguising himself as a large banking corporation or popular online auction site by replicating of target web sites. However, over the decade the definition of phishing has expanded. Phishers today use attack vectors, such as QR code, email, Trojan horse key loggers and man-in-the-middle attacks to trick the victims.

Phishing activity is naive, but the caused damage is tremendous. According to recent security reports of APAC in China, 45 million adults lost a total of 30 billion RMB directly due to phishing every year [3]. But the damage caused by phishing does not only apply to monetary property alone. Indirect losses are much higher, including loss of productivity, cost of maintaining a helpdesk to field calls, recovery costs, or damage to an online organization's reputation. This in turn causes a significant loss in money, resources and time.

Another phenomenon is that only small set of targeted sites are imitated by phishers. In order to exploit the financial profit, phishers usually select famous online e-commerce websites. For instance, Feb. 2016 saw the total number of unique phishing submitted to APAC in China is 17,116. Four brands, such as Taobao, ICBC, CBC and China Mobile, hijacked by phishing campaigns, and comprised 99.05 % of the volume [4].

© Springer International Publishing AG 2016
X. Sun et al. (Eds.): ICCCS 2016, Part I, LNCS 10039, pp. 156–165, 2016.
DOI: 10.1007/978-3-319-48671-0_15

Quite a number of solutions to mitigate phishing attacks have been proposed to date [5–9]. Generally, past works can be classified into browser-side-based solution and server-side-based solution. Browser-side-based solution usually embeds anti-phishing measures "plug-in" into end-user's browsers. Taking the advantage of heuristics, similarity, identity and machine learning, the measures can automatically detect phishing sites, and warn the end-user to go away from phishing trick. However, it is entirely passive; its effectiveness hinges on user's ability. As we all know, end-users may also be ill-equipped to identify phishing attacks.

An alternative that has been widely adopted is server-side-based solution, which refers to require online organization authentication to defend against phishing attacks [10–16]. Typical approach attempts to eliminate the phishing problem at the server side by trying to prevent phishing e-mails from reaching the potential victims. Industry relies heavily on manually-verified URL black-lists in combating phish. Another authentication approach is to share a secret between server and end-user, e.g. an image, a watermark, a fingerprint or a password. However, email filter and black-list verification will unavoidably cause false positive and false negative, and secret share requires user awareness and prior knowledge.

These methods had obtained certain achievement, but increase the cost of user experience, and in the face of today's high speed change to phishing, exquisite technology for counterfeit and huge amounts of network data, the accuracy of the detecting results is always unsatisfactory. In this paper, a novel phishing webpage detecting algorithm using the webpage noise and n-gram was proposed. Firstly, the webpage noise from suspicious websites is extracted, and then expressed as a feature vector by using n-gram. Lastly, the similarity of feature vector between the protected website and suspicious is calculated. Experimental results on detecting phishing sites samples data show that: webpage features is stability in the processing of this algorithm, and this algorithm obtain a more effective, accurate and quickly to judge whether a site for phishing website algorithm system than existing algorithms.

2 Algorithm Model

Today, the defense of phishing attacks mainly focus on taking text or picture page as feature to study the defense. Such method not only increases the cost of the user experience, and most of the algorithms cannot keep high detection rate and accurate rate in the Internet era, which face high speed change and at the same time contain huge amount of data. Based on the advantages and disadvantages of all kinds of phishing website defense methods, they usually have shortcomings of inefficiency, complicated process, low precision and accuracy.

In order to deal with the increasingly serious network security problems by developing of the Internet, this paper proposes a new kind of phishing detection algorithm using webpage noise and n-gram.

Definition 1. Webpage noise refers to the page content that is not in conformity with the applied purpose, such as navigation bars, logo and contact information, banner ad and image, etc. Usually, the webpage noise means this information frequently appear in the all webpages where from the same organization.

Through the research we found that each webpage containing about 20 %–40 % of the template, and each page template is relatively fixed [17]. At the same time, n-gram language model can simply and directly express the probabilistic relationship between each element word. The webpage noise is extracted as features to describe website, and then the n-gram language model deal with it. Comparing with those methods which take the page text as the webpage feature, the data need to process is greatly reduced in this method. This algorithm using the noise data to express webpage feature can more clearly and briefly with a lower cost and a high efficiency. So, the feature similar rule between phishing and protected website is calculated with the testing threshold value for detecting phishing websites.

2.1 Webpage Noise Extraction Model

Researching a lot of noise sample has found that the content of webpage total noise is small and stable. If use word features and choose webpage noise as webpage features to describe, it will save amount of storage space and greatly improve the efficiency of web processing, also it can let the final detection result is more accurate.

In extracting noise model, HTML is a simple label language which has certain relationship between the tree structure itself and define a series of tags (such as <head>, <title>, <script>, <style>, <img>, <table>, etc.) to depict the content of websites. So that, webpage can be simply and intuitively described through making up the main label in websites in accordance with the nested relationship into DOM (Document Object Model) tree structure. And, the experimental observation of the large number of sample data found that the content of webpage usually won't appear in <script>, <style>, <img> tags. These tags usually contain a large number of links and descriptions of web information. Thus, in this paper with the analysis of noise in the tag, the noise of the webpage source code can be divided into three categories, are shown in following Table 1:

Analyzing web sample data has been collected in this study, the total amount of noise in the I class label and the II class label is about 98 % of all websites. But according to the statistical sample features, the labels of the II class have fewer occurrences in the sample source; even occurrences of some labels are 0. And the III class labels contain all theme and content related to the topic.

Table 1. The classification of the labels

Categories	Tags
The I class	<script>,<noscript>,<style>,<image>,<input>,<form>,<object>,<label>, <option>,<a>
The II class	<param>,<meta>,<optgroup>,<textarea>,<area>,<map>,<ifram>,<embed>
The III class	<head>,<table>,<span>,<body>,<tbody>,<p>,<Hr>, ,<tr>,<td>,<dt>, <dd>,<dl>,<div>,<ol>,<ul>

So we firstly parse the protected webpage code and tested webpage code into the DOM tree structure. After parsing, the contents of the I class label nodes are extracted directly from the DOM tree act as the experimental data for this new algorithm.

2.2   N-Gram

N-gram is a kind of language model which can calculate the sentence probability in the text information. Using n-gram language model, text information can be described in the form of a probability for ease of studying and computing. Assuming that the webpage features are extracted, the appearance of the nth word is relevant to the former $n - 1$ words. If it is only relevant to the former words, the $n - 1$th word, so it called 2-gram, denote as bigram.

Definition 2. In the extracted web page feature, we set the emergence of the nth term is only related to $(n - 1)$ words which in front of it, and has nothing relationship with the any other word, so that the probability of the whole sentence you can use the product of each word occurrence probability. If web features have a sentence T, and sentence T by W1, W2,..., Wn, several words composition, so the probability of sentence T in the text is:

$$P(T) = P(W_1 W_2 W_3 \ldots W_n) = \Pi_{i=1}^{n} P(W_n | W_1 W_2 \ldots W_{n-1}).$$

Similarly, if the element word is related to both the former one and later one, then it so called 3-gram. Through the observation, bigram and trigram have been widely applied in practice. And the quaternary or higher than the quaternary algorithm model, as it needs quite a lot of corpus to training and imprecise, applicable fields are relatively few. According to this characteristic, selects the bigram to calculate in each label the probability of appearances for a word and its former word. Let the result as noise feature matrix, and the dimension of the matrix is determined by the number of appeared words.

Because of testing the English website, will remove the English words and digital sign as the word segmentation identification. Take out letters or numbers between two characters each word as a unit element word. In view of the differences between texts, selects the frequency of the each element word appearance as elements for characteristic matrix. Traverse the noise text, record the frequency of all words appears is $m + 1$. The frequency of the mth + 1 element word and the mth element word appear at same time is denoted by am. So the frequency of the $(m + 1)$th element word and the mth element word appear in the text at same time is:

$$Fm = am/m + 1.$$

Definition 3. Assuming that a noise text is composed of $n + 1$ element words, the feature word frequency matrix is expressed as m = (f1,f2,....,fm), in which fm is expressed as the frequency of the $(m + 1)$th element word and the mth element word appear in the text at same time. For example, the text is consisting of four words in turn

– "This", "is", "a", "book".Which the probability of "this" and "is" appear at the same time is 0.2,the frequency of "is" and "a" appear at the same time is 0.4, the frequency of "a" and "book" appear at the same time is 0.7. Hence, obtain the feature matrix for this text: m = (0.2, 0.4, 0.7).

To choose an experiment website sample data after noise extraction. Then, the text of the previously extracted node to have string segmentation, get all the words. Statistics "the frequency of one word after another word appears" and save it into the dictionary as "features".

Processing the webpage noise data through this language model, it can get the noise feature frequency matrix for all tested websites. When all samples are obtained through this method, the results will classify and save as sample data for the following experiments.

2.3   Similarity Algorithm

We select cosine law to detect the text similarity. Assuming that the feature frequency matrix of the protected website is x, and the feature frequency matrix of the ith tested website is yi. Fxt and fyitare denoted the ith element of protected site's characteristic frequency matrix and the ith element of the ith monitored website's characteristic frequency matrix, respectively. The angle of cosine between the two website feature frequency vectors are calculated, and then the similarity of the protected and tested website is determined. Assume the protected website is x, the tested website is yi, the computation formula is as follows:

$$\cos(x, y_i) = sim1 = \cos(\theta) =$$
$$\frac{\vec{x} \cdot \vec{y}_i}{\|\vec{x}\| \times \|\vec{y}_i\|} = \frac{\sum_{t=1}^{m+1} f_{xt} \cdot f_{y_it}}{\sqrt{\sum_{t=1}^{m+1} f_{xt}^2} \sqrt{\sum_{t=1}^{m+1} f_{y_it}^2}} \tag{1}$$

3   Experimental Results and Analysis

Relevant experiments verifying, and it is concluded that precision rate and recall rate of the algorithm to identify the reliability of the algorithm. In addition, based studying on the experimental results using the algorithm found that for the same protected sites abound with similar similarity of phishing sites. Through clustering analysis the new phishing web site data of experimental results, objective and true verified the possibility of phishing attacks team, at the same time more progress to confirm in the experiment the phishing site threshold has high practical value.

3.1 The Experimental Data Collection

Through PhishTank website (http://www.phishtank.com/) [18], we fetch the identified phishing website URL links and related Whois information which reported by users to classify and save. This experiment mainly aimed at PayPal and eBay website to collect the data for research. Currently, it has saved total 4812 phishing website from Phish-Tank, including 2610 from PayPal, 2202 from eBay. After label selecting, involved in the testing of actual phishing website is 2490 from PayPal and 1699 from eBay.

3.2 The Similarity Results and Analysis

Collecting the PayPal and eBay phishing website data, the similarity values between their office websites and tested phishing websites is calculated by Formula 1. Distribution is shown in Fig. 1.

In the Fig. 1(a) and (b), abscissa is the value between 0 and 1 calculated by cosine formula, namely similarity, and ordinate is the numbers of this website have same similarity. Through Fig. 1(a) found that PayPal protected website and phishing website similarity intensively distribute in the vicinity of 0.67 and accounts for about 60 % of the total sample data. In the range of the similarity value between 0 and 0.65 points, the number of websites is relatively rare, only at 0.32. The number of websites with the same similarity value rose slightly. Figure 1(b) shows, eBay protected website and phishing website similarity intensively distribute in 0.56, 0.57 and 0.69, these three values, especially in 0.57 and 0.69. While between 0 and 0.3, the number of it is very few. Site numbers distribute intensively between 0.3 and 0.56, but in the vicinity of 0.56, corresponding similarity value website count more. In the range of more than 0.7 similarity values, the number of websites is min. Thus, PayPal protected and tested websites similarity values mainly concentrate on 0.67 or between 0.65 and 0.67. And then, eBay protected websites and tested websites similarity values distribute in 0.56, 0.57 and 0.69, the numbers of these three values are more.

3.3 Detecting Similarity

In order to observe the data of this experiment more directly and clearly, through this experimental observation know that similarity value data is 2 dimensional continuous spaces. Based on all above, using the K-means average method which is usually use for detecting objects in n-dimensional continuous space to analysis this experiment's data. As a result, it can determine the threshold of phishing website more accurately.

The characteristic of basing on the K-means mean clustering and the characteristic of basing on the prototype category, we choose k = 7. In this data which obtained from calculating, considering the similarity value of 0 and over 0.8 that their number of website is very few, therefore it not be considered. Based on this, the similarity value is set 0 between to 0.8, and divided into eight equal parts as an initial state. We choose interval point as the initial cluster center similarity value point. Followed by processing experimental data through K-Mean average clustering algorithm, the algorithm steps are divided into the following three steps:

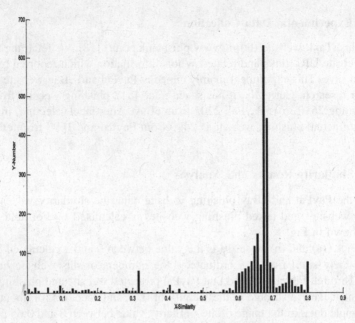

(a) *PayPal* Similarity Histogram

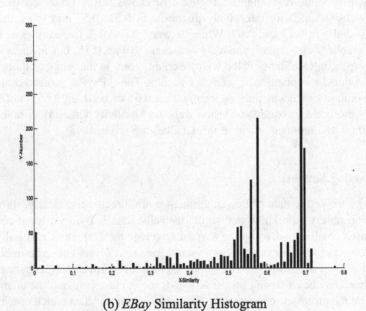

(b) *EBay* Similarity Histogram

Fig. 1. Protected website and tested website similarity point figure

(1) Take an arbitrary similarity value between the initial center point corresponding to each center point and the similarity value for distance, and calculation its Manhattan distance. Then, find the shortest distance. Locate the similarity value points into the shortest distance of its corresponding center.

(2) When all objects distributing is completed, calculated for each class average distance from all similarity point to the center similarity point, set it as the new center point.

(3) Repeat steps 2 and 3, until there no similarity value data would be redistributed.

Because samples of collected phishing website in this experiment, some Website source code do not contain any required experimental HTML labels. Therefore, get rid of those websites do not as experimental subject. The results of the detected data are shown in Tables 2 and 3.

Table 2. Result of detecting of PayPal

Classification	Number	The center point of similarity
0	110	0.1
1	50	0.179733203789006
2	107	0.30579304313606
3	77	0.426420700418534
4	171	0.592828124464023
5	497	0.635070781276205
6	1578	0.690915230136077

Table 3. Result of detecting of eBay

Classification	Number	The center point of similarity
0	62	0.0265207649943965
1	47	0.20707073028211
2	106	0.339163534778367
3	97	0.430406891337013
4	242	0.512931517614603
5	432	0.56898435015218
6	713	0.686381847541975

Analyzed the results of comprehensive observation of the figure above, in the phishing website and protected sites alignment similarity, there is appeared a lot of similarity values similar or consistent phishing website. According to the feature of phishing can speculate that may be composed of one or a plurality of groups of the same protected sites, repeated and targeted, strong purpose malignant phishing behavior. Therefore, aiming at the specific site can set the similarity threshold corresponding to detect whether it is phishing website. Comprehensive experimental results, set the PayPal phishing site screening for threshold range: $\{0.65 \leq \alpha\_PayPal \leq 0.67\}$, set the eBay phishing site screening for threshold range: $\{0.55 \leq \alpha\_eBay \leq 0.57 \cup \alpha\_eBay = 0.68\}$.

3.4   The Detection of the Precision

In order to detect the accuracy of the threshold, using precision by the reaction of the accuracy of algorithm, the recall rate of reaction algorithm has false negative features and F value to evaluate the detection results. The specific calculation formula is as follows. The P represents the precision of the ith class in data. The R represents the recall rate of the ith class in data. Nc denotes the number of phishing sites which have been judge right. Np denotes the number of phishing sites which actual participate in comparing. N is the whole sample number of website.

$$P = Nc/Np \tag{2}$$

$$R = Nc/N \tag{3}$$

$$F = 2P * R/(P+R) \tag{4}$$

The corresponding data were substituted into the Formulas 2 and 3, the results is shown as follows: Ppaypal = 0.8863, RpayPal = 0.8550; PeBey = 0.8964, ReBay = 0.8299. From the Formula 4, we can get FpayPay = 0.91, FeBay = 0.86.

4   Conclusion

This algorithm uses the Webpage noise and n-gram to detect phishing sites. Compared with the existing anti-phishing method, this algorithm costs lowly. What's more, we selected the web noise which relatively stable in websites as the feature to describe the whole website, could enhance the performance of the algorithm and as well the corresponding stability is better. At the sometime, set a phishing website investigation threshold which aims to PayPal and eBay to against its phishing website malicious attacks detection more effectively and efficiency. Comparing with Other algorithms, this algorithm has fewer amounts of calculation and higher veracity. Also, it is better to cope with today's Internet rapidly changes and larger quantities of data. Considering that the development trend of large data and cloud computing is brought by the Internet now, the future work will be to make the phishing website defense to achieve large data, intelligent, and balance of efficiency and performance in the detection.

In the next work, we should find the general artifact and design more accurate and sensitive detection algorithm as well.

Acknowledgment. This study is supported by National Natural Science Foundation of China (No. 61304208), Hunan Province Natural Science Foundation of China (No. 13JJ2031); Youth Scientific Research Foundation of Central South University of Forestry & Technology (No. QJ2012009A).

References

1. APWG. http://www.antiphishing.org. Accessed 3 Mar 2015
2. Hong, J.: The state of phishing attacks. Commun. ACM **55**(1), 74–81 (2012)
3. APAC. http://www.apac.org.cn/. Accessed 3 Mar 2016
4. APAC. http://www.apac.org.cn/gzdt/qwfb/201602/P020160225393465225017.pdf. Accessed 3 Mar 2016
5. Abbasi, A., Zhang, Z., Zimbra, D., et al.: Detecting fake websites: the contribution of statisitical learning theory. MIS Q. **34**(3), 435–461 (2010)
6. Huang, H.J., Qian, L., Wang, Y.J.: A SVM-based technique to detect phishing URLs. Inf. Technol. J. **11**(2), 921–925 (2012)
7. Yue, C., Wang, H.N.: BogusBiter: a transparent protection against phishing attacks. ACM Trans. Internet Technol. **11**(7), 6–36 (2010)
8. Zhang, H., Liu, G., Chow, T.W.S., et al.: Textual and visual content-based anti-phishing: a Bayesian approach. IEEE Trans. Neural Netw. **22**(10), 1532–1546 (2011)
9. Huang, C., Ma, S., Yeh, W.: Mitigate web phishing using site signatures. In: Proceedings of TENCON 2010, pp. 803–808. IEEE (2010)
10. Huang, H.J., Wang, Y.J., Xie, L.L., et al.: An active anti-phishing solution based on semi-fragile watermark. Inf. Technol. J. **12**(1), 198–203 (2013)
11. Wardman, B., Stallings, T., Warner, G., Skjellum, A.: Automating phishing website identification through deep MD5 matching. In: eCrime Researchers Summit, pp. 1–7 (2008)
12. Dunlop, M., Groat, S., Shelly, D: GoldPhish: using images for content-based phishing analysis. In: Proceedings of the Fifth International Conference on Internet Monitoring and Protection, pp. 123–128. IEEE (2010)
13. Whittaker, C., Ryner, B., Nazif, M: Large-scale automatic classification of phishing pages. In: Network and Distributed Systems Security Symposium, pp. 1–10 (2010)
14. Gu, B., Sheng, V.S., Tay, K.Y., Romano, W., Li, S.: Incremental support vector learning for ordinal regression. IEEE Trans. Neural Netw. Learn. Syst. **26**(7), 1403–1416 (2015)
15. Gu, B., Sun, X., Sheng, V.S.: Structural minimax probability machine. IEEE Trans. Neural Netw. Learn. Syst. (2016). doi:10.1109/TNNLS.2016.2544779
16. Bin, G., Sheng, V.S., Wang, Z., Ho, D., Osman, S., Li, S.: Incremental learning for ν-support vector regression. Neural Netw. **67**, 140–150 (2015)
17. Mao, X.L., He, J., Yan, H.F.: A survey of web page cleaning research. J. Comput. Res. Dev. **47**(12), 2025–2036 (2010)
18. Phishtank. http://www.phishtank.com/. Accessed 3 Mar 2015

A Construction Scheme of Steganographic Codes Based on Matrix Unwrapping

Weiwei Liu[1,2(✉)], Guangjie Liu[1], Jiangtao Zhai[3], and Yuewei Dai[1,3]

[1] School of Automation, Nanjing University of Science and Technology,
Nanjing, China
{lwwnjust,gjieliu}@njust.edu.cn
[2] School of Computer and Software,
Nanjing University of Information Science and Technology, Nanjing, China
[3] School of Electrical and Computer Engineering,
Jiangsu University of Science and Technology, Zhenjiang, China

Abstract. As the most efficient matrix embedding scheme, syndrome-trellis codes (STCs) has been widely used in the field of data hiding, it is implemented based on syndrome trellis structure of convolutional codes and the Viterbi algorithm. In this paper, a new construction scheme of STCs is proposed based on a family of time-varying periodic convolutional codes, the parity-check matrix is constructed by matrix unwarpping. The proposed scheme can enhance the parameter recognition of STCs efficiently while maintaining similar performance with STCs. Moreover, their construction method is more systematic.

Keywords: Steganography · Time-varying periodic · Time-invariant · Matrix unwrapping

1 Introduction

Steganography is the technology of invisible communication. It can be realized as embedding a secret message in an appropriate multimedia carrier, e.g., image, audio and video files. The ultimate purpose of steganography is to convey the information in some other medium without being exposed [1]. Syndrome-trellis codes (STCs) [2] have been widely used as the core embedding strategy in the state-of-the-art steganographic schemes [3–6]. The suggested method to construct the good parity-check matrices used in STCs is just the brute-force searching, which is commonly time-consuming and also faces to the inconvenience to share the parity-check matrix between both communication sides. The practical method is to find the good fixed parity-check matrices for the typical embedding

W. Liu—This study was supported by NSF of Jiangsu province (Grant nos. BK20160840, BK20150472), and NSF of China (Grant nos. 61272421, 61472188) and A Project Funded by the Priority Academic Program Development of Jiangsu Higer Education Institutions (PAPD), and Jiangsu Collaborative Innovation Center on Atmospheric Environment and Equipment Technology (CICAEET).

X. Sun et al. (Eds.): ICCCS 2016, Part I, LNCS 10039, pp. 166–177, 2016.
DOI: 10.1007/978-3-319-48671-0_16

rates beforehand and bind them to the steganographic tools. Moreover, the convolutional codes employed in STCs are time-invariant, that is, their parity-check matrices are all composed of repeated submatrices, which may bring in some security vulnerabilities. A parameter recognition scheme of STCs has been proposed for further steganalysis [7], and the secret key space for parameter recognition is analyzed under two strong attack conditions [8]. Thus, it is necessary to find a systematic method for constructing a family of time-varying convolutional codes, which can achieve similar performance when compared with those good time-invariant convolutional codes adopted in STCs.

In this paper, we propose a family of time-varying periodic convolutional codes based on matrix unwrapping, which can also be utilized for syndrome trellis coding and capable of performing close to the bounds derived from appropriate rate-distortion bounds. Their time-varying periodic structure can enhance the secrecy security.

2 Fundamental of Time-Varying Convolutional Codes

Since Costello firstly threw the conjecture that non-systematic time-varying convolutional codes may attain larger free distance than non-systematic time-invariant ones, the searching for such codes has attracted more and more researchers attentions, despite that the irregularity of such codes led to few related achievements [9,10]. Recently, its worth noting that Low-Density Parity-check (LDPC) convolutional codes have become a research hotspot because of their remarkably good performance [10–12], they have been shown to be capable of achieving capacity-approaching performance in channel coding with iterative message-passing decoding. Whats more, the time-varying periodic LDPC convolutional codes also have certain advantages compared to time-invariant LDPC convolutional codes. In fact, time-varying periodic LDPC convolutional codes are a particular class of time-varying convolutional codes. In [12], time-varying convolutional codes are defined by parity-check matrices. A semi-infinite binary parity-check matrix $\mathbf{H}_{conv}$ as Eq. (1) defines a time-varying convolutional code $C_{conv}(N, K)$.

$$
\mathbf{H}_{conv} =
\begin{bmatrix}
\hat{\mathbf{H}}_0(0) & & & & & \\
\hat{\mathbf{H}}_1(1) & \hat{\mathbf{H}}_0(1) & & & & \\
\vdots & \vdots & \ddots & & & \\
\hat{\mathbf{H}}_{m_s}(m_s) & \hat{\mathbf{H}}_{m_s-1}(m_s) & \cdots & \hat{\mathbf{H}}_0(m_s) & & \\
& \hat{\mathbf{H}}_{m_s}(m_s+1) & \hat{\mathbf{H}}_{m_s-1}(m_s+1) & \cdots & \hat{\mathbf{H}}_0(m_s+1) & \\
& & \ddots & \ddots & & \ddots \\
& & \hat{\mathbf{H}}_{m_s}(t) & \hat{\mathbf{H}}_{m_s-1}(t) & \cdots & \hat{\mathbf{H}}_0(t) \\
& & & \ddots & & \ddots
\end{bmatrix}
\tag{1}
$$

The submatrices $\hat{\mathbf{H}}_i(j), i = 0, 1, \ldots, m_s, j = 0, 1, \ldots, t$ are all sized $(N - K) \times N$ with $K < N$, the parameter m_s denotes the syndrome former memory. With the structure of the parity-check matrix, we know that the maximal number of nonzero submatrices per block row of $\mathbf{H}_{conv}$ is $m_s + 1$ and the constraint length v_s which measures the maximal width of the nonzero area of $\mathbf{H}_{conv}$ is $(m_s + 1) \cdot N$. If there is a positive integer T_s such that $\hat{\mathbf{H}}_i(j) = \hat{\mathbf{H}}_i(j + T_s)$ for all $i = 0, 1, \ldots, m_s$ and $j = 0, 1, \ldots, t$, then T_s is called the period of $\mathbf{H}_{conv}$, and $C_{conv}(N, K)$ is periodically time-varying. Particularly, when the period $T_s = 1$, $\mathbf{H}_{conv}$ is called time-invariant, and the parity-check matrix has been adopted in STCs.

3   The Proposed Construction Scheme

3.1   Properties of Good Time-Varying Convolutional Codes for Syndrome Coding

Two properties for good time-invariant convolutional codes have been mentioned in [10,11] with experience in experiments: The first row or the last row of the submatrix $\hat{\mathbf{H}}$ should not be all zero and it should not have identical columns. However, more detail and convincing explains for the properties of good convolutional codes should be given. With the introduction in Sect. 3.2, we know that time-invariant convolutional codes are a particular class of time-varying periodic convolutional codes with the period $T_s = 1$. Thus, in this section, we extend the two properties to time-varying convolutional codes and give detailed explanations. Without loss of generality, we rewrite the parity-check matrix $\tilde{\mathbf{H}}_{conv}(t)$ in Eq. (1) as the form like Eq. (2).

$$\tilde{\mathbf{H}}_{conv}(t) = \begin{bmatrix} \mathbf{H}_1(1) & & & & & \\ \mathbf{H}_2(1) & & & & & \\ & \ddots & \mathbf{H}_1(i) & & & \\ \mathbf{H}_h(1) & \ddots & \mathbf{H}_2(i) & & & \\ & & \ddots & & \\ & & \mathbf{H}_h(i) & \ddots & \\ & & & & \mathbf{H}_1(t) \end{bmatrix} \tag{2}$$

where $\mathbf{H}_j(i) = \begin{bmatrix} h_i(j,1) & h_i(j,2) & \cdots & h_i(j,N) \end{bmatrix}$, $i = 1, 2, \ldots, t$ and $j = 1, 2, \ldots, h$. The syndrome trellis of time-varying convolutional codes consists of different trellis modules constructed by different submatrix. Here, we analyze the property of good time-varying convolutional codes based on trellis module, the i-th trellis module corresponds to the i-th submatrix $\hat{\mathbf{H}}(i) = \begin{bmatrix} \mathbf{H}_1(i) \\ \vdots \\ \mathbf{H}_h(i) \end{bmatrix}$ as shown in Eq. (2).

The trellis module constructed by $\hat{\mathbf{H}}(i)$ is represented by $\Omega(\mathbf{E}, \mathbf{V})$, $\mathbf{E}$ and $\mathbf{V}$ are the sets of the edges and states respectively. $v_{j,k} \in \mathbf{V}$ denotes the $(k+1)$-th state in the $(j+1)$-th column, $j = 0, 1, \ldots, N$ and $k = 0, \ldots, 2^h - 1$. We call the state active state if there exists edge arriving at it, only these states can be used to implement the Viterbi algorithm, otherwise, we call it inactive state, the weight of which is defined as infinite. It is the well-known conclusion that the performance of convolutional codes always arise along with the memory degree length h, which means more paths through the trellis and more active states in each column. In general, there are at most 2^{h-1} initial states in the first column of each trellis module, and in the last column, only the paths arriving at the states with the last bit equaling to the embedding bit can be reserved, the accumulated distortion weight of these states will be transferred to the initial states in the first column of the next trellis module. Thus, the number of active states in the first column of the $(i+1)$-th trellis module is determined by the number of active states in the last column of the i-th trellis module. In each trellis module, the number of the path through the trellis module is $N_a : 2^N$, where N_a is the number of the active states in the first column. Thus, the conclusion can be drawn that a good submatrix $\hat{\mathbf{H}}(i)$ must have as more as possible active states in the last column of the corresponding trellis module. To begin with the following discussion, a simple related theorem is given beforehand. In the i-th trellis module, we denote the set of the paths from the state $v_{0,j}$ to the state $v_{N,k}$ as $\Theta(j,k)$, and $|\Theta(j,k)|$ denotes the cardinality of $\Theta(j,k)$.

Theorem 1. When there exist no nonzero solution for the equation $\hat{\mathbf{H}}(i) \cdot \lambda = \mathbf{0}$, for arbitrary j and k, if $\Theta(j,k) \neq \emptyset$, then $|\Theta(j,k)| = 1$. Otherwise, when there exist nonzero solution λ^*, for arbitrary j and k, if $\Theta(j,k) \neq \emptyset$, we have $|\Theta(j,k)| = 2$ and $\sum_{\mu \in \Theta(j,k)} \mu = \lambda^*$.

Proof. When $\Theta(j,k) \neq \emptyset$,

$$j \oplus k = \begin{bmatrix} h_i(h,1) & \cdots & h_i(h,N) \\ \vdots & \ddots & \vdots \\ h_i(1,1) & \cdots & h_i(1,N) \end{bmatrix} \begin{bmatrix} \lambda_1 \\ \vdots \\ \lambda_N \end{bmatrix} \tag{3}$$

If there exist two different solutions $\lambda_1 = (\lambda_1,\ldots,\lambda_N)^T$ and $\lambda_2 = (\lambda'_1,\ldots,\lambda'_N)^T$ both satisfying Eq. (3), which correspond to two paths through the trellis module, then we must have

$$\begin{bmatrix} h_{v1}(i) & \cdots & h_{vN}(i) \\ \vdots & \ddots & \vdots \\ h_{11}(i) & \cdots & h_{1N}(i) \end{bmatrix} \begin{bmatrix} \lambda_1 \oplus \lambda'_1 \\ \vdots \\ \lambda_N \oplus \lambda'_N \end{bmatrix} = \mathbf{0} \tag{4}$$

Which means $\lambda^* = (\lambda_1 \oplus \lambda'_1,\ldots,\lambda_N \oplus \lambda'_N)^T$ is the nonzero solution of $\hat{\mathbf{H}}(i) \cdot \lambda = \mathbf{0}$. Thus if $|\Theta(j,k)| = 2$, there must exist a nonzero solution of $\hat{\mathbf{H}}(i) \cdot \lambda = \mathbf{0}$, obviously, this is a necessary and sufficient condition. Q.E.D. Based on the theorem, we explain the two properties of good time-varying convolutional codes for syndrome coding.

The First Row or the Last Row of Each Submatrix Should Not be All Zero. Without loss of generality, suppose that there exist 2^{h-1} active

states in the first column of the trellis module constructed by submatrix
$\hat{\mathbf{H}}(i) = \begin{bmatrix} \mathbf{H}_1(i) \\ \vdots \\ \mathbf{H}_h(i) \end{bmatrix}$, and they are labeled with $0, 1, \ldots, 2^{h-1} - 1$ in order from
top to bottom. If $\mathbf{H}_h(i) = \mathbf{0}$, we have $k \leq 2^{h-1} - 1$ according to Eq. (27), which
means the number of active states in the last column of the trellis module is
2^{h-1} at most. Moreover, the number of active states in the first column of the
(i + 1)-th trellis module is at most 2^{h-2}, that means the number of the paths
through the (i + 1)-th trellis module is at most 2^{N+h-2}, this always drops the
performance of syndrome coding. And if $\mathbf{H}_1(i) = \mathbf{0}$, we have $(j \oplus k) \bmod 2 = 0$
according to Eq. (27), which means all paths leaving from the state $v_{0,j}$ satisfying
$(j - m_i) \bmod 2 = 0$ will be removed at the end of the trellis module, m_i denotes
the i-th message bit. It can be equivalent to the condition that the number of
active states in the last column of the (i − 1)-th trellis module is 2^{h-1} at most,
which is similar to the condition when $\mathbf{H}_h(i) = \mathbf{0}$. Thus, $\mathbf{H}_h(i)$ or $\mathbf{H}_1(i)$ should
not be all zero for each submatrix $\hat{\mathbf{H}}(i)$.

Each Submatrix Should not have Identical Columns. We rewrite the
i-th submatrix $\hat{\mathbf{H}}(i)$ to column vector form $\hat{\mathbf{H}}(i) = (\mathbf{H}_1^*(i), \ldots, \mathbf{H}_N^*(i))$, where
$\mathbf{H}_j^*(i) = \begin{bmatrix} h_i(1, j) & h_i(2, j) & \cdots & h_i(h, j) \end{bmatrix}^T$, $i = 1, 2, \ldots, t$ and $j = 1, 2, \ldots, N$.
Without loss of generality, suppose that $\mathbf{H}_\alpha^*(i) = \mathbf{H}_\beta^*(i)$, $\alpha \neq \beta$, then there
must exist a nonzero solution $\lambda' = \left(0, \ldots, 0, \underset{\alpha-th}{1}, 0, \ldots, 0, \underset{\beta-th}{1}, 0, \ldots, 0 \right)^T$ which
satisfies $\hat{\mathbf{H}}(i) \cdot \lambda' = \mathbf{0}$. According to Theorem 1, we know that for arbitrary j
and k, if $\Theta(j, k) \neq \emptyset$, then $|\Theta(j, k)| = 2$, which means there are at least two
path connecting the state $v_{0,j}$ to the state $v_{N,k}$. For given number of the path
through the trellis module, that will drop the number of the active states in the
last column of the trellis module. Thus, each submatrix $\hat{\mathbf{H}}(i)$ should not contain
identical columns.

3.2   Construction of Time-Varying Periodic Syndrome-Trellis Codes

The main task of constructing time-varying periodic syndrome-trellis codes is to
find the good time-varying periodic convolutional codes, which can be described
with their parity-check matrices. Several graph-cover-based methods for deriving families of time-invariant and time-varying LDPC convolutional codes from
LDPC block codes have been discussed in [12]. There are two typical methods for
constructing LDPC convolutional codes: Tanners method and JFZ method. The
Tanners method exploits similarities between quasi-cyclic block codes and time-
invariant convolutional codes; The JFZ method uses a matrix-based unwrapping procedure to obtain the parity-check matrix of a time-varying periodic
convolutional code from the parity-check matrix of a block code. Unfortunately,
these LDPC convolutional codes achieve poor performance when adopted in

syndrome coding. Combining the construction methods of these LDPC convolutional codes with the property analysis, we propose a family of time-varying periodic convolutional codes based on matrix unwrapping which can achieve good performance when adopted in syndrome coding, their construction method is flexible and systematic. The procedure of constructing these time-varying periodic convolutional codes can be depicted as follows. For a binary proto-matrix $\mathbf{A} \in \{0,1\}^{m_{\mathbf{A}} \times n_{\mathbf{A}}}$, let $\{\mathbf{A}_l\}_{l \in \mathbf{L}}$ be a collection of matrices such that $\mathbf{A}_l \in \{0,1\}^{m_{\mathbf{A}} \times n_{\mathbf{A}}}$ and $\sum_{l \in \mathbf{L}} \mathbf{A}_l = \mathbf{A}$, where $\mathbf{L}$ denotes a finite set. For some positive integer r, let $\{\mathbf{K}_l\}_{l \in \mathbf{L}}$ be a collection of size-$r \times r$ binary matrices, and each $\mathbf{K}_l$ is a right-shifted matrix of the matrix $\mathbf{Z}$.

$$\mathbf{Z} = \sum_{i=0}^{\kappa} \mathbf{I}_i \tag{5}$$

Where $\kappa = \lfloor r/2 \rfloor$ and $\mathbf{I}_i$ is an i times right-shifted identity matrix of size-$r \times r$, that means each matrix $\mathbf{K}_l$ contains $\kappa + 1$ 1s per column, $\kappa + 1$ 1s per row. Then, an intermediary matrix $\mathbf{B}$ can be defined as Eq. (6) with the collections of matrices $\{\mathbf{A}_l\}_{l \in \mathbf{L}}$ and $\{\mathbf{K}_l\}_{l \in \mathbf{L}}$.

$$\mathbf{B} = \sum_{l \in \mathbf{L}} (\mathbf{A}_l \otimes \mathbf{K}_l) \tag{6}$$

Where $\mathbf{M} \otimes \mathbf{N}$ denote the Kronecker product of the matrices $\mathbf{M}$ and $\mathbf{N}$, $\mathbf{B}$ is a binary matrix of size-$m_{\mathbf{A}}r \times n_{\mathbf{A}}r$. Let $\eta = \gcd(m_{\mathbf{A}}r, n_{\mathbf{A}}r)$ and the diagonal cut is performed by alternately moving $N = n_{\mathbf{A}}r/\eta$ units to the right and $N - K = m_{\mathbf{A}}r/\eta$ units down with the intermediary matrix $\mathbf{B}$, two cutting matrices $\bar{\mathbf{B}}_0$ and $\bar{\mathbf{B}}_1$ of size-$m_{\mathbf{A}}r \times n_{\mathbf{A}}r$ can be obtained by the cutting line such that $\bar{\mathbf{B}}_0 + \bar{\mathbf{B}}_1 = \mathbf{B}$. We consider Toeplitz matrices $\mathbf{T}_0$ and $\mathbf{T}_1$, where $\mathbf{T}_k$ is a bi-infinite matrix with zeros everywhere except for ones in the k-th diagonal below the main diagonal, i.e., $[\mathbf{T}_k]_{j,i} = 1$ if $j = i + k$ and $[\mathbf{T}_k]_{j,i} = 0$ otherwise. For example

$$\mathbf{T}_1 = \begin{bmatrix} 0 & 0 & 0 & 0 & \\ 1 & 0 & 0 & 0 & \ddots \\ 0 & 1 & 0 & 0 & \ddots \\ 0 & 0 & 1 & 0 & \ddots \\ & \ddots & \ddots & \ddots & \ddots \end{bmatrix} \tag{7}$$

Then, the matrix $\mathbf{B}'$ can be calculated with cutting matrices and Toeplitz matrices.

$$\begin{aligned} \mathbf{B}' &= \mathbf{T}_0 \otimes \bar{\mathbf{B}}_0 + \mathbf{T}_1 \otimes \bar{\mathbf{B}}_1 \\ &= \begin{bmatrix} \bar{\mathbf{B}}_0 & 0 & 0 & 0 & \\ \bar{\mathbf{B}}_1 & \bar{\mathbf{B}}_0 & 0 & 0 & \ddots \\ 0 & \bar{\mathbf{B}}_1 & \bar{\mathbf{B}}_0 & 0 & \ddots \\ 0 & 0 & \bar{\mathbf{B}}_1 & \bar{\mathbf{B}}_0 & \ddots \\ & \ddots & \ddots & \ddots & \ddots \end{bmatrix} \end{aligned} \tag{8}$$

At last, adding all 1 row vector $\mathbf{W} \in \{1\}^N$ to the top and the bottom of each block in

$$\mathbf{B}',$$

the resulting parity-check matrix $\tilde{\mathbf{H}}$ for time-varying periodic convolutional code $C(N, K)$ can be obtained with Eq. (9).

$$\tilde{\mathbf{H}} = \begin{bmatrix} \mathbf{W} & 0 & 0 & 0 & \\ \bar{\mathbf{B}}_0 & \mathbf{W} & 0 & 0 & \ddots \\ \bar{\mathbf{B}}_1 & \bar{\mathbf{B}}_0 & \mathbf{W} & 0 & \ddots \\ \mathbf{W} & \bar{\mathbf{B}}_1 & \bar{\mathbf{B}}_0 & \mathbf{W} & \ddots \\ & \mathbf{W} & \bar{\mathbf{B}}_1 & \ddots & \ddots \\ & & \ddots & \ddots & \ddots & \ddots \\ & & & & & \mathbf{W} \end{bmatrix} \tag{9}$$

Where the code rate of the resulting time-varying periodic convolutional code is $R = K/N = (n_{\mathbf{A}} - m_{\mathbf{A}})/n_{\mathbf{A}}$, the period $T_s = r$. This family of convolutional codes can be utilized in syndrome coding as indicated in Sect. 4, which we call time-varying periodic syndrome-trellis codes (TP-STCs), the convolutional code with code rate R can be used for matrix embedding with relative payload $\alpha = 1 - R$. We give an example to depict the construction procedure, consider the proto-matrix $\mathbf{A} = \begin{bmatrix} 1 & 1 & 1 \end{bmatrix}$ with $m_{\mathbf{A}} = 1$ and $n_{\mathbf{A}} = 3$. Let the finite set $\mathbf{L} = \{1\} \times \{1, 2, 3\}$, the collection of matrices $\{\mathbf{A}_l\}_{l \in \mathbf{L}}$ is given by $\{\mathbf{A}_{m,n}\}, m = 1, 2, \ldots, m_{\mathbf{A}}, n = 1, 2, \ldots, n_{\mathbf{A}}$, $\mathbf{A}_{m,n}$ is the binary matrix of size-$m_{\mathbf{A}} \times n_{\mathbf{A}}$, it can be defined as Eq. (10).

$$[\mathbf{A}_{m,n}]_{i,j} = \begin{cases} A_{i,j}, & \text{if}(m, n) = (i, j) \\ 0, & \text{otherwise} \end{cases} \tag{10}$$

Moreover, let $r = 5$, the matrix $\mathbf{Z}$ can be obtained according to Eq. (5), $\mathbf{Z}_i$ denotes i times right-shifted matrix of $\mathbf{Z}$.

$$\mathbf{Z} = \begin{bmatrix} 1 & 1 & 0 & 0 & 0 \\ 0 & 1 & 1 & 0 & 0 \\ 0 & 0 & 1 & 1 & 0 \\ 0 & 0 & 0 & 1 & 1 \\ 1 & 0 & 0 & 0 & 1 \end{bmatrix} \tag{11}$$

And the collection of matrices $\{\mathbf{K}_l\}_{l \in \mathbf{L}}$ can be given by $\{\mathbf{K}_{m,n}\}, m = 1, 2 \ldots, m_{\mathbf{A}}, n = 1, 2, \ldots, n_{\mathbf{A}}$. Suppose that

$$\mathbf{K}_{m,n} = \mathbf{Z}_{\bmod (a^{m-1}b^{n-1}, r)} \tag{12}$$

where a and b are both small primes, in this paper, we concentrate on high rate convolutional codes $C(N, N-1)$, so the parameter $a \triangleq 1$. For simplicity, we set $b = 1$. Then, the intermediary matrix $\mathbf{B}$ can be obtained according to Eq. (6).

$$\mathbf{B} = \begin{bmatrix} \mathbf{Z}_1 & \mathbf{Z}_1 & \mathbf{Z}_1 \end{bmatrix} \tag{13}$$

$$
\begin{array}{cccccccccccccccc}
0 & 1 & 1 & 0 & 0 & 0 & 1 & 1 & 0 & 0 & 0 & 1 & 1 & 0 & 0 \\
0 & 0 & 1 & 1 & 0 & 0 & 0 & 1 & 1 & 0 & 0 & 0 & 1 & 1 & 0 \\
0 & 0 & 0 & 1 & 1 & 0 & 0 & 0 & 1 & 1 & 0 & 0 & 0 & 1 & 1 \\
1 & 0 & 0 & 0 & 1 & 1 & 0 & 0 & 0 & 1 & 1 & 0 & 0 & 0 & 1 \\
1 & 1 & 0 & 0 & 0 & 1 & 1 & 0 & 0 & 0 & 1 & 1 & 0 & 0 & 0 \\
\end{array}
$$

Fig. 1. The structure of the intermediary matrix **B**.

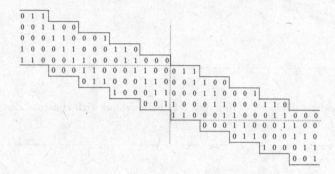

Fig. 2. The structure of the matrix **B′**.

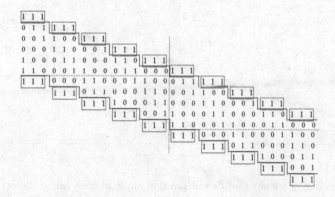

Fig. 3. The structure of the resulting parity-check matrix **Ĥ**.

The diagonal cut performed with **B** is shown in Figs. 1, 2 and 3. As shown in Fig. 6, we know that the code rate of the resulting time-varying periodic convolutional code is $R = (n_{\mathbf{A}} - m_{\mathbf{A}})/n_{\mathbf{A}} = 2/3$, the periodic $T_s = 5$ and the memory degree length $h = r + 2 = 7$.

4   Experimental Results

In order to benchmark the proposed codes, three distortion profiles are used. They are the constant profile $\rho_i = 1$, the linear profile $\rho_i = 2i/n$ and the square

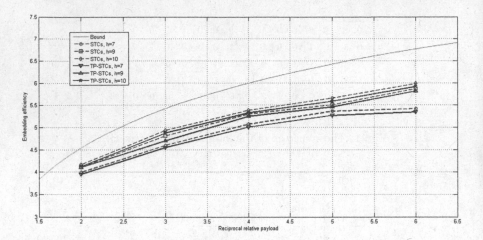

Fig. 4. Embedding efficiency of different relative payload with constant distortion profile.

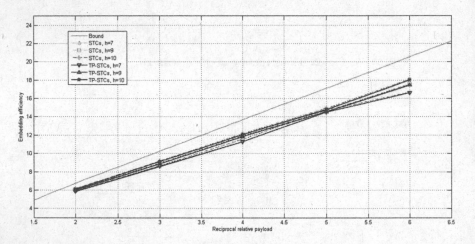

Fig. 5. Embedding efficiency of different relative payload with linear distortion profile.

profile: $\rho_i = 3(i/n)^2$. In order to make the comparison, the C++ and Matlab source codes of STCs are downloaded from the site http://dde.binghamton.edu/download/syndrome/. Embedding efficiency of two schemes (STCs and TP-STCs) are computed with three distortion profiles in different memory degree length h and relative payload α. The cover object $\mathbf{X} \in \{0,1\}^n$ and the embedding message $\mathbf{M} \in \{0,1\}^m$ are both provided by a pseudo-random bits generator. The code length n = 6000, the parameter b in Eq. (36) is set to 3, the relative payload $\alpha = \{1/2, 1/3, 1/4, 1/5, 1/6\}$ and the proto-matrix $\mathbf{A} \in \{1\}^{1/\alpha}$. The results have been shown in Figs. 4, 5 and 6. As shown in Figs. 4, 5 and 6, we can find that the constructed time-varying periodic syndrome-trellis codes only have little loss of

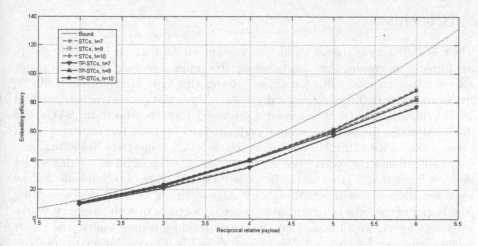

Fig. 6. Embedding efficiency of different relative payload with square distortion profile.

performance when compared with STCs from the overall perspective, they are both capable of performing close to the bounds, which reports the good performance of the proposed codes. Besides, because of employing the same type of trellis, the computation complexity of the two methods are also the same. Then, we also compare the embedding efficiency for different parameter b. The relative payload $\alpha = \{1/2, 1/3, 1/4, 1/5, 1/6\}$, and the memory degree length h is fixed to 10. The results with constant distortion profile have been shown in Fig. 7. With Fig. 7, we can find that for different parameter b, the embedding efficiency are almost the same, it means the large choosability of the matrix $\mathbf{K}_l$, which can ensure the flexibility of the construction methods.

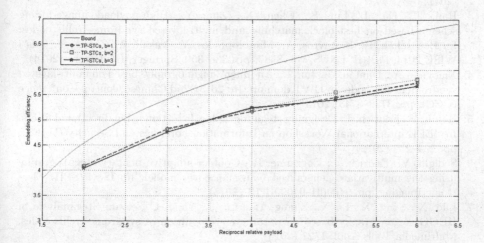

Fig. 7. Embedding efficiency for different parameter b with constant distortion profile.

5   Conclusion

STCs is the state-of-the-art syndrome coding method which has been widely used in steganography, they are based on the trellis structure of time-invariant convolutional codes. In this paper, we extend this type of syndrome trellis to time-varying periodic convolutional codes, a systematic construction method for this family of codes is proposed. Compared with time-invariant STCs, the proposed codes can achieve similar performance. Besides, the construction of these codes is more flexible and easier than STCs brute-force searching, and they can enhance the secrecy security for resisting attacks on recovering secret key. We know that STCs and the proposed TP-STCs are both implemented by convolutional codes with small memory degree length, because the computing complexity of the Viterbi algorithm grows exponentially over the memory degree length. However, we all know that the larger memory degree length, the better performance can be achieved. We believe that LDPC convolutional codes can also be adopted for syndrome coding and may reach a compromise between reasonable computing complexity and higher embedding efficiency because the computing complexity of their corresponding message passing algorithms are not influenced by the memory degree length, which needs the further studies in the future work.

References

1. Xia, Z., Wang, X., Sun, X., Liu, Q., Xiong, N.: Steganalysis of LSB matching using differences between nonadjacent pixels. Multimedia Tools Appl. **75**(4), 1947–1962 (2016)
2. Filler, T., Judas, J., Fridrich, J.: Minimizing additive distortion in steganography using syndrome-trellis codes. IEEE Trans. Inf. Forensics Secur. **6**(3), 920–935 (2011)
3. Han, T., Fei, J., Liu, S., Chen, X., Zhu, Y.: High-payload image-hiding scheme based on best-block matching and multi-layered syndrome-trellis codes. In: Benatallah, B., Bestavros, A., Manolopoulos, Y., Vakali, A., Zhang, Y. (eds.) WISE 2014, Part II. LNCS, vol. 8787, pp. 336–350. Springer, Heidelberg (2014)
4. Xiaoyuan, Y., Duntao, G., Jun, L.: An image steganography based on multi-layered syndrome-trellis codes in DWT domain. In: 2013 32nd Chinese Control Conference (CCC), pp. 3738–3743 (2013)
5. Holub, V., Fridrich, J.: Designing steganographic distortion using directional filters. In: IEEE International Workshop on Information Forensics and Security (WIFS), pp. 234–239 (2012)
6. Sedighi, V., Fridrich, J., Cogranne, R.: Content-adaptive pentary steganography using the multivariate generalized Gaussian cover model. In: IS&T/SPIE Electronic Imaging, pp. 94090H–94090H-13 (2015)
7. Luo, X., Song, X., Li, X., Zhang, W., Lu, J., Yang, C., et al.: Steganalysis of HUGO steganography based on parameter recognition of syndrome-trellis-codes. Multimedia Tools Appl. 1–27 (2015)
8. Liu, W., Liu, G., Dai, Y.: On recovery of the stego-key in syndrome-trellis codes. ICIC Express Lett. **8**(10), 2901–2906 (2014)

9. Palazzo Jr., R.: A time-varying convolutional encoder better than the best time-invariant encoder. IEEE Trans. Inf. Theor. **39**(3), 1109–1110 (1993)
10. Lee, P.J.: There are many good periodically time-varying convolutional codes. IEEE Trans. Inf. Theor. **35**(2), 460–463 (1989)
11. Mu, L., Liu, X., Liang, C.: Construction of binary LDPC convolutional codes based on finite fields. IEEE Commun. Lett. **16**(6), 897–900 (2012)
12. Pusane, A.E., Smarandache, R., Vontobel, P.O., Costello, D.J.: Deriving good LDPC convolutional codes from LDPC block codes. IEEE Trans. Inf. Theor. **57**(2), 835–857 (2011)

A Technique of High Embedding Rate Text Steganography Based on Whole Poetry of Song Dynasty

Yanchen Liu$^{(\boxtimes)}$, Jian Wang, Zhibin Wang, Qifeng Qu, and Shun Yu

College of Computer Science and Technology,
Nanjing University of Aeronautics and Astronautics, Nanjing 210016, China
{liuyanchen,wangjian}@nuaa.edu.cn

Abstract. Text steganography is a kind of technique which can transmit secret information using text as carrier. Compared with other types of carriers such as image and video, the embedding rate and capacity of text steganography algorithm is generally lower due to its low redundancy. A text steganography algorithm using single Ci-Pai of song poetry as a template and the embedding rate of it reaches 16.1 %. This paper presents a new text steganography algorithm based on song poetry with a higher embedding rate 27.1 %. In our proposed scheme, by selecting and processing 2538 pieces of song poetry which from 145 pieces of different Ci-Pai, a system which includes the template, the large capacity of lexicon, the encoder and the decoder is constructed. According to users' needs, the proposed scheme can generate arbitrary Ci-Pai to make the secret messages hidden in the song poetry which metrical patterns, rhyme words completely accord with the Ci-Pai. Additionally, we confirm our high embedding rate through theoretical analysis and extensive experiments.

Keywords: Information hiding · Chinese information processing · Text steganography · Data security · Embedding rate

1 Introduction

With the rapid development and the increasing popularity of Internet and information technology, the online communication has reached an unprecedented depth and breadth. People transmit a large number of text data through the Internet every day and using text data for steganography has become a very important secret communication channel [1]. It is more difficult for attackers to find concealed information by using the methods of text steganography. At present, there are a few text information hiding algorithms and software. A ratio which named embedding rate, information embedded in the text divided by the amount of cover text, should be as high as possible [2, 3]. And in the meanwhile, the conceal text should be as close to natural language text as possible. The above two principles are key points to conceal text message [4–6].

The Text hiding technology based on content syntax is mainly operated on the grammar content of the text itself. The synonym substitution method proposed by Atallah is widely used at present [7–9]. This kind of algorithm also includes the hiding method based on Markov chain, the hiding method based on sentence template and the

© Springer International Publishing AG 2016
X. Sun et al. (Eds.): ICCCS 2016, Part I, LNCS 10039, pp. 178–189, 2016.
DOI: 10.1007/978-3-319-48671-0_17

hiding method based on text style [10, 11]. The text hiding technology based on the semantic generation, which means that the integrity of the overall text is maintained, the concealed information embedded in the text through the replacement of words and phrases, the transformation of syntax and the change of sentence structure [13, 14]. The representative software, led by Nicetext, controls the text style template and dictionary through the text steganography algorithm, making the text more natural [12]. Based on the Nicetext method, Yu Zhenshan et al. proposed an information hiding algorithm in 2009 named "Ci-Steg" by using single Ci-Pai as a template and generated a Song poetry accord to the Ci-Pai [15]. The method uses a single template and extract the terms as a dictionary. Compared with common method, although the embedding rate of information is improved, the security and embedded information capacity of this methods unable to meet the current technology applications due to the continuous progress of Natural Language Processing Technology.

1.1 Our Contribution

The contributions of this paper are:

1. Use metres of Song poetry to create templates and select 145 pieces of Ci-Pai, which are moderate-in-length from the whole poetry of song, and then split 2538 pieces of Song poetry among Ci-Pai names, so a lexicon made up of selected words corresponding to the rhythm of "Ping" and the rhythm of "Ze" can be achieved. This dictionary contains over 30000 words from a variety of Song poetry.
2. We present an effective and high reliable text steganography scheme. The proposed method can generate arbitrary Ci-Pai to make the secret messages hidden in the song poetry which metrical patterns, rhyme words completely accord with the Ci-Pai.

According to the test, compared with "Ci-Steg" scheme in literature [15], our proposed method achieves significantly better performance. Furthermore, the capacity of lexicon is expanded; the secretiveness is greatly improved and the embedding rate can maintained at around 20.6 % to 27.1 %, which is different owing to different Song poetry metre template.

1.2 Organization

The second section describes the process of splitting words in Song poetry, generating dictionary and hash resetting. Also the detail scheme and proposal of text steganography algorithm is given in the second section. The third section evaluates and illustrates the security and performances of the algorithm. Experiments are carried out to verify the performance of it in the fourth section. Here, we test many metre templates which have different capacities and compare their embedding rates. And the last section summarize the works and future prospects.

2   New Scheme of Song-Steg Steganography

Song poetry is a kind of new poetry in ancient China. Each song Poetry has a musical tune called "Ci-Pai". Such as "Man Jianghong", "Yong Yuye", etc. There are four kinds of tone in Chinese characters, however, only three kinds of rhythm in Ci-Pai. The rhythm "Ping" expresses affection and endless charming; the rhythm "Ze" usually lasts short. The rhythm "Zhong" for "Ping"and "Ze".

2.1   Partition of Metre Templates and Construction of Lexicon of Rhythms

Similar to Nicetext, we select Song poetry: the intrinsic metre template included in genre of Chinese poetry as text to create templates. Choose moderate-in-length Song poetry from the whole poetry of song as a set C. Then, we classify selected Song poetry by Ci-Pai names so metre template sets $T = \{T_i | i = 1, 2, \cdots n\}$ corresponding to Ci-Pai names are created. For sets corresponding to specified metres T_i we mark these as C_{T_i}. Take "Man Jianghong" for instance, the poetry set corresponding to its metre template is denoted by $C_{T_i} = \{A_k | k = 1, 2, \cdots poemsnum\}$. After that, we manually partition words in poetry into two-word or three-word prosodic blocks according to specific poetic rhymes. Table 1 indicates the partition process of "Man Jianghong", each word in lines strictly corresponds to the rhythms of "Ping", "Ze", or "Zhong". The rhythm combination such as "ZhongZe", "PingPing", represents different kinds of rhythm block.

Table 1. Partition process of Man Jianghong

"Man Jianghong"	Metre template of "Man Jianghong"
怒发冲冠，凭栏处、潇潇雨歇。	ZhongZe/PingPing,/PingZhongZe,/ZhongPing/ZhongZe./
抬望眼，仰天长啸，壮怀激烈。	PingZeZe,/ZePing/PingZe,/ZePing/ZhongZe./
三十功名尘与土，八千里路云和月。	ZhongZe/ZhongPing/PingZeZe,/ZhongPing/ZhongZe/PingPingZe./
莫等闲、白了少年头，空悲切！	ZhongZhongZhong,/ZhongZe/ZePingPing,/PingPingZe./
靖康耻，犹未雪。臣子恨，何时灭！	ZhongZhongZe,/PingZeZe./PingZeZe,/PingPingZe./
驾长车，踏破贺兰山缺。	ZePingPing,/ZhongZe/ZePing/PingZe./
壮志饥餐胡虏肉，笑谈渴饮匈奴血。	ZhongZe/ZhongPing/PingZeZe,/ZhongPing/ZhongZe/PingPingZe./
待从头、收拾旧山河，朝天阙。	ZhongZhongZhong,/ZhongZe/ZePingPing,/PingPingZe./

According to the rhythm characteristics of Song poetry, we use sets R to represent rhythms like "ZhongZe", "PingPing". We use numbers to represent the rhythms, that is to say, "Ping = 1", "Ze = 2", "Zhong = 3". Besides, it is essential to separate every prosodic block with '/' and remove all the punctuations including line breaks from the partitioned Song poetry A_k. Table 2 gives a typical example of metre template and word partition.

Table 2. Metre template and word partition

"Man Jianghong" (Inserted into IN.txt)
怒发冲冠凭栏处潇潇雨歇抬望眼仰天长啸壮怀激烈三十功名尘与土八千里路云和月莫等闲白了少年头空悲切靖康耻犹未雪臣子恨何时灭驾长车踏破贺兰山缺壮志饥餐胡虏肉笑谈渴饮匈奴血待从头收拾旧山河朝天阙
Metre template(Inserted into FORMAT.txt)
32/11/132/31/32/122/21/12/21/32/32/31/122/31/32/112/333/32/211/112/332/122/122/112/211/32/21/12/32/31/122/31/32/112/333/32/211/112/

Similarly, we processed all the poems which accorded with the Ci-Pai of "Man Jianghong" into the file of "IN.txt" after doing some formatting and put digitized metre template T_i into file of "FORMAT.txt". Then, we divide each Song poetry A_k of C_{T_i} into sequence of words $(w_k R_1, w_k R_2, \cdots w_k R_{rhythm})$ by using algorithm that split words.

Next, putting the words $w_k R_j$ which have same rhythm into dictionary D_j. Finally, we get preliminary dictionary $D_j = (w_k R_j | k = 1 \cdots poemsnum)$. There are 15 Song poetry whose Ci-Pai is "Man Jianghong" in this example, that is to say, $poemsnum = 15$. According to the above operations, we deal with 15 poems of the same Ci-Pai of "Man Jianghong" and obtain part of rhythm dictionary showed on Table 3.

Table 3. Rhythm-dictionary coding in chapter 2.1

	D_1 ZhongZe			D_2 PingPing		D_3 PingZhongZe		D_4 ZhongPing		
雨歇	0000	初展	1000	中原	000	荒烟外	000	功名	0000	最怜	1000
激烈	0001	遥望	1001	深庭	001	露红晚	001	八千	0001	东风	1001
风物	0010	翠幕	1010	西楼	010	怕天放	010	饥餐	0010	旧痕	1010
回首	0011	龙阁	1011	芙蓉	011	一番过	011	笑谈	0011	眉间	1011
壮志	0100	收拾	1100	东流	100	愁目断	100	许多	0100	南山	1100
依旧	0101	江北	1101	朱栏	101	高楼下	101	山前	0101	风摇	1101
世事	0110	秋色	1110	离愁	110	纱窗外	110	蓬壶	0110	从容	1110
烟雨	0111	如昨	1111	江南	111	池亭畔	111	金鳞	0111	暗随	1111

We artificially develop a metre template documents "FORMAT.txt" and "IN.txt" which the format of the poetry is processed in advance, and then get the Ci-Pai Rhyming Dictionary by running the split program. Word splitting algorithm WordSplit ( ) are shown as Algorithm 1.

Algorithm 1: Split all the Poetry of Song accord with template T and generate the Rhythm Dictionary D
Input: All the Song poetry to be split in set C :Metre template set T in different kinds of Ci-Pai
Output: Rhythm dictionary set D
1.   int k=0:
2. D =null
3.   **for each** *poem* $\in C$ **do**
4.   **for each** $t_i \in T$ **do**
5.   **if** (poem.name== t_i .name)
6.   // t_i .name is the name of ith metre template.
7.   //poem.name represents the Ci-Pai name of this Song poetry
8.   k=i;// k records the information of corresponding position i
9.   **break;**
10.   **end if;**
11.   **end for;**
12.   **for each** *block* $\in t_i$ **do**
13. D [rhythm].add(word[j])
14.   //word[j] is the jth word in Song poetry
15.   // rhythm represents the rhythm block which position is "j"
16.   // D [rhythm]is the rhythm dictionary of certain rhythm block
17.   **end for;**
18.   **end for;**
19.   **return** D :

Similarly, we deal with the other Ci-Pai such as "Shuidiao Getou", "Nian Nujiao" etc. In total *metrenum* $= 144$. We split all the Song poetry $C_T = \{C_{T_i}|i = 1 \cdots metrenum\}$ according to Ci-Pai by running the split algorithm WordSplit ( ) and put the words into the generated rhythm dictionary. After statistics, we get a total of 36 blocks of the rhythm such as "PingPing", "ZeZe" etc., that is to say *rhythmnum* $= 36$. However there are repetitive words as a result of a large amount of Song poetry, so we put all words into one set, and then output back to the original document after the combined operation of the collected words. Finally, we get the dictionary $D = \{D_j|j = 1 \cdots rhythmnum\}$ after sorting according to the order of normal dictionary, which has 30279 words in total.

2.2   The Generation of Dictionary and Relocation with Hash

In the proposed scheme, the resource of Song poetry is open to all the users. Hash function is used to relocate the metre dictionary in order to make sure the security of dictionary in the algorithm. Dictionary structure D is defined as follows: the words included in the same rhythmical block is saved for one row in the dictionary and D_j represents one row of the metre dictionary. And we make $poem[W_j]$ represent dictionary D_j. (W_j Stands for words in jth row of the dictionary). Read all content of dictionary files by file stream and write them to corresponding location i to obtain the dictionary. Assume the Hash function is $H( )$, and every word in the dictionary is relocated with Hash function. Each word's MD5 value has been hashed and all words are sorted by hash values $H(word)$. Finally, the relocation of the dictionary is finished. Senders and receivers use the same Whole Song poetry library, fixed pattern template and dictionary when secret information transfer in information channel.

2.3   Secret Information Steganography

After we got dictionary D and pattern templates T, a piece of Song poetry S can be generated by steganography from secret information m. Therefore, a piece of Song poetry with fixed rhythm will be generated. And then, if one template T_i has totally $K = \{1 \cdots blocknum\}$ rhythmical partition blocks, there are W_j words corresponding in the row D_j of the dictionary for each location in the partition. So $\left\lfloor \log_2^{W_j} \right\rfloor$ bits information can be embedded in each location at least and the amount of information contained in every block is expressed as $blockcap_k = \left\lfloor \log_2^{W_j} \right\rfloor$. Owing to different quantities of D_j, the total quantity of information to be hidden in the Song poetry equals the sum of that of each partition. And then, it's expressed as follows: $CAPACITY = \sum_{K=1}^{blocknum} capacity_K$. Take "Man Jianghong" in chapter 2.1 as example, the first row of the pattern template T_i: "ZhongZe/PingPing, /PingZhongZe, /ZhongPing/ZhongZe./" is selected and it has $blocknum = 5$ blocks. Among them, $D_1 : ZhongZe$ has $W_1 = 149$ words in total, $D_2 : PingPing$ and $D_3 : PingZhongZe$ has $W_2 = W_3 = 14$ words and $D_4 : ZhongPing$ has $W_4 = 74$ words in total. In consideration of convenience, the exponent of '2' is chosen to be the capacity of dictionary. The dictionary is encoded as Table 3.

Algorithm 2: Secret Information Steganography Algorithm of SongSteg ( )

Input: Secret message m :metre template set T ; rhythm block R_j of each position should be written into metre template set T

Output: A complete Song poetry S which contains conceal messages
1. $m' = 0$
2.   Len=0
3. $m' = $strToBinstr($m$)// m is converted to binary code m'
4.   **if**(m' .getLength( )<L)
5. $m' = m'$ .append( ):// append 0 at the end of m'
6.   **for each** *block* $\in t_i$ **do**
7.   Len= $\log(W_j)$:
8.   // W_j is the number of words in rhythm dictionary:
9.   //Len is the length of this position that can be accommodated by the binary encoding.
10.   B=the next Len binary number in m' :
11.   // B is the binary string of length Len in the next position of m'
12.   n=binToDec(B)://B is converted into decimal number
13.   word[i]=n://word[i] is the ith word in rhythm dictionary
14.   S.add(word[i]): // Fill every word into each position in of Song poetry
15.   **end for**
16.   **return** S :

And then, assuming that secret sentence transformed into a binary string "100101000100110110", and it can be divided into "1001", "010", "001", "0011", "0110" according to the pattern template and the capacity of every location, and the corresponding words in D_j are "遥望", "西楼", "露红晚", "笑谈" and "世事", which form a poem in form of pattern template. As a result, the first sentence of new Song poetry "Man Jianghong" is rewritten as "遥望西楼, 露红晚, 笑谈世事". As is shown, 18 bits information is embedded in this sentence. In this example, the amount of information can be hidden is $CAPACITY' = \sum_{K=1}^{5} capacity_K$, adding up to 26 bits if the whole sample dictionary is used. If we use Song poetry to generate dictionary, for instance there are 4583 words in the dictionary "PingPing", 12 bits information can be embedded in this location. If the scope of dictionary increases, more information can be hidden. If the length of the input text is not enough to generate a steganography Song poetry, binary number 0 is supplemented at the end of binary string to meet the capacity of the Song poetry. SongSteg (z) is shown as Algorithm 2.

2.4   Extraction of Steganographic Information

Only when you use the same dictionary D and metre template T can the secret information m' be restored through the extractor by using retrieving algorithm Extraction ( ) after receiving the steganographic Song poetry S from information channel. According to Chapter 2.3, when the receiver gets a piece of steganographic Song poetry S that is "遥望西楼, 露红晚, 笑谈世事", we can divide this sentence into "遥望/西楼, /露红晚, /笑谈/世事" according to the metre template of "Man Jianghong" that the corresponding position of the sentence is divided to T_i: "ZhongZe/PingPing,/PingZhongZe,/ZhongPing/ZhongZe./". So this piece of Song poetry is partitioned to "遥望/西楼, /露红晚, /笑谈/世事".

Algorithm 3: Extract the secret information m' from steganography in Song poetry

Input: Metre template set T; Song poetry S which contains conceal messages

Output: secret message m

```
1.   m =null
2.   for each block ∈ tᵢ do
3.       for each word ∈ D[rhythm] do
4.           if (word[i]==blockword)
5.           // word[i] is the ith word in rhythm dictionary
6.               k=i; //k records the information of corresponding position i
7.               break;
8.           end if;
9.       end for;
10.      Len= log(Wⱼ);
11.      k'=decToBin(k); //put k turns to binary string k' of length Len
12.       m' = m' .add(k')// binary string m' is generated in the iterative way
13.  end for
14.  m =binToStr( m' );// m' turns into binary string ASCII m
15.  return m;
```

According to Table 3, we can find that "遥望" correspond to the binary code "1001" in the dictionary D_1, "西楼" correspond to the binary code "010" in the dictionary D_2, "露红晚" correspond to the binary code "001" in the dictionary D_3, "笑谈" correspond to the binary code "0011" in the dictionary D_4, and "世事"

correspond to the binary code "0110" in the dictionary D_1. Consequently, we can get the secret information $m' = (100101000100110110)$. Due to the operation of removing duplicate word in dictionary generation, there is no duplicate word in the rhyming dictionary, which means it can avoid ambiguity. The detail extraction algorithm Extraction ( ) is shown as Algorithm 3.

3 Analysis of Security and Capability

In the proposed scheme, we input all the Song poetry texts and generate the dictionary we need manually. Operations in the scheme include breaking up the Song poetry according to metre templates, merging the set, hash resetting and sorting. The time complexity of the proposed algorithm is $O(n \log n)$, in which "n" represents the number of Song poetry. In the process of coding dictionary, we fill each partition block with words in accordance with decimal index of templates and dictionary. And the number of the block called *blocknum* is usually a multiple of 100 and the time complexity of this operation is $O(1)$. In the process of extraction of steganographic information, we extract the corresponding index from the dictionary in accordance with metre template partition and the time complexity of this operation is $O(n)$.

  Song poetry, generated by our scheme containing secret messages, is hard to discover and to identify through the machine for the attacker. If the attacker intercepts a piece of Song poetry with steganographic information and tries to extract the steganographic information embedded in it, he needs a dictionary the same as the decoder. Although the attacker can sort out and extract the whole Song poetry included by the created Ci-Pai names to restore the dictionary, our dictionary is made up of over 2500 pieces of Song poetry by 145 Ci-Pai names and each Ci-Pai name selects pieces of Song poetry freely instead of literature [15] which creates the dictionary according to single metre template's partition. Once the attacker attempts to decipher steganographic information, he has to get the entire selected dictionary, partition of metre templates and the same hash resetting operation. In the meanwhile, the time complexity is the factorial of the total number of dictionary when trying to enumerate words of the dictionary after hash resetting operation. So the attacker will find it hard to use exhaustive classification to do statistical analysis. Furthermore, our scheme creates the dictionary strictly on the basis of metre templates and then classifies all the words that corresponding to a certain rhyme. When creating steganographic Song poetry, use words corresponding to the same rhyme makes Song poetry read more smoothly. Compared with literature [15], its concealment of secret information is better with less possibility to cause the attacker's attention.

4 Performance Evaluation

4.1 Experimental Results

We have processed ten Song poetry "Man Jianghong", "Shuidiao Getou", "Gui Zhixiang", "Sheng Shengman", "Shui Longyin", "Man Tingfang", "Han Gongchun",

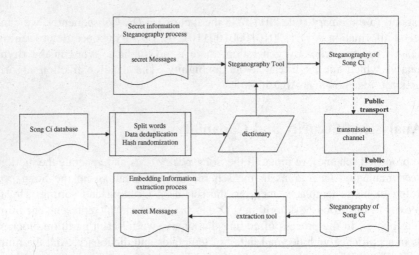

Fig. 1. Workflow of "Song-Steg" text steganography

"He Xinlang", "Mo Yu'er", "Yong Yuye" and saved them as Song poetry metre template in our experiment. We select 2,538 pieces of Song poetry which origin from 145 Ci-Pai and split them. After removing the rarely used words, the vocabulary of the dictionary reach 32,079 words and we get the final dictionary which is used in the experiment after the operation of de-duplication and hash relocation. The workflow about "Song-Steg" scheme is shown as Fig. 1 below.

After secret information concealing by algorithm 3, the *blocknum* of the Song poetry metre template "Man Jianghong" is 38 (*blocknum* = 38), and the quantity of secret information of one pieces of Song poetry is $CAPACITY = \sum_{K=1}^{38} capacity_K = 397$ bit. The Song poetry "Man Jianghong" includes 93 Chinese characters and each character consumes 2 bytes, so the whole poem consumes 1,904 bits (including punctuations and title). The embedding rate of have reached to 20.9 % in this experiment. If using a metre template which has longer length and more blocks such as "Yong Yuye", the quantity of information be hidden can reach to 567 bits and 27.1 % in embedding rate. Therefore, we choose prosodic word library which have high capacity to build artificial metre template according to the feature of metre template and the rhyme of Song poetry, named "Zhe Xinliu". The embedding rate reaches to 26.5 %.

The input information will be converted to binary string, so it has nothing to do with languages. When the two pieces of secret messages are "When i was young I'd listen to the radio waiting for my favorite songs" and,"夏日消溶, 江河横溢, 人或为鱼鳖。 千秋功罪, 谁人曾与评说?" the results of steganography using the Song poetry "Man Jianghong" and "Yong Yuye" are shown as Table 4 follows.

It can be seen that the generated Song poetry has the proper length and rhymes correspond to the rule of Song poetry, with almost no difference between normal "Song Ci", and makes it confusing to the attackers. Only the semantic analysis can distinguish between normal and steganography Song poetry. The non-steganography Song poetry

Table 4. Generate steganographic Song poetry

"Man Jianghong"	"Yong Yuye"
红驻藏花，人春困，八音吹断。	更向闺情，棠郊千载，欢事阴里。
应忘却，同是前梦，旧巢闻鸡。	顾曲观鱼，翻云声度，扇底荆湘路。
牡丹安石裙带草，临江拨刺莲花并。	千首圣子，春幡弄影，梦觉晓霜啼落。
更荒寒，逝水绿云中，秋汀暮。	更尊荣，荷香趁得。沈思此情虹架。
控宝马，寒尚浅。想当时，春光巧。	红颜佩解，青衫登临，或遇寿星料燕。
不须河桥路，得知钓台。	古驿乌台，藏丝荣事，翅薄丹青手。
浪遏开花皇恩溥，黄流天气披衣起。	雨侵不受，津亭何逊，梦断揉香不许。
空分垒，无主两山春，榴花吐。	顿容易，卧看惹梦，相看倦柳。

usually have links between its words and sentences, and have meaningful expressions in each paragraph. While steganography Song poetry have the shortcomings of lacking the overall topic. However, as a classical theme, Song poetry has a variety of writing metre. It's very hard to distinguish between normal and steganography Song poetry artificially without strong literary skills. As the natural language processing technology is inadequate nowadays, it's difficult for the attackers to detect with computer programs, so the proposed scheme has a high level security.

4.2   Comparison with Existing Schemes

When we use Nicetext to hide the sentence whose size is 70 bytes, the sentence "when i was young I'd listen to the radio waiting for my favorite songs", we can get a steganography text of 5096 bytes, but its embedding rate is only 1.37 %. By contrast, we generate 11 different kinds of steganography Song poetry whose text size is totally only 230–280 bytes with "Song-Steg" scheme.

In the proposed scheme, we hide information using 10 kinds of template of the Song poetry lyrics and 1 man-made template "Zhe Xinliu". And different partition and different size of template will lead to different amount of hidden information. What is more, the embedding rate is different if using the different templates to hide the same information. The embedding rates of different metre templates are given in Fig. 2.

We also compare the embedding rate of Song-Steg (generate 11 samples by using ten pattern templates and one man-made template) with Nicetext, Ci-Steg and T-lex. We input the data in length of 70 bytes, and Fig. 3 shows the comparison of embedding rates of the 11 samples.

As we can see in the Fig. 3, the embedding rate of Song-Steg is around 27.1 %, while that of Nicetext is about 1.5 %–2 % and that of T-lex is only around 1 %. Compared with 16.1 % of the literature [15], which uses single pattern, the embedding rate of the scheme in literature [15] increases about 10 %, so our scheme achieves significantly better performance.

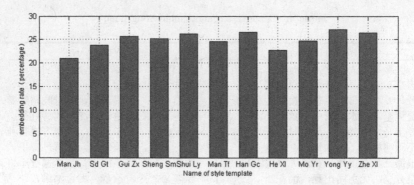

Fig. 2. Comparison of algorithm embedding rate using different metre template ("Man Jh" is short for "Man Jianghong")

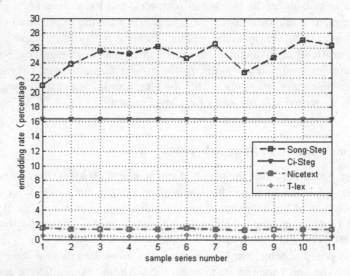

Fig. 3. Embedding rate comparison of Song-Steg steganography scheme and other text steganography scheme

5   Conclusions

This paper proposes a new kind of text steganography algorithm, it protects secret information by generating a specified pattern of Song poetry. Compared with other existing steganographic tools, the embedding rate is higher. So the proposed algorithm is practical in the real application. If expand the rhyming dictionary capacity including the Tang Dynasty and modern themes of tonal patterns in poetry words into the dictionary, the capacity will be greatly improved. If we classify the different characteristic of words when divide the dictionary. And then we distinguish them according to the characteristic when generate the dictionary in order to increase the relevance that will make the way of composing a Song poetry more coherent. Future work will aim to improve this two aspects.

Acknowledgements. This work is partly supported by the Fundamental Research Funds for the Central Universities (NZ2015108), the fifth graduate student innovation experiment competition breeding project base of Nanjing University of Aeronautics and Astronautics, Natural Science Foundation of Jiangsu province (BK20150760), the China Postdoctoral Science Foundation funded project (2015M571752), Jiangsu province postdoctoral research funds (1402033C), and NSFC (61472470, 61370224).

References

1. Moulin, P., O'Sullivan, J.A.: Information-theoretic analysis of information hiding. J. Inf. Theor. **49**, 563–593 (2003)
2. Gupta S, Jain R.: An innovative method of Text Steganography In: Proceedings of the 2015 Third International Conference on Image Information Processing (ICIIP), pp. 60–64. IEEE (2015)
3. Kingslin, S., Kavitha, N.: Evaluative Approach towards Text Steganographic Techniques. Indian J. Sci. Technol. **8**(1), 29 (2015)
4. Zhi-li, C., Liu-sheng, H., Zhen-shan, Y.: An information hiding algorithm based on double text segments. J. Electr. Inf. Technol. **31**(11), 2725–2730 (2009)
5. Xia, Z., Wang, X., Sun, X., Liu, Q., Xiong, N.: Steganalysis of LSB matching using differences between nonadjacent pixels. Multimedia Tools Appl. **75**(4), 1947–1962 (2016)
6. Rana, M.S., Sangwan, B.S., Jangir, J.S.: Art of hiding: an introduction to steganography. J. Int. J. Eng. Comput. Sci. **1**(1), 11–23 (2012)
7. Xia, Z., Wang, X., Sun, X., Wang, Q.: A secure and dynamic multi-keyword ranked search scheme over encrypted cloud data. IEEE Trans. Parallel Distrib. Syst. **27**(2), 340–352 (2015)
8. Uddin, M.P., Saha, M., Ferdousi, S.J., et al.: Developing an efficient solution to information hiding through text steganography along with cryptography. In: Proceedings of the 2014 9th International Forum (IFOST) Strategic Technology, pp. 14–17. IEEE (2014)
9. Fu, Z., Ren, K., Shu, J., Sun, X., Huang, F.: Enabling personalized search over encrypted outsourced data with efficiency improvement. IEEE Trans. Parallel Distrib. Syst. (2015). DOI:10.1109/TPDS.2015.2506573
10. Shu-Feng, W., Liu-Sheng, H.: Research on information hiding. J. Degree Master. University of Science and Technology of China (2003)
11. Maher, K.: TEXTO (2008, unpublished). ftp://funet.fi/pub/crypt/steganography/texto.tar.gz
12. Chapman, M., Davida, G.: Hiding the hidden: a software system for concealing ciphertext as innocuous text. In: Han, Y., Quing, S. (eds.) ICICS 1997. LNCS, vol. 1334, pp. 335–345. Springer, Heidelberg (1997)
13. Winstein, K.: Lexical steganography through adaptive modulation of the word choice hash (1998, unpublished). http://www.imsa.edu/~keithw/tlex
14. Yuling, L., Xingming, S., Can, G., et al.: An efficient linguistic steganography for Chinese text. In: Proceedings of Multimedia and Expo 2007 IEEE International Conference, pp. 2094–2097. IEEE (2007)
15. Zhenshan, Yu., Liusheng, H., Zhili, C., et al.: High embedding ratio text steganography by ci-poetry of the song dynasty. J. Inf. Process. **23**(4), 55–62 (2009)

Cloud Computing

Multi-objective Ant Colony Optimization Algorithm Based on Load Balance

Liwen Zhu[1](✉), Ruichun Tang[1](✉), Ye Tao[2], Meiling Ren[1], and Lulu Xue[1]

[1] College of Information Science and Engineering, Ocean University of China,
Qingdao 266100, China
840512702@qq.com, tangruichun@ouc.edu.cn
[2] Qingdao University of Science and Technology, Qingdao 266061, China
http://www.springer.com/lncs

Abstract. Virtual machine (VM) placement is a process of mapping VMs to physical machines. The optimal placement is important for improving power efficiency and resource utilization in a cloud computing environment. In this paper, we propose a multi-objective ant colony optimization algorithm based on load balance (MACOLB) for the VM placement problem. Firstly, the algorithm for a multi-objective context is to efficiently obtain a set of non-dominated solutions (the Pareto set) that simultaneously minimize total resource wastage and power consumption. Secondly, the pheromone adjustment factor (PAF) is given according to the load of physical machine (PM) and the pheromone update rule is transformed correspondingly. Finally, the effectiveness of the proposed algorithm is evaluated by the simulation.

Keywords: Cloud data center · VM placement · Multi-objective optimization · Ant colony algorithm · PAF

1 Introduction

The emergence of cloud computing has changed the traditional computing resource delivery model, which is widely used in the application. The adoption and deployment of cloud computing platforms have many attractive benefits, such as reliability, quality of service and robustness. There are a number of key technologies [1] that make cloud computing possible. One of the most important is virtualization. Virtualization enables dynamic sharing of physical resources in cloud computing environments, allowing multiple applications to run in different performance-isolated platforms called VMs in a single physical server. Through virtualization, a cloud provider can ensure the quality of service (QoS) delivered to the users while achieving a high server utilization and energy efficiency. As virtualization is a core technology of cloud computing, the problem of VM placement has become a hot topic recently. This VM placement is an important approach for improving power efficiency and resource utilization in cloud infrastructures. In [2], in order to improve the resource utilization of the PM,

X. Sun et al. (Eds.): ICCCS 2016, Part I, LNCS 10039, pp. 193–205, 2016.
DOI: 10.1007/978-3-319-48671-0_18

the author proposed ant colony algorithm to solve the problem of resource utilization and energy consumption. In [3], the VM placement problem was defined as a multi-objective optimization problem. A modified genetic algorithm for decreasing the number of PMs and reducing the migration times of VM is proposed. To solve the problem of creating the new VM requests and host allocation for the minimum energy consumption, an improved best fit decreasing (BFD) algorithm was given by Anton et al. [4]. All papers above have studied the problem of resource utilization and energy consumption of VM placement in the cloud computing environment, but none of them considered the issue of the PM load balance.

Recently, many scholars have studied the problem of load balance for the VM deployment. In [5], in order to achieve the PM load balance, the authors adopted the genetic algorithm for VM placement. However, as for large scale of nodes in cloud computing environment, the result needs to be validated. Nishant K et al. [6] proposed an ant colony algorithm based on load balance of PM, where each ant only conducts the partial update of the pheromone after establishing their own set of results, which led to slow convergence speed.

In summary, considering the complexity of cloud computing resources, the improvement should be conducted from both scheduling performance and load balance. Therefore, a MACOLB algorithm is proposed in this paper. We define the problem of VM placement as a multi-objective combinatorial optimization problem. The goal is to efficiently obtain a set of the Pareto set that simultaneously minimize total resource wastage and power consumption. We propose the PAF according to the load of PM and the pheromone update rule is transformed correspondingly, which lowers the imbalance load of PMs.

The remainder of this paper is organized as follows. Section 1 is the research environment in cloud and problem description of virtual machine placement. Section 2 formulates the multi-objective optimization model. The MACOLB of cloud data center scheduling algorithm is proposed in Sect. 3. Finally the simulation is carried out in Sect. 2 and Sect. 5 is the conclusion.

2   Research Environment and Problem Description

2.1   Research Environment

Cloud data center [7] is a service platform for cloud computing applications which contains a large number of PMs, VMs, storage devices, network equipment. Cloud data center uses virtualization technology to abstract the physical resource pool. The user's resource request is encapsulated in one or more VMs which run in a data center or PM cluster. The cloud data center resource scheduling is shown in Fig. 1.

Firstly, the user dynamically applies for resources through the network. Secondly, the scheduling algorithm builds multi-objective model for VM placement and uses ant colony optimization algorithm to efficiently search for good solutions. Finally, the VM is deployed on the PM correspondingly.

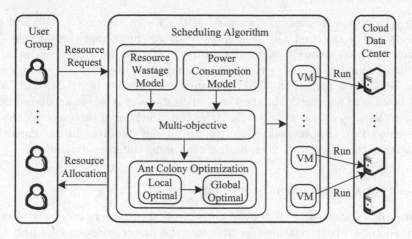

Fig. 1. Cloud data center resource scheduling

2.2   Problem Description

In a certain period of time, assuming that there are n VMs to be deployed, the $VM = \{vm_1, vm_2, \ldots, vm_n\}$ represents a collection of VMs to be placed, the $i-th$ VM resource demand is described as $(R_{pi}, R_{mi}, R_{bwi})$. Let R_{pi}, R_{mi} and R_{bwi} be CPU, memory resource and bandwidth demand of each VM. The available number of PMs in the data center is m, the $PM = \{pm_1, pm_2, \ldots, pm_m\}$ represents a collection of PMs in the data center. VM placement is a process of mapping virtual machines to physical machines.

3   Multi-objective Optimization Model for VM Placement

In this paper, the problem of VM placement is formulated as a multi-objective combinatorial optimization problem aiming to simultaneously optimize total resource wastage and power consumption. The goal of the majority of existing multi-objective optimization algorithms is to find Pareto-optimal solutions. A solution is said to be Pareto-optimal if it is not dominated by any other possible solution. Pareto-optimal sets are the solutions that cannot be improved in one objective function without deteriorating their performance in at least one of the remaining objective functions.

3.1   Resource Wastage Modeling

The remaining resources available on each server may vary greatly with different VM placement solutions. To fully utilize multidimensional resources, the following equation is used to calculate the potential cost of wasted resources:

$$W_j = \frac{L_j^p + L_j^m + L_j^{bw}}{U_j^p + U_j^m + U_j^{bw}}. \tag{1}$$

where W_j denotes the resource wastage of the $j - th$ server, U_j^p, U_j^m and U_j^{bw} represent the normalized CPU, memory resource and bandwidth usage (i.e., the ratio of used resource to total resource). L_j^p, L_j^m and L_j^{bw} represent the normalized remaining CPU, memory and bandwidth resource. For example, let (20 %, 30 %) be a pair of the CPU and memory requests of a VM, and (35 %, 40 %) be that of another VM. Then, the utilizations of a server accommodating the two VMs are estimated at (55 %, 70 %), i.e., the sum of the vectors. The key idea behind Eq. (1) is to make effective use of the resources in all dimensions and balance the resources left on each server along different dimensions.

3.2   Power Consumption Modeling

Recent studies show that the power consumption of servers can be accurately described by a linear relationship between the power consumption and CPU utilization [8]. In order to save energy, servers are turned off when they are idle. Hence, their idle power is not part of the total energy consumption. Finally, we defined the power consumption of the $j - th$ server as a function of the CPU utilization as shown in Eq. (2).

$$
P_j = \begin{cases} (P_j^{busy} - P_j^{idle}) \times U_j^p + P_j^{idle}, & U_j^p > 0 \\ 0, & otherwise \end{cases}
\tag{2}
$$

where P_j^{busy} and P_j^{idle} are the average power values when the $j - th$ server is idle and fully utilized.

3.3   Optimization Formulation

Next, we formalize the VM placement optimization problem. Suppose that we are given n VMs (applications) $i \in I$ that are to be placed on m servers $j \in J$. For simplicity, we assume that none of the VMs requires more resource than can be provided by a single server. We use two binary variables y_j and χ_{ij}. The binary variable χ_{ij} indicates if VM i is assigned to server j and the binary variable y_j indicates whether server j is in use or not. The placement problem can therefore be formulated as:

$$
Min \sum_{j=1}^{m} W_j = \sum_{j=1}^{m} [y_j \times \frac{L_{pj} + L_{mj} + L_{bwj}}{\sum_{i=1}^{n}(\chi_{ij} \cdot R_{pi}) + \sum_{i=1}^{n}(\chi_{ij} \cdot R_{mi}) + \sum_{i=1}^{n}(\chi_{ij} \cdot R_{bwi})}].
\tag{3}
$$

$$
Min \sum_{j=1}^{m} P_j = \sum_{j=1}^{m} [y_i \times ((P_j^{busy} - P_j^{idle}) \times (\chi_{ij} \cdot R_{pi}) + P_j^{idle})].
\tag{4}
$$

Subject to:

$$
\sum_{j=1}^{m} \chi_{ij} = 1 \qquad\qquad \forall i \in I.
\tag{5}
$$

$$\sum_{i=1}^{n} R_{pi} \cdot \chi_{ij} \leq T_{pj} \cdot \chi_{ij} \qquad \forall j \in J. \tag{6}$$

$$\sum_{i=1}^{n} R_{mi} \cdot \chi_{ij} \leq T_{mj} \cdot \chi_{ij} \qquad \forall j \in J. \tag{7}$$

$$\sum_{i=1}^{n} R_{bwi} \cdot \chi_{ij} \leq T_{bwj} \cdot \chi_{ij} \qquad \forall j \in J. \tag{8}$$

$$y_j, \chi_{ij} \in 0,1 \qquad \forall i \in I \ and \ j \in J. \tag{9}$$

Equations (3) and (4) are the objective function. Constraint (5) assigns a VM i to only one of the servers. Constraints (6), (7) and (8) model the capacity constraint of the server. Constraint 9 defines the domain of the variables of the problem. Given a set of n VMs and a set of m PMs, there are a total of m^n possible VM placement solutions. It is therefore typically impractical to make a complete enumeration of all possible solutions to find the best solutions. The following shows how to apply an MACOLB algorithm to efficiently search for good solutions in large solution spaces.

4   The MACOLB Algorithm

The proposed MACOLB algorithm is based on ACS, which uses a unique ant colony to simultaneously minimize all functions. All objectives share the same pheromone trails. In every iteration, an ant k receives all VM requests and constructs one feasible solution. This rule is based on the information about the current pheromone concentration on the movement and a heuristic which guides the ants towards choosing the most promising PMs. A local pheromone update is performed once an artificial ant has built a movement. After all ants have constructed their solutions, a global update is performed with each solution of the current Pareto set. The pseudocode of the proposed MACOLB Algorithm is depicted as follows:

4.1   Definition of the Pheromone Trail and the Heuristic Information

The quality of an ACO implementation depends greatly on the definition of the meaning of the pheromone trail. It is crucial to choose a definition which conforms to the feature of the problem. In this paper, the pheromone trail τ_{ij} will be defined as the favorability of packing VM i into host j. In the initialization phase, initial pheromone level is calculated by (10).

$$\tau_0 = \frac{1}{n \times (P(S_0) + W(S_0))}. \tag{10}$$

where n is the number of VMs, S_0 is the solution generated by the FFD heuristic and $W(S_0)$, $P(S_0)$ is the resource wastage and power consumption of the solution S_0.

Algorithm 1. The MACOLB Algorithm.

Require: Set of VMs and set of PMs with their associated resource demand, set of parameters.

Ensure: a Pareto set P.

1: Initilize: τ_0, α, β, q_0, ρ_l, ρ_g, I_{Num}(number of iteration), N_A(number of ants).
2: **for** $k = 1$ to N_A **do**
3:   **while** all VMs are not placed **do**
4:     construct a solution using Eq.(12) and Eq.(13);
5:     record the solution to LP;
6:     apply the local updating rule(Eq.(18));
7:   **end while**
8: **end for**
9: Calculate the values of the two objectives for each solution in LP.
10: If a solution in the current ant population is not dominated by any other solutions in the current population and the non-dominated solutions in LP, this solution is added to the set P. Then all solutions dominated by the added one are eliminated from the set P.
11: **for** each non-dominated solution in the Pareto set P **do**
12:   Apply the global updating rule(Eq.(19)).
13: **end for**
14: until the maximum number of iterations is reached.

Apart from pheromone trails, another important factor in an ACO application is the choice of a good heuristic, which will be used in combination with the pheromone information to build solutions. It guides the probabilistic solution construction of ants with problem-specific knowledge. The heuristic information is denoted by η_{ij}. This information indicates the desirability of assigning VM i into host j. In order to accurately assess the desirability of each move, the heuristic information is dynamically computed according to the current state of the ant as follows:

$$\eta_{ij} = \frac{1}{\sum_{j=1}^{m} P_j} + \frac{1}{\sum_{j=1}^{m} W_j}. \tag{11}$$

4.2 Constructing a Solution

After defined the pheromone and heuristic information, according to the heuristic function and pheromone function the ants will calculate the probability of the VM i to the PM j.

$$p_{ij}^k = \begin{cases} \dfrac{[\tau_{ij}]^{\alpha} * [\eta_{ij}]^{\beta}}{\sum_{j=1}^{m} [\tau_{ij}]^{\alpha} * [\eta_{ij}]^{\beta}}, & j \in \Omega_k(i) \\ 0, & otherwise \end{cases} \tag{12}$$

where the pheromone value τ_{ij} is given in Eq. (14) below. η_{ij} is defined in Eq. (11) above. $\Omega_k(i)$ is the set of PMs that meet the demand of the VM. α is a parameter that allows a user to control the relative importance of pheromone trail.

The greater the value, the more inclined to choose the path. And β is a parameter that allows a user to control the relative importance of heuristic information.

In the process of making assignments, the ant k selects a PM j to deploy the VM according to the following pseudo-random-proportional rule.

$$j = \begin{cases} \max_{\mu \in \Omega_k(i)} p_{ij}^k, & q \le q_0 \\ S, & otherwise \end{cases} \quad (13)$$

where q is a random number uniformly distributed in $[0, 1]$. q_0 is a fixed parameter $(0 \le q_0 \le 1)$ determined by the relative importance of exploitation of accumulated knowledge about the problem versus exploration of new movements. If q is equal or less than q_0, this process will choose a PM with a maximum value according to the Eq. (13). Otherwise, it will randomly select of a PM to meet the needs of the $i - th$ VM.

4.3   Pheromone Trail Update Rule

Another vital component of MACOLB is the update of pheromone trails. The pheromone trail value can either increase, as ants deposit pheromone, or decrease, due to pheromone evaporation. When ants for VM assigned to the physical machine, the original pheromone will be evaporate with the increase of the number of iterations. In our proposed algorithm, the pheromone updating process includes two steps: a local pheromone update and a global pheromone update. While constructing an assignment of VM i to host j, an ant transforms the pheromone trail level between VM i to host j by applying the following local updating rule:

$$\tau_{ij}(t) = (1 - \rho_l)\tau_{ij}(t - 1) + \rho_l * \tau_0. \quad (14)$$

where τ_0 is the initial pheromone level and $\rho_l(0 < \rho_l < 1)$ is the local pheromone evaporating parameter.

The global updating rule is applied after all ants have finished building a solution. In each iteration, the solution found by each ant is recorded to a set P. After all ants for VM assigned to the PM, the non-dominated set of solutions LP, are found from P. Each solution in LP is compared with the solutions in P in order to check if it is non-dominated. If it is a new Pareto-optimal solution, it is added to P and all solutions dominated by the added one are erased from P. Therefore, the global update is performed for each solution S of the current Pareto set by applying the following rule:

$$\tau_{ij}(t) = (1 - \rho_g)\tau_{ij}(t - 1) + \frac{\rho_g * \lambda}{P(S) + W(S)}. \quad (15)$$

where

$$\lambda = \frac{N_A}{t - I_{Num} + 1}. \quad (16)$$

In Eq. (15), $\rho_g(0 < \rho_g < 1)$ is the pheromone evaporation parameter of global updating. In Eq. (16), N_A is the number of ants and I_{Num} represents the number of iterations.

4.4   Realizing the Load Balance

Since the resource fragments originate from the imbalanced use of resources over different dimensions, the placement of VMs on PMs should be executed in a resource-balanced manner. To achieve this, in this paper, we propose PAF according to the load of PM and the pheromone update rule is transformed correspondingly. PAF is described as follows:

$$PAF = 1 - \frac{T_i^j - T_{avg}^j}{\sum_{j=1}^m T_i^j}. \tag{17}$$

where T_i^j is the running time of assignment VM i to host j. T_{avg}^j is the average value of running time of assignment VM i to host j. The local and global updating rule is transformed as follows:

$$\tau_{ij}(t) = (1 - \rho_l)\tau_{ij}(t-1) + \rho_l * \tau_0 * PAF. \tag{18}$$

$$\tau_{ij}(t) = (1 - \rho_g)\tau_{ij}(t-1) + (\frac{\rho_g * \lambda}{P'(S) + W(S)}) * PAF. \tag{19}$$

If the $j - th$ PM in the previous iteration process under the heavy load, T_i^j will be greater than T_{avg}^j. At this time, the PAF of $j-th$ PM becomes smaller. So in the next iteration, the probability of the virtual machine assigned to physical machine will decrease. After several iterations, the MACOLB can maintain load balancing.

5   Simulation and Performance Evaluation

In order to evaluate the performance of the algorithm presented in this paper, we implement this algorithm by the CloudSim toolkit [9]. The genetic algorithm (GA) [10], the ant colony algorithm (ACO) [11], the round robin algorithm (RR) [12] and the multi-objective grouping genetic algorithm (MGGA) [13] are used to compare with MACOLB algorithm.

5.1   Simulation Parameter Settings

The simulation parameters set seriously affect the performance of the algorithm. The experiment is carried out under various combinations parameters. The value ranges of these parameters are as follows. $\alpha = 1$, $\beta \in \{1, 2\}$, $q_0 \in \{0.1, 0.6, 0.9\}$, $\rho_l \in \{0.01, 0.10, 0.40, 0.80\}$, $\rho_g \in \{0.01, 0.10, 0.40, 0.80\}$. The average result in 10 running times is taken as the distance index of each parameter combination, which is used to evaluate the uniformity of the algorithm. The parameters in MACOLB algorithm are given in Table 1. The smaller the distance index, the more uniform the Pareto optimal solution.

Therefore, the algorithm parameter is set to $\alpha = 1$, $\beta = 1$, $q_0 = 0.9$, $\rho_l = 0.10$, $\rho_g = 0.10$.

Table 1. The simulation parameter setting

α	β	q_0	ρ_l	ρ_g	Distance index
1	1	0.1	0.01	0.01	0.526559
1	1	0.6	0.10	0.10	0.311924
1	1	0.9	0.10	0.10	0.295726
1	2	0.1	0.10	0.10	0.495358
1	2	0.6	0.40	0.40	0.321079
1	2	0.9	0.80	0.80	0.448130

5.2   The Response Time

In order to verify the response time of the algorithm, the GA, ACO and RR are taken as a comparison with MACOLB algorithm. Specific simulation results are as follows:

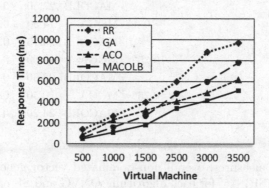

Fig. 2. Response time comparison

It can be seen in Fig. 2 that the running time of each algorithm is different from the number of VMs, but with the increase of the number of VMs, the time of RR algorithm will be more and more. The search time of GA for optimal solution increases with the expansion of the search range. The MACOLB algorithm has a good performance with the increase number of VMs.

5.3   Algorithm Performance Analysis

In this section, we use some simulation experiments to evaluate the proposed algorithm with respect to performance. To evaluate the effectiveness of the proposal VM placement algorithm, its performance is compared to that of the MGGA algorithm, which is used as the benchmark because it is an effective and efficient method used to solve multi-objective VM placement problems.

Table 2. ONVG and SP performance comparison of MACOLB and MGGA.

Reference value	Corr	Algorithm	ONVG	SP
$\bar{U}_p = \bar{U}_m = \bar{U}_{bw} = 20\,\%$	−0.75	MGGA	15.10	0.60
		MACOLB	19.86	0.20
	−0.35	MGGA	16.50	0.50
		MACOLB	22.25	0.16
	−0.05	MGGA	11.50	0.40
		MACOLB	23.10	0.15
	0.35	MGGA	13.80	0.30
		MACOLB	18.35	0.12
	0.75	MGGA	15.00	0.16
		MACOLB	24.20	0.06
$\bar{U}_p = \bar{U}_m = \bar{U}_{bw} = 50\,\%$	−0.75	MGGA	16.20	0.19
		MACOLB	20.50	0.10
	−0.35	MGGA	19.40	0.20
		MACOLB	27.50	0.12
	−0.05	MGGA	14.50	0.30
		MACOLB	25.15	0.14
	0.35	MGGA	12.00	0.16
		MACOLB	23.60	0.06
	0.75	MGGA	10.50	0.10
		MACOLB	24.20	0.05

We compute two measures, overall non-dominated vector generation (ONVG) [14] and Spacing (SP) [15] for each algorithm. ONVG and SP can be calculated as:

$$ONVG = |P_f|_c. \tag{20}$$

$$SP = \sqrt{\frac{1}{|P_f|_c - 1} \sum_{i=1}^{|P_f|_c} (\bar{d} - d_i)^2}. \tag{21}$$

where P_f denotes the calculated Pareto front, $|\;\;|_c$ denotes cardinality, $d_i = min_j(\sum_{k=1}^{m} ||f_m^i - f_m^j||)$, $i, j = 1,...|P_f|_c$, f is the objection function, m is the number of objectives and $\bar{d}$ is the mean of all d_i. The higher the value of the ONVG the better for understanding Pareto front details. A good solution set should have a value close to 0 for the SP metric. Table 2 shows ONVG and SP under MACOLB and MGGA. The column "Corr." indicates the correlation coefficients for the CPU, memory and bandwidth utilizations. $\bar{U}_p$, $\bar{U}_m$ and $\bar{U}_{bw}$ represent the reference CPU, memory and bandwidth utilization. Two kinds of the reference values and five probabilities were used in the experiments. We set $\bar{U}_p$, $\bar{U}_m$ and $\bar{U}_{bw}$ to 20\,% and then 50\,%. And correlation coefficients correspond

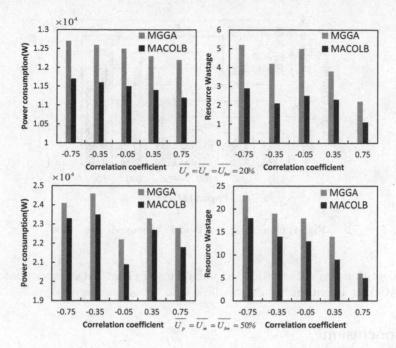

Fig. 3. Power consumption and resource wastage comparison of MACOLB and MGGA

to strong-negative, weak-negative, no, weak-positive, and strong-positive correlations.

Figure 3 compares the total resource wastage and power consumption for each of the algorithms under consideration. From the results, we can clearly see that the MACOLB algorithm outperforms MGGA. The reason is that VM placement under MACOLB algorithm combines the partial solution information under construction and the feed information of the reserved time of a non-dominated solution in the external set and simultaneously incorporates continuous updating of pheromone, therefore it can find more appropriate VM placement and achieve better performance.

5.4 Degree of Load Imbalance

In this paper, the degree of load imbalance (DI) is presented as follows:

$$DI = \frac{T_{max}^j - T_{min}^j}{T_{avg}^j}. \tag{22}$$

where T_{avg}^j represent the run time average value of assignment VM i to host j. T_{max}^j and T_{min}^j are the maximum and minimum values of the run time.

It can be seen in Fig. 4 that the degree of load imbalance of RR algorithm is very high, which reflects the difference between PMs. The GA algorithm and

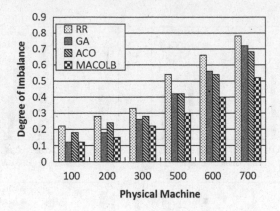

Fig. 4. Comparison of load imbalance degree

ACO algorithm can reduce the load imbalance of cloud data center. But only the MACOLB algorithm has the smallest load imbalance degree.

6　Conclusion

With the increasing prevalence of large scale cloud computing environments, how to efficiently place VMs into available computing servers has become an essential research problem. The MACOLB algorithm for the VM placement problem is proposed in this paper. The goal is to efficiently obtain a set of non-dominated solutions that simultaneously minimizes total resource wastage and power consumption. And according to the load condition of the PM, the PAF is proposed to improve the pheromone update rule and realize load balance. Experimental results illustrate that the MACOLB algorithm is efficient for VM placement problem.

Acknowledgment. This work was supported by National Science and Technology Support Program Project under grant No. 2015BAF28B01.

References

1. Ren, Y., Shen, J., Wang, J., Han, J., Lee, S.: Mutual verifiable provable data auditing in public cloud storage. J. Internet Technol. **16**(2), 317–323 (2015)
2. Gao, Y., Guan, H., Qi, Z., et al.: A multi-objective ant colony system algorithm for virtual machine placement in cloud computing. JCSS **79**(8), 1230–1242 (2013)
3. Xu, J., Fortes, J.A.B.: Multi-objective virtual machine placement in virtualized data center environments. In: GreenCom, pp. 179–188 (2010)
4. Beloglazov, A., Abawajy, J., Buyya, R.: Energy-aware resource allocation heuristics for efficient management of data centers for cloud computing. FGCS J. **28**(5), 755–768 (2012)

5. Hu, J., Gu, J., Sun, G., et al.: A scheduling strategy on load balancing of virtual machine resources in cloud computing environment. In: PAAP, pp. 89–96 (2010)
6. Nishant, K., Sharma, P., Krishna, V., et al.: Load balancing of nodes in cloud using ant colony optimization. In: UKSim, pp. 3–8 (2012)
7. Xia, Z., Wang, X., Sun, X., Wang, Q.: A secure and dynamic multi-keyword ranked search scheme over encrypted cloud data. IEEE Trans. Parallel Distrib. Syst. $27(2)$, 340–352 (2015)
8. Wen, X., Shao, L., Xue, Y., Fang, Y.: A rapid learning algorithm for vehicle classification. Inf. Sci. $295(1)$, 395–406 (2015)
9. Calheiros, R.N., Ranjan, R., Beloglazov, A., et al.: CloudSim: a toolkit for modeling and simulation of cloud computing environments and evaluation of resource provisioning algorithms. Pract. Exp. J. $41(1)$, 23–50 (2011)
10. Jianhua, G.U., Jinhua, H.U., Zhao, T., et al.: A new resource scheduling strategy based on genetic algorithm in cloud computing environment. J. Comput. $7(1)$, 42–52 (2012)
11. Shen, J., Yuan, S.: QoS-aware peer services selection using ant colony optimisation. In: Abramowicz, W., Flejter, D. (eds.) BIS 2009. LNBIP, vol. 37, pp. 362–374. Springer, Heidelberg (2009)
12. Zohar, Y., Gafni, A., Morris, J., et al.: Eucalyptus plantations in Israel: an assessment of economic and environmental viability. New Forest. J. $36(2)$, 135–157 (2008)
13. Xu, J., Fortes, J., et al.: Multi-objective virtual machine placement in virtualized data center environments. In: CGCC, pp. 179–188 (2010)
14. Veldhuizen, V., et al.: Multi-objective evolutionary algorithms: classifications, analyses, and new innovations. Evol. Comput. $8(2)$, 125–147 (1999)
15. Schott, J.R., et al.: Fault tolerant design using single and multi-criteria genetic algorithm optimization. massachusetts Inst. Technol. $11(2)$, 25–47 (1995)

A Novel Spatio-Temporal Data Storage and Index Method for ARM-Based Hadoop Server

Laipeng Han[1], Lan Huang[1], Xueyi Yang[1], Wei Pang[2], and Kangping Wang[1(✉)]

[1] College of Computer Science and Technology,
Jilin University, Changchun 130012, Jilin, China
wangkp@jlu.edu.cn
[2] School of Natural and Computing Sciences,
University of Aberdeen, Aberdeen AB24 3UE, UK

Abstract. During the past decade, a vast number of GPS devices have produced massive amounts of data containing both time and spatial information. This poses a great challenge for traditional spatial data-bases. With the development of distributed cloud computing, many high-performance cloud platforms have been built, which can be used to process such spatio-temporal data. In this research, to store and process data in an effective and green way, we propose the following solutions: firstly, we build a Hadoop cloud computing platform using Cubieboards2, an ARM development board with A20 processors; secondly, we design two types of indexes for different types of spatio-temporal data at the HDFS level. We use a specific partitioning strategy to divide data in order to ensure load balancing and efficient range query. To improve the efficiency of disk utilisation and network transmission, we also opti-mise the storage structure. The experimental results show that our cloud platform is highly scalable, and the two types of indexes are effective for spatio-temporal data storage optimisation and they can help achieve high retrieval efficiency.

1 Introduction

In recent years, with the advancement of mobile technologies, smart phones are becoming more and more popular. This greatly enriches the way people access to information and thus huge amounts of data have been generated. A survey shows that the scale of China's mobile Internet users had reached 620 million by the end of 2015, and many enterprises have accumulated a vast amount of personal location information. It is also pointed out that 74 % of the smart phone users use geographic information [1], which makes the related technologies and application model of LBS (Location-based Service) develop more and more rapidly [2].

With the development of LBS applications and recommender systems [3], the spatio-temporal data to be dealt with show a trend of rapid growth in terms of both quantity and complexity. Some researchers use NoSQL databases [4] (such as BigTable, HBase, and Cassandra) to store spatio-temporal data, but

© Springer International Publishing AG 2016
X. Sun et al. (Eds.): ICCCS 2016, Part I, LNCS 10039, pp. 206–216, 2016.
DOI: 10.1007/978-3-319-48671-0_19

these databases do not consider the particularity of geographical information, and they do not support spatio-temporal query very well. Other researchers who study data storage hope to solve the problem of massive storage of spatio-temporal data, such as PIST database [5] and TrajStore database [6], both of which can deal with spatio-temporal data. However, these systems analyse the spatio-temporal data in non-distributed storage environments, and they cannot process big data effectively.

Indexing is very important for massive data querying and manipulation. R-tree [7] is a highly balanced tree structure which can be effective when dealing with spatial data. On the basis of R-tree, some researchers put forward many improved approaches, such as R*-tree [8]. Beckman *et al.* [8] improved the R-tree algorithm in inserting and deleting. Singh *et al.* [9] proposed a hybrid index method based on inverted index and R-tree. All of the above research built index and query methods in a single machine and they did not consider how to make use of such indexes and query methods in a distributed environment. Ahmed Eldawy *et al.* developed SpatialHadoop [10], a system that is based on Hadoop [11] and uses distributed storage space to greatly improve the efficiency of retrieval. This system changes at the HDFS level and has pioneering significance in building the Grid spatial data, R-tree, and R+-tree index. However, this system is only effective for the spatial data and it is not effective for spatio-temporal data.

In this paper, we built a green ARM-based spatio-temporal database which employs the distributed storage technology, distributed index technology, as well as the distributed computing algorithm based on the Hadoop system. We proposed two distributed indexing mechanisms for spatio-temporal data, and our research has the following three novel contributions: (1) we design two new spatio-temporal partition algorithms, TGrid (the spatio-temporal grid algorithm) and QaDTree (Quadtree-3Drtree algorithm), and apply these two algorithms to different distributions of spatio-temporal data; (2) in the local index phase, we improve the query efficiency by building a one-dimensional time index and a multidimensional R-tree index; (3) we improve the efficiency of network transmission by optimising the storage structure and reducing disk I/O.

The ARM board is cost effective and energy-efficient, but it has low performance and slow network speed. In order to adapt to such a platform, we use the column storage and a compression algorithm to process spatio-temporal data. This greatly reduces the amount of data to be processed and improves the utilisation efficiency of disks and the network transmission.

The rest of this paper is organised as follows: the mechanism of distributed spatio-temporal index is introduced in Sects. 2, and 3 describes the storage optimisation of the two kinds of indexes for spatio-temporal data. The experimental procedure and the experimental results are reported in Sect. 4. Finally, Sect. 5 concludes the paper.

2   Distributed Spatio-Temporal Index

2.1   A Spatio-Temporal Data Storage Model

In order to support efficient spatio-temporal index, we define a novel spatio-temporal data storage model. This model is very convenient for describing both time and space dimension, and it can reduce the workload of index retrieval and data quering. We define a record Q in the following format:

$$Q = (Timestamp, Lon(longitude), Lat(latitude), Attr1, Attr2, ..., AttrN)$$

The above format indicates that the record is at a certain time and a specific location. In Q, *Timestamp* represents the timestamp of the record which we also use T to represent later for ease of description, and *(Lon, Lat)* is the spatial location which is generally the longitude and latitude ; *Attr1, Attr2, ..., AttrN* are the other attributes of the record Q. The first three properties of Q are the core components of a spatio-temporal data object. As shown in Fig. 1, a cuboid C (A, B) specified by A (t1, lon1, lat1) and B (t2, lon2, lat2) represents a time range between t1 and t2 and a spatial range between (lon1, lat1) and (lon2, lat2), and C is called MBC (the minimum bounding cuboid) which is similar to the minimum bounding rectangle (MBR) [10] in traditional spatial data representation.

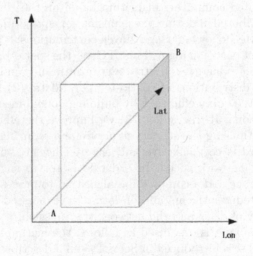

Fig. 1. MBC: the minimum bounding cuboid

2.2   The TGrid Algorithm

The traditional grid index partitions data into different subspace units in accordance with different lengths and widths of the space, and different spatial data are partitioned into different cells. But for spatio-temporal data, if the partitioning method is still in this way and in different time periods the degree of data aggregation is different, the data will not be distributed evenly and some nodes may have very heavy load. Considering this, we improve the segmentation algorithm called spatio-temporal grid algorithm (TGrid), and the segmentation process has five steps, as detailed below.

Step 1. In the division of MBC, divide the time period. In this research, we will set the default size of time to 10 s.

Step 2. Calculate the time period of MBC and the number of partitions. We use the following formula:

$$N = \left\lceil \frac{S(1+\alpha)}{B} \right\rceil \tag{1}$$

In the above, S is the total size of spatio-temporal data in the input file; B is the HDFS block size (the default value is 64 MB); α is the load factor, with a default value of 0.2, which makes the actual storage capacity of each data block less than the default size of a HDFS block.

Step 3. Calculate the partition boundaries. According to the number of the partitions N, we will uniformly divide the MBC in spatial range. Each unit is calculated by considering the space coordinates which are the coordinates of lower left corner and the coordinate of upper right corner.

Step 4. If there are still some space to be partitioned, return to Step 2; otherwise, go to Step 5.

Step 5. According to the partition method of spatio-temporal grids, store the spatio-temporal data into the corresponding partitions.

In the division process, some of the data grid cells may be larger than the size of the data blocks. So we need to set a threshold (a little less than 64 MB) during the actual division. When the data are beyond the threshold limit, the data will be assigned to a new block.

After obtaining the number of blocks, the next step is to start a MapReduce assignment. Then, the spatio-temporal data will be divided within the scope of each MBC grid into different partitions, and an index of one-dimensional time is created during the reduce phase. Finally, the results will be output into the HDFS, and the local indexes are put together to the master node to constitute a global index.

Because the grid index is a plane index, the contents of the grid cells in this index are stored disorderly. However, we will use one dimensional time index in the data block, essentially, which divides the minimum bounding rectangles of the data block into small MBCs and marks each MBC according to the time dimension. The format of storage is shown in Table 1. In this table, (T1, T2) is the time interval and (T1, T2) is marked C which represents the offset value of the data block in the MBC, such as (201402070223122, 3.21, 12334.34, C1), which represents the location of the spatio-temporal data at time 201402070223. We will introduce the methods of storing the spatio-temporal data in the next section.

Table 1. One-dimensional time index and data storage structure

Temporal interval (T1,T2)	Offset value
(201402030112, 201403050223)	C1
(201403050223, 201404050645)	C2
.....	.....

2.3   The QaDTree Algorithm

In order to make uniform distribution of the spatial data and ensure the node load balance, we improve the quadtree algorithm [12] and design a better partitioning strategy for spatio-temporal data, and we term this algorithm the QaDTree algorithm, which generates the global index using the improved quadtree algorithm to partition the spatio-temporal data and the local indexes using 3DR-tree index to manage the spatio-temporal data [13]. The tree non-leaf node of the global index contains four children, each of which represents a subspace area. Then each child space area is divided into four again and this is done recursively until the end of the division. The leaf node points to the local index tree. In order to partition efficiently in large-scale spatio-temporal data, we run a MapReduce assignment and build the quadtree according to the following five steps.

Step 1. According to different time intervals, the MBCs of spatio-temporal data are divided and the total size of MBCs is recorded.

Step 2. If the size of the spatio-temporal objects is lower than the threshold value (the default value is 60 MB) in each MBC, a partition is output directly.

Step 3. We divide data into smaller MBCs in accordance with the extent of space. If in an MBC the total size of the spatio-temporal objects is below the threshold value (the default value is 60 MB), all the data in the MBC are output to the same partition. And we continue to divide the MBC region into four smaller MBCs uniformly.

Step 4. Divide each child MBC as in Step 3 until all the data in the MBC meet the divided value.

Step 5. Repeat Step 2 until all the spatio-temporal data objects have been processed.

The size (60 MB) which we set is smaller than the default size of HDFS block (64 MB) so that we can have enough room in the data block to store the local index file. But the dividing value cannot be too small because it will cause the time of dividing spatio-temporal data to be long, and it will also increase the number of data blocks and decrease the retrieval efficiency. Through the above steps, the data divided are physically adjacent in the HDFS blocks of the same database, and at the same time the distribution of data is more uniform than others.

Finally, we construct local indexes for each block of the data file. Once the job of MapReduce is completed, we initialise the HDFS command and all the local indexes are written to a file and this file is the global index. The Master node then records this global index. The global index is constructed by the bulk load and is stored in the memory of the master node. Once the master node fails or restarts, global indexes can be recreated through the local indexes.

In order to improve the throughput of I/O and reduce the limit of I/O and network bandwidth, it is very important to use a good index technology and store the data which are physically adjacent and improve the retrieval efficiency. Multi-dimensional indexing technology can provide technical support for the spatio-temporal index and the time serves as another dimension of space objects. 3DR-tree index can query historical data effectively and it is very suitable for one-time writing and reading a lot of spatio-temporal data. The index structure is simple and it is superior to the other index structures when dealing with a long time period of the query. In the job of MapReduce, spatio-temporal data are divided into different partitions after the Map tasks, and then we start to build the local 3DR-tree index in each partition in the Reduce task. The leaf node of the index is the MBC and the non-leaf node is a rectangle containing all the children nodes. At the end, we construct a tree structure which is similar to the 3DR-tree.

2.4   The Storage Structure of Spatio-Temporal Data

The column-based database is different from the traditional relational database which stores data in row. In the table of a typical relational database, each row contains a record of field values, so every piece of spatio-temporal data sequence is stored together. However, the column-based database will store a column with the same attribute. In this research we use the column storage, which has the following advantages: (1) we query historical spatio-temporal data, so we slightly modify the data. Although it is time consuming to store spatio-temporal data by splitting the records of each row, the retrieval is more efficient than others and the data redundancy is reduced. (2) Due to the fact that the data attribute stored in each column is the same, it is highly beneficial for data analysis. Compared to the storage in row, we need to analyse multiple attributes of each record. (3) Each column attribute is the same and the compression algorithm is more efficient.

Each column has similar properties. If we want to find certain spatio-temporal data, such as Id, we can just scan the Id column. And it also makes the compression ratio very high. It can use less space for storage to reduce the disk I/O requirements, and at the same time it has more advantages in terms of the network transmission. Similar to RCFile [14], in the spatio-temporal grid index, we will store the data of the same period of time in column and will store the data of the different periods of time in row. In the QaDTree index, we will write the MBC data of leaf nodes according to the column into data block. Each MBC writes into the file according to the column and each MBC is stored in normal order.

We add the gzip data compression method when constructing a column to store and write to a file. This data compression algorithm has the following advantages:

(1) The HDFS stores spatio-temporal data files by compressing data, which can reduce the storage space.
(2) The communication between a Hadoop cluster is dependent on the network. We can transmit the compressed data to improve the network traffics.
(3) Based on spatio-temporal data storage, the compression effect is better.

We start the MapReduce and need to partition the data which will be queried in HDFS when we query spatio-temporal data. Due to the fact that the type of data which are stored based on column is consistent and the characteristics are similar, it can efficiently compress data. When the data in storage are stable or change a little, the compression of data can greatly reduce the storage space. In this paper, we use the generic gzip compression algorithm. After storage, all the data use the gzip compression algorithm.

3   Experimental Results

In the experiments, we adopt fifteen ARM-based Cubieboards2 [15] development boards to set up the Hadoop cloud computing platform. Cubieboard2 is developed by the Zhuhai Cubietech team. It adopts the A20 processor development board and runs on Android, Ubuntu, and other Linux systems. Cubieboard2 adopts the CortexTM - A7 dual-core processor and the memory of the board is 1 GB, so its function is more powerful. This cluster has Hadoop 1.2.1 deployed on it and running on Lubuntu. Unless mentioned otherwise, we use the data set based on the format of the raw GPS taxi data in a region. We design the process which generates simulation data: we generate 100 GB simulated GPS spatio-temporal data randomly. We then perform the data pre-processing according to the definition of the spatio-temporal data model.

3.1   Storage Performance

Figure 2 shows the size of the data after using different storage methods for the 2 GB GPS data. In this figure, the size is the sum of the data size and index size. The spatio-temporal grid construction method has used 0.641 GB storage space for the 2 GB data. We take the storage solution which is based on column and use the compression algorithm to compress data. This greatly reduces the storage space. The size of QaDRtree index is bigger than the size of grid index, so the storage space of QaDRtree index is relatively larger but there is no much difference. Compared with the storage methods, the size of SequenceFile is about 5 to 6 times larger than the size of our storage solution. While compared with the traditional PostGIS database, the cost of space for storing 2 GB spatio-temporal data is 10 to 12 times higher than the column-based database. So the advantages of our storage solution are very obvious. The storage space of 100 GB spatio-temporal data is about 31.3 GB and the compression ratio is 31.3 %. So our solution has great advantages on saving storage space when dealing with the huge amounts of data.

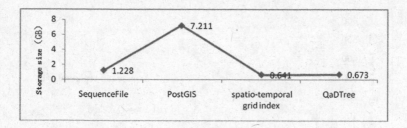

Fig. 2. The comparison of different storage solutions in terms of storage used

3.2   The Time for Spatio-Temporal Data Index Generation

Figure 3 shows the analysis of two index structures. The data have been generated in advance. The construction process of the index is as follow: (1) read the data from the HDFS, (2) perform one-time construction after executing two MapReduce tasks. The index can be read many times to retrieve the spatio-temporal data contents. As data ranges from 1 GB to 20 GB, the construction time for the indexes increases with the increase of data size. Due to the hardware limitation, such as CPU, memory, and network card performance, we use the compression mechanism in network transmission of the clusters. So the time of disk I/O transmission and network transmission is greatly reduced when the index is built and the data are retrieved. The construction method of the spatio-temporal grid index is simple and the cost of time is less than that of constructing the QaDTree index. However, with the increase of the amount of data, the number of map tasks and reduce tasks which execute concurrently also increase in the MapReduce tasks and thus the efficiency of the index building is improved.

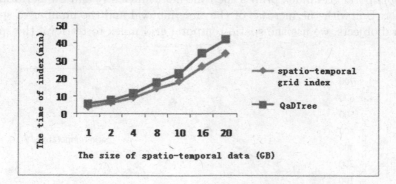

Fig. 3. The time used for index construction of different data sizes

3.3   Spatio-Temporal Data Retrieval Performance

In order to evaluate the retrieval performance of the indexes, we use the simulated taxi data of 100 GB and select multiple retrieval scopes of space and

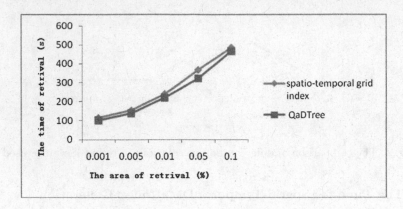

Fig. 4. The time used for retrieval under different space areas with the same fixed time interval

time range to carry out a series of experiments. In Fig. 4, we retrieve different scopes of space within a fixed time 100 s. The horizontal space area increases from 0.001 % to 1 % of the total space with respect to all the data. In terms of the spatial retrieval, the performance of QaDTree is better than taht of the spatio-temporal grid index. But with the decrease of the search space, the performance of these two kinds of retrievals is almost unanimous. In Fig. 5, the x-axis represents that the time range that we retrieve data from increases from 0.01 % to 0.2 % of the whole range of time spanned by all data. We found that when the time interval was small, the retrieval performance of using spatio-temporal grid index is better than that of using the QaDTree index. This is because the spatio-temporal grid index prunes the time more efficiently and the performance is higher. But with the increase of the time interval and the number of spatio-temporal objects, we use the spatio-temporal grid index to retrieval the spatial

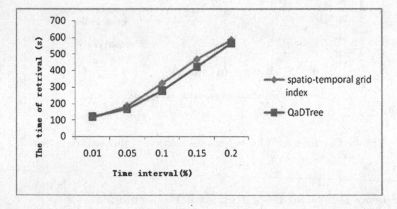

Fig. 5. The time used for retrieval under different time intervals with the same space area

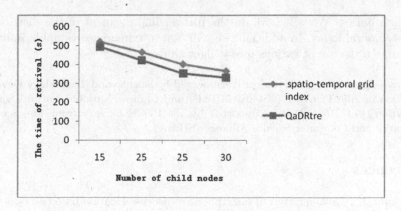

Fig. 6. The scalability of the cloud computing platform

attributes is slowly. In contrast, QaDTree is more applicable in retrieving data from a bigger time interval.

Figure 6 demonstrates the scalability of our cloud computing platform and the stability of the index. The number of cluster nodes increases from 15 to 30 and the scope of retrieval is 1 % of the total time spanned by all data and 0.1 % of the total spaces occupied by all data. With the increase of the number of nodes, the performance of the system in terms of the time used for retrieval is improved significantly, especially under the cloud computing platform. Because the performance of single node is too low and the processing ability is limited, we need to share the MapReduce tasks among multiple nodes.

4   Conclusion and Future Work

In this research, we proposed a novel storage and retrieval solution for spatio-temporal data based on the ARM development boards, which are cost effective and green. In this solution we use one-dimensional time index and 3DR-tree index. The former can quickly locate the query time interval, and the latter is based on the R-tree. Thus we proposed the concept of MBC which is based on the minimum bounding rectangular (MBR). Considering the fact that the hardware performance of the cloud computing platform we used is low and the network transmission speed is slow, in order to adapt to such a platform we use the column storage and a compression algorithm to deal with the spatio-temporal data. This greatly reduces the amount of data to be processed and thus improves the utilization efficiency of disk and the transmission efficiency of networks.

In future work, our research can be improved in the following three aspects: (1) we will further improve the temporal data retrieval functions. (2) We need to further strengthen the spatio-temporal indexing learning. In addition, we will learn the latest technology, such as Storm and Spark. (3) We can study the visualization modules of spatio-temporal data, and analyse the spatio-temporal data distribution. We will work on the further improvement of the distributed spatio-temporal index. In addition, we will aim to mine more valuable information through the use of various query algorithms.

Acknowledgements. This project is supported by Science and Technology Development Plan of Jilin Province (20140204010SF) and Chinese National Natural Science Foundation (61472159). WP is supported by the PECE bursary from The Scottish Informatics and Computer Science Alliance (SICSA).

References

1. Zickuhr, K.: Three-quarters of smartphone owners use location-based services. Pew Internet and American Life Project (2012)
2. Dhar, S., Varshney, U.: Challenges and business models for mobile location based services and advertising. Commun. ACM **54**(5), 121–128 (2011)
3. Ma, T., Zhou, J., Tang, M., Tian, Y., Al-Dhelaan, A., Al-Rodhaan, M., Lee, S.: Social network and tag sources based augmenting collaborative recommender system. IEICE Trans. Inf. Syst. **E98–D**(4), 902–910 (2015)
4. Cattell, R.: Scalable SQL and NoSQL data stores. ACM SIGMOD Rec. **39**(4), 12–27 (2011)
5. Botea, V., Mallett, D., Nascimento, M.A., et al.: PIST: an efficient and practicalindexing technique for historical spatio-temporal point data. GeoInformatica **12**(2), 143–168 (2008)
6. Cudre-Mauroux, P., Wu, E., Madden, S.: Trajstore: an adaptive storage system for very large trajectory data sets. In: 2010 IEEE 26th International Conference on Data Engineering (ICDE), pp. 109–120. IEEE (2010)
7. Guttman, A.: R-trees: a dynamic index structure for spatial searching. In: Proceedings of Meeting, pp. 47–57, Boston, Massachusetts, June 1984
8. Schneider, R., Seeger, B., Beckmann, N., et al.: The R*-tree: an efficient and robustaccess method for points and rectangles. In: Proceedings of ACM SIGMOD Symposium on Principles of Database Systems, pp. 322–331 (1990)
9. Singh, S., Mayfield, C., Prabhakar, S., et al.: Indexing uncertain categorical data. In: IEEE 23rd International Conference on Data Engineering, ICDE 2007, pp. 616–625. IEEE (2007)
10. Apache Hadoop. http://wiki.apache.org/hadoop/. Accessed 28 Nov 2015
11. Eldawy, A., Mokbel, M.F.: SpatialHadoop: a MapReduce framework for spatialdata. In: Proceedings of the IEEE International Conference on Data Engineering (ICDE 2015), pp. 1352–1363. IEEE (2015)
12. Eldawy, A., Alarabi, L., Mokbel, M.F.: Spatial partitioning techniques in SpatialHadoop. Proc. VLDB Endowment **8**(12), 1602–1605 (2015)
13. Gong, J., Zhu, Q., Zhong, R., et al.: An efficient point cloud management method based on a 3D R-tree. Photogram. Eng. Remote Sens. **78**(4), 373–381 (2012)
14. He, Y., Lee, R., Huai, Y., et al.: RCFile: a fast and space-efficient data placement structure in MapReduce-based warehouse systems. In: 2011 IEEE 27th International Conference on Data Engineering (ICDE), pp. 1199–1208. IEEE (2011)
15. http://docs.cubieboard.org/products/. Accessed 30 Mar 2015

An Efficient Hierarchical Comparison Mechanism for Cloud-Based Heterogeneous Product Lifecycle Management Systems

Mikayla Cohen and Yanzhen Qu[✉]

Colorado Technical University, Colorado Springs, CO, USA
{mcohen,yqu}@coloradotech.edu

Abstract. Cloud computing has enabled various product lifecycle management (PLM) systems from different parts venders to form a heterogeneous system to facilitate joint product development. To avoid the performance issue caused by traversal multiple different PLM systems in hierarchical comparison, in this research we have developed an efficient hierarchical comparison mechanism for cloud-based heterogeneous PLM systems. We have used this mechanism to convert the traditional hierarchical comparison by traversal through the tree type data structure into a string comparison. Our approach is very simple but scalable, and also very suited to the cloud-based heterogeneous PLM system because the method itself is independent to the details of data stores. Therefore we have offered an efficient solution for a specific interoperability problem in cloud-based heterogeneous product lifecycle management systems.

Keywords: Bill of materials · Cloud computing · Heterogeneous · Product lifecycle management · Hierarchical comparison · Interoperability

1 Introduction

1.1 Background

Product engineering companies and manufacturers represent their product structure data in the form of a bill of materials (BOM). A BOM is a hierarchical list of all the components and subcomponents that make up a top level product structure. This hierarchical structure is used by a manufacturing organization's product engineers for many purposes, including product design (as in an "As-Engineered" BOM), part and materials procurement, product assembly (as in an "As-Built" BOM), configuration management, and product maintenance (as in an "As Maintained" BOM) [1]. The activity of maintaining the structure of a BOM is called product data management (PDM). PDM is part of a larger concept called product lifecycle management (PLM), which is the activity of tracking a product's state from its conception through any necessary maintenance all the way to its eventual decommission and disposal. There are many benefits to being able to track a product through its entire life cycle including improved process control, fewer defects, accurate materials management, efficient field maintenance, and the reduction of waste [1].

© Springer International Publishing AG 2016
X. Sun et al. (Eds.): ICCCS 2016, Part I, LNCS 10039, pp. 217–228, 2016.
DOI: 10.1007/978-3-319-48671-0_20

Now that cloud computing technology has matured, more and more companies are migrating their traditional PLM systems into cloud-based PLM systems. This new type of PLM system has one extra advantage over traditional PLM systems: it is much easier to integrate many in-house PLM systems, belonging to different internal organizations and product vendors, together to facilitate an engineering project involving the parts made by multiple venders. This allows a company to easily produce a customized replica of any portion of their PLM database in the cloud for their partners use without affecting their own continued development activities at home.

To achieve this great benefit, developers of cloud-based PLM must overcome some new challenges such as integrated authentication, integrated query processing, integrated data security, as well as integrated data visualization, etc.

Figure 1 shows what a typical physical product structure could look like. Figure 2 shows the same structure as a hierarchical bill-of-materials. Note that BOM structures are not just limited to physical, tangible parts. For example, rocket engines must be calibrated and tuned for their specific launch mission. Configuration settings for mission characteristics such as trajectory and orbit may also be defined as a part of the BOM structure as a child of the component they mechanically affect.

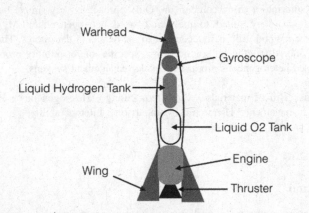

Fig. 1. A typical physical product structure

Product engineers often must compare different versions or configurations of a BOM structure. For example, a rocket engineer may want to re-purpose some of the hardware and software designs from the rocket of a previous launch mission and may perform a comparison analysis to determine which features are similar to the current mission's launch vehicle. In cloud-based PLM systems, BOM data may be distributed across heterogeneous data stores, making the comparison operation depend on a complex structured query involving iterating through one tree-like data structure through many different data stores while performing a search in another. This consumes $O(mn)$ time, where m is the number of columns involved in the query filter and n is the number of records in the tree. Obviously, when m and n are both very large numbers, such operations become very slow.

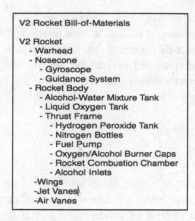

Fig. 2. Example of bill-of-materials

1.2 Problem Statement

Characteristics of the hierarchical (or tree) data structure require traversal through multiple heterogeneous data stores connected through the cloud that reduce the performance of hierarchical comparisons on the cloud-based PLM systems.

1.3 Hypothesis Statement

If a compression algorithm can be developed that (1) eliminates the need for going through heterogeneous data stores connected through the cloud and (2) reduces the size of a hierarchical data structure, performance of hierarchical comparisons on the cloud-based PLM systems can be improved.

1.4 Research Questions

The problem statement above raises the following research questions:

Q1: What factors individually impact hierarchical comparison performance?
Q2: Will compression of hierarchical data structures significantly improve the performance of hierarchical comparisons?
Q3: What combination of factors must exist before hierarchical data compression benefits hierarchical comparison operations?

1.5 Research Objectives

There are two research objectives. The primary research objective is to devise a compression algorithm for hierarchical data residing in the heterogeneous data stores of the cloud-based PLM systems. This algorithm can then be used to improve the performance of hierarchical comparisons. The secondary objective is to define a predictive formula to determine when the hierarchical compression algorithm should be used.

The remainder of this paper will be organized as the follows: Sect. 2 will review the current literature on methodologies related to this research. Section 3 will outline the methodology used to conduct this research on. Section 4 will discuss the experiments for answering research questions and present the results of the experiments. Finally, Sect. 5 will discuss the contributions of this research to the body of knowledge.

2   Related Work

2.1   Merkle Tree

In computer science, an index is implemented with a "lookup table" with the intended purpose of substituting a large piece of data with a smaller piece of data (the index key). Merkle [2] defined a method of validating a digital signature using a tree data structure in which each tree node is labelled with a key consisting of the concatenated keys of all its children nodes (Fig. 3). One tree can be validated against another by comparing the keys of the root nodes. The Merkle tree was originally intended for verifying a finite number of digital signatures. However, information assurance is just one type of use for Merkle trees. Amazon's Dynamo storage system methodology [3] utilizes Merkle trees to identify inconsistencies between synchronized datasets. Apache Cassandra, an opensource "NoSQL" database management system originally developed by Facebook to power an inbox search utility, borrowed this strategy from Dynamo.

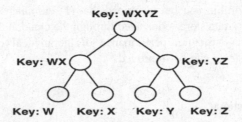

Fig. 3. A Merkle tree

2.2   String Comparisons

There is literature specifically related to the global alignment of two genetic nucleotide sequences. A "global" alignment is when entire sequences are aligned, whereas a "local" alignment is only concerned with a common subsection occurring in the sequences. Obviously, a local alignment would be much faster since it is concerned with only a piece of the entire sequence. This is interesting since where a BOM is concerned, a local alignment might be desirable over a global alignment in cases where only a sub-assembly within the total BOM is compared. Furthermore, if entire BOM structures are being compared, rather than use a global alignment approach, it is plausible using a local alignment method to compare the sub-assemblies within the BOMs in a "divide-and-conquer" approach might be more efficient.

Needleman and Wunsch [4] devised an algorithm for aligning textual patterns representing nucleotide sequences in proteins. The purpose of their research was to automate the comparison of two different proteins. This involves scoring the chances of a particular nucleotide alignment and assigning the alignment penalties in the case of evolutionary nucleotide insertions or deletions (called "indels" in the microbiology realm). The K-align algorithm [5] is unique in that it employs both global and local alignment strategies. A global alignment algorithm, Wu-Manber, is first used to identify sub-sequences within the total sequence and then a dynamic programming algorithm is used to locally align sub-sequences. A variation of the Needleman and Wunsch algorithm is then used to verify accuracy. It might be possible to build a custom scoring matrix based on what components can reside under certain assemblies within a BOM. Needleman and Wunsch's sequence alignment algorithm has already been adapted to problems in other domains. Abbot [6] explores "sequences" in the broad sense of the term and related problems found in psychology, economics, archaeology, linguistics, political science, and sociology. Abbot proposes that, since all of the sequencing-related problems are all very similar to biological problems, the same biological sequencing algorithms can be used to solve them with minor modifications. [6] is relevant because this theory should also apply to the manufacturing information technology subdomain of computer science. If the product structure representing a BOM can be converted into a textural or binary sequence of parts and subsequently converted into binary code and then nucleotide nomenclature, the same algorithms used to capture biological sequences can be used to compare two different BOMs.

2.3 Cloud-Based Heterogonous PLM Systems

In recent years, cloud computing has transformed into a reliable and scalable computing platform. With greatly enhanced operational resource scheduling and utilization maturity, accessibility and security [12–17], many business in the engineering and manufacturing sectors have started looking into the possibility of converting traditional product lifecycle management (PLM) systems into cloud-based heterogonous systems that provide great interoperability within or beyond the borders of the immediate organization to achieve improved engineering and manufacturing capabilities, resources componentization, integration, and global optimization [10]. However, most of the current research has only been done at a high level such as framework [7, 8] and requirements analysis [9, 11], rarely touching the specific technologies that can be explored with cloud-based heterogonous PLM systems. In contrast, our research is an effort to solve a specific interoperability issue: how to compare the parts-hierarchy efficiently in cloud-based heterogonous PLM systems.

3 Methodology

The root cause of the performance hit to hierarchical comparisons in cloud-based PLM systems is mainly due to two aspects: (1) operation has to go through multiple heterogeneous data stores; and (2) the very large numbers of data node in a very deep hierarchy data structure. Any effective solution must remove the negative impact of both aspects. Therefore, we have proposed a method to uniquely identify all nodes in a hierarchy based on the definition of a simple unique identifier rule as specified below.

Definitions: Assume that we have a parts-hierarchy consists of total n "data nodes". We define such hierarchy as a set H, and $H = \{h_1, h_2, \ldots, h_n\}$.

We also define another set I, such that:
$I = \{(i_1, l_1, c_1), (i_2, l_2, c_2), \ldots \ldots (i_n, l_n, c_n)\}$, where each element tuple (i_j, l_j, c_j) is called the "element tuple of data node h_j" such that i_j is called "unique identifier of node h_j"; l_j is called "the highest level of node h_j''; and c_j as "the total number of children nodes of node h_j", where $j = 1, 2, \ldots\ldots, n$; and n is an integer.

We define the notation "$\blacklozenge$" as an "concatenation operator" such that if we apply $\blacklozenge$ to any given two stings s_1 and s_2, we will call the result of "$s_1 \blacklozenge s_2$" as "the concatenation of s_1 and s_2". Now we can define the "node identifier" for any given data node h_j in H based on the following convention:

If h_j is a node, and we cannot find any existing node which has the same content, then we will use the following string as the node identifier for node h_j: $[h_j] = [i_j] = l_j \blacklozenge i_j \blacklozenge c_j$.

If h_j is a leaf node, $l_j = 1$, $c_j = 0$, we will have $[h_j] = [i_j] = 1 \blacklozenge i_j \blacklozenge 0 = i_j$.

Example 1. An example Parts-Hierarchy is shown in Fig. 4.

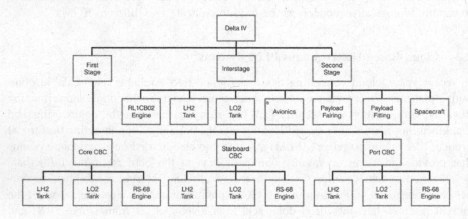

Fig. 4. An example of parts-hierarchy

In this hierarchy we can quickly assign the nodes' identifiers as the following:

Leaf Nodes:
[LH2Tank] = LH2Tank
[LO2Tank] = LO2Tank
[RS-68Engine] = RS-68Engine
[InterStage] = InterStage
[RL1CB02Engine] = RL1CB02Engine
[Avionics] = Avionics
[PayloadFairing] = PayloadFairing

[PayloadFitting] = PayloadFitting
[Spacecraft] = Spacecraft

None Leaf Nodes:
[StandardCBC] = 2♦StandardCBC♦3♦[LH2Tank]♦[LO2Tank]♦[RS-68Engine]
[CoreCBC] = 2♦CoreCBC♦ 3♦ [LH2Tank]♦[LO2Tank]♦[RS-68Engine]
[PortCBC] = 2♦PortCBC♦ 3♦ [LH2Tank]♦[LO2Tank]♦[RS-68Engine]
[FirstStage] = 3♦FirstStage♦3♦[CoreCBC]♦[StandardCBC]♦[PortCBC]
[SecondStage] = 2♦SecondStage♦7♦[RL1CB02Engine]♦[LH2Tank]♦[LO2Tank]♦
                [Avionics]♦[PayloadFairing]♦[PayloadFitting]♦[Spacecraft]
[DeltaIV] = 4♦DeltaIV♦3♦[FirstStage]♦[InterStage]♦[SecondStage]

One of benefits after having built up such node identifier for each node in the hierarchy, to query if a given parts-hierarchy is in a targeted parts-hierarchy in fact has been transformed into a search if a string is contained in another string. If we denote the given parts-hierarchy as H1 and the targeted parts-hierarchy as H2, and we also assume that the total number of data nodes in H1 is k_1, and the total number of data nodes in H2 is k_2, then we can easily approve that the complexity of such string comparison is $O(k_2 - k_1)$. If $k_2 \gg k_1$ it is $O(k_2)$. Compared with original complexity $O(k_1k_2)$, it is a significant improvement.

4 Experiments and Results

4.1 Experiments to Answer Research Question 1

We have identified three variables as having a plausible impact on hierarchical comparison rate: (a) depth, (b) number of children per node, and (c) number of filtered fields.

Depth: There is a visible positive correlation between hierarchical depth and mean comparison time (Fig. 5). As hierarchical structures approach 8 levels deep, there is a spike in the mean comparison time.

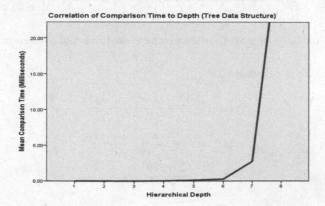

Fig. 5. Correlation of mean comparison time to depth.

The covariance is calculated as:

$$cov(x, y) = \frac{\sum_{i=1}^{n} (x_i - \bar{x})(y_i - \bar{y})}{(N - 1)}$$

$$cov(x, y) = \frac{\sum_{i=1}^{100} (x_i - \bar{x})(y_i - \bar{y})}{(99)}$$

$$= \frac{1825.537}{99}$$

$$= 18.44$$

The covariance above confirms a positive correlation between hierarchical depth and mean comparison time.

Number of Children per Node: Mean comparison time started to spike when the number of children per node reached 6 (Fig. 6). However, the mean comparison time appears to drop sharply when there are 7 children per node. This can be explained by the data in that there were not enough randomly created structure samples with 7 children.

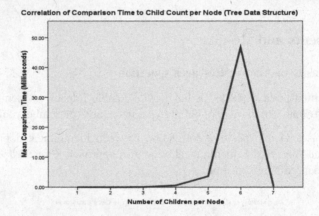

Fig. 6. Correlation of mean comparison time to the number of children per node

The covariance is calculated as:

$$cov(x, y) = \frac{\sum_{i=1}^{n} (x_i - \bar{x})(y_i - \bar{y})}{(N - 1)}$$

$$cov(x, y) = \frac{\sum_{i=1}^{100} (x_i - \bar{x})(y_i - \bar{y})}{(99)}$$

$$= \frac{1209.339}{99}$$

$$= 12.22$$

The covariance above confirms a positive correlation between the number of children per node and comparison time.

Number of Filtered Fields: There was not a visible correlation between the number of filtered fields and mean comparison time (Fig. 7).

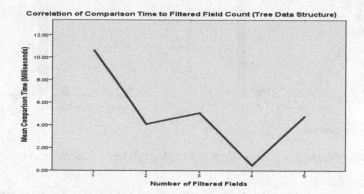

Fig. 7. Correlation of mean comparison time to the number of children per node

The covariance is calculated as:

$$cov(x, y) = \frac{\sum_{i=1}^{100} (x_i - \bar{x})(y_i - \bar{y})}{(N-1)}$$

$$cov(x, y) = \frac{\sum_{i=1}^{100} (x_i - \bar{x})(y_i - \bar{y})}{(99)}$$

$$= \frac{-343.281}{99}$$

$$= -3.47$$

The negative covariance above confirms that there is no any correlation between the number of filtered fields and mean comparison time. This is in agreement with the earlier visual observation.

4.2   Experiments to Answer Research Question 2

It was clear that comparison times significantly improved after the parts hierarchies were transformed into a compressed binary string. Neither the depth nor the number of children per node (Fig. 8) had the same impact on comparison time as it did when the hierarchies resided in a tree data structure.

4.3   Experiments to Answer Research Question 3

A multiple regression analysis was performed with IBM SPSS. Depth and child count were observed to have similar significant, positive correlations to hierarchical

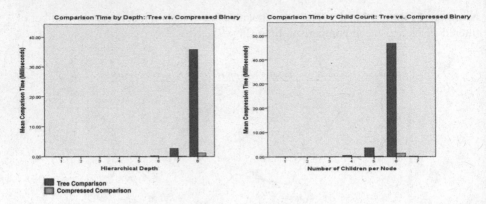

Fig. 8. Comparison time by depth and child count: tree vs. compressed binary

comparison execution times while the number of filtered fields did not appear to have any significant correlation to hierarchical comparison times (Table 1).

It was observed that as depth or child count increased in the hierarchical data structures, so did the execution times for hierarchical comparisons. This was especially evident as hierarchical structures approached a depth of 8 levels and the child count per node reached 6 children (Fig. 9).

In fact, it was observed that as depth increased by one unit, hierarchical comparison execution time increased by approximately 2.77 units. As the number of children per node increased by one unit, comparison time increased by approximately 3.12 units (Table 2).

The coefficients above were incorporated into a predictive model:

$$Comparision\_time_i = b_0 + b_1 depth_i + b_2 no\_of\_children\_per\_node_i$$
$$- 18.44 + 2.77(depth_i) + 3.12(no\_of\_children\_per\_node_i)$$

Table 1. SPSS correlation output

Correlations					
		RelationalTime	Depth	ChildCount	FieldCount
Pearson correlation	RelationalTime	1.000	.274	.243	−.087
	Depth	.274	1.000	.167	.147
	ChildCount	.243	.167	1.000	−.009
	FieldCount	−.087	.147	−.009	1.000
Sig. (1-tailed)	RelationalTime	.	.003	.007	.194
	Depth	.003	.	.048	.073
	ChildCount	.007	.048	.	465
	FieldCount	.194	.073	.465	.
N	RelationalTime	100	100	100	100
	Depth	100	100	100	100
	ChildCount	100	100	100	100
	FieldCount	100	100	100	100

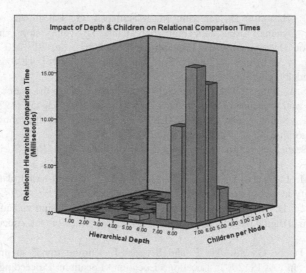

Fig. 9. Observed impact of depth and children on comparison times

Table 2. SPSS coefficient output

Model	Unstandardized coefficients		Standardized coefficients	t	Sig.	95.0 % confidence interval for B		Correlations			Collinearity statistics	
	B	Std. error	Beta			Lower bound	Upper bound	Zero-order	Partial	Part	Tolerance	VIF
(Constant)	−18.44	7.257		−2.541	.013	−32.842	−4.036					
Depth	2.765	1.113	.241	2.483	.015	.555	4.975	.274	.245	.237	.972	1.029
ChildCount	3.12	1.489	.203	2.095	.039	.165	6.075	.243	.208	.200	.972	1.029

5 Conclusion

In this research we have developed an efficient hierarchical comparison mechanism for cloud-based heterogeneous product lifecycle management systems. We have used this mechanism to convert the traditional hierarchical comparison by traversal through the tree type data structure into a string comparison. Our approach is very simple but scalable, and also very suited to cloud-based heterogeneous product lifecycle management systems because the method itself is independent to the details of data stores. Therefore we have offered an efficient solution for a specific interoperability problem in cloud-based heterogeneous product lifecycle management systems.

References

1. Grieves, M.: Product Lifecycle Management: Driving Next Generation of Lean Thinking. McGraw-Hill, New York City (2006)
2. Merkle, R.C.: Secrecy, authentication, and public key systems. Doctoral dissertation, Stanford University (1979)

3. DeCandia, G., Hastorun, D., Jampani, M., Kakulapati, G., Lakshman, A., Pilchin, A., Vogels, W.: Dynamo: Amazon's highly available key-value store. In: 21st ACM Symposium on Operating System Principles (SOSP 2007), pp. 205–220 (2007). Nagel, W.E., Walter, W.V. Lehner, W. (eds.): Euro-Par 2006. LNCS, vol. 4128, pp. 1148–1158. Springer, Heidelberg (2006)

4. Needleman, S.B., Wunsch, C.D.: A general method applicable to the search for similarities in the amino acid sequence of two proteins. J. Mol. Biol. **48**, 443–453 (1970)

5. Lassmann, T., Sonnhammer, E.L.: KALIGN–an accurate and fast multiple sequence alignment algorithm. BMC Bioinform. **6**(1), 298 (2005)

6. Abbott, A.: Sequence analysis: new methods for old ideas. Ann. Rev. Sociol. **21**, 93–113 (1995)

7. Khalfallah, M., Figay, N., Da Silva, C.F., Ghodous, P.: A cloud-based platform to ensure interoperability in aerospace industry. J. Intell. Manufact. **27**(1), 119–129 (2016)

8. Wu, D., Rosen, D.W., Wang, L., Schaefer, D.: Cloud-based design and manufacturing: a new paradigm in digital manufacturing and design innovation. Comput. Aided Des. **59**, 1–14 (2015)

9. Staisch, A., Peters, G., Stueckl, T. and Sergua, J.: Current trends in product lifecycle management. In: ACIS 2012: Location, Location, Location: Proceedings of the 23rd Australasian Conference on Information Systems, pp. 1–10. ACIS, January 2012

10. Wang, X.V., Xu, X.W.: An interoperable solution for cloud manufacturing. Robot. Comput.-Integr. Manufact. **29**(4), 232–247 (2013)

11. Ali, S.I.: Adoption of cloud computing in manufacturing industry supply chains, a hype or a myth? In: 2013 Second International Conference on Future Generation Communication Technology (FGCT), pp. 69–72. IEEE (2013)

12. Qu, Y., Xiong, N.: RFH: a resilient, fault-tolerant and high-efficient replication algorithm for distributed cloud storage. In: 2012 41st International Conference on Parallel Processing (ICPP), pp. 520–529. IEEE (2012)

13. Zhou, Y., Zhang, Y., Xie, Y., Zhang, H., Yang, L.T., Min, G.: TransCom: a virtual disk-based cloud computing platform for heterogeneous services. IEEE Trans. Netw. Serv. Manag. **11**(1), 46–59 (2014)

14. Johnson, B., Qu, Y.: A holistic model for making cloud migration decision: a consideration of security, architecture and business economics. In: 2012 IEEE 10th International Symposium on Parallel and Distributed Processing with Applications (ISPA), pp. 435–441. IEEE (2012)

15. Fu, Z., Sun, X., Liu, Q., Zhou, L., Shu, J.: Achieving efficient cloud search services: multi-keyword ranked search over encrypted cloud data supporting parallel computing. IEICE Trans. Commun. **E98-B**(1), 190–200 (2015)

16. Ren, Y., Shen, J., Wang, J., Han, J., Lee, S.: Mutual verifiable provable data auditing in public cloud storage. J. Internet Technol. **16**(2), 317–323 (2015)

17. Xia, Z., Wang, X., Sun, X., Wang, Q.: A secure and dynamic multi-keyword ranked search scheme over encrypted cloud data. IEEE Trans. Parallel Distrib. Syst. **27**(2), 340–352 (2015)

Automatic Classification of Cloud Service Based on Weighted Euclidean Distance

Yanqiu Lou, Yi Zhuang[✉], and Ying Huo

College of Computer Science and Technology,
Nanjing University of Aeronautics and Astronautics,
Nanjing, Jiangsu Province, People's Republic of China
joyceqiu@163.com, {zyl6,huoying}@nuaa.edu.cn

Abstract. Because the wide use of cloud computing has led to vast amounts of service information in the network, the quick identification and the automatic classification of cloud services have become the key to the quick and accurate location of the expected service.

In this paper, a new method of automatic classification of cloud services based on weighted Euclidean distance is proposed. Firstly, we perform the service pretreatment on the collected dataset, and extract features to build a text model based on VSM (Vector Space Model). Further on, a new algorithm named WT_K-means algorithm is proposed by improving the distance function of the original K-means algorithm. Experiments have been carried out under two-dimensional test set and real service dataset, respectively. The results show that the pretreatment of service can abstract the functional characteristics of the original WSDL (Web Service Description Language) documents, and the proposed WT_K-means algorithm can effectively classify services according to these characteristics.

Keywords: Cloud computing · Cloud service · Automatic classification · Service cluster

1 Introduction

The emergence of cloud computing [1] has promoted the development of SOA [2] (Service-Oriented Architecture). The vast amount of cloud services has brought great challenges to the management and organization of services in cloud [3]. To accelerate their search efficiency, services can be classified into different categories according to their functional characteristics.

At present, the most widely used registration center standard is UDDI [4] (Universal Description Discovery and Integration). It is a description specification based on XML, which enables global enterprises to publish various services on the Internet. UDDI also provides service release and discovery mechanism [5]. During the service registration in UDDI, service providers can label the category of services by using a variety of standard classification systems, such as NAICS, UNSPSC, etc. During the service searching, service requesters can scan or search by the categories, which can greatly improve the efficiency.

X. Sun et al. (Eds.): ICCCS 2016, Part I, LNCS 10039, pp. 229–239, 2016.
DOI: 10.1007/978-3-319-48671-0_21

However, due to the large amount of cloud services, the manual service category tagging will become complex and time-consuming. Besides, the services discovery mechanism using UDDI to extract keys is not comprehensive thus will seriously restrict the development of SOA. Therefore, it is necessary to study automatic service classification technology.

In this paper, a new method of automatic classification of cloud services based on weighted Euclidean distance is proposed. We perform the service pretreatment on the collected dataset, and extract features to build a text model based on VSM (Vector Space Model). Further on, a new algorithm named WT_K-means algorithm is proposed by improving the distance function of the original K-means algorithm. Experiments have been carried out under two-dimensional test set and real service dataset, respectively, and the results have been analyzed.

The rest of the paper is organized as follows. Section 2 discusses the related work. Section 3 presents our service classification method based on WT_K-means, including the service classification process, service pretreatment, feature extraction, and text modeling based on VSM. Section 4 describes and analyzes the experiments under two-dimensional test set and real service dataset. Finally, Sect. 5 concludes this paper.

2   Related Work

2.1   Service Classification

In order to realize the automatic classification of services, we need to predefine the service training set, which can be implemented using clustering algorithms. Service classification [6] is applied on the clustering results in order to find the most suitable new service category. With the development of the cloud service [7], the amount of services on the Internet are rapidly increasing. The quick identification and the automatic classification of cloud services have become the key to the quick and accurate location of the expected service. The first step of identifying cloud services is to classify them accurately. It has become a huge challenge to classify a large number of services, more importantly, to classify them automatically.

At present, there are many methods of service classification, such as the methods proposed by Pan and Crasso. Pan's method separates the WSDL document using terms in brackets, uses the Binary, Times, Tf-idf to perform the feature extraction, and uses the Naive Bayes and SMO algorithms to perform the classification [8]. The accuracy of their method is between 27 % and 41 %. Crasso's method firstly segments the elements of WSDL and removes the deactivated words, then does the stemming and uses different classification algorithms to perform classification [9]. Their experiments were carried out on small data sets. The accuracy of their method is between 70 % and 80 %. Liang from Singapore Management University presents a new method of Web service clustering. The method considers the combination of elements in the WSDL document and the potential semantic information of the different combinations [10]. However, these studies only consider the information of part of the elements in the WSDL documents and ignore other important elements or attributes. It doesn't take the inheritance of ontology concept and the property categories into consideration in structure, which can affect the accuracy of clustering. Also, some of them use the traditional algorithms to do the classification, which could take a lot of time and space.

2.2 Clustering Algorithm

There are many mature clustering algorithms at present, such as K-means algorithm based on partition, COBWEB based on model, STING based on grid, CURE based on hierarchy and so on. K-means is one of the most commonly used methods and its clustering criterion function is the error square. However, K-means has its own limitations. Its clustering results are easily influenced by the initial clustering centers, and it is extremely easy to converge to local optimal solutions. To solve these problems, many improvements on K-means based on global optimization have been presented, such as the combination with simulated annealing algorithm and genetic algorithm. Xie from Shaanxi Normal University presents an improved global K-means algorithm. They use the fast K centers to determine the initial centers of the improved clustering algorithm. This strategy can avoid the situation of selecting a noise point as the optimal initial center [11]. Meanwhile, it can also shorten the clustering time. Zhang from Chongqing University presents an improved K-means algorithm based on sampling partition [12]. This algorithm can reduce the phenomenon in which the large cluster is separated when using the function of error sum of the K-means algorithm. Al-Mohair proposes a Multilayer Perceptron artificial neural network, which is a universal classifier, is combined with the k-means clustering method to accurately detect skin. The experimental results show that the method can achieve high accuracy [13]. Jiangyan proposes an improved k-means algorithm which uses two algorithms to obtain the initial clustering with high accuracy and adaptability [14].

But under the environment of cloud computing, we need to consider the multiple attributes of cloud services. These methods have not considered the priority of attributes according to their degrees of importance. The attributes of the service in the cloud computing environment often include the information that which field it belongs to and which function it can complete. Furtherly, through the analysis of the multiple attributes, we can get the category of the service more quickly and correctly. What's more, the equal status of the attributes in clustering cannot accurately reflect the similarity between samples.

3   Service Classification Based on WT_K – Means

3.1   Service Classification Process

The proposed service classification process is shown in Fig. 1.

The detailed processes are as follows:

(1) Get cloud service dataset through manual collection and web crawlers;
(2) Perform pretreatment for every WSDL document;

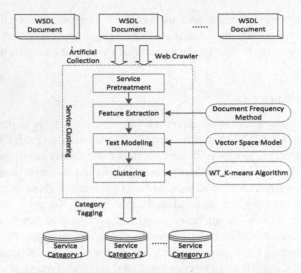

Fig. 1. Service classification process

(3) Perform feature extraction using document frequency method for every WSDL document that has been pretreated;
(4) Based on the set of key words, model the set of WSDL documents as a matrix R of $M \times N$;
(5) WT_K-means algorithm is used to cluster the services.

3.2 Service Pretreatment

In real life, we can observe that key information lies within a lot of redundant information. How to identify and locate the key information? How to reduce the space of information? To solve these problems, we need to carry out some measures of information pretreatment before further actions. WSDL documents are mainly used as the carrier of service information. WSDL documents are able to describe the access interface and function of services in an accurate and comprehensive way. Usually, WSDL documents contain the following elements: Import, Type, PortType, Message, Binding, Operation and Service [9]. In order to extract effective service information but maintain minimum storage space, it is necessary to perform pretreatment on WSDL documents.

The main operations of the pretreatment are as follows:

(1) Get the contents under the labels "operation name" and "service name" from the WSDL documents;
(2) Change the capital letters into lowercase letters in the contents, and divide the words accordingly;
(3) Remove the preposition and form words according to the stopwords list;
(4) Perform the stemming.

For example, in the WSDL document of a service named "StadiumData", the first term tagged as "operation name" is <wsdl: operation name = "IsStadiumActive">. We can get three words "is", "stadium", "active" from the obtained interface name "IsStadiumActive", by identifying the capital letters and changing them into lowercase letters. The second term tagged as "operation name" is <wsdl: operation name = "GetAllStadiums">. Similarly, we can get three words "get", "all", "stadiums". Process the rest of the WSDL document accordingly. Remove the preposition and form words according to the stopwords list, such as a, of, by, to, with and so on. Then, perform the stemming for these words combine the cognate words and sum up the appearance frequence. The result of pretreatment is a set of key words formed as follows.

WSDL_Keywords = {stadium, version, event, active}

3.3   Feature Extraction

The purpose of feature extraction is to establish a mathematical model of all kinds of features to help classification. Features for classification should have the following four characteristics [15]:

(1) Features for classification should have great separability, that is, a large amount of information for the classifier to identify;
(2) Features for classification should have great reliability. The specious or amphibolous features should be abandoned;
(3) Features for classification should have strong independences as much as possible. For those appear repeatedly or strongly correlated, choose only one of them;
(4) Keep a minimum set of features, while maintain a minimum loss of information.

We have extracted information about the operation and service in WSDL documents after the service pretreatment, because they describe the function and field information of the service. For example, a service named "CinemaData", whose interface is "GetCinemaInfo", has a clear relationship with cinema.

However, the set of key words we have obtained from the pretreatment and preliminary feature extraction of the WSDL documents are not minimized. There are many words that are not distinguishable enough in the interface of WSDL documents, including "info", "result" and so on. Due to the existence of such words, the similarity of some different categories of WSDL documents is increased during clustering, thus the accuracy of classification is greatly reduced.

In this paper, we adopt the DF (Document Frequency) method to minimize the set of features, removing the words that appear less than three times or more than 80 % in the documents. This method reduces the set of key words and gets more simplified phrases, which will improve the accuracy greatly. For instance, the key words we obtain for the service named "CinemaData" after adopting the DF method are {stadium, event}, which is more representative comparing with the original set {version, stadium, active, event, performance, ata}.

3.4   Text Modeling Based on VSM

After the feature extraction, we can get sets of key words for each WSDL document.

Based on the sets of key words, we can model the WSDL documents as a matrix R for $M \times N$. In this matrix, each column stands for a WSDL document, while each row corresponds to a different keyword. We can express the matrix as $R = [r_{ij}]$, where r_{ij} is a nonnegative value. In this paper, we calculate the weight values for keywords using the TF-IDF method. During the calculation, we consider the degree of representation of each word and the amount of information it carries, which is shown in formula (1).

$$\omega(i,j) = tf(i,j) \times idf_i = tf(i,j) \times \log(1 + \frac{N}{n_i}) \qquad (1)$$

In formula (1), $\omega(i,j)$ denotes the weight value, $tf(i,j)$ denotes the appearance frequency of the i th word in the j th document, idf_i denotes the inverse document frequency of the i th word, N denotes the amount of all the WSDL documents, while n_i denotes the amount of the WSDL documents that contain the i th word.

3.5   WT_K-Means Algorithm

This paper presents an improved WT_K-means algorithm to perform the service clustering. We use the weighted Euclidean distance as a distance function, using weight values to reflect the different status of keywords in the clustering to improve the effectiveness and accuracy. The new distance function is shown in formula (2).

$$D_{ij} = \sqrt{\sum_{k=1}^{n} \omega_k \left(x_{ik} - x_{jk} \right)^2} \qquad (2)$$

$$\omega_k = \frac{S_k}{|\overline{X_k}|} \Bigg/ \sum_{t=1}^{m} \frac{S_k}{|\overline{X_t}|} \qquad (3)$$

$$\overline{X_k} = \frac{1}{m} \sum_{t=1}^{m} x_{tk} \qquad (4)$$

$$S_k = \sqrt{\frac{1}{m} \sum_{t=1}^{m} \left(x_{tk} - \overline{X_k} \right)^2} \qquad (5)$$

In formula (2), ω_k denotes the mutation weights of the k th column for all m vectors, which is calculated using formula (3). x_{ik} and x_{jk} denote the values of two documents in the k th column. In formula (3), $\overline{X_k}$ denotes the average value of the k th column for all m vectors, which is calculated using formula (4). S_k denotes the standard deviation of k th column for all m vectors, which is calculated using formula (5).

The proposed WT_K-means algorithm is described as Table 1.

Table 1. WT_K-means algorithm description

Algorithm: WT_K-means algorithm

Input: $X_1, X_2, ..., X_M$, where $X_i = (\mathrm{x}_{i1}, \mathrm{x}_{i2}, ..., \mathrm{x}_{in})$, M means the number of samples, and n means the dimension of each sample; the number of clusters K.

Output: the clustering results.

Begin

Step 1:Choose the initial K clustering centers as:

$Z_1(1), Z_2(1), ..., Z_K(1), \mathrm{K} < M$, where $Z_i(1)$ means the i th cluster center.

Step 2: Use formula (2) to perform the clustering.

Step 3: Calculate the new center $Z_i(k+1), \mathrm{i} = 1, 2, ..., \mathrm{K}$, where

$$Z_i(k+1) = \frac{1}{M_i} \sum_{X \in S_i(k)} X \cdot$$

Step 4: If $Z_i(k+1) \neq Z_i(k)$, $\mathrm{i} = 1, 2, ..., \mathrm{K}$, then go back to Step 2, else the algorithm is convergent and the calculation is completed.

End

---

4   Experiment and Analysis

4.1   Experimental Environment and Dataset

In this paper, the experimental environment is Windows 7, the CPU is Inter(R) Core (TM) i3/3.19 GHz, and the memory is 4 GB. The data sets used are described as follows:

(1) Two-dimensional test set: In a two-dimensional area, create 200 data randomly as a test set to evaluate the performance of the clustering algorithm. Data is generated independently by a random data generator.

(2) Real service dataset: WS-DREAM (Distributed Reliability Assessment Mechanism for Web Services) is collected by the Chinese university of Hong Kong, including 1.5 million service calling records for 10258 Web Services, by 150 service users from 24 countries worldwide. Each record includes three attributes, which are response time, response datasize and failure probability.

In this paper, we choose Dataset4 [16], which includes: (1) A document named readme.txt describing the dataset; (2) A document named wslist.txt, which includes 3738 records about the information of services; and (3) A folder named WSDL including 3738 WSDL documents.

4.2   Clustering Experiment on Two-Dimensional Test Set

In this paper, 200 two-dimensional data samples are used as the test set to compare the performance of the basic K-means algorithm and the improved WT_K-means algorithm.

Figure 2 shows the result of dividing the two-dimensional dataset into 5 categories using K-means algorithm, while Fig. 3 shows the result using WT_K-means algorithm. The points denoted by different shapes in Figs. 2 and 3 belong to different categories.

We can see from these two figures that most of the data are classified similarly, but the boundaries between categories are different and Fig. 3 has better results. This is because the WT_K-means algorithm takes into account the relationship and difference between categories according to their attributes.

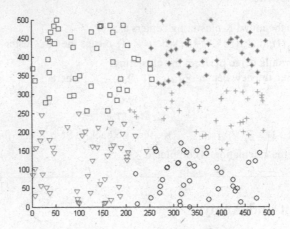

Fig. 2. The result using K-means algorithm (K = 5)

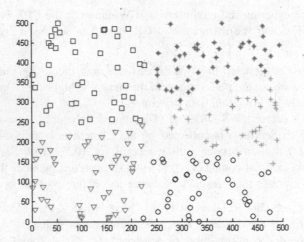

Fig. 3. The result using WT_K-means algorithm (K = 5)

4.3   Clustering Experiment on Real Service Dataset

In this paper, we use 202 WSDL documents of the data set. In order to elaborate the service clustering experiment, this section takes two services, i.e., Service 1 "CinemaData" and Service 3 "CinemaSinchronization", as a case study.

Firstly, we perform the service pretreatment and extract the keywords of the WSDL documents. The results related to our two services in the case study are shown in Fig. 4.

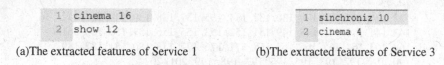

```
1  version 3
2  cinema 16
3  active 3
4  show 12
5  performanc 3
6  data  1
```

```
1  sinchroniz 10
2  cinema 4
3  show 3
4  performanc 3
```

(a) The pretreatment result of Service 1   (b) The pretreatment result of Service 3

Fig. 4. The pretreatment results of the case study

Secondly, we perform the feature extraction, and the results for our case study are shown in Fig. 5.

```
1  cinema 16
2  show 12
```

```
1  sinchroniz 10
2  cinema 4
```

(a)The extracted features of Service 1   (b)The extracted features of Service 3

Fig. 5. The feature extraction results of the case study

Similarly, we are able to get 490 keywords from the 202 WSDL documents and after the feature extraction, we get 72 features as shown in Table 2.

Table 2. The features extracted from 202 WSDL documents

web	version	system	method	mode	supplier	send	remove	code
term	message	instanc	filter	authentic	upload	content	referral	engine
show	obtener	entity	descriptor	list	file	summari	twitter	fetch
lob	sinchronize	for	login	search	rpc	device	client	lodg
repli	white	link	tip	categori	promo	bak	pcce	solicitacao
multi	board	call	warn	ticker	ic	save	export	taxi
team	buddy	zone	cat	kijker	lolli	winter	mensagem	ref
hit	cinema	dimer	sign	min	mold	ecake	pedido	pack

We perform the clustering using the proposed WT_K-means algorithm. The number of clusters K is set as 10. The clustering result is shown as Table 3.

We can see from Table 3 that Service 1 and Service 3 are in the same category due to their high similarity.

Table 3. The clustering result (K = 10)

Cluster ID	Result	Cluster size
C0	4, 5, 6, 7, 8, 9, 11, 12, 13, 23, 25, 30, 31, 39, 41, 42, 43, 44, 45, 65, 46, 47, 49, 50, 51, 60, 55, 56, 59, 35, 61, 67, 71, 80, 36, 81, 28, 82, 64, 83, 84, 38, 85, 86, 87, 88, 89, 90, 91, 66, 92, 93, 94, 95, 96, 99, 32, 100, 101, 102, 103, 104, 62, 105, 79, 106, 107, 40, 108, 109, 110, 70, 111, 37, 113, 68, 114, 115, 69, 116, 117, 121, 122, 124, 133, 29, 150, 170, 172, 173, 174, 175, 179, 188, 194, 63, 200	97
C1	1, 2, 3	3
C2	14, 16, 18, 53, 72, 74, 76, 97, 118	9
C3	26, 33, 57, 78	4
C4	24, 27, 131, 136, 158, 182	6
C5	112	1
C6	15, 17, 19, 20, 21, 22, 54, 73, 75, 77, 98, 119, 120	13
C7	52, 125, 145, 154, 169, 183, 184, 185, 186	9
C8	10, 34, 48, 58	4
C9	123, 126, 127, 128, 129, 130, 132, 134, 135, 137, 138, 139, 140, 141, 142, 143, 144, 146, 147, 148, 149, 151, 152, 153, 155, 156, 157, 159, 160, 161, 162, 163, 164, 165, 166, 167, 168, 171, 176, 177, 178, 180, 181, 187, 189, 190, 191, 192, 193, 195, 196, 197, 198, 199, 201, 202	56

5 Conclusion

In this paper, we propose an systematic process of classification towards cloud services. As an essential step of the classification process, we propose an improved WT_K-means algorithm to perform the automated clustering. We illustrate our method and evaluate its performance using both simulated dataset and real service dataset. The results show that the proposed algorithm, compared with the traditional service classification methods, takes less time and has better accuracy on the simulated datasets. The results on real service dataset also shows the effectiveness of WT_K-means algorithm. We believe that our algorithm is promising in both theoretical and practical aspects.

References

1. Fu, Z., Sun, X., Liu, Q., Zhou, L., Shu, J.: Achieving efficient cloud search services: multi-keyword ranked search over encrypted cloud data supporting parallel computing. IEICE Trans. Commun. **E98-B**(1), 190–200 (2015)
2. Surhone, L.M., Timpledon, M.T., Marseken, S.F.: Service Component Architecture. Betascript Publishing (2010)
3. Xia, Z., Wang, X., Sun, X., Wang, Q.: A secure and dynamic multi-keyword ranked search scheme over encrypted cloud data. IEEE Trans. Parallel Distrib. Syst. **27**(2), 340–352 (2015)

4. Adams, C., Boeyen, S.: UDDI and WSDL extensions for Web service: a security framework. In: ACM Workshop on XML Security, Fairfax, VA, USA, pp. 30–35, November 2002

5. Fu, Z., Ren, K., Shu, J., Sun, X., Huang, F.: Enabling personalized search over encrypted outsourced data with efficiency improvement. IEEE Trans. Parallel Distrib. Syst. (2015). doi:10.1109/TPDS.2015.2506573

6. Yahyaoui, H., Own, H., Malik, Z.: Modeling and classification of service behaviors. Expert Syst. Appl. 42(21), 7610–7619 (2015)

7. Addis, B., et al.: Autonomic management of cloud service centers with availability guarantees. IEEE International Conference on Cloud Computing, pp. 220–227. IEEE (2010)

8. Zhang, J., Pan, D.: Web Service Classification (2011)

9. Crasso, M., Zunino, A., Campo, M.: AWSC: an approach to Web service classification based on machine learning techniques. Intel. Artif. 12(37), 25–36 (2008)

10. Wu, J., et al.: Clustering Web services to facilitate service discovery. Knowl. Inf. Syst. 38(1), 207–229 (2014)

11. Xie, J.Y., et al.: An improved global K-means clustering algorithm. J. Shaanxi Normal Univ. 38(2) (2010)

12. Fang, Z.Y., Li, M.J., Yang, X.Z.: An improved K-means algorithm. Comput. Appl. (2003)

13. Al-Mohair, H.K., Saleh, J.M., Suandi, S.A.: Hybrid human skin detection using neural network and K-means clustering technique. Appl. Soft Comput. 33(C), 337–347 (2015)

14. Jiangyan, S.: An improved K-means clustering algorithm for the community discovery. J. Softw. Eng. 9, 242–253 (2015)

15. Duda, R.O., Hart, P.E., Stork, D.G.: Pattern Classification, 2nd edn. Wiley, New York (2001)

16. Zhang, Y., Zheng, Z., Lyu, M.R.: WSExpress: a QoS-aware search engine for Web services. In: IEEE International Conference on Web Services, ICWS 2010, Miami, Florida, USA, pp. 91–98, 5–10 July 2010

A Conflict Prevention Scheduling Strategy for Shared-State Scheduling in Large Scale Cluster

Libo He[1], Zhenping Qiang[1], Lin Liu[1], Wei Zhou[2],
and Shaowen Yao[2(✉)]

[1] School of Information Science and Engineering,
Yunnan University, Kunming, China
22013000170@mail.ynu.edu.cn, qzp@swfu.edu.cn,
liulinrachel@163.com
[2] School of Software, Yunnan University,
No. 2 Cuihu North Rd, Kunming, Yunnan, China
{zwei,yaosw}@ynu.edu.cn

Abstract. The scheduling strategy is being challenged by the scaling cloud size and more complicated application requirements. Omega provides a share state scheduling architecture to achieve flexible and scalable performance. However, there is few studies aim at the scheduling strategy for shared-state scheduling architecture. So it is worthy further research. In this paper, we present a conflict prevention scheduling strategy for shared-state scheduling architecture. Conflict prevention scheduling strategy gives a feasible solution to reduce conflict and improve efficient for parallel schedulers in shared-state scheduling architecture. We implement it in Omega's public simulator, experiments results show that conflict prevention scheduling strategy is effective and can significantly improves the efficiency of scheduler with long decision time.

Keywords: Shared-state scheduling · Conflict prevention scheduling strategy · Multiple choices approach

1 Introduction

With the growth of big data, nowadays the size of cloud-scale computing clusters is growing rapidly to run complicating data-parallel computation jobs. In monolithic scheduling architecture, such as Hadoop Fair Scheduler [1], it only has one scheduler for all jobs submitted to cluster management system. However, the scaling cluster size and more complicated application requirements let efficient scheduling by monolithic scheduler to be a scalability bottleneck. Therefore, many scheduling architectures, such as Mesos [2], YARN [3], Omega [4], Sparrow [5], Apollo [6] and Borg [7], Tarcil [8] have proposed many approaches to overcome this challenge. Omega, whose approach has been adopted in Google's current cluster management system Borg, achieves efficient and flexible scheduling based on the notion of sharing entire cluster state to parallel schedulers to make schedule decisions. In the shared-state scheduling architecture, at least two parallel schedulers are in charge of finding the suitable machines to place tasks of jobs. The scheduling algorithm of those parallel schedulers should

X. Sun et al. (Eds.): ICCCS 2016, Part I, LNCS 10039, pp. 240–250, 2016.
DOI: 10.1007/978-3-319-48671-0_22

consider many factors, such as task's constraints, user-specified preferences and so on. Since it is flexible for schedulers to choose scheduling strategy, no strategy considers alleviating conflicts as a scheduling goal. However, in this architecture, because scheduling decisions have been made by parallel schedulers concurrently, so conflict is the mainly factor to effect scheduling efficiency. In this paper, we propose a new specific scheduling strategy for schedulers to try to avoid conflicts between parallel schedulers. The contributions of this paper are as follows:

1. We propose a novel conflict prevention scheduling strategy for shared-state scheduling in large cluster. To the best of our knowledge, it is the first work to explore to use scheduling strategy to reduce conflicts between schedulers for shared-state scheduling architecture.
2. The conflict prevention scheduling strategy is somewhat akin to the power of two choices load balancing technique [9] and multiple choices approach [10]. Instead of probing to machine to get load information of cluster machines, our strategy uses placement array which is like cell state to record concurrent schedule transactions information to help schedulers make decisions.
3. We rewrite the Omega's simulator and implement proposed conflict prevention scheduling strategy in the simulator. A series of experiments is developed to evaluate the effectiveness of this method.

The rest of this paper is organized as fellows. Section 2 presents background of scheduling architectures and scheduling strategies adopted in those architectures. Section 3 describes the basic mechanisms of our scheduling strategy and the detail of this algorithm. We further compare the performance of our approach to the original in Sect. 4. We conclude our work and describe future work in Sect. 5.

2   Background

With the advent of the era of big data, a lot of people pay attention to the security of the cloud recently [11–14], at the same time, scheduling in large-scale clusters has become another hot research area. Due to the decentralized decisions, the distributed schedulers such as Omega, Sparrow, Apollo, Tarcil and Borg are better to benefit for large scale cluster. By sharing cluster's entire allocation state to parallel schedulers, Omega's approach achieve flexible and efficient scheduling. However the scheduling algorithm is not the focus of the paper [4] which proposed Omega's approach. In this paper, we deeply research on scheduling strategy for shared-state scheduling architecture.

So far, in monolithic schedulers and two-level schedulers, more and more scheduling strategies have been proposed. Such as delay scheduling, FIFO scheduling, Fair Scheduling [1], Capacity Scheduling, Quincy [15], Condor [16], and so on. In the distributed schedulers, especially Omega's approach, some of those scheduling strategies are no longer applicable.

Sparrow uses batch sampling strategy to schedule lower-latency jobs. Its goal is to schedule millions of tasks per second. So scheduling efficiency is its focus. Sparrow's schedulers schedule tasks on machines with the shortest queue through probing to machines.

Apollo adopts a variant of the stable matching algorithm [17] to schedule tasks to servers according by wait time matrices and uses some correction mechanisms to alleviate conflicts. For each tasks in a group, scheduler finds the machine with the earliest estimated completion time as a candidate machine for that task.

Borg adopts a scheduling algorithm which concludes feasibility checking and scoring phases. Schedulers firstly choose a set of candidate machine which meet the task's constraints and have enough resources, then chose one from them by their score.

Tarcil adopts interference-aware scheduling algorithm. It is focus on reducing interference which is brought by collocated tasks in a server. Its schedulers need rich information on the resource preferences and interference sensitivity of incoming jobs to make scheduling decisions.

All of above scheduling algorithm are based on the specific application architecture. Our research is based on Omega's shared-state scheduling architecture. However, none Borg's and Omega's scheduling strategy consider using strategy to avoid conflicts. Furthermore, our scheduling strategy can be considered as a score factor in Borg's scoring phase.

Spired the power of two choices load balancing technique [9], multiple choices approach [10] and Sparrow's batch sampling, we propose a conflict prevention scheduling strategy for shared-state scheduling architecture. Sparrow uses information which is gotten by probing to machines to make scheduling decision. Our approach uses logically centralized data objects to record machine's state and concurrent claims information and use them to make scheduling decision. Compare to Sparrow's batch sampling, our approach is more freedom of choosing machines.

In Google's cluster management system which adopts Omega's approach, a cluster can be divided into many cells, and a median cell size is 10 K. Then, A data object which called cell state is used to records the resource allocations information of machines in the cell. Therefore, parallel schedulers copy the cell state to local and synchronize it at the beginning of job's scheduling process. Then schedulers use scheduling strategy to concurrently make scheduling decisions for their scheduling tasks. Subsequently, those scheduling decisions are committed by transactions. Finally, whether those scheduling decisions really valid or not is according to the OCC method [18] which maintains serial equivalence [19, 20] of those concurrent transactions.

Omega's lightweight simulator uses a linear function to model scheduler decision time of schedulers and uses randomized first fit strategy to make scheduling decision. It is no doubt that this simulator simplifies the scheduling strategy of a real scheduling system. Through studying the scheduling strategy of Borg, we think the real scheduling strategy of schedulers in Google's cluster management system has two parts: feasibility checking and scoring. In feasibility checking, the scheduler makes sure a set of candidate machines that have enough resources and meets task's constraints. In the scoring phase, the scheduler chooses one of the suitable machines by scoring the candidate machines with user-specified preferences. Since the conflicts are rare in their current scheduling system, so both Omega's and Borg's schedulers don't consider using scheduling strategy to reduce conflict. However, with scaling of workload and schedulers, conflicts may not rare as Omega hopes. Besides, in shared-state scheduling architecture, because of conflicts, the efficient of scheduler with long decision time is not ideal. So using scheduling strategy to prevent conflicts beforehand is very necessary, that is the motivation of proposing our approach.

3   The Conflict Prevention Scheduling Strategy

3.1   Basic Mechanisms of Conflict Prevention Scheduling Strategy

Since the intent of using the conflict prevention scheduling strategy is avoiding conflicts in advance. When a scheduler schedules a task, if it knows other concurrent scheduler has made scheduling decision to its wanted machine with the same cell state before, it can choose other candidate machine to place task to avoid conflict. So under this demand, beside cell state, we add another data object (placement array) to record the concurrent resource requirement information about each machine. The maintenance and update mechanisms are like the cell state. At the beginning of the schedule phase, schedulers concurrently synchronize cell state and placement array to local and use those information to make decision. Then after schedule phase of each scheduler, schedulers commit their scheduling transactions and update information of placement array. The function of placement array is that schedulers can use it to make decision to avoid conflicts. However, because of placement array is periodically synchronized, so conflicts may not been completely eliminated. Our conflict prevention scheduling strategy gives a feasible solution to use placement array to reduce conflicts. We will detailed describe the schedule algorithm which adopts the conflict prevention scheduling strategy in Sect. 3.2.

3.2   Basic Mechanisms of Conflict Prevention Scheduling Algorithm

Algorithm 1 describes the detail of conflict prevention scheduling strategy, it can be provide to schedulers to concurrently and separately choose candidate machines for tasks submitted to them.

Schedulers in shared-state scheduling architecture periodically copies shared cell state and placement array to local. Therefore, when a scheduler schedules a job, if the job still has unscheduled tasks, it firstly chooses $m(m \geq 1)$ unscheduled tasks into a group TG by task's constraints and some other reasons (line 1–3). For this task group, scheduler randomly selects at most $d*m(d \geq 2)$ candidate machines which have passed the feasibility checking (line 4–11). Here the function RandomizedChoose-Machines (TG,LC) is used to randomly select a feasible machine from candidate machines pool. The maximum number of candidate machines is $d*m$. We limit the number of running this function to *count* (*count* $\geq d*m$) tries. So, the function will be terminated when $d*m$ candidate machines have been found or only less than $d*m$ candidate machines have been found after *count* tries. Subsequently, for each task T_j in TG, the scheduler preliminarily lays claim to the machine whose concurrent claims is least among those candidate machines MP according by local placement array (line 12–15), deletes this machine from candidate machines and delete this task from remaining tasks (line 16–18). For function ChooseLeastConcurrentClaimsMachine (MP,LP) in line 14, if number of concurrent claims of machines in MP are equal, then the scheduler randomized chooses one machine to lay claim. Otherwise, the scheduler chooses the machine that has the least concurrent claims to lay claim. Here, if the job still has remaining tasks, the scheduler repeats the process of line 3–19. Then if all remaining tasks in the job have been scheduled once, the scheduler commits all claims by a transaction (line 21). Finally, whether those placement claims are succeed or not is according by OCC, if some claims are not succeed, those claims related tasks will be marked as unscheduled and this job is added to the pending queue to wait for another scheduling. In our experiments, we also limit any single job to 1,000 scheduling attempts, and abandon job when it has not been completely scheduled after 1000 tries or when none task of a job is successfully scheduled after 100 tries.

Algorithm1. ConflictPreventionScheduling (J, LC, LP, m, d, count)

```
Input: J - a job include a set of unscheduled tasks
   LC - a local cell state
   LP - a local placement array
   m - tasks number in a group
   d - multiples of candidate machine
Output: Cclaims- a set of task-machine claims
 1:  Cclaims = Null
 2:  while J. numRemainingTasks!=null
 3:    TG=DivideTaskGroup(m,J)
 4:    i = 0
 5:      While( i< =count)
 6:       MP = RandomizedChooseMachines(TG,LC, d)
 7:        If MP.number != d*m
 8:          i++;
 9:        Else
10:          Break;
11:      End while
12:    If MP != null
13:      foreach Tj in TG
14:        Mk = ChooseLeastConcurentClaimsMachine(MP,LP)
15:        Cclaims.add (CreatClaim (Tj, Mk))
16:        MP = MP. delete(Mk)
17:        J. numRemainingTasks -= Tj
18:      end foreach
19:    end if
20:  end while
21:  return Cclaims
```

4 Experimental Evaluation

In this section, to evaluate the performance of our approach, we extended the Omega's lightweight simulator which is written in Scale and implement our scheduling strategy. The runtime environment of our experiments is JVM (openjdk-6-jdk) and Scala 2.9.0 based on a 32 bit Ubuntu 10.04 Server. The hardware environment is setup on one Intel (R) Core(TM) i7-3612QM CPU with total 4 cores, and 6 GB of RAM.

Based on previous analysis [21, 22] about cluster's jobs, we synthesize two workloads (batch and service) like some experiments in paper [4] by considering some job's characteristics: the number of tasks per job, the per-task resources, task duration and job inter-arrival times.

In order to simulate scheduling jobs in a cell, we construct a cell environment as following: 10000 machines, each machine have 4 CPU cores and 16 GB memory.

We use the fellow three metrics to evaluate our approach:

✓ Conflict fraction

Conflict fraction is the number of failed scheduling transactions divided by all scheduling transactions.

✓ Job queuing time

We use the same linear function as Omega's simulator to model scheduler decision time, $t_{decision} = t_{job} + t_{task} *$ *tasks per job*. This model is based on Google's current cluster scheduling logic that most jobs in their workloads have tasks with identical requirements [23]. In this paper, we define the job queuing time as the average time jobs takes to queue in pending queue till jobs have been fully scheduled. In our experiments except varying t_{job} (service) experiments, we set $t_{job} = 0.1$ s and $t_{task} = 5$ ms which is same as experiments in paper [4].

✓ Scheduler busyness

Scheduler busyness is defined as the fraction of time which the scheduler is busy in making scheduling decisions. It is influenced by the per-job decision time and the time of redone scheduling work which caused by conflicts takes.

For conflict prevention scheduling algorithm, when a parallel scheduler picks a machine from candidate machines pool, it may exist the following three cases:

✓ Equal case

The number of concurrent claims in those candidate machines is the same, so the scheduler randomly chooses one from them to place task.

✓ Not equal case

The number of concurrent claims in those candidate machines is different, so the scheduler chooses the one whose number of concurrent claims is least to place task.

✓ No- candidate machine case

After trying a giving number of times, the scheduler doesn't find any feasible machine from the candidate machine pool for a task.

Figure 1 shows the statistics about those three cases. As it shown, the not equal case is not trivial from λ to 7λ. For this part of scheduling decisions, parallel schedulers can avoid conflict by choosing machines with least concurrent claims. On the other hand, most of scheduling decisions are under the equal case from λ to 5λ. For this part of scheduling decisions, parallel schedulers can alleviate conflicts by randomly choosing a machine from at most d*m machines. When arrival rate of batch jobs bigger than 7λ, the average resource usage of machine is bigger than 90 %, the proportion of no-candidate machine case is increase obviously. Figure 2 shows the situation of no-candidate machine case by using first fit and conflict prevention. Except 9λ and 10λ cases, the proportion of no-candidate machine case by using conflict prevention strategy is smaller than by using first fit strategy.

It is no doubt, the time complexity of conflict prevention scheduling algorithm is much higher than the first fit strategy. However, its effect of reducing the potential cost

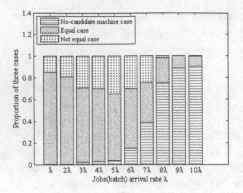

Fig. 1. Proportion of three cases of scheduling decision by using conflict prevention scheduling strategy in Omega's simulator.

Fig. 2. Proportion of no-candidate machine case comparison between Omega's scheduling strategy and prevention scheduling strategy

of redoing work compensates this degradation. The fellow experiments focus on evaluate the conflicts and performance situation of parallel schedulers.

As the purpose of using conflict prevention scheduling strategy is to reduce conflicts between schedulers, so we do experiments to further verify it. For Google's like workloads, shared-state scheduling approach should be good at support the scalability for batch jobs and placing long decision service jobs. So we do experiments by varying arrival rate of batch jobs and decision time of service scheduler to evaluate the performance of our approach. As Fig. 3 shown, the conflict fraction is increased with more schedulers. However, compare to Omega's randomized first fit scheduling strategy, the mean conflict fraction of batch schedulers by using conflict prevention scheduling strategy is always smaller from λ to 10λ under the same workload and cluster environment. In most time the conflict fraction by using Omega's approach is nearly 0.1

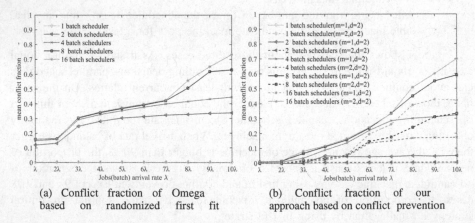

(a) Conflict fraction of Omega based on randomized first fit

(b) Conflict fraction of our approach based on conflict prevention

Fig. 3. Mean conflict fraction comparison of batch schedulers by varying arrival rate of batch jobs. 1.0 is the default rate.

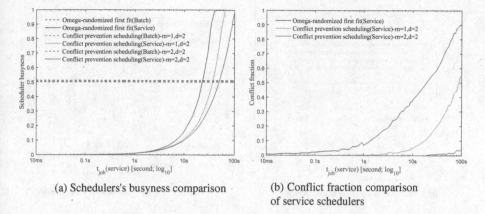

(a) Schedulers's busyness comparison

(b) Conflict fraction comparison of service schedulers

Fig. 4. Schedulers busyness comparison and conflict fraction comparison by varying tjob of service scheduler (1 service scheduler, 2 batch schedulers).

bigger than by using our approach by setting m = 1 and d = 2. For m = 2 and d = 2 case, the conflict prevention scheduling strategy reduces nearly 0.2 conflict fraction. This means conflict prevention scheduling strategy is effective for reduce conflicts between batch schedulers.

Figure 4(a) shows that the busyness of service scheduler scales quickly when t_{job} is bigger than 10 s. It has proved the increase of busyness is caused by conflicts. Figure 4(b) further verify it, the conflict increase obviously when t_{job} is bigger than 10 s. However, both busyness and conflict fraction by using conflict prevention scheduling strategy is obviously lower than Omega's randomized first fit scheduling strategy. Especially under the m = 2 and d = 2 case, the efficiency of service scheduler is improved significantly.

Beside scheduler's busyness, we also use another metric to evaluate our approach. Generally, users evaluate the quality of schedulers by task startup latency which is the time from job submission to a task running, and a common production service level objective (SLO) for this time is 25 s. This time is influence by job's decision time and job's queuing time. Since job's decision time in the simulator is a defined by the linear function, so it is a fixed value. The job's queuing time is the viable part of the time. So we use job's queuing time as a metric to evaluate the performance of schedulers. As Fig. 5 shown, mean job queuing time of service jobs by using conflict prevention scheduling strategy is obviously smaller than by using Omega's randomized first fit scheduling strategy when t_{job} of service scheduler is bigger than 10 s. Compared to first fit scheduling strategy, conflict prevention scheduling strategy reduces median job wait time by 2–3× and reduces max job wait time by over 2× (Fig. 5(b)) when m = 1 and d = 2. When m = 2 and d = 2, conflict prevention scheduling strategy reduces median job wait time by bigger than 10×.

All experiments illustrate that using scheduling strategy to reduce conflict can improve efficiency of schedulers and conflict prevention scheduling strategy is a feasible solution for parallel schedulers in shared-state scheduling architecture.

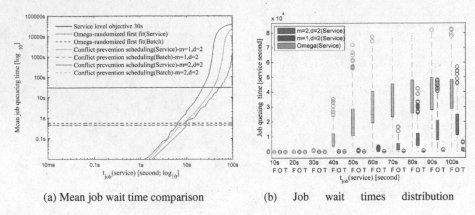

(a) Mean job wait time comparison   (b)   Job   wait   times   distribution

Fig. 5. Service jobs' mean job wait time comparison. Black horizontal lines indicate service level objective 30 s. Whiskers of (b) depict min and max, boxes depict median, 25th, and 75th percentiles, circles depict outliers.

5   Conclusions and Future Work

In this paper, our work explores how to alleviate interference between schedulers through scheduling strategy. We propose and implement a new strategy which called conflict prevention scheduling strategy in the simulator of Omega and found it can reduce conflicts between parallel schedulers and improve efficiency of schedulers, especially it significantly improves the efficiency of scheduler to place long decision time jobs.

Our Future work could usefully focus on those things:

Even we propose a new scheduling strategy for preventing conflicts, conflicts still exists in share-state scheduling system. We think conflicts are closely related to the usage of resources and they are difficult to be completely eliminated. In conflict prevention scheduling strategy, we only based on avoiding conflicts to choose machine, but not consider other scheduling goals, such as minimizing the number of abandoned tasks, picking machines that already have a copy of the task's packages and so on. Our future work will explore how to combine our scheduling strategy with Borg's scoring mechanism. Besides, in this paper, we only focus on propose an idea, however, in real scheduling system, how to give value to m and d is needed further investigation.

Acknowledgments. This work is supported by National Natural Science Foundation of China (No. 61363021, No. 61540061). We would like to thank the authors of Omega for their selflessness to public the simulator of Omega. This simulator make up for our lack of experimental environment.

References

1. Zaharia, M., Borthakur, D., Sen Sarma, J., Elmeleegy, K., Shenker, S., Stoica, I.: Delay scheduling: a simple technique for achieving locality and fairness in cluster scheduling. In: Proceedings of the 5th European Conference on Computer Systems (EuroSys 2010), pp. 265–278. ACM (2010)
2. Hindman, B., Konwinski, A., Zaharia, M., Ghodsi, A., Joseph, A.D., Katz, R., Shenker, S., Stoica, I.: Mesos: a platform for fine-grained resource sharing in the data center. In: Proceedings of the 8th USENIX Conference on Networked Systems Design and Implementation (NSDI 2011), pp. 295–308. ACM (2011)
3. Vavilapalli, V.K., Murthy, A.C., Douglas, C., Agarwal, S., Konar, M., Evans, R., Graves, T., Lowe, J., Shah, H., Seth, S., Saha, B., Curino, C., O'Malley, O., Radia, S., Reed, B., Baldeschwieler, E.: Apache Hadoop YARN: yet another resource negotiator. In: Proceedings of the 4th Symposium on Cloud, pp. 1–16. ACM (2013)
4. Schwarzkopf, M., Konwinski, A., Abd-El-Malek, M., Wilkes, J.: "Omega: flexible, scalable schedulers for large compute clusters. In: Proceedings of the 8th ACM European Conference on Computer Systems (EuroSys 2013), pp. 351–364. ACM (2013)
5. Ousterhout, K., Wendell, P., Zaharia, M., Stoica, I.: Sparrow: distributed, low latency scheduling. In: Proceedings of the Twenty-Fourth ACM Symposium on Operating Systems Principles (SOSP 2013), pp. 69–84. ACM (2013)
6. Boutin, E., Ekanayake, J., Lin, W., Shi, B., Zhou, J., Qian, Z., Wu, M., Zhou, L.: Apollo: scalable and coordinated scheduling for cloud-scale computing. In: Proceedings of the 11th USENIX Symposium on Operating Systems Design and Implementation (OSDI 2013), pp. 285–300. ACM (2013)
7. Verma, A., Pedrosa, L., Abd-El-Malek, M., Korupolu, M., Oppenheimer, D., Tune, E., Wilkes, J.: Large-scale cluster management at Google with Borg. In: Proceedings of the Tenth European Conference on Computer Systems (EuroSys 2015), p. 18. ACM (2015)
8. Delimitrou, C., Sanchez, D., Kozyrakis, C.: Tarcil: reconciling scheduling speed and quality in large shared clusters. In: Proceedings of the Sixth ACM Symposium on Cloud Computing (SoCC 2015), pp. 97–110. ACM (2015)
9. Mitzenmacher, M.: The power of two choices in randomized load balancing. IEEE Trans. Parallel Distrib. Comput. 12(10), 1094–1104 (2001)
10. Park, G.: Eneralization of multiple choice balls-into-bins. In: Proceedings of the 30th Annual ACM SIGACT-SIGOPS Symposium on Principles of Distributed Computing, pp. 297–298. ACM (2011)
11. Ren, Y., Shen, J., Wang, J., Han, J., Lee, S.: Mutual verifiable provable data auditing in public cloud storage. J. Internet Technol. 16(2), 317–323 (2015)
12. Shen, J., Tan, H., Wang, J., Wang, J., Lee, S.: A novel routing protocol providing good transmission reliability in underwater sensor networks. J. Internet Technol. 16(1), 171–178 (2015)
13. Guo, P., Wang, J., Li, B., Lee, S.: A variable threshold-value authentication architecture for wireless mesh networks. J. Internet Technol. 15(6), 929–936 (2014)
14. Xia, Z., Wang, X., Sun, X., Wang, Q.: A secure and dynamic multi-keyword ranked search scheme over encrypted cloud data. IEEE Trans. Parallel Distrib. Syst. 27(2), 340–352 (2015)
15. Isard, M., Prabhakaran, V., Currey, J., Wieder, U., Talwar, K., Goldberg, A: Quincy: fair scheduling for distributed computing clusters. In: Proceedings of the ACM SIGOPS 22nd Symposium on Operating Systems Principles, pp. 261–276. ACM (2009)

16. Bradley, D., Clair, T.S., Farrellee, M., Guo, Z., Livny, M., Sfiligoi, I., Tannenbaum, T.: An update on the scalability limits of the condor batch system. J. Phys: Conf. Ser. **331**(6), 062002 (2011)
17. Gale, D., Shapley, L.S.: College admissions and the stability of marriage. Am. Math. Mon. **69**(1), 9–15 (1962)
18. Kung, H.T., Robinson, J.T.: On optimistic methods for concurrency control. ACM Trans. Database Syst. (TODS) **6**(2), 213–226 (1981)
19. Papadimitriou, C.H.: Serializability of concurrent updates. J. ACM **26**(4), 631–653 (1979)
20. Eswaran, K.P., Gray, J.N., Lorie, R.A., Traiger, I.L.: The notions of consistency and predicate locks in a database system. Commun. ACM **19**(11), 624–633 (1976)
21. Chen, Y., Ganapathi, A.S., Griffith, R., Katz, R.H.: Design insights for MapReduce from diverse production workloads. Technical report UCB/EECS–2012–17, UC, Berkeley, January 2012
22. Kavulya, S., Tan, J., Gandhi, R., Narasimhan, P.: An analysis of traces from a production MapReduce cluster. In: Proceedings of 10th IEEE/ACM International Conference on (CCGrid 2010), pp. 94–103. IEEE (2010)
23. Reiss, C., Tumanov, A., Ganger, G.R., Katz, R.H., Kozuch, M.A.: Heterogeneity and dynamicity of clouds at scale: Google trace analysis. In: Proceedings of the Third ACM Symposium on Cloud Computing (SoCC 2012). ACM (2012)

Design and Performance Comparison of Modular Multipliers Implemented on FPGA Platform

Khalid Javeed[1,2], Daniel Irwin[2], and Xiaojun Wang[2(✉)]

[1] Electrical Engineering Department, COMSATS Institute of Information Technology Abbottabad, Abbottabad, Pakistan
[2] School of Electronic Engineering, Dublin City University, Dublin, Ireland
xiaojun.wang@dcu.ie

Abstract. Modular multiplier is the most critical component in many data security protocols based on public key cryptography (PKC). To provide data security in many real time applications, a high performance modular multiplier is of utmost importance. Two techniques mostly used for high speed modular multiplication are Montgomery Modular Multiplication (MMM) and Interleaved Modular Multiplication (IMM). This paper presents radix-2 hardware implementation of the MMM and IMM methods with detailed performance analysis. The designs are implemented in Verilog HDL and synthesized targeting Xilinx Virtex-6 FPGA platform. Synthesized results indicate that the radix-2 MMM design is better in terms of computation time, FPGA slice area and throughput as compared to the radix-2 IMM design.

Keywords: Public-key cryptography · Modular multiplication · Montgomery multiplicaiton · Interleaved multiplicaion

1 Introduction

With a plethora of Internet of Things (IOT), many new cryptographic protocols have evolved to provide data security in systems ranging from hand-held devices to large servers. These systems have different computing power, area, storage space, and bandwidth limitations. For example, hand-held devices are limited with resources as compared to the servers.

Traditional ways to construct security protocols are based on RSA techniques [16]. RSA based cryptosystems are not suitable for hand-held or resource constrained devices due to large key sizes that are typically in the range of 1024–3072 bits. During the last decade another PKC scheme has received tremendous attention, with key sizes in the range 160–256 bits which can provide the same level of security capability as RSA [1]. This scheme is based on manipulating points on suitably chosen elliptic curves, this is known as elliptic curve cryptography (ECC) [12,13]. Due to its potential of much higher security strength per bit as compared to RSA, its implementation on several new platforms has been explored.

© Springer International Publishing AG 2016
X. Sun et al. (Eds.): ICCCS 2016, Part I, LNCS 10039, pp. 251–260, 2016.
DOI: 10.1007/978-3-319-48671-0_23

Security protocols based on either RSA or ECC involves certain finite field operations such as modular addition, modular subtraction, modular multiplication, and modular division. Out of these finite field primitives, modular multiplication is a rigorous operation in RSA based cryptosystems. It is also a bottleneck in ECC implementation especially using projective coordinates, the technique which replaces modular division with more number of modular multiplication operations [6]. So, a modular multiplication is the component that limits the performance of data security protocols, therefore to meet speed requirements of many real time applications it is critical to have an optimized modular multiplier in an overall data security infrastructure.

The classical approach to perform a modular multiplication of given operands a, b modulo p is computed in two steps: integer multiplication and reduction modulo p given as follows:

$$d = a \cdot b$$

$$R = d \text{ modulo } p$$

The reduction modulo p step usually involves a division operation, which is a very time consuming operation on many software or hardware platforms. Therefore, to avoid the division operation, several techniques have been proposed which can mainly be categorised into three groups given as follows:

- Specialized primes
- Montgomery method [14]
- Interleaved method [3, 18]

Specialized primes are important to reduce the computational complexity of a modular multiplication operation in ECC implementation [6]. However, RSA implementation can not be benefited from the specialized primes. Interleaved Modular Multiplication (IMM) method is based on repeated additions and reduction of partial products. Partial products are accumulated and reduced individually to eliminate the final division. The idea is to reduce intermediate results below the modulus value in each iteration so that the final division can be omitted. The Montgomery Modular Multiplication (MMM) replaces the costly division operation by a cheap division by a power of 2 i.e., a right shift operation. MMM method is only applicable to operands in the Montgomery domain. Thus, to perform a modular multiplication using MMM method, operands and result must be converted from binary to Montgomery and from Montgomery to binary domains before and after the multiplication in Montgomery domain respectively. So this method requires extra computations beside the actual operation and are not suitable for a single modular multiplication. However, in RSA and ECC several consecutive modular multiplications are required. As the conversions in to and out of Montgomery domain is carried out only once, so the MMM method is very useful in ECC and RSA applications.

Several modifications of the IMM algorithm have been proposed [2, 5, 8, 9]. A radix-2 parallel architecture of IMM algorithm is introduced in [5]. The introduced parallelism perform the IMM critical operations concurrently. It computes a 256-bit modular multiplication operation in 3.2 us and consumes 3475 Virtex II pro

---

Algorithm 1. Interleaved Modular Multiplication (IMM)

Input: $a = \sum_{i=0}^{n-1} x_i \cdot 2^i$, $b = \sum_{i=0}^{n-1} y_i \cdot 2^i$, $p = \sum_{i=0}^{n-1} p_i \cdot 2^i$
Output: $c = a \times b \bmod p$
// n: number of bits in p //
1 $z := 0$
2 **for** $(i = n - 1;\ i \geq 0;\ i = i - 1)$ **do**
3 $\quad z := 2z \bmod p$
4 $\quad$ **if** $b_i = 1$ **then**
5 $\quad\quad | \quad z = z + a \bmod p$
6 **return** z

FPGA slices. [2] incorporated a sign detection and carry save reduction techniques to enhance the operating frequency of the IMM method. [8,9] utilized higher-radix and Booth encoding techniques to decrease the total number of loop iterations in the IMM algorithm. There are a lot of modifications to the MMM method since it was first published. A number of possible implementation strategies are discussed in [11]. Some of the modular multipliers based on MMM are presented in [7,10,17]. Comparison of IMM and MMM methods are discussed in [15].

This work presents radix-2 implementations of IMM and MMM methods on the same FPGA platform. The designs are evaluated on the basis of critical path delay, design space complexity, computation time, FPGA area consumption and throughput rate. This study is very useful to the cryptosystems designers in selection between IMM and MMM methods depending upon their applications.

This paper is organized as follows: IMM method and its hardware architecture is presented in Sect. 2. Section 3 described the MMM method with its hardware architecture. Implementation results and performance evaluation are presented in Sect. 4 while the Sect. 5 concludes the overall paper.

2   Interleaved Modular Multiplication

The Interleaved Modular Multiplication (IMM) is given in Algorithm 1. The algorithm starts traversing a multiplier from the most-significant-bit (MSB) to the least-significant bit (LSB). The internal operations in IMM algorithm are simple. In radix-2 (bit-wise) implementation there are a total of n iterations, where n is the bit length of the modulus p. In every iteration two operations are required: A single bit left-shift modulo p (step 3) and addition modulo p (step 5).

Accumulator contents z is left shifted and reduced by modulo p, then a multiplicand a is added if the respective multiplier bit (b_i) is equal to one. Therefore, in every iteration of the loop there are a single n-bit addition and two n-bit subtractions.

2.1 IMM Hardware Architecure

A hardware architecture to execute the IMM algorithm is shown in Fig. 1. It is comprised of a n-bit adder, two n-bit subtractors, one n-bit register z and some multiplexers to control the correct flow of data. Step 2 of the algorithm is controlled by a counter which is a part of a control unit not shown in Fig. 1.

Initially register z is loaded with zero. Then, an operation $z = 2z$ modulo p is executed in two steps: First z is single left shifted ($<<$). If the result is greater than or equal to a modulus p, then the modulus p is subtracted from the result. The $z = 2z$ modulo p operation is carried out by the first subtractor and a multiplexer.

An operation $z = z + a \bmod p$ is performed by the adder and the second subtractor of Fig. 1. The adder adds $z + a$ depending on the respective i^{th} bit of the multiplier b. The second subtractor subtracts the modulus p from the result and finally the desired value is loaded into the register z for the next iteration. Each iteration of Algorithm 1 on hardware architecture in Fig. 1 is executed in a single clock cycle. Therefore, the presented hardware architecture performs an n-bit modular multiplication operation in $n + 1$ clock cycles. The extra clock cycle is consumed for the final result output.

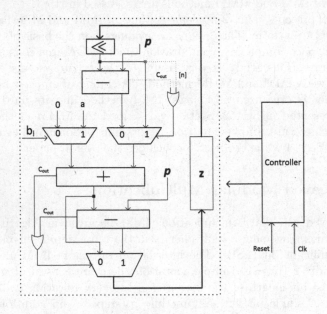

Fig. 1. Radix-2 hardware IMM architecture

3 Montgomery Modular Multiplication

As Montgomery Modular Multiplication (MMM) method works on operands in the Montgomery domain. Operands a and b have to be converted into Montgomery domain as follows:

Algorithm 2. Montgomery Multiplication [15]

Input: $a = \sum_{i=0}^{n-1} x_i \cdot 2^i$, $b = \sum_{i=0}^{n-1} y_i \cdot 2^i$, $p = \sum_{i=0}^{n-1} p_i \cdot 2^i$, $2^{n-1} < p < 2^n$
Output: $z = a \times b \times 2^{-n} \bmod p$
// n: number of bits in p //

1 $z := 0$
2 **for** $(i = 0; \ i \leq n - 1; \ i = i + 1)$ **do**
3 $\quad$ $z := z + a \cdot b_i$
4 $\quad$ **if** $z[0] = 1$ **then**
5 $\quad\quad$ $z = z + p$
6 $\quad$ $z = z$ div 2
7 **if** $z \geq p$ **then**
8 $\quad$ $z = z - p$
9 **return** z

$$\overline{a} = ar \text{ modulo } p$$

$$\overline{b} = br \text{ modulo } p$$

where $\overline{a}, \overline{b}$ are the Montgomery representations of a and b for some constant r and normally r is in powers of 2 i.e. $r = 2^n$.

A method described in Algorithm 2 is the radix-2 version of the MMM method [14]. Unlike the IMM method, it scanned a multiplier from right to left i.e. from the LSB to MSB. In every loop iteration there are two additions and one division operations. As the division by 2 is a free of cost right shift operation so only two additions per iteration of the loop are required. A final subtraction (step 8) is outside of the loop and executed only once. Note that for each iteration, the IMM algorithm requires two subtractions and one addition operations but in the MMM only two additions are required. A modified design reported in [4] reduced the required number of adders from two to one by pre-computing $a + p$ and in each iteration an appropriate value from $(0, a, p, a + p)$ is added.

3.1 MMM Hardware Architecture

Hardware architecture to execute Algorithm 2 is shown in Fig. 2. It is comprised of two $n + 1$-bit adders, two multiplexers and one data register z. Initially register z is loaded with zero. The first adder performs addition of accumulator z and respective partial product $(a \cdot b_i)$. Then the result of the first adder is conditionally added with a modulus p if it is an odd number which is true if LSB is equal to one and false otherwise. Note that $>>$ represents a single bit right shift operation which is required to divide z by 2 in step 6 of Algorithm 2.

This process is repeated in every loop iteration. As the total number of iterations in Algorithm 2 is n, so the given architecture takes n clock cycles to complete the loop iterations. In the last step (step 8) of the algorithm a conditional subtraction operation is required. This operation can be achieved

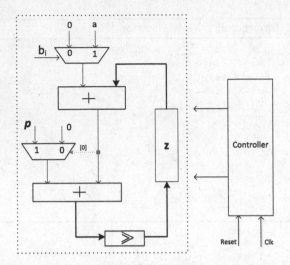

Fig. 2. Radix-2 hardware MMM architecture

by any of the integrated adder. It takes an extra two clock cycles, therefore the MMM method performs an n-bit modular multiplication operation in $n+2$ clock cycles. For example, a 512-bit modular multiplication is performed in 514 clock cycles.

4   Implementation Results

The IMM and MMM multiplier designs presented in this paper are coded in Verilog HDL and simulations of the designs are carried out using Modelsim. Synthesis of the designs are performed using Xilinx ISE 14.2 Design Suite targeting Virtex-6 FPGA devices. Synthesis results of the presented designs are demonstrated in Table 1 for a number of different bit sizes. The IMM architecture computes a 256-bit modular multiplication in 2.72 µs, consumes 1540 Virtex-6 FPGA Look-Up-Tables (LUTs). It can run at a maximum frequency of 94 MHz. For the same bit length, the MMM architecture takes 1.675 µs, consumes 1534 LUTs and achieves a maximum frequency of 154 MHz. Which shows that the IMM multiplier is almost 62 % slower than the MMM multiplier.

A parallel IMM multiplier design reported in [5] is based on Montgomery powering ladder approach. Carry select approach is adopted to reduce the long carry propagation delay in the adder circuit. The parallel IMM multiplier computes a 256-bit modular multiplication operation in 1.48 µs, consumes 3072 LUTs and operates at a maximum frequency of 174 MHz on the same platform. These performance results of [5] are observed by our implementation of [5] on Virtex-6 FPGA. It is almost 84 % and 13 % faster than the IMM and MMM designs, respectively. In [8], radix-4 and radix-8 Booth encoded interleaved multipliers are presented. The radix-4 Booth encoded multiplier reduced 50% of the

Table 1. Virtex-6 FPGA implementation results of modular multipliers

Design	Bit-length	Frequency (MHz)	Slice LUTs	Time (μs)
IMM	160	128	961	1.24
IMM	192	114	1153	1.68
IMM	224	103	1348	2.17
IMM	256	94	1540	2.72
IMM	384	69	2309	5.56
IMM	512	55	3077	9.30
IMM	1024	30	6149	34.2
MMM	160	207	958	0.78
MMM	192	186	1150	1.04
MMM	224	169	1342	1.34
MMM	256	154	1534	1.68
MMM	384	115	2302	3.36
MMM	512	92.5	3070	5.56
MMM	1024	51	6142	20.1
[5]	160	191	2002	0.84
	192	184.6	2401	1.04
	224	179.1	2787	1.25
	256	174	3207	1.48
[8]	160	91.6	2911	0.88
	192	89	3511	1.08
	224	87.3	4053	1.29
	256	85.5	4606	1.5

total number of loop iterations in the IMM algorithm. It is 81 % faster than the IMM and 12 % faster than the MMM multipliers, respectively.

A straight forward comparison on the basis of computation time and resource consumption may not be adequate for the detailed performance analysis, other factor needs to be considered. Designs optimized to meet different targets can not be compared directly. Another performance metric is known as area-delay product described as AT/B. AT/B is the product of area and computation time per bit. In Table 2, IMM and MMM designs are compared on the basis of AT/B value and throughput rate. It is evident from Table 2 that the MMM multiplier design has higher throughput rate and lower AT/B value as compared to the IMM multiplier. However, the parallel IMM multiplier [5] and radix-4 Booth encoded IMM multiplier [8] are better than the MMM multiplier in terms of throughput rate, however, they have higher AT/B value which depicts that they require more hardware resources than the MMM multiplier.

Table 2. Virtex-6 FPGA implementation results of modular multipliers

Design	Bit-length	AT/B	Throughput (Mbps)
IMM	160	7.44	129
IMM	192	10.08	144.2
IMM	224	13	103.2
IMM	256	16.36	94.11
IMM	384	33.4	69
IMM	512	55.89	55
IMM	1024	205.36	29.9
MMM	160	4.67	205
MMM	192	6.23	184.6
MMM	224	8.03	167.2
MMM	256	10.03	152.8
MMM	384	20.14	114.28
MMM	512	33.33	92.1
MMM	1024	120.56	50.9
[5]	224	5.55	179.2
	256	6.92	171.8
[8]	224	8.33	173.6
	256	9.02	171.8

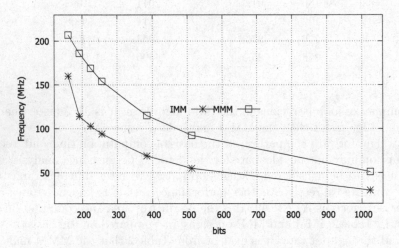

Fig. 3. IMM vs MMM frequency comparison

On a concluding remark, the experimental results shown in Figs. 3 and 4 reveal that the MMM method without any optimization is better than the IMM method for repeated modular multiplication operations. The results did not

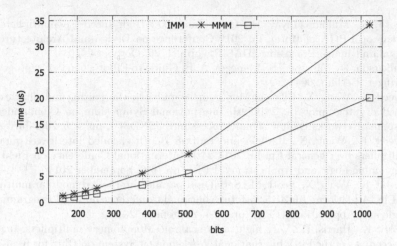

Fig. 4. IMM vs MMM computation time comparison

include the conversion cost which is required in the case of MMM multiplier. Hence, applications where only one or few modular multiplications are required then the IMM method is a better choice to avoid the conversion cost.

5   Conclusion

This paper introduced two bit-level hardware implementations to perform modular multiplication operation over a finite field of prime characteristics. The proposed architectures are based on Montgomery and Interleaved Multiplication algorithms. The proposed designs have been implemented in Verilog HDL and have been synthesized on Xilinx Virtex-6 FPGA platform. The presented designs are evaluated on the basis of computation time, FPGA resource consumption and throughput rate. The experimental results revealed that Montgomery based multiplier design is better in terms of computation time, resource consumption and throughput rate.

References

1. IEEE standard specifications for Public-Key cryptography - amendment 1: Additional techniques. IEEE Std 1363a–2004 (Amendment to IEEE Std 1363–2000), pp. 1–167, September 2004
2. AbdelFattah, A.M., El-Din, A.M.B., Fahmy, H.M.: An efficient architecture for interleaved modular multiplication
3. Blakely, G.: A computer algorithm for calculating the product AB modulo M. IEEE Trans. Comput. **C–32**(5), 497–500 (1983)
4. Bunimov, V., Schimmler, M., Tolg, B.: A complexity-effective version of Montgomery's algorithm. In: Workshop on Complexity Effective Designs, ISCA 2002, May 2002

5. Ghosh, S., Mukhopadhyay, D., Chowdhury, D.: High speed Fp multipliers and adders on FPGA platform. In: 2010 Conference on Design and Architectures for Signal and Image Processing (DASIP), pp. 21–26, October 2010
6. Hankerson, D., Vanstone, S., Menezes, A.J.: Guide to Elliptic Curve Cryptography. Springer, Berlin (2004)
7. Javeed, K., Wang, X.: Efficient Montgomery multiplier for pairing and elliptic curve based cryptography. In: 2014 9th International Symposium on Communication Systems, Networks Digital Signal Processing (CSNDSP), pp. 255–260, July 2014
8. Javeed, K., Wang, X.: Radix-4 and radix-8 Booth encoded interleaved modular multipliers over general Fp. In: 2014 24th International Conference on Field Programmable Logic and Applications (FPL), pp. 1–6, September 2014
9. Javeed, K., Wang, X., Scott, M.: Serial and parallel interleaved modular multipliers on FPGA platform. In: 2015 25th International Conference on Field Programmable Logic and Applications (FPL), pp. 1–4, September 2015
10. Kelley, K., Harris, D.: Very high radix scalable Montgomery multipliers. In: 2005 Proceedings of the Fifth International Workshop on System-on-Chip for Real-Time Applications, pp. 400–404, July 2005
11. Koç, C., Acar, T., Kaliski Jr., B.S.: Analyzing and comparing Montgomery multiplication algorithms. IEEE Micro **16**(3), 26–33 (1996)
12. Koblitz, N.: Elliptic curve cryptosystems. Math. Comput. **48**(177), 203–209 (1987)
13. Miller, V.S.: Use of elliptic curves in cryptography. In: Williams, H.C. (ed.) CRYPTO 1985. LNCS, vol. 218, pp. 417–426. Springer, Heidelberg (1986)
14. Montgomery, P.L.: Modular multiplication without trial division. Math. Comput. **44**(170), 519–521 (1985)
15. Narh Amanor, D., Paar, C., Pelzl, J., Bunimov, V., Schimmler, M.: Efficient hardware architectures for modular multiplication on FPGAs. In: 2005 International Conference on Field Programmable Logic and Applications, pp. 539–542, August 2005
16. Rivest, R., Shamir, A., Adleman, L.: A method for obtaining digital signatures and public-key cryptosystems. Commun. ACM **21**, 120–126 (1978)
17. Shigemoto, K., Kawakami, K., Nakano, K.: Accelerating Montgomery modulo multiplication for redundant radix-64k number system on the FPGA using dual-port block rams. In: 2008 IEEE/IFIP International Conference on Embedded and Ubiquitous Computing, EUC 2008, vol. 1, pp. 44–51. IEEE (2008)
18. Sloan Jr., K.R.: Comments on a computer algorithm for calculating the product AB modulo M. IEEE Trans. Comput. **34**(3), 290–292 (1985)

Cloud-Based Video Surveillance System Using EFD-GMM for Object Detection

Ce Li[1], Jianchen Su[1], and Baochang Zhang[2(✉)]

[1] China University of Mining and Technology, Beijing, China
{celi,jcsu}@cumtb.edu.cn
[2] Beihang University, Beijing, China
bczhang@buaa.edu.cn

Abstract. Nowadays, new generation of video surveillance systems integrates lots of heterogeneous cameras to collect, process, and analyze video for detecting the objects of potential security threats. The existing systems tend to reach the limit in terms of scalability, data access anywhere, video processing overhead, and massive storage requirements. A novel cloud computing can provide scalable and powerful techniques for large-scale storage, processing, and dissemination of video data. Furthermore, the integration of cloud computing and video processing technology offers more possibilities for efficient deployment of surveillance systems. This paper deploys the framework of a cloud-based video surveillance system and proposes an EFD-GMM approach for object detection in the overhead video processing. A prototype surveillance system is also designed to validate the proposed approach. It finally shows that the proposed approach is more efficient than GMM in video processing of cloud-based system.

Keywords: Video surveillance · Cloud computing · Object detection · EFD-GMM

1 Introduction

Modern video surveillance systems are composed of lots of heterogeneous cameras distributed over variety of sites [1]. The systems collect, process, and analyze different video streams to detect objects of potential security threats. Despite of significant benefit, there are important problems concerned in systems which are scalability, resource utilization, ubiquitous access, searching, processing, and storage to support large-scale surveillance. To solve the issues, a novel cloud-based surveillance systems [2] has been possessed and developed with improved processing capability and storage.

The existing work studies design and implement of the cloud-based surveillance system, for example, dependability characteristics [3], resource allocation [4], video recording [5], cloud storage mechanism [2], and cloud computing suitability for video surveillance [6]. However, there are also some significant research challenges to develop a cloud-based video surveillance system. For instance, the strategy for video acquisition and storage over the cloud, the technique for effective processing of video data and its manifold structure. Therefore, a whole cloud-based video surveillance framework is in need to address two abovementioned challenges.

© Springer International Publishing AG 2016
X. Sun et al. (Eds.): ICCCS 2016, Part I, LNCS 10039, pp. 261–272, 2016.
DOI: 10.1007/978-3-319-48671-0_24

Some researchers have attempted potential directions for cloud-based video surveillance systems. But cost [7] and security [8] make some organizations difficulty to choose cloud-based solutions. Even some may argue that a cloud approach may seem not needed on account of strong local control in surveillance data acquired [9]. Nevertheless, with the availability of cloud-based video surveillance solutions and strong research on cloud technology, the signs of its potential growth become obvious. In this paper, the framework of a cloud-based video surveillance system is designed and deployed, and a novel approach is proposed for object detection in video processing.

Gaussian Mixture Model (GMM) has been widely applied in background model and video processing [15]. However, it have some weakness of convergence, sensitive to ambient noise and sudden light change, and prone to detect false target. Inspired by the edge information with efficient noise suppression, an improved algorithm based on Edge Frame Difference and GMM (EFD-GMM) is proposed to model the background and detect the moving object. The paper validates it on a deployed prototype surveillance system, and further discuss the detecting performance on two public datasets.

The remainder of this paper is organized as follows. Section 2 describes the related work, and Sect. 3 introduces the framework of a cloud-based video surveillance system. Section 4 explains the proposed method for object detection in video processing. Experimental result and analysis are given in Sect. 5, and conclusion in Sect. 6.

2 Related Work

Video surveillance over cloud is an emerging research area. Literature review shows that there is a growing interest in adopting the cloud technology in this new area [10]. A cloud-based video surveillance system is first proposed in [2] with emphasis on storage. The paper analyzed the storage requirements of a cloud-based surveillance system different with the traditional one, and also investigated a secure cloud storage system and a video transmission optimization. Karimaa [3] studied the dependability of video surveillance technologies over cloud, such as the authority, security, maintainability and reliability characteristics of the cloud-based video surveillance solutions.

Recently, Neal [7] explored whether cloud computing is suitable for high-resolution video surveillance management system, and cloud computing is considered a suitable application for video surveillance management system. However, there are issues of cost and other threats to study. Next, Hossain [6] discussed the solutions of cloud-based video surveillance with some reservation to security and privacy aspects. In the paper [5], Lin not only designed a Hadoop distributed file system for recording system, but also provided store backups and monitoring features for video processing tasks. Cucchiara [11] concentrated on the deployment of a software to realize video service platform and object detection in multicamera surveillance system. Hossain proposed a dynamic resource allocation mechanism for service composition in cloud afterwards [4], and suggested that a number of virtual machines need to be optimally utilized for multiple surveillance services. All the above works demonstrate different aspects of system, and some especially focus on the strategy for video acquisition and storage to the cloud.

As for video processing in the cloud-based surveillance system, the results of object detection play important roles in providing information for better video processing. From the multiple cameras, images quality in video are always impacted even being corrupted by noise. There is a challenging work in object detection. Several previous works have been carried out on object detection, in particular like clustering approach, mean shift-based method [12], graph-based method [13], Bayesian-based method [14]. Gaussian Mixture Model (GMM) [15] is well known, but the main drawback of GMM is that the prior distribution does not depend on the pixel index and not on the spatial relationship between the labels of neighboring pixels. Thus, the object detection is extremely noise prone and illumination dependent, even prone to detect false target.

To overcome these disadvantages, Liu employed K-means clustering for GMM initialization to increase the function convergence rate [16], there is still the problems of poor anti-interference ability and easily noise prone when modeling background when coping with videos in complicated environment. Wei introduced three frame difference into GMM to restrain error detection rate of moving object [17]. However, this approach is difficult to adapt the light change and easily get incomplete object because of the three frame difference. Similarly, Mahnood [18] applied the frame difference in edge detection. Although it eliminate the influence of illumination change, the approach has low accuracy of detecting moving object for it is hard to get a complete object in the foreground. Overall, the above works improve the technique of effective video processing from different aspects, so this paper concentrates to develop a distinctive algorithm which is contribute to dealing with the issues of noise prone, illumination dependent and false target in detection.

3 Framework for a Cloud-Based Video Surveillance System

In view of a cloud-based video surveillance system, there are several issues to explore for framework deployment. System requirements analysis, system architecture design, core system modules and system prototype deployment are described as follows.

3.1 System Requirements Analysis

By analyzing the cloud-based video surveillance system, four main function requirements are listed in Fig. 1, user manager, system setting, cloud-based video manager and video surveillance service. User manager module is composed of the operations of creating, updating, retrieval, and deleting system users. The users usually access to the system by heterogeneous devices from anywhere and subscribe the abnormal event happening on heterogeneous video providers, so the system setting module is necessary to include the providers, networks and devices. Cloud-based video manager module is the overall management of cloud-based operations, which bridges between users and video surveillance service. Besides, the functions in video surveillance service include object detection, event analysis and abnormal warning.

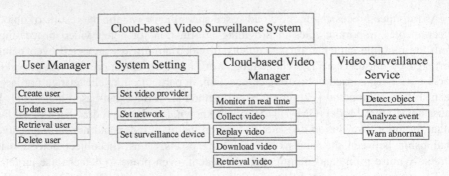

Fig. 1. The chart of system requirements analysis

3.2   System Architecture Design

Figure 2 shows the architecture of the designed cloud-based video surveillance framework. The system can be deployed on a private cloud in the system used by our single organization at present. Two core system modules are in the cloud, cloud video manager and video surveillance service. Located in the cloud side, notification and sharing mechanism is a vital part of the framework, which facilitates acquiring video streams as well as spreading the events of interest to the appropriate clients. It can provide high scalability for ubiquitous video surveillance service, connect and deliver video streams to various video providers and surveillance users [6]. In this architecture, some types of video providers exists, such as fixed cameras, IP cameras, and PTZ cameras. The video stream from multiple devices is transmitted to the cloud through the notification and sharing mechanism. System users with proper authentication can configure the connected devices and control video capturing and delivering.

3.3   Core System Modules

In the cloud architecture, there are two core system modules in Fig. 2, cloud video manager and video surveillance service. The following paragraphs elaborate the modules.

Cloud Video Manager. In the framework, the overall management of the cloud based operations are cloud providers, resource allocation and monitoring statistic.

1. *Cloud Providers.* To encounter high demand for large storage and huge amount of data to process continuous videos [2, 3], cloud providers connect different types of network storage devices to meet specific requirements of system [19].
2. *Resource Allocation.* Cloud resources are computational in the form of virtual machines (VMs) [20]. Various VMs are managed and allocated to run associated services [21] by dynamically configuring capacities following the current workload.
3. *Monitoring Statistic.* Because of the readily available resource usage whenever, the monitoring statistic component is responsible for system monitoring and usage tracking of cloud resources, and provides statics of requests and usage cost.

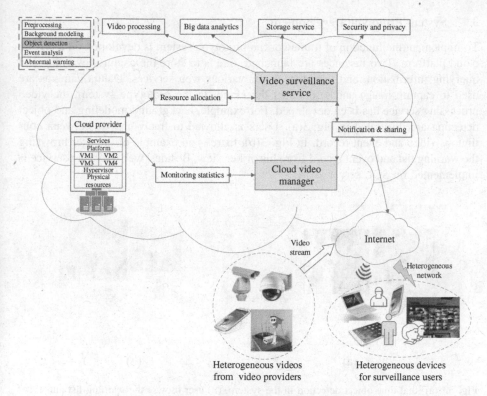

Fig. 2. The designed architecture for a cloud-based video surveillance system.

Video Surveillance Service. The system is a service oriented system in essence, so all function components are designed as services over the internet, including video processing, big data analytics, storage, security and privacy.

1. *Video Processing.* The cloud-based processing seems promising due to the enormous video processing capability that can be leveraged. The tasks of video processing are preprocessing, background modeling, object detection, event analysis, and abnormal warning, in Fig. 2. Due to different video types, networks and devices, object detection is the first and foremost task to identify abnormal events and generate warnings.
2. *Big Data Analytics.* Big data analytics service is used to determine that whether it improves the fidelity of information or timelines of response.
3. *Storage Service.* Storage service provides a database for intelligent video processing. Important factors like vendor lock-in, disaster recovery capability, elasticity, and payment structure are concerned.
4. *Security and Privacy.* Security and privacy policy must be in place for deployment to secure videos, identify authentication and enforce privacy for access control.

3.4   System Prototype Development

To implement the function of framework, a prototype system is developed on a private cloud platform. Two instances are launched, one is to store the captured warning and querying information, and the other is for various web services. Dahua cameras are used to capture image and to connect the cloud. In the prototype system, the video processing service has been developed. For example, background modeling and object detecting are illustrated in Fig. 3(a). Users is allowed to freely choose between continuous video and event record. In Fig. 3(b), there is an example of the user browsing the warning list and event record from his or her view. Besides, web querying service is implemented on SQL server 2014.

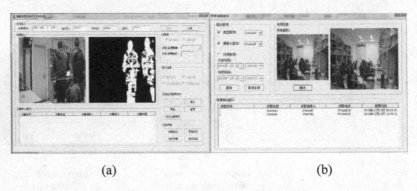

(a)   (b)

Fig. 3. (a) Real-time object detection in the system, (b) user browse the warning list and event record in the system.

4   Proposed Method for Object Detection in Video Processing

As mentioned above, object detection is one of the key task for video processing service in the system. During video processing, GMM has been widely applied in background model and object detection. However, it have some weakness of convergence, sensitive to ambient noise and sudden light change, and prone to detect false target. Therefore, to overcome the disadvantages, we improve traditional GMM in OpenCV library and propose a novel EFD-GMM approach for object detection.

The flowchart of method is described in Fig. 4. Firstly, frame difference is introduced into GMM background model, which quickly distinguishes the background and moving region to extract the foreground. Then, the background model is mixed with the edge frame difference, and different updating rates are adopted during modeling to accelerate the speed of convergence for noise suppression and illumination independent. Finally, image AND operation is performed among the foreground information detected by background model, the blob information calculated by frame difference, and contour information gotten from edge frame difference. The approach has improvements on noise suppression, shadow removal and false target elimination, because of the processes of adding frame difference to GMM and integrating edge frame difference.

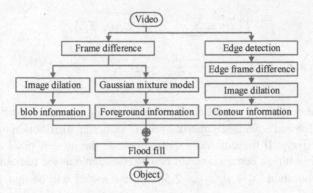

Fig. 4. Flowchart of proposed method.

4.1 Adding Frame Difference to GMM

GMM uses several frames to model background at the beginning. In the complicated scene, the background could hardly be modeled, for the background is shaded by the moving objects in most of the time. Thus, we consider the frame difference method [22] as the compensation for foreground extraction, and then rectify it using the blob information dilated from the frame difference image.

We first calculate the difference image among successive frames, using a threshold T to get a binary image to distinguish background and foreground coarsely. The process is described as follows. A count value C for each pixel ($0 \leq C \leq m$) is initialized as $m/2$ (m is the upper limit of C), two frames f_t and f_{t-1} are used to detect the foreground in

$$C = \begin{cases} C - 1/\beta & |f_t(i,j) - f_{t-1}(i,j)| \leq T \\ C + 1 & |f_t(i,j) - f_{t-1}(i,j)| > T \end{cases},$$

$$\alpha = \frac{2C}{m} \times \alpha \qquad (0 \leq C \leq m) \tag{1}$$

where β is a coefficient determined by camera parameters. The pixel is identified as the background and the count C increases if the difference between two frames are not more than T, and vice versa. The updating rate α is dynamic according with the C. If the frame variation is great, α will increase. The threshold T consists of T_c and T_r. T_r is a fixed empirical value 30, and T_c is an optimum factor with the change of frame.

$$T = T_c + T_r, \qquad T_c = \frac{1}{N} \sum_{i,j} |f_t(i,j) - f_{t-1}(i,j)|. \tag{2}$$

Moreover, if the pixels changes rapidly in the video frame, GMM will be updated sooner with the updating rate α for background modeling. To construct GMM, each pixel is modeled by a mixture of K Gaussian distributions. The sample value of a certain pixel point $P(x,y)$ is $\{X_1, X_2, \ldots, X_t\}$, the probability of the present observed pixel value X_t in t^{th} time is

$$P(X_t) = \sum_{i=1}^{k} \omega_{i,t} \eta \left(X_t, \mu_{i,t}, \Sigma_{i,t} \right), \tag{3}$$

$$\eta(X_t, \mu_{i,t}, \Sigma_{i,t}) = \frac{1}{(2\pi)^{n/2} |\Sigma_{i,t}|^{1/2}} e^{-\frac{1}{2}(X_t - \mu_{i,t})^T \sum_{i,t}^{-1} (X_t - \mu_{i,t})}. \tag{4}$$

Where, K is the quantity of model components, and $\omega_{i,t}$, $\mu_{i,t}$ and $\Sigma_{i,t}$ are the weighted value, mean value and covariance matrix of the ith Gaussian distribution of the model in t^{th} time, respectively. If the difference value between the present pixel and the background model is within a certain range, it can be considered as the background. That is, if it meet the condition $\left| X_t - \mu_{i,t-1} \right| > 2.5\sigma_{i,t-1}$, the model will be updated by

$$\begin{cases} \omega_{k,t} = (1-\alpha)\omega_{k,t-1} + \alpha \left(M_{k,t} \right) \\ \mu_t = (1-\rho)\mu_{t-1} + \rho X_t \\ \sigma_t^2 = (1-\rho)\sigma_{t-1}^2 + \rho(X_t - \mu_t)^T (X_t - \mu_t) \\ \rho = \alpha\eta(X_t | \mu_k, \sigma_k) \end{cases}. \tag{5}$$

The updating speed of GMM mainly depends on learn rate α. $M_{k,t}$ is 1 for the matched model or 0 for the remaining distributions. If none of them match the current pixel, the least probable distribution will be replaced by a new with the current mean, the initialized high variance, and a low prior weight. α is determined by the frame difference process, the learning rate ρ, μ and σ are updated. Finally, for background estimation [24], we can sort order of K Gaussian distributions according to ω/θ, and suppose the first B distributions as the background models.

$$B = \arg \min \left(\sum_{k=1}^{b} \omega_{k,t} > T \right). \tag{6}$$

4.2 Integrating Edge Frame Difference

Although the combination of frame difference and GMM make the convergence of model better, the updating and estimation of model is still vulnerable to the sudden light change. We adopt the method of Canny edge detection [22] on frame difference image, then integrate the contour information from edge frame difference (EFD) to the foreground mask for sake of removing the false target. The basic idea is that the edge frame difference in false area is robust to the moving object in foreground, displayed in Fig. 5. Surely, there is a drawback of edge frame difference that the foreground contour has some inner cavity. Therefore, we perform the image AND operation among the blob, foreground and contour information, then flood fill the foreground to get a complete object. In fact, the experimental result in the next section validate that the EFD and GMM are really mutual reinforcing to suppress noise, remove shadow and eliminate false target. Moreover, the performance of EFD-GMM can pave the basis for the next steps of event analysis and abnormal warning. In our system, a LIB linear SVM [23] classifier is learned to determine whether the event of object is abnormal or not.

Fig. 5. The original image and edge frame difference image.

5 Experimental Result and Analysis

To verify the proposed algorithm, the comparison experiments are made in video sequences from different scenes. They are carried out on the client of the developed system prototype. We run the experiments on Pentium(R) E700@3.2 GHz CPU unit, dual CPU core, 2 GB memory, drive with 64-bit windows file system in Microsoft server. Two datasets belong to Kyushu University and Institute of Automation of Chinese Academy of Sciences are used to test various situations, such as sudden light changes, a pedestrian comes into the scenery and stay for a while, and ambient noise. Besides, we set the parameters of our algorithm K, α and T to 5, 0.03 and 0.85 in trials.

In Fig. 6, we compare the original GMM [19], EFD [27] and the proposed EFD-GMM methods to validate the performance on an indoor video with quick lighting changes. The examples from the 25th frame, 541th frame, 857th frame in the original video are located in the first column (corresponding to Fig. 6(a1, (b1) and (c1), respectively). The results of object detection by original GMM are in second column in Fig. 6, the results of EFD are in the third column, and the EFD-GMM results are in fourth column. It is obvious that the method of EFD-GMM gets the best performance in the extracted foreground and object detection, for we exclude lots of unnecessary moving points in background updating. Moreover, by comparison between the second and third column, EFD can indeed perform better than GMM when light is changing.

In Fig. 7, we also compare the GMM, EFD and EFD-GMM to validate the performance on an outdoor video while a pedestrian starts walking instead of squatting. The example from the 100th frame in the original video are Fig. 7(a), and the results of object detection by GMM, EFD and EFD-GMM are in Fig. 7(b), (c) and (d), respectively. It shows that there is a false target around the object detected by GMM, because pixels of the long-time stationary target are gradually recognized as the background, and part of them is left in the foreground once the target moves suddenly. In contrast, our proposed EFD-GMM can update model timely to remove the false target.

In Fig. 8, the results in a complicated outdoor situation with waving leaves are compared. The example from the 331th frame in the video are Fig. 8(a), and the results of object detection by GMM, EFD and EFD-GMM are in Fig. 8(b), (c) and (d), respectively. In Fig. 8(b) and (c), the leaves are detected as the object, but they are ambient noise in fact. EFD-GMM is robust on this situation and has the ability of noise suppression in Fig. 8(d) compared with the other methods. In total, 3338 frame videos

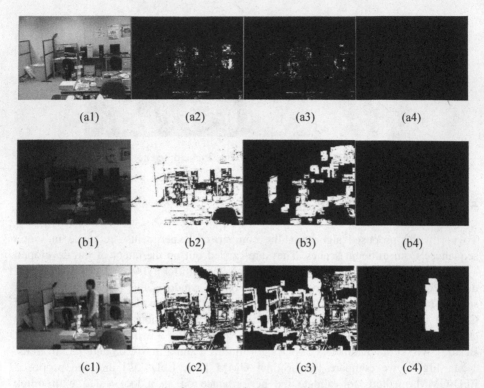

Fig. 6. The examples from the 25th frame, 541th frame, 857th frame with sudden light changes.

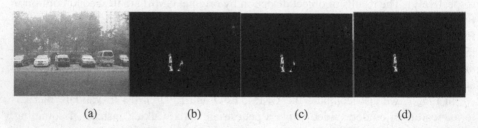

Fig. 7. The example from the 100th frame while a pedestrian starts walking instead of squatting.

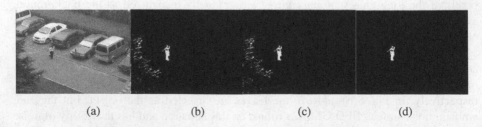

Fig. 8. The example from the 331th frame with waving leaves.

are involved in the experiments. The object detection rate (DR) and false alert rate (FAR) of EFD-GMM is 98 % and 2 %, and DR has an increase of 14 % and FAR has a decrease of 7 %. To sum up, the proposed EFD-GMM method for object detection in video processing service of our developed system prototype.

6 Conclusion

To integrate lots of heterogeneous cameras and analyze numerous video for detecting the objects of potential security threats, this paper develop a new cloud-based video surveillance system. Based on the system requirements analysis, the architecture framework is designed with two core system modules. In the video surveillance service, to fulfill the key task of video processing, a novel EFD-GMM approach is proposed for object detection. A prototype system is developed on the designed cloud architecture to validate the proposed approach. The experimental results show that the approach is effective and robust than GMM in complicated scenes from various video providers. However, the classifier for abnormal analysis needs improvement, and the cost remains a decisive factor to embrace the cloud-based surveillance. Therefore, future works may be directed to these issues for video surveillance application.

Acknowledgement. The work was supported in part by the Natural Science Foundation of China under Contract 61272052, 61473086, 61672079, 61601466, in part by PAPD, in part by CICAEET, and in part by the National Basic Research Program of China under Grant 2015CB352501. The work of B. Zhang was supported by the Program for New Century Excellent Talents University within the Ministry of Education, China, and Beijing Municipal Science & Technology Commission Z161100001616005. Ba-chang Zhang is the corresponding author.

References

1. Raty, T.D.: Survey on contemporary remote surveillance systems for public safety. IEEE Trans. Syst. Man Cybern. C Appl. Rev. **40**(5), 493–515 (2010)
2. Ren, Y.J., Shen, J., Wang, J., Han, J., Lee, S.: Mutual verifiable provable data auditing in public cloud storage. J. Internet Technol. **16**(2), 317–323 (2015)
3. Karimaa, A.: Video surveillance in the cloud: dependability analysis. In: Proceedings of 4th International Conference on Dependability, pp. 92–95 (2011)
4. Hossain, M.S., Hassan, M.M., Qurishi, M.A., Alghamdi, A.: Resource allocation for service composition in cloud-based video surveillance platform. In: Proceedings of IEEE International Conference on Multimedia and Expo Workshops, pp. 408–412 (2012)
5. Lin, C.F., Yuan, S.M., Leu, M.C., Tsai, C.T.: A framework for scalable cloud video recorder system in surveillance environment. In: Proceedings of 9th International Conference on Ubiquitous Intelligence & Computing and Autonomic & Trusted Computing, pp. 655–660 (2012)
6. Hossain, M.A.: Analyzing the suitability of cloud based multimedia surveillance systems. In: Proceedings of 15th IEEE International Conference on High Performance Computing and Communications (2013)

7. Neal, D., Rahman, S.: Video surveillance in the cloud. J. Crypt. Inf. Secur. **2**(3) (2015)
8. Sabahi, F.: Cloud computing security threats and responses. In: Proceedings of 3rd International Conference on Communication Software and Networks, pp. 245–249 (2011)
9. Venters, W., Whitley, E.A.: A critical review of cloud computing: researching desires and realities. J. Inf. Technol. **27**(3), 179–197 (2012)
10. Hossain, M.A.: Framework for a Cloud-based Multimedia Surveillance System. J. Distrib. Sens. Netw. (2014)
11. Cucchiara, R., Prati, A., Vezzani, R.: Designing video surveillance systems as services. In: Proceedings of 2nd Workshop on Video Surveillance Projects, Italy (2011)
12. Li, J., Li, X.L., Yang, B., Sun, X.M.: Segmentation-based image copy-move forgery detection scheme. IEEE Trans. Inf. Forensics Secur. **10**(3), 507–518 (2015)
13. Shi, J., Malik, J.: Normalized cuts and image segmentation. IEEE Trans. PAMI **22**(8), 888–905 (2000)
14. Li, S.Z.: Markov Random Field Modeling in Image Analysis. Springer, Heidelberg (2009)
15. Zhang, B.C., Perina, A., Li, Z.G., Murino, V., Liu, J.Z., Ji, R.R.: Bounding multiple gaussians uncertainty with application to object tracking. IJCV **118**, 364–379 (2016)
16. Zhang, B.C., Li, Z.G., Perina, A., Bue, A.D., Murino V.: Adaptive local movement modelling (ALMM) for object tracking. In: IEEE Transactions on CSVT (2016)
17. Zhang, B.C., Perina, A., Murino, V., Bue, A.D.: Sparse representation classification with manifold constraints transfer. In: Proceedings of CVPR, pp. 4557–4565 (2015)
18. Mahmood, A.M., Maras, H.H., Elbasi, E.: Measurement of edge detection algorithms in clean and noisy environment. In: Proceedings of 8th International Conference on Application of Information and Communication Technologies, pp. 1–6 (2014)
19. Shen, R.: Building a cloud-enabled file storage infrastructure. Tech Republic White Paper, F5 Network (2013)
20. Sotomayor, B., Montero, R.S., Lorente, I.M., Foster, I.: Virtual infrastructure management in private and hybrid clouds. IEEE Internet Comput. **13**(5), 14–22 (2009)
21. Beloglazov, A., Buyya, R.: Energy efficient resource management in virtualized cloud data centers. In: Proceedings of 10th IEEE ACM International Symposium on Cluster, Cloud, and Grid Computing, pp. 826–831 (2010)
22. Liu, X.D., Yu, Y., Liu, B., Li, Z.: Bowstring-based dual-threshold computation method for adaptive canny edge detector. In: Proceedings of International Conference of Image and Vision Computing, New Zealand, pp. 13–18 (2013)
23. Gu, B., Sheng, V.S., Tay, K.Y., Romano, W., Li, S.: Incremental support vector learning for ordinal regression. Trans. Neural Netw. Learn. Syst. **26**(7), 1403–1416 (2015)
24. Pan, Z.Q., Kwong, S., Sun, M.T., Lei, J.J.: Early MERGE mode decision based on motion estimation and hierarchical depth correlation for HEVC. IEEE Trans. Broadcast. **60**(2), 405–412 (2014)

Enhanced Edge Detection Technique
for Satellite Images

Renu Gupta(✉)

Department of Computer Science and Engineering,
ITM University, Gwalior, Gwalior, India
renugupta1248@gmail.com

Abstract. Traditional Canny edge detection algorithm is sensitive to noise, therefore when filtering out this noise weak edge information gets lose easily. In response of these problems an improved canny edge detection algorithm was proposed by Weibin Rong, Zhanjing Li, Wei Zhang and Lining Sun. The improved canny algorithm introduces the concept of gravitational field intensity to obtain the gravitational field intensity operator while replacing image gradients. Based on standard deviation and the mean of image gradient magnitude were put forward for two kinds of typical image among which one has the rich edge information and another has relatively poor edge information. The experimental results says that algorithm preserve more edge information but it's computing speed was relatively slow. In response of these problem this paper proposes an Enhanced edge detection algorithm which uses the concept of double derivative Gaussian filter and is much faster than the improved canny algorithm. The Experimental Analysis has been done based on time, peak-signal to noise-ratio (PSNR) and entropy which states that algorithm preserves more edge information and is more robust to noise.

1 Introduction

Edges provide important information towards human image understanding. It is the most essential processing step in human picture recognition system. Now-a-days, in image processing research a key problem is Edge detection. With the help of edge detection method find out change in material properties, discontinuities in surface orientation, discontinuities and different variations in scene illumination. There are different ways to implement edge detection. But, most of the methods may be grouped into either Gradient and Laplacian, Derivative Approach and Pattern Fitting Approach, or search-based and zero-crossing based. Several existing edge detection methods include [1] such as Sobel, Canny, Prewitt, Laplician of Gaussian, Robert edge detection method. The detection methods commonly applied differ in smoothing filter's types and the way the measures of edge strength are computed. Various detection methods were based on computation of image gradients, they also differ in the types of filters used for computing gradient estimates in the x- and y-directions [2]. For this paper work we are taking satellite images as the data set. Satellite images are being used in many fields of research and information gathering. Satellites today are prime source of capturing information and making conclusions by corporate houses, research

X. Sun et al. (Eds.): ICCCS 2016, Part I, LNCS 10039, pp. 273–283, 2016.
DOI: 10.1007/978-3-319-48671-0_25

organizations and government departments like weather forecasting, agricultural monitoring etc. Satellite images can prove helpful in reliable decisions regarding weather forecast, geographical monitoring. In many different formats information received by satellite images. The most generally used weather satellite channels used are visible, infrared, and water vapor satellites. Among them every Channel on the satellite sensors is sensitive to energy (electromagnetic energy) at a specific range of frequencies; therefore each type gives a different vision of the Earth, its oceans and its atmosphere. Analysts depend on every one of the three sorts of information, and regularly utilize them together to better comprehend the communications between the Earth's surface, climate and seas. Brief description of these types of images is done below (Table 1).

Table 1. Type of satellite image

Types of satellite images		
Visible imagery	Infrared imagery	Water Vapor imagery
These images can be viewed at the day time only because the sunlight reflects through clouds. On visible images, the cloud shown in white, ground in grey and water in dark color. At the time of winter season the ground is covered of snow which makes more difficult to distinguish from clouds. Looping images is solution that differentiates between clouds and snow; clouds can move from one place to another while the snow can't.	In this kinds of images show clouds at both time in day and night. Infrared satellite images show clouds in both day and night. In infrared images clouds are recognized by satellite sensors that measures heat radiating off from them. Sensors also calculate heat radiating off the earth surface. It can also used for fog and low clouds identification	In this kind of image amount of moisture present in troposphere (nearly from 15,000 to 30,000 ft). The white area represents the high humidity while dark color represent Water vapor images are useful for indicating where heavy rain is possible.

1.1 Existing Edge Detection Algorithm

Several existing edge detection methods include [1] Sobel, Prewitt, Robert, Canny etc. among which canny method preserves more useful edge information and is more robust to noise. The process of traditional canny edge detection method is explained here with its advantages and limitations.

1.1.1 Traditional Canny Edge Detector
Canny filter was developed by John F. Canny (JFC) in 1986 [3]. Canny filter is optimal with regards the following-

Canny is an edge detection operator, which uses a multi-stage algorithm to find out the wide range of edges in image. The algorithm follows the steps given below-

1) Smoothing: Smoothing refers to blur the image to remove the noise presented in the image.

2) Finding Gradients: When the gradients of the image have large magnitudes, the edge should be marked.

3) Non-Maximum Suppression: According to the Canny's algorithm, only local maxima should be marked as edge. And remove the pixels which are not the part of the edge.

4) Double Thresholding: The algorithm uses two thresholds Upper threshold and Lower threshold. If the pixel gradient have the higher value than the upper threshold, then the pixel will be marked as an edge. And the pixel will be discarded, if the gradient value is below the lower threshold. And if the threshold value lies between the two threshold then only that pixel is marked as an edge which is connected above the upper threshold.

5) Edge Tracking by Hysteresis: At the last step of algorithm, final edges are determined by suppressing all the edges that are not connected to very strong edges.

1.1.2 Problem of Traditional Canny Edge Detector Algorithm

Although the traditional canny edge detection algorithm is more widely used in practical engineering, there are still two aspects to improve.

The first one is that, to calculate image's gradient value, the traditional canny edge detection algorithm accepts the first order limited difference of 2×2 neighboring area [4]. This algorithm was simple and easy to realize but was more sensitive to noise due do the fact that deviation on the direction of $45°$ and $135°$ was not joint so weak edge information gets lost easily. And the second one is that canny set a fixed value for double threshold. The traditional canny algorithm shows poor adaptability for those images having rich edge information. And it is easy to lose local characteristics edge information.

In response to these problems improved canny edge detection algorithm was introduced which uses the concept of gravitational field intensity to replace the image gradient and also proposed two adoptive threshold selections.

1.1.3 Improved Canny Edge Detector Algorithm

The gravitational field intensity was introduced in this paper to replace image gradient, and the 2×2 operator was extended to 3×3 operator [4]. This paper put forward two adaptive double-threshold selection methods for two kinds of typical images based on the mean and standard deviation of image gradient. The improved algorithm not only keeps the advantages of the traditional Canny algorithm, but also it enhances the ability of noise suppression and keeps more edge information, i.e. it has higher SNR. This algorithm can obtain threshold automatically, which has higher practical value in the practical engineering application.

1.1.4 Problem of Improved Canny Edge Detector Algorithm

The detection results of algorithm are superior to the ordinary first-order, second-order edge detection algorithm (Roberts, Sobel, Laplacian, etc.) and the traditional Canny algorithms, but its computing speed is relatively slow, which need to be further improved.

2 Literature Survey

Lots of work towards edge detection for satellite images has been done. This section represents the analysis of some pre-research's towards the particular area and explains the advantages and limitations.

Two adaptive double-threshold selection methods has been put forward [4] for two kinds of typical images based on the mean and standard deviation of image gradient. The improved algorithm not only keeps the advantages of the traditional Canny algorithm, but also it enhances the ability of noise suppression and keeps more edge information, i.e. it has higher SNR. This algorithm can obtain threshold automatically, which has higher practical value in the practical engineering application. The detection results of algorithm are superior to the ordinary first-order, second-order edge detection algorithm (Roberts, Sobel, Laplacian, etc.) and the traditional Canny algorithms, but its computing speed is relatively slow, which need to be further improved.

A hybrid approach for edge detection presented in [5]. By this technique, edge detection is performed in two phase. In first phase, for image smoothing applied canny algorithm and in second phase neural network is to detecting actual edges. Neural network is a wonderful tool for edge detection. As it is a non-linear network with built-in thresholding capability. Neural Network can be trained with back propagation technique using few training patterns but the most important and difficult part is to identify the correct and proper training set.

Edge detection is developed [6] for satellite image using fuzzy logic concept. Fuzzy logic helps to find and highlight all the edges associated with an image by checking the relative pixel values. Scanning of an image using the windowing technique takes place which is subjected to a set of fuzzy conditions for the comparison of pixel values with adjacent pixels to check the pixel magnitude gradient in the window. After the testing of fuzzy conditions the appropriate values are allocated to the pixels in the window under testing to provide an image highlighted with all the associated edges.

A novel approach for edge detection in satellite images based on cellular neural networks proposed in [7]. CNN based edge detector in used conjunction with image enhancement and noise removal techniques, in order to deliver accurate edge detection results, compared with state of the art approaches. Thus, considering the obtained results, a comparison with optimal Canny edge detector is performed. The proposed image processing chain deliver more details regarding edges than canny edge detector. The proposed method aims to preserve salient information, due to its importance in all satellite image processing applications.

An algorithm that depends on type-2 fuzzy sets to manage automatically selects threshold values uncertainties is proposed in [8]. Algorithm is required to divide the gradient image using existing Canny's edge detection algorithm. Results of their proposed work well in different medical images (hand radiography images).

A new image mosaic method is proposed [9] based on the performance limitations of the SIFT descriptor of a square area, as well as a matching time that is too long because of the complex descriptor. The new method devises an improved 18-dimensional feature descriptor consisting of 12-gradient values in a circular window, a three-cumulative gray-scale value and a three-gray-scale difference in a concentric circular window.

This descriptor reduces the computing complexity and decreases the dimensions of descriptor. It also retains the feature points in a 16-neighborhood near the Canny edges and requires less computing time. The new method improves the quality of the image mosaic and the stitching efficiency and robustness. The results indicate that the efficiency of image mosaic can be improved even alongside variations in scale, parallax and rotation. It is a stable, high precision and automatic image mosaic method and can be applied practically.

The study in [10] implementing a gray-level transformation and the Canny edge detector into the work flow for discontinuity characterization. The gray level transformation generates newzero-Mean data for recharacterizing seismic features with non-zero mean amplitude variation, and the Canny edge detector helps more effectively capture amplitude changes associated with dis- continuities. The added value of the new algorithm is verified through applications to a fluvial channel system in Stratton field (Texas) and fracture dresser or sat Teapot Dome (Wyoming) and offshore Netherlands (North Sea). Compared to the traditional similarity, amplitude-gradient, and semblance schemes, the new algorithm produces better images of channels, faults, and fractures Along with their orientation in the subsurface.

A new edge detection algorithm [11] decomposes the source image firstly by wavelet lifting transform, and during ED for high-frequency information use of the wavelet modulus maximum algorithm, and for low-frequency information the Canny operator is used. Lifting algorithm speeds the image decomposition; the self-adaptive processing of update operators well reserves the local structural feature information; when the image is decomposed, column and row transformations decrease the computational complexity and memory requirement the different algorithms being respectively used for high-frequency and low-frequency component make higher edge detection precision. The proposed result is more accurate and faster than Canny operator and traditional wavelet algorithm in edge extraction.

3 Proposed Algorithm

To overcome with the problems of traditional canny algorithm and improved canny algorithm explained above, An enhanced edge detection algorithm have been proposed. This proposed algorithm uses the double derivative Gaussian filter to enhance the computing speed. The algorithm follows the given steps-

The proposed process starts with selecting an image w[350 350]. If selected image is in RGB format convert it into gray by using function rgb2gray(w) and if image is gray, no further action required. Then apply two dimensional median filter medfilt2(w, [3 3]) for smoothing. Set the thresholding parameter Alfa = 0.125 and fixed the value of sigma at 1. Then at step 5, to find the value of filter apply d2gauss function for x-axis direction and y-axis direction edge detection and assign the values of x and y respectively to the filter. Assume the Gaussian-like function G is written as:

$$G(x, y) = e^{\frac{-(x^2+y^2)}{\sigma^2}} \tag{1}$$

Where $\sigma^2$is the variance of the Gaussian-like function. The oriented Gaussian-like second derivative $G_{2\ominus}$ is defined as:

$$G_{2\theta} = cos^2(\theta)G_{xx} - 2\cos(\theta)G_{xy} + sin^2(\theta)G_{yy} \qquad (2)$$

After this at step 6, convolution is used to find out the derivative of both Ix and Iy direction. For this input image w is convolved with the oriented Gaussian-like second derivative filter, and the resultant image is

$$I_X = G_{2\theta} * w \qquad (3)$$

$$I_y = G_{2\theta} * w \qquad (4)$$

After above process, fint out the magnitude of Ix and Iy for that normalization of gradient has been done by combining the x and y directional derivatives.

$$NVI = sqrt(Ix. * Ix + Iy. * Iy) \qquad (5)$$

Then thresholding is done by finding the max and min value of I and do leveling.

$$level = alfa * (I_{max} - I_{min}) \qquad (6)$$

where I_max and I_min is the maximum and minimum value of I and alfa is predefine above 0.125.

After thresholding process the thinning has been done using interpolation to discover pixels where the gradient norms are local maximum.

Then find out the PSNR with the help of the given formula.

$$PSNR = 10 * \log((double(m)^2)/e \qquad (7)$$

Where m = max(max(pic1)); e = MeanSquareError (pic1, pic2); pic1 = origImg and pic2 = distImg.

And compute the entropy of the difference image (I-y).

$$E = -\sum_{(i=0)}^{(N-1)} p(xi)logp(xi) \qquad (8)$$

Where E: Entropy; N: Maximum gray level values; p(xi): Probability of occurrence of xi.

4   Experimental Analysis

For the experiments, this paper used *MATLAB* to test the performance of improved Canny algorithm and Enhanced algorithm for satellite images and carried out the research experiments on the three types of color satellite images (visible, infrared and water vapor).

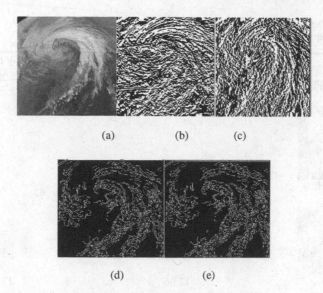

(a)   (b)   (c)

(d)   (e)

Fig. 1. Experiments for visible satellite image: (a) Original image, (b) Horizontal gradient image, (c) Vertical gradient image, (d) Improved canny method image, (e) Proposed method image (Color figure online)

Figure 1 shows the edge detection results on visible satellite image which is an RGB image. Figure 1(a) shows the original visible satellite image. Figure 1(b) and (c) shows the horizontal and vertical gradient images respectively. Figure 1(d) shows the output of edge detection by improved canny method and Fig. 1(e) shows the output of enhanced edge detection technique for satellite images.

Comparison has been done in terms of PSNR, Time and Entropy and the results says proposed algorithm is more robust to noise and it can preserve more useful edge information. The proposed algorithm has better edge detection results so it is more competitive. The proposed algorithm has great practical values in microscopic visual Edge Detection engineering.

Table 2 Shows the comparison between PSNR values of canny algorithm, improved canny algorithm and proposed algorithm. PSNR is a ratio often used as the quality measurement between the original and the compressed image. The more PSNR, the better quality of reconstructed or compressed image. The results of proposed algorithm gives the more PSNR values so the better quality of image as compared with the other two.

Table 3 shows the computing time taken by the improved canny algorithm and proposed algorithm. The comparative results shows that the computing speed of improves canny algorithm was relatively slow, which has been improved by the proposed algorithm.

Edge Detection Technique for satellite Images

Table 4 shows the comparison of Entropy values of improved canny algorithm and proposed algorithm. Image entropy is used to describe the amount of coded information in an image. Any image having high entropy has a great deal of contrast from one pixel

Table 2. Shows comparison of PSNR between improved Canny algorithm and enhanced edge detection technique for satellite images

Images	PSNR of Improved Canny Algorithm	PSNR of Enhanced Canny Algorithm
Visible Satellite Imagery	11.27	25.14
Infrared Satellite Imagery	9.12	20.60
Water Vapor Satellite Imagery	12.06	23.84

Table 3. Shows comparison of TIME between improved Canny algorithm and enhanced edge detection technique for satellite image.

Images	Time of Improved Canny Algorithm	Time of Enhanced Canny Algorithm
Visible Satellite Imagery	16.56	3.13
Infrared Satellite Imagery	16.48	3.61
Water Vapor Satellite Imagery	20.10	7.08

Table 4. Shows comparison of entropy between improved Canny algorithm and enhance

Images	Entropy of Improved Canny Algorithm	Entropy of Enhanced Canny Algorithm
Visible Satellite Imagery	0.5670	0.4374
Infrared Satellite Imagery	0.7145	0.5896
Water Vapor Satellite Imagery	0.5905	0.4156

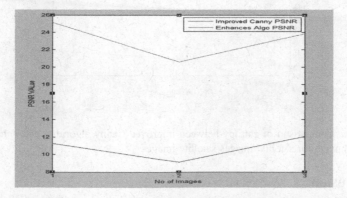

Fig. 2. Shows comparison of PSNR between improved Canny algorithm and enhanced edge detection technique for satellite images satellite images

to another and consequently cannot be compressed as much as the low entropy image. It means more information can be compressed to the image having low entropy as compare to the image that is having high entropy value. And the comparative results shows that the proposed algorithm having low entropy that means the reconstructed image by proposed algorithm can have more compressed information (Figs. 2, 3, and 4).

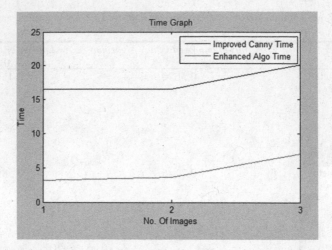

Fig. 3. Shows comparison of TIME between improved Canny algorithm and enhanced edge detection technique for satellite images satellite images

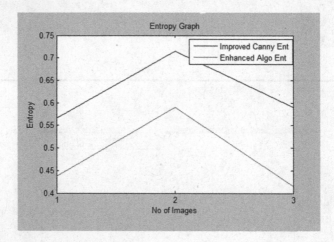

Fig. 4. Shows comparison of entropy between improved Canny algorithm and enhanced edge detection technique for satellite images satellite images

5   Conclusion

The proposed algorithm in this paper uses the two dimensional Gaussian filter to reduce the computing time for edge detection. The improved algorithm not only keeps the advantages of the existing Canny algorithm, but also it enhances the ability of noise suppression and keeps more edge information, i.e. it has higher PSNR and lower Entropy. This algorithm can obtain threshold automatically, which has higher practical value in the practical engineering application. The detection results of algorithm are superior to the ordinary first-order, second-order edge detection algorithms (Roberts, Sobel, prewitt etc.) and the existing Canny algorithms.

References

1. Bustince, H., Barrenechea, E., Pagola, M., Orduna, R.: Construction of interval type-2 fuzzy images to represent images in grayscale: false edges. In: Proceedings of IEEE International Conference Fuzzy System, London, U.K., pp. 73–78 (2007)
2. Bustince, H., Barrenechea, E., Pagola, M., Fernandez, J.: Interval-valued fuzzy sets constructed from matrices: application to edge detection. IEEE Trans. Fuzzy Sets Syst. **160**, 1819–1840 (2009)
3. Canny, J.: A computational approach to edge detection. IEEE Trans. Pattern Anal. Mach. Intell. **8**, 679–714 (1986)
4. Rong, W., Li, Z., Zhang, W., Sun, L.: An improved canny edge detection algorithm. In: Proceedings of 2014 IEEE International Conference on Mechatronics and Automation, August 3–6, Tianjin, China (2014)
5. Rani, P., Tanwar, P.: A nobel hybrid approach for edge detection. IJCSES **4**(2), 27–38 (2013)
6. Shenbagavalli, R., Ramar, K.: Satellite image edge detection using fuzzy logic. IJES **2**(1), 47–52 (2013)
7. Gazi, O.B., Belal, M., Abdel-Galil, H.: Edge detection in satellite image using cellular neural network. IJACSA **5**(10), 61–70 (2014)
8. Biswasa, R., Sil, J.: An Improved Canny Edge Detection Algorithm Based on Type-2 Fuzzy Sets, 2212-0173 © 2012 Published by Elsevier Ltd. doi:10.1016/j.protcy.2012.05.134
9. Chena, Y., Xua, M., Liub, H.-l., Huanga, W.-N., Xing, J.: An improved image mosaic based on Canny edge and an 18-dimensional descript. http://dx.doi.org/10.1016/j.ijleo.2014.04.069, 0030-4026/© 2014 Elsevier Gmb
10. Di, H., Gao, D.: Gray-level transformation and Canny edge detection for 3D seismic discontinuity enhancement. http://dx.doi.org/10.1016/j.cageo.2014.07.011 0098-3004/Published by Elsevier Ltd
11. Zhang, X., Zhang, Y., Zheng, R.: Image edge detection method of combining wavelet lift with Canny operator 1877-7058 © 2011 Published by Elsevier Ltd. doi:10.1016/j.proeng.2011.08.247

Phone Call Detection Based on Smartphone Sensor Data

Huiyu Sun$^{(\boxtimes)}$ and Suzanne McIntosh

Department of Computer Science, New York University, New York, NY 10012, USA
{hs2879,sm4971}@nyu.edu

Abstract. Smartphones are now equipped with as many as 30 embedded sensors, which have been widely used in human activity recognition, context monitoring, and localization. In this paper, we propose a phone call detection scheme using smartphone sensor data. We design Android applications to record, upload and display smartphone sensor data. We show how proximity and orientation sensors together can be used to accurately predict phone calls. Furthermore, the activity state during a phone call can be classified into three categories: sitting/standing, lying down, and walking. Features are extracted from proximity and orientation sensors to determine the range of values satisfying each state. Our system achieves an overall accuracy of 85 %.

Keywords: Human activity recognition · Smartphone sensors · Phone call detection

1 Introduction

Smartphones nowadays are equipped with embedded sensors, some are equipped with as many as 30 different types. They can be separated into three broad categories: motion sensors, environmental sensors, and position sensors. Motion sensors such as accelerometer, gravity sensor, gyroscope, and rotational vector sensor measure acceleration forces and rotational forces along three axes. Environmental sensors such as barometer, photometer, and thermometer measure various environmental parameters like air temperature and pressure, illumination, and humidity. Position sensors such as orientation sensor and magnetic field sensor measure the physical position of the smartphone.

Smartphone sensors have been applied to various areas of research such as human activity recognition (HAR) [1–3,7–9], environmental context monitoring [4,11], and localization [5,13,17]. They are powerful compared to traditional sensors in that a smartphone is rechargeable solving the power restriction problem, it has decent computing ability, and it has a decent storage capacity. The most used sensors are accelerometer, magnetic sensor, orientation sensor, and gyroscope sensor.

The current human activity recognition research based on smartphones mainly classifies human activities into one of the following broad categories:

© Springer International Publishing AG 2016
X. Sun et al. (Eds.): ICCCS 2016, Part I, LNCS 10039, pp. 284–295, 2016.
DOI: 10.1007/978-3-319-48671-0_26

sitting, standing, walking, and running. There are very few researches on phone call recognition based on smartphone sensors. Phone call detection satisfies the research demand and the user demand. Also through phone call detection, we can perform deeper analyses on human activities. We first show that proximity and orientation sensor can be effectively used to determine phone calls, then we extract features and classify phone calls into three states: sitting/standing, lying down, and walking.

The remainder of this paper is organized as follows. Section 2 discusses related works. Section 3 shows how smartphone sensors can be used to successfully detect phone calls. Section 4 describe our experimental setting and results. Section 5 presents potential future research areas. Section 6 concludes with a summary of our findings.

2 Related Works

Shoaib et al. [1] proposed a physical activity recognition schema using the less commonly used smartphone sensors gyroscope and magnetometer. They used seven classifiers and recognized six physical activities: walking, jogging, ascending stairs, descending stairs, sitting, and standing. They also showed that the accelerometer and gyroscope complement each other, making the recognition process more reliable.

Bedogni et al. [2] used accelerometer and gyroscope sensors data collected by smartphones to detect a user's motion type: walking, by train or by car. They found the existence of specific sensors data patterns associated with each motion type and extracted features as such. Then they compared different classification algorithms and showed that utilizing multiple sensors inputs significantly improve the accuracy of the classifiers. They also integrated their algorithm into an Android application, allowing specific smartphone configuration to each detected motion type.

Wang et al. [8] proposed a game theory-based feature selection method to evaluate the features of human activity recognition. Relevant and distinguished features that are robust to the placement of sensors are selected. They trained a k-nearest neighbor and support vector machine classifiers to recognize the human activities from waist and ankle. Dai et al. [3] proposed a highly efficient system to achieve early detection of dangerous vehicle maneuvers typically related to drunk driving and alert users. They used acceleration based sensor readings and compared patterns with real driving tests. Jalal et al. [7] proposed a real-time life logging systems that provide monitoring, recording and recognition of daily human activities using video cameras, offering life-care and health-care services at homes. Liu et al. [9] proposed a human activity recognition method based on the p-Laplacian regularization to preserve the local geometry, which is a non-linear generalization of standard graph Laplacian and has tighter isoperimetric inequality.

Douangphachanh et al. [4] used accelerometer, GPS sensor and camera sensor to estimate road surface roughness conditions to achieve low cost and easy to implement. Their model is based on experiments and frequency domain analysis, which they found the 3-axis acceleration and speed, has a linear relationship with road surface roughness condition. Majethia et al. [11] uses external and smartphone-interfaced wireless sensors to evaluate the sensitivity and accuracy of the ambient temperature sensor under various circumstances and measure its performance against standardized weather monitoring equipment. Ongenae et al. [12] envisions an ambient-intelligent patient room containing numerous devices to sense and adjust the environment, monitor patients and support caregivers. The also developed a smartphone application to receive and assess calls.

Zhang et al. [5] proposed a location tracking service that leverages the sensor hints on the smartphone to reduce the usage of GPS. They utilized orientation and accelerometer readings to achieve selective sampling of the GPS, and utilized the Gaussian process regression to reconstruct the trajectory from the recorded location samples. They showed that their system can significantly reduce the usage of GPS at the same time achieving a high tracking accuracy. Liu et al. [12] proposed an economic and easy-to-deploy indoor localization model suitable for ubiquitous smartphone platforms. They processed embedded inertial sensors readings through a inertial localization system, and a particle filter is developed to integrate the building map constraints and inertial localization results to estimate the user's location. He et al. [13] presents an adaptive motion model for tracking the movement of smartphone users by using the accelerometer, gyroscope and magnetometer sensors. They used a particle filter based estimator to fuse the motion model with a WiFi based indoor localization system.

Mizouni et al. [6] proposed a business service model based on smartphone sensors. They proposed a service using many smartphone sensors to form a smartphone sensor network, replacing traditional wireless sensor networks (WSN) based on the insufficiencies of existing WSNs: power restriction, limited computational abilities, and storage restriction. Lin et al. [15] proposed a proximity sensor based no-touch mechanism for smartphones by applying proximity sensors to initiate mobile applications without the need of touching the screen. Li et al. [17] developed a navigation algorithm, which fuses the WiFi received single strength indicator and smartphone inertial sensor measurements. A sequential Monte Carlo filter is developed for inertial sensor based tracking.

3   Phone Call Detection

In this section, we show how proximity and orientation sensor together can be used to determine whether a phone call is taking place.

Proximity and orientation sensor are monitored on a real-time basis, and data is uploaded onto our server where analyses are taken place. On the server, if the proximity sensor readings satisfy our predefined range of values (P-thresholds), we then analyze the three axes readings of the orientation sensor (O-thresholds). And if they all satisfy their set of range of values, we arrive at the preliminary conclusion that a phone call has been detected. Next we describe the set of features extracted from each sensors to achieve phone call detection.

3.1   Feature Extraction

We recorded the proximity sensor and orientation sensor readings before, during and after 48 phone calls. For proximity sensor, the only feature is its value. Since a non-zero value indicates an object is close to the phone's screen, we just use this as the feature. For orientation sensor, we extracted four features from the y-axis and z-axis readings in each of the 48 phone calls that we recorded: average, maximum, minimum, and standard deviation.

After features have been extracted, we first carry out feature reduction. Redundant value in the y-axis and z-axis of the orientation sensor are removed. We used a window size of 0.5 s, if the previous reading and the reading after 0.5 s are substantially different, it is counted as redundant feature and is removed. Figure 1 shows the result after redundant features have been removed. Substantial difference is when the absolute difference between the previous and current value is greater than $90°$, and the sum of the two values are close to $180°$, which is described by the following equations:

$$|y(i-1) - y(i)| > 90 \tag{1}$$

$$170 < |y(i-1) + y(i)| < 190 \tag{2}$$

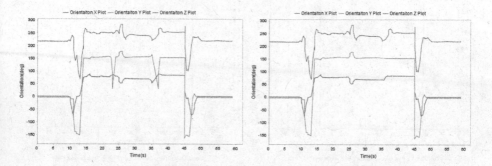

Fig. 1. Orientation sensor x, y, z-axis readings before (*left*) and after (*right*) redundant features have been removed.

3.2   Call State Classification

We classify the state during a phone call into three classes: sitting/standing, lying down, and walking. We calculated feature values of the orientation sensor readings in the y-axis for each of the three classes for the data from the 48 phone calls we recorded. This is shown in Table 1. Each entry has a range of between 10 to $25°$ in either direction. This is to be expected since the range of motions during a phone call varies and hence the orientation sensor reading varies accordingly. The feature values here are used as the O-thresholds when

Table 1. Feature values (°) for each of the three states for orientation sensor y-axis readings

	Sitting/standing	Lying down	Walking
Average	−92	150	−87
Maximum	10	13	18
Minimun	−45	170	−40
Std. Dev	−135	130	−140

determining whether a phone call has taken place. The proximity threshold, P-threshold, is any non-zero value, which indicate that an object is close to the phone's screen.

The maximum and standard deviation feature values in the table overlaps quite a bit, therefore using these two features alone we would not be able to classify phone calls into the states. The minimum feature values for sitting/standing and walking also overlaps, so classifying into these two states using the minimum

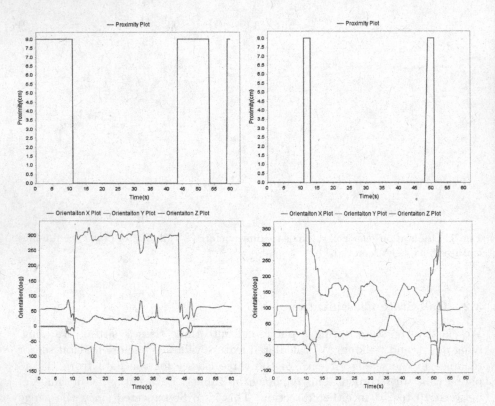

Fig. 2. Proximity sensor (*top two*) and orientation sensor (*bottom two*) readings used to detect phone calls and is classified into the sitting/standing state.

is also not possible. However, the average feature values in the table for the three different states are mostly mutually exclusive. Together, we can confidently classify each detected phone call into one of these three categories based on the four feature values.

Figure 2 shows the orientation and proximity sensor readings for two phone calls recorded that was classified into the sitting/standing state. The left two graphs are associated with one phone call, and the right two graphs are associated with the other. A sliding window of 1 min is used here. The top left graph show that the proximity sensor satisfied the P-threshold between 11 to 44 s, and 54 to 58 s. And then analyze the orientation sensor readings during those two periods. The bottom right graph shows the corresponding orientation sensor readings. Between 11 and 44 s, each of the four features (avg, min, max, and SD) are all within their range of values for sitting/standing, therefore the O-threshold is satisfied. And We deduce that between 11 and 44 s, the user was in a phone conversion in which he/she was sitting or standing. Now, between 54 and 58 s, we see that the average for the y-axis reading is 0, which does not satisfy the O-threshold, therefore, the possibility of a phone call is eliminated.

The top right graph satisfies the P-threshold between 0 and 11 s, 13 and 47 s, and 51 and 60 s. We see from the bottom right graph that of the three intervals, only 13–47 s satisfy the O-threshold features of sitting/standing. Therefore, a phone call was taken place during 13 and 47 s in which the user was sitting or standing.

4   Experimental Result

In this section, we describe our system architecture of collecting and analyzing smartphone sensor data, and describe the stages of data acquisition, processing, display and storage. We then compare our system's performance against others. We also present our two Android smartphone applications used to collect and display the data. The system architecture is shown in Fig. 3.

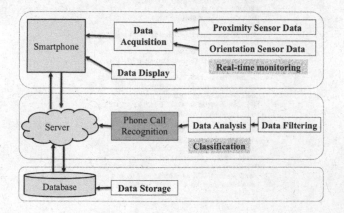

Fig. 3. System architecture.

Smartphone sensor data is acquired from the user's phone and is uploaded onto our server where analyses are taken place. At the server, data is also being stored onto our database for training purposes. There is also a user interface provided to the smartphone users.

4.1 Data Acquisition

We designed an Android application to read smartphone's sensor data. Our application reads the proximity sensor and orientation sensor reading among others in a sampling window of size T seconds. We also acquire the user's current location via GPS. Figure 4. shows the user interface used for data acquisition. The sensor readings are monitored on a real-time basis and uploaded onto our server. Here the user can choose the upload frequency T in seconds, for the purpose of phone call detection, the default is set to 0.2 s, meaning 5 samples are uploaded onto our server every second. However, uploading this many samples per second drains the battery very fast and uses up valuable network bandwidth. So when the purpose is to monitor the user's smartphone regularly, we can choose a much smaller upload frequency, such as 60 s, meaning a sample is uploaded every minute.

Data acquired from smartphones are uploaded onto our server, which is then stored onto our database. All data acquired are persisted to the database. At the server, relevant data is retrieved from the database. Data is filtered and then analyses are done on the real-time data and if a phone call has been detected, the event is recorded.

Fig. 4. Androd app user interface showing readings acquired from smartphone's sensors.

4.2 Data Display

We also designed an Android application displaying results on data collected from different users. The app displays useful information regarding a user's current state and his/her current surrounding environments. This is achieved through collecting and analyzing the data obtained from sensors embedded in the user's smartphone. Figure 5 shows the user interface presenting many features of the application.

User's current locations are displayed on Google maps using Google maps API, where the blue and red markers show the current location of users on the map. After clicking on a user on the map or selecting one from the drop-down menu, it takes the user to the sensor data display page where real-time sensor data from the user's smartphone are displayed. Historic data from sensors are also plotted and displayed in graphs. The sensor data here are all obtained from our server, which can access the database storing the current and history data regarding the user and his/her respective phone sensors.

An alert system is also implemented into the application alerting the users in various cases. For example, if a phone call has been detected, the user's icon on the map will change as shown by the red markers in the figure. Also, using the Light sensor data, we could deduce what kind of an environment the client's in: whether he/she is indoor or outdoor, in a dimly lit room or a bright room, and so on. If we have detected that the light sensor data has exceeded a pre-determined harmless threshold, the app will notify the user in a timely fashion and advice him to take necessary actions.

Fig. 5. Androd app for displaying user locations and smartphone historic data showing the map page (*left*), sensor data display page (*middle*), and sensor data history graphs (*right*). (Color figure online)

4.3   Performance

For each classification state (sitting/standing, lying down, and walking), we conducted 20 tests where in 10 of them a phone call took place, and in the other 10 a phone call did not take place. This totals to 60 test cases. We extracted features from proximity and orientation sensors during these cases, and used our classifier to detect whether a phone call has taken place or not.

Table 2 shows our system compared to other HAR systems. But since we used different sensors and that the detection is for completely different motions, the comparison is just for reference. Our method achieves the highest accuracy of 90 % for sitting/standing, and the overall accuracy is 85 %. Our accuracy for all states are above 80 %, but the other methods when detecting running, descending and ascending stairs, has a very low accuracy between 40–80%.

Table 2. Accuracy of our method compared to other methods in classifying states

	Sitting/standing	Lying down	Walking
Our method (%)	90	85	80
Shaoib's (%)	**99**	N/A	92
Kwapisz's (%)	94.5	N/A	**93.6**

5   Future Work

We extracted features that are relatively simple. There could be many more in depth features that might provide us with new aspects of evaluation. For example, the maximum and minimum values could be extracted at different intervals, forming multiple local maximum and minimum values, and together they can be used as features. Also, the low-pass filtering method we used calculated the smoothed values weighing the previous and current values. Many other more complex filtering method such as Fourier transform and Gaussian method could be investigated.

6   Conclusion

In this paper, we presented a method to detect whether a user is on the phone or not using real-time proximity and orientation sensor data from the user's smartphones. Real-time sensor data is uploaded onto our server for analyses. We designed Android applications to display real-time and historic data on the user's smartphone. When proximity sensor is reading a value of 0, we know that an object is close to the phone's screen, then we analyze the three axes of the orientation sensor. If the features extracted from the orientation sensor readings satisfy our predefined range of values, we conclude that a phone call has been detected. We further classify each phone call into three states: sitting/standing, lying down, and walking. We showed that our method has a overall detection accuracy of 85 %. The most errors occur when detecting phone calls in the walking state, since the orientation sensor readings have a much larger fluctuations compared to the other two, increasing the number of false negatives and false positives. Overall, our method achieves a detection accuracy of over 80 % for all classes.

References

1. Shoaib, M., Scholten, H., Havinga, P.J.M.: Towards physical activity recognition using smartphone sensors. In: IEEE 10th International Conference on Ubiquitous Intelligence and Computing (2013)
2. Bedogni, L., Felice, M.D., Bononi, L.: By train or by car? Detecting the user's motion type through smartphone sensors data. In: Wireless Days (2012)
3. Dai, J., Teng, J., Bai, X., Shen, Z., Xuan, D.: Mobile phone based drunk driving detection. In: Pervasive Computing Technologies for Healthcare (2010)
4. Douangphachanh, V., Oneyama, H.: Formulation of a simple model to estimate road surface roughness condition from android smartphone sensors. In: IEEE 9th Conference on Intelligent Sensors (2014)
5. Zhang, L., Liu, J., Jiang, H., Guan, Y.: SensTrack: energy-efficient location tracking with smartphone sensor. IEEE Sens. J. **13**(10), 3775–3784 (2013)
6. Mizouni, R., Barachi, M.E.: Mobile phone sensing as a service: business model and use cases. In: Seventh International Conference on Next Generation Mobile Apps, Services and Technologies (2013)
7. Jalal, A., Kamal, S.: Real-time life logging via a depth silhouette-based human activity recognition system for smart home services. In: 11th IEEE International Conference on Advanced Video and Signal Based Surveillance (2014)
8. Wang, Z., Wu, D., Chen, J., Ghoneim, A., Hossain, M.: A triaxial accelerometer-based human activity recognition via EEMD-based features and game-theory-based feature selection. IEEE Sens. J. **16**(9), 3198–3207 (2016)
9. Liu, W., Zha, Z., Wang, Y., Lu, K., Tao, D.: p-laplacian regularized sparse coding for human activity recognition. IEEE Trans. Ind. Electron. (99) (2016)
10. Majethia, R., Mishra, V., Pathak, P., Lohani, D., Acharya, D., Sehrawat, S.: Contextual sensitivity of the ambient temperature sensor in smartphones. In: 7th International Conference on Communication Systems and Networks (2015)
11. Ongenae, F., Duysburgh, P., Verstraete, M., Sulmon, N., Bleumers, L., Jacobs, A., Ackaert, A., De Zutter, S., Verstichel, S., De Turck, F.: User-driven design of a context-aware application: an ambient-intelligent nurse call system. In: 6th International Conference on Pervasive Computing Technologies for Healthcare (PervasiveHealth) and Workshops (2012)
12. Liu, Y., Dashti, M., Rahman, M., Zhang, J.: Indoor localization using smartphone inertial sensors. In: 11th Workshop on Positioning, Navigation, and Communication (WPNC) (2014)
13. He, X., Li, J., Aloi, D.: WiFi based indoor localization with adaptive motion model using smartphone motion sensors. In: International Conference on Connected Vehicles and Expo (ICCVE) (2014)
14. Kwapisz, J.R., Weiss, G.M., Moore, S.A.: Activity recognition using cell phone accelerometers. In: SensorKDD, 25 July 2010

15. Lin, C., Chen, Y., Wang, L., Tseng, Y.: A proximity sensor based no-touch mechanism for mobile applications on smart phones. In: IEEE Vehicular Technology Conference (VTC Fall) (2012)

16. Curone, D., Bertolotti, G.M., Cristiani, A., Secco, E.L., Magenes, G.: A real-time and self-calibrating algorithm based on triaxial accelerometer signals for the detection of human posture and activity. IEEE Trans. Inf. Technol. Biomed. **14**(4), 1098–11054 (2010)

17. Li, W.W., Iltis, R.A., Win, M.Z.: A smartphone localization algorithm using RSSI and inertial sensor measurement fusion. In: Signal Processing for Communications Symposium, Globecom (2013)

18. Herranen, H., Kuusik, A., Saar, T., Reidla, M., Land, R., Martens, O., Majak, J.: Acceleration data acquisition and processing system for structural health monitoring. In: IEEE Metrology for Aerospace (2014)

19. Yurur, O., Labrador, M., Moreno, W.: Adaptive and energy efficient context representation framework in mobile sensing. IEEE Trans. Mob. Comput. **13**(8), 1681–1693 (2014)

20. Baranasuriya, N., Gilbert, S., Newport, C., Rao, J.: Aggregation in smartphone sensor networks. In: IEEE International Conference on Distributed Computing in Sensor Systems (2014)

21. Abdullah, M., Negara, A., Sayeed, M., Choi, D., Muthu, K.: Classification algorithms in human activity recognition using smartphones. World Acad. Sci. Eng. Technol. **6** (2012)

22. Ishida, Y., Thepvilojanapong, N., Tobe, Y.: WINFO+: identification of environment condition using walking signals. In: 10th International Conference on Mobile Data Management: Systems, Services and Middleware (2009)

23. Li, J., Li, X., Yang, B., Sun, X.: Segmentation-based image copy-move forgery detection scheme. IEEE Trans. Inf. Forensics Secur. **10**(3), 507–518 (2015)

24. Xia, Z., Wang, X., Sun, X., Wang, Q.: A secure and dynamic multi-keyword ranked search scheme over encrypted cloud data. IEEE Trans. Parallel Distrib. Syst. **27**(2), 340–352 (2015)

25. Fu, Z., Ren, K., Shu, J., Sun, X., Huang, F.: Enabling personalized search over encrypted outsourced data with efficiency improvement. IEEE Trans. Parallel Distrib. Syst. (2015)

26. Sun, H., Mcintosh, S., Li, B.: Detection of in-progress phone calls using smartphone proximity and orientation sensors. Int. J. Sens. Netw. (to appear)

27. Won, J., Ryu, H., Delbruck, T., Lee, J., Hu, J.: Proximity sensing based on a dynamic vision sensor for mobile devices. IEEE Trans. Ind. Electron. **62**(1), 536–544 (2015)

28. Gu, B., Sun, X., Sheng, V.S.: Structural minimax probability machine. IEEE Trans. Neural Netw. Learn. Syst. (2016)

29. Fu, Z., Sun, X., Liu, Q., Zhou, L., Shu, J.: Achieving efficient cloud search services: multi-keyword ranked search over encrypted cloud data supporting parallel computing. IEICE Trans. Commun. **E98–B**(1), 190–200 (2015)

30. Xia, Z., Wang, X., Sun, X., Liu, Q., Xiong, N.: Steganalysis of LSB matching using differences between nonadjacent pixels. Multimedia Tools Appl. **75**(4), 1947–1962 (2016)

31. Weiss, G.M., Lockhart, J.W., Pulickal, T.T., McHugh, P.T., Ronan, I.H., Timko, J.L.: Actitracker: a smartphone-based activity recognition system for improving health and well-being. In: KDD, 24–27 August, New York (2014)

32. Sun, H., Grishman, R., Wang, Y.: Active learning based named entity recognition and its application in natural language coverless information hiding. J. Internet Technol. (to appear)
33. Xia, Z., Wang, X., Sun, X., Wang, B.: Steganalysis of least significant bit matching using multi-order differences. Secur. Commun. Netw. **7**(8), 1283–1291 (2014)
34. Sun, H., Mcintosh, S.: Big data mobile services for New York city taxi riders and drivers. In: 2016 IEEE International Conference on Mobile Services, San Francisco (to appear)
35. Chen, B., Shu, H., Coatrieux, G., Chen, G., Sun, X., Coatrieux, J.: Color image analysis by quaternion-type moments. J. Math. Imaging Vis. **51**(1), 124–144 (2015)
36. Tamura, T., Yoshimura, T., Sekine, M., Uchida, M., Tanaka, O.: A wearable airbag to prevent fall injuries. IEEE Trans. Inf. Technol. Biomed. **13**(6), 910–914 (2009)
37. Yurur, O., Liu, C., Perara, C., Chen, M., Liu, X., Moreno, W.: Energy-efficient and context-aware smartphone sensor employment. IEEE Trans. Veh. Technol. **64**(9), 4230–4244 (2014)

A Survey of Speculative Execution Strategy in MapReduce

Qi Liu[1,2(✉)], Dandan Jin[2,3], Xiaodong Liu[4], and Nigel Linge[5]

[1] Jiangsu Collaborative Innovation Center of Atmospheric Environment
and Equipment Technology (CICAEET), Nanjing University of Information
Science and Technology, Nanjing 210044, China
qi.liu@nuist.edu.cn
[2] School of Computer and Software,
Nanjing University of Information Science and Technology, Nanjing, China
1005949332@qq.com
[3] Jiangsu Engineering Centre of Network Monitoring,
Nanjing University of Information Science and Technology, Nanjing, China
[4] School of Computing, Edinburgh Napier University,
10 Colinton Road, Edinburgh EH10 5DT, UK
[5] The University of Salford, Salford, Greater Manchester M5 4WT, UK

Abstract. MapReduce is a parallel computing programming model designed to process large-scale data. Therefore, the accuracy and efficiency for computing are needed to be assured and speculative execution is an efficient method for calculation of fault tolerance. It reaches the goals of shortening the execution time and increasing the cluster throughput through selecting slow tasks and speculative copy these tasks on a fast machine to be executed. Hadoop naïve speculative execution strategy assumes that the cluster is homogeneous, and this assumption leads to the poor performance in heterogeneous environment. Several speculative execution strategies which aim to improve the MapReduce Performance in the heterogeneous environments are reviewed in this paper like LATE, MCP, ex-MCP and ERUL, then the comparison between these methods are listed.

Keywords: Hadoop · MapReduce · Speculative execution · Heterogeneous environment

1 Introduction

With the innovation of internet technology, not only the network transmission rate is rising, but the number of internet users grows explosively, which fully shows that the era of big data is coming [1]. Former Yahoo! Engineer Doug Cutting combined his search engine project with the three Google published papers [2–4] to achieve a distributed parallel computing system called "Hadoop" [5], and completely open from the Apache Software Foundation.

Hadoop is an open source framework for storing and processing large-scale data sets, it uses a distributed file system called HDFS to storage data blocks in the Data-Node, which obtains a high fault tolerance feature and uses MapReduce for processing

© Springer International Publishing AG 2016
X. Sun et al. (Eds.): ICCCS 2016, Part I, LNCS 10039, pp. 296–307, 2016.
DOI: 10.1007/978-3-319-48671-0_27

these data in parallel on many cheap nodes. With the continuous development and perfection of Hadoop platform, the upper applications based on HDFS and MapReduce become more and more abundant, such as the distributed database called HBase, Hive and Pig [6–10].

MapReduce is a specialized parallel processing mode for massive data computing, which will be calculated into Map and Reduce stages, Map is for processing <key, value> pairs based on a data collection, and puts out the intermediate <key, value>, while then Reduce merges all intermediate values with the same intermediate key values [3]. The MapReduce framework consists of three parts: Client, JobTracker, and TaskTracker. The Client is used to submit jobs; JobTracker is responsible for are decomposing jobs into Map and Reduce tasks and allocate them to each TaskTracker, TaskTracker performs these tasks in parallel [11].

Task Scheduler is the core component of task allocation in MapReduce, which aims to schedule the overall tasks to run in proper order and shorten the execution time through obtaining the running state of the TaskTracker. While JobTracker does not access to all real-time execution information and it is difficult to predict the future running status of tasks. Therefore, it can only let the job perform fastest at the time of task allocation and does not guarantee that the allocation still maintains its superiority in the subsequent implementation [12]. To improve the bad performance resulting from unexpected problems that exist in the node or task scheduler and reduce the loss caused by these problems, MapReduce launches speculative execution, which backing up a slow task on alternative nodes with the hope that the whole job execution time can reduce. Google applies the naïve speculative execution and observes that speculative execution can decrease the job execution time by 44 % [3]. Apart from Hadoop, speculative execution is also implemented in Microsoft Dryad [13].

Considering the importance of speculative execution in MapReduce, this paper reviews some of the recent research done on speculative execution to enhance the performance of MapReduce including its relative strong and weak points. The paper is organized as follows: Sect. 2 presents the overview of speculative execution. Many strategies that have been designed to optimize the speculative execution in heterogeneous environments are introduced in Sect. 3. Section 4 analyzes the advantages and limitations of these methods. Finally, we conclude this paper in Sect. 5.

2 Overview of Speculative Execution

2.1 Speculative Execution

Due to software bugs, unbalanced load or uneven distribution of resources and other reasons, it will result in inconsistent speed between multiple tasks running the same job, some task runs significantly slower than other tasks (such as the progress of a task is only 10 %, while all other tasks have finished running), these tasks will slow down the overall progress in the implementation of the job, which are called "Stragglers". To prevent this from happening, MapReduce uses speculative execution mechanism [3]; MapReduce will start a backup task and let the backup task run with the original simultaneously; then MapReduce takes the first tasks performed output as the final result of the task. As it can be seen, this mechanism is the idea of "space for time." From the description, three key points of speculative execution can be found:

1. Find "Stragglers," this requires MapReduce system to find out the Stragglers in an efficient way. If the normal task is judged to be straggler and backup it on another node to perform, it will increase the execution time and consume cluster resources.
2. Launch the backup task on a faster node. MapReduce system needs an effective mechanism to measure node processing tasks ability to find the faster node to launch backup tasks.
3. Ensure that the backup task execution brings effectiveness to the cluster. Backup-task execution should be able to reduce the job execution time and increase cluster throughput.

2.2 Hadoop Naïve Strategy

To select the slow tasks, Hadoop implements the most original speculative execution, called Hadoop-NAÏVE [14]. In this strategy, MapReduce calculates the progress of every task in the current stage according to the returned heartbeat package information, denoted by P_{st}, that can be calculated using the formula (1):

$$P_{st} = \frac{Y}{N} \tag{1}$$

Where, Y is the number of k/v pairs that have been processed in this stage and N is the overall number of k/v pairs needed to be processed in this stage.

MapReduce contains Map and reduce tasks. For example, if t is a map task, then its progress can be calculated by (1). However, if t is a reduce task and has finished first M ($M \in (0,1,2)$) stages of the reduce task which contains three stages called shuffle, sort and reduce and each stage accounts for one third of the progress, then its progress need to be calculated separately. The progress of the task t, denoted by P_t can be calculated using (2). So the Average progress of all tasks in a job, denoted by P_{avg}, which can be computed by the formula (3).

$$P_t = \begin{cases} P_{st} & t \ is \ map \ task \\ \left(\left(\frac{1}{3}\right) \times M\right) + \left(\left(\frac{1}{3}\right) \times P_{st}\right) & t \ is \ a \ reduce \ task \end{cases} \tag{2}$$

$$P_{avg} = \sum_{i=1}^{K} \frac{P_t[i]}{K} \tag{3}$$

Where K is the number of tasks, $P_t[i]$ is the progress of task i.

Naïve finds the Straggler by comparing the progress of the task with the average progress of all the tasks. When the task runs more than 60S and meets the following requirements (4), then it a Straggler:

$$P_{avg} - P_t \geq 20\% \tag{4}$$

Since that Naïve assumes that the entire cluster is homogeneous, it is necessary to find the "Stragglers" by the formula (4), but this strategy has many pitfalls in a heterogeneous cluster environment. Therefore, it is needed to improve the Hadoop's Speculative Execution strategy to adapt to the heterogeneous environment.

3 Speculative Execution Optimization in Heterogeneous Environments

To improve the performance of speculative execution in the heterogeneous environment. Many researchers discuss the defects of speculative execution and put forward a series of solutions to improve it. In this section, several improved speculative execution strategies are summarized.

3.1 Longest Approximate Time to End Algorithm

Zaharia et al. proposed a Longest Approximate Time to End (LATE) algorithm to improve the performance in the heterogeneous environment [15]. The main idea of LATE is choosing the task with the longest remaining time as a "straggler" and re-executed on the fast node. The progress rate of the task t_k, denoted by PR_k is used to compute the remaining time of the task t_k using (5), so the remaining time, marked by RT_k, can be evaluated by (6), where T is the execution time.

$$PR_k = \frac{P_k}{T} \tag{5}$$

$$RT_k = \frac{(1 - P_k)}{PR_k} \tag{6}$$

3.2 Maximum Cost Performance Strategy

Chen et al. proposed Maximum Cost Performance (MCP) strategy [16], which determines whether it is worth to launch backup tasks by ensuring that speculative execution can bring higher benefits to the cluster.

In the MCP, the Exponentially Weighted Moving Average (EWMA) rate is used to predict the progress rate of the task in the future, rather than to use the average rate. The EWMA rate can be calculated by (7), where the $E(t)$ and $Y(t)$ represent the evaluated and observed progress rate at time t, λ reflects the weight of historically measured value and is set to be 0.2 according to the experiment.

$$E(t) = \lambda * Y(t) + (1 - \lambda) * E(t - 1) \, 0 < \lambda < 1 \tag{7}$$

Different from the LATE, the remaining time (RT) in MCP is the sum of the remaining time of the current phase (RT_{cp}) and following phases (RT_{fp}), which is shown in (8) and (9). The est_time_p is evaluated by the average progress rate of the following phases and the $factor_d$ is the radio of the input size of the task to the average input size of all tasks.

$$RT = RT_{cp} + RT_{fp} = \frac{rem\_data_{cp}}{bandwith_{cp}} + \sum_{p \, in \, f_p} est\_time_p * factor_d \tag{8}$$

$$factor_d = \frac{data_{input}}{data_{avg}} \tag{9}$$

Also, the execution time of the backup task, marked by T_{backup}, can be estimated by the est_time_p using (10).

$$T_{backup} = \sum_p est\_time_p * factor_d \tag{10}$$

MCP established a cost-benefit model to ensure the efficiency of the speculative execution, where cost represents the slots that task occupied and profit marks the time saved. Launching a backup task will cost two slots T_{backup} and save one slot $RT\text{-}T_{backup}$, while not launching a backup task will occupy one slot for RT and save nothing. Therefore, the profit of the two actions can be expressed as follows:

$$profit_{backup} = \alpha * (RT - T_{backup}) - 2 * \beta * T_{backup} \tag{11}$$

$$profit_{not\_backup} = -\beta * RT \tag{12}$$

Where α and β are the weight of benefit and cost. Then if the task satisfies the (13), it can be selected as a backup candidate.

$$profit_{backup} > profit_{not\_backup} \Leftrightarrow \frac{RT}{T_{backup}} > \frac{\alpha + 2\beta}{\alpha + \beta} \tag{13}$$

The formula can be simplified by using γ to replace β/α, and it becomes (14). γ is set as the $load\_factor$ of the Hadoop cluster and can be computed by (15), where $number_{pendingtasks}$ and $number_{freeslots}$ mark the number of pending tasks and free slots.

$$\frac{RT}{T_{backup}} > \frac{1 + 2\gamma}{1 + \gamma} \tag{14}$$

$$\gamma = load\_factor = \frac{number_{pending\_tasks}}{number_{free\_slots}} \tag{15}$$

A set of backup candidates can be get by iterating through all the running tasks which satisfy the following condition (16), then the candidate that has the longest remaining time (*RT*) will be backed up finally.

$$profit_{backup} > profit_{not\_backup} \Leftrightarrow \frac{RT}{T_{backup}} > \frac{1 + 2load\_factor}{1 + load\_factor} \qquad (16)$$

3.3 Extensional Maximum Cost Performance Strategy

Huang et al. improved the MCP strategy and designed the extensional Maximum Cost performance (ex-MCP) strategy [17]. The following aspects include the main improvements of this strategy:

- Divide the map tasks into three classes based on data distribution, which is Data—local, Rack—local and Off rack, then analyze the task execution information more effectively and judge the "straggler" more accurately
- Consider the value of slots occupied by tasks that aims to calculate the real cluster resource cost
- Choose fast node first, and then use the ex-MCP model to determine whether a task is worth to back up on the node. Rather than Choose slow task using MCP model first, and then find the fast node to execute. The former is more accurate and convenient

The novel contribution of ex-MCP is to take the value of each slot, which can be represented by the reciprocal of the task execution time (*1/t*). Similar to MCP, the profit of *backup* and *not_backup* can be modeled as follows:

$$profit_{backup} = \alpha * \left(RT - T_{backup}\right) * \frac{1}{T_{original}} - \beta * \left(\frac{1}{T_{original}} + \frac{1}{T_{backup}}\right) \qquad (17)$$

$$profit_{not\_backup} = -\beta * RT * \frac{1}{T_{original}} \qquad (18)$$

Where *RT* is the remaining time of task on the original node, which can be obtained from the formula (8) in MCP, $T_{original}$ represents the execution time of the task on the original node which can be estimated by the average process rate of each phase, T_{backup} marks the execution time on the backup node calculated by Eq. (10). α and β are the weight of benefit and cost.

The ex-MCP obtain a conclusion as follows, where γ is the *load_factor* of the Hadoop cluster and formulated in Eq. (15). Then whether speculative execution should be launched is determined by applying the Eq. (19).

$$profit_{backup} > profit_{not\_backup} \Leftrightarrow RT > T_{backup} + \frac{\gamma}{1 + \gamma} * T_{original} \qquad (19)$$

3.4   Estimate Remaining Time Using Linear Relationship Model

In the previous study among speculative execution, researchers do not consider the impact of system load on the execution time. Estimate Remaining time Using Linear relationship model (ERUL) [17, 18] was put forward by Huang et al. This strategy estimates the remaining execution time using a roughly linear relationship between system load and execution time, which is formulated as follows:

$$RT_{est} = \frac{(1 + \overline{Z_{est}})RT_{now}}{1 + \overline{Z_{now}}} \tag{20}$$

Where RT_{est} marks the estimated remaining time, the remaining time is denoted as RT_{now} when the system load is maintained as $\overline{Z_{now}}$, while $\overline{Z_{est}}$ is the average load.

MCP model is also utilized to guarantee the effectiveness of speculative execution, and a slow task candidate should satisfy the Eq. (21), where the RT is calculated by ERUL and T_{backup} is computed based on the following expression (22), γ is also the load_factor of Hadoop cluster.

$$\frac{RT}{T_{backup}} > \frac{1 + 2\gamma}{1 + \gamma} \tag{21}$$

$$backup\_time = \begin{cases} procCap * Data_{total} & for\ map\ task \\ procCap & for\ reduce\ task \end{cases} \tag{22}$$

Where $procCap$ represents the processing capability of nodes that have been selected to execute this kind of backup tasks. The node is judged as a fast node when its $procCap$ is higher than the average $procCap$ of all nodes; the opposite is a slow node. $procCap$ is calculated in two conditions: one is the node has never processed this type of tasks, and another is the node has processed same type of tasks. $procCap$ can be expressed using (23), where T_{cost} is the time spent by the first running task in this type and the RT is computed by ERUL.

$$procCap = \begin{cases} \frac{(T_{cost} + RT)}{Data_{total}} & for\ map\ task \\ T_{cost} + RT & for\ reduce\ task \end{cases} \tag{23}$$

On the contrary, $procCap$ can be formulated as follows:

$$procCap = \begin{cases} \theta * preCap + (1 - \theta) * \frac{exeTime}{Data_{total}} & for\ map\ task \\ \theta * preCap + (1 - \theta) * exeTime & for\ reduce\ task \end{cases} \tag{24}$$

Where $preCap$ is the previous processing capability of the backup node processing this kind of task, the execution time of a task is marked by $exeTime$ and θ is a smoothing factor and set at 0.3.

In summary, if applying the ERUL strategy, the whole process is as follows:

- Select the "Straggler" candidate with the high priority according to the order of non-rack map task, non-locality map task, locality map task, and reduce task.
- Estimate the type of the task on this node and determine *procCap* of this node
- Determine whether the node is fast node, if not, return the first step
- Use MCP model to verify the effectiveness of launching backup task on this node, if not, return the first step
- Launch a backup task on this node.

4 Comparison of Several Optimization Strategies

4.1 Advantages and Limitations of Each Strategy

There are several strategies proposed in the research of MapReduce speculative execution, each of them has advantages and pitfalls, which will introduce one by one in this section.

In general, naïve regards task of which progress has been too far behind the average progress as a low task and launch a backup task on a new node, it assumes that the cluster is a homogeneous so will not be able to obtain good results in the heterogeneous environments.

LATE was designed to robust to node heterogeneity and backup tasks that have the longest remaining time, which is more fair than just according to the task progress, but it also has some limitations:

- LATE sets the constant values of three child phases of reducing phase as 1/3, 1/3 and 1/3, which will change in the actual execution environment, it will result in inaccuracy progress calculation and unable to find the real slow task since the remaining time is calculated inaccurately.

MCP model uses the EWMA rate to replace the average process rate and calculates the remaining time by adding the remaining time of each phase, applying MCP model ensures that speculative execution brings benefits to cluster, however, it still has some limitations:

- MCP thinks cluster resources are reflected by slots and embody cost of the backup task through the consumption of slots, but different nodes have different performance, leading to the different value of each slot, so it is unreasonable to think that all slots are with same values in MCP.
- Using the average execution time in each phase of known tasks and a *factor_d* to estimate the *backup_time* will cause some errors.
- In the map task, task satisfying data localization executes faster than those, not satisfying data localization, so it is unfair to compare these tasks at the same level.

ex-MCP was designed to overcome drawbacks of MCP. The value of slots are considered in the calculation of cost-performance model, and ex-MCP divides the map tasks into three classes based on data distribution, which is Data local, Rack local and Off rack, then analyze the task execution information and judge the "straggler" more effectively. However, the estimation of *backup_time* still uses the method of MCP, which will cause estimation errors.

ERUL found the relationship between system load and execution time, and evaluated the remaining time using a linear relationship between them, and it also provides some improvements to solve the data skew in map tasks. However, from the results of the experiment, ERUL is more suitable for CPU-bound tasks and it may probably because the linear relationship of system load and the execution time is more obvious in computationally intensive tasks.

In summary, all of these strategies obtain good performance to some extent, the main strengths and weaknesses of approaches are listed in Table 1. Also, time complexity is a very important factor to judge the pros and cons of an algorithm and shown in Table 2. MCP, ex-MCP, and ERUL only need to verify whether each of tasks meets the model or not, so all the time complexity is $O(n)$, while LATE needs to prioritize tasks based on remaining time, so the time complexity is $O(nlogn)$.

Table 1. Strengths and weaknesses of strategies

Strategies	Strength	Weakness
Naive	No particular	No adaption to heterogeneity
LATE	Robustness to heterogeneity	Progress computed Inaccurately
MCP	Ensuring cluster effectiveness	Estimation error of *backup_time*
ex-MCP	Consideration of slots' value	
ERUL	Linear relationship more accurate	Suit CPU-bound

Table 2. Time complexity of each Strategy

Strategies	LATE	MCP	ex-MCP	ERUL
Time complexity	$O(nlogn)$	$O(n)$	$O(n)$	$O(n)$

4.2 Performance Comparison

The performance metrics of Mapreduce are always defined as the job execution time and cluster throughput. Job execution time is the completion time of all tasks in a job, while cluster throughput is the amount of jobs that the cluster can process per unit time. Figure 1 shows the execution time of each strategy in the implementation of Word-Count at the best, worst and average case. Gridmix2 is always used to evaluate the cluster throughput, Fig. 2 shows the cluster throughput of each strategy at the best, worst and average case. As can be seen from these two figures, Hadoop-naïve did not bring many benefits to the cluster, so several strategies have been proposed to enhance the performance of MapReduce compared with Hadoop-none and Hadoop-naive. Overall, we can learn that ex-MCP shows fewer advantages than other strategies both in execution time and cluster throughput.

Nevertheless, researchers do not only compare with Hadoop-naïve and Hadoop-none but with some existing strategies to fully show their advantages. To prove the superiority of MCP, authors compared it with LATE that was proposed

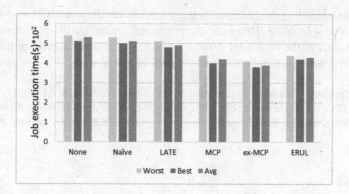

Fig. 1. Comparisons of job execution time of wordcount under different strategies

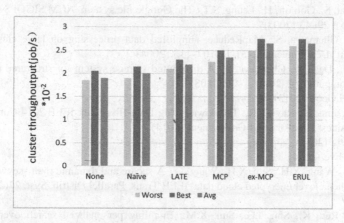

Fig. 2. The Hadoop cluster throughput under different strategies

before it and found that MCP reduces the job execution time by 14 % and improves the cluster throughput by 9 % over LATE on average. ex-MCP was proposed to optimize MCP, so researchers made a comparison of MCP and ex-MCP, and experiments proved that ex-MCP reduces the job execution time by 8 % over MCP and 21 % over LATE and enhances the cluster throughput by 10 % over MCP and 20 % over LATE. The job execution time with ERUL is decreased by 12.5 % less than LATE, and the cluster throughput is increased by 10 % more than LATE.

5   Conclusion

In this paper, basic principles of speculative execution and Hadoop naïve Strategy are introduced. Due to the bad performance that naïve shows in the heterogeneous environments, We reviewed some of the exiting Strategies that have been proposed to enhance the performance of MapReduce speculative execution in heterogeneous environments, including the heuristic strategy LATE, ERUL and MCP, ex-MCP based on the resource guarantee. However, there are still many challenges existing in the MapReduce such as the data skew in reduce phase, the estimation error of backup time and so on. We will put these challenges as part of future work.

Acknowledgements. This work is supported by the NSFC (61300238, 61300237, 61232016, 1405254, 61373133), Marie Curie Fellowship (701697-CAR-MSCA-IFEF-ST), Basic Research Programs (Natural Science Foundation) of Jiangsu Province (BK20131004) and the PAPD fund.

References

1. Armbrust, M., Fox, A., Griffith, R., Joseph, A., Katz, R., Konwinski, A., Zaharia, M.: A view of cloud computing. Commun. ACM **53**(4), 50–58 (2010)
2. Ghemawat, S., Gobioff, H., Leung, S.T.: The Google file system. ACM SIGOPS Oper. Syst. Rev. **37**(5), 29–43 (2003)
3. Dean, J., Ghemawa, S.: MapReduce: simplified data processing on large clusters. Proc. Oper. Syst. Des. Implement. **51**(1), 107–113 (2004)
4. Chang, F., Dean, J., Ghemawa, S.: A distributed storage system for structured data. ACM Trans. Comput. Syst. **26**(2), 1–26 (2008)
5. Apache Hadoop (2013). http://Hadoop.Apache.Org/
6. Vijayalakshmi, B., Ravi, P.R.: The down of big Data-Hbase. In: IEEE 2014 Conference on IT in Business, Industry and Government (2014)
7. Apache Pig (2014). http://pig.apache.org/
8. Apache Hive (2014). https://hive.apache.org/
9. Xia, Z.H., Wang, X.H., Sun, X.H., Wang, Q.: A secure and dynamic multi-keyword ranked search scheme over encrypted cloud data. IEEE Trans. Parallel Distrib. Syst. **27**(2), 340–352 (2015)
10. Fu, Z.J., Ren, K., Shu, J.G., Sun, X.M.: Enabling personalized search over encrypted outsourced data with efficiency improvement. IEEE Trans. Parallel Distrib. Syst. (in press)
11. Fu, Z.J., Sun, X.M., Li, Q., Zhou, L., Shu, J.G.: Achieving efficient cloud search services: multi-keyword ranked search over encrypted cloud data supporting parallel computing. IEICE Trans. Commun. **E98-B**(1), 190–200 (2015)
12. Yoo, D.G., Sim, K.M.: A comparative review of job scheduling for MapReduce. In: IEEE International Conference on Cloud Computing and Intelligence Systems (CCIS), pp. 353–358. IEEE (2011)
13. Isard, M., Budiu, M., Yu, Y., Birrel, A., Fetterly, D.: Dryad: distributed data-parallel programs from sequential building blocks. Proceedings of the 2nd ACM SIGOPS/EuroSys European Conference on Computer Systems, pp. 59–72. ACM (2007)
14. Nenavath, S.N., Atul, N.: A review of adaptive approaches to MapReduce scheduling in heterogeneous environments. In: International Conference on Advances in Computing, Communications and Informatics, pp. 677–683. IEEE (2014)
15. Zaharia, M., Konwinski, A., Joseph, A., Katz, R., Stoica, I.: Improving MapReduce performance in heterogeneous environments. Proceedings of the 8th USENIX Conference on Operating Systems Design and Implementation (OSDI), pp. 29–42 (2008)
16. Chen, Q., Liu, C., Xiao, Z.: Improving MapReduce performance using smart speculative execution strategy. IEEE Trans. Comput. **63**(4), 954–967 (2014)

17. Huang, X., Zhang, L.X., Li, R.F., Wan, L.J., Li, K.Q.: Novel heuristic speculative execution strategies in heterogeneous distributed environments. Comput. Electr. Eng. **50**, 166–179 (2015)
18. Wu, H.C., Li, K., Tang, Z., Zhang, L.: A heuristic speculative execution strategy in heterogeneous distributed environments. In: 2014 Sixth International Symposium on Parallel Architectures, Algorithms and Programming (PAAP), pp. 268–273 (2014)

Cloud Security

Cryptanalysis and Improvement of a Smart Card Based Mutual Authentication Scheme in Cloud Computing

Qi Jiang[1]([⊠]), Bingyan Li[1], Jianfeng Ma[1], Youliang Tian[2], and Yuanyuan Yang[3]

[1] School of Cyber Engineering, Xidian University, Xi'an, China
jiangqixdu@gmail.com
[2] Guizhou Provincial Key Laboratory of Public Big Data, Guiyang, Guizhou, China
[3] The Third Research Institute of Ministry of Public Security, Shanghai, China

Abstract. Cloud computing enables the users to access and share the data as and when required at anytime from anywhere. Due to its open access, one of the major issues faced by cloud computing is how to prevent the outsourced data from being leaked to unauthorized users. Therefore, mutual authentication between the user and the cloud service provider is a necessity to ensure that sensitive data in the cloud are not available to illegal users. Recently, Li et al. proposed a two-factor authentication protocol based on elliptic curve cryptosystem which enables the cloud users to access their outsourced data. However, we first show that their scheme suffers from the problem of wrong password login. Secondly, their scheme is prone to denial of service attack in the password-changing phase. Thirdly, it fails to provide user revocation when the smart card is lost or stolen. To remedy these flaws, we propose an improved two-factor authentication and key agreement protocol, which not only guards various known attacks, but also provides more desired security properties.

Keywords: Authentication · Key agreement · Password · Smart card · Privacy · Cloud computing

1 Introduction

Cloud computing is a promising computing paradigm where computing and storage resources are provided by third-party service providers with remarkable cost reduction [1–4]. Users are relieved from the cost of buying and maintaining hardware and software platforms. Besides, the users can access and share the data as and when required at anytime from anywhere. However, one of the major issues hindering the adoption of cloud computing is the privacy of outsourced data in cloud may be leaked to unauthorized users, including malicious insiders and outsiders, which renders authentication mechanisms of crucial importance [5–9].

Choudhur et al. [10] proposed a smart card and password based user authentication framework for cloud computing. Hao et al. proposed a time-bound ticket-based mutual authentication scheme for cloud environment using smart card [11]. Although

© Springer International Publishing AG 2016
X. Sun et al. (Eds.): ICCCS 2016, Part I, LNCS 10039, pp. 311–321, 2016.
DOI: 10.1007/978-3-319-48671-0_28

Hao et al. claimed that the authentication scheme was secure; Pippal et al. found it was vulnerable to Denial-of-Service (DOS) attack and the password change phase was insecure [12]. To resist these weaknesses, Pippal et al. proposed an enhancement to Hao et al.'s scheme. Jiang et al. proposed a three-factor authentication scheme for healthcare cloud [13].

However, these authentication protocols [10–13], which are designed for single server environment, are not suitable for multiple-server cloud environment in which a user generally access different types of cloud services from different cloud servers. A user needs to remember the pairs of identity and password corresponding to different servers, the mechanism will bring about a lot of inconvenience to users. Therefore, in the multiple-server cloud environment, it is preferable for a user to use a single pair of identity and password to access different servers. Hwang and Sun proposed a single sign-on scheme for multiple cloud services [14]. Tsai and Lo proposed a privacy aware authentication scheme for distributed mobile cloud computing services [15]. However, Jiang et al. identified that their scheme is vulnerable to the service provider impersonation attack [16]. Recently, Li et al. [17] proposed a two-factor multi-server authentication protocol based on elliptic curve cryptosystem (ECC) which enables the cloud users to access their outsourced data across multiple cloud servers.

However, we find that Li et al.'s protocol is flawed. Specifically, we first show that their scheme suffers from the problem of wrong password login. Secondly, their scheme is prone to DOS attack in the password-changing phase. Thirdly, it fails to provide user revocation when the smart card is lost or stolen. Then, we put forward a robust two-factor authentication scheme. Our new scheme makes up the missing security features necessary for cloud computing while maintaining the desired features of the original scheme. We show that the proposed scheme can withstand various known attacks and provide more security features than Li et al.'s scheme.

The remainder of this paper is organized as follows. The next section briefly reviews Li et al.'s scheme. Section 3 elaborates on the flaws of their scheme. Section 4 presents the improved authentication scheme. In Sect. 5, the security and efficiency of the proposed scheme is analyzed and compared. Finally, the paper is concluded.

2   Review of Li et al.'s Scheme

We review Li et al.'s authentication protocol based on ECC [17], which is composed of three phases, i.e., registration, authentication, and password update. The elliptic curve equation is defined in the form: $E_p(a, b) : y^2 = x^3 + ax + b \pmod{p}$ over a prime finite field F_p, where $a, b \in F_p$, and $4a^3 + 27b^2 \neq 0 \pmod{p}$ [18]. The notations used in the paper are listed in Table 1.

2.1   Registration Phase

The registration phase involves users and the cloud service provider. When a user A wants to get cloud services, he needs to register in the service provider SP.

Table 1. Notations

Notation	Description
G	A group with order q
P	The generator of G
l	The security length parameter for hash values and random numbers
q	A large prime
A	A user
CS_i	The cloud server
SP	The service provider
ID_A	A's identity
PW_A	A's password
s	SP's private key
sP	SP's public key
K_{CS_i-SP}	The key shared between CS_i and SP
$h(\cdot)$	One-way hash functions: $\{0,1\} \rightarrow \{0,1\}^l$
K_{CS_i-A}, K_{A-CS_i}	The session key established between A and CS_i
$E_k(\cdot)/D_k(\cdot)$	The symmetric encryption/decryption algorithm with a key k
$\|\|$	The concatenation operation;
$\oplus$	The bitwise XOR operation

Step 1. User A first selects PW_A as his/her password. Then, A chooses a random number $r \in Z_q^*$ and computes $h(PW_A\|\|r)$. A sends $\{ID_A, h(PW_A\|\|r)\}$ to the service provider SP through a secure channel.

Step 2. When receiving the message, SP selects a random value $R \in \{0,1\}^{64}$ and computes $C_A = h(s\|\|ID_A\|\|R) \oplus h(PW_A\|\|r)$ for A. SP maintains the value R in database and issues a smart card which contains $\{ID_A, C_A\}$ to A.

Step 3. When receiving the smart card, A stores r into the card. The security parameters in the smart card are $\{ID_A, r, C_A\}$.

2.2 Authentication and Key Exchange Phase

When A wants to get the cloud service, he/she needs to complete a mutual authentication and key exchange with the ith cloud server CS_i.

Step 1. $A \rightarrow CS_i$
A inserts his/her card and inputs his/her password PW_A. Then, he/she selects two random values, $a, r_1 \in Z_q^*$. A computes $K = h(a \cdot sP)$ and $M_A = h(K\|\|r_1) \oplus ID_A$. Next, A reveals $X_A = h(PW_A\|\|r) \oplus C_A$, computes $N_A = h(K\|\|r_1\|\|X_A)$ as the authentication message, and sends $\{aP, r_1, M_A, N_A\}$ to the cloud server CS_i.

Step 2. $CS_i \rightarrow SP$
On receiving $\{aP, r_1, M_A, N_A\}$, CS_i selects a random value $b \in Z_q^*$ and computes $M_{CS_i} = E_{K_{CS_i-SP}}(aP, bP, r_1, M_A, N_A)$. Then, CS_i sends $\{ID_{CS_i}, M_{CS_i}\}$ to the service provider SP.

Step 3. $SP \rightarrow CS_i$

On receiving $\{ID_{CS_i}, M_{CS_i}\}$, SP first decrypts M_{CS_i} and obtains $\{aP, bP, r_1, M_A, N_A\}$. Then, SP computes $K = h(s \cdot aP)$ and $ID_A = h(K||r_1) \oplus M_A$. SP computes $X_A = h(s||ID_A||R)$. After that, SP verifies whether $N_A = h(K||r_1||X_A)$ holds. If it does, SP rejects it. Otherwise, SP selects a random value $s_1 \in Z_q^*$, and computes $Auth_{SP} = h(K||s_1||aP)$ and $M_{SP} = E_{K_{CS_i-SP}}(ID_A, aP, bP, s_1, Auth_{SP})$. SP sends M_{SP} to CS_i.

Step 4. $CS_i \rightarrow A$

On receiving M_{SP}, CS_i first decrypts M_{SP} and obtains $\{ID_A, aP, bP, s_1, Auth_{SP}\}$. Then CS_i verifies whether bP is equal to the random value it chooses. If it is not equal, CS_i rejects it. Otherwise, CS_i computes its authentication message $Auth_{CS_i} = h(b \cdot aP||bP||ID_{CS_i})$ and the session key between CS_i and A, $K_{CS_i-A} = h(abP||aP||bP||ID_A||ID_{CS_i})$. CS_i sends $\{ID_{CS_i}, bP, s_1, Auth_{SP}, Auth_{CS_i}\}$ to A.

Step 5. On receiving the messages from CS_i, user A computes and verifies whether $Auth_{SP} = h(K||s_1||aP)$ and $Auth_{CS_i} = h(b \cdot aP||bP||ID_{CS_i})$ hold. If one of them does not hold, A rejects them. Otherwise, A computes $K_{A-CS_i} = h(abP||aP||bP||ID_A||ID_{CS_i})$ as the session key between A and CS_i.

2.3   Password-Changing Phase

Step 1. If A wants to change the password, he/she performs the authentication phase first. After a successful authentication, A gets the secret information $h(K||s_1)$ shared with SP. Then, A inputs the new password PW_{new}, selects a random value $r' \in Z_q^*$ and submits $E_{h(K||s_1)}(ID_A, h(PW_{new}||r'))$ to SP.

Step 2. On receiving the message, SP decrypts it and obtains the new password of A. Then, SP selects another random value $R' \in \{0,1\}^{64}$ and computes $C_A' = h(s||ID_A||R') \oplus h(PW_{new}||r')$ for A. SP sends $E_{h(K||s_1)}(ID_A, C_A')$ to A.

Step 3. A decrypts $E_{h(K||s_1)}(ID_A, C_A')$ and updates the information in the smart card with $\{ID_A, r', C_A'\}$.

3   Weaknesses of Li et al.'s Scheme

We suppose that the adversary may intercept, insert, delete, or modify any message transmitted through the channel between the user and the server. Moreover, the secret information stored in the smart card may be exposed when the card is lost or stolen, since the secret information in it can be extracted by side channel attacks [19, 20]. Truly two-factor authentication should still be secure even either one of two factors are compromised.

Although Li et al.'s scheme is claimed to be secure against various attacks, we observe that the scheme suffers from wrong password login, DOS attack in the password-changing phase, and no provision for revocation.

3.1 Wrong Password Login

As is noted in [21], it is desired that there is an authentication test (also known as local password verification) to reject the login request if a legal user A enters a wrong password. In Li et al.'s scheme, if A mistakenly enters a wrong password, say PW'_A ($PW'_A \neq PW_A$), then Step 1 of authentication phase is still performed. Specifically, the smart card still computes $X'_A = h(PW'_A||r) \oplus C_A$ instead of $X_A = h(PW'_A||r) \oplus C_A$. In this case, A will send a wrong message $\{aP, r_1, M_A, N'_A\}$ instead of the valid message $\{aP, r_1, M_A, N_A\}$. Thus, no authentication test is in place to reject wrong password, which shows the inefficiency of scheme in terms of the detection of incorrect input. This leads to unnecessarily extra communication and computational overheads during the login and authentication phase.

3.2 DOS Attack in the Password-Changing Phase

We also identify that Li et al.'s scheme suffers from DOS attack, also known as de-synchronization attack, in the password-changing phase [22]. An adversary I can mount this attack by blocking the second message in this phase. The details of the procedure are presented as follows.

Step 1. A follows the specification of password-changing phase, and submits $E_{h(K||s_1)}(ID_A, h(PW_{new}||r'))$ to SP.

Step 2. SP obtains the new password of A by decrypting the received message. Then, SP selects $R' \in \{0,1\}^{64}$ and computes $C'_A = h(s||ID_A||R') \oplus h(PW_{new}||r')$ for A. SP stores the new value R' instead of the old one R, and sends $E_{h(K||s_1)}(ID_A, C'_A)$ to A.

Step 3. I intercepts the message $E_{h(K||s_1)}(ID_A, C'_A)$. A cannot receive the message. The information in A's smart card with is still $\{ID_A, r, C_A\}$, where $C_A = h(s||ID_A||R) \oplus h(PW_A||r)$.

At this point, the value maintained by SP is the new value R', while the value stored in the smart card is $C_A = h(s||ID_A||R) \oplus h(PW_A||r)$, which is computed by the old value R. As a result, the authentication between A and SP is destined to fail when A initiates a new session to be authenticated by SP.

3.3 No Provision for Revocation

In practice, revocation of lost/stolen smart card is one of the important security demands of smart card based authentication protocols [21]. If A's smart card is lost/stolen, some mechanism is needed to prevent the misuse of lost/stolen smart card. Otherwise, an attacker can impersonate A because the registration phase is incapable to detecting the re-registration with the old identity. To address this issue, the identity table must be maintained in the server's database, through which the invalid smart card will be detected. However, most of the existing smart card based authentication schemes including Li et al.'s scheme fail to take revocation into consideration in their schemes.

4 Our Improved Scheme

To remedy these flaws presented in Sect. 3, we adopt the concept of fuzzy verifier proposed by Wang et al. [23, 24] to achieve wrong password detection and local password update. Specifically, we improve the authentication scheme of Li et al. in the following aspects. (1) The registration and authentication phase is revised to enable wrong password detection and revocation. (2) The password-changing phase is revised to avoid DOS attack. (3) Revocation and re-registration phase is added to prevent the misuse of lost/stolen smart card.

Our scheme consists of 4 phases: registration, authentication, password update, and revocation and re-registration.

4.1 Registration Phase

In the registration phase of our improve scheme, Step 1 is the same as Li et al.'s scheme. Step 2 and 3, which are different from Li et al.'s scheme, is given as follows.

Step 2. When receiving the messages, SP selects a random value $R \in \{0, 1\}^{64}$ and computes $C_A = h(s||ID_A||R) \oplus h(PW_A||r)$ for A. SP updates its identity information table with the new entry $\{ID_A, R\}$, and issues a smart card which contains $\{ID_A, C_A\}$ to A.

Step 3. When receiving the smart card, A computes $HPW_A = h(h(PW_A||r) \bmod m)$, where m is a medium integer, $2^8 \leq m \leq 2^{16}$, which determines the capacity of the pool of the PW_A against offline password guessing attack [21]. Then A stores r, HPW_A into the card. The security parameters in the smart card are $\{ID_A, r, HPW_A, C_A\}$.

4.2 Authentication and Key Exchange Phase

When A wants to access the ith cloud server CS_i, he/she needs to complete the authentication and key exchange phase. Steps 2–5 are the same as Li et al.'s scheme. Step 1, which is different from Li et al.'s scheme, is given as follows.

Step 1. $A \rightarrow CS_i$

A inserts his/her card and inputs his/her password PW_A. Then, The smart card computes $HPW_A' = h(h(PW_A||r) \bmod m)$. If the equation $HPW_A? = HPW_A'$ does not hold, the card rejects the request. Otherwise, it continues to selects two random values $a, r_1 \in Z_q^*$. A computes $K = h(a \cdot sP)$ and $M_A = h(K||r_1) \oplus ID_A$. Next, A reveals $X_A = h(PW_A||r) \oplus C_A$, computes $N_A = h(K||r_1||X_A)$ as the authentication message, and sends $\{aP, r_1, M_A, N_A\}$ to the cloud server CS_i.

4.3 Password Change Phase

In this phase, A update the password through the following steps.

Step 1. If A needs to change his password, he inserts his card into a terminal, and enters PW_A.

Step 2. The smart card computes $HPW'_A = h(h(PW_A||r) \bmod m)$. If the equation $HPW_A? = HPW'_A$ does not hold, the card rejects the request. Otherwise, A selects a new password PW_{new}, and calculates $C'_A = C_A \oplus h(PW_A||r) \oplus h(PW_{new}||r)$ and replace C_A with C'_A.

4.4   Revocation and Re-Registration Phase

In this phase, A can revoke his/her account and re-register without changing his/her identity ID_A.

1. For revocation of A's account, SP verifies his/her personal identities, such as personal identification card, and then simply removes the random number R from the identity information table. After the revocation of A's account, SP rejects the login request since the corresponding random value R is not presented in the identity Table
2. In the case of re-registration of A with the same identity ID_A, SP verifies whether ID_A matches with any existing entry in the identity information table. If so, SP continues to check whether the status of A is inactive. If it is true, that is, A has been already registered but the status is inactive. SP executes the registration phase to reactivate A's account. Otherwise, the re-registration request is rejected.

5   Security and Efficiency Analysis

In this section, we present the security analysis of the proposed protocol. Due to limited space, we only show that the improved protocol can resist the attacks and provide the missing features presented in Sect. 3.

5.1   Wrong Password Login Freeness

As is presented in Sect. 3.1, there is no authentication test to reject the login request when a legal user A enters a wrong password, which will lead to inefficiency and unnecessary communication and computational overheads during the login and authentication phase. However, there is an inevitable tradeoff between wrong password detection and the resistance to offline password guessing attack when the smart card is lost/stolen. In the improved scheme, we adopt the concept of fuzzy verifier proposed by Wang et al. [23, 24]. On the one hand, it can be used to provide timely wrong password and fingerprint detection when login. Specifically, the smart card checks the validity of user input password PW_A before the authentication phase. Since the smart card computes $HPW'_A = h(h(PW_A||r)\bmod m)$ and compares it with the stored value of HPW_A in its memory to verify the legitimacy of the user before the smart card proceeds to the following operations. On the other hand, the adversary has to perform online guessing to determine the correct password from as high as 2^{12} candidates, which can be relatively easily detected and thwarted by the server by using rate-limiting and/or lockout policy [16]. Therefore, the problem of wrong password login is thwarted.

5.2   Immunity from DOS Attack in the Password-Changing Phase

In Li et al.'s scheme, if a legitimate user A wants to change her password, she has to send the new password in the request to SP, and then waits for the reply from SP to update the user-specific security information stored in the smart card. This interactive process enables the adversary to de-synchronize the information stored in the smart card and that maintained by SP. In our improved scheme, A can change her password without interacting with SP. That is, the user-specific security parameters stored in the smart card can be updated locally. Moreover, the user-specific security parameters maintained by SP do not need to be updated during the password-changing phase. Thus, the risk of in-consistence is eliminated, and the adversary cannot de-synchronize the information of the smart card and SP. Moreover, the fuzzy verifier mechanism is in place to resist wrong password entry. Therefore, DOS attack in the password-changing phase is thwarted.

5.3   Provision for Revocation and Re-Registration

In our scheme, the identity table is maintained by the service provider, through which the invalid smart card will be detected, as is presented in Sect. 4.4. As a result, revocation of lost/stolen smart card is accomplished, and the re-registration with the old identity is also detected.

5.4   Feature and Efficiency Comparison

We compare our proposed authentication scheme with existing authentication schemes [17, 25] in terms of security features. The results of comparison are shown in Table 2. From Table 2, it is obvious that our scheme is the only one which is capable of resisting all known attacks and fulfills the desirable security features.

For efficiency analysis, we compare the time complexity of our scheme and the related schemes, including the registration phase, login phase and authentication phase. The following notations are defined to facilitate the analysis.

m: the time complexity for scalar multiplication of ECC;
e: the time complexity for symmetric key encryption/decryption;
h: the time complexity of hash function.

The results of efficiency comparison are summarized in Table 3. Although the computation cost of our scheme is higher than that of [17, 25], we argue that this is because our scheme ensures the robustness of the authentication scheme and provides more security features. From Table 2, we can see that the scheme of Li et al. [25] fails to provide user anonymity and untraceability, and the scheme of Li et al. [17] cannot resist cloud server impersonation attack and denial of service attack. The additional computational cost is worthwhile in view of the security strength and features accomplished.

Table 2. Comparison of security features

Functionality\Scheme	Li et al.'s [25]	Li et al.'s [17]	Ours
Privileged insider attack	Yes	Yes	Yes
Stolen-verifier attack	Yes	Yes	Yes
Online password guessing attack	Yes	Yes	Yes
Offline password guessing attack	No	Yes	Yes
Wrong password login	No	No	Yes
Modification attack	Yes	Yes	Yes
User impersonation attack	Yes	Yes	Yes
Cloud server impersonation attack	Yes	Yes	Yes
Service provider impersonation attack	Yes	Yes	Yes
DOS attack	Yes	No	Yes
Mutual authentication	Yes	Yes	Yes
Known key security	Yes	Yes	Yes
Perfect forward secrecy	No	Yes	Yes
User anonymity	No	Yes	Yes
User untraceability	No	Yes	Yes
Provision for revocation and re-registration	No	No	Yes

Table 3. Comparison of computation cost

Schemes	Li et al.'s [36]	Li et al.'s [47]	Ours
Registration phase	$6h$	$2h$	$3h$
Authentication phase	$28h$	$6m + 4e + 14h$	$6m + 4e + 15h$
Overall computation cost	$34h$	$6m + 4e + 16h$	$6m + 4e + 18h$

6 Conclusion

Authentication is a necessity to ensure that sensitive data in the cloud are not available to illegal users. In this paper, we have used the authentication protocol of Li et al. as a case study and demonstrated the subtleties and challenges in designing a two-factor authentication and key agreement protocol. We have shown that their scheme is susceptible to the problem of wrong password login. Furthermore, their scheme is prone to DOS attack in the password-changing phase. Finally, it fails to provide user revocation when the mobile device is lost or stolen. Then, we have proposed an improved authentication and key agreement protocol to remedy these drawbacks in Li et al.'s scheme. We have shown that the proposed protocol can withstand various known attacks and provide more security features compared with Li et al.'s protocol.

Acknowledgements. This work is supported by Supported by National Natural Science Foundation of China (Program No. 61672413, U1405255, U1536202, 61372075, 61472310), National High Technology Research and Development Program (863 Program) (Program No. 2015AA016007), Natural Science Basic Research Plan in Shaanxi Province of China

(Program No. 2016JM6005), Fundamental Research Funds for the Central Universities (Program No. JB161501), and Specific project on research and development platform of Shanghai Science and Technology Committee (Program No. 14DZ2294400).

References

1. Ardagna, A., Asal, R., Damiani, E., et al.: From security to assurance in the cloud: a survey. ACM Comput. Surv. (CSUR) **48**(1), 2:1–50 (2015)
2. Li, H., Yang, Y., Luan, T., Liang, X., Zhou, L., Shen, X.: Enabling fine-grained multi-keyword search supporting classified sub-dictionaries over encrypted cloud data. IEEE Trans. Dependable Secure Comput. **13**(3), 312–325 (2015)
3. Ren, Y., Shen, J., Wang, J., Han, J., Lee, S.: Mutual verifiable provable data auditing in public cloud storage. J. Internet Technol. **16**(2), 317–323 (2015)
4. He, D., Zeadally, S., Wu, L.: Certificateless public auditing scheme for cloud-assisted wireless body area networks. IEEE Syst. J. (2015). doi:10.1109/JSYST.2015.2428620
5. Jiang, Q., Ma, J., Li, G., Yang, L.: Robust two-factor authentication and key agreement preserving user privacy. Int. J. Netw. Secur. **16**(3), 229–240 (2014)
6. Jiang, Q., Ma, J., Lu, X., Tian, Y.: An efficient two-factor user authentication scheme with unlinkability for wireless sensor networks. Peer-to-Peer Netw. Appl. **8**(6), 1070–1081 (2015)
7. Shen, J., Tan, H., Moh, S., et al.: Enhanced secure sensor association and key management in wireless body area networks. J. Commun. Netw. **17**(5), 453–462 (2015)
8. Jiang, Q., Wei, F., Fu, S., Ma, J., Li, G., Alelaiwi, A.: Robust extended chaotic maps-based three-factor authentication scheme preserving biometric template privacy. Nonlinear Dyn. **83**(4), 2085–2101 (2016)
9. Fushan, W., Jianfeng, Ma., Aijun, G., Guangsong, L., Chuangui, Ma.: A provably secure three-party password authenticated key exchange protocol without using server's public-keys and symmetric cryptosystems. ITC **44**(2), 195–206 (2015)
10. Choudhury, A.J., et al.: A strong user authentication framework for cloud computing. In: Proceedings of IEEE Asia-Pacific Services Computing Conference, 12–15, pp. 110–115 (2011)
11. Hao, Z., Zhong, S., Yu, N.: A time-bound ticket-based mutual authentication scheme for cloud computing. Int. J. Comput. Commun. Control **6**(2), 227–235 (2011)
12. Pippal, R.S., Jaidhar, C.D., Tapaswi, S.: Enhanced time-bound ticket-based mutual authentication scheme for cloud computing. Informatica **37**(2), 149–156 (2013)
13. Jiang, Q., Khan, M.K., Lu, X., Ma, J., He, D.: A privacy preserving three-factor authentication protocol for e-health clouds. J. Supercomput. (2016). doi:10.1007/s11227-015-1610-x
14. Hwang, M.S., Sun, T.H.: Using smart card to achieve a single sign-on for multiple cloud services. IETE Tech. Rev. **30**(5), 410–416 (2013)
15. Tsai, J.L., Lo, N.W.: A privacy-aware authentication scheme for distributed mobile cloud computing services. IEEE Syst. J. **9**(3), 805–815 (2015)
16. Qi, J., Jianfeng, Ma., Fushan, W.: On the security of a privacy-aware authentication scheme for distributed mobile cloud computing services. IEEE Syst. J. (2016). doi:10.1109/JSYST.2016.2574719
17. Li, H., Li, F., Song, C., et al.: Towards smart card based mutual authentication schemes in cloud computing. KSII Trans. Internet Inf. Syst. **9**(7), 2719–2735 (2015)
18. Hankerson, D., Menezes, A., Vanstone, S.: Guide to Elliptic Curve Cryptography. Springer Professional Computing. Springer, Berlin (2004)

19. Kocher, P.C., Jaffe, J., Jun, B.: Differential power analysis. In: Wiener, M. (ed.) CRYPTO 1999. LNCS, vol. 1666, pp. 388–397. Springer, Heidelberg (1999)
20. Messerges, T.S., Dabbish, E.A., Sloan, R.H.: Examining smart-card security under the threat of power analysis attacks. IEEE Trans. Comput. **51**(5), 541–552 (2002)
21. Odelu, V., Das, A.K., Goswami, A.: A secure biometrics-based multi-server authentication protocol using smart cards. IEEE Trans. Inf. Forensics Secur. **10**(9), 1953–1966 (2015)
22. Jiang, Q., Ma, J., Li, G., et al.: An efficient ticket based authentication protocol with unlinkability for wireless access networks. Wireless Pers. Commun. **77**(2), 1489–1506 (2014)
23. Wang, D., He, D., Wang, P., Chu, C.H.: Anonymous two-factor authentication in distributed systems: certain goals are beyond attainment. IEEE Trans. Dependable Secure Comput. **12** (4), 428–442 (2015)
24. Wang, D., Wang, P.: On the usability of two-factor authentication. In: Tian, J., Jing, J., Srivatsa, M. (eds.) International Conference on Security and Privacy in Communication Networks. LNICS, vol. 152, pp. 141–150. Springer, Heidelberg (2014)
25. Li, X., Xiong, Y., Ma, J., Wang, W.: An efficient and security dynamic identity based authentication protocol for multi-server architecture using smart cards. J. Netw. Comput. Appl. **35**(2), 763–769 (2012)

Another SPA Key Recovery Against Random Order Countermeasures for AES Key Expansion

Mengting Chen[1,2], Yang Li[1,2(✉)], and Jian Wang[1,2]

[1] College of Computer Science and Technology,
Nanjing University of Aeronautics and Astronautics, Nanjing, China
chenmengting0601@163.com, {li.yang,wangjian}@nuaa.edu.cn
[2] Collaborative Innovation Center of Novel Software Technology and
Industrialization, Nanjing, China

Abstract. To increase the resistance against power analysis, random order countermeasure applied to AES key expansion was proposed and evaluated by Clavier et al. in CHES 2014. The proposed column-wise random order countermeasure showed certain resistance when the power consumption of the key expansion part is used for key recovery. For further evaluation, Clavier et al. analyzed the improvement of key recovery attack using fault injection as additional information. As for the acceleration of the key recovery, this work argues that extracting power information of AES state is more preferred than performing fault injections for practical attackers. This work comprehensively evaluates the random order countermeasure assuming the attackers use the power consumptions of AES state to accelerate the key recovery. We studied the relationship between key recovery result and the amount of information from AES state via both theoretical analysis and key recovery simulations. The results (a) demonstrate a set of effective key extractions with no fault injections and (b) discover the most cost-effective attack is extracting Hamming weight of 12 bytes for 2 AES executions, whose key extraction averagely finishes in 1 min.

Keywords: Power analysis · AES key expansion · Countermeasures

1 Introduction

The security of cryptographic protocols and primitives are the key basis for constructing, maintaining and providing a secure cloud computing service. Nowadays, for a well designed cryptographic application, the attackers can bypass the mathematical resistance and use physical attacks to practically break it. Non-invasive physical attacks including side-channel attacks [1] and fault attacks [2] have practically broken the implementations of cryptographic primitives in the real word. Thus, evaluating the resistance of an implemented cryptographic primitive against the physical attacks becomes a necessity.

This work focuses on a specific security evaluation for Advanced Encryption Standard (AES) [3], which is the most studied block cipher in literatures.

© Springer International Publishing AG 2016
X. Sun et al. (Eds.): ICCCS 2016, Part I, LNCS 10039, pp. 322–334, 2016.
DOI: 10.1007/978-3-319-48671-0_29

The physical security of AES implementation has been largely discussed in academic [4–8]. In CHES 2014, the security of AES key expansion against simple power analysis was discussed considering two possible countermeasures [9]. The first type of countermeasure is boolean masking, and the second countermeasure is random order for the storage of the AES round keys. This work extends the security evaluation for the random order countermeasure. Previous work found that the key extraction using only power traces could fail after all kinds of optimization. Then it was proposed to use fault injection in additional with power traces to accelerate the key recovery. We believe fault injection discussed in [9] is not the first choice of a side-channel attacker. A more practical way is try to extract more information from the power traces, for example the Hamming weight of AES state, to accelerate the key recovery.

The contributions of this work can be summarized as follows.

Contribution

- We point out that using Hamming weight of AES state can help attackers to accelerate the key recovery against AES key expansion with random order countermeasure. Extracting a few Hamming weight information of the AES state works as an alternate method to accelerate the key recovery that does not require fault injections.
- We study the possible techniques and variations that the attackers could apply in practice for the key recovery. All the discussed attack scenarios are verified via key recovery simulations. The results show that with the Hamming weight of an AES state from 1 or 2 AES executions, the key recovery can be accelerated to different extend.
- We discuss the trade-off between the additional information extracted from power traces and the key recovery efficiency via key recovery simulations. A cost-effective key recovery uses Hamming weights of 12 bytes for 2 AES executions, whose average key recovery time is less than 1 min. This work shows even without fault injections, the attacker can efficiently extract AES key against random order countermeasure.

The rest of this paper is organized as follows. In Sect. 2, we review AES and briefly introduce the existing power analysis attacks against AES key expansion and their countermeasures. In Sect. 3, we propose a new fast key recovery method for random order countermeasure. Section 4 shows the experimental verification of the proposed attack. Section 5 concludes this paper.

2 Preliminaries

2.1 Review AES Key Expansion

Advanced Encryption Standard (AES) was selected by the U.S. National Institution of Standard and Technology (NIST) in 2001 to replace the Data Encryption Standard (DES). The block size of AES is fixed to 128 bits, and the key size can be 128, 192 or 256 bits, corresponding to 10, 12 or 14 rounds of encryption and decryption. The 128-bit data block in encryption, decryption and round keys are usually considered as a 4×4 byte matrix. The byte matrix of intermediate date of 128 bits, which is called state, represents a block of data with 128 bits or 16 bytes.

This paper mainly discusses the 128-bit version of AES as AES-128. Figure 1 depicts the encryption flow of AES-128. Each AES round consists of four operations including SubBytes, ShiftRows, MixColumns and AddRoundKey except the final round which is without MixColumn.

We denote K as the initial key. Each round uses its round key K_r for $r = 0, 1, \ldots, 15$ and we have $K_0 = K$. All the round keys are the results of the key expansion based on the initial key K. The 16 key bytes of K_r are expressed as $k_{r,i}$ and $i = 0, 1, \ldots, 15$. The key expansion of AES-128 is based on the following formulas

$$\begin{cases} k_{r,i} = k_{r-1,i} \oplus S\big(k_{r-1,12+((i+1) \bmod 4)}\big) \oplus c_r, & \text{for } i = 0,\ldots,3 \quad (1) \\ k_{r,i} = k_{r-1,i} \oplus k_{r,i-4}, & \text{for } i = 4,\ldots,15 \quad (2) \end{cases}$$

where S is the AES substitution-box (S-box) and c_r is the round constant with variable r. Note that S-box is the only non-linear operation in the AES key expansion. For AES key expansion, each round key, e.g. K_0, can be expanded to all the other round keys.

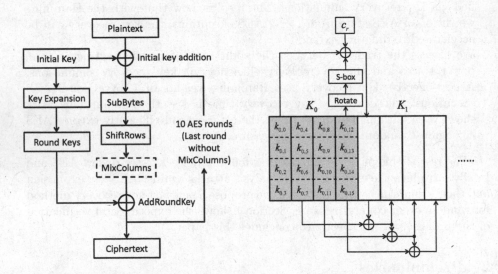

Fig. 1. AES encryption flow.   Fig. 2. AES key expansion.

The process of key expansion from K_0 to K_1 is shown in Fig. 2. The round keys can be computed column by column. For a round key, the computation of the first column is different from the other three columns, which involves S-box, byte rotate and round constant c_r.

2.2 AES Key Expansion Under SPA

When considering the security of AES against physical attacks, most of the literatures focus on the round function of AES. However, there are some works mentioned that the AES key can be extracted with Simple Power Analysis (SPA) from the key expansion part of AES. In contrast to Differential Power Analysis (DPA), SPA observes only a few or only one power trace for the key extraction. Among the SPA attacks on AES key expansion, most of them assumed the target to be an AES implementation on a 8-bit micro controller. Furthermore, the leakage model for a 8-bit micro controller is usually considered to fit the Hamming weight model. In other words, the attacker can extract the Hamming weight of the operated 8-bit value from the power traces. As for the key expansion, it is assumed that the Hamming weight of key bytes of all the round keys can be extracted [10–12].

In 2003, Mangard [13] first described this key recovery problem as the SPA attack on AES key expansion. It is found that the Hamming weight extracted from the power consumption of smart cards can be used to reveal the initial key of AES. The key recovery process is essentially a continuously reduction of the key space using Hamming weight information and the internal computational relations between round key bytes. To make the key recovery effective and efficient, the key recovery algorithm has to use several techniques in accelerating the process of key recovery.

In 2005, VanLaven et al. [14] improved the key recovery process for the SPA attack on AES key expansion. They proposed a key search algorithm as the guess-compute-and-backtrack algorithm. After guessing a key byte value, some related key bytes could be computed with guessed keys, then all the computed key byte values can be checked with the Hamming weight information. If all the key byte values are correct, the next key byte value will be guessed. Otherwise, the algorithm backtrack to a previous stage. Another important contribution of [14] is that the author discussed how to optimize the guess sequence of the key bytes to maximize the number of computable key bytes during recover process. As the result of the optimized guess sequence, the attack efficiency is largely improved. In [14], the key of AES-128 can be recovered as fast as 16 ms.

2.3 Random Order as a Countermeasure for AES Key Expansion

In 2014, Clavier et al. [9] first conducted the security evaluation of AES key expansion considering two approaches of countermeasures. As the countermeasure increases the difficulty of SPA key recovery, boolean masking and a column-wise random order storage of key bytes have been considered. It is shown that for the boolean masking countermeasure, a 11-byte entropy masking and a 16-byte entropy masking are still vulnerable to the improved SPA attacks. In this paper, we concentrate on the random order countermeasure, since it seems to be more effective than boolean masking as a power analysis countermeasure.

The applied random order countermeasure in [9] is a column-wise random order. As mentioned in Sect. 2.1, AES round keys could be computed column by column. Based on this property, it is reasonable to randomly shuffle the key bytes which are inside the same column of a round key. After applying the column-wise countermeasure, the sequence of the 4 key bytes is in a random order. For each column, although 4 Hamming weight could still be obtained using SPA, the attacker cannot ensure the exact position for the 4 non-ordered Hamming weight. Figure 3 is an example of the available information of SPA attack for random order countermeasure. The attackers get 4 non-ordered Hamming weight for each column of round key, e.g. K_{10}.

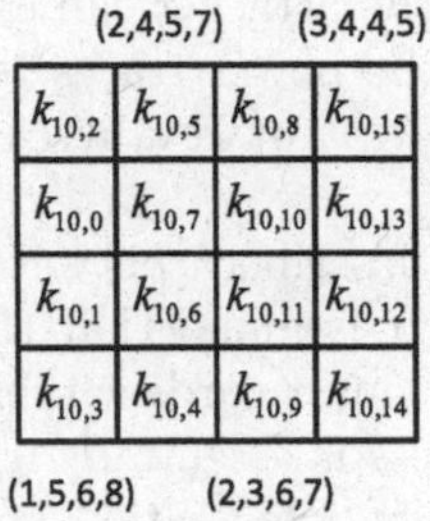

$$(2,4,5,7) \qquad (3,4,4,5)$$

$k_{10,2}$	$k_{10,5}$	$k_{10,8}$	$k_{10,15}$
$k_{10,0}$	$k_{10,7}$	$k_{10,10}$	$k_{10,13}$
$k_{10,1}$	$k_{10,6}$	$k_{10,11}$	$k_{10,12}$
$k_{10,3}$	$k_{10,4}$	$k_{10,9}$	$k_{10,14}$

$$(1,5,6,8) \qquad (2,3,6,7)$$

Fig. 3. Example of random order countermeasure.

Basic Key Recovery Attack Against Random Order Countermeasure. In [9], Clavier et al. first tried to apply the key recovery using Hamming weight information of random ordered key bytes as the basic attack. Basic attack adopts the idea of a booking system combined with the guess-compute-and-backtrack algorithm. That is, to every position, attackers will book a candidate Hamming weight for it and then determine its value either by guessing or computing. If one position could be directly calculated with already determined key bytes, then compute it and compare it with the candidate Hamming weight list. If couldn't, guess the value of it which should satisfy the constraint of its booked Hamming weight. Once the Hamming weight of the computed position is not in the candidate list, or all available values of the guessed position are exhausted, it will backtrack to the previous guessed position. For instance, Fig. 3 shows the Hamming weight of K_{10} that the attackers get. Among the 4 candidates (1, 5, 6, 8), first book $HW(k_{10,0}) = 1$ and guess its value $k_{10,0} = 1$. Similarly, book $HW(k_{10,4}) = 2$ and guess its value $k_{10,4} = 3$. Then compute the $k_{9,4} = k_{10,0} \oplus k_{10,4} = 2$ and check it with its candidate Hamming weight list. If $HW(k_{9,4}) = 1$ is in the list, then book value 1 as the Hamming weight of $k_{9,4}$ and update the candidate Hamming weight list of the other 3 key bytes in the same column with $k_{9,4}$. If $HW(k_{9,4}) = 1$ is not in the list, backtrack to $k_{10,4}$ and re-guess another value satisfying $HW(k_{10,4}) = 2$. If no more available value satisfies $HW(k_{10,4}) = 2$, then book Hamming weight of $k_{10,4}$ with another candidate.

Table 1 shows the result of basic attack over 100 runs of experiments in [9]. About 27 % of the key recovery experiments cannot finish within a reasonable time limit, which implies that the computation effort of the key recovery for random order countermeasure is non-negligible. Only 41 % cases ended in 1 h and we estimate the average runtime is as long as 2 h.

Table 1. Basic attack result against random order in [9]

Time elapsed	⩽30 min	⩽1 h	⩽2 h	⩽3 h	⩽4 h	⩽5 h	⩽6 h	+6 h
# Over 100 runs	6	25	41	55	66	71	73	27

Fault Injection Key Recovery Attack. In order to accelerate the key recovery, in [9] Clavier et al. considers an attack that combines fault attack (FA) with SPA. The idea is that the attackers could randomly induce a fault into a key byte. The fault model is a random modification of the chosen byte value. Due to key expansion, the induced fault will cause differential in some round key bytes and also their corresponding Hamming weight. By SPA, attackers could observe the differentials in Hamming weight and infer the position of these changed key bytes. For example, Fig. 4 shows the changed positions in K_{10} when $k_{9,0}$ is modified. The attackers will compare the original Hamming weight to the fault-induced Hamming weight and observe the changes. Then, attackers could deduce out the position of the changed key bytes and reduce the number of candidate Hamming weight of other 3 bytes in the same column. Afterwards, attackers will retrieve the round keys using the idea of basic attack, that is the booking system with guess-compute-and-backtrack algorithm.

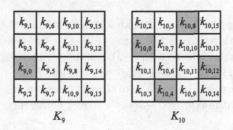

Fig. 4. Fault propagation in round keys.

The experiment result of fault injection key recovery attack indicates that the average attack time is reduced to 20 min using 1 fault injection. However, we notice that this attack pattern uses two kinds of attack techniques as SPA and FA. It requires more knowledge from attackers and increases the cost and equipment difficulty of the attack.

3   Fast Key Recovery Without Fault Injection Against Column-Wise Random Order Countermeasure

In [9], two types of key recovery attacks have succeeded in attacking the AES key expansion with the column-wise random order countermeasure. The basic attack complete the key recovery using 2 h in average and there are still 27 % of experiments cannot finish within a reasonable timeout. Then, fault injection is combined with basic attack so that the average key recovery time is reduced to 20 min and the success rate is improved. However, the usage of two kinds of attack techniques, SPA and FA, inevitably require more expertise from attackers and increases the cost of the attack. Furthermore, since there are key recovery attacks that use the fault injections to key expansion only [15], the attack method that combines fault analysis and power analysis makes less sense.

In this paper, we propose an attack method that only uses the power consumption information to perform the security evaluation of column-wise random order. The basic idea is to use additional Hamming weight information of AES state to help recover the round keys. Our attack pattern is based on the circumstance that attackers could get Hamming weight of some bytes of the AES state. Hereafter, from an attacker's perspective, we discuss the practical key recovery strategy including the choice of start point of the attack, the choice of the AES state and the key guessing sequence.

3.1   Choice of Start Point

For a target chip that executes the AES encryption, the attackers could have access to both the plaintext and the corresponding ciphertext. The start point of our attack must start near these public data, i.e. plaintext and ciphertext. The power trace of the calculations near the public data are easier to extract even with random delay countermeasure that adds random delays during AES execution.

Under the assumption that plaintext, ciphertext and the related power consumption can be achieved with the same difficulty, we select ciphertext as the start point for a faster key recovery. To explain the reasons, we review the graphed representation of AES-128 key expansion from [14] to describe the computational relationship between round key bytes. In [14], the optimized key guessing sequence that maximized the key recovery efficiency was discussed using this graph.

Figure 5 shows the graphed representation of key expansion for AES-128, in which each circle represents a key byte. The label $k_{N,i}$ on the left side stands for the position of every key byte, where N is the round number and i represents the key byte position. For example, the 11 circles of the top line from left to right correspond to $k_{0,0}, k_{1,0}, \ldots$ until $k_{10,0}$. For each grey triangle, the 3 vertexes have an exclusive-or computational relationship, while for each black triangle, the 3 vertexes have the computational relationship using S-box. Note that given any two vertexes of a triangle, the other one can be computed. For example, the

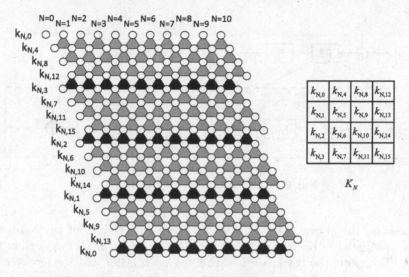

Fig. 5. Graphed representation of key expansion for AES-128.

second circle of the top line is $k_{1,0}$ and the first two circles of the second line are $k_{0,4}$ and $k_{1,4}$. Since $k_{1,4} = k_{1,0} \oplus k_{0,4}$, knowing any two of them, the other one can be directly computed.

In key recovery process, the attackers guess key byte values according to the Hamming weight in a certain sequence, while obtaining the key bytes which can be calculated with the initially identified key bytes. When the directly computed key byte value does not match the Hamming weight of its position, the current guessed key byte is wrong, the key recovery algorithm backtracks to the previous stage. For each guess of a key byte, itself and the key bytes that can be calculated from it can be used to check the Hamming weight information. Therefore, for each key guess, the more key bytes can be calculated with known key bytes, the faster the key space shrinks and the higher the key recovery efficiency is.

We use Fig. 5 to explore the optimized recovery sequence for the start point near plaintext or ciphertext. If the start point is set to plaintext, K_0 is the main target for key recovery. When guessing each byte of K_0, one of the best guess sequence is $k_{0,13}, k_{0,0}, k_{0,4}, k_{0,8}, \ldots, k_{0,5}, k_{0,9}$. Starting with guessing $k_{0,13}$, the number of key values that can be additionally calculated for each key value guess is $1, 1, 1, 1, 2, 2, 2, 2, 3, 3, 3, 3, 4$ and 4. After guessing $k_{0,9}$, all remaining key bytes can be calculated.

If the start point is set to ciphertext, K_{10} is the main target for key recovery. When guessing each byte of K_{10}, one of the best guess sequence is $k_{10,0}, k_{10,4}, k_{10,8}, k_{10,12}, \ldots, k_{10,9}, k_{10,13}$. Starting with guessing $k_{10,0}$, the number of key values that can be additionally calculated for each key value guess is $1, 2, 3, 3, 4, 5, 6, 6, 7, 8, 9, 9, 10$ and 10. After guessing $k_{10,13}$, all remaining key bytes can be calculated.

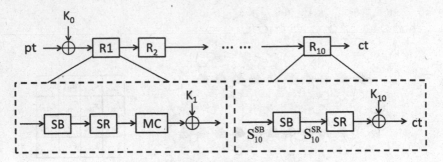

Fig. 6. State location for S_{10}^{SB} and S_{10}^{SR}.

Based on the above analysis, it is clear that the number of key bytes that can be calculated in the key recovery process for K_{10} is much larger than that for K_0. Therefore, the key space is shrinking much faster and the key recovery efficiency is much higher when using ciphertext as the start point.

3.2   Choice of AES State

There are two AES states near ciphertext can be chosen, i.e. the state before SubBytes S_{10}^{SB} and the state before ShiftRows S_{10}^{SR}, as shown in Fig. 6. Note that the state after ShiftRow is essentially equivalent to S_{10}^{SR} since they can be linearly transformed into each other. If the Hamming weight of S_{10}^{SR} is used, some candidates of Hamming weight ordering directly fail the linear calculation among K_{10}, ciphertext and S_{10}^{SR}. If the Hamming weight of S_{10}^{SB} is used, the non-linear part S-box could enable a faster restriction of Hamming weight than that of S_{10}^{SR}. The reason is that S-box is the only non-linear part in AES key expansion, which confuses the relationship between input bits and output bits. By a preliminary experiment, we find out that the key space restricted using S_{10}^{SB} is about 49.4 % smaller than that of S_{10}^{SR}. Thus, we consider the attackers will choose Hamming weight of S_{10}^{SB} to pursue the best key recovery complexity.

3.3   Key Recovery Algorithm with AES State Hamming Weight

The key recovery problem becomes a restriction process of key space using 176 Hamming weight of round keys with column-wise random order denoted as HW_K, the Hamming weight of AES state S_{10}^{SB} denoted as HW_S and the ciphertext denoted as CT. In the key recovery process, first a function GETHW is called to return all the possible Hamming weight sequences of K_{10} with exact positions as $\mathrm{HWSET}_{K_{10}}$. Then, for every possible Hamming weight sequence $\mathrm{HW}_{K_{10}}^t$ in $\mathrm{HWSET}_{K_{10}}$, two functions KEYRECOVER and KEYVERIFY are used to recover the round keys. The function KEYRECOVER uses $\mathrm{HW}_{K_{10}}^t$, which is a possible Hamming weight sequence of K_{10}, Hamming weight of AES state HW_S and CT as inputs to obtain the possible values of K_{10}. The function KEYVERIFY verifies the correctness of K_{10} with the byte-wise Hamming weight of other 10 round keys. Algorithm 1 outlines the process of recovering AES round keys.

Algorithm 1. Key Recovery Algorithm with AES State Hamming Weight

---
Input: HW_S, HW_K, CT
Output: K
1: $HWSET_{K_{10}} \leftarrow \text{GetHW}(HW_K)$
2: **for all** $HW_{K_{10}}^t \in HWSET_{K_{10}}$ **do**
3:     $K_{10}^t \leftarrow \text{KeyRecover}(HW_S, HW_{K_{10}}^t, CT)$
4:     $K \leftarrow \text{KeyVerify}(K_{10}^t, HW_K)$
5: **end for**

In function KeyRecover, it should be noticed that not all 16 Hamming weight of state S_{10}^{SB} are necessary in recovery process. We consider the situation that attackers probably only get a part of Hamming weight of state S_{10}^{SB}. Thus, first the number and position of the obtained Hamming weight of S_{10}^{SB} should be confirmed. For every confirmed position of the state, the corresponding position's possible value set of K_{10} could be initially determined with its Hamming weight. Then, with the calculation relationship $HW(CT_i \oplus k_{10,i}) = HW(SR(SB(S_{10,i}^{SB})))$, we could further shrink the value set of K_{10}. Compared with the "brute force" technique, the value set is relatively acceptable to deal with. In order to further improve the computational efficiency, in function KeyVerify we use the optimized sequence, i.e. $k_{10,0}, k_{10,4}, k_{10,8}, k_{10,12}, \ldots, k_{10,9}, k_{10,13}$, to verify the correctness of each possible value of K_{10}. When guessing each byte of K_{10} in the possible value set, the optimized sequence could maximize the number of computable bytes and therefore, more quickly to remove false key values.

4 Experimental Verification

Our experiments are implemented on a normal PC with Intel Core I3-3220 CPU and 4.0 GB of RAM. The key recovery algorithm is written in python. The keys are randomly generated and 176 Hamming weight of round key bytes are used as the input to the key recovery algorithm. We simulated the situation of getting 1 power trace and 2 power traces, separately. Note that, we consider 2 traces since at least two AES executions are necessary to get the differential when fault injection is used to accelerate the key recovery. Our experiments verify the relationship between the key recovery results and the number of key bytes whose Hamming weight are used in the key recovery. Table 2 summarizes the result of the performed key recovery simulations. Note that the last 5 lines of Table 2 are the fault injection attack results from [9] for comparison.

As shown in Table 2, we set the simulation timeout as 600 or 2,000 s. Each line represents the key recovery result for an attack scenario. For example, line 1 means that 500 times of runs on 16 bytes for 2 traces are executed, 100 % of them terminated in 600 s and the average run time of terminated runs is 37.33 s.

Table 2. Result of fast key recovery without fault injection

No. of traces	No. of bytes	No. of runs (N)	Simulation timeout (s)	Percentage of finished runs	Average time (s)	Average residual entropy (bits)
2	16	500	600	100	37.33	0.009
2	15	500	600	99.8	55.98	0.014
2	14	500	600	99.8	56.96	0.012
2	13	500	600	99.6	56.01	0.012
2	**12**	**500**	**600**	**99.6**	**59.08**	**0.13**
2	11	100	2000	95	314.83	0.12
2	10	100	2000	91	308.85	0.15
2	9	100	2000	91	363.98	0.15
2	8	100	2000	86	382.80	0.19
1	16	100	2000	90	519.05	0.08
1	15	100	2000	48	860.31	0.12
1	14	100	2000	39	892.97	0

No. of fault injections in [9]	Average time (s)
0 fault, 1 AES execution	7200
1 fault, at least 2 AES executions	1200
5 fault, at least 6 AES executions	300
10 fault, at least 11 AES executions	180
20 fault, at least 21 AES executions	120

Similarly, with 15 Hamming weight of state bytes extracted, the recover success rate decreases to 99.8 % and the average of recovery time rises to 55.98 s. When the knowing state bytes decrease to 8, the recover success rate decreases to only 86 % and the average of recovery time rises to 382.80 s. When only 1 power trace is used, the success rate and average time of 16 bytes are 90 % and 519.05 s, respectively.

The experiment results show that 2 traces will extremely increase the efficiency of key recovery. Among all simulations, getting 12 bytes for 2 traces is a good option for the attackers, which uses relatively less number of key bytes to achieve a high success rate, a low running time and acceptable residual entropy. Compared with the fault injection attack in [9], we can see that getting 2 traces 10 bytes of our attack pattern is close to 5 fault injections of [9]. Getting 12 bytes for 2 traces in our attack pattern is much better than all the attack result in [9].

5   Conclusion

This paper focused on the key recovery problem for AES key expansion when random order countermeasure is applied. In [9], the random order countermeasure shows certain resistance against the basic power analysis. Then, fault injection is used together with power analysis to further discuss the security of random order countermeasure. As a more practical approach, we consider that the attackers could use power traces to get a few Hamming weight of an AES state to accelerate the power analysis. This work studied the most possible strategy of the attack and quantitatively evaluated the relationship between the additional information from the AES state and the key recovery efficiency. When the attacker could get Hamming weights of 12 bytes for 2 AES traces, a very fast key recovery can be achieved with a high success rate even though no fault injection is required.

Acknowledgments. This work is supported by Chinese Postdoctoral Science Foundation (No. 2015M581795), Jiangsu Province Postdoctoral Science Foundation (No. 1501014A), and Foundation of Graduate Innovation Center in NUAA (kfjj20151609).

References

1. Goodwin, J., Wilson, P.R.: Advanced encryption standard (AES) implementation with increased DPA resistance and low overhead. In: IEEE International Symposium on Circuits and Systems, ISCAS 2008, pp. 3286–3289. IEEE (2008)
2. Piret, G., Quisquater, J.-J.: A differential fault attack technique against SPN structures, with application to the AES and KHAZAD. In: Walter, C.D., Koç, Ç.K., Paar, C. (eds.) CHES 2003. LNCS, vol. 2779, pp. 77–88. Springer, Heidelberg (2003)
3. National Institute of Standards and Technology: Advanced Encryption Standard. NIST FIPS PUB 197 (2001)
4. Kocher, P., Jaffe, J., Jun, B.: Differential power analysis. In: Wiener, M. (ed.) CRYPTO 1999. LNCS, vol. 1666, pp. 388–397. Springer, Heidelberg (1999). doi:10.1007/3-540-48405-1_25
5. Brier, E., Clavier, C., Olivier, F.: Correlation power analysis with a leakage model. In: Joye, M., Quisquater, J.-J. (eds.) CHES 2004. LNCS, vol. 3156, pp. 16–29. Springer, Heidelberg (2004). doi:10.1007/978-3-540-28632-5_2
6. Herbst, C., Oswald, E., Mangard, S.: An AES smart card implementation resistant to power analysis attacks. In: Zhou, J., Yung, M., Bao, F. (eds.) ACNS 2006. LNCS, vol. 3989, pp. 239–252. Springer, Heidelberg (2006)
7. Chari, S., Rao, J.R., Rohatgi, P.: Template attacks. In: Kaliski, B.S., Koç, K., Paar, C. (eds.) CHES 2002. LNCS, vol. 2523, pp. 13–28. Springer, Heidelberg (2003). doi:10.1007/3-540-36400-5_3
8. Gierlichs, B., Batina, L., Tuyls, P., Preneel, B.: Mutual information analysis. In: Oswald, E., Rohatgi, P. (eds.) CHES 2008. LNCS, vol. 5154, pp. 426–442. Springer, Heidelberg (2008). doi:10.1007/978-3-540-85053-3_27
9. Clavier, C., Marion, D., Wurcker, A.: Simple power analysis on AES key expansion revisited. In: Batina, L., Robshaw, M. (eds.) CHES 2014. LNCS, vol. 8731, pp. 279–297. Springer, Heidelberg (2014). doi:10.1007/978-3-662-44709-3_16
10. Mayer-Sommer, R.: Smartly analyzing the simplicity and the power of simple power analysis on smartcards. In: Koç, Ç.K., Paar, C. (eds.) CHES 2000. LNCS, vol. 1965, pp. 78–92. Springer, Heidelberg (2000). doi:10.1007/3-540-44499-8_6
11. Biham, E., Shamir, A.: Power analysis of the key scheduling of the AES candidates. In: Proceedings of the Second AES Candidate Conference, pp. 115–121 (1999)

12. Messerges, T.S., Dabbish, E.A., Sloan, R.H.: Investigations of power analysis attacks on smartcards. Smartcard **99**, 151–161 (1999)
13. Mangard, S.: A simple power-analysis (SPA) attack on implementations of the AES key expansion. In: Lee, P.J., Lim, C.H. (eds.) ICISC 2002. LNCS, vol. 2587, pp. 343–358. Springer, Heidelberg (2003). doi:10.1007/3-540-36552-4_24
14. VanLaven, J., Brehob, M., Compton, K.J.: A computationally feasible SPA attack on AES via optimized search. In: Sasaki, R., Qing, S., Okamoto, E., Yoshiura, H. (eds.) Security and Privacy in the Age of Ubiquitous Computing, pp. 577–588. Springer, Berlin (2005)
15. Ali, S.S., Mukhopadhyay, D.: A differential fault analysis on AES key schedule using single fault. In: 2011 Workshop on Fault Diagnosis and Tolerance in Cryptography (FDTC), pp. 35–42. IEEE (2011)

A Note on "IPad: ID-Based Public Auditing for the Outsourced Data in the Standard Model"

Wenting Shen[1], Jia Yu[1,2(✉)], Hui Xia[1], and Rong Hao[1]

[1] College of Computer Science and Technology,
Qingdao University, Qingdao 266071, China
yujia@qdu.edu.cn
[2] Institute of Big Data Technology and Smart City,
Qingdao University, Qingdao 266071, China

Abstract. Cloud storage is an increasingly popular data storage manner which allows cloud data owners to outsource their data to the cloud for storage and maintaining. However, users will lose their physical control over their data after their data are outsourced to the cloud. To ensure the integrity of data stored in the cloud, many public auditing schemes have been proposed. Recently, Zhang et al. proposed an ID-based public auditing scheme for the outsourced data in the standard model. In this note, we prove this scheme is not secure. We show that the malicious cloud can pass the auditor's verification even if it has deleted or modified the users' data in this scheme.

Keywords: Cloud storage · Public auditing · Security analysis · ID-based auditing

1 Introduction

Cloud storage service allows data owners to outsource their data to the cloud, which not only reduces the users' burden of local data storage and maintenance, but also provides universal on-demand data access for users [1]. Though the cloud storage provides great advantages and conveniences for users, it also brings some new security concerns because the users will lose their physical control over their cloud data once their data are outsourced to the cloud. Thus, the data stored in the cloud might be lost or corrupted due to the inevitable hardware/software failures and human errors [2–5]. What is more serious, the cloud might deliberately delete the rarely used data to get more storage space [6]. Therefore, checking the integrity of data stored in the cloud periodically is very important and necessary for users.

In order to check the integrity of cloud data for users, some cloud storage auditing [7–16] has been proposed. In these cloud storage auditing schemes, a third party auditor (TPA) is introduced to help users to verify the integrity of data efficiently without downloading the entire data from the cloud which is termed as public auditing. In addition, these public auditing schemes are mainly based on traditional public key infrastructure (PKI) system. However, most of them exist the problem of complex

© Springer International Publishing AG 2016
X. Sun et al. (Eds.): ICCCS 2016, Part I, LNCS 10039, pp. 335–342, 2016.
DOI: 10.1007/978-3-319-48671-0_30

certificate management in the PKI-based auditing system. As Zhang and Dong analyzed in [17], in the traditional public key infrastructure, the verifier needs to validate the certificates of user when it verifies the integrity of cloud data. Therefore, it results in a large amount of computation cost. In addition to heavy certificate verification, the considerable overheads come from the certificates generation, revocation, delivery and so on. To solve above problem, the ID-based cryptosystem is introduced, which uses data users' identity to replace his public key and simplifies certificate management in traditional PKI. Wang et al. [18] proposed an ID-based public auditing scheme which can eliminate the certificate management. Tan and Jia [19] also proposed a public auditing scheme based on identity. But both of them are only proven secure in the random oracle model. However, the security in the random oracle models does not imply security in the real world. To overcome this problem, Zhang et al. [20] propose an ID-based public auditing scheme for the outsourced data in the standard model. In this note, we review Zhang et al.'s ID-based public auditing scheme [20] and demonstrate this scheme is not secure. As long as the malicious cloud stores a data block and its corresponding valid authentication tag, it can generate a valid proof to pass the auditor's verification even if it has arbitrarily deleted or modified the users' data.

2   Review Zhang et al.'s Scheme in [20]

2.1   The System Model and Security Definition of Zhang et al.'s Scheme

The system model includes four kinds of different entities: data users, the cloud server, the third party auditor (TPA) and private key generation center (PKG), as shown in Fig. 1. The data user has a great quantity of data files stored in the cloud. The cloud server has unlimited computation capability and storage space. It can offer scalable and on-demand outsourcing data services for data users. TPA is a public verifier who is able to audit the integrity of cloud data on behalf of data users. PKG is responsible to produce the whole system parameter and issues private key for each data users.

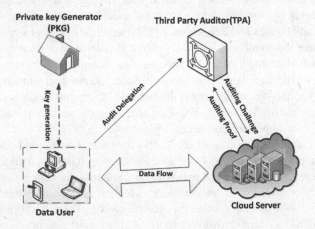

Fig. 1. The system model

Security Definition. For the cloud, it is computationally infeasible to generate a forgery of auditing proof. The cloud passes the auditor's verification only if it truly possesses the challenged blocks [21, 22].

2.2   The Algorithms of Zhang et al.'s Scheme

Zhang et al.'s scheme includes the following six algorithms: *Setup*, *Key − extract*, *TagGen*, *Challenge*, Pr *oof* and *Verifying*.

(1) Algorithm *Setup*: Assume (G_1, G_2) are two multiplicative cyclic groups of the prime order q, and $e : G_1 \times G_1 \rightarrow G_2$ is a bilinear map. Let $g \in_R G_1$ be a generator of group G_1, and $h, g_2 \in_R G_1$ be two different random generators of group G_1. Define $H_1 : \{0,1\}^* \rightarrow Z_q$ and $H_v : \{0,1\}^* \rightarrow \{0,1\}^{n_v}$ be two collision-resistant hash functions, where $n_v \in Z$. Randomly choose the following elements: $v' \in_R G_1$ and $v_i \in_R G_1$ for $i \in [1, n_v]$. Set $V = \{v_i\}_{i \in [1, n_v]}$. PKG randomly selects $\alpha \in Z_q$ as its master key, and calculates its public key $P_{pub} = g^\alpha$. And then the PKG secretly keeps his master secret key α and publishes the system parameters $Param = (G_1, G_2, q, e, v', V, g, h, H_1, H_v, g_2, P_{pub})$.

(2) Algorithm *Key − extract*: When a user wants to register his identity ID_j to the *PKG*, he does the following steps:
   1. The user firstly submits his identity ID_j to the PKG.
   2. Then, PKG calculates $\wp_j = H_v(ID_j)$. Let $\wp_j[i]$ be the i-th bit of $\wp_j$ and $V_j \subset \{1, 2, \ldots, n_v\}$ be the set of indices such that $\wp_j[i] = 1$.
   3. Finally, PKG randomly chooses $a_{uj} \in_R Z_q$, and calculates

   $$d_j = (d_{j1}, d_{j2}) = \left(g_2^\alpha \left(v' \prod_{i \in V_j} v_i\right)^{a_{uj}}, g^{a_{uj}}\right)$$

   as the private key of the data user with identity ID_j.

(3) Algorithm *TagGen*: Assume a file M with name *Name* is divided into n blocks $(m_1, m_2, \ldots, m_n)$ and each block is divided into s sectors $(m_{i1}, m_{i2}, \ldots, m_{is})$. The data user with identity ID_j chooses $s + 1$ random values $r_0, r_1, \ldots, r_s \in_R Z_q$ to calculate $u_i = g_2^{r_i}$ for each $0 \le i \le s$.
   The user computes authentication tag as follows:
   1. Firstly, he calculates $(pk_s, sk_s) \leftarrow \sum.KGen(1^k)$ to obtain a pair of public/private keys, where $\sum$ is a secure signature algorithm.
   2. Then he calculates $\phi = \sum.sign(sk_s, \tau_0)$ to obtain a signature on string τ_0, where $\tau_0 = $ "*Name* $\| n \| u_0 \| u_1 \| \cdots \| u_s$".
   3. For each data block $m_i (1 \le i \le n)$, he calculates

   $$\omega_i = r_0 H_1(Name\|i) + \sum_{j=1}^s r_j m_{ij}$$

   4. Finally, he calculates

$$ti = \left(ti1 = (dj1)^{\omega_i} = g_2^{\xi_1} \left(v' \prod_{i \in V_j} v_i \right)^{\xi_2}, ti2 = d_{j2}^{\omega_i} = g^{\xi_2} \right)$$

as the authentication tag on data block m_i, where $\xi_1 = \alpha \cdot \omega_i$ and $\xi_2 = a_{uj} \cdot \omega_i$. (Note that to produce a probabilistic signature, the data user with identity ID_j chooses a element $\hat{r} \in Z_q$ to calculate

$$ti = \left(ti1 = (dj1)^{\delta i} \left(v' \prod_{i \in v_j} v_i \right)^{\hat{r}}, ti2 = d_{j2}^{\delta_i} \cdot g^{\hat{r}} \right)$$

The data user uploads the data file M along with all the authentication tag $t_i (1 \le i \le n)$ to the cloud. And then, he deletes the above random values $r_0, r_1, \ldots, r_s$, private key sk_s of signature algorithm $\sum$ and the local file M from local storage.

(4) Algorithm *Challenge:* The auditor firstly verifies whether the signature ϕ is valid or not by invoking $\sum .verify(\phi, pk_s)$. If it is valid, the auditor recovers the file name *Name*, n and $u_0, u_1, \ldots, u_s$ by parsing τ. Then, he randomly chooses an l-element subset I of the set $[1, n]$ and a number $\rho \in Z_q$ to construct challenging message $Chall = \{\rho, I\}$. Finally, he sends this challenging message to the cloud.

(5) Algorithm *Proof:* After receiving the auditing challenge $Chall = \{\rho, I\}$ from auditor, the cloud firstly produces a l-element set $Q = (i, \beta_i)$, where $i \in I$ and $\beta_i = \rho^i \mod q$. And then the cloud calculates

$$\delta_1 = \prod_{i \in I} t_{i1}^{\beta_i}$$

$$\delta_2 = \prod_{i \in I} t_{i2}^{\beta_i}$$

and he calculates

$$\mu_j = \sum_{i \in I} \beta_i m_{ij} \ (j \in [1, s])$$

Finally, the cloud sends the proof $Prf = (\delta_1, \delta_2, \{\mu_j\}_{j=1,2,\ldots,s})$ to the auditor.

(6) Algorithm *Verifying:* After receiving the proof $Prf = (\delta_1, \delta_2, \{\mu_j\}_{j=1,2,\ldots,s})$ from the cloud, the auditor firstly calculates

$$\hat{h} = \sum_{i \in I} \beta_i \cdot H_1(Name \| i)$$

And then he checks the correctness of this auditing proof as follows:

$$e\left(u_0^{\hat{h}}\cdot\prod_{j=1}^{s}u_j^{\mu_j},P_{pub}\right)e\left(v'\prod_{i\in V_j}v_i,\delta_2\right)=e(\delta_1,g) \tag{1}$$

If the above equation holds, the auditor outputs "accept"; otherwise, outputs "reject".

The correctness of the above verification equation can be shown as follows:

$$
\begin{aligned}
e(\delta 1,g) &= e\left(\prod_{i\in I}t_{i1}^{\beta_i},g\right)\\
&= e\left(\prod_{i\in I}\left(g_2^{\xi_1}\left(v'\prod_{i\in V_j}v_i\right)^{\xi_2}\right)^{\beta_i},g\right)\\
&= e\left(\prod_{i\in I}g_2^{\xi_1},g^{\beta_i}\right)e\left(\prod_{i\in I}\left(v'\prod_{i\in V_j}v_i\right)^{\xi_2},g^{\beta_i}\right)\\
&= e\left(\prod_{i\in I}g_2^{\xi_1},g^{\beta_i}\right)e\left(\left(v'\prod_{i\in V_j}v_i\right),\prod_{i\in I}g^{\xi_2\beta_i}\right)\\
&= e\left(\prod_{i\in I}g_2^{\xi_1\cdot\omega_i},g^{\alpha}\right)e\left(\left(v'\prod_{i\in V_j}v_i\right),\prod_{\in I}(t_{i2})^{\beta_i}\right)\\
&= e\left(\prod_{i\in I}g_2^{\beta_i\cdot(r_0 H_1(Name\|i)+\sum_{j=1}^{s}r_j m_{ij})},g^{\alpha}\right)e\left(\left(v'\prod_{i\in V_j}v_i\right),\prod_{\in I}(t_{i2})^{\beta_i}\right)\\
&= e\left(u_0^{\hat{h}}\cdot\prod_{j=1}^{s}u_j^{\mu_j},P_{pub}\right)e\left(v'\prod_{i\in V_j}v_i,\delta_2\right)
\end{aligned}
$$

3 Analysis of Zhang et al.'s Scheme

According to the above security definition, we know that if the cloud does not truly store data users' intact data, it cannot pass the verification from the auditor in a public auditing scheme. In [20], the authors think the proposed scheme is secure. Unfortunately, it cannot satisfy this basic security in the standard model. The cloud can arbitrarily delete or modify other data files as long as it possess a valid data block and its corresponding valid authentication tag, which can pass auditor's verification by forging a valid proof. We give the following analysis:

When the data user with identity ID_j sends data file $M(m_1, m_2, \ldots, m_n)$ and their corresponding valid authentication tags $(t_1, t_2, \ldots, t_n)$ to the cloud. The cloud can select to store only one data block m_i and its corresponding valid authentication tag t_i, and then deletes all other data blocks and authentication tags. Because the data block m_i's authentication tag t_i is valid, it can pass the auditor's verification. That is to say, the following equation holds.

$$e\left(u_0^{\hat{h}_i}\cdot\prod_{j=1}^{s}u_j^{\mu'_j},P_{pub}\right)e\left(v'\prod_{i\in V_j}v_i,\delta_{2i}\right)=e(\delta_{1i},g) \tag{2}$$

Where $\hat{h}_i = \beta_i\cdot H_1(Name\|i)$ and $\mu'_j = \beta_i m_{ij}(j\in[1,s])$.

Now, the cloud possess m_i **and** t_i **for the data user with identity** ID_j, **and can know** $\hat{h}_i$ **and** $\mu'_j(j \in [1, s])$ **according to above messages.** Below, we describe how a malicious cloud forges a valid proof to pass the auditor's verification even if it has arbitrarily deleted or modified any data file of any user.

When the auditor wants to verify the integrity of data file $M'(m'_1, m'_2, \ldots, m'_n)$ on behalf of the data user with identity ID'_j, he will send an auditing challenge to the cloud. And then the cloud can forge a valid proof message to reply the auditor's auditing challenge by doing the following algorithm.

(1) The auditor generates the challenging message $Chall = \{\rho', I'\}$ by randomly choosing a l-element subset I' of the set $[1, n]$ and a number $\rho' \in Z_q$, and then sends this challenging message $Chall = \{\rho', I'\}$ to the cloud. When the cloud receives the challenging message from auditor, it firstly calculates $\beta'_j = (\rho')^j \mod q$, for each $j \in I'$.

(2) Then, the cloud calculates $\hat{h}' = \sum\limits_{j \in I'} \beta'_j \cdot H_1(Name\|j)$.

(3) Finally, the cloud forges a poof message that can pass the auditor's verification from the messages it has known about m_i.

    ① The cloud calculates $\varphi = \hat{h}'/\hat{h}_i$;
    ② The cloud sets $\delta'_1 = \delta^\varphi_{1i}$, $\delta'_2 = \delta^\varphi_{2i}$, and $\mu''_j = \varphi \cdot \mu'_j$, for $j = 1$ to s.
    ③ The cloud sends the proof message $Prf = (\delta'_1, \delta'_2, \{\mu''_j\}_{j=1,2,\ldots,s})$ to the auditor.

According to Eq. (2), we know the following relations follow.

$$
\begin{aligned}
e\left(\delta'_1, P\right) &= e\left(\delta^\varphi_{1i}, P_{pub}\right) \\
&= e\left(\delta_{1i}, P_{pub}\right)^\varphi \\
&= e\left(u_0^{\hat{h}_i} \cdot \prod\nolimits_{j=1}^s u_j^{\mu'_j}, P_{pub}\right)^\varphi e\left(v' \prod\nolimits_{i \in V_j} v_i, \delta_{2i}\right)^\varphi \\
&= e\left(u_0^{\hat{h}_i \cdot \varphi} \cdot \prod\nolimits_{j=1}^s u_j^{\mu'_j \cdot \varphi}, P_{pub}\right) e\left(v' \prod\nolimits_{i \in V_j} v_i, \delta^\varphi_{2i}\right) \\
&= e\left(u_0^{(\hat{h}'/\hat{h}_i) \cdot \hat{h}_i} \cdot \prod\nolimits_{j=1}^s u_j^{\mu'_j \cdot \varphi}, P_{pub}\right) e\left(v' \prod\nolimits_{i \in V_j} v_i, \delta'_2\right) \\
&= e\left(u_0^{\hat{h}'} \cdot \prod\nolimits_{j=1}^s u_j^{\mu''_j}, P_{pub}\right) e\left(v' \prod\nolimits_{i \in V_j} v_i, \delta'_2\right)
\end{aligned}
$$

It means the proof $Prf = (\delta'_1, \delta'_2, \{\mu''_j\}_{j=1,2,\ldots,s})$ can pass the checking Eq. (1). Therefore, $Prf = (\delta'_1, \delta'_2, \{\mu''_j\}_{j=1,2,\ldots,s})$ is a valid proof.

From above analysis, we can know the malicious cloud can pass the auditor's verification by forging a valid proof even if it does not actually store users' data.

4   Conclusion

In this note, we review the Zhang et al.'s ID-based public auditing scheme for the outsourced data in the standard model, and give a detailed demonstration to prove this scheme is not secure. We demonstrate that a malicious cloud can pass the auditor's verification by forging a valid proof even if it does not keep users' intact data in this scheme.

Acknowledgement. This research is supported by National Natural Science Foundation of China (61572267, 61272425, 61402245).

References

1. Armbrust, M., Fox, A., Griffith, R., Joseph, A.D., Katz, R.H., Konwinski, A., Lee, G., Patterson, D.A., Rabkin, A., Stoica, I., Zaharia, M.: Above the clouds: a Berkeley view of cloud computing. EECS Department University of California Berkeley, vol. 53, no. 4, pp. 50–58 (2015)
2. Ren, K., Wang, C., Wang, Q.: Security challenges for the public cloud. IEEE Internet Comput. 16(1), 69–73 (2012)
3. Song, D., Shi, E., Fischer, I., Shankar, U.: Cloud data protection for the masses. IEEE Comput. 45(1), 39–45 (2012)
4. Arrington, M.: Gmail Disaster: Reports of Mass Email Deletions (2006). http://techcrunch.com/2006/12/28/gmail-disaster-reports-of-mass-email-deletions/
5. Amazon S3 Team: Amazon S3 Availability Event: July 20, 2008 (2008). http://status.aws.amazon.com/s3-20080720.html
6. Wang, Q., Wang, C., Ren, K.: Enabling public auditability and cloud data dynamics for storage security in cloud computing. IEEE Trans. Parallel Distrib. Syst. 22(5), 847–859 (2011)
7. Yu, Y., Zhang, Y., Ni, J., Au, M., Chen, L., Liu, H.: Remote data possession checking with enhanced security for cloud storage. Future Gener. Comput. Syst. 52, 77–85 (2015)
8. Yuan, J., Yu, S.: Public integrity auditing for dynamic data sharing with multiuser modification. IEEE Trans. Inf. Forensics Secur. 10(8), 1717–1726 (2015)
9. Yu, J., Ren, K., Wang, C., Varadharajan, V.: Enabling cloud storage auditing with key-exposure resistance. IEEE Trans. Inf. Forensics Secur. 10(6), 1167–1179 (2015)
10. Zhang, Y., Blanton, M.: Efficient dynamic provable possession of remote data via balanced update trees. In: Department of 8th ACM SIGSAC Symposium on Information, Computer and Communications Security, pp. 183–194. ACM (2013)
11. Guan, C., Ren, K., Zhang, F., Kerschbaum, F., Yu, J.: Symmetric-key based proofs of retrievability supporting public verification. In: Pernul, G., Ryan, P.Y.A., Weippl, E. (eds.) ESORICS. LNCS, vol. 9326, pp. 203–223. Springer, Heidelberg (2015). doi:10.1007/978-3-319-24174-6_11
12. Wang, H.: Proxy provable data possession in public clouds. IEEE Trans. Serv. Comput. 6(4), 551–558 (2013)
13. Yang, K., Jia, X.: Data storage auditing service in cloud computing: challenges, methods and opportunities. World Wide Web-Internet Web Inf. Syst. 15(4), 409–428 (2012)

14. Wang, B., Li, H., Li, M.: Privacy-preserving public auditing for shared cloud data supporting group dynamics. In: 2013 IEEE International Conference on IEEE Communications (ICC), pp. 1946–1950 (2013)

15. Yu, Y., Li, Y., Ni, J., Yang, G., Mu, Y., Susilo, W.: Public integrity auditing for dynamic data sharing with multiuser modification. IEEE Trans. Inf. Forensics Secur. 11(3), 658–659 (2016)

16. Yang, G., Yu, J., Shen, W., Su, Q., Zhang, F., Hao, R.: Enabling public auditing for shared data in cloud storage supporting identity privacy and traceability. J. Syst. Softw. 113, 130–139 (2016)

17. Zhang, J., Dong, Q.: Efficient ID-based public auditing for the outsourced data in cloud storage. Inf. Sci. 6(6), 1–14 (2016)

18. Wang, H., Wu, Q., Qin, B., Ferrer, D.: Identity-based remote data possession checking in public clouds. Inf. Secur. 8(2), 114–121 (2014)

19. Tan, S., Jia, Y.: NaEPASC: a novel and efficient public auditing scheme for cloud data. J. Zhejiang Univ. Sci. C 15(9), 794–804 (2014)

20. Zhang, J., Li, P., Mao, J.: IPad: ID-based public auditing for the outsourced data in the standard mode. Cluster Comput. 19(1), 1–12 (2015)

21. Shacham, H., Waters, B.: Compact proofs of retrievability. J. Cryptol. 26(3), 442–483 (2014)

22. Ateniese, G., Burns, R., Curtmola, R., Herring, J., Kissner, L., Peterson, Z., Song, D.: Provable data possession at untrusted stores. In: Proceedings of ACM CCS 2007, pp. 598–610 (2007)

Supervised Nonlinear Latent Feature Extraction and Regularized Random Weights Neural Network Modeling for Intrusion Detection System

Jian Tang[1,2(✉)], Liu Zhuo[2], Meiying Jia[1], Chunlai Sun[1], and Chaowen Shi[1]

[1] Research Institute of Computing Technology,
Beifang Jiaotong University, Beijing 100029, China
tjan001@126.com
[2] State Key Laboratory of Synthetical Automation for Process Industries,
Northeaster University, Shenyang 110004, China
liuzhuo@ise.neu.edu.cn

Abstract. Colinearity and latent relation among different input features of net work intrusion detection system (IDS) have to be addressed. The strong non-linearity and uncertain mapping between input features and network intrusion behaviors lead to difficulty to built effective detection model for IDS. In this paper, a new supervised nonlinear latent feature extraction and fast machine learning algorithm based on global optimization strategy is proposed to solve these problems. Specifically, for diminishing colinearity among input variables, kernel partial least squares (KPLS) algorithm is employed to extract nonlinear latent features. Then, regularized random weights neural networks (RRWNN) is utilized to construct the intrusion detection model. To optimize the proposed system, the modeling parameters of KPLS and RRWNN are selected in terms of global optimization. Experiments on KDD99 data show that the proposed approach is effective.

Keywords: Supervised nonlinear latent feature extraction · Fast machine learning algorithm · Global optimization strategy · Intrusion detection system

1 Introduction

Recently, researches on intrusion detection techniques for network fundamental infrastructures relative to national security have become one of the most essential issues. These researches have been widely used in detecting, identifying and tracking intruders. In this sense, it is very important to develop an intrusion detection technology with high detection accuracy and low training time for intrusion detection system (IDS). In fact, the main objective of intrusion detection is to distinguish the normal activities from the malicious activities. It can be looked as classified identification problem [1]. Thus, various machine learning methods can be introduced to construct intrusion detection model in many studies [2, 3].

© Springer International Publishing AG 2016
X. Sun et al. (Eds.): ICCCS 2016, Part I, LNCS 10039, pp. 343–354, 2016.
DOI: 10.1007/978-3-319-48671-0_31

Naturally, a solution of network intrusion detection model with well prediction performance should be an effective classifier. Thus, the first problem is dimension reduction. Two approaches, feature selection and feature extraction, can be used. The former selects only the most relevant elements for the classification tasks. And these discarded variables may decrease generalization performance of the classification model. On the contrary, the later can use a linear or nonlinear way to determine an appropriate low dimensional data to replace the original one. The best known feature extraction method is principal component analysis (PCA), which can effectively approximate the original data by a linear sub-space using the mean squared error criterion. However, PCA don't take into account the correlation between inputs and outputs variables [4]. As a result, the extracted latent variables (LVs) may have little correlation with the output data [5]. Supervised feature extraction method, such as PLS, can extract LVs correlative to the input and the output data simultaneously. However, most of the complex processes are nonlinear. Kernel method has become one of the simple and elegant approaches to extract these nonlinear latent features [6]. Through employing kernel PLS (KPLS) method, input features' dimension of intrusion detection model can be reduced. But, how to select kernel parameters and number of latent features is still an open issue.

The most used construction methods of network intrusion detection model are artificial neural network (ANN) and support vector machines (SVM) [7]. Although back propagation neural networks (BPNN) have been used widely with different application backgrounds, it still suffers from local optima, uncontrolled convergence speed and over-fitting problems. As far as SVM, it has to solve quadratic program (QP) problem in terms of long leaning time. Some on-line versions of SVM are proposed [8, 9] and only sub-optimized solution can be obtained. A single-hidden layer feed-forward networks with random weights algorithm (SLFNrw) was proposed, in which weights and biases of the hidden layer nodes are chosen randomly with uniform distribution in $[-1,1]$. However, it cannot guarantee the universal approximation capability (in the sense of probability one) of the resulting random weights neural network (RWNN) model, duo to its way to randomly assign the input weights and biases [10]. Random vector functional-link nets (RVFLs) was proposed to overcome shortcomings that caused by the gradient-based learning algorithm [11, 12]. Theoretical justification of the universal approximation capability of RVFLs (without direct link case) shows that the scope of randomly assigned input weights and biases are data dependent [12]. The most appealing property of randomized techniques for RWNN lies in the possibility of the fast learning. A smaller training error and a smaller norm of weights imply a better generalization performance of feed forward networks [13]. Thus, regularized RWNN (RRWNN) is employed in most of the recent stuides [14]. A regularizing factor should be optimal selected for different modeling data. Therefore, three modeling parameters of RRWNN, i.e., number of nods at hidden layer, range of random input weights and bias, and regularizing factor, are data dependent.

Obviously, it is necessary to select latent features and build intrusion detection model in terms of global optimization. Motivated by this problem, a new nonlinear latent feature extraction and fast machine learning algorithm-based global optimization strategy for modeling IDS is proposed in this paper. KPLS is used to extract nonlinear latent features hidden in the modeling data. RRWNN is used to construct intrusion detection model with these extracted nonlinear features. Modeling parameters KPLS and RRWNN are selected jointly. KDD99 data are use to validate the proposed approach.

2 Modeling Strategy

Based on the above analysis, the proposed KPLS- and RRWNN-based network instruction detection modeling strategy in terms of global optimization consists of three parts, which are supervised nonlinear latent feature extraction module, intrusion detection model construction module and modeling parameters optimized selection module. It is shown in Fig. 1.

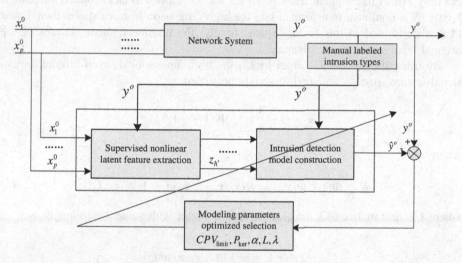

Fig. 1. The proposed modeling strategy

In Fig. 1, $\{x_1^o, \ldots, x_p^o\}$ and y^o represent the input data and output data of the network system, respectively; $\{z_1, \ldots, z_{h'}\}$ stands for the selected nonlinear latent features; h' indicates the number of the latent features; CPV_{limit} is the upper limit of cumulative percent variance (CPV) of input data block; P_{ker} is the kernel parameters of KPLS; α is the range of random input weights and bias; L is the number of nodes at hidden layer, and λ is the regularizing factor.

Figure 1 shows that the modeling parameters optimized selection module should select the nonlinear latent feature extraction parameters (CPV_{limit}, P_{ker}) and intrusion detection model learning parameters (α, L, λ) simultaneously. Detailed realization is shown in the following section.

3 Modeling Algorithm Realization

3.1 Supervised Nonlinear Latent Features Extraction

Feature extraction method uses a linear/nonlinear way to determine an appropriate low dimensional data to replace the original high dimensional one. The objective of PLS algorithm is to maximize the covariance between the input variables $X = \{x_l\}_{l=1}^k$ and output variables $Y = \{y_l\}_{l=1}^k$. The first PLS latent score t_1 is obtained from the solution process of covariance between X and Y, which can be looked as the first be extracted feature (latent variable, LV). Each subsequent latent score is computed using the residuals of X and Y from the previous step. As a result, a small number of LVs can be used to replace the large number of original input variables. However, PLS algorithm can only extract linear latent features. KPLS was developed to tackle data nonlinearity. Firstly, X is nonlinear transformed into the high dimension features space; then, linear PLS is performed in this feature space; finally, the nonlinear latent features of the original input variables are obtained.

By using the so-called "kernel trick", the high-dimensional, even infinite dimensional feature space is obtained. It should be scaled as:

$$\tilde{\mathbf{K}} = (\mathbf{I} - \frac{1}{k} 1_k 1_k^T)\mathbf{K}(\mathbf{I} - \frac{1}{k} 1_k 1_k^T), \tag{1}$$

where

$$K = \Phi(x_l)^T\Phi(x_m) = K(x_l, x_m), \quad l, m = 1, 2, \ldots, k, \tag{2}$$

where $\mathbf{I}$ is unit matrix of k dimension; 1_k is a vector with value 1 and length k.

Table 1. The KPLS algorithm

Let h be the desired number of kernel LVs (KLVs).   Repeat for $i = 1$ to $h = rank(X)$.
Step(1): Set $i =1$, $\tilde{K}_1 = \tilde{K}$, $Y_1 = Y$;   Step(2): Random initialized $\mathbf{u}_i$ equal to any column of Y_i;   Step(3): $t_i = \tilde{K}_i^T u_i, t_i \leftarrow t_i / \|t_i\|$;   Step(4): $c_i = Y_i^T t_i$;   Step(5): $\mathbf{u}_i = Y_i c_i, c_i \leftarrow c_i / \|c_i\|$;   Step(6): If t_i converges, go to Step (7); else return to Step (3);   Step(7): Calculate the residual: $K_i \leftarrow (I - t_i t_i^T)\tilde{K}_i(I - t_i t_i^T), Y_i \leftarrow Y_i - t_i t_i^T Y_i$;   Step(8): Set $i = i+1$, if $i \geq h$, terminate; else return to Step (2).

The KPLS algorithm is outlined in Table 1.

After extracting the desired KLVs, the low dimensional score matrixes $T = [t_1, t_2, \ldots, t_h]$ and $U = [u_1, u_2, \ldots, u_h]$ are obtained, respectively. Thus, the dimension of the original matrix X is reduced to h. The extracted features can be calculated as:

$$Z^{\text{all}} = \tilde{K}U(T^{\text{T}}\tilde{K}U)^{-1} \tag{3}$$

The extracted features from testing sample $X^{\text{test}} = \{x_l^{\text{test}}\}_{l=1}^{k_t}$ can be calculated by:

$$(Z^{\text{test}})^{\text{all}} = \tilde{K}_t U(T^{\text{T}}\tilde{K}U)^{-1} \tag{4}$$

where $\tilde{K}_t$ is the scaled kernel matrix of K_t, i.e.,

$$\tilde{K}_t = (K_t I - \frac{1}{k}1_{kt}1_k^{\text{T}}K)(I - \frac{1}{k}1_k1_k^{\text{T}}) \tag{5}$$

$$K_t = K((x'_t)_l, (x')_m) \tag{6}$$

where 1_{kt} is a vector with value 1 and length k_t. Finally, KLVs of Z^{all} and $(Z^{\text{test}})^{\text{all}}$ are treated as the low dimensional input features of the training and testing datasets.

Normally, the desired number of KLV (h') is less than that of the original number (h). In this paper, cumulate percent variance (CPV) of the input data block is used to determine h' by the following criterion:

$$\begin{cases} CPV_{h'} \geq CPV_{\text{limit}} \\ CPV_{h'} = \sum_{i_{h'}=1}^{h'} \lambda_{i_{h'}} \Big/ \sum_{i_h=1}^{p} \lambda_{i_h} \end{cases} \tag{7}$$

where λ_{i_h} is the eigenvalue of covariance matrix that transformed from the input and output data. Thus, it is important to select appropriate kernel parameters (P_{ker}) and CPV's upper limit (CPV_{limit}) to obtain effective latent features.

In this study, the selected latent features from X are represented as:

$$Z = \{z\}_{l=1}^k \{z_1, \ldots, z_{h'}\}_{l=1}^k. \tag{8}$$

3.2 Intrusion Detection Model Construction

Random weights neural networks (RWNN) are the universal approximator for any continuous functions on compact sets. An RWNN network can be represented as:

$$f(z; \beta) = \sum_{i=1}^{L} \beta_i g(w_i^{\text{T}}z + b_i) \tag{9}$$

where $\boldsymbol{\beta} = [\beta_1, \beta_1, \ldots, \beta_L] \in R^L$ is the output layer weights; L is the hidden nodes' number; $z \in R^{h'}$ is the input features vector; $w \in R^{h'}$ and $b \in R$ are the input weights and hidden layer's biases with certain ranges $[-\alpha, \alpha]$, respectively; p is the number of the input features, i.e., the number of RWNN network inputs.

Given training data set, let $w \in R^{h'}$ and $b \in R$ be chosen randomly from the uniform distribution and fixed in advance. The following linear system can be obtained

$$H\boldsymbol{\beta} = Y \tag{10}$$

where,

$$H = \begin{bmatrix} g(w_1^T z_1 + b_1) & \cdots & g(w_L^T z_1 + b_L) \\ \cdots & \cdots & \cdots \\ g(w_1^T z_k + b_1) & \cdots & g(w_L^T z_k + b_L) \end{bmatrix} \tag{11}$$

In most of cases, H is not full column rank or even ill-conditioned. Therefore, the output weights can be estimated:

$$\hat{\boldsymbol{\beta}} = \underset{\beta}{\arg\min} \frac{1}{k} \sum_{l=1}^{k} \frac{1}{2}(f(z_l) - y_l)^2 \tag{12}$$

The solution can be analytically determined by solving least mean square problem:

$$\hat{\boldsymbol{\beta}} = H^+ Y \tag{13}$$

where H^+ is the Moore-Penrose generalized inverse of matrix H. When $H^T H$ is nonsingular, we have $H^+ = (H^T H)^{-1} H^T$.

However, the least squares problem is usually ill-posed. The regularized model is normally employed to find a solution. The regularized RWNN (RRWNN)-based learning problem can be formulated as:

$$\min_{\beta} \sum_{l=1}^{k} \left(f(z_l) - \sum_{i=1}^{L} \beta_i g(z_l; w_i, b_i) \right)^2 + \lambda ||\boldsymbol{\beta}||_2^2 \tag{14}$$

which can be rewritten as:

$$\min_{\beta} ||H\boldsymbol{\beta} - Y||^2 + \lambda ||\boldsymbol{\beta}||_2^2 \tag{15}$$

where $\lambda > 0$ is used to adjust the trade-off between the training accuracy and the penalty. Thus, generalization performance and stability of the learner model are improved further. Its solution can be denoted as:

$$\hat{\beta} = (H^{\mathrm{T}}H + \lambda I)^{-1}H^{\mathrm{T}}Y \qquad (16)$$

The RRWNN algorithm is described in Table 2.

Table 2. The RRWNN algorithm

Input: Training data of samples Z and targets Y, random weights and biases range α, number of neurons at hidden layer L, regularizing factor λ.
Output: Given input weights w and biases b, output weights β.
Steps: Step 1: Randomly choose w and b between $[-\alpha, \alpha]$; Step 2: Calculate the output matrix of the hidden layer $H_{k \times L}$; Step 3: Calculate the output weights $\hat{\beta} = (H^{\mathrm{T}}H + \lambda I)^{-1}H^{\mathrm{T}}Y$.

The above analysis shows that three modeling parameters of RRWNN, i.e., L, α and λ, need to be refined.

3.3 Modeling Parameters Optimized Selection

As shown in the above subsections, it is very necessary to select latent features and construct intrusion detection model in terms of global optimization. Thus, based on the optimized selection of modeling parameters set $\{CPV_{\mathrm{limit}}, P_{\mathrm{ker}}, \alpha, L, \lambda\}$, maximum accuracy of the intrusion identification model can be formulated as the following optimization problem:

$$\mathrm{Max} \quad Accuracy = \frac{Num\left\{ \left((y_l^o - \hat{y}_l^o) = 0 \right)_{l=1}^{k} \right\}}{k}$$

$$s.t. \begin{cases} 0 < P_{\mathrm{ker}} \leq (P_{\mathrm{ker}})_{\mathrm{limit}} \\ \min(h'), CPV_{h'} \geq CPV_{\mathrm{limit}} \\ 1 \leq h' \leq h, h = rank(X) \\ 0 \leq \alpha \leq \alpha_{\mathrm{limit}} \\ 0 \leq \lambda \leq 1 \\ h' < L < L_{\mathrm{limit}}, L \in R^N \end{cases} \qquad (17)$$

where $Num\left\{ \left((y_l^o - \hat{y}_l^o) = 0 \right)_{l=1}^{k} \right\}$ represents the number of the correct identified samples; $(P_{\mathrm{ker}})_{\mathrm{limit}}$, α_{limit} and L_{limit} are the upper limits of P_{ker}, α and L, respectively.

The above optimization problem can be solved with grid search approach or heuristic intelligent optimization methods. Therefore, this proposed KPLS-RRWNN based intrusion detection algorithm can be described in Table 3.

Table 3. The proposed intrusion detection identification algorithm

Input: Training data of samples X and targets Y, upper limit of kernel parameters $(P_{ker})_{limit}$, upper limit CPV for select latent features CPV_{limit}, upper limit of random weights and biases α_{limit}, upper limit of nodes of hidden layer L_{limit}.
Output: Given input weights w and biases b, output weights β.
Steps:
Step (1): Extract all the latent features with given P_{ker} by algorithm in Table 1;
Step (2): Calculate the desired latent features with given CPV_{limit} by Eq. (7) and (8);
Step (3): Calculate the input weights, input biases and output weights by algorithm in Table 2;
Step (4): Repeat the Step (1) to Step (3) with the grid search algorithm or heuristic intelligent optimization methods until satisfy the pre-set criterion.
Step 5: Select the best modeling parameters based on Eq. (18) and obtain final model.

4 Experimental Results

4.1 Data Description

The simulation of the proposed method is made on KDD CUP99 data. The data are divided into five categories, which are normal, denial of service (DoS), unauthorized access from a remote machine (Remote to Local, R2L), unauthorized access to local supervisor privileges (User to Root, U2R) and Probe. Each network record contains 41 attributes, of which 34 attributes are continuous and 7 ones are discrete. These discrete attributes should be converted to numerical attributes before being used. Take "protocol type", "service" and "flag" for example, the transform codes are shown in Table 4.

Table 4. Transform codes of the "protocol type", "service" and "flag" attributes

Protocol type	TCP, UDP, ICMP	1001 ~ 1003
service	'auth', 'bgp', 'courier', 'csnet_ns', 'ctf', 'daytime',…,…, …,, 'exec', 'finger', 17'ftp', 'ftp_data', 'gopher', 'harvest', 'hostnames', 'http',	100001 ~ 100070
flag	'OTH', 'REJ', 'RSTO', 'RSTOS0', 'RSTR', 'S0', 'S1', 'S2', 'S3', 'SF', 'SH'	1001 ~ 1011

. In this study, the training and testing samples are obtained by random sampling 0.5 % and 1 % from the original training and testing data with size 2470 and 3110.

4.2   Feature Extraction Results

In this section, the popular radius basis function (RBF) is used in KPLS for latent features extraction. Contribution of the former 10 KLVs with different kernel parameters (e.g. P_{ker} = 0.1, 1, 10 and 100) are shown in Fig. 2.

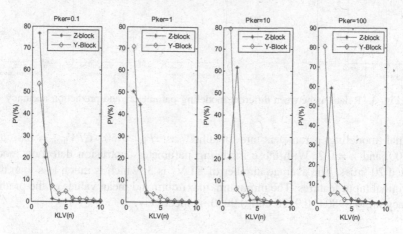

Fig. 2. Contributions of the form 10 KLVs with different kernel parameters

Figure 2 shows that a few of the nonlinear KLVs can represent most of changes of the original input features. Moreover, with different kernel parameters, the contributions (captured PV) of different KLVs are different. With different CPV_{limit}, the numbers of latent features to construct intrusion detection model are also different. Normally, CPV_{limit} is selected bigger than 85 %. It is necessary to select optimum P_{ker} and CPV_{limit} for improving prediction accuracy of the intrusion detection model.

4.3   Model Construction Results

Initial values of the five modeling parameters are selected as: P_{ker} = 1, CPV_{limit} = 90, α = 1, L = 200, λ = 0.2. Prediction accuracy based on testing samples is exploited to evaluate model performance, which is defined as

$$Accuracy = \frac{Num\left\{ ((y_l^o - \hat{y}_l^o) = 0)_{l=1}^{k_{test}} \right\}}{k_{test}} \tag{18}$$

In this study, grid search method is employed to select the modeling parameters. We change these parameters one by one to show their influence to prediction accuracy. Considered random selection process of the training and testing samples, and randomized initialization characteristics of RRWNN, intrusion detection model is repeated 20 times. The relations between different modeling parameters and prediction performance are shown in Fig. 3.

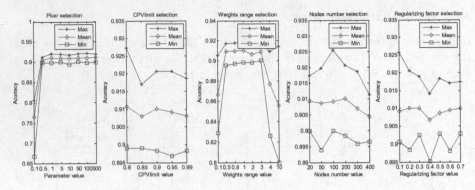

Fig. 3. Relations between different modeling parameters and prediction accuracy

Final modeling parameters are obtained as: $P_{ker} = 50$, $CPV_{limit} = 0.8$, $\alpha = 1$, $L = 200$, and $\lambda = 0.2$. With these modeling parameters, intrusion detection model is repeated 20 times. The average number of KLVs is 3, which is much less than that of the original input features. The minimum, maximum and mean values of the prediction accuracy are 0.89804, 0.9170 and 0.9090, respectively.

4.4   Comparison Results

The proposed method is compared with different dimension reduction approaches, such as supervised linear latent feature extraction (based on PLS) method and unsupervised linear latent feature extraction (based on PCA) method. These approaches are repeated 20 times. Prediction accuracy and statistical results of these methods are shown in Fig. 4 and Table 5.

Figure 4 shows that PLS/KPLS-based methods have higher prediction accuracy (Mean Accuracy) and better prediction stability (Max and Min Accuracy) than that of

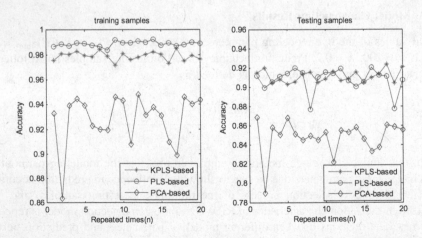

Fig. 4. Prediction accuracy of 20 repeated times with different feature extraction-based methods

Table 5. Statistical results of different latent feature extraction-based methods

	CPV(%)			Latent features		Prediction accuracy		
	Number	X-Block	Y-Block	Type	Number	Type	Training	Testing
PCA-based	1PC	31.19	NaN	Max	11	Max	0.9477	0.8684
	2PC	45.77	NaN	Mean	9	Mean	0.9282	0.8480
	3PC	56.33	NaN	Min	7	Min	0.8635	0.7893
PLS-based	1LV	12.91	14.82	Max	13	Max	0.9927	0.9205
	2LV	41.75	15.39	Mean	11	Mean	0.9887	0.9076
	3LV	51.36	16.27	Min	9	Min	0.9838	0.8768
KPLS-based	1KLV	18.47	80.40	Max	3	Max	0.9854	0.9237
	2KLV	78.70	85.71	Mean	3	Mean	0.9789	0.9111
	3KLV	90.25	89.24	Min	3	Min	0.9716	0.9028

PCA-based approach. The main reason is that PCA-based method belongs to unsupervised feature extraction method. PLS-based method has better prediction accuracy on training samples; however, its average prediction accuracy on testing samples is lower than that of KPLS-based method. Thus, there is a little over fitting for PLS-based method. For example, the former three LVs of PLS only represent 51.36 % and 16.27 % CPV(%) of X-blcock and Y-block. However, the former three KLVs of KPLS represent 90.25 % and 89.24 %, respectively. Therefore, with the same $CPV_{limit} = 0.8$, i.e., 80 %, the average number of latent features are 11 and 3, respectively.

5 Conclusion

Aiming at network intrusion detection model construction problem, a new method combined supervised nonlinear latent feature extraction with regularized random weights neural networks (RRWNN) algorithms for intrusion detection system is proposed in this paper. Kernel partial least squares (KPLS) algorithm is used to address colinearity and complex nonlinear mapping of the input features. These features are fed into RRWNN algorithm to construct intrusion detection model with fast learning speed and well generalization performance. Global optimization strategy algorithm is exploited to select modeling parameters of KPLS-RRWNN-based intrusion detection model. Simulate results based on KDD99 data show that this study is effective.

Acknowledgment. This work is partially supported by the post doctoral National Natural Science Foundation of China (2013M532118, 2015T81082), National Natural Science Foundation of China (61573364, 61273177, 61305029, 61503066), State Key Laboratory of Synthetical Automation for Process Industries, China National 863 Projects (2015AA043802), and the Project Funded by the Priority Academic Program Development of Jiangsu Higer Education Institutions (PAPD) and Jiangsu Collaborative Innovation Center on Atmospheric Environment and Equipment Technology (CICAEET) fund.

References

1. Tsai, C.F., Hsu, Y.F., Lin, C.Y., Lin, W.Y.: Intrusion detection by machine learning: a review. Expert Syst. Appl. **36**(10), 11994–12000 (2009)
2. Zheng, Y.H., Jeon, B.W., Xu, D.H., Wu, Q.M.J., Zhang, H.: Image segmentation by generalized hierarchical fuzzy C-means algorithm. J. Intell. Fuzzy Syst. **28**(2), 961–973 (2015)
3. Gianluigi, F., Pietro, S.: Ensemble based collaborative and distributed intrusion detection systems: a survey. J. Netw. Comput. Appl. **66**, 1–16 (2016)
4. Tang, J., Yu, W., Chai, T., Liu, Z., Zhou, X.: Selective ensemble modeling load parameters of ball mill based on multi-scale frequency spectral features and sphere criterion. Mech. Syst. Signal Process. **66**, 485–504 (2016)
5. Tang, J., Chai, T., Zhao, L., Yu, W., Yue, H.: Soft sensor for parameters of mill load based on multi-spectral segments PLS sub-models and on-line adaptive weighted fusion algorithm. Neurocomputing **78**(1), 38–47 (2012)
6. Motai, Y.: Kernel association for classification and prediction: a survey. IEEE Trans. Neural Netw. Learn. Syst. **26**(2), 208–223 (2015)
7. Wang, G., Hao, J.X., Ma, J., Huang, L.H.: A new approach to intrusion detection usingartificial neural networks and fuzzy clustering. Expert Syst. Appl. **37**(9), 6225–6232 (2010)
8. Gu, B., Sheng, V.S., Wang, Z., Ho, D., Osman, S., Li, S.: Incremental learning for v-support vector regression. Neural Netw. Off. J. Int. Neural Netw. Soc. **67**, 140–150 (2015)
9. Gu, B., Sheng, V.S., Tay, K.Y., Romano, W., Li, S.: Incremental support vector learning for ordinal regression. IEEE Trans. Neural Netw. Learn. Syst. **26**(7), 1403–1416 (2015)
10. Cao, F.L., Wang, D.H., Zhu, H.: An iterative learning algorithm for feedforward neural networks with random weights. Inf. Sci. **328**, 546–557 (2016)
11. Pao, Y.H., Takefuji, Y.: Functional-link net computing: theory, system architecture, and functionalities. Computer **25**(5), 76–79 (1992)
12. Igelnik, B., Pao, Y.H.: Stochastic choice of basis functions in adaptive function approximation and the functional-link net. IEEE Trans. Neural Netw. **6**(6), 1320–1329 (1995)
13. Bartlett, P.L.: The sample complexity of pattern classification with neural networks: the size of the weights is more important than the size of the network. IEEE Trans. Inf. Theory **44**(2), 525–536 (1998)
14. Cao, F.L., Tan, Y.P., Cai, M.M.: Sparse algorithms of random weight networks and applications. Expert Syst. Appl. **41**(5), 2457–2462 (2014)

A Revocable Certificateless Signature Scheme Without Pairing

Yinxia Sun[1]([⊠]), Zhuoran Zhang[2], and Limin Shen[1]

[1] School of Computer Science and Technology,
Nanjing Normal University, Nanjing 210023, China
bela_suno@163.com
[2] School of Mathematics Science,
Nanjing Normal University, Nanjing 210023, China

Abstract. In a public key cryptosystem, an important problem is how to revoke a user. As we know, the certificateless public key cryptography (CLPKC) unites the qualities of the traditional public key system and the identity-based public key system. It is free of complicated certificate management and key escrow. However, there are few solutions to the revocation problem in CLPKC. In this paper, we present an efficient revocable certificateless signature scheme. Moreover, this new scheme is free of bilinear pairing. Under the assumption of Discrete Logarithm problem, our scheme is provably secure.

Keywords: Revocation · Certificateless signature · Without pairing · DL problem

1 Introduction

The invention of public key cryptography in 1976 opens a new era in the history of cryptography. Public key cryptography provides new and effective technology to solve the information security problem [5,6,14], especially the technology of digital signature. In a public key cryptosystem, a necessary problem is how to guarantee the authenticity of public keys. The traditional public key system issues a public certificate to authenticate a public key. However, the management of certificates is very costly. In 1984, Shamir [11] presented the notion of identity based public key cryptography (IDPKC). In this public key system, the unique identity (such as phone number, IP address and email address) of a user is used as the public key, thus avoiding the need of a certificate.

However, a shortcoming of IDPKC is that a user's private key SK is fully generated by the PKG, so the PKG can use SK to decrypt any ciphertext and do signature on behalf of the user. In some practical situation, this cannot be accepted. To overcome the problems of costly certificate management and key escrow, in 2003, Al-Riyami and Paterson [2] presented certificateless public key cryptography (CLPKC). Actually, this public key system can be viewed as a nice combination of the former two public key systems. In CLPKC, a user's private

© Springer International Publishing AG 2016
X. Sun et al. (Eds.): ICCCS 2016, Part I, LNCS 10039, pp. 355–364, 2016.
DOI: 10.1007/978-3-319-48671-0_32

key is composed of two parts: one part computed by KGC and the other chosen by the user. So, CLPKC avoids the need of certificate and the problem of key escrow. Though a bit more computation is required in certificateless algorithms, CLPKC can get better comprehensive performance than the traditional public key system and IDPKC.

For any public key cryptosystem, an important problem is how to revoke a user when a user's authority is expired or his/her private key is compromised. In traditional public key system, the revocation technique has been well designed, such as CRLs, OCSP [9] and Novomodo [8]. In the certificate-free public key system, the main revocation technique is to update private keys for all non-revoked users periodically just as mentioned by Boneh-Franklin [3]. All these new keys should be transmitted over secret channels, which adds heavy burdens to the system. So, it is very necessary to design efficient revocation methods. In IDPKC, there emerges a lot of revocation schemes. Boldyreva et al. designed a scalable and revocable identity based encryption scheme [4]. Libert and Vergnaud [7] improved the scheme. Other identity-based revocation schemes are e.g. [13]. Seo et al. presented a revocable identity-based scheme against decryption exposure [10]. In 2015, we proposed an efficient revocable certificateless encryption scheme against decryption key exposure [12].

Nevertheless, there are few solutions to the revocation problem in certificateless public key cryptosystem. Though a lot of similarities exist between IDPKC and CLPKC, techniques in IDPKC cannot be directly moved to CLPKC. The trivial revocation method which was mention by Al-Riyami in [1] is that the KGC updates partial private keys for all non-revoked users. But secret channels are needed for the transmission of all the new partial private keys, which inevitably introduces more computations.

Our Contributions. In this paper, we present an efficient revocation method by giving a revocable certificateless signature scheme without pairings. The partial private key is generated by using Schnorr signature, and the KGC refreshing users' time keys periodically. Only public channels are needed to transmit these new keys. The system revokes a private key via stopping generating new time keys for the user. Without a new time key, the user cannot do valid signatures. The efficiency of our signature scheme is comparable to that of a conventional certificateless signature scheme. In addition, there is no need for the terminals to do the costly paring computations. Our scheme is provably secure under the discrete logarithm assumption. We also give a solution to the signing key exposure problem.

2   Definitions

2.1   Revocable Certificateless Signature

In this section, we introduce the definition of a revocable certificateless signature scheme. A revocable certificateless signature (RCLS) scheme consists of the following eight algorithms:

- Setup: Taking a security parameter k as input, the KGC runs this algorithm to generate a master key mk and a list of public system parameters params.
- Extract-Partial-Private-Key: Taking params, mk and an identity ID as input, the KGC runs this algorithm to compute a partial private key D_{ID}. D_{ID} is transmitted to the user via a secret channel.
- Update-Time-Key: Taking params, mk, an identity ID and a time period t as input, the KGC runs this algorithm to produce a time key D_{IDt}. D_t is transmitted to the user via a public channel.
- Set-Secret-Value: Taking params and ID as input, the user with ID runs this algorithm to generate a secret value s_{ID}.
- Set-Private-Key: Taking params, D_{ID}, D_{IDt} and s_{ID} as input, the user runs this algorithm to set a private key SK_{IDt}.
- Set-Public-Key: Taking params and s_{ID} as input, the user runs this algorithm to set a public key PK_{ID}.
- Sign: Taking params, SK_{IDt}, ID, t and a message M as input, this algorithm outputs a signature σ.
- Verify: Taking params, PK_{ID}, ID, t and a signature σ as input, this algorithm verifies the signature to output "accept" or "reject".

2.2 Security Model

The security of a certificateless scheme is defined against adversaries who even hold partial secret information (secret value or partial private key) of the target user. So, the adversaries are divided into two classes: *Type I adversaries* can replace a user's public key with a new value of its own choice; *Type II adversaries* have knowledge of system master secret key (but cannot replace a public key). In the scenario of RCLS, a third adversary – a malicious revoked user should be taken into consideration.

Let $\mathcal{A}_I$, $\mathcal{A}_{II}$ and $\mathcal{A}_{re}$ denote a Type I, a Type II adversary and a revoked-user adversary, respectively. We consider three games Game I, Game II and Game III where $\mathcal{A}_I$, $\mathcal{A}_{II}$ and $\mathcal{A}_{re}$ interact with their challengers. Note that the challengers will keep a history of query-answer in these games.
Game I (for a Type I adversary)

- **Setup:** The challenger runs Setup to generate a master secret key mk and a list of public system parameters params. It gives params to the adversary $\mathcal{A}_I$ and keeps mk secret.
  Next, $\mathcal{A}_I$ may make some queries; the challenger responses with answers.
- **Queries:**
  Partial Private Key Extraction query(ID): The challenger runs Extract-Initial-Partial-Private-Key to generate the initial partial private key D_{ID}, then returns it to $\mathcal{A}_I$.
  Time Key query(ID, T): The challenger runs Update-time-key to generate the time key $D_{ID,T}$, then returns it to $\mathcal{A}_I$.
  Secret Value query(ID): The challenger runs Set-Secret-Value to generate s_{ID}, then returns it to $\mathcal{A}_I$.

Public Key request(ID): The challenger runs Set-Public-Key to generate the public key PK_{ID}. It returns PK_{ID} to $\mathcal{A}_I$.

Public Key Replacement: The adversary $\mathcal{A}_I$ can replace any public key with any value of its choice. The current public key is used by the challenger in any subsequent computation or response to $\mathcal{A}_I$'s requests.

Signature query(M, ID, T): The challenger responds with the signature of M by using the private key of ID in the time period T.

- **Forge**: Finally, $\mathcal{A}_I$ outputs a signature on the tuple (M^*, ID^*, T^*) which is not an output of the signature oracle.

Game II (for a Type II adversary)

- **Setup**: The challenger runs Setup to generate a master key mk and a list of public parameters params. It gives mk to the adversary $\mathcal{A}_{II}$ as well as params. Next is the query phase. As $\mathcal{A}_{II}$ knows mk, it can compute any partial private key and any time key.
- **Queries**:

Secret Value query(ID): The challenger runs Set-Secret-Value to generate s_{ID}, then returns it to $\mathcal{A}_I$.

Public Key request(ID): The challenger runs Set-Public-Key to generate the public key PK_{ID} which is then returned to $\mathcal{A}_{II}$.

Signature query(M, ID, T): The challenger responds with the signature of M for the user ID in the time period T.

- **Forge**: Finally, $\mathcal{A}_{II}$ outputs a signature on a message M on the tuple (M^*, ID^*, T^*) which is not an output of the signature oracle.

Game III (for a revoked user)

- **Setup**: The challenger runs Setup to generate a master secret key mk and a list of public parameters params. It gives params to the adversary $\mathcal{A}_{re}$.

Query phase acts as follows:
- **Queries**:

Partial Private Key Extraction query IPPK(ID): The Challenger runs Extract-Initial-Partial-Private-Key to generate the initial partial private key D_{ID}, then returns it to $\mathcal{A}_{re}$.

Time Key query(ID, T): The Challenger runs Update-time-key to generate the time key $D_{ID,T}$, then returns it to $\mathcal{A}_{re}$.

Secret Value query(ID): The challenger runs Set-Secret-Value to generate s_{ID}, then returns it to $\mathcal{A}_{re}$.

Public Key request(ID): The challenger runs Set-Public-Key to generate the public key PK_{ID}. It returns PK_{ID} to $\mathcal{A}_{re}$.

Signature query(M, ID, T): The challenger responds with the signature of M under for the user ID in the time period T.

- **Forge**: At the end of the game, $\mathcal{A}_{re}$ outputs a signature on the tuple (M^*, ID^*, T^*) which is not an output of the signature oracle.

If the forgery is valid, $\mathcal{A}_i$ wins, $i \in \{I, II, re\}$. An RCLS scheme is said to be existentially unforgeable against chosen message attacks (EUF-CMA secure) if no probabilistic polynomial-time adversary has non-negligible probability to win the above games.

2.3 Difficult Problem

As below, we introduce an assumption of a difficult problem that our scheme is based on.

Discrete Logarithm (DL) problem. *Given* $g^x \in Z_p^*$ *where* p *is prime, to compute* x. The DL assumption states that the DL problem is difficult.

3 The Construction

This section is our concrete construction of a revocable certificateless signature scheme without pairing.

- Setup: Choose two primes p and q where $p = 2q + 1$, g is a generator of Z_p^* with order q. Select $x \in Z_q^*$ at random and compute $y = g^x$. Choose three hash functions: $H_1 : \{0,1\}^* \to Z_q^*$, $H_2 : \{0,1\}^* \to Z_q^*$, $H_3 : \{0,1\}^* \to Z_q^*$, The system public parameters are $(p, q, g, y, H_1, H_2, H_3)$. The master secret key is x.
- Extract-Partial-Private-Key: Taking as input an identity ID, this algorithm chooses a random $r \in Z_q^*$ and computes $w_{ID} = g^r$ and $d_{ID} = r + xH_1(ID, w_{ID})$. The partial private key $D_{ID} = (w_{ID}, d_{ID})$.
- Update-Time-Key: Taking as input an identity ID and a time period T, this algorithm chooses a random $r' \in Z_q^*$ and computes $w_{ID,T} = g^{r'}$ and $d_{ID,T} = r' + xH_2(ID, T, w_{ID,T})$. The time key is $D_{ID,T} = (w_{ID,T}, d_{ID,T})$.
- Set-Secret-Value: Choose a secret value $v_{ID} \in Z_q^*$ for the user ID.
- Set-Private-Key: The full private key $SK_{ID,T}$ is $(D_{ID} + D_{ID,T}, v_{ID})$.
- Set-Public-Key: The public key of the user is $PK_{ID} = g^{v_{ID}}$.
- Sign: This algorithm takes as input a message M, a time tag T and a signer's private key $SK_{ID,T}$, then does the following:
    1. Choose $t \in Z_q^*$ at random and compute $\gamma = g^t$.
    2. Compute $h = H_3(\gamma, PK_{ID}, ID, T, M)$ and $\delta = t + (v_{ID} + d_{ID} + d_{ID,T})h$
    3. Output the signature $\sigma = (h, \delta, w_{ID}, w_{ID,T})$.
- Verify: This algorithm takes as input a message-signature pair $(M, \sigma = (h, \delta, w_{ID}, w_{ID,T}))$, a time tag T and the signer's public key ID and PK_{ID}. Compute $h_1 = H_1(ID, w_{ID})$, $h_2 = H_2(ID, T, w_{ID,T})$ and $\gamma' = (PK_{ID}w_{ID}y^{h_1}w_{ID,T}y^{h_2})^{-h}g^{\delta}$. If the equation

$$H_3(\gamma', PK_{ID}, ID, T, M) = h \text{ holds, output "accept", else output "reject".}$$

4   Security and Efficiency Analysis

4.1   Security Proof

In this section, we give formal analysis to show that our RCLS scheme is existentially unforgeable against chosen message attacks from all kinds of adversaries.

Theorem 1. Suppose there exists a Type I EUF-CMA adversary $\mathcal{A}_I$ against the RCLS scheme with probability ϵ. Then, there exists an algorithm $\mathcal{B}$ to solve the DL problem with probability $\epsilon' \geqslant \epsilon/q_1$ where q_1 denotes the times for querying H_1.

Proof. Let B be an algorithm to solve the DL problem with an instance $g^a \in Z_p^*$. It intends to compute a by interacting with the adversary A_I.

B plays the role of the challenger. It firstly setups the system parameters (p, q, y, H_1, H_2, H_3). The three hash functions are viewed as random oracles. y is computed via $y = g^x$ where x is randomly selected from $\mathbb{Z}_q^*$. Then $\mathcal{A}_I$ begins to attack. It will make a list of queries before giving its forgery. Suppose $\mathcal{A}_I$ is allowed to make q_1 queries to H_1. B randomly chooses an index $I \in [1, q_1] \cap \mathbb{Z}$.

Except for hash queries, A_I may make queries to the oracles of partial private key, time key, secret values, public key and signature. In addition, A_I can replace any public key with a different value of its own choice. All query-answers are maintained in corresponding lists.

$H_i(i = 1, 2, 3)$ queries: When receiving an $H_i(i = 1, 2, 3)$ query, B picks a random element from Z_q^* as the answer.

Now we assume that A_I always makes the appropriate $H_i(i = 1, 2, 3)$ queries before making other related queries.

Partial Private Key Extraction queries: When $\mathcal{A}_I$ makes a partial private key query on an identity ID_i, if $i \neq I$, B does the following:

- randomly choose $r \in \mathbb{Z}_q^*$ and compute $w_{ID_i} = g^r$;
- compute $d_{ID_i} = r + xH_1(ID_i, w_{ID_i})$;
- return (w_{ID_i}, d_{ID_i}) as the answer.

Otherwise, abort the game.

Time Key queries: When $\mathcal{A}_I$ queries a time key on (ID_i, T), B does the following:

- randomly choose $r' \in \mathbb{Z}_q^*$ and compute $w_{ID_i, T} = g^{r'}$;
- compute $d_{ID_i, T} = r + xH_1(ID_i, T, w_{ID_i})$;
- return $(w_{ID_i, T}, d_{ID_i, T})$ as the answer.

Secret Value queries: For a secret value query, B responds with an x randomly chosen from Z_q^*.

Public Key queries: When receiving a public key query, B firstly checks the secret value list for a corresponding x then computes g^x as the answer. If there is no matched x, B selects an x at random. Then add the x to the secret value list and compute the public key g^x.

Public Key Replacement: A_I can replace any public key with a new value chosen by itself.

Signature queries: When receiving a signature query on (M, ID_i, t),

- if $i \neq I$ and the public key of PK_{ID_i} remains unplaced, B signs normally to output a signature.
- otherwise,
  - B pick $\delta, h \in_R Z_q^*$;
  - compute $\gamma = (PK_{ID_i} w_{ID_i} y^{h_1} w_{ID,T} y^{h_2})^{-h} g^{\delta}$, where $w_{ID_I} = g^a$, and set $h = H_3(\gamma, PK_{ID_i}, ID_i, T, M)$;
  - return the signature $\sigma = (h, \delta, w_{ID_i}, w_{ID_i,T})$.

Forge: Finally, A_I outputs a message-signature pair (M^*, σ^*) on behalf of the identity ID_I at the time T^*. Since the hash function H_3 is viewed as a random oracle, according to the forking lemma, A_I can obtain another signature $\sigma^{*'}$. So, B can calculate $a = (\delta^* - \delta^{*'})(h^* - h^{*'})^{-1} - v_{ID_I} - d_{ID_I,T^*} - xh_1$.

Analysis. It is not difficult for us to obtain the advantage for B to solve the DL problem $\epsilon' \geqslant \frac{1}{q_1} \epsilon$.

Theorem 2. Suppose there exists a Type II EUF-CMA adversary A_{II} against the RCLS scheme with advantage ϵ. Then, there exists an algorithm B to solve the DL problem with advantage $\epsilon' \geqslant \frac{1}{q_1} \epsilon$ where q_1 is the times of queries to the random oracle H_1.

Proof. Let B be an algorithm to solve the DL problem with an instance $g^a \in Z_p^*$. It intends to compute a by interacting with the adversary A_{II}.

B plays the role of the challenger. It firstly setups the system parameters (p, q, y, H_1, H_2, H_3). The three hash functions are viewed as random oracles. y is computed via $y = g^x$ where x is randomly selected from $\mathbb{Z}_q^*$. Then A_{II} begins to attack. It will make a list of queries before giving its forgery. Suppose A_{II} is allowed to make q_1 queries to H_1. B randomly chooses an index $I \in [1, q_1] \cap \mathbb{Z}$.

Except for hash queries, A_{II} may make queries to the oracles of secret values, public key and signature. All query-answers are kept in corresponding lists.

$H_i(i = 1, 2, 3)$ queries: When receiving an $H_i(i = 1, 2, 3)$ query, B picks a random element from Z_q^* as the answer.

Now we assume that A_{II} always makes the appropriate $H_i(i = 1, 2, 3)$ queries before making other related queries.

Secret Value queries: For a secret value query, B responds with an x randomly chosen from Z_q^*.

Public Key queries: When receiving a public key query, if $i = I$, B returns $PK_{ID_i} = g^a$; otherwise B chooses an x at random and computes $PK_{ID_i} = g^x$.

Signature queries: When receiving a signature query on (M, ID_i, T),

– if $i \neq I$, B signs normally to output a signature.
– otherwise,
  - B pick $\delta, h \in_R Z_q^*$;
  - compute $\gamma = (PK_{ID_i} w_{ID_i} y^{h_1} w_{ID,T} y^{h_2})^{-h} g^{\delta}$, where $w_{ID_i} = g^a$, and set $h = H_3(\gamma, PK_{ID_i}, ID_i, T, M)$;
  - return the signature $\sigma = (h, \delta, w_{ID_i}, w_{ID_i,T})$.

Forge: Finally, A_{II} outputs a message-signature pair (M^*, σ^*) on behalf of the identity ID_I at the time T^*. Since the hash function H_3 is viewed as a random oracle, according to the forking lemma, A_{II} can obtain another signature $\sigma^{*'}$. So, B can calculate $a = (\delta^* - \delta^{*'})(h^* - h^{*'})^{-1} - d_{ID^*} - d_{ID^*,T^*}$.

Analysis. It is clear that the advantage for B to solve the DL problem $\epsilon' \geqslant \frac{1}{q_1} \epsilon$.

Theorem 3. Suppose there exists a revoked user A_{re} who can break the EUF-CMA security of the RCLS scheme with advantage ϵ. Then, there exists an algorithm B to solve the DL problem with advantage $\epsilon' \geqslant \frac{1}{q_2} \epsilon$ where q_2 denotes the times of queries to the random oracle H_2.

Proof. Let B be an algorithm to solve the DL problem with an instance $g^a \in Z_p^*$. It intends to compute a by interacting with the adversary A_{re}.

B plays the role of the challenger. It firstly setups the system parameters (p, q, y, H_1, H_2, H_3). The three hash functions are viewed as random oracles. y is computed via $y = g^x$ where x is randomly selected from $\mathbb{Z}_q^*$.

Now A_{re} begins to attack. It will make a list of queries before giving its forgery. Suppose A_I is allowed to make q_2 queries to H_2. B randomly chooses an index $I \in [1, q_2] \cap \mathbb{Z}$.

Except for hash queries, A_{re} may make queries to the oracles of partial private key, time key, secret values, public key and signature. All query-answers are maintained in corresponding lists.

$H_i(i = 1, 2, 3)$ **queries:** When receiving an $H_i(i = 1, 2, 3)$ query, B picks a random element from Z_q^* as the answer.

Now we assume that A_{re} always makes the appropriate $H_i(i = 1, 2, 3)$ queries before making other related queries.

Partial Private Key Extraction queries: When A_{re} makes a partial private key query, B runs the Extract-Partial-Private-Key algorithm to output a partial private key.

Time Key queries: When A_{re} queries a time key on (ID_i, T), if (ID_i, T) is equal to the that of an H_2 query, aborts the game. Otherwise, B runs the update-time-key algorithm to output a time key.

Secret Value queries: For a secret value query, B responds with an x randomly chosen from Z_q^*.

Public Key queries: When receiving a public key query, B firstly checks the secret value list for a corresponding x then computes g^x as the answer. If there is no matched x, B selects an x at random. Then add the x to the secret value list and compute the public key g^x.

Signature queries: When receiving a signature query on (M, ID_i, T),

- if (ID_i, T) is not the Ith H_2 query, B acts normally by running the signing algorithm to yield a signature.
- otherwise,
  - B pick $\delta, h \in_R Z_q^*$;
  - compute $\gamma = (PK_{ID_i} w_{ID_i} y^{h_1} w_{ID,T} y^{h_2})^{-h} g^\delta$, where $w_{ID_I} = g^a$, and set $h = H_3(\gamma, PK_{ID_i}, ID_i, T, M)$;
  - return the signature $\sigma = (h, \delta, w_{ID_i}, w_{ID_i,T})$.

Forge: Finally, A_{re} outputs a message-signature pair (M^*, σ^*) on behalf of the identity ID^* at the time T^*. Since the hash function H_3 is viewed as a random oracle, according to the forking lemma, A_{re} can obtain another signature $\sigma^{*'}$. So, B can calculate $a = (\delta^* - \delta^{*'})(h^* - h^{*'})^{-1} - v_{ID^*} - d_{ID^*} - xh_2$.

Analysis. The advantage for B to solve the DL problem $\epsilon' \geqslant \frac{1}{q_2}\epsilon$.

Efficiency Analysis. The conventional revocation problem in certificateless cryptosystem is to update users's partial private key periodically. These new keys must be transmitted via secret channels thus consuming a lot of computation resources. Another method is to set a trusted mediator to realize revocation. Compared with these existing revocation solutions, our method performs better since the periodic time keys are delivered on public channels and no trusted third party is needed.

Extension. The above construction does not consider signing key exposure (also called decryption key exposure in [10]). This threat captures a realistic attack that the signing key may be leaked. It is better that even if a signing key is compromised, the other signing keys still remains secure. The following algorithm is to design the generation of a signing key (instead of the original Set-Private-Key):

- Set-Signing-Key: Randomly select $k \in Z_q^*$, computes $u = g^k$ and $sk_{ID,T} = kH_3(u, ID, T) + d_{ID} + v_{ID} + d_{ID,T}$. The signing key is $(u, sk_{ID,T})$.

The algorithms of Setup, Extract-Partial-Private-Key, Update-Time-Key, Set-Secret-Value, Set-Public-Key, Sign and Verify are similar to that of the above scheme.

5   Conclusion

A necessary problem in public key cryptosystem is how to revoke a user. The traditional certificate public key system employs e.g. CRLs to solve the revocation problem. Though there are many solutions in the identity-based public key system, there are few methods proposed to solve this problem in certificateless public key system.

Early in 2003, Al-Riyami and Paterson suggested that the KGC update the partial private keys for all non-revoked user. However, this method requires secret channels for the transmission of these new-produced partial private keys. Obviously, secret channels consume more resources of computation. In contrast, our scheme outputs new time keys periodically for every non-revoked user, and these time keys only require public channels. Moreover, there is no bilinear pairing in the whole construction. We give formal security proofs to show that our scheme satisfies existential unforgeability against chosen message attacks under the DL assumption. Finally, we consider the threat of signing key exposure.

Acknowledgement. This work is supported by the Nature Science Foundation of China [No. 61502237], NSF of Jiangsu Province [No. BK20130908].

References

1. Al-Riyami, S.S.: Cryptographic schemes based on elliptic curve pairings. Ph.D. thesis, Royal Holloway, University of London (2004)
2. Al-Riyami, S.S., Paterson, K.G.: Certificateless public key cryptography. In: Laih, C.-S. (ed.) ASIACRYPT 2003. LNCS, vol. 2894, pp. 452–473. Springer, Heidelberg (2003)
3. Boneh, D., Franklin, M.: Identity-based encryption from the weil pairing. In: Kilian, J. (ed.) CRYPTO 2001. LNCS, vol. 2139, pp. 213–229. Springer, Heidelberg (2001)
4. Boldyreva, A., Goyal, V., Kumar, V.: Identity-based encryption with efficient revocation. In: Proceedings of CCS 2008, pp. 417–426. ACM (2008)
5. Fu, Z., Ren, K., Shu, J., Sun, X., Huang, F.: Enabling Personalized Search over Encrypted Outsourced Data with Efficiency Improvement. IEEE Trans. Parallel Distrib. Syst. (2015). doi:10.1109/TPDS:2015.2506573
6. Bin, G., Sheng, V.S., Tay, K.Y., Romano, W., Li, S.: Incremental support vector learning for ordinal regression. IEEE Trans. Neural Netw. Learn. Syst. **26**(7), 1403–1416 (2015)
7. Libert, B., Vergnaud, D.: Adaptive-ID secure revocable identity-based encryption. In: Fischlin, M. (ed.) CT-RSA 2009. LNCS, vol. 5473, pp. 1–15. Springer, Heidelberg (2009)
8. Micali, S.: Novomodo: scalable certificate validation and simplified PKI management. In: Proceedings of 1st Annual PKI Research Workshop, pp. 15–25 (2002)
9. Myers, M., Ankney, R., Alpani, A., Galperin, S., Adams, C.: X.509 Internet public key infrastructure: online certificate status protocol (OCSP). RFC 2560
10. Seo, J.H., Emura, K.: Revocable identity-based encryption revisited: security model and construction. In: Kurosawa, K., Hanaoka, G. (eds.) PKC 2013. LNCS, vol. 7778, pp. 216–234. Springer, Heidelberg (2013)
11. Shamir, A.: Identity-based cryptosystems and signature schemes. In: Blakely, G.R., Chaum, D. (eds.) CRYPTO 1984. LNCS, vol. 196, pp. 47–53. Springer, Heidelberg (1985)
12. Sun, Y., Zhang, F., Shen, L.: Efficient revocable certificateless encryption secure against decryption key exposure. IET Inf. Secur. **9**(3), 158–166 (2015)
13. Tseng, Y.M., Tasi, T.T.: Efficient revocable ID-based encryption with a public channel. Comput. J. **55**(4), 475–486 (2012)
14. Xia, Z., Wang, X., Sun, X., Wang, Q.: A secure and dynamic multi-keyword ranked search scheme over encrypted cloud data. IEEE Trans. Parallel Distrib. Syst. **27**(2), 340–352 (2015)

Privacy Protection of Digital Speech Based on Homomorphic Encryption

Canghong Shi, Hongxia Wang$^{(\boxtimes)}$, Qing Qian, and Huan Wang

School of Information Science and Technology, Southwest Jiaotong University,
Chengdu 611756, China
canghongshi@163.com, hxwang@swjtu.edu.cn

Abstract. This paper presents a digital speech encryption scheme based on homomorphic encryption, which uses a symmetrical key cryptosystem (MORE-method) with probabilistic statistics and fully homomorphic properties to encrypt speech signals. In the proposed scheme, each sample of speech signal is firstly multiplied one weight, and then encrypted, the normalization is exploited to make the data expend lossy compression. Finally, a recombination method of the cipher-text is proposed to obtain the corresponding speech cipher-text with good performances. Experimental results show that the proposed scheme is homomorphism, which has strong diffusibility and a large key-space. What's more, it is robustness to statistical analysis attacks, decreased the residual intelligibility as small as possible. Moreover, the encrypted speech can be decrypted completely. Compared with two dimensional chaotic and Paillier cryptosystem, the proposed scheme is more security and lower complexity, so the proposed scheme especially meets the sensitive speech security in the cloud.

Keywords: Fully homomorphic symmetrical encryption · Digital speech · Speech security · Normalization · Homomorphism

1 Introduction

Digital speeches are widely used in many territories, more and more speech files are produced and stored in the cloud. And, the integrity, confidentiality and availability of digital speeches become more and more important in the cloud storage. The problems how to protect the integrity and confidentiality of digital speeches arise. In [1], it shows a method which is used to protect the integrity of data in public cloud storage. But protecting the confidentiality of digital speeches is still a problem in public cloud storage, even users can accurately acquire the recommendations of digital speeches with a recommender approach in [2]. The traditional way of encrypting speech signal is permutation-based [3–8], the encryption methods just change the seats of samples but not change the samples themselves. When the original digital speech is needed to process, the encrypted speech must be decrypted, which will leak confidential information to the public. However, using homomorphic cryptographic algorithms can protect privacy and enable computation on encrypting data. In [9], it shows that solving these types of problems by processing the signals in an encrypted form using fully

© Springer International Publishing AG 2016
X. Sun et al. (Eds.): ICCCS 2016, Part I, LNCS 10039, pp. 365–376, 2016.
DOI: 10.1007/978-3-319-48671-0_33

homomorphic encryption. In recent years, because of the good properties of homomorphic encryption, the encrypted multimedia signals can be stored in the cloud and be processed by the third party. Some scholars do some works on image homomorphic encryption [10–13], and speech homomorphic encryption [14], the homomorphic cryptosystem which they use mostly is the Paillier cryptosystem [15], but it is a asymmetrical and partly homomorphic encryption which has high computation complexity. In this paper, we proposed a practical implementation speech encryption scheme based on homomorphic encryption which can be exploited to encrypt digital speech effectively.

The remainder of this paper is organized as follows. The MORE-method is described in Sect. 2. In Sect. 3, the proposed scheme is given. In Sect. 4, algorithm performance analysis and comparison are given. The conclusions are drawn in Sect. 5.

2 The MORE-Method Cryptosystem

The concept of probabilistic secure cryptosystem was proposed in [16]. Cryptosystems that satisfy both the homomorphic and probabilistic properties do exist. One of them is MORE-method cryptosystem [17]. According to Refs. [16, 17], it is known that MORE-method cryptosystem is probabilistic symmetrical fully homomorphic cryptosystem. A brief introduction of MORE-method cryptosystem is presented below:

Symmetric-Key Generation. Selects two large prime numbers p and q randomly. Computes their product N and Z_N (Z_N is integer in N), choose four numbers in Z_N randomly to form one invertible matrix S as the symmetric key for encryption.

Encryption. For each plain-text X_i, select a random large-number Y_i in Z_N. The encryption process of X_i is defined as Eq. (1).

$$C_i = E_k[X_i, Y_i] = S \cdot \begin{bmatrix} X_i & 0 \\ 0 & Y_i \end{bmatrix} \cdot S^{-1} = \begin{bmatrix} c_{11} & c_{12} \\ c_{21} & c_{22} \end{bmatrix} \tag{1}$$

the cipher-text can be regarded as the four values $c_{11}, c_{12}, c_{21}, c_{22}$.

Decryption. Let $c_{11}, c_{12}, c_{21}, c_{22}$ be the cipher-texts. The decryption process of $c_{11}, c_{12}, c_{21}, c_{22}$ is defined as Eq. (2).

$$D_k(C_i) = D_k[c_{11}, c_{12}, c_{21}, c_{22}] = S^{-1} \cdot \begin{bmatrix} c_{11} & c_{12} \\ c_{21} & c_{22} \end{bmatrix} \cdot S = \begin{bmatrix} X_i & 0 \\ 0 & Y_i \end{bmatrix} \tag{2}$$

after decryption, the decrypted plain-text can be obtained from the first element X_i of the decrypted matrix.

Using MORE-method cryptosystem to encrypt digital speech can protect the privacy and the confidential of digital speech content in the cloud, the proposed practical scheme is described in the following section.

3 The Proposed Speech Encryption Scheme Based on Homomorphic Encryption

3.1 Speech Encryption

Suppose that an original speech signal $X = \{a(i)|i = 1,2,\ldots,I\}$ with I samples is quantified in 16 bits, where the quantified value $a(i)$ belongs to $(-1,1)$. The details of the proposed encryption scheme is illustrated as following:

Step 1: Encrypt speech signal. In this phase, the speech signal $X = \{a(i)|$ $i = 1,2,\ldots,I.\}$ is encrypted by MORE-method cryptosystem. For two large primes p and q, calculate $N = pq$, choose four numbers in Z_N randomly to form one invertible matrix S as the symmetric key matrix as Eq. (3). MORE-method only works on real integer values, if a speech is needed to encrypt by MORE-method, all the speech samples must be quantized to integers. In order to satisfy that demand, the original speech signal should be converted into another signal $X' = \{Ma(i)|i = 1,2,\ldots,I\}$, which all samples are real integer values, by multiply one weight $M = N/10^2$ (a estimated value), where $Ma(i)$ belongs to $\left(-N/10^2, N/10^2\right)$. For each sample value, the encrypted value of each sample is calculated as Eq. (4).

$$S = \begin{bmatrix} s_{11} & s_{12} \\ s_{21} & s_{22} \end{bmatrix}, \quad 0 \le s_{11}, s_{12}, s_{21}, s_{22} \le N \tag{3}$$

$$C_i = E_k[M \cdot a(i), r(i)] = S \cdot \begin{bmatrix} M \cdot a(i) & 0 \\ 0 & r(i) \end{bmatrix} \cdot S^{-1} = \begin{bmatrix} c_{11} & c_{12} \\ c_{21} & c_{22} \end{bmatrix} \tag{4}$$

where $r(i)$ is a randomly selected larger-number in Z_N, and $c_{11}, c_{12}, c_{21}, c_{22}$ are the speech cipher-text values, all the speech signal samples of cipher-text values are collected to form four encrypted speech signal. The data extension will occur after encryption, and one sample will become quadruple and the size of each encrypted speech signal become much bigger than the original speech signal.

Step 2: Compress speech cipher-texts by normalization. In the proposed scheme, the biggest elements of $c_{11}, c_{12}, c_{21}, c_{22}$ are taken and defined as $C_{11}, C_{12}, C_{21}, C_{22}$, respectively; the round up of $C_{11}, C_{12}, C_{21}, C_{22}$ can be expressed as $C'_{11}, C'_{12}, C'_{21}, C'_{22}$. The normalization results are $d_{11} = c_{11}/C'_{11}$, $d_{12} = c_{12}/C'_{12}$, $d_{21} = c_{21}/C'_{21}$, and $d_{22} = c_{22}/C'_{22}$.

Step 3: Recombine compressed speech cipher-texts. Firstly, the odd number $f_o = \{f_1, f_3, \cdots, f_{n-1}\}$ of cipher-text $d_{11} = \{f_1, f_2, f_3, \cdots, f_n\}$ and the even number $g_e = \{g_2, g_4, \cdots, g_n\}$ of cipher-text $d_{21} = \{g_1, g_2, g_3, \cdots, g_n\}$ can be taken to constitute one new encrypted signal $d'_{11} = \{f_1, g_2, f_3, g_4, \cdots, f_{n-1}, g_n\}$; and the remind cipher-texts constitute another new encrypted signal $d'_{21} = \{g_1, f_2, g_3, f_4, \cdots, g_{n-1}, f_n\}$. Meanwhile, the odd number $h_o = \{h_1, h_3, \cdots, h_{n-1}\}$ of cipher-text $d_{12} = \{h_1, h_2, h_3, \cdots, h_n\}$, and the even number

$j_e = \{j_2, j_4, \cdots, j_n\}$ of cipher-text $d_{22} = \{j_1, j_2, j_3, \cdots, j_n\}$ can also be taken to constitute a new encrypted signal $d'_{12} = \{h_1, j_2, h_3, j_4, \cdots, h_{n-1}, j_n\}$, and the remainder do the same operation to constitute another new encrypted signal $d'_{22} = \{j_1, h_2, j_3, h_4, \cdots, j_{n-1}, h_n\}$. Then, we can get four encrypted signals $d'_{11}, d'_{12}, d'_{21}, d'_{22}$.

3.2 Speech Decryption

The details of decryption speech scheme are illustrated as follows:

Step 1: Recover compressed speech cipher-text. Because of the properties of homo-morphic encryption, a receiver obtains cipher-texts $d'_{11}, d'_{12}, d'_{21}, d'_{22}$, who can get the cipher-texts $d_{11}, d_{12}, d_{21}, d_{22}$ with the inverse process of method mentioned in step 3 of Sect. 3.1.

Step 2: Decompress speech cipher-texts. After got the speech cipher-texts $d_{11}, d_{12}, d_{21}, d_{22}$, the speech receiver performs the inverse process of step 2 in Sect. 3.1 to get the cipher-texts $c_{11}, c_{12}, c_{21}, c_{22}$.

Step 3: Decrypt speech cipher-text. With the symmetric key S, the principal content of original speech can be reconstructed by using inverse process of step 1 in Sect. 3.1. The details are as follows, the receiver knows the symmetric key S can decrypt the cipher-text matrix C_i and recover the plain-text $a(i)$ by simple matrix multiplication as Eq. (5).

$$D_k(C_i) = D_k[c_{11}, c_{12}, c_{21}, c_{22}] = S^{-1} \cdot \begin{bmatrix} c_{11} & c_{12} \\ c_{21} & c_{22} \end{bmatrix} \cdot S = \begin{bmatrix} Ma(i) & 0 \\ 0 & r(i) \end{bmatrix} \quad (5)$$

after decryption, take the first element $Ma(i)$ of the decrypted matrix as the plain-text. The decrypted speech signal $a(i)$ can be obtained by moving the weight M by $a(i) = Ma(i)/M$.

4 Performance Analysis and Comparison

In order to illuminate the proposed scheme for homomorphic encryption of digital speech, series of experiments are given with the following examples. In our all tests, speech signals are all adopted by 16-bit quantified mono speech files sampled at 8 kHz with WAVE format, the number of sampling points is 3000, the weight is set as 10^{56}. All of the experiments are performed on a PC with 3.40 GHZ CPU and 4.00 GB main memory.

4.1 Properties of Speech Encryption and Decryption

In the proposed scheme, the digital speech signals are encrypted in time domain, and the encrypted results are shown in Fig. 1(b, c, d, e). Form Fig. 1 (b, c, d, e), we can see that the waveforms of the encrypted speech are uniform distribution, and the encrypted

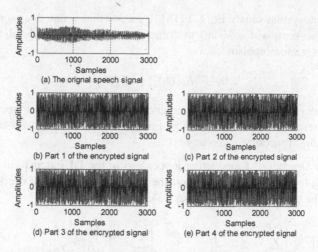

Fig. 1. Homomorphic encryption of speech. (a) Original signal. (b, c, d, e) Encrypted speeches.

speech is similar to the noise. It indicates that the proposed scheme has a good diffusibility and encryption performance. Meanwhile, the decrypted speech is similar to the original speech signal shown in Fig. 2(f).

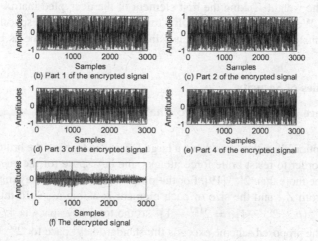

Fig. 2. Homomorphic decryption of speech. (b, c, d, e) Encrypted speeches. (f) Decrypted speech.

4.2 Property of Homomorphism

The DFT of a sequence $x(n)$ is defined as

$$X(k) = \sum_{n=0}^{M-1} x(n) \cdot e^{-j\frac{2\pi}{M}nk}, \quad k = 0, 1, \ldots, M-1 \tag{6}$$

where $x(n)$ is a finite duration sequence with length M.

If one cryptosystem satisfy Eq. (7) [18], it means that if one does some operation on speech cipher-text, who amounts to doing the corresponding operation on speech plain-text, it is homomorphism.

$$D_k\{F'[E_k(O_i)]\} = F(O_i) \tag{7}$$

where O_i is the plain-text, E_k, D_k are the encryption and decryption operation of the cryptosystem respectively, F represents an operation function for plain-text, and F' is the corresponding function for cipher-text.

Homomorphic Operation. Considering a scenario in the DFT transform as Eq. (6) is done on encrypted speech C_i, and obtain the transform result, then decrypt the transform result. The process is shown as Eq. (8).

$$D_k\{D[C_i]\} = S^{-1} \cdot \left[\sum_{i=0}^{I-1} C_i \cdot e^{-j\frac{2\pi}{I}ik}\right] \cdot S = S^{-1} \cdot \left[\sum_{i=0}^{I-1} S \cdot \begin{bmatrix} Ma(i) & 0 \\ 0 & r(i) \end{bmatrix} \cdot S^{-1} \cdot e^{-j\frac{2\pi}{I}ik}\right] \cdot S$$

$$= \sum_{i=0}^{I-1} S^{-1} \cdot S \cdot \begin{bmatrix} Ma(i) & 0 \\ 0 & r(i) \end{bmatrix} \cdot S^{-1} \cdot S \cdot e^{-j\frac{2\pi}{I}ik} = \begin{bmatrix} \sum_{i=0}^{I-1} Ma(i)e^{-j\frac{2\pi}{I}ik} & 0 \\ 0 & \sum_{i=0}^{I-1} r(i)e^{-j\frac{2\pi}{I}ik} \end{bmatrix} \tag{8}$$

where D stands for the DFT transform, $\{a(i)|i = 1, 2, ..., I\}$ are samples of original speech, M is the weight. Taking the first element of the decrypted matrix of Eq. (8) as the plain-text. We can see that doing DFT transform on encrypted speech amounts to doing DFT transform on original speech using the proposed scheme as Eq. (7).

4.3   Properties of Security

A.   Key-Space and Cipher-Text Size Analysis

A good encryption algorithm must have a large key space to make the brute-force attack infeasible. In order to resist brute force attacks, the key space for the encryption algorithm should be more than 2^{128} [19]. For the proposed scheme, the key matrix elements are selected from Z_N, and the size of each element is as big as N. In this paper, N is selected as 2^{194} $(p = 2^{67} - 1, q = 2^{127} - 1)$, so the total key space is 4×2^{196}, so the key space of the proposed scheme exceeds the standard key space for 2^{66}. According to the proposed scheme, the size of the speech plain-text, key and inverse of key are all as big as $N = 2^{194}$; the cipher-texts $c_{11}, c_{12}, c_{21}, c_{22}$ are the product of the plain-text, the key and inverse of key; therefore, the sizes of $c_{11}, c_{12}, c_{21}, c_{22}$ are all $N^3 = 2^{582}$.

B.   Residual Intelligibility

Time-varying spectrum behavior of a significative speech signal can be shown intuitively in speech spectrograms. Using the proposed scheme can change a significative speech spectrograms completely. The speech spectrograms of the original and encrypted speech are shown in Fig. 3. It is evident that the encrypted speech in the

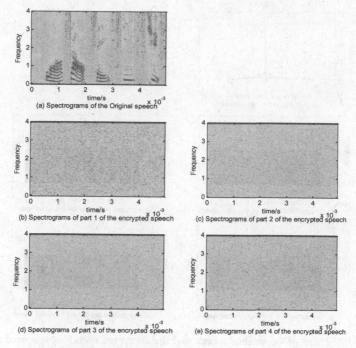

Fig. 3. Spectrograms of the original signal and the encrypted speech signal.

proposed scheme is obviously similar to white noise without any talk spurts, the intonation of original speech has been removed, which indicates that residual intelligibility of encrypted speech is useless for eavesdroppers at the communication channel.

C. Statistical Analysis and Histogram Comparison

When multimedia are protected by the encryption or steganography method, if the histograms of protected multimedia have not changed or changed little, one can reveals the histograms to attack the protected multimedia [20]. Statistical analysis has been performed on the proposed scheme to demonstrate its superior confusion and diffusion properties, which strongly resist the statistical attacks. In the proposed scheme, the sample values of original speech have been changed. The histograms of encrypted speech are shown in Fig. 4(b, c, d, e), the attacker can not know the original histogram from the encrypted speech. However, the original speech is encrypted by two dimensional chaotic maps in [5], the sample positions are permuted and the sample values are not masked in the encrypted phase pseudorandomly, the histogram of encrypted speech using the two dimensional chaotic maps is shown in Fig. 5. The original and encrypted speech have the same statistical characteristic according to Figs. 4(a) and 5(f), an attacker without the key can know the original histogram from encrypted values. Therefore, the security of our scheme is better than the scheme proposed in [5].

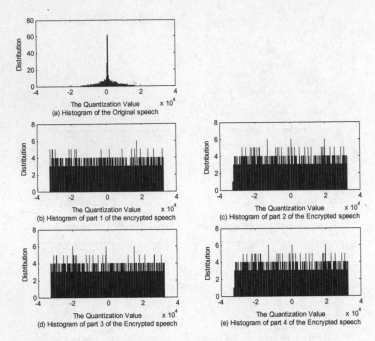

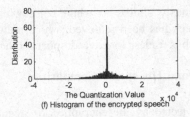

Fig. 4. Histograms of the original speech and the encrypted speech in proposed scheme

Fig. 5. Histogram of encrypted speech in [5].

D. Correlation Test

A useful measure to assess the encryption quality of any cryptosystem is the correlation coefficient between the original signal and the encrypted signal. It can be calculated as Eq. (9).

$$r(x, y) = \frac{\text{cov}(x, y)}{\sqrt{D(x)}\sqrt{D(y)}} \tag{9}$$

where $\text{cov}(x, y) = 1/N \sum_{i=1}^{N} (x_i - E(x))(y_i - E(y))$ is the covariance between the adjacent sampling points of digital speech signal, $D(x) = 1/N \sum_{i=1}^{N} (x_i - E(x))^2$ is the variances of the signals x, $D(y)$ is the variances of the signals y, and

$E(x) = 1/N \sum_{i=1}^{N} x_i$, N is the number of speech samples involved in the calculations. The small value of the correlation coefficient r indicates a good encryption quality.

To test the correlation between two adjacent samples (AS) quantitative value (QV) in the original speech and the encrypted speech, the following procedure was carried out. Firstly, randomly select 1500 pairs of adjacent quantitative value from a speech. The correlation distribution of two adjacent quantitative value in original speech and encrypted speech is shown in Fig. 6, and the correlation coefficients are 0.7386 and 0.0115 respectively. Then, the correlation coefficients of two adjacent quantitative value in original speech and in encrypted speech of four types selected speeches are tabulated in Table 1. These correlation analysis above prove that the proposed encryption speech scheme satisfy low correlation.

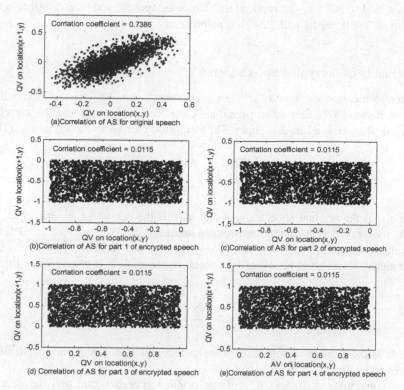

Fig. 6. Correlations of two adjacent QV in the original speech and the encrypted speech

E. Computation Complexity and Time-Consuming

According to the proposed scheme, its encryption and decryption algorithm computation complexity are all $O(n^2)$, however, the encryption algorithm computation complexity of using the Paillier cryptosystem [10, 12–14] is $O(g^n)$ (g is a constant in Paillier cryptosystem); and the decryption algorithm computation complexity of the

Table 1. Correlation coefficients of two adjacent quantitative values

	Original speech	Encrypted speech
Man (Chinese)	0.9943	−0.0070
Woman (Chinese)	0.9850	−0.0010
Man (English)	0.9953	0.0014
Woman (English)	0.9488	0.0027

Paillier cryptosystem is $O(n^{\log n})$. So the proposed scheme has lower computation complexity than Paillier cryptosystem.

In the encryption and decryption test, time-consuming of encryption a 513 ms Chinese speech file and a 215 ms English speech file by the proposed scheme are 0.2466 s and 0.3075 s, decryption the Chinese speech and the English speech cipher-texts are 0.7990 s and 1.2481 s, respectively.

4.4 Quality of Decrypted Speech Signal

In order to measure the quality of decrypted speech signals. The traditional Signal to-Noise Ratio (*SNR*), segmental Signal-to-Noise Ratio (*SNRseg*) and the correlation coefficient $R_{aa'}$ are used in this paper. The definition of *SNR* is shown as Eq. (10).

$$SNR = 10 \lg \left(\sum_{i=1}^{N} a^2(i) \middle/ \sum_{i=1}^{N} \left(a(i) - a(i)' \right)^2 \right) \tag{10}$$

where $a(i)$ is the original speech signal and $a(i)'$ is the decrypted speech signal.

The most popular one of the time domain metrics is the *SNRseg*, which is defined as the average of the *SNR* values. The *SNRseg* values come from short segments of the output signal. It is a good estimator for speech signal quality. It is defined as Eq. (11).

$$SNRseg = \frac{10}{W} \sum_{m=0}^{M-1} \lg \sum_{i=Km}^{Km+k-1} \left(\frac{a^2(i)}{a(i) - a'(i)} \right)^2 \tag{11}$$

where W is the number of segments in the output signal, and K is the length of each segment ($K = 5$).

The correlation coefficient $R_{aa'}$ of the original speech signal and the decrypted signal is defined as Eq. (12). As the value of $R_{aa'}$ is close to 1, the decrypted speech becomes similar to the original speech signal.

$$R_{aa'} = \frac{\text{cov}(a(i), a'(i))}{\sqrt{D(a(i))}\sqrt{D(a'(i))}} \tag{12}$$

In this paper, the *SNR*, *SNRseg* and $R_{aa'}$ of decrypted speech are listed in Table 2. Form Table 2, we can see that the decrypted speech are similar as the original speech, which indicates the original speech signal can be recovered accurately.

Table 2. Quality metrics values for the decrypted speech signals

Quality metrics	Value
$SNR(dB)$	45.0206
$SNRseg(dB)$	45.2222
$R_{aa'}$	1.0000

5 Conclusion

In this paper, one practical and effective fully homomorphic symmetrical encryption scheme of speech signal is proposed. Firstly, we introduce the fully homomorphic symmetrical encryption arithmetic, then we give out a speech encryption scheme using the fully homomorphic symmetrical encryption arithmetic. The algorithm analysis and experimental results show that the proposed scheme is homomorphism, which has large key space, good diffusibility, perfect randomness of cipher-text. It is also robustness to statistical analysis attacks. Moreover, this encryption algorithm not only wipe off original intonations character but also has a lower complexity, and it is more security.

Acknowledgments. This work was supported by the National Natural Science Foundation of China (NSFC) under the grant No. U1536110.

References

1. Ren, Y., Shen, J., Wang, J., Han, J., Lee, S.: Mutual verifiable provable data auditing in public cloud storage. J. Internet Technol. **16**(2), 317–323 (2015)
2. Ma, T., Zhou, J., Tang, M., Tian, Y., Al-Dhelaan, A., Al-Rodhaan, M., Lee, S.: Social network and tag sources based augmenting collaborative recommender system. IEICE Trans. Inf. Syst. **E98-D**(4), 902–910 (2015)
3. Kanhe, A., Aghila, G., Kiran, C.Y.S., Ramesh, C.H., Jadav, G., Gowtham Raj, M.: Robust audio steganography based on advanced encryption standards in temporal domain. In: IEEE ICACCI 2015, pp. 1449–1453 (2015)
4. Eldin, S.M.S., Khamis, S.A., Hassanin, A.A.I.M., Alsharqawy, M.A.: New audio encryption package for TV cloud computing. Int. J. Speech Technol. **18**(1), 131–142 (2015)
5. Mostafa, A., Soliman, N.F., Abdalluh, M., El-samie, F.E.A.: Speech encryption using two dimensional chaotic maps. In: IEEE ICENCO 2015, pp. 235–240 (2015)
6. Zeng, L., Zhang, X., Chen, L., Fan, Z., Wang, Y.: Scrambling-based speech encryption via compressed sensing. EURASIP J. Adv. Signal Process. http://asp.eurasipjournals.com/content/2012/1/257
7. Wang, H., Zhou, L., Zhang, W., Liu, S.: Watermarking-based perceptual hashing search over encrypted speech. In: Shi, Y.-Q., Kim, H.J., Pérez-González, F., Echizen, I. (eds.) IWDW 2015. LNCS, vol. 9569, pp. 423–434. Springer, Heidelberg (2014). doi:10.1007/978-3-662-43886-2_30
8. García-Martínez, M., Ontañón-García, L.J., Campos-Cantón, E., Celikovský, S.: Hyper-chaotic encryption based on multi-scroll piecewise linear systems. Appl. Math. Comput. **270**, 413–424 (2015)

9. Shortell, T., Shokoufandeh, A.: Secure signal processing using fully homomorphic encryption. In: Battiato, S., Blanc-Talon, J., Gallo, G., Philips, W., Popescu, D., Scheunders, P. (eds.) ACIVS 2015. LNCS, vol. 9386, pp. 93–104. Springer, Heidelberg (2015). doi:10. 1007/978-3-319-25903-1_9

10. Zhang, X., Long, J., Wang, Z., Cheng, H.: Lossless and reversible data hiding in encrypted images with public key cryptography. IEEE Trans. Circuits Syst. Video Technol. **PP**, 1 (2015)

11. Yang, P., Gui, X., An, J., Tian, F., Wang, J.: An encrypted image editing scheme based on homomorphic encryption. In: IEEE INFOCOM Workshops, pp. 109–110 (2015)

12. Zhang, Y., Zhuo, L., Peng, Y., Zhang, J.: A secure image retrieval method based on homomorphic encryption for cloud computing. In: 19th International Conference on Digital Signal Processing, pp. 269–274. IEEE (2014)

13. Li, Y., Zhou, J., Li, Y., Au, O.C.: Reducing the ciphertext expansion in image homomorphic encryption via linear interpolation technique. In: IEEE GlobalSIP, pp. 800–804 (2015)

14. Hendriks, R.C., Erkin, Z., Gerkmann, T.: Privacy-preserving distributed speech enhancement for wireless: sensor networks by processing in the encrypted domain. In: IEEE ICASSP, pp. 7005–7009 (2013)

15. Paillier, P.: Public-key cryptosystems based on composite degree residuosity classes. In: Stern, J. (ed.) EUROCRYPT 1999. LNCS, vol. 1592, pp. 223–238. Springer, Heidelberg (1999). doi:10.1007/3-540-48910-X_16

16. Goldwasser, S., Micali, S.: Probabilistic encryption. J. Comput. Syst. Sci. **28**(2), 270–299 (1984)

17. Kipnis, A., Hibshoosh, E.: Efficient methods for practical fully homomorphic symmetric key encryption, randomization and verification. http://eprint.iacr.org/2012/637

18. Gentry, C.: Computing arbitrary functions of encrypted data. Commun. ACM **53**(3), 97–105 (2010)

19. ECRYPT II yearly report on algorithms and keysizes. In: European Network of Excellence in Cryptology. http://cordis.europa.eu/docs/projects/cnect/6/216676/080/deliverables/002-DSPA20

20. Xia, Z., Wang, X., Sun, X., Liu, Q., Xiong, N.: Steganalysis of LSB matching using differences between nonadjacent pixels. Multimed. Tools Appl. **75**(4), 1947–1962 (2016)

Two Factor Authenticated Key Exchange Protocol for Wireless Sensor Networks: Formal Model and Secure Construction

Fushan Wei[1]([⊠]), Ruijie Zhang[1], and Chuangui Ma[2]

[1] State Key Laboratory of Mathematical Engineering and Advanced Computing,
Zhengzhou, China
{weifs831020,rjz_wonder}@163.com
[2] Department of Basic Courses, Army Aviation Institute, Beijing, China
chuanguima@sina.com

Abstract. Two-factor authenticated key exchange (TFAKE) protocols are critical tools for ensuring identity authentication and secure data transmission in wireless sensor networks (WSNs). Until now, numerous TFAKE protocols based on smart cards and passwords are proposed for WSNs. Unfortunately, most of them are found insecure against various attacks. Researchers focus on cryptanalysis of these protocols and then fixing the loopholes. Little attention has been paid to design rationales and formal security models of these protocols. In this paper, we first put forward a formal security model for TFAKE protocols in WSNs. We then present an efficient TFAKE protocol for WSNs without using expensive asymmetric cryptology mechanisms. Our protocol can be proven secure in the random oracle model and achieves user anonymity. Compared with other TFAKE protocols, our protocol is more efficient and enjoys provable security.

Keywords: Two-factor authenticated key exchange · Password · Smart card · Provable security · Wireless sensor networks

1 Introduction

With the rapid development of the micro electronic mechanism system, wireless communications and low-power technologies in embedded systems, wireless sensor networks (WSNs) are now widely used in many applications, such as military surveillance, environment monitoring, health care monitoring, disaster relief and natural disaster prevention. WSNs are usually composed of thousands even millions of sensor nodes. Due to its ubiquitous nature, sensor nodes are randomly

F.Wei—This work is supported by the National Natural Science Foundation of China (Nos. 61309016, 61379150, 61501515), Postdoctoral Science Foundation of China (Grant No. 2014M562493), Postdoctoral Science Foundation of Shanxi Province, and Key Scientific Technological Project of Henan Province (Grant Nos. 122102210126, 092101210502).

© Springer International Publishing AG 2016
X. Sun et al. (Eds.): ICCCS 2016, Part I, LNCS 10039, pp. 377–388, 2016.
DOI: 10.1007/978-3-319-48671-0_34

deployed in unattended environments and collect valuable data of interest. In order to protect these valuable data from unauthorized users or even malicious adversaries, user authentication and data confidentiality are primary concerns in WSNs before accessing data from sensor nodes [1–4]. User authentication ensures the validity of the user while data confidentiality requires the user and the sensor node to establish a common secret key to encrypt the collected data.

Typically, an authenticated key exchange protocol in WSNs involves a user, a gateway node and a sensor node. When a user wants to access real-time data from a sensor node, he will send a query to the gateway node. The gateway node will verify the validity of the user. If the user is a qualified one, then the gateway will assist the user and the sensor node to establish a common secret key to realize data integrity and confidentiality for the upcoming data transmission. Currently, two-factor authenticated key exchange (TFAKE) protocols based on smart card and password are the most popular authentication mechanism in WSNs. TFAKE protocol is an approach to authenticate someone which requires the presentation of two different kinds of authentication factors (smart card and password in this case). The adversary has to compromise both the smart card and the password to impersonate the user. By combining the advantages of smart cards and passwords, TFAKE protocols achieve high-level security without additional computation cost.

In 2009, Das [5] presented the first two-factor user authentication scheme using smart card and password. Das claimed his scheme can resist replay attack, stolen-verifier attack, guessing attack, and impersonation attack. However, Das's scheme is found to be insecure against various attacks. Nyang et al. [6] demonstrated that Das's scheme is insecure against off-line dictionary attack, sensor node compromising attack, and does not protect query response messages. They also proposed an improved scheme to overcome the drawbacks of Das's scheme. Chen et al. [7] showed that Das's scheme does not provide mutual authentication and proposed their improvement. He et al. [8] found that Das's scheme is vulnerable to the insider attack and the derived impersonation attack. Khan et al. [9] pointed out that Das's scheme is vulnerable to the gateway node bypassing attack and privileged insider attack, it does not provide methods to change users' passwords, and it does not achieve mutual authentication between the GW-node and the sensor node. Khan et al. also presented an improved scheme to overcome the security weaknesses of Das's scheme. Unfortunately, Sun et al. [10] showed that Khan et al.'s scheme still suffers from the GW-node impersonation attack, the GW-node bypassing attack, and the privileged insider attack. They proposed a new user authentication scheme which is proved to be secure under the security model of Bellare and Rogaway [11]. Recently, Yuan [12] also found that in Khan et al's scheme, there is no provision of non-repudiation, it is susceptible to attack due to a lost smart card, and mutual authentication between the user and the GW-node does not attained. To fix these weaknesses, Yuan proposed an improved scheme using user's biometrics and proved the security of the new scheme by the GNY logic [13]. Nevertheless, Wei et al. [14] pointed out several secure loopholes of Yuan's scheme and also presented their improvement.

Although there are many TFAKE protocols proposed in the literature, most of them only have heuristic security arguments and are found to be insecure. Researchers show great interest to cryptanalyze the existing TFAKE protocols for WSNs and fix the shortcomings. Little attention has been paid to formal security analysis of TFAKE protocols for WSNs. Until now, to the best of our knowledge, there are only two TFAKE protocols for WSNs which have rigorous security proof. The first one is Sun et al.'s protocol [10]. However, their protocol is proven secure in Bellare and Rogaway's security model, which is a security model for key exchange protocols rather than a model for TFAKE protocols. Their protocol employs "challenge-response" technique which makes it inefficient in term of communication. Moreover, their protocol does not provide session key establishment for the user and the sensor node. Another provably secure TFAKE protocol is due to Nam et al. [15]. Their protocol is the first provably secure TFAKE protocol for WSNs with user anonymity. Nevertheless, their protocol uses computation-expensive public key operations, which makes their protocol unsuitable for WSNs because of the resource-constrained nature of sensor nodes. Furthermore, it is easier for TFAKE protocols to achieve two-factor security and user anonymity when public key cryptosystems are employed.

In this paper, we investigate how to design provably secure TFAKE protocols for WSNs without using computation-expensive public key operations. We first present a security model for TFAKE protocols in WSNs based on the security models of [16,17]. We then propose an efficient TFAKE protocol with user anonymity by using symmetric encryptions and hash functions. We also explain the design rationales for a better understanding of our protocol. The novel TFAKE protocol is proven secure in the random oracle model. Based on the security proof and the performance evaluation, we believe that the proposed TFAKE protocol is more secure and efficient than other related protocols.

The remainder of this paper is organized as follows. In Sect. 2, we summarize the attacks and security requirements of TFAKE protocols in WSNs. In Sect. 3, our proposed TFAKE protocol is described. The security proof of our protocol is conducted in Sect. 4. We compare the efficiency and security features of our protocol with related protocols in Sect. 5. In Sect. 6, we conclude the paper with a brief summary.

2   Attacks and Security Requirement

In this section, we first describe the communication model for TFAKE protocols in WSNs. We then summarize the attacks against TFAKE protocols in WSNs and present the security requirements for these protocols.

2.1   Communication Model

A TFAKE protocol in WSNs involves three kinds of participants: users, gateway nodes and sensor nodes. Plenty of resource-constrained sensor nodes are deployed in unattended environments to collect information of interest. These sensor nodes

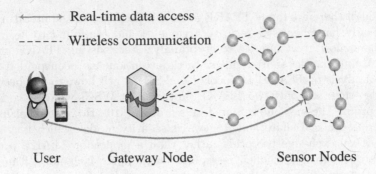

Fig. 1. Communication model

communicate with each other through multi-hop transmissions. In order to get access to the collected data of the sensor nodes, a user should first register himself to the gateway node. Whenever a registered user wants to get real-time data from the sensor nodes, he first sends a query to the gateway node and the gateway node will authenticate the validity of the user. If the user is an enrolled one, the gateway node will further help the user and the target sensor node to establish a common secret session key. The gateway node can be viewed as an interface between the user and the sensor node. A typical communication model for TFAKE protocol in WSNs is shown in Fig. 1.

2.2 Summary of Attacks

In this subsection, we summarize all the attacks against TFAKE protocols in WSNs. The attacks against TFAKE protocols in WSNs are listed and explained in the following:

1. **Privileged-Insider Attack.** It is a common practice that a user only remembers several passwords and uses the same password in different application scenarios for convenience. In a TFAKE protocol in WSNs, if the gateway node knows the password of the user, he can use the password to impersonate the user to get access to other servers. So it is desirable the gateway node does not know the password of the user to thwart the privileged-insider attack.
2. **Impersonation Attack.** The adversary impersonates a participant to deceive other protocol participants. Many attacks can be classified as the impersonation attack.
3. **Stolen-Verifier Attack.** Typically, the gateway node maintains a password verifier table of all the registered users. If the adversary compromises the gateway node and steals the password verifier table, he can extract the password from the verifier table and impersonate all the users at will. Consequently, it is desirable the gateway node does not maintain such a password-related verifier table.

4. **Replay Attack.** The adversary records a valid protocol messages and later replays the intercepted message to impersonate the legal user to the gateway node. The replay attack can be viewed as a special kind of impersonation attack.

5. **Password Guessing Attack/Dictionary Attack.** The password is human-memorable and low-entropy. If an adversary can get a verification equation of the password, he can enumerate all the passwords from the dictionary and verify its guess until the corrected password is found. Password guessing attack can be classified into on-line attack and off-line attack. It is desirable that the off-line password guessing attack should be impossible and the on-line password guessing attack can be detected by the victim participant.

6. **Node Capture Attack.** Since sensor nodes are usually deployed in unattended or hostile environments, the adversary can easily compromise a sensor node and extract the secret information stored in it. However, the adversary should not impersonate other protocol participants (such as un-compromised sensor nodes or a user) by the captured sensor node.

7. **GW-Node Bypassing Attack.** The gateway node shares different secrets with the users and the sensor nodes, respectively. GW-node bypassing attack details that the adversary can compromise a user's secret and authenticates himself directly to the sensor node. In other words, the gateway node is bypassed during the authentication. This attack is a special kind of impersonation attack.

8. **Password Guessing Attack by Insiders.** This attack basically belongs to the password guessing attack. If an TFAKE protocols in WSNs is not well-designed, the insiders (e.g. other users, the gateway node) have some advantage in guessing the victim user's password. It is desirable that the insiders should not get the password information.

9. **Parallel Session Attack.** The adversary executes two protocol sessions in parallel. The adversary tries to use the transcripts of one session to impersonate a valid participant in another session. This attack is basically an impersonation attack.

10. **Stolen Smart Card Attack/The Smart Card Breach Attack.** The adversary steals a user's smart card and then extracts all the information stored in the smart card via side channel attacks. It is desirable that the adversary cannot impersonate the victim user with the breached smart card. In other words, the adversary should not compromise the password by the stolen smart card.

11. **Many Logged-in Users with the Same Login-ID Attack.** When the users register to the gateway node, the gateway node may store the same secret in different smart cards which are belong to different users. As a result, a malicious user can use the common secret to log in the name of other users.

12. **Reflection Attack.** In this attack, The adversary simply sends back (reflect) the message generated by the target participant to himself. The essential idea of the attack is to trick the target into providing the response to its own challenge.

Some ordinary attacks, such as the man-in-the-middle attack and the denial of service attack, are omitted. The reason is that these attacks are either included in another attack (i.e. the man-in-the-middle attack belongs to impersonation attack) or cannot be solved by cryptology methodology (i.e. denial of service attack is always possible no matter how the protocol is designed). It also should be noted that our summary of attacks is based on earlier work of [18,19]. However, our summary is more comprehensive and tailers to TFAKE protocol in WSNs. Based on the summary of the attacks, we present a formal security model for TFAKE protocols in WSNs. The security model will be presented in the full version due to lack of space.

3   Our Proposed Protocol

In this section, we propose an efficient TFAKE protocol for WSNs based on robust authenticated encryption (RAE) schemes [20]. Unlike traditional symmetric encryption schemes which only ensure data confidentiality, an RAE scheme can achieve both data confidentiality and authenticity. The authenticity of the ciphertext enables us to prove the security of our protocol rigorously. For a better understanding of the paper, we briefly introduce the definition of RAE schemes. Fix an alphabet Σ. Typically Σ is $\{0,1\}$ or $\{0,1\}^8$. An RAE scheme is defined as a triple $\Pi = (\mathcal{K}, \mathcal{E}, \mathcal{D})$. The key space $\mathcal{K}$ is a set of strings with an associated distribution. The encryption algorithm $\mathcal{E}$ is deterministic and maps a five-tuple $(K, N, A, M, \lambda) \in (\Sigma^*)^3 \times N \times \Sigma^*$ to a string $C = \mathcal{E}_K^{N,A,\lambda}(M)$ of length $|M| + \lambda$, where K is the encryption key, N is a nonce, A is the associated data, M is the message and λ is the ciphertext expansion. λ can be 0 and thus can be omitted sometimes. The decryption algorithm $\mathcal{D}$ is deterministic and takes a five-tuple (K, N, A, M, λ, C) to a value $\mathcal{D}_K^{N,A,\lambda}(C) \in \Sigma^* \cup \{\perp\}$. It is required that $\mathcal{D}_K^{N,A,\lambda}(\mathcal{E}_K^{N,A,\lambda}(M)) = M$ for all K, N, A, M, λ. If there is no M such that $C = \mathcal{E}_K^{N,A,\lambda}(M)$, then $\mathcal{D}_K^{N,A,\lambda}(C) = \perp$. For more details, refer to [20].

There are three phases in our protocol: the registration phase, the authentication and key exchange phase and the password updating phase.

3.1   Registration Phase

When registering with the gateway node GW, the user U_i chooses his own low-entropy password PW_i and a high-entropy random number b, then U_i computes $PW_i^* = h(PW_i\|b)$ and sends the message (ID_i, PW_i^*) to the gateway node through a secure channel, where ID_i is U_i's real identity. Upon receiving the message, the gateway node GW computes $V_i = h(ID_i\|K)$ and $N_i = V_i \oplus h(ID_i\|PW_i^*)$. The GW-node GW also chooses U_i's pseudo identity DID_i for user anonymity and records the list (DID_i, ID_i) in its data base. At last, GW generates a smart card with parameters $(DID_i, N_i, h(\cdot))$, and sends the user's smart card to U_i through a secure channel. Upon receiving the smart card, U_i updates the parameters by adding the random number b to the smart card.

User U_i	Gateway Node GW
choose password PW_i choose a random number b $PW_i^* = h(PW_i\|b)$	

$$\xrightarrow{\quad ID_i, PW_i^* \quad}$$

$V_i = h(ID_i\|K)$
$N_i = V_i \oplus h(ID_i\|PW_i^*)$
choose U_i's pseudo identity DID_i
record (ID_i, DID_i)
generate a smart card with parameters DID_i, N_i, $h(\cdot)$

$$\xleftarrow{\quad \text{smart card} \quad}$$

write b to the smart card

Fig. 2. Registration phase of the proposed scheme

3.2 Authentication and Key Exchange Phase

When a user U_i wants to access the real-time data from a sensor node SN_j, U_i invokes the authentication and key exchange phase with the gateway node GW. If U_i is a valid user, he will share a common secret key with the sensor node SN_j at the end of this phase. For a pictorial description, refer to Fig. 3.

1. U_i inserts his smart card into the card reader, inputs his identity ID_i and password PW_i. The smart card computes $PW_i^* = h(PW_i\|b)$ and recovers $V_i^* = N_i \oplus h(ID_i\|PW_i^*)$. After this, the smart card computes an encryption key $k_1 = h(V_i^*\|T_1)$, where T_1 is the current timestamp in U_i's system. The smart card also chooses a random number R_1 from the space $\{0,1\}^l$ and encrypts the random number (R_1) using a robust authenticated encryption scheme to get the ciphertext $C_1 = E_{k_1}^{T_1, DID_i}(R_1)$, where the timestamp T_1 is used as the nonce and the pseudo identity DID_i of U_i is the associated data. Finally, the smart card sends the message (DID_i, SN_j, C_1, T_1) to the gateway node GW.

2. Upon receiving the message (DID_i, C_1, T_1) at time T_1^*, the gateway node GW checks whether $T_1^* - T_1 \leq \triangle T$ or not, where $\triangle T$ denotes the upper bound of time interval for the transmission delay. If it is true, GW finds U_i's real identity ID_i in the data base using the pseudo identity DID_i and computes the decryption key $k_1 = h(h(ID_i\|K)\|T_1)$. GW then decrypts the ciphertext C_1 and computes $R_1 = D_{k_1}^{T_1, DID_i}(C_1)$. If the decryption operation succeeds, U_i is authenticated by the gateway node GW. GW computes an encryption key $k_2 = h(ID\|h(K\|SN_j)\|T_2)$, where T_2 is the current timestamp of the GW-node's system. Finally, GW encrypts the random number R_1 using the robust authenticated encryption scheme to get the ciphertext $C_2 = E_{k_2}^{T_2, ID}\{R_1\}$, where the timestamp T_2 is used as the nonce and $ID = (DID_i\|GW\|SN_j)$ is the associated data. Finally, GW sends the message (ID, C_2, T_2) to the sensor node SN_j.

3. Upon receiving the message (ID, C_2, T_2) at time T_2^*, the sensor node SN_j checks if $T_2^* - T_2 \leq \triangle T$. If it is true, S_n computes $k_2 = h(ID\|x_j\|T_2)$ and decrypts C_2 and computes $R_1 = D_{k_2}^{T_2, ID}\{C_2\}$. If the decryption operation

succeeds, SN_j computes the encryption key $k_3 = h(ID\|R_1\|T_3)$, where T_3 is the current timestamp of SN_j's system. After that, S_n chooses a random number R_2 from the space $\{0,1\}^l$ and encrypts R_2 using k_3 to get the ciphertext $C_3 = E_{k_3}^{T_3,ID}\{R_2\}$, where the timestamp T_3 is used as the nonce and $ID = (DID_i\|GW\|SN_j)$ is the associated data. SN_j sends the message (C_3, T_3) to the user U_i. Finally, SN_j computes the session key $sk = h(ID\|T_3\|R_1\|R_2)$ for future communications with the user U_i and accepts the session.

4. Upon receiving the message (C_3, T_3) at time T_3^*, U_i checks if $T_3^* - T_3 \leq \triangle T$. If it is true, GW computes $k_3 = h(ID\|R_1\|T_3)$ and decrypts $R_2 = D_{k_3}^{T_3,ID}\{C_4\}$. If the decryption operation succeeds, U_i accepts the session and computes the session key $sk = h(ID\|T_3\|R_1\|R_2)$ for future communications with the sensor node SN_j.

Finally, U_i and SN_j could use the common session key sk in upcoming private communications.

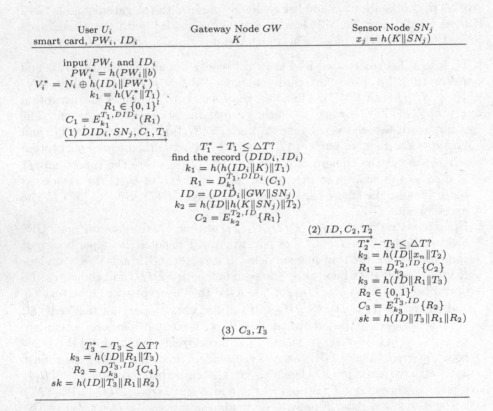

Fig. 3. Authentication and key exchange phase

3.3 Password Updating Phase

This phase is invoked whenever U_i wants to change his password PW_i with a new one, say PW_i'. U_i inserts his smart card into the terminal and inputs his identity ID_i, the old password PW_i and the new password PW_i'. The smart card computes $N_i' = N_i \oplus h(ID_i\|h(PW_i\|b)) \oplus h(ID_i\|h(PW_i'\|b))$ and replaces N_i with N_i'.

4 Security Proof

In this section, we present the security proof of our protocol within the security model given in Sect. 3. Due to lack of space, the security proof of Theorem 1 will be presented in the full version.

Theorem 1. *Let $\mathcal{P}$ be our TFAKE protocol. If the encryption scheme used in our protocol achieves RAE security, and the hash function used in our protocol is a random oracle. Let $\mathcal{A}$ be an PPT adversary, then the adversary's advantage in attacking the session key security and authentication security of the proposed protocol is negligible.*

5 Performance Analysis

In this section, we compare the performance of our protocol with other related protocols [5,6,8–10,15]. The comparison of computation and communication costs are demonstrated in Table 1. In terms of computation, let "H" denote the

Table 1. Comparisons of efficiency

	Our protocol	Das's protocol [5]	N-L protocol [6]	H-G-C protocol [8]	K-A protocol [9]	S-L-F protocol [10]	N-K-P protocol [15]
E1	H	0	0	H	H	0	H
E2	2H	3H	3H	5H	2H	2H	T_{sym}
E3	$5H+2T_{sym}$	4H	$7H+T_{sym}$	5H	4H	2H	$5H+3T_{pub}$
E4	$4H+2T_{sym}$	4H	$8H+T_{sym}$	5H	5H	5H	$6H+T_{pub}$
E5	$3H+2T_{sym}$	H	$4H+2T_{sym}$	H	2H	2H	$3H+2T_{pub}$
E6	4H	N/A	N/A	6H	4H	2H	2H
E7	832 bits	832 bits	1344 bits	928 bits	992 bits	1056 bits	2144 bits
E8	3	3	3	3	3	8	4

E1: Computation cost of the registration phase for a user
E2: Computation cost of the registration phase for a GW-node
E3: Computation cost of the authentication phase for a user
E4: Computation cost of the authentication phase for a GW-node
E5: Computation cost of the authentication phase for a sensor node
E6: Computation cost of the password updating phase for a user
E7: Bandwidth of the authentication phase
E8: Message flows of the authentication phase
N/A: Not Available

computation cost of one hash operation, "T_{pub}" denote the computation cost of one public key operation, "T_{sym}" denote the computation cost of one symmetric key encryption/decryption. Note that the encryption/decryption cost of an RAE scheme is the same as that of symmetric key encryption/decryption. In terms of communication, we consider bandwidth and round complexity. We assume the identifications can be represented with 32 bits, the output size of secure hash functions/Nonces is 160 bits, the timestamp can be represented with 64 bits. The ciphertext is the same size with the plaintext in symmetric encryptions, and the size of the ciphtext is usually doubled in public key encryptions.

We can see from Table 1 that the computation costs of the registration phase and the password updating phase are more or less the same. Consequently, we focus on the computation cost of the authentication phase. Our protocol needs 12 hash operations and 6 symmetric encryption/decryption operations in the authentication phase. The symmetric encryption/decryption operations arise from the distribution of the session key. Without the symmetric encryption/decryption cost, our protocol is as efficient as other protocols. Nam et al.'s protocol [15] uses public key operation, so it is very inefficient compared with other protocols. In terms of communication, our protocol is the most efficient with respect to bandwidth and achieves optional round complexity. In wireless sensor networks, transmitting radio signals on resource-constrained wireless devices usually consumes much more power than computation does, so it is more important to reduce the communication cost than the computation cost. As a result, our protocol is very attractive in terms of efficiency.

Table 2. Comparisons of security features

	Our protocol	Das's protocol [5]	N-L- protocol [6]	H-G-C- protocol [8]	K-A- protocol [9]	S-L-F- protocol [10]	N-K-P protocol [15]
C1	Yes	Yes	Yes	Yes	Yes	Yes	Yes
C2	Yes	No	No	Yes	No	Yes	Yes
C3	Yes	No	No	Yes	No	Yes	Yes
C4	Yes	Yes	Yes	Yes	Yes	Yes	Yes
C5	No	No	No	No	No	No	Yes
C6	Yes	No	Yes	Yes	Yes	Yes	Yes
C7	Yes	No	No	No	No	Yes	Yes
C8	Yes	No	No	No	No	Yes	Yes
C9	Yes	No	Yes	No	No	No	Yes
C10	Yes	No	No	No	No	No	Yes
C11	Yes	No	Yes	No	No	No	Yes

C1: Resist the replay attack
C2: Resist the privileged insider attack
C3: Resist the impersonation attack
C4: Resist the stolen verifier attack
C5: Resist the stolen smart card attack
C6: Resist the off-line dictionary attack
C7: Resist the node capture attack
C8: Mutual authentication
C9: Session key distribution
C10: User anonymity
C11: Provable security

Table 2 summarizes security features of our protocol with related protocols [5,6,8–10,15]. We can see from Table 2 that our protocol provides more security features than other related protocols. The only disadvantage of our protocol is its vulnerability against the stolen smart attack. However, it is noted in [19] that it is impossible to resist the stolen smart card attack merely using symmetric cryptology mechanism.

Considering the computation cost, communication cost and security features as a whole, our protocol achieves provable security and outperforms other related protocols. Therefore, our protocol is more secure than related scheme while preserving high efficiency. As a result, it is more suitable for real-life applications in WSNs.

6 Conclusions

In this paper, we summarize the security requirements of TFAKE protocols in WSNs and present a formal security model to evaluate their security. We also put forward an efficient TFAKE protocol based on robust authenticated encryption schemes and prove the security of our protocol in the random oracle model. Comparison shows that our protocol not only enjoys provable security but also has high efficiency in terms of communication and computation. To the best of our knowledge, our protocol is the first TFAKE protocol which introduces robust authenticated encryption schemes to achieve provable security.

References

1. Guo, P., Wang, J., Li, B., Lee, S.: A variable threshold-value authentication architecture for wireless mesh networks. J. Internet Technol. 15(6), 929–936 (2014)
2. Shen, J., Tan, H., Wang, J., Wang, J., Lee, S.: A novel routing protocol providing good transmission reliability in underwater sensor networks. J. Internet Technol. 16(1), 171–178 (2015)
3. Xie, S., Wang, Y.: Construction of tree network with limited delivery latency in homogeneous wireless sensor networks. wirel. Pers. Commun. 78(1), 231–246 (2014)
4. He, D.B., Kumar, N., Chen, J.H., et al.: Robust anonymous authentication protocol for health-care applications using wireless medical sensor networks. Multimedia Syst. 21(1), 49–60 (2015)
5. Das, M.L.: Two-factor user authentication in wireless sensor networks. IEEE Trans. Wirel. Commun. 8(3), 1086–1090 (2009)
6. Nyang, D.H., Lee, M.K.: Improvement of Das's two-factor authentication protocol in wireless sensor networks. Cryptology, ePrint archive. http://eprint.iacr.org/2009/631.pdf
7. Chen, T.H., Shih, K.K.: A robust mutual authentication protocol for wireless sensor networks. ETRI J. 32(5), 704–712 (2010)
8. He, D.J., Gao, Y., Chan, S.: An enhanced two-factor user authentication scheme in wireless sensor networks. Ad Hoc Sens. Wirel. Netw. 10(4), 1–11 (2010)

 9. Khan, M.K., Alghathbar, K.: Cryptanalysis and security improvements of two-factor user authentication in wireless sensor networks. Sensors 10(3), 2450–2459 (2010)
10. Sun, D.Z., Li, J.X., Feng, Z.Y.: On the security and improvement of a two-factor user authentication scheme in wireless sensor networks. Pers. Ubiquit. Comput. 17(5), 895–905 (2013)
11. Bellare, M., Rogaway, P.: Entity authentication and key distribution. In: Stinson, D.R. (ed.) CRYPTO 1993. LNCS, vol. 773, pp. 232–249. Springer, Heidelberg (1994)
12. Yuan, J.J.: An enhanced two-factor user authentication in wireless sensor networks. Telecommun. Syst. 55(1), 105–113 (2014)
13. Gong, L., Needham, R., Yahalom, R.: Reasoning about belief in cryptographic protocols. In: Proceedings of 1990 IEEE Computer Society Symposium Research in Security and Privacy, pp. 234–246 (2009)
14. Wei, F.S., Ma, J.F., Jiang, Q., et al.: Cryptanalysis and improvement of an enhanced two-factor user authentication scheme in wireless sensor networks. Inf. Technol. Control 45(1), 62–70 (2016)
15. Nam, J., Kim, M., Paik, J., et al.: A provably-secure ECC-based authentication scheme for wireless sensor networks. Sensors 14(11), 21023–21044 (2014)
16. Pointcheval, D., Zimmer, S.: Multi-factor authenticated key exchange. In: Bellovin, S.M., Gennaro, R., Keromytis, A., Yung, M. (eds.) ACNS 2008. LNCS, vol. 5037, pp. 277–295. Springer, Heidelberg (2008)
17. Bellare, M., Pointcheval, D., Rogaway, P.: Authenticated key exchange secure against dictionary attacks. In: Preneel, B. (ed.) EUROCRYPT 2000. LNCS, vol. 1807, pp. 139–155. Springer, Heidelberg (2000). doi:10.1007/3-540-45539-6_11
18. Alsaleh, M., Mannan, M., Van Oorschot, P.C.: Revisiting defenses against large-scale online password guessing attacks. IEEE Trans. Dependable Secure Comput. 9(1), 128–141 (2012)
19. Wang, D., He, D., Wang, P., et al.: Anonymous two-factor authentication in distributed systems: certain goals are beyond attainment. IEEE Trans. Dependable Secure Comput. 12(4), 428–442 (2015)
20. Hoang, V.T., Krovetz, T., Rogaway, P.: Robust authenticated-encryption AEZ and the problem that it solves. In: Oswald, E., Fischlin, M. (eds.) EUROCRYPT 2015. LNCS, vol. 9056, pp. 15–44. Springer, Heidelberg (2015). doi:10.1007/978-3-662-46800-5_2

Outsourced Data Modification Algorithm with Assistance of Multi-assistants in Cloud Computing

Jian Shen[1,2,3(✉)], Jun Shen[1], Xiong Li[4], FuShan Wei[5], and JiGuo Li[6]

[1] School of Computer and Software, Nanjing University of Information Science
and Technology, Nanjing, China
s_shenjian@126.com, sj310310@qq.com

[2] Department of Jiangsu Engineering Center of Network Monitoring,
Nanjing, Jiangsu, China

[3] Technology and Engineering Center of Meteorological Sensor Network,
Jiangsu Collaborative Innovation Center on Atmospheric Environment
and Equipment Technology, Nanjing, China

[4] Hunan University of Science and Technology, Hunan, China
lixiongzhq@163.com

[5] The PLA Information Engineering University, Henan, China
weifs831020@163.com

[6] Hohai University, Nanjing, China
ljg1688@163.com

Abstract. The rapid development of cloud storage in these years has caused a wave of research craze. To improve the cloud user experience, a large amount of schemes are proposed with various practical performances, for instance, long term correct data storage and dynamic data modification. In most works, however, the authors seem to completely ignore the hard fact that data owner alone could not have enough energy to discover and correct all the inappropriate data outsourced in cloud. Others did consider it, and gave more than one user both read and write permissions, which leads to chaotic management of multiusers. In this paper, we propose a novel algorithm, in which the data owner and several authenticated assistants form a team to support dynamic data modification together. Assistants are in charge of detecting problems in cloud data and discussing a corresponding modification suggestion, while data owner is responsible for the implementation of the modification. In addition, our algorithm supports identity authentication, efficient malicious assistant revocation, as well as lazy update. Sufficient numerical analysis validates the performance of our algorithm.

Keywords: Cloud storage · Assistants · Data modification · Identity authentication · Assistant revocation · Lazy update

1 Introduction

So far, an increasing number of people have accepted cloud as a practical tool, for the rapid development of cloud computing at an unimaginable speed [1–12]. More and more Neo-Generations of people, who are called "cloud users", prefer to employ cloud

© Springer International Publishing AG 2016
X. Sun et al. (Eds.): ICCCS 2016, Part I, LNCS 10039, pp. 389–408, 2016.
DOI: 10.1007/978-3-319-48671-0_35

for their data storage and then delete the local copy. With a great demand of satisfying cloud users, cloud services develop a lot, especially the storage one. However, we observed that there were very few people caring about the details of cloud data modification, which is mentioned sometimes in auditing schemes.

In real-world scene, the outsourced data in cloud could not be always right or kept pace with the times. As a result, data owner or data users may discover some problems of the cloud data. In particular, with time going by, the data might be out of date and should be replaced by something new, which may lead to data users' misunderstandings. Obviously, such data of no sense should be deleted, rather than be stored in cloud to waste room. Besides, since the new data may take place of the old one, the function of data insertion is needed. What's more, nobody is perfect, even the great people can make mistakes. Therefore, the outsourced data might be incorrect at the very beginning, which may not be discovered by the data owner because of his/her subjective consciousness.

As we can see from the above, to modify the cloud data cannot be simply done by merely one person — the data owner, who may not discover so many problems as well as update them. However, most of the previous works on cloud storage ignored the fatal weakness, which assign such heavy a task to the original data owner, who uploaded the cloud data. Other works did consider the practical scene, so they assume that there are more than one data owner who upload the cloud data [13–19]. Obviously, this assumption is not practical to a certain extend. Most of the rest extend cloud users' permission to the read and write one as well. Nevertheless, this method is not so perfect to some degree. Now that the data is shared in cloud, its aim can be to be shared by as many people as possible in a large part. Obviously, the more people, the more difficult to manage, and the more risks of privacy leakage. Besides, the modification that a certain data owner does is not so persuasive, and it could be incorrect because of subjective consciousness. On the other hand, if the number of users were cut down to exchange for privacy protection, the scene will contrary the original intention of data sharing. Hence, a much more practical scene is urgently needed.

In this work, we design a novel scene containing several assistants, and propose a solution to efficient data modification which could address the following challenges: (1) quality assurance of data modification. As we all know, a certain person's judgement could be subjective, but the masses have sharp eyes. In this paper, the data modification is done after the discussion of a group of assistants, which will be further described in Sect. 5. With the agreement of all assistants equipped with corresponding professional knowledge, the quality of data modification could be much higher than the one under just a certain person's judgement. (2) no conflict between read permission and read and write permission. As mentioned in the above paragraph, previous works did not deal with this problem very well. In our work, the entities in the whole system are divided into three categories, in which only the original data owner have read and write permission. But a group of assistants can help data owner to detect and modify errors of the cloud data. (3) efficient and secure assistant revocation. When a certain assistant is attacked by external attackers or goes bad itself, it should be revoked immediately [20–23]. In previous works, there are no assistants but several data owners. So once any of them is attacked, the data in cloud is in danger. Because the rights of all data owners are equal, and anyone can access and modify the cloud data by itself. In our work, however, whenever an assistant is disloyal, the cloud owner could detect and revoke it efficiently. Besides, data modification is finally done by the original data owner, and assistants just play a supporting role. Hence, even if a certain assistant is unsafe, the cloud data will not be in danger immediately as long as the assistant is revoked in time. (4) lazy update. In practical, the data owner who can update the data in cloud might be not online at every moment. Consequently, the modification suggestions may be backlogged in the data owner side. Then, such a practical scene requires the system to deal with the above problem appropriately. In this paper, the data owner could batch update several modifications if necessary, which trades off the efficiency of the system. (5) low communication and computational costs. What is known to us all is that the communication and computational costs are significant principles for measuring a certain technique, which should be controlled in an appropriate range. In our work, the cost of bringing in several assistants to help cloud data modification is relatively low.

The rest of this paper is organized as follows: Sect. 2 introduces some related works concerning our works. Following immediately are the models, which consists of system model and threat model. In Sect. 4, some technique preliminaries are presented, including Symmetric Balanced Incomplete Block Design primarily. The next comes the main part of this paper — our algorithms, which contains some notations and the detailed algorithm. Performance along with the corresponding analysis of our works are introduced in Sect. 6, while security analysis and the cost of our algorithm are presented in Sects. 7 and 8 respectively. The last section is a brief conclusion of this paper.

2 Related Works

Efficient data outsourcing in cloud has been extensively studied these years. Many aspects of cloud data are in heated discussions, such as security, privacy, and correctness. Actually, dynamic operations on cloud data is a focus as well, which is what we will discuss later in our paper.

To support dynamic operations, Yang et al. in 2013 [24] employed index table of abstract information of cloud data, which costs more obviously to use such a tool. In 2009, Wang et al. [25] proposed a dynamic operation solution based on Merkle Hash Tree. Later, in [26], their team proposed a protocol that could support dynamic operations as well, however, its security worries us. Their solution introduced a third party auditor, which could compute the cloud data via linear combinations of data blocks to have a knowledge of the specific content of data files stored in cloud.

Though many works have been done to update the data outsourced in cloud, most of them did not consider the practical scene that data owner who possesses both read and write permissions is not competent to discover and correct all the errors in cloud data. Some works aim to give more than one person write permission. Wang et al. [27] employed ring signature to support multi-writers, which ignores the revocation of malicious writers however. After that, Wang et al. [28] awarded the above defect and made their scheme supporting writer revocation. But [28] suffers from secret key leakage. Yuan et al. [29] proposed a solution for dynamic data sharing services among multiusers. Their works employed (k, n)-Shamir's Secret Sharing Scheme to support multiusers, which is not flexible for the limit of at least k users.

Different from all the above solutions, our algorithm is a totally new one, which employs several assistants to help dynamic update of cloud data.

3   Models

In this section, we will introduce the system models of our algorithm briefly, as well as the threat models.

3.1   System Models

As shown in Fig. 1, we consider a cloud system consisted of three major entities in this work: the cloud server, the original data owner, and a group of assistants. The cloud server is widely known to us, which provides various cloud services to its users. In our model, the cloud server is mainly responsible for data storage. As to the original data owner, it is a cloud user different from others, who possesses the cloud data at the very beginning and outsources it into cloud. Certainly, the data owner can access and modify the cloud data. The group of assistants are several cloud users, who are different from normal data users. They are equal to each other, and their primary responsibility is to cooperate with each other to help the data owner to discover and modify wrong data in cloud. As for their relationship with the data owner, data owner looks like their group leader, who manages all the assistants. We picture five assistants in Fig. 1, which is not the specific number of assistants. Data owner may nominate several assistants that he can trust to help himself, and a certain cloud user can apply for this job himself,

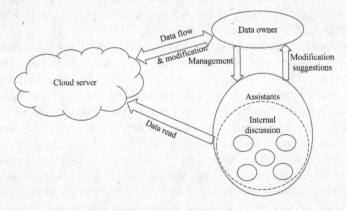

Fig. 1.   System models

which is beyond the scope of our study. Besides, in this work, we assume that the cloud data is stored in form of files, which can be further divided into a number of blocks or even sectors if the block is too large.

3.2 Threat Models

In this work, we consider that the primary threats in our system are the attacks which may take place in the process of internal discussion among assistants. Specifically, when the assistants are contact with each other to decide a certain modification, the conversation among them may be attacked.

Such attacks could be divided into two categories: the passive attacks and the active ones [30–43]. The passive attacks mean that an attacker stays aside quietly and tries to hear the session key. In another word, passive attackers are eavesdroppers practically, who may tell others what he heard or use it for other purposes. Fortunately, passive attacks make no effects on the process of a certain conversation. On another hand, the active attacks are much more complex than the passive ones, which try to influence or destroy a certain conversation. Specifically, the active attackers will not only record what he heard, but involve himself in the discussion among assistants to mess it in various ways. Alteration, injection, interception, and replay of data are all included. Data alteration and injection are easy to understand, which is what they literally mean. Data interception may stop the discussion from continuing by blocking communication among assistants. And replay is sending what the attackers captured once again to camouflage himself.

4   Technique Preliminaries

In this section, some technique preliminaries will be introduced. The primary is the technique for assist phase in Sect. 5.2.

4.1   Symmetric Balanced Incomplete Block Design

In our work, we employ a basic mathematical method called Symmetric Balanced Incomplete Block Design (SBIBD), which is a special case of Balanced Incomplete Block Design (BIBD) [44–51]. And the definition of a SBIBD is as follows:

Definition 1. Given a finite set with v elements $X = \{x_1, x_2, \cdots, x_v\}$. let b be the number of blocks in the block design, while k is the number of elements in the subsets of X. Besides, r and λ are parameters of the block design. The Symmetric Balanced Incomplete Block Design (SBIBD) of X is the set of b subsets of k elements, in which the k-element subsets are denoted as $B_1, B_2, \cdots, B_b$. In another word, the size of each block in this design is k. Additionally, the design should satisfy the following requirements:

1. Each element should appear in exactly r of the b blocks, which represents the number of repeated elements.
2. Every pair of elements should appear in exactly λ of the b blocks, which identifies the number of encounters.
3. b = v and r = k. This is where SBIBD differs from BIBD.

BIBD consists of five parameters — b, v, r, k, and λ, while SBIBD consists of three — v, k, and λ. As a result, an SBIBD could be denoted as (v, k, λ)-design.

5   Our Algorithm

This section is the main part of the whole paper, which includes some notations will be used in our algorithm and the detailed design.

5.1   Notations

As is shown in Table 1, we will introduce some notations used in this paper. Suppose p is a big prime, and $p = 6q - 1$, in which q is a prime as well. The primes p and q are the orders of G_1 and G_T respectively. And g is the generator of G_1. Z_p is a set of non-negative integers less than p, which is the conventional interpretation of Z_p. $H_1(\cdot)$: $\{0,1\}^* \to G_1$ is a one-way hash function, which maps some strings to the elements in G_1. e: $G_1 \times G_1 \to G_T$ is a Weil pairing map, which satisfies three characteristics: bilinear property, non-degeneracy, and computability. $H_2(\cdot)$: $G_T \to Z_p$ is a one-way hash function as well, which maps the elements in G_T to Z_p. In addition, F is the joint name of files to be stored in cloud, which may be divided into several data blocks denoted by m_y, or even data sectors denoted by m_{yz}.

Table 1. Notation

G_1, G_T	A cycle group
g	The generator of G_1
Z_p	A set of non-negative integers less than p
p	Prime order of group G_1
q	Prime order of G_T
$H_1(\cdot)$: $\{0,1\}^* \to G_1$	One-way hash function
e: $G_1 \times G_1 \to G_T$	A Weil pairing map
$H_2(\cdot)$: $G_T \to Z_p$	One-way hash function
F	Data file outsourced in cloud
m_y	Blocks of a certain data file
m_{yz}	Sectors of a certain block m_y

5.2 Threat Models

In this section, we will describe our algorithm in details. Totally, there are four primary phases: setup phase, assist phase, inform phase and update phase. First, the setup phase is in charge of the preparation works at the very beginning of the algorithm, such as outsourcing the data file in cloud and so on. Then, in the assist phase, we assume that a certain assistant proposes a modification suggestion and discuss the feasibility of it with the rest $(v - 1)$ assistants. After this phase, the assistant who proposed the modification will inform the data owner such suggestion in inform phase. The final is update phase. After receiving the modification suggestion, data owner will update the data file in cloud. And the following are the details:

Setup Phase. This phase consists of two parts: data outsourcing and assistants nominating. First, data owner divides the file to be stored in cloud into several blocks

$$F = \{m_1, m_2, \cdots, m_y, \cdots, m_n\},$$

where m_y is the name of each block for y from 1 to n and n is the total number of the blocks in a certain file. Besides, if the file blocks are too large for later data modification, each of them could be divided into several sectors

$$F = \{\{m_{11}, m_{12}, \cdots, m_{1z}, \cdots, m_{1k}\}, \{m_{21}, m_{22}, \cdots, m_{2z}, \cdots, m_{2k}\},$$
$$\cdots, \{m_{y1}, m_{y2}, \cdots, m_{yz}, \cdots, m_{yk}\}, \cdots, \{m_{n1}, m_{n2}, \cdots, m_{nz}, \cdots, m_{nk}\}\},$$

where m_{yz} is the name of each data sector in block my and k is the total number of sectors in each data block. No matter dividing the data block into sectors or not, the later processes are all similar. For each data block, data owner selects random $u \rightarrow G_1$ and $x \rightarrow Z_p$ and generates a corresponding authenticator

$$\sigma_y = (H_1(name||y) \cdot u^{my})^x,$$

where name is the name of file stored in cloud. As a result, each data block possesses its own identity now. All these authenticators form a set Φ. After that, data owner uploads the data file along with the set of authenticators Φ to cloud server and deletes its local copy to save resources. All the above are the data outsourcing part.

Next is the assistants nominating part, which gives the assistants authority to help data modification. Firstly, data owner selects random $s \in Z_p$ as a secret key, which is known by the data owner itself merely and is exactly secure. Besides, the corresponding public key is $p_s = sg$. Then, data owner publishes

$$\{p, q, G_1, G_T, g, e, p_s, H_1, H_2\}$$

to all the assistants.

In addition, to support assistant revocation, another parameter $c \in Zp$ should also be published to each assistant, which will be discussed in Sect. 6. Our algorithm assigns each assistant an ID, which denoted as $ID_i \in \{0,1\}^*$ and $i \in [1, v]$. For each i, data owner computes its corresponding public and secret key pair

$$(P_i = H_1(ID_i), \ S_i = sP_i),$$

where P_i is the public key of a certain assistant i, and S_i is the secret one. After that, data owner distributes the key pairs to assistants, which symbolizes the authorization. Besides, to ensure that a certain message is exactly from a certain assistant, data owner selects random primes p^* and q^*, and then computes $n = p^*q^*$ for all assistants. In addition, data owner distributes random prime e_i to each assistant, where e_i is coprime to $(p^* - 1)(q^* - 1)$. After that, each assistant possesses a pair (e_i, n), which is only known by themselves respectively except the data owner. For e_i $d_i = 1$ mod $(p^* - 1)(q^* - 1)$, each assistant could compute its own d_i, and further compute $X_i = (Y_i)^{di} = (H_2(H_1(ID_i)))^{di}$. Finally, each assistant keeps (d_i, X_i) secret.

Assist Phase. In this phase, we employ SBIBD to achieve modification assistance. With SBIBD, a common conference key could be gained among all assistants, which makes it easy for assistants to discuss with each other upon discovering a problem. As for how these assistants judge whether a certain modification is appropriate, we assume that they are all equipped with professional knowledges, which needs no worries. In another word, if they are not able to judge a modification accurately, how could data owner give the authority to them?

With the above assumption, the following are the details of this phase. The whole scene is a (v, k, λ)-design, where v is the number of both assistants and blocks, k is the number of both elements in a certain block and repeated elements, λ is the number of encounters. SBIBD uses an incidence matrix to identity whether a block i includes element j. If so, $l_{ij} = 1$, while if not, $l_{ij} = 0$. At the very beginning, assistant i selects a random r_i as the secret key of their conference, and then computes $M_i = e(g, e_i, r_i, S_i)$. When $l_{ij} = 1$ and $j \neq i$, there is $C_{ij} = \prod_{x \in B_i - \{j\}} M_x$. Besides, to realize identity authentication, some auxiliary information should be computed. Therefore, assistant i computes $T_i = X_i \cdot e(g, w_i, r_i, S_i)$, where $w_i = H_2(H_1(M_i, t_i))$ and t_i denotes a timestamp. So that, we let

$$D_j = \{Y_j, (M_j)^{ei}, T_j, t_j\}.$$

When $l_{ij} = 1$ and $j \neq i$, assistant i could receive $E_{ji} = \{D_j, (C_{ji})^{ei}\}$ from j, where $(C_{ji})^{ei}$ is for conference key generation and D_j is for identity authentication.

Finally, for assistant i, the conference key could be computed as follows:

$$K = M_i^{\lambda} \left(\prod_{l_{ji} = 1} C_{ji} \right)$$
$$= e\left(g, \lambda \sum_{i=1}^{v} e_i r_i S_i \right).$$

If all assistants are honest, they can get a common conference key and employ it to communicate with each other to discuss the modification suggestion if necessary.

The modification suggestions are divided into three categories: insertion suggestion, deletion suggestion, and alteration one. No matter which kind it is, there is a corresponding procedure to be performed. The following are the details:

1. Insertion: Firstly, we assume that the assistant who proposed the modification is i. Then, assistant i should inform the rest assistants its insertion suggestion, which may contain the information such as the operation "insert", where to insert, as well as what to be inserted in. With the common conference key K among assistants, they could communicate with each other without worrying about content leakage. Thus, assistant i could transmit $(y, insert, I_s, I)$ to others boldly, in which the first two are easy to understand, while I_s is the exact place to insert in and I is the specific content.

2. Deletion: Similarly, assistant i ought to inform others who will discuss with him the specific deletion suggestion, such as the "delete" operation, where to delete, and the content. What is slightly different is the message to be transmitted to other assistants. This time, assistant i sends $(y, delete, D_s, D_e)$. Obviously, y and delete are the sequence number of data block and the name of operation, while D_s is where the deletion starts and D_e is the point to end.

3. Alteration: As for the last kind of modification suggestion, what the rest assistants need to know are still how to operate, where to operation, and what to be operated on. In this procedure, assistant i spreads $(y, alter, T_p, T_l)$ to the rest, in which the latter three are different from the previous two operations. There is no point to explain the first two elements, while the latter two are not. T_p is the previous part in a certain block in cloud data, while T_l is the content to replace T_p afterwards.

Upon receiving the modification suggestion from assistant i, the others access the certain data block m_y in cloud indicated by suggestion to judge whether the proposed modification is correct and responsible. It is clear to see that using y here to indicate the block to be modified saves much resources than using m_y directly, though the rest assistants need to access the cloud data by themselves rather than analyzing the received data straightly. Of course, y could be replaced by (y, z) if the data block is too large, which could improve access rate and locate the point to be modified much more quickly. As for the responses to assistant i, they are made by the rest assistants using their own professional knowledges. In addition, it is a yes or no question merely. In another word, the rest require to respond "agree" or "disagree", without making a list of ideas or reasons. Specifically, with the common conference key K, other assistants return back $R_x = 1$ or $R_x = 0$ (here $x \in [1, i-1] \cup [i + 1, v]$) to the one who proposed the modification secretly. Once receiving all the responses from others, assistant i computes

$$R = R_1 \& R_2 \& R_3 \& \cdots \& R_{(i-1)} \& R_{(i+1)} \& \cdots \& R_v.$$

If $R = 1$, the modification is adopted, while $R = 0$ means that there is at least one assistant who questions the rationality of the modification, making the modification cancelled.

Inform Phase. Once the discussion results come out, the assistant i who proposed the modification suggestion would be busy informing the data owner who has the permission to both read and write the data in cloud the modification. It looks that all the assistants and data owner work as a team. As seen in setup phase, data owner computes (P_i, S_i) pair for each assistant, where S_i is kept secret by each assistant. Besides, to compute S_i, it involves s, which is only known by data owner itself in the whole scene. Thus, (S_i, s) could be used in this phase, which is the right key pair we use in our work. Certainly, for three different categories of modification, there are corresponding notification methods.

1. Insertion: If assistant i aims to inform data owner the insertion suggestion, he would employ S_i to encrypt (y, insert, I_s, I) first, which is sent to other assistants to judge on. Finally, assistant i sends

$$M_{insert} = Enc_{Si}(\text{insert}, y, I_s, I)$$

   to data owner as a suggestion.
2. Deletion: As an equivalent operation of insertion notification, the variation of deletion is only on the result rather than the process. Hence, assistant i ought to encrypt its suggestion (y, delete, D_s, D_e) as well. Then,

$$Mdelete = EncSi(delete, y, Ds, De)$$

   could be generated by assistant i and would be transmitted to data owner.
3. Alteration: What is predictable via the above two suggestion notifications is that the process concerning altering will not be too far away from the two. Naturally, here assistant i needs to encrypt (y, alter, T_p, T_l) as well. In this operation, it will be

$$M_{alter} = Enc_{Si}(alter, y, T_p, T_l),$$

   acting as the information to inform data owner.

This phase is in charge of delivering the modification suggestion to data owner, which is the bridge between assist phase and the following update one.

Update Phase. This phase is performed by data owner who possesses both read and write permissions, which is the final phase of the whole algorithm. Once receiving the modification suggestion, data owner starts to think about renewing the cloud data file according the suggestion. No matter data owner receives M_{insert}, M_{delete}, or M_{alter}, he could always decrypt the message via secret key s to get the essential information. In addition, to support lazy update, we could employ a queue to store the modification suggestions, which follows the principle of first in first out. For simplicity, we will discuss the scene of only one modification needing update, and the detailed support for lazy update will be described in Sect. 6.

After knowing how to modify the cloud file, data owner would put it into action subsequently. As a result of deleting the local copy of the data outsourced in cloud, data owner no longer possesses the data file. Hence, data owner is supposed to depend on cloud for data block to be modified. In another word, data owner ought to download the certain data block from cloud, which needs essential overhead. Nevertheless, we could minimize the consumption by using a relatively small data sector instead of a block when the modification suggestion was just launched. With the original data block or sector (for convenience, we still use data block my here to describe the whole process), data owner modifies the appointed points in the specified place. Thus far, a novel block m_y^* is formed. Then, data owner follows the same steps in setup phase to generate a novel authenticator σ_y^* for m_y^*. Finally, data owner uploads the new pair (m_y^*, σ_y^*) to cloud server to replace the ancient one, which symbolizes the finish of a complete modification process.

6 Performance of Our Algorithm

In this Section, we will introduce the performance of our algorithm, including some detailed challenges mentioned in Sect. 1 along with the corresponding analysis. The primary three challenges are identity authentication in assist phase, efficient revocation of dishonest assistants, and support of lazy updating. Table 2 indicates the comparison with [29] in aspects of performance. It clearly shows that our algorithm is equipped with the above three performances, while [29] considered only user revocation of the three. The following are the details.

Table 2. Modification performance comparison

	Yuan et al. [29]	Our algorithm
Lazy update	N	Y
User revocation (assistant revocation)	Y	Y
Identity authentication	N	Y

6.1 Identity Authentication

As mentioned above, the identity authentication here mainly aims at assist phase. Simultaneously, in assist phase, there exists some parameters for this performance indeed. As for the requirements of authentication, it owes to the uncertainty of correctness of messages from other assistants, which may influence the whole process of modification assistance. Besides, what we use here is $D_j = \left\{ Y_j, \left(M_j\right)^{ei}, T_j, t_j \right\}$ from assistant j to i when $l_{ij} = 1$ and $i \neq j$, which was introduced in assist phase previously. What we define here for a successful authentication is that

$$\frac{T_j^{e_j}}{M_j^{w_j^*}} = Y_j$$

which indicates that the message assistant i receives is indeed from j. However, if the equation does not hold, the authentication fails.

In this paragraph, we will show some brief proofs. From the above equation, we can see that w_j^* is the only parameter not included in D_j. As a matter of fact, assistant j could compute $w_j = H_2(H_1(M_j, t_{jj}))$ by itself as described in assist phase, meanwhile, assistant i could compute $w_j^* = H_2 (H_1 (M_j, t_{jj}))$ as well, for the knowledge of M_j from assistant j and t_j from the reception time point. Obviously, we could get $w_j^* = w_j$. Besides, $X_i = (Y_i)^{d_i} = (H_2(H_1(ID_i)))^{d_i}$ and $e_i d_i = 1 \mod (p^* - 1)(q^* - 1)$, which are already mentioned in setup phase. Thus,

$$X_i = Y_i^{d_i}$$
$$= Y_i^{1/e_i}.$$

Then,

$$Y_i = X_i^{e_i}$$
$$= ((Y_i)^{d_i})^{e_i}.$$

Additionally, in the process of formula derivation, we will employ the bilinear property of bilinear map. Finally, we deduced the following formula

$$\frac{T_j^{e_j}}{M_j^{w_j}} = \frac{\left(X_j \cdot e\left(g, w_j r_j S_j\right)\right)^{e_j}}{e\left(g, e_j r_j S_j\right)^{w_j}}$$
$$= \frac{((Y_i)^{d_i})^{e_i} \cdot e\left(g, w_j r_j S_j\right)^{e_j}}{e\left(g, e_j r_j S_j\right)^{w_j}}$$
$$= \frac{Y_j \cdot e(g, w_j r_j S_j e_j)}{e(g, e_j r_j S_j w_j)}$$
$$= Y_j$$

In summary, if the above formula holds, the massage is indeed from assistant j to assistant i, otherwise not.

6.2 Assistant Revocation

Efficient assistant revocation is the challenge previously mentioned in Sect. 1. This performance in our works does not only indicate the discovery and revocation of dishonest assistants, but also the smooth later process with assistant revocation. To be equipped with this performance, with the additional parameter c mentioned in setup phase, each assistant x is supposed to upload a parameter $A_x = M_x^c$ to data owner in addition.

The process and principle of assistant revocation is shown in Algorithm 1, in which some code names need to be explained. First of all, BM in line two is the broadcasted massage from data owner to all assistants, where BM = $\{(N, ID_{dataowner}, A_x) \mid 1 \leq x \leq v\}$ and N = H_2 (H_1 ($ID_1, ID_2, \cdots, ID_v, ID_{dataowner}, t$)). Formula 1 in line three is $K^c = \prod_{x=1}^{v} A_x^\lambda$, which is used to verify the correctness of common conference key K. As for the fault report FR_i and FR_x, they are both special cases of FR_x, where x is from 1 to v. Besides, $FR_x = \{N, ID_x, r_x, \{M_x \mid l_{xi} = 1, x \neq i\}\}$. The next is formula 2, which is $M_x^c = e(g, e_x r_x S_x)^c = A_x$ specifically and x is from 1 to v. And the last is formula 3, which aims to check whether $\{M_s\}$ computed and uploaded by assistant s equals to $\{M_s{'}\}$ indeed from assistant j.

Once all malicious assistants are revoked, the assist phase ought to continue smoothly anyway. In our work, we employ some empty participants to replace the revoked assistants. Thus, a novel common conference key K_{new} could be generated for assist phase.

6.3   Lazy Update

In practical scene, data owner may not be online whenever and wherever, which could lead to a backlog of modification suggestions. Thus, lazy update is supported in our works to adapt to this scene, which may trade off for timeliness however. In update phase, data owner would download the corresponding data block and modify it according the modification suggestion and re-upload the block finally if there is only one modification backlogged. However, how about more than one modifications waiting for uploading?

As mentioned in update phase, a queue could be employed to support this performance. When data owner is not online for a period of time, the modification suggestions are stored in the queue in turns. For the first in first out principle of queue, the order of modifications will not be disrupted. Take a certain data block m_y for example, if the first modification is to inset a sector into it, and the second aims to alter the inserted sector, the two operations would not be reversed, which avoids a mess.

7   Security Analysis of Our Algorithm

In this section, we will present the security analysis of our proposed algorithm, which is pre-mentioned in threat models in Sect. 3. The analysis will be conducted in two aspects — the active attacks as well as the passive ones. The details are summarized as follows.

Algorithm 1 Assistant Revocation

BEGIN

    data owner broadcasts massage BM to all assistants;

assistant i verifies formula 1;

    if (*formula* 1 *holds*) **then**

        K is established correctly;

        goto EXIT;

    else

        assistant i asks data owner to resend BM;

    end if

    while ($1 \leq resending\ times \leq T_{threshold}$) **do**

        if (*formula* 1 *holds*) **then**

            K is established correctly;

            goto EXIT;

        else

            resending times ++;

    end if

    end while

    assistant i sends fault report FR_i to data owner;

    data owner verifies formula 2 for i;

    if (*formula* 2 *for i doesn't hold*) **then**

        data owner asks assistant i to resend FR_i;

    if (*no resend for a longtime* || *fault for many times*) **then**

            data owner revokes assistant i;

    end if

    else

        data owner asks the rest assistants to send FR_s;

        data owner verifies formula 2 for each assistant s;

        if (*formula* 2 *for some s doesn't hold*) **then**

            data owner asks assistant s to resend FR_s;

        if (*no resend for a longtime* || *fault for many times*) **then**

            data owner revokes assistant s;

        end if else

            data owner verifies formula 3;

            if (*formula* 3 *does't hold*) **then**

                data owner revokes assistant s;

            else

                data owner revokes assistant i;

            end if

        end if

    end if

    EXIT

END

7.1 Resistance to Active Attacks

Active attacks aim to destruct a certain conference via alteration, injection, interception, and replay of data. In Sect. 6.1, we show the performance of identity authentication in our algorithm, which ensures the consistency of the assistant sending message to and the one receiving message from. As a result, active attackers are unable to pretend the authenticated assistants to communicate with others. Besides, as shown in Sect. 6.2, malicious assistant revocation keeps the assistants who are suffering from denial of service or go bad themselves out. What's more, our algorithm supports forward security perfectly. Specifically, S_i is distributed to each assistant by data owner, which is valid for a long term. Once an active attacker gains S_i, the parameter r_i could not be computed anyway, which thanks to the intractability discrete logarithm problem. As a result, the previous common conference key could not be computed by attacker, which indicates the forward security of our algorithm.

7.2 Resistance to Passive Attacks

What is known to us all is that passive attackers act like eavesdroppers, who aim to know what is transmitted in communications. When a passive attacker would like to obtain the common conference key, it would intercept and record as well as analyze the public information $\{g, P_s, R_v\}$, where R_v is the set of public keys P_i $(1 \leq i \leq v)$ of all assistants. For a random $1 \in Z_p$, we set $L = (g, P_s, R_v, 1)$. In our works, $X = (g, P_s, R_v, e(g, \lambda \sum_{i=1}^{v} e_i r_i S_i))$ and the two tuples of L is hard to be distinguished, so our algorithm is passive attacks resisted.

8 Cost Analysis of Our Algorithm

In this section, we analyze our proposed algorithm from the numerical point of view specifically. It is widely accepted that the cost of a certain scheme is divided into computational cost and communication cost. For simplicity, we abbreviate point multiplication as MUL, and modular exponentiation as EXP. Besides, we use Enc and Dec to denote encryption and decryption separately. For the cost of Hash operation and AND operation is quite small compared with the above several operations, Hash and AND could be ignored in our analysis.

8.1 Computational Cost

Throughout Sect. 5, our algorithm is consisted of four primary phases — setup phase, assist phase, inform phase, and update phase. Hence, the computational cost will be analyzed phase by phase.

Setup phase includes cloud data outsourcing and assistants nominating. The computational cost in cloud data outsourcing mainly focuses on the authentication generation for each data block, which performs (1 MUL + 2 EXP) for each data block, and the total is (n MUL + 2n EXP). On the other hand, distributing secret and public key pairs to assistants needs v MUL altogether. Besides, as the preparations for subsequent identity authentication, data owner performs 1 MUL, while assistants perform (v MUL + v EXP).

As for assist phase, some operations are supposed to be finished before the formation of the common conference key, which requires (1 Pairing + k MUL). And the final generation of K contains (1 Pairing + (v + 1) MUL). In addition, this phase involves some preparatory works for identity authentication as well, and (1 Pairing + 2 MUL + (k-1) EXP) are needed. For the negligible cost of AND operation, the $(v - 2)$ AND operations performed in the process of confirmation of the validity of modification suggestion could be ignored.

The inform phase is responsible for the transmission of modification suggestions from assistant i who proposed it to data owner, which performs 1 Enc merely.

And the final phase is the update one, which should be divided into two circumstances to be discussed. When there is only one modification waiting for updating, (1 Dec + 1 MUL + 2 EXP) would be performed. However, when it comes to lazy update, we assume that there are m modification suggestions in a queue, in which m_s suggestions are related to the same data block in total. As a tradeoff for timeliness, such a lazy update performs $(m \text{ Dec} + (m - m_s) \text{ MUL} + 2(m - m_s) \text{ EXP})$.

In addition, the process of identity authentication requires $(2(k - 1) \text{ EXP})$, while assistant revocation performs only one extra EXP.

In this paragraph, we will compare the computational cost of our design with the existing [29] proposed by Yuan et al. in 2015. The general results are shown in Table 3, in which s is the number of sectors in a certain data block in [29], n is number of blocks in a cloud data file and k is the number of users in their scene who possess both read and write permissions and are called "multiusers". In file pre-processing before data outsourcing, [29] performs ((s + 2)n EXP + sn MUL), which is more than (2n EXP + n MUL) in our algorithm. In file pre-processing, we let sectors in a certain block share one authenticator if necessary. Even though there is only one sector in a block in [29], the computational cost is 1 EXP more than ours. As for key distribution, which is a process of nominating valid users or assistants, the cost of [29] is higher than our algorithm if we assume that the number of users in [29] equals the number of assistants in ours. The next is the computational cost of update after the finish of modification, [29] costs (s EXP + s MUL) more than ours. When it comes more than

Table 3. Computational cost comparison

	File pre-processing	Key distribution (assistant nominating)	Modification update	Follow-ups of user revocation
Yuan et al. [29]	(s + 2)n EXP + sn MUL	(s + k + 4) EXP	(s + 2) EXP + (s + 1) MUL	Y EXP + Y Pairing
Our algorithm	2n EXP + n MUL	(v + 1) MUL + 1 Pairing	2 EXP + 1 MUL	None

one modification update, the computational cost will reduce further for the support of lazy update. The final are the follow-up operations after user revocation. In [29], (Y EXP + Y Pairing) are needed to update the corresponding Y authenticators last modified by the revoked user, while no operation is necessary in our algorithm for no write permission of assistants and the support of identity authentication, which makes attackers have no ability to imitate as a valid assistant.

8.2 Communication Cost

In our algorithm, the communication cost mainly comes from the common conference key generation among assistants, discussion of modification suggestion, and the inform of modification. In the process of common conference key generation, $v(k-1)$ $E_{ji} = \{D_j, (C_{ji})^{ei}\}$ are transmitted in channel to cooperate with each other. As for the discussion of modification suggestions among assistants, $(v-1)$ groups of modification suggestions including the detailed modification information are sent from assistant i to the rest assistants. After that, v Boolean values would be returned back to i. The final is informing of modification, where only one encrypted modification suggestion would be transmitted in the whole process. In summary, the communication complexity of our algorithm is O(vk).

9 Conclusion

In this paper, we propose a novel algorithm for dynamic update of data files in cloud, which employs several assistants to help error discovery and modification discussion. We point out the shortcomings of the impractical scene that only data owner could participate in cloud data modification, and overcome the chaotic management of the scene with multiusers who possess both read and write permissions. In our algorithm, assistants provide modification suggestions to data owner, and data owner is the only one who can update cloud data indeed. Besides the orderly process of dynamic operations, our algorithm supports identity authentication, malicious assistant revocation, and lazy update as well. Extensive numerical analysis validates the performance of our works.

Acknowledgments. This work is supported by the National Science Foundation of China under Grant No. 61300237, No. U1536206, No. U1405254, No. 61232016 and No. 61402234, the National Basic Research Program 973 under Grant No. 2011CB311808, the Natural Science Foundation of Jiangsu province under Grant No. BK2012461, the research fund from Jiangsu Technology & Engineering Center of Meteorological Sensor Network in NUIST under Grant No. KDXG1301, the research fund from Jiangsu Engineering Center of Network Monitoring in NUIST under Grant No. KJR1302, the research fund from Nanjing University of Information Science and Technology under Grant No. S8113003001, the 2013 Nanjing Project of Science and Technology Activities for Returning from Overseas, the 2015 Project of six personnel in Jiangsu Province under Grant No. R2015L06, the CICAEET fund, and the PAPD fund.

References

1. Mell, P., Grance, T.: The NIST definition of cloud computing. Commun. ACM **53**(6), 50 (2011)
2. Xiao, Z., Xiao, Y.: Security and privacy in cloud computing. IEEE Commun. Surv. Tutor. **15**(15), 843–859 (2013)
3. Dudin, E.B., Smetanin, Y.G.: A review of cloud computing. Sci. Tech. Inf. Process. **38**(38), 280–284 (2011)
4. Zeng, W., Zhao, Y., Ou, K., Song, W.: Research on cloud storage architecture and key technologies. In: Proceedings of the International Conference on Interaction Sciences: Information Technology, Culture and Human 2009, Seoul, Korea, 24–26 November, pp. 1044–1048 (2009)
5. Wang, Q., He, M., Du, M., Chow, S.S.M., Lai, R.W.F., Zou, Q.: Searchable encryption over feature-rich data. IEEE Trans. Dependable Secure Comput. **PP**(99), 1 (2016). doi:10.1109/TDSC.2016.25934446
6. Buyya, R., Yeo, C.S., Venugopal, S., Broberg, J., Brandic, I.: Cloud computing and emerging IT platforms: vision, hype, and reality for delivering computing as the 5th utility. Future Gener. Comput. Syst. **25**(6), 599–616 (2009)
7. Velte, T., Velte, A., Elsenpeter, R.: Cloud Computing, A Practical Approach. McGraw-Hill, New York (2009)
8. Yang, K., Jia, X.: Data storage auditing service in cloud computing: challenges, methods and opportunities. World Wide Web-Internet Web Inf. Syst. **15**(4), 409–428 (2011)
9. Xiao, Z., Xiao, Y., Chen, H.: An accountable framework for sensing-oriented mobile cloud computing. J. Internet Technol. **15**(5), 813–822 (2014)
10. He, D., Zeadally, S., Kumar, N., Lee, J.: Anonymous authentication for wireless body area networks with provable security. IEEE Syst. J. **PP**(99), 1–12 (2016)
11. Zhang, Q., Chen, Z., Len, Y.: Distributed fuzzy c-means algorithms for big sensor data based on cloud computing. Int. J. Sens. Netw. **18**(1/2), 32–39 (2015)
12. Ren, Y., Shen, J., Wang, J., Lee, S.: Mutual verifiable provable data auditing in public cloud storage. J. Internet Technol. **16**(2), 317–323 (2015)
13. Yuan, J., Yu, S.: Efficient public integrity checking for cloud data sharing with multi-user modification. In: Proceedings of the IEEE International Conference on Computer Communication, pp. 2121–2129 (2014)
14. Rakesh, J., Krishna, J.V.: A novel approach for secure data sharing in multi-owner groups in cloud. Int. J. Comput. Trends Technol. **16**(1), 20–23 (2014)
15. He, D., Zeadally, S.: Authentication protocol for ambient assisted living system. IEEE Commun. Mag. **35**(1), 71–77 (2015)
16. Baskar, H.: Fully secure and efficient data sharing with attribute revocation for multi-owner cloud storage. Int. J. Adv. Res. Educ. Technol. **3**(2), 835–838 (2015)
17. Wang, B., Li, H., Liu, X., Li, X., Li, F.: Preserving identity privacy on multi-owner cloud data during public verification. Secur. Commun. Netw. **7**(11), 2104–2113 (2013)
18. Suba, J.: Multi owner data sharing with privacy preserving in cloud security mediator. Int. J. Sci. Res. **3**(3), 41–44 (2014)
19. Tasmiya, S.K., Kausar, F.: An efficient approach to share data in cloud with multi-owner groups. Int. J. Comput. Technol. **1**(3), 137–141 (2014)
20. Wang, G., Liu, Q., Wu, J., Guo, M.: Hierarchical attribute-based encryption and scalable user revocation for sharing data in cloud servers. Comput. Secur. **30**(5), 320–333 (2011)

21. Sun, D., Chang, G., Miao, C., Wang, X.: Modelling and evaluating a high serviceability fault tolerance strategy in cloud computing environments. Int. J. Secur. Netw. **7**(4), 196–210 (2012)
22. Femilshini, F., Ganeshkarthikeyan, V., Janani, S.: Privacy preserving revocation update protocol for group signature in cloud. In: Proceedings of the IEEE International Conference on Engineering and Technology, pp. 1–5. IEEE (2015)
23. Zagade, P., Yadav, S., Shah, A., Bachate, R.: Group user revocation and integrity auditing of shared data in cloud environment. Int. J. Comput. Appl. **128**(12), 22–25 (2015)
24. Yang, K., Jia, X.: An efficient and secure dynamic auditing protocol for data storage in cloud computing. IEEE Trans. Parallel Distrib. Syst. **24**(9), 1717–1726 (2013)
25. Wang, Q., Wang, C., Li, J., Ren, K., Lou, W.: Enabling public verifiability and data dynamics for storage security in cloud computing. In: Backes, M., Ning, P. (eds.) ESORICS 2009. LNCS, vol. 5789, pp. 355–370. Springer, Heidelberg (2009)
26. Wang, Q., Wang, C., Ren, K., Lou, W., Li, J.: Enabling public auditability and data dynamics for storage security in cloud computing. IEEE Trans. Parallel Distrib. Syst. **22**(5), 847–859 (2011)
27. Wang, B., Li, B., Li, H.: Oruta: privacy-preserving public auditing for shared data in the cloud. IEEE Trans. Cloud Comput. **2**(1), 295–302 (2012)
28. Wang, B., Li, B., Li, H.: Public auditing for shared data with efficient user revocation in the cloud. In: Proceedings of the 32nd IEEE International Conference on Computer Communication, Turin, Italy, pp. 2904–2912 (2013)
29. Yuan, J., Yu, S.: Public integrity auditing for dynamic data sharing with multi-user modification. IEEE Trans. Inf. Forensics Secur. **10**(8), 1 (2015)
30. Green, M.: The threat in the cloud. IEEE Secur. Priv. **11**(1), 86–89 (2013)
31. Fu, Z., Ren, K., Shu, J., Sun, X., Huang, F.: Enabling personalized search over encrypted outsourced data with efficiency improvement. IEEE Trans. Parallel Distrib. Syst. (2015). doi:10.1109/TPDS.2015.2506573
32. Hu, S., Wang, Q., Wang, J., Qin, Z., Ren, K.: Securing SIFT: privacy-preserving outsourcing computation of feature extractions over encrypted image data. IEEE Trans. Image Process. **25**(7), 3411–3425 (2016)
33. He, D., Zeadally, S., Wu, L.: Certificateless public auditing scheme for cloud-assisted wireless body area networks. IEEE Syst. J. **PP**(99), 1–10 (2015)
34. Shen, J., Tan, H., Wang, J., Wang, J., Lee, S.: A novel routing protocol providing good transmission reliability in underwater sensor networks. J. Internet Technol. **16**(1), 171–178 (2015)
35. Santos, D., Nascimento, T., Westphall, C., Leandro, M., Westphall, C.: Privacy-preserving identity federations in the cloud: a proof of concept. Int. J. Secur. Netw. **9**(1), 1–11 (2014)
36. Khorshed, M.T., Ali, A.B.M.S., Wasimi, S.A.: A survey on gaps, threat remediation challenges and some thoughts for proactive attack detection in cloud computing. Future Gener. Comput. Syst. **28**(6), 833–851 (2012)
37. Fernandes, D.A.B., Soares, L.F.B., Gomes, J.V., Freire, M.M., Incio, P.R.M.: Security issues in cloud environments: a survey. Int. J. Inf. Secur. **13**(2), 113–170 (2014)
38. Soares, L.F.B., Fernandes, D.A.B., Gomes, J.V., Freire, M.M., Incio, P.R.: Cloud Security: State of the Art, Security, Privacy and Trust in Cloud Systems, pp. 3–44. Springer, Heidelberg (2014)
39. Chraibi, M., Harroud, H., Maach, A.: Classification of security issues and solutions in cloud environments. In: Proceedings of the International Conference on Information Integration and Web-Based Applications & Services. ACM (2013)
40. Chen, Y., Paxson, V., Katz, R.H.: What's new about cloud computing security. Univ. Calif. Berkeley Rep. **20**(2010), 2010–2015 (2010)

41. Ju, H.: Intelligent disaster recovery structure and mechanism for cloud computing network. Int. J. Sens. Netw. **16**(2), 70–76 (2014)
42. Barua, M., Liang, X., Lu, R., Shen, X.: ESPAC: enabling security and patient-centric access control for eHealth in cloud computing. Int. J. Secur. Netw. **6**(2/3), 67–76 (2011)
43. Boampong, P.A., Wahsheh, L.A.: Different facets of security in the cloud. In: Proceedings of the 15th Communications and Networking Simulation Symposium. Society for Computer Simulation International (2012)
44. Shen, J., Moh, S., Chung, I.: Identity-based key agreement protocol employing a symmetric balanced incomplete block design. J. Commun. Netw. **14**(14), 682–691 (2012)
45. Xiao, Z., Xiao, Y.: Achieving accountable MapReduce in cloud computing. Future Gener. Comput. Syst. **30**(1), 1–13 (2014). (Elsevier)
46. Lawal, B.: Incomplete block design. In: Lawal, B. (ed.) Applied Statistical Methods in Agriculture, Health and Life Sciences, pp. 639–659. Springer International Publishing, Heidelberg (2014)
47. Lee, O., Yoo, S., Park, B., Chung, I.: The design and analysis of an efficient load balancing algorithm employing the symmetric balanced incomplete block design. Inf. Sci. **176**(15), 2148–2160 (2006)
48. Shen, J., Moh, S., Chung, I.: Enhanced secure sensor association and key management in wireless body area networks. J. Commun. Netw. **17**(5), 453–462 (2015)
49. Xiao, Z., Xiao, Y.: Accountable MapReduce in cloud computing. In: IEEE Conference on Computer Communications Workshops (INFOCOM WKSHPS), pp. 1082–1087 (2011)
50. Mbegbu, J.I.: Some designs from symmetric balanced incomplete block design. J. Niger. Assoc. Math. Phy. **17**, 363–366 (2013)
51. Shen, J., Zheng, W., Wang, J., Zheng, Y., Sun, X.: An efficient verifiably encrypted signature from Weil pairing. J. Internet Technol. **14**(6), 682–691 (2012)

Location Privacy Protected Recommendation System in Mobile Cloud

Haiyan Guan[✉], Hongyan Qian, and Yanchao Zhao

College of Computer Science and Technology,
Nanjing University of Aeronautics and Astronautics, Nanjing 211106, China
{ghy_nuaa,qhy98,yczhao}@nuaa.edu.cn

Abstract. As the core of location-based services (LBS), the LBS-oriented recommendation systems, which suggest the points-of-interest (POIs) to users by analyzing the distribution of the user's previous points-of-interest, have attracted great interest from both academia and industry. Despite the convenience brought by the LBS-oriented recommendation systems, most of current systems require users to expose their locations, which give rise to a big concerning of the location privacy issues. Meanwhile, as the defacto LBS infrastructure, the mobile-cloud computing paradigm introduces new opportunities and challenges to solve the privacy issues in LBS-oriented recommendation systems. To this end, we propose a novel location-privacy protected scheme for mobile-cloud based recommendation system. The scheme consists of two parts. (1) The server analyzes the user behavior pattern and then makes a list of sketchy recommendation, named as the recommended candidate list. (2) Mobile phone downloads the recommended candidate list from the server and refines the recommendation by taking the current geographical position, current time and location popularity into consideration. With the result from real data driven simulations, the scheme is proved to solve the problem of location privacy risks and improve the accuracy of recommendation.

Keywords: LBS-oriented recommendation system · Points-of-interest · Location-based social networks · Check-in data · Privacy risks

1 Introduction

Nowadays, the location based services (LBSs) have brought great convenience to improve the quality of life. As the core of the LBSs, LBS-oriented recommendation is the task of suggesting unvisited POIs to the users and mining the potential customers for businesses effectively. According to the user's check-in history, LBS-oriented recommendation system makes analysis when and where the user prefers to go [1]. Traditionally, most of the work endeavour to improve the accuracy of recommendation. For example, Lian, et al. exploited weighted matrix factorization for the task of sparse check-in data [2]. Yin et al. proposed

© Springer International Publishing AG 2016
X. Sun et al. (Eds.): ICCCS 2016, Part I, LNCS 10039, pp. 409–420, 2016.
DOI: 10.1007/978-3-319-48671-0_36

a unified probabilistic generative model, Topic-Region Model (TRM), to simultaneously discover the semantic, temporal and spatial pattern of users' check-in activities, and to model their joint effect on users' decision-making for POIs [3].

Although the accuracy of LBS-oriented recommendation system has been improved, the concern of privacy protection in location based services keeps rising. Some recommendation systems require users to expose their current position to the server and recommend POIs based on users' check-in history. Hence, there are great risks of location privacy-leaking due to insecure transmission or compromised cloud end, as is shown in Fig. 1. Recently some of the works focus on protecting the location privacy while still provides the cloud services. Jin et al. in [4] proposed a user-centric device-cloud architecture for intelligently managing user data. The architecture allowed users to keep the confidential data on their mobile devices and decided what to be shared with the service providers on the cloud which reduced the pressure on processing users' information. Some systems protected user privacy by using encryption, pseudonym, K-anonymity [5,6], or cache pushing [7].

However, the state-of-the-art work have following limitations. Firstly, most of these works ignore the location privacy issues in LBS-oriented recommendation system. Secondly, the computation capacity of mobile devices has not been fully explored to achieve both high quality services and location privacy protection.

Meanwhile, the LBSs trend to be implemented in the mobile-cloud computing paradigm [8]. This paradigm utilizes both the computation power of cloud end and mobile devices to achieve best performance by offloading certain computation. Based on this paradigm, how to balance the recommendation system and achieve location privacy is still lack of research efforts.

To alleviate the above limitations, we propose a novel scheme to achieve the cloud-based LBS-oriented recommendation which is designed to solve the problem of location privacy risks and improve the accuracy of recommendation. Our main contributions are summarized as following.

- We propose a location uploading-free recommendation system architecture which can still provide accurate recommendation results.
- We design a location-protected transport protocol by using k-anonymity, which introduced by Sweeney in [5] and the pseudonym in [9] to avoid the real information was leaked during transmission.
- We exploit a new algorithm by combining the temporal pattern, geographical correlation, categorical correlation and social influence to improve the accuracy of the recommendation.

The rest of this paper is organized as following. We introduce the related work in Sect. 2. In Sect. 3, the framework of our system is designed. Then experiments on the kinds of datasets and the discussion of results are presented in Sect. 4. Section 5 concludes this paper.

2   Related Work

2.1   Privacy Preservation

K-anonymity is the most commonly used model for privacy preservation which attackers cannot distinguish one user from a k user group [5]. Submission of fake position [10] is similar to K-anonymity which is the model that sends fake positions to the server while Spatio-Temporal cloaking [11–13] is the model that sends a region instead of their accurate position. Chen et al. [7] proposed a Location Privacy Preservation Scheme (LPPS) based on distributed cache pushing which was based on Markov Chain. And the cache pushing strategy in their system divided cache content into group and broadcast the cache items in batch, which was shown to guarantee k-anonymity of location privacy. Kong et al. [6] proposed a novel Privacy Preserving Compressive Sensing (PPCS) scheme, which encrypted a trajectory with several other trajectories while maintaining the homomorphic obfuscation property for compressive sensing.

2.2   Recommendation Accuracy

The existing LBS-oriented recommendation systems mainly consider the following four factors, which have major impact on the recommendation accuracy:

Geographical Correlation. Geographical correlation refers to the movement of the user who will be biased in the vicinity of their work place or home. In other words, if the unvisited POIs are closer to the user historical footprints, the easier they are to be accepted by users [14]. In order to model the geographical check-in distribution of POIs for each user over the latitude and longitude coordinates, [15,16] used kernel density estimation method with the fixed bandwidth. For further research, an adaptive kernel estimation method was used in [14].

Social Correlation. Social correlation refers to the impact of social relationships on the recommendation. In fact, a user will likely accept the recommendations made by friends who have the similar interest. Some researches took the users' similarity as a potential factor to make recommendations [1,17]. In our system, we compute the proximity between unvisited POIs of users and visited POIs of the users' friends.

Categorical Correlation. The category of a POI reflects its usual business activities and nature. Systems can obtain the users' trajectory by taking the categorical correlation into consideration [14,18,19]. For example, if a user frequently appears in restaurants during a specified time period, it means that the user will likely to accept the LBS-oriented recommendation related the food and beverage. Hu et al. leveraged the matrix factorization technique to associate each category and deduced the relevance of a user to a POI based on the latent vectors of the categories of the POI [20].

Locational Popularity. The location popularity has impact on LBS-oriented recommendation. If the location is popular, the user will prefer to accept it than that unknown. On the other hand, nearest neighboring locations tending to the famous places will also attract more tourists. Zhang et al. [14] devised a new method to combine the category bias of a user and the popularity of a POI into a relevance score between the user and the POI so as to personalize the effect of the popularity of the POI on the user.

3   System Architecture

In this section, we introduce our scheme, which is illustrated in Fig. 2. The whole system consists of two modules: the cloud server module and mobile terminal module. This scheme automatically deals with the non-sensitive data e.g. social relational data and check-in history on cloud server while the sensitive data e.g. the current position is utilized on terminal.

Fig. 1. Privacy protection and information theft

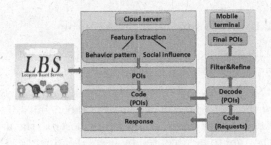

Fig. 2. System architecture

3.1   Cloud Server Module

This module mainly contains three parts:

- The server gains user's behavior model by analyzing the user's check-in data. Then computes the correlation score $S_G(u, l, c, t)$ of the user's spatial and temporal distribution.
- The server computes the correlation score $S_F(u, l, c, t)$ of K-Top POIs recommended from the similar and close friends by analyzing the social relationship data and check-in data.
- The server makes the recommended candidate list by merging the user's spatial and temporal distribution and the social influence. Because the recommended candidate list contains the sensitive information of the users' behavior model which should be protected, we employ a strategy to hide the sensitive information through pseudonyms.

A. User Behavior Pattern. In this section, we analyze the user behavior pattern which is represented by the spatial and temporal distribution. Firstly we analyze the categorical popularity which is aimed to get the categorical correlation. Secondly, we analyze the geographical correlation of the locations. Last, we merge the categorical correlation and geographical correlation, and compute the score of location l being recommended to the user.

Step 1: Estimating the categorical correlation. The category of a POI indicates the activities of a user in the POI. For example, if a user often goes to a cinema on Saturday evening, we can recommend a cinema to the user at that time. Further more, popularity of a POI indicates the quality of service or goods in the POI. In fact, customers will prefer to buy high-quanlity goods so that the popularity of category is useful for making LBS-oriented recommendation.

We assume that category $c_g \ \varepsilon \ C$ where C is the set of categories of POIs that is often predefined in the LBSN. $P(c,t)$ is the popularity of category c and $f_{c_g}(x)$ is the probability density function of the categorical popularity, defined as following.

$$f_{c_g}(x) = (\varpi - 1)(1 + x)^{-\varpi}, x >= 0, \varpi > 1 \tag{1}$$

In which ϖ can be learned from the popularity matrix $P(c,t)$ and the frequence $R_{u,c}$ of visiting category c by user u.

$$\varpi = 1 + |U||C|[\sum_{u \varepsilon U} \sum_{c \varepsilon C} ln(1 + R_{u,c} \cdot P(c,t))] \tag{2}$$

It is obvious that the probability density function of the categorical popularity $f_{c_g}(x)$ defined in Eq. (1) is monotonically decreasing regarding the categorical popularity $P(c,t)$. In order to obtain the categorical relevance score of $P(c,t)$, which is monotonically increasing respecting the categorical popularity, we employ the cumulative distribution function of $f_{c_g}(x)$, defined by

$$C_G(P(c,t);t) = \int_0^{P(c,t)} f_{c_g}(x)dx = 1 - (1 + P(c,t))^{1-\varpi} \tag{3}$$

where $1 - \varpi < 0$ and $C_G(P(c,t);t)$ is an increasing function with respect to the categorical popularity $P(c,t)$.

Step 2: Estimating the point of interest. The geographical region will be defined at two levels:

- Geographical region sharing similar user preferences. Users would like to accept the recommendation if the location is similar to their preferences. For example, a food aficionado would like to go to a restaurant or food street.
- Geographical region nearby the visited POIs of a user. In fact, it is convenient for users to go to the places where are near to their work place or home so that users often accept the location in the region where is nearby their POIs. For example, a user would like to have dinner and then go to a cinema where is not too far away from the restaurant.

We exploit kernel density estimation to compute the geographical correlation.

$$S_{Gl}(l; t; u) = \frac{1}{N} \sum_{i=1}^{n} (R_{u,l_i}.T(u, l_i|t).(K_H(l - l_i) + K'_H(Simi(c_l, c_{l_i})))) \qquad (4)$$

$$N = \sum_{i=1}^{n} R_{u,l_i} \qquad (5)$$

where R_{u,l_i} is the frequence of visiting the location l_i by user u, $T(u, l_i|t)$ is the temporal pattern, K_H is the kernel function, $K_H(l - l_i)$ is aimed to compute the correlation of geographical region nearby the visited POIs and $K'_H(Simi(c_l, c_{l_i}))$ is used to compute the correlation of geographical region sharing similar user preferences, $Simi(c_l, c_{l_i})$ is the similarity of the category c_l and c_{l_i}.

Step 3: Merging categorical correlation and geographical correlation. We compute the score of location l being recommended to the user based on the analysis of user behavior pattern.

$$S_G(u, l, c, t) = S_{Gl}.C_G \qquad (6)$$

B. Influence of Users. We analyze the influence of friends by using the social relationship data and check-in data, then compute the correlation score of K-Top POIs from the similar and close friends.

Firstly, we calculate the similarity of users. The similarity of users was defined at two levels: the similarity based on the social relationship and the similarity based on the POIs. Here we utilize Pearson similarity method to compute the similarity of two users as showed in the following.

$$PCS(u, u') = \frac{cov(u, u')}{\delta_u \delta_{u'}} \qquad (7)$$

Secondly, we take social actions such as '@', comments and similarity into consideration to calculate the influence of the friends.

$$Rl_{u,u'} = \alpha.PCS(u, u') + \beta.CLO(u, u') \qquad (8)$$

where $\alpha + \beta = 1$ and $CLO(u, u')$ is the influence of social action.

Last, we obtain the score of location l being recommended to a user based on the social influence.

$$S_F(u, l, c, t) = \sum_{u' \in U} Rl_{u,u'}.R_{u',l} \qquad (9)$$

C. Merging. Here we merge the user behavior pattern and social influence to make a list of recommended candidates.

$$S(u, l, c, t) = \mu S_G(u, l, c, t) + \lambda S_F(u, l, c, t) \qquad (10)$$

where $\mu + \lambda = 1$.

The cloud server responses to requests from mobile terminal and sends the recommended candidate list showed as Eq. (13) to the mobile. However, the information of the list is sensitive and users are averse to being leaked. In order to deal with the problem, we code the information of $List : (u_i, L, T, S, C)$ anonymously, such as $u_i \longmapsto code(u_i)$.

$$u_i^{'} = code(u_i) = reverse(u_i) + Parameter \tag{11}$$

$$u_i = decode(u_i^{'}) = reverse(u_i^{'} - Parameter) \tag{12}$$

For example, $reverse(123) = 321$ and $Parameter$ is a constant.

$$List^{'} = code(List : (u_i, L, T, S, C)) \tag{13}$$

where u_i is the user id, L is recommended location set $\{(x_{it_1}, y_{it_1}), (x_{it_2}, y_{it_2}), (x_{it_3}, y_{it_3}), \cdots , (x_{it_n}, y_{it_n})\}$, T is the time set $\{t_{i1}, t_{i2}, t_{i3}, \cdots , t_{in}\}$, S is the score set $\{s_{i1}, s_{i2}, s_{i3}, \cdots , s_{in}\}$ for LBS-oriented recommendation and C is the set of category which represents the user's favorite categories.

3.2   Mobile Terminal Module

Firstly, the mobile terminal sends requests to server for the recommended candidate list and downloads it. The transport protocol from mobile terminal to cloud server works by coding the requests $[code(userID), code(Position)]$. The $Position$ is the set of five positons within 5 Km from the current position of the user which does not include the current position by using k-anonymity. In order to hide the identities of users, we use our transport protocol to send the requests to sever. After receiving the requests, the server extracts the POIs by filtering the recommended candidate list with the $userID$ and $Position$. The POIs in the same city with the $Position$ will be sent to the mobile terminal. If there are no POIs fit the requests, we send the representative POIs which can indicate the behavior pattern of the user. Secondly the mobile obtains the final recommended results by filtering and refining the recommended candidate list.

Step 1: Filtering the recommended candidate list. In this step, we first decode the recommended candidate list by using Eq. (12), then we filter the LBS-oriented recommendation with the current position and time. The result of the filtering will have two cases. If the user's POIs in the recommended candidate list is in the same city with the current position which means that we can get the final recommendation from the recommended candidate list, because we have recommended the POIs nearby the visited POIs based on user's preferences and the location popularity. However, there is another case. If the current position is too far away from the user's POIs which means that there are no visited history about the geographical region and its neighbour. In this case, we have to mine the user's preferences from the recommended candidate list (in step 2) and then make the final recommendation according to the preferences and the popularity of the current geographical region (in step 3).

Step 2: Mining the user's preferences. Due to the limitation of power, storage and computation capability of mobile terminal, we prefer to mine the user's preferences from the $List : (u_i, L, T, S, C)$ than mine the user's preferences from the check-in history. Here, we mainly consider the category-time distribution of the user which we can easily obtain from $List : (u_i, L, T, S, C)$. The category-time distribution is shown as $List(T, S, C)$

Step 3: Refining the LBS-oriented recommendation. In this step, we refine the LBS-oriented recommendation with the location popularity and user's preferences:

$$Refine(List(T, S, C), (C_{current}, L_{current})) \tag{14}$$

$$Score(c, t, l) = \frac{1}{N} \sum_{i=1}^{n} (P(c, t).(K_H(l - l_p) + K_H'(Simi(c_i', c)))) \tag{15}$$

where $List(T, S, C)$ indicates the user's preferences, $(C_{current}, L_{current})$ are the category and location of the current geographical region and its neighbor, $c \varepsilon C_{current}$, $c_i' \varepsilon C$, $l \varepsilon L_{current}$ and $N = |C|$, l_p is the current position of the user. The score in Eq. (15) is larger, the location will be more likely recommended to the user.

4   Evaluation

In order to discuss the experimental results, we conduct the experiment to investigate the effect of different LBS-oriented recommendation systems. Compared with these experiments by using different algorithms and models, we find that our novel scheme works better. In order to get a dataset including the user ID, location ID, location latitude, location longitude, time stamp of the check-in, and location category that are useful to improve the performance, we choose the Gowalla dataset.

4.1   System Evaluation Metrics

The scheme mentioned in this paper will be compared with GeoSoCa [14], sPCLR [1], GeoMF [2], CoRe [15] based on the following performance metrics:

$$Precision = \frac{\sum_{u \in U} |R(u) \cap T(u)|}{\sum_{u \in U} R(u)} \tag{16}$$

$$Recall = \frac{\sum_{u \in U} |R(u) \cap T(u)|}{\sum_{u \in U} T(u)} \tag{17}$$

where $R(u)$ is the number of recommendation candidates for user u, $T(u)$ is the number of samples of a user's POIs, $R(u) \cap T(u)$ is the accepted number of recommendation. The aim of the recommendation system is to get larger precision and recall at the same time.

4.2   Simulation Results

The values of parameters referred in this paper are given as showed in Table 1. Our experiment starts with the analysis of the user's habits in daily life. Figure 3 shows the temporal distribution of three different users towards one category. It is obvious that the three users have different habits in daily life. For example, User 1 would like to go to the category in the early morning while User 2 and User 3 would like to go at night. User 2 and User 3 have the similar living habits, which indicate the two users have the similar preference.

Table 1. Settings of parameters

Parameters	α	β	μ	λ
Value	0.65	0.35	0.75	0.25

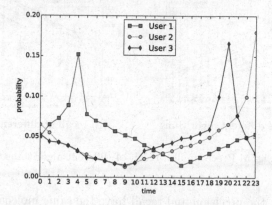

Fig. 3. Temporal curves for different users towards one category

Figure 4(a) and (b) depict the results of our cloud server module and mobile terminal module respectively. The best precision and recall in cloud server module are 0.247 and 0.112 while in mobile terminal module are 0.295 and 0.148. The precision in cloud server is smaller than that in mobile terminal because cloud server only makes a sketchy recommendation without considering the current position and time of the user and the popularity of the current geographical region.

Figure 5 shows the precision and recall of our experiments compared with GeoSoCa, sPCLR, GeoMF, CoRe. It is obvious that our novel scheme works better than those algorithms. The most important reason is that we filter and refine the recommendation with the current position, current time and the popularity of the current geographical region. We take these steps in mobile in order to protect user privacy. Figure 5 shows that the greater number of the recommendation, the smaller precision and the larger recall. From Eqs. (16) and (17),

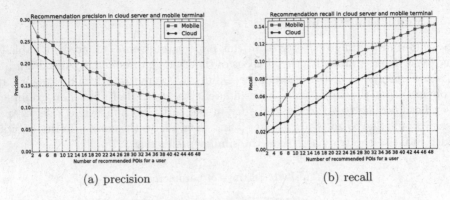

(a) precision

(b) recall

Fig. 4. Precision and recall in cloud server and mobile terminal

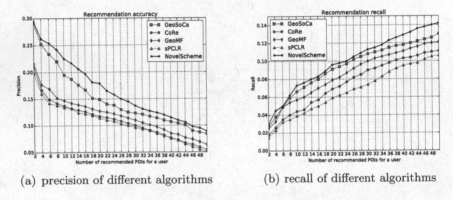

(a) precision of different algorithms

(b) recall of different algorithms

Fig. 5. Precision and recall of different algorithms

we can learn that the precision and recall have the same molecule $R(u) \cap T(u)$. $R(u)$ is the number of LBS-oriented recommendation candidates for user u which is changing from 1 to 50 in our experiments, $T(u)$ is the number of samples of a user's POIs which is static. That is why precision is smaller and recall is larger when the number of the recommendation is larger.

5   Conclusion

In this paper, we propose a location-privacy protected scheme for mobile-cloud based LBS-oriented recommendation system. In cloud server module, we take the geographical correlation, categorical correlation and location popularity into consideration to analyze the user behavior pattern by exploiting kernel density estimation. Then we merge the social influence and the user behavior pattern to obtain recommended candidate POIs. In order to protect user privacy, we encode the recommended candidate POIs on cloud server and use an encrypted transport protocol for the transmission between mobile terminal and cloud server. We refine the recommendation with the user' current position and time on mobile terminal to improve the accuracy of the LBS-oriented recommendation system. The experimental results show that our scheme can improve the accuracy and privacy protection of the current state-of-the-art LBS-oriented recommendation approaches. In the future, we will further focus on the duration of time a user stayed in a place and the views on POIs which can reflect the degree of a user's interest in the places.

References

1. Zhou, D., Wang, X.: Probabilistic category-based location recommendation utilizing temporal influence and geographical influence. In: Proceedings of DSAA, pp. 115–121 (2014)
2. Lian, D., Zhao, C., Xie, X., Sun, G., Chen, E., Rui, Y.: GeoMF: joint geographical modeling and matrix factorization for point-of-interest recommendation. In: Proceedings of ACM SIGKDD, pp. 831–840. ACM (2014)
3. Yin, H., Cui, B., Huang, Z., Wang, W., Wu, X., Zhou, X.: Joint modeling of users' interests and mobility patterns for point-of-interest recommendation. In: Proceedings of ACMMM, pp. 819–822. ACM (2015)
4. Jin, H., Saldamli, G., Chow, R., Knijnenburg, B.P.: Recommendations-based location privacy control. In: Proceedings of PERCOM Workshops, pp. 401–404 (2013)
5. Sweeney, L.: K-anonymity: a model for protecting privacy. Int. J. Uncertainty, Fuzziness Knowl.-Based Syst. **10**(5), 557–570 (2002)
6. Kong, L., He, L., Yang Liu, X., Gu, Y., Wu, M.Y., Liu, Y.: Privacy-preserving compressive sensing for crowdsensing based trajectory recovery. In: Proceedings of ICDCS, pp. 31–40 (2015)
7. Chen, M., Li, W., Li, Z., Lu, S.: Preserving location privacy based on distributed cache pushing. In: Proceedings of WCNC, pp. 3456–3461 (2014)
8. Li, W., Zhao, Y., Sanglu, L., Chen, D.: Mechanisms and challenges on mobility-augmented service provisioning for mobile cloud computing. IEEE Commun. Mag. **53**(3), 89–97 (2015)
9. Espinoza, F., Persson, P., Sandin, A., Nyström, H., Cacciatore, E., Bylund, M.: GeoNotes: social and navigational aspects of location-based information systems. In: Abowd, G.D., Brumitt, B., Shafer, S. (eds.) UbiComp 2001. LNCS, vol. 2201, pp. 2–17. Springer, Heidelberg (2001)
10. Kido, H., Yanagisawa, Y., Satoh, T.: Protection of location privacy using dummies for location-based services. In: Proceedings of ICDEW, p. 1248. IEEE Computer Society (2005)
11. Gruteser, M., Grunwald, D.: Anonymous usage of location-based services through spatial and temporal cloaking. In: Proceedings of MobiSys, pp. 31–42. ACM (2003)
12. Gedik, B., Liu, L.: Location privacy in mobile systems,: a personalized anonymization model. In: Proceedings of ICDCS, pp. 620–629. IEEE Computer Society (2005)
13. Mokbel, M.F., Chow, C.-Y., Aref, W.G.: The new Casper: query processing for location services without compromising privacy. In: Proceedings of VLDB, pp. 763–774. VLDB Endowment (2006)
14. Zhang, J.-D., Chow, C.-Y.: GeoSoCa: exploiting geographical, social and categorical correlations for point-of-interest recommendations. In: Proceedings of ACM SIGIR, pp. 443–452. ACM (2015)
15. Zhang, J.D., Chow, C.Y.: CoRe: exploiting the personalized influence of two-dimensional geographic coordinates for location recommendations. Inf. Sci. **293**, 163–181 (2015)

16. Zhang, J.-D., Chow, C.-Y., Li, Y.: LORE: exploiting sequential influence for location recommendations. In: Proceedings of ACM SIGSPATIAL, pp. 103–112. ACM (2014)
17. Zhao, Y.-L., Nie, L., Wang, X., Chua, T.-S.: Personalized recommendations of locally interesting venues to tourists via cross-region community matching. ACM Trans. Intell. Syst. Technol. 5(3), 50:1–50:26 (2014)
18. Liu, Y., Wei, W., Sun, A., Miao, C.: Exploiting geographical neighborhood characteristics for location recommendation. In: Proceedings of ACM CIKM, pp. 739–748. ACM (2014)
19. Liu, X., Liu, Y., Aberer, K., Miao, C.: Personalized point-of-interest recommendation by mining users' preference transition. In: Proceedings of CIKM, pp. 733–738. ACM (2013)
20. Longke, H., Sun, A., Liu, Y.: Your neighbors affect your ratings: on geographical neighborhood influence to rating prediction. In: Proceedings of ACM SIGIR, pp. 345–354. ACM (2014)

An Extended Chaotic Maps Based Authenticated Key Agreement Protocol Without Using Password

Xiong Li[1($\boxtimes$)], Junguo Liao[1], Wei Liang[1], and Jingqiang Zhao[2]

[1] School of Computer Science and Engineering,
Hunan University of Science and Technology, Xiangtan 411201, China
lixiongzhq@163.com
[2] Network and Information Center, Hunan University of Science and Technology,
Xiangtan 411201, China

Abstract. Chaotic maps have been used in the design of cryptosystem due to its excellent properties. Recently, researchers have proposed many authenticated key agreement protocols based on the chaotic maps. However, most of those protocols use the password to achieve the key agreement, and it will lead some security problems. First, the server has to store a sensitive verification table, and it is dangerous if the server has been compromised or the verification table was stolen. Besides, the low entropy passwords are vulnerable to some password related attacks, such as insider attack and password guessing attack. To resolve the aforementioned problems, this paper propose an extended chaotic maps based authenticated key agreement protocol without using password, where the server just needs to maintain a master secret key and the user just needs to hold a secret key, then they can achieve the key agreement. Compared with other related protocols, the proposed protocol not only keeps the efficiency, but also enhances the security. So, it is more suitable for client/server environment.

Keywords: Chaotic maps · Key agreement · Authentication · Password

1 Introduction

Along with the development of the information and communication technology, security problem has become an important issue in many applications such as wireless mesh networks [1], wireless sensor networks [2] and cloud computing [3]. Chaotic systems have features of randomness and ergodicity, and the output is sensitive to initial condition that a tiny change and disturbance in the current trajectory will lead to significant difference of the subsequent states. These features of the chaotic systems just meet the confusion and diffusion principles of

---

This work was supported by the National Natural Science Foundation of China under Grant Nos. 61300220, 61572013 and 61572188, and the Scientific Research Fund of Hunan Provincial Education Department under Grant Nos. 16B089 and 10C0688.

X. Sun et al. (Eds.): ICCCS 2016, Part I, LNCS 10039, pp. 421–431, 2016.
DOI: 10.1007/978-3-319-48671-0_37

the design of cryptosystem, and chaotic systems are widely used in the design of cryptosystem, such as in symmetric cryptographic algorithm, hash function and stream cipher.

Due to its low computational complexity and easy to be implemented, symmetric cryptography is widely used for the secure of network communications. However, in symmetric cryptography based communication systems, encryption key and decryption key are the same or easily to get one from another. Therefore, how to generate a secret key and share it between two communication parties become an important issue in information security. Authenticated key agreement protocol can solve this problem which allows two communication parties agree on a shared secret key through the open network, and the shared secret key can be used to guarantee the secure of the following communications. Since Diffie and Hellman proposed the first key exchange protocol over an insecure channel [4], many key agreement protocols based on traditional public key cryptography have been proposed [5–8]. Recently, due to the excellent cryptographic properties of chaotic systems, researchers have designed some chaotic maps based key agreement protocols. In 2007, Xiao et al. [9] proposed an authenticated key agreement protocol based on the semi-group property of chaotic maps. However, Han [10] pointed out the weaknesses of Xiao et al.'s protocol [9] that an adversary can block a user and a server to agree on a session key even if the adversary has not any secret information of the user and the server. Besides, Xiang et al. [11] found Xiao et al.'s protocol [9] is vulnerable to stolen verifier attack and offline password guess attack. Later, Xiao et al. [12] presented two chaotic maps based authenticated key agreement protocols, where one is utilized the timestamp, and the another is not used the timestamp. In 2009, Tseng et al. proposed a chaotic maps based authenticated key agreement protocol with user anonymity [13]. However, Niu and Wang [14] found that Tseng et al.'s protocol [13] cannot achieve user anonymity really, and it also cannot resist man-in-the-middle attack. To address the security weaknesses of Tseng et al.'s protocol [13], Niu and Wang [14] proposed an enhanced authenticated key agreement protocol based on chaotic maps. However, Yoon [15] pointed out that Niu and Wang's protocol [14] is inefficient since it uses traversal method to identify user's identity, and their protocol is vulnerable to denial-of-service attack. To enhance the security, Yoon [15] proposed an improved protocol. Almost at the same time, Xue and Hong [16] also pointed out the weaknesses of Niu and Wang's [14] protocol, and they designed an enhanced one. However, Xue and Hong's protocol [16] was found cannot achieve user anonymity and it suffers from man-in-the-middle attack. Recently, Lee et al. [17] indicated that Xiao et al.'s protocol [9] cannot resist stolen verifier attack and offline password guessing attack, and they proposed an improved authenticated key agreement protocol based on chaotic maps. However Lee et al.'s protocol [17] was found cannot resist insider attack and denial-of-service attack [18]. Most of above mentioned authenticated key agreement protocols using chaotic maps for client/server environments are designed based on the smart card. Although smart card based protocols are easy to implement, the cost of tamper-proof smart card is still high. In 2010, Guo and Zhang [19] proposed a chaotic maps based authenticated key agreement protocol without using smart card, it has low computational costs, but it was found cannot resist stolen verifier attack. Gong et al. [20] also proposed a chaotic maps based authenticated key agreement protocol without using smart card, but it is pointed out cannot resist stolen verifier attack [21]. Recently, Shu [22] proposed a new chaotic maps based authenticated key agreement protocol without using smart card, it keeps high computational efficiency with clever design. However, it is vulnerable to insider attack and stolen verifier attack. Most of aforementioned protocols achieve key agreement between user and server by using password, and a password related verification table should be stored in the server side. In this type of protocols, it will face huge security threats if the server was compromised or the verification table was stolen. Besides, the low entropy passwords are often vulnerable to password related attacks, such as insider attack and password guessing attack. In order to resolve these security problems, an extended chaotic maps based authenticated key agreement protocol without using password is proposed in this paper, where the server only needs to maintain a system master secret key and the user just needs to hold a secret information to agree on a shared session key between them. Analysis shows that compared with other related protocols, the proposed protocol keeps computational efficiency and improves the security.

The rest of the paper are arranged as follows. Section 2 introduces some preliminaries about Chebyshev chaotic maps. Shu's chaotic maps based authenticated key agreement protocol is reviewed in Sect. 3, and the corresponding security weaknesses are analyzed also in this section. The proposed chaotic maps based authenticated key agreement protocol and its security analysis are given in Sects. 4 and 5, respectively. At last, we conclude the full paper in Sect. 6.

2   Chebyshev Chaotic Maps

In this section, some preliminaries about Chebyshev chaotic maps, and the corresponding chaotic maps based intractable problems are introduced.

Definition 1. Chebyshev polynomial. Let n be an integer, and x be a variable belonging to the interval $[-1, 1]$. The Chebyshev polynomial $T_n(x) : [-1, 1] \to [-1, 1]$ is defined as $T_n(x) = \cos(n \cdot \arccos(x))$.

According to the Definition 1, the Chebyshev polynomial satisfies the following recursive relationship: $T_n(x) = 2xT_{n-1}(x) - T_{n-2}(x)$, $n \geq 2$, where the initial conditions $T_0(x) = 1$, $T_1(x) = x$, and the first few Chebyshev polynomials are: $T_2(x) = 2x^2 - 1$, $T_3(x) = 4x^3 - 3x$, $T_4(x) = 8x^4 - 8x^2 + 1$, $T_5(x) = 16x^5 - 20x^3 + 5x$.

Definition 2. Chaotic property of Chebyshev polynomials. When $n > 1$, the Chebyshev polynomial map $T_n(x) : [-1, 1] \to [-1, 1]$ of degree n is a chaotic map with invariant density $f^*(x) = 1/(\pi\sqrt{1 - x^2})$ for positive Lyapunov exponent $\lambda = \ln n > 0$.

Definition 3. Semi-group property of Chebyshev polynomials. $T_r(T_s(x)) = \cos(r\cos^{-1}(\cos(s\cos^{-1}(x)))) = \cos(rs\cos^{-1}(x)) = T_{sr}(x) = T_s(T_r(x))$, where r and s are two positive integers, and $x \in [-1, 1]$.

Zhang [23] further demonstrated that the semi-group property holds for Chebyshev polynomials on the interval $(-\infty, +\infty)$, which can enhance the property as follows: $T_n(x) = (2xT_{n-1}(x) - T_{n-2}(x)) \bmod p$, where $n \geq 2$, $x \in (-\infty, +\infty)$, and p is a large prime number.

Therefore, $T_r(T_s(x)) \equiv T_{rs}(x) \equiv T_{sr}(x) \equiv T_s(T_r(x)) \bmod p$.

Definition 4. Chaotic maps based discrete logarithm problem (DLP): Given parameters x and y, DLP is to find an integer r such that $T_r(x) = y$.

Definition 5. Chaotic maps based Diffie-Hellman problem (DHP): Given x, $T_r(x)$ and $T_s(x)$, DHP is to compute the value $T_{rs}(x)$.

It is generally believed that these two problems are intractable, i.e., there are no polynomial-time algorithms to solve these problems with non-negligible probability, and it provides the possibility to design information security protocols using these two intractable problems.

3   Review and Cryptanalysis of Shu's Protocol

In this section, we first review Shu's chaotic maps based authenticated key agreement protocol [22], and then analyze its security weaknesses.

3.1   Review of Shu's Protocol

Shu's protocol [22] contains two phases, i.e. the registration phase and authentication phase.

Registration Phase. When a user U_i wants to register as a valid user, he/she needs to interact with server S as follows:
Step 1: User U_i chooses an identity ID_i and a low entropy password PW_i, and then sends (ID_i, PW_i) to the server S via a secure channel.
Step 2: The server S computes $S_i = H(ID_i \| PW_i)$, and stores (ID_i, S_i) into server list L.
Step 3: S submits a hash function $H(\cdot)$ to user U_i.

Authentication Phase. In order to agree on a shared session key, the following steps should be performed between the user U_i and the server S:
Step 1: U_i inputs a password PW_i, and computes $P_i = H(ID_i \| PW_i)$. Meanwhile, U_i chooses a random integer x and a large prime number P, and computes $X = T_x(P_i) \bmod P$. Then, U_i submits message $M_1 = \{ID_i, X, P\}$ to server S.
Step 2: When receiving the message M_1, S acquires S_i by checking the list L according to identity ID_i. Then S chooses a random integer y, and computes $Y = T_y(S_i) \bmod P$, $K_B = T_y(x) \bmod P$, $MAC_1 = H(Y, K_B)$. At last, S sends the message $M_2 = \{Y, MAC_1\}$ to user U_i.

Step 3: Upon receiving the message M_2, U_i computes $K_A = T_x(Y) \bmod P$, and checks whether $H(Y, K_A) = MAC_1$. If they are not equal, the session is terminated by U_i. Otherwise, if they are equal, S is authenticated by U_i. Then, U_i computes $MAC_2 = H(X, Y, K_A)$, $SK_A = H(K_A)$, and submits $M_3 = \{MAC_2\}$ to the server S.

Step 4: When receiving the message M_3, S verifies whether $H(X, Y, K_B) = MAC_2$. If the equation does not hold, the session is stopped by S. Otherwise, U_i is authenticated by S. At last, S computes the session key $SK_B = H(K_B)$.

3.2 Cryptanalysis of Shu's Protocol

In this subsection, we show that Shu's protocol [22] is vulnerable to insider attack and stolen verifier attack.

Insider Attack. In real-world applications, people usually use same identity and password to access different services since it is hard for people to remember so many identities and passwords for different services. However, if the system administrator or privileged insider obtains user's identity and password, he/she can impersonate the user to login to other services where the user had registered using the same identity and password. Generally, in order to avoid insider attack, user's password cannot be transmitted as plaintext form in any phase of the protocol. However, in the registration phase of Shu's protocol, U_i submits the password PW_i as plaintext form to server S. So the system administrator or privileged insider can get the user's identity and password, and Shu's protocol [22] is suffer from insider attack.

Stolen Verifier Attack. In authentication and key agreement protocols, server usually needs to store a user related verification table to verify the validity of the user. Generally, the verification table stores user's password or hashed password. However, if the server was compromised or the verification table was stolen, it will face serious security problems. In Shu's protocol [22], the verification table stores user U_i's information (ID_i, S_i), where $S_i = H(ID_i \| PW_i)$. If the verification table L was stolen, an adversary can guess the user's real password PW_i by using password guessing attack, and then he/she can impersonate as the user U_i to negotiate a session key with server S using the guessed password. Besides, the adversary can impersonate any user to negotiate a session key with server S using the stolen verification table. Here, we illustrate this attack that the adversary A impersonates user U_j to share a session key with server when he/she gets the verification table L. First, A finds out data pair (ID_j, S_j) from the verification table L, and then he/she performs the following interaction with server S:

Step 1: The adversary A generates a random integer x' and a large prime number P', and computes $X' = T'_x(S_j) \bmod P'$. Then A submits message $M'_1 = \{ID_j, X', P'\}$ to server S.

Step 2: When receiving the message M_1', S acquires S_j from verification table L according the identity ID_j. Then S generates a random integer y', and computes $Y' = T_y'(S_j) \bmod P'$, $K_B' = T_y'(X') \bmod P'$, $MAC_1' = H(Y', K_B')$. At last, S submits the message $M_2' = \{Y', MAC_1'\}$ to A.

Step 3: When A receiving the message M_2', he/she computes $K_A' = T_x'(Y') \bmod P'$, and gets the equation $H(Y', K_A') = MAC_1'$. Then A computes $MAC_2' = H(X', Y', K_A')$ and a session key $SK_A' = H(K_A')$. At last, A submits $M_3' = \{MAC_2'\}$ to S.

Step 4: When receiving the message M_3', S can verify the equation $H(X', Y', K_B') = MAC_2'$ is hold. Then, S computes a session key $SK_B' = H(K_B')$.

From the above description, we can see that the adversary A can impersonate as a user U_j to agree a session key $H(T_{x'y'}(S_j) \bmod P')$ with server S if he/she obtained the verification table of the server, and Shu's protocol [22] is vulnerable to stolen-verifier attack.

4   The Prosed Extended Chaotic Maps Based Authenticated Key Agreement Protocol

In this section, we propose a new extended chaotic maps based authenticated key agreement protocol without using password. Compared with other related protocols, the user does not need a password to achieve the key agreement with the server. So, it not only can avoid the password related attacks, such as insider attack and password guessing attack, but also can avoid stolen verifier attack since there are not any verification table stored in server side. The proposed protocol contains two phase, i.e. the initialization phase and authentication and key agreement phase.

4.1   Initialization Phase

In this phase, server S chooses the system parameters and accepts the registration of users. We assume that the communication channel between user and server is secure in this phase. First, server S chooses a high entropy random number x as the master secret key of the system, and generates a larger prime number p. Then, S generates a random seed X of a Chebeshev polynomial. Besides, S chooses a hash function $h(\cdot)$, and a symmetric cryptographic encryption/decryption algorithms pair $E_k(\cdot)/D_k(\cdot)$. At last, the server publishes the system parameters $\{p, X, H(\cdot), E_k(\cdot)/D_k(\cdot)\}$.

When user U_A wants register as a valid user of the system, he/she chooses the identity ID_A freely, and submits ID_A to server S for registration. S first checks the validity of ID_A, if it is repeated with the identities of the database, U_A is requested to choose a new identity. If ID_A is valid, S computes $h(ID_A\|x)$, and sends it to U_A via a secure channel. U_A should store the secret information $h(ID_A\|x)$ securely, and cannot reveal it to any other entities.

4.2 Authentication and Key Agreement Phase

In order to share a session key with server S, U_A and S need perform the following steps.

Step 1: $U_A \rightarrow S : \{ID_A, M_1\}$

U_A generates a random number a, and computes $K_A = T_a(X) \bmod p$, $M_1 = E_{h(ID_A\|x)}(ID_A, K_A)$. Then, U_A submits $\{ID_A, M_1\}$ to server S.

Step 2: $S \rightarrow U_A : \{M_2\}$

When receiving the message $\{ID_A, M_1\}$, server S first checks whether ID_A in the database. If so, S computes $h(ID_A\|x)$, $D_{h(ID_A\|x)}(M_1) = (ID_A, K_A)$. When gets (ID_A, K_A), the server S can check the validity of ID_A again. Then, S chooses a random number b, and computes $K_S = T_b(X) \bmod p$, $SK = T_b(K_A) \bmod p$, $H_S = h(K_S\|SK)$, $M_2 = E_{h(ID_A\|x)}(K_S, H_S)$, and submits $\{M_2\}$ to U_A.

Step 3: $U_A \rightarrow S : \{M_3\}$

Upon receiving the message $\{M_2\}$, U_A computes $D_{h(ID_A\|x)}(M_2) = (K_S, H_S)$, $SK' = T_a(K_S) \bmod p$, $H_S' = h(K_S\|SK')$, and checks whether H_S' equals to H_S. If they are not equal, U_A terminates the session. Otherwise, server S is authenticated by U_A. Then, U_A computes $M_3 = h(K_A\|K_S\|SK')$, and sends $\{M_3\}$ to server S.

Step 4: When receiving the message $\{M_3\}$, server S computes $M_3' = h(K_A\|K_S\|SK)$, and verifies whether M_3' equals to M_3. If they are not equal, the session is terminated by server S. Otherwise, S is authenticated by U_A.

Because $T_b(K_A) \bmod p = T_b(T_a(X)) \bmod p = T_{ab}(X) \bmod p = T_a(T_b(X)) \bmod p = T_a(K_S) \bmod p$, U_A and S share a session key $SK' = T_{ab}(X) \bmod p = SK$ at last.

5 Analysis of the Proposed Protocol

In this section, the security and performance features of the proposed protocol are analyzed, and the comparisons with other related protocols are given.

5.1 Perfect Forward Secrecy

In the proposed protocol, the generation of the shared session key $SK = T_{ab}(X) \bmod p$ between U_A and S is relied on the random numbers a and b, where they are generated by U_A and S, respectively. Obviously, the adversary can eavesdrop the message $\{ID_A, M_1\}$, $\{M_2\}$ and $\{M_3\}$ from the public channel. We suppose that the system master secret key x is compromised by the adversary, then he/she can decrypt $\{M_1\}$ and $\{M_2\}$ to get K_A and K_S. However, in order to calculate the session key $SK = T_{ab}(X) \bmod p$, the adversary has to solve chaotic maps based discrete logarithm problem and chaotic maps based Diffie-Hellman problem. Therefore, the proposed protocol has the property of perfect forward secrecy.

5.2 Known-Key Security

If the session key of current session cannot be compromised by an adversary even though he/she already know other session keys beyond of this session, we can say that the protocol has the property of known-key security. In the proposed protocol, the session key $SK = T_{ab}(X) \bmod p$ is relied on the random numbers a and b, which are generated by user and server, respectively. Since the random numbers a and b in one session are different from those of other sessions, and they are just valid for only one session. Therefore, the known of other session keys have no use to reveal the session key of current session, and the proposed protocol has the property of known-key security.

5.3 Mutual Authentication

In the authentication and key agreement phase, when receiving the message $\{M_2\}$, U_A decrypts $\{M_2\}$ by using the secret key $h(ID_A\|x)$ to get (K_S, H_S), and computes $SK' = T_a(K_S) \bmod p$, $H'_S = h(K_S\|S'_K)$. Then U_A can verify the validity of S by check whether $H'_S = H_S$. On the contrary, when receiving the message $\{M_3\}$ from U_A, S computes $M'_3 = h(K_A\|K_S\|SK)$, and can authenticate U_A by check whether $M'_3 = M_3$. Therefore, the proposed protocol achieves the feature of mutual authentication between the user and the server.

5.4 Resist Replay Attack

In the proposed protocol, random number method is used to assure the freshness of the messages and resist replay attack. In order to impersonate as user U_A by using replay attack, the adversary replays U_A's previous used message $\{ID_A, M_1\}$, and the adversary would receive S's response message M_2. However, the adversary cannot generate the valid mutual authentication message M_3 without known U_A's secret key $h(ID_A\|x)$. Besides, the new random numbers a and b are generated for each session, so the replayed message M_2 cannot pass the authentication of user. Therefore, the proposed protocol is free from replay attack.

5.5 Resist Impersonation Attack

In the proposed protocol, the messages exchanged between U_A and S are encrypted by the secret key $h(ID_A\|x)$, where $h(ID_A\|x)$ is hold by U_A secretly, and can be calculated by S using ID_A and x. Any adversary cannot impersonate as the user U_A without known the secret key $h(ID_A\|x)$. Meanwhile, without known the system master secret key x, any adversary cannot impersonate as the server to communicate with the user. Therefore, the proposed protocol can resist impersonation attack.

5.6   Resist Password Related Attacks

In password based authenticated key agreement protocols, the server has to store user's password table or hashed password table, and the verification table becomes a main object of attack. The compromise of the server or the stolen of the verification table will deduce serious security problems. Besides, in password based authenticated key agreement protocols, the low entropy password is vulnerable to password related attack, such as password guessing attack and insider attack. However, the proposed protocol does not rely on the password to achieve the key agreement, and the server does not need to store user's password table or hashed table. In the proposed protocol, the server only needs to maintain a system master secret key x and the user U_A just needs to hold a secret information $h(ID_A\|x)$, and then they can complete the key agreement. Therefore, the proposed protocol is free from password related attacks.

5.7   Analysis and Comparisons of Performance

In order to analyze the computational cost of authenticated key agreement protocol, the following notations are defined. Compared with other operations, the time cost of X-OR operation is ignorable, and we omit this operation in the analysis and comparisons of performance.

T_C: the time cost of one Chebeshev polynomial operation;
T_H: the time cost of one hash operation;
T_E: the time cost of one symmetrical encryption/decryption operation.

Generally, T_C is far great than T_E and T_H. According to reference [24], under the environment of 2.4 GHz Intel Core i5 CPU and 4.0 G RAM, T_C, T_E and T_H are 32.9 ms, 0.042 ms and 0.02 ms, respectively.

The security and performance comparisons of the proposed protocol with other related protocols are shown in Table 1. From Table 1, we can see that the proposed protocol almost in the same level in total computation costs with other

Table 1. Performance and security comparisons with other related protocols

	GZ protocol [19]	GLS protocol [20]	Shu's protocol [22]	Our protocol
User computational cost	$2T_C + 4T_H$	$2T_C + 4T_H$	$2T_C + 4T_H$	$2T_C + 2T_H + 2T_E$
	65.88 ms	65.88 ms	65.88 ms	65.924 ms
Server computational cost	$2T_C + 5T_H$	$2T_C + 3T_H$	$2T_C + 3T_H$	$2T_C + 3T_H + 2T_E$
	65.9 ms	65.86 ms	65.86 ms	65.944 ms
Total computational cost	$4T_C + 9T_H$	$4T_C + 7T_H$	$4T_C + 7T_H$	$4T_C + 5T_H + 4T_E$
	131.78 ms	131.74 ms	131.74 ms	131.87 ms
Mutual authentication	Yes	Yes	Yes	Yes
Perfect forward secrecy	Yes	Yes	Yes	Yes
Known-key security	Yes	Yes	Yes	Yes
Resist replay attack	Yes	Yes	Yes	Yes
Resist insider attack	Yes	Yes	No	Yes
Resist password guessing attack	No	No	Yes	Yes
Resist stolen verifier attack	No	No	No	Yes

related protocols. However, GZ protocol [19], GLS protocol [20] and Shu's protocol [22] are all based on password, the server has to store a security sensitive verification table. So, GZ protocol [19] and GLS protocol [20] are both vulnerable to password guessing attack and stolen verifier attack, and Shu's protocol [22] is vulnerable to insider attack and stolen verifier attack. However, in the proposed protocol, the server only needs to store the user's identity information and the user just needs to store a secret key to achieve the key agreement. It not only can reduce the possibility the server to be attacked, but can also avoid password related attacks. Therefore, the proposed protocol is more secure than other related protocols.

6   Conclusions

This paper analyzed the security weaknesses of Shu's extended chaotic maps based authenticated key agreement protocol [22], and pointed out that his protocol is vulnerable to insider attack and stolen verifier attack. In order to resolve the security flaws of password based authenticated key agreement protocol, this paper proposed a new extended chaotic maps based authenticated key agreement protocol without using password. In the proposed protocol, the server does not needs to maintain a password table and the user just needs to store a secret information, and then they can complete the key agreement process. Compared with other related protocols, our protocol has the same computational complexity. However, the proposed protocol is free from stolen verifier attack, insider attack and password guessing attack, and is more security than other related protocols. Therefore, the proposed protocol is more fit for client/server environments.

References

1. Guo, P., Wang, J., Li, B., Lee, S.Y.: A variable threshold-value authentication architecture for wireless mesh networks. J. Internet Technol. 15(6), 929–936 (2014)
2. Shen, J., Tan, H.W., Wang, J., Wang, J.W., Lee, S.Y.: A novel routing protocol providing good transmission reliability in underwater sensor networks. J. Internet Technol. 16(1), 171–178 (2015)
3. Ren, Y.J., Shen, J., Wang, J., Han, J., Lee, S.Y.: Mutual verifiable provable data auditing in public cloud storage. J. Internet Technol. 16(2), 317–323 (2015)
4. Diffie, W., Hellman, M.E.: New directions in cryptography. IEEE Trans. Inf. Theor. 22(6), 644–654 (1976)
5. Xiong, H., Chen, Z., Li, F.: New identity-based three-party authenticated key agreement protocol with provable security. J. Netw. Comput. Appl. 36(2), 927–932 (2013)
6. He, D., Padhye, S., Chen, J.: An efficient certificateless two-party authenticated key agreement protocol. Comput. Math. Appl. 64(6), 1914–1926 (2012)
7. Hölbl, M., Welzer, T., Brumen, B.: An improved two-party identity-based authenticated key agreement protocol using pairings. J. Comput. Syst. Sci. 78(1), 142–150 (2012)

8. He, D., Chen, J., Hu, J.: An ID-based client authentication with key agreement protocol for mobile client-server environment on ECC with provable security. Inf. Fusion **13**(3), 223–230 (2012)
9. Xiao, D., Liao, X., Deng, S.: A novel key agreement protocol based on chaotic maps. Inf. Sci. **177**(4), 1136–1142 (2007)
10. Han, S.: Security of a key agreement protocol based on chaotic maps. Chaos, Solitons Fractals **38**(3), 764–768 (2008)
11. Xiang, T., Wong, K.W., Liao, X.: On the security of a novel key agreement protocol based on chaotic maps. Chaos, Solitons Fractals **40**(2), 672–675 (2009)
12. Xiao, D., Liao, X., Deng, S.: Using time-stamp to improve the security of a chaotic maps-based key agreement protocol. Inf. Sci. **178**(6), 1598–1602 (2008)
13. Tseng, H.R., Jan, R.H., Yang, W.: A chaotic maps-based key agreement protocol that preserves user anonymity. In: Proceedings of 2009 IEEE International Conference on Communications (ICC 2009), pp. 1–6. IEEE, June 2009
14. Niu, Y., Wang, X.: An anonymous key agreement protocol based on chaotic maps. Commun. Nonlinear Sci. Numer. Simul. **16**(4), 1986–1992 (2011)
15. Yoon, E.J.: Efficiency and security problems of anonymous key agreement protocol based on chaotic maps. Commun. Nonlinear Sci. Numer. Simul. **17**(7), 2735–2740 (2012)
16. Xue, K., Hong, P.: Security improvement on an anonymous key agreement protocol based on chaotic maps. Commun. Nonlinear Sci. Numer. Simul. **17**(7), 2969–2977 (2012)
17. Lee, C.C., Chen, C.L., Wu, C.Y., Huang, S.Y.: An extended chaotic maps-based key agreement protocol with user anonymity. Nonlinear Dyn. **69**(1–2), 79–87 (2012)
18. He, D., Chen, Y., Chen, J.: Cryptanalysis and improvement of an extended chaotic maps-based key agreement protocol. Nonlinear Dyn. **69**(3), 1149–1157 (2012)
19. Guo, X., Zhang, J.: Secure group key agreement protocol based on chaotic hash. Inf. Sci. **180**(20), 4069–4074 (2010)
20. Gong, P., Li, P., Shi, W.: A secure chaotic maps-based key agreement protocol without using smart cards. Nonlinear Dyn. **70**(4), 2401–2406 (2012)
21. Wang, X.Y., Luan, D.P.: A secure key agreement protocol based on chaotic maps. Chin. Phys. B **22**(11), 110503 (2013)
22. Shu, J.: An authenticated key agreement protocol based on extended chaotic maps. Acta Phys. Sinica **63**(5), 050507 (2014)
23. Zhang, L.: Cryptanalysis of the public key encryption based on multiple chaotic systems. Chaos, Solitons Fractals **37**(3), 669–674 (2008)
24. Jabbari, A., Bagherzadeh, J.: A revised key agreement protocol based on chaotic maps. Nonlinear Dyn. **78**(1), 669–680 (2014)

A Privacy-Preserving Online Reverse Multi-attributes Auction Scheme Based on Degree-Matching

Mingfan Ma[1], Jun Gao[1], Ning Lu[2], and Wenbo Shi[2(✉)]

[1] Department of Computer Science and Engineering,
Northeastern University, Shenyang, China
[2] School of Computer and Communication Engineering,
Northeastern University at Qinhuangdao, Qinhuangdao, China
swb319@hotmail.com

Abstract. In recent years, online auction system obtains the widespread application with the vigorous development of e-commerce. During the process of an auction, numbers of qualified suppliers propose their own bidding according to procurements demands. Then the winner is generated by comparing and sorting all of degree-matching between procurers ideal solution and suppliers' bidding, we remind it as Ideal Degree-Matching Determined Solution (IDDS). IDDS requires suppliers to provide their private information to the auction servers. However, suppliers usually do not expect the real information of the bid leaked out, especially known by other competitors. In this paper we propose a Privacy-Preserving Online Reverse Multi-Attributes Auction Scheme based on Degree-Matching (PRMA). IDDS is used as the basis of determining the auction winner. Impressively based on the difficulty of integer factorization assumption, our scheme ensures data security of all suppliers. Compared with previous work, our scheme also gains higher security performance by eliminating the participation of third party.

Keywords: Reverse multi-attribute auction · Privacy-preserving · Degree-matching · Integer factorization assumption

1 Introduction

E-commerce has made considerable progress with the rapid development of the Internet. As one of the important part of e-commerce, theoretical research about the electronic auction has achieved fruitful results [1]. In terms of the bidding form, online auction can be divided into two categories: increasing bidding and decreasing bidding. English auction is the most common form of increasing auction [2], in which the auctioneer opens the auction by announcing a Suggested Opening Bid, a starting price or reserve for the item on sale and then accepts increasingly higher bids from the floor consisting of buyers with possible interests in the item. Decreasing bidding auctions have a series of types including reverse

© Springer International Publishing AG 2016
X. Sun et al. (Eds.): ICCCS 2016, Part I, LNCS 10039, pp. 432–442, 2016.
DOI: 10.1007/978-3-319-48671-0_38

auctions, Dutch auctions and first-price sealed-bid (FPSB), or sometimes even a combination of multiple auctions, taking elements of one and forging them with another. On the other hand, auction protocols can be classified into two types: one-sided auction and two-sided auction. A single seller (or buyer) accepts bids from multiple buyers (or seller) in one-sided auction protocols, and multiple buyers and sellers are permitted to bid/ask for designated goods in two-sided or double auction protocols [3–6]. FPSB and reverse auction are both becoming a mainstream way of purchasing for government and enterprises, which is benefited from the change that the global market to a buyer's market, wide application of Business-to-Business and the comprehensive upgrade of logistics industry [7]. In FPSB all bidders simultaneously submit sealed bids so that no bidder knows the bid of other participants. The highest bidder pays the price they submitted. Sealed first-price auctions are commonly used in tending, particularly for government contracts and auctions for mining leases. Sealed-bid second-price auction, also known as Vickrey auction, is identical to the FPSB except that the winning bidder pays the second-highest bid rather than his own. The most obvious disadvantages of the Vickrey auction are the complexity of the problem it poses to bidders: the reluctance of bidders to reveal their values, and the strategic issues posed by budget constraints. But Vickrey auctions are still important in auction theory, and commonly used in automated contexts such as real-time bidding for online advertising [8].

With the development of market demands, price is not only factor of determining auction winner. To filter suppliers by a variety of attributes and reduce the likelihood of nonperformance, the buyer may have to use multi-attribute reverse auction (MARA) to determine a winner based on price and non-price attributes. In contrast to the price-oriented reverse auctions, MARA leads to a more satisfying outcome through effective information exchange between buyer's preferences and suppliers' offerings. Naturally, MARA has been widely used for the centralized procurements of large enterprise groups [9,10]. For instance, we will take it not only the price but also memory and hard disk capacity and other properties into account when purchasing a computer; when the building company is going to purchase building materials, price is not only considered, but also quality and transportation costs.

In addition to the functionality and efficiency, security issue is also one of the main issues of online auction protocol. Technologies like one-to-many authentication [11], encrypted outsourced data search [12], key-management [13], one-to-many authentication social network based augment collaborative recommender system [14] and multi-keyword ranked search [15] are proposed to ensure the process confidential and to avoid malicious tampering. So far for the MARA related research is still very lacking. Srinath et al. [16] proposed a simple MARA protocol, which uses score function to compute the rank of bidding and the digital pseudonym generation algorithm from [17] to implement the anonymity in bidding process. The bid privacy is weak because bids need to be opened and computed according to score function, it does not provide bid privacy after the biding phase. Later, Srinath et al. [18] adopts ElGamal cryptosystem and range protocol from the protocol of Parkes *et al.* [19] to achieve bid privacy and public verifiability. However, this protocol has low efficiency because there are too much communication rounds, and the involvement of the third party also reduces the security. In [16,18,19], winner determination secure computation of qualitative-attribute-based bid structure is analyzed and solved. Still, we need to consider and solve winner determination secure computation problem of qualitative-attribute-based bid structure from the perspective of information security.

In this paper, we design a PRMA scheme using thoughts of interest matching. Zhu *et al.* [20] proposed an Efficient Weight-based Private Matching Scheme for mobile social networks (EWPM) using confusion matrix transformation algorithm, which carries out private matching with consideration of both the number of common interests and the related weights on them. We get the idea from EWPM and have made some pivotal improvements to get the rank of the bidding. The main contributions of our scheme are shown as follows:

a. The auction winner is decided by securely calculating all of the degree-matching between the buyer's ideal bidding and the optional bidding submitted by suppliers, whose idea is similar to interest matching. And trusted third party is not involved in our scheme.
b. The attribute weight is taken into account in auction process which can measure the relative importance of attributes. Moreover, a classification method is also designed in information matrix so that we can calculate bidding ranking scores in case the attribute sets submitted by bidders simultaneously having qualitative and quantitative based attributes.

The organization of the paper is as follows. Section 2 presents the preliminaries of the algorithm. Then we will present PRMA scheme and some security analysis in Sect. 3. Finally, Sect. 4 concludes this paper.

2   Preliminaries

2.1   Problem Statement

There is a purchaser initiating a bidding in an online MARA platform, n of suppliers supply optional schemes which can form the set $P = \{p_1, p_2, ..., p_n\}$, each of p_i has m of different attributes that also is a set $A = \{a_1, a_2, ..., a_m\}$. a_i denotes different attributes in A. A has a corresponding weight set $W = \{w_1, w_2, ..., w_m\}$ to weight the attributes in one bidding, satisfying $\sum_{i=1}^{m} w_i = 1$. $W(a_i)$ is the weighted attribute for a_i. By sorting $W(a_i)$ with score function f, we compute and select the winner who has the highest scores, namely $f_{\max}(W(a_i))$. However, every partial process of this auction could be tampered maliciously because it's all on the status of plaintext. Both the purchaser and bidders want to bid in a safe and fair environment. As shown in Fig. 1, our proposed scheme in semi-honest model not only can determine the bidding winner but also ensure the fairness and privacy in the bidding process. Firstly, buyer generates an ideal

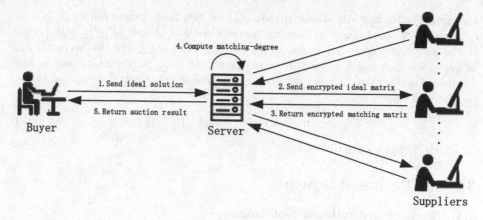

Fig. 1. The diagram of PRMA

matrix consists of encrypted and weighted attributes and sends it to the auction server. Then every supplier calculates the matching matrix according to encrypted ideal matrix and returns it to the server. Next, sever calculates and sorts all of the degree-matching between the ideal bidding and the optional bidding. Finally the sever will publish the bidding results and the buyer can choose the optimal bidding as the winner. In the following, we are going to introduce some prior knowledge which will be helpful in reading this paper.

2.2   Semi-honest Model

In the semi-honest model, all parties are assumed to perform computations and send messages according to their prescribed actions in the protocol. They may record all information from the protocol execution and try to infer as much information as possible in the process of the protocol, but the intermediate results in the process of the protocol cannot be modified [21]. Based on the semi-honest models, we define the following privacy levels.

Definition 1. Level-I privacy: when the protocol ends, clients learn nothing about the information matrix of ideal scheme, and sever also learns nothing about the information matrix of alternative scheme.

2.3   Integer Factorization [22]

For $\forall N \in (0, +\infty)$, the problem of integer factorization is to find out all prime factors of N that can be described mathematically as:

$$N = p_1^{e_1} p_2^{e_2} ... p_l^{e_l} \tag{1}$$

p_i is a distinct prime number which satisfies $p_1 < p_2 < ... < p_l$ and $e_i \geq 1$.

Integer Factorization Assumption. Given two large prime numbers P and Q having the same length, then we have $N = P * Q$ and $|P|_2 = |Q|_2 = \lambda$. If the adversary does not know $\varphi(N) = (P-1) * (Q-1)$, this assumption is based on that finding out the prime factor of N in polynomial time is not feasible. Furthermore, for any adversary A's advantage Adv_A^{IFP} in probabilistic polynomial time:

$$Adv_A^{IFP} := \Pr[(A(N) = s) \wedge (s \in \{[P,Q]\} \leq l(\lambda) \tag{2}$$

In which $l(\lambda)$ is a negligible value.

3   Our Proposed Scheme

3.1   Some of Instantiated Notations

In our scheme, a public vector of quantitative and qualitative attributes needs to be pre-generated according to the needs of the buyer's, this set can be defined as $A = \{a_1, a_2, ..., a_n\}$. For each of a_i, its attribute value $v(a_i)$ belongs to a fixed interval within $\bar{b}_i = [v(a_i)_{min}, v(a_i)_{max}]$. Meanwhile we use an interval χ to map the overall range of all attributes, namely $\chi \to \bigcup_{i=1}^{n} \bar{b}_i$. Now, let's classify χ into several levels with a set of positive integers $[1, L]$, so that we could distinguish the different importance-degree among all biddings for the same attribute (L is the maximum level for each of a_i). For example, there are three attributes in a buying laptop solution $\tilde{A}$ where $v(\tilde{a}_1) = 3225, v(\tilde{a}_2) = 2048, v(\tilde{a}_3) = 1215$ represents price, memory size and graphics card's price respectively. We initialize the price attribute having four levels, and each i level maps attribute interval $\bar{b}_i$, then we can classify $\tilde{A}$ into several levels. That is to say the minimum level can correspond to $\bar{b}_1 = [1000, 2000)$, similarly the second level maps the $\bar{b}_2 = [2000, 3000)$ and so on. Based on the above definition, the level of $\tilde{a}_1$ is 3, the level of $\tilde{a}_2$ is 2, and the level of $\tilde{a}_3$ is 1. Also, we can illustrate this by an information matrix $M_{L \times n} = \begin{bmatrix} m_{11} & \cdots & m_{1n} \\ \vdots & \ddots & \vdots \\ m_{l1} & \cdots & m_{Ln} \end{bmatrix}$ (m_{ij} keeps the first two digits after the decimal point). M completely describe an procurement/supply scheme's profile, in which the row index indicate the level of the attribute and column number means the attribute index in A. In the previous instance, information matrix $M_{4 \times 3} = \begin{bmatrix} 0 & 0 & 1215 \\ 0 & 2048 & 0 \\ 3225 & 0 & 0 \\ 0 & 0 & 0 \end{bmatrix}$. In the following, we present the other essential notations which will be used in our scheme in Table 1.

3.2   The Algorithms for Our PRMA Scheme

In this section, we'll present our proposed PRMA scheme in details. For simplicity, we'll introduce a σ_i calculating process between A^{ideal} and A_i^{opt}.

Table 1. Notations used in our scheme.

p, p'	p, p' are two large prime numbers generated randomly. p only be saved on the server as the private key
q	q is used as the public key in the algorithm, it needs to meet the requirement that $q = p * p'$, and $q > L^2 * p * (p+1)$
A^{ideal}, A_i^{opt}	A is the attribute-set of one good, namely $A = \{a_1, a_2, ..., a_n\}$. A^{ideal} is the ideal bidding generated by buyer, and A_i^{opt} denotes the ith optional bidding from suppliers
$\phi(\sigma), \sigma$	σ represents degree-matching between A^{ideal} and A_i^{opt}, $\phi(\sigma)$ is the set for all of biddings' σ, namely $\phi(\sigma) = \{\sigma_i \mid i \in [1, 2, ..., n]\}$
W	W is the weight vector of A, W_i means the ith attribute's weight satisfying $\sum_{i=1}^{n} W_i = 1, W_i \in (0, 1)$. With a view to simplify the calculation, we let W_i keep the first digit after the decimal point
$M_{L \times N}^1, M_{L \times N}^{1*}$	$M_{L \times N}^1$ denotes ideal scheme matrix from buyer, its element m_{ij}^1 indicates the jth attribute's level is i, and $M_{L \times N}^{1*}$ is the encrypted matrix of $M_{L \times N}^1$
$M_{L \times N}^2$	$M_{L \times N}^2$ represents the information matrix of alternative scheme from suppliers, and m_{ij}^2 indicates jth attribute's level is i
$M_{L \times L}^3$	The matching matrix between $M_{L \times N}^1$ and $M_{L \times N}^2$, m_{ij}^3 means the matching result of the ith row of $M_{L \times N}^1$ and the jth row of $M_{L \times N}^2$
$M_{L \times n}^{R1}, M_{L \times n}^{R2}, M_{L \times n}^{R3}$	$M_{L \times n}^{R1}, M_{L \times n}^{R2}, M_{L \times n}^{R3}$ are three random matrix during the computational process of transmission between the buyer and suppliers, satisfying $\sum_{i=1}^{L} \sum_{j=1}^{n} m_{ij}^{R1} < p - L * n$, $m_{ij}^{R2} < L * n$, $\|m_{ij}^{R3} * q\| \approx 1024$. The matrix elements $m_{ij}^{R1}, m_{ij}^{R2}, m_{ij}^{R3} \in Z^+$

Before carrying the bidding process out, we are supposed to do some data-preprocessing for the information matrix M. In order to uniformly handle the values of different attributes in A^{ideal} and A_i^{opt}, all attributes should be unified in the same interval. As a result, a new attribute's range is available which actually a union set of all attributes' ranges, namely the interval χ as mentioned in Sect. 3.1. The maximum and minimum bounds of χ can be denoted by χ^{max} and χ^{min} separately. Since there are usually having two types of attributes in one attribute set: quantitative and qualitative based attributes, and we need to mix the quantitative based attributes into quantitative computation process, we set a series of levels can map the qualitative based attribute into a quantitative interval. The partial interval χ_i of χ mapping level l can be calculated as following formula:

$$\chi_i = \left[\chi^{min} + (l-1) \left(\chi^{max} - \chi^{min} \right) / (L-1), \chi^{min} + l \left(\chi^{max} - \chi^{min} \right) / (L-1) \right) \tag{3}$$

And the left and end endpoint of χ_i satisfy $\chi_i^{right} / \chi_i^{left} \leq 2$.

Moreover, the new value $v'(a_i)$ mapping into new range χ for the original $v(a_i)$ can be obtained by formula as follows:

$$v'(a_i) = (v(a_i) - v(a_i)_{min})/(v(a_i)_{max} - v(a_i)_{min}) * (\chi^{max} - \chi^{min}) + \chi^{min} \quad (4)$$

Next, we can initiate the jth column of elements in M by:

$$m_{ij} = \begin{cases} if \ \ v'(a_i) \in \chi_i : \mu \\ else: \ \ 0 \end{cases} \quad (5)$$

Where

$$\mu = v'(a_i)/(\chi^{min} + (\chi^{max} - \chi^{min})/(L-1) * (i-1)) \quad (6)$$

Now, M's initialization has been completed. Next we need to obtain the interactions between A^{ideal} and A_i^{opt}. In Algorithm 1 (described in Table 2), we're going to calculate the encrypted ideal matrix $M_{L \times N}^{1*}$ and vector k_i ($i \in [1, L]$). Then, the sever sends encrypted ideal matrix $M_{L \times N}^{1*}$ to the client, and keeps private key p and vector k_i ($i \in [1, L]$) secretly.

After receiving encrypted matrix $M_{L \times N}^{1*}$, the client calculates matching matrix $M_{L \times L}^{3}$ according Algorithm 2 (described in Table 3), and send it back to the server.

After receiving matching matrix $M_{L \times L}^{3}{}'$ from the client, the auction sever is prepared to calculate σ by executing Algorithm 4. Before that, we need to carry the Algorithm 3 (in Table 4) out to compute an intermediate matrix T, in which each of elements t_{ij} could be calculated with formula (7):

$$\sum_{x=1}^{n} m_{jx}^2 \cdot j \cdot (p^{m_{ix}^1} \cdot^i \cdot m_{ix}^1 \cdot i \cdot W_x + m_{ix}^{R1}) - m_{ix}^{R1} \quad (7)$$

Table 2. Algorithm 1

Algorithm 1 Encrypt the ideal matrix $M_{L \times N}^1$.

Input: The ideal matrix $M_{L \times n}^1$ a weight vector W and a temporary vector k
Output: Encrypted ideal matrix $M_{L \times N}^{1*}$
1: **for** $(i = 1; i \leq L; i++)$ **do**
2:    $k_i = 0;$
3:    **for** $(j = 1; j \leq n; j++)$ **do**
4:       $m_{ij}^{1*} = p^{m_{ij}^1} \cdot^i \cdot m_{ij}^1 \cdot i \cdot W_j + m_{ij}^{R1};$
5:       $k_i = k_i + (m_{ij}^{R3} \cdot q + m_{ij}^{R1});$
6:    **end for**
7: **end for**

Table 3. Algorithm 2

Algorithm 2 Calculate matching matrix $M^3_{L \times L}$

Input: Encrypted ideal matrix $M^{1*}_{L \times N}$ and information matrix of optional scheme $M^2_{L \times N}$

Output: The matching matrix $M^3_{L \times L}$

1: **for** $(i = 1; i \leq L; i++)$ **do**
2:    **for** $(j = 1; j \leq L; j++)$ **do**
3:      $m^3_{ij} = 0;$
4:      **for** $(t = 1; t \leq n; t++)$ **do**
5:        $m^3_{ij} = m^3_{ij} + (m^2_{jt} \cdot j + m^{R2}_{jt} \cdot q) \cdot m^{1*}_{it}$
6:      **end for**
7:    **end for**
8: **end for**

There is calculation process of t_{ij} in detail:

$$t_{ij} = (m^3_{ij} + k_i) \bmod q$$

$$= (\sum_{x=1}^{n} (m^2_{jx} \cdot j + m^{R2}_{jx} \cdot q) \cdot (p^{m^1_{ix} \cdot i} \cdot m^1_{ix} \cdot i \cdot W_x + m^{R1}_{ix}) + m^{R3}_{ix} \cdot q$$

$$- m^{R1}_{ix}) \bmod q$$

$$= (\sum_{x=1}^{n} m^2_{jx} \cdot j \cdot (p^{m^1_{ix} \cdot i} \cdot m^1_{ix} \cdot i \cdot W_x + m^{R1}_{ix}) - m^{R1}_{ix}) \bmod q$$

$$= (\sum_{x=1}^{n} m^2_{jx} \cdot j \cdot (p^{m^1_{ix} \cdot i} \cdot m^1_{ix} \cdot i \cdot W_x + m^{R1}_{ix}) - m^{R1}_{ix}) \bmod q$$

$$= \sum_{x=1}^{n} m^2_{jx} \cdot j \cdot (p^{m^1_{ix} \cdot i} \cdot m^1_{ix} \cdot i \cdot W_x + m^{R1}_{ix}) - m^{R1}_{ix}$$

We can compute t_{ij} in several following steps and continue to execute the Algorithm 4 (in Table 5) using the intermediate matrix T:

Table 4. Algorithm 3

Algorithm 3 Calculate intermediate matrix $T = (t_{ij})_{L*L}$

Input: Matching matrix $M^3_{L \times L}$, vector k_i, public key q

Output: Matrix $T = (t_{ij})_{L*L}$

1: **for** $(i = 1; i \leq L; i++)$ **do**
2:    **for** $(j = 1; j \leq L; j++)$ **do**
3:      $t_{ij} = (m^3_{ij} + k_i) \bmod q$
4:    **end for**
5: **end for**

Table 5. Algorithm 4

Algorithm 4 Calculate matrix and degree-matching σ

Input: Matching matrix $T = (t_{ij})_{L*L}$, max level L, private key p
Output: Matrix $T^* = \left(t_{ij}^*\right)_{L*L}$ and degree-matching σ
1: **for** $(i = 1; i \leq L; i + +)$ **do**
2:    **for** $(j = 1; j \leq L; j + +)$ **do**
3:       $t_{ij}^* = (t_{ij} - (t_{ij} * 10^3 \bmod Lp^L)/10^3)/p^L;$
4:       $\sigma = \sum\limits_{i=1}^{L} \sum\limits_{j=1}^{L} t_{ij}^*;$
5:    **end for**
6: **end for**

σ_i can be obtained by the procedure elaborated above. Generally, we need to repeat the computing steps to gain $\phi(\sigma)$ to rank the bidding. Finally, we choose the auction winner by select the bidder who has the highest degree-matching, namely satisfying $\phi_{\max}(\sigma_i)$. In the following, we'll give some security proofs about the proposed scheme.

3.3   Security Analysis

In this section, the security analysis of ideal matrix $M_{L\times n}^1$'s privacy preserving and the security analysis of degree-matching σ's privacy preserving will be described in details.

3.3.1   The Security Analysis of the Ideal Matrix $M_{L\times n}^1$'s Privacy-Preserving

Theorem 1. Level- I privacy can be realized if Algorithm 1 is secure.

Proof. In Algorithm 1, the auction sever encrypts the ideal matrix $M_{L\times n}^1$ then sends the encrypted matrix $M_{L\times n}^{1*}$ to the client. For each of element in $M_{L\times n}^{1*}$, $m_{ij}^{1*} = p^{m_{ij}^1 \cdot i} \cdot m_{ij}^1 \cdot i \cdot W_j + m_{ij}^{R1} + m_{ij}^{R3} \cdot q,\ (m_{ij}^{R1} \in M_{L*n}^{R1}, m_{ij}^{R3} \in M_{L*n}^{R3})$. Since M_{L*n}^{R1} and M_{L*n}^{R3} are randomly generated, $m_{ij}^{R1} and m_{ij}^{R3}$ can't be predicted by adversaries. Due to the key information $p^{m_{ij}^1 \cdot i} \cdot m_{ij}^1 \cdot i \cdot W_j$ is masked by random numbers $m_{ij}^{R1} + m_{ij}^{R3} \cdot q$, it cannot be known by others unless the random matrix M_{L*n}^{R3} has been exposed on purpose. Thus our scheme can realize the Level- I privacy.

3.3.2   The Security Analysis of σ's Privacy-Preserving

Theorem 2. σ's security can be guaranteed if Algorithms 3 and 4 both are secure.

Proof. The private key p used in our algorithm is a large integer, its corresponding factorization method is the number field sieve, and the time complexity of NFS is $O\left(\exp\left((64/9)^{1/3}(\ln p)^{1/3}(\ln\ln p)^{2/3}\right)\right)$. The private key p is used in Algorithm 4 at $t_{ij}^* = (t_{ij} - (t_{ij}*10^3 \bmod Lp^L)/10^3)/p^L$ and its time complexity is $O(L \cdot n)$. It's obvious that $O(L \cdot n) \ll O\left(\exp\left((64/9)^{1/3}(\ln p)^{1/3}(\ln\ln p)^{2/3}\right)\right)$, that means the time attacker crack private key p is much longer than the time of running Algorithm 4, hence the degree-matching σ which is the results of Algorithm 4 would not be exposed to the attacker before the end of Algorithm 4, therefore, the security of the degree-matching σ can be guaranteed.

4 Conclusions

In this paper we propose a PRMA scheme, which choose the winner of the auction by securely computing and ranking the degree-matching between ideal solution supplied by purchaser and bidding submitted by supplies. PRMA can strongly preserve the information privacy of every participant. In addition, without the participation of any trusted third party, our scheme gains better security assurance.

Acknowledgement. The authors thank the editors and the anonymous reviewers for their valuable comments. This research was supported by National Natural Science Foundation of China (Nos. 61472074, 61401083), the Doctoral Fund of Northeastern University of Qinhuangdao (Grant No. XNB201410); the Fundamental Research Funds for the Central Universities (Grant No. N130323005, L1523009); the Natural Science Foundation of Hebei Province of China (Grant No. F2014501139, F2015501122); the Doctoral Scientific Research Foundation of Liaoning Province (Grant No. F201501143).

References

1. Carbonneau, R., Vahidov, R.: A Multi-attribute bidding strategy for a single-attribute auction marketplace. Expert Syst. Appl. **43**, 42–50 (2016)
2. Wu, T.C., Lin, T.Y., Wu, T.S., et al.: Efficient english auction scheme without a secure channel. Int. Arab J. Inf. Technol. **12**(3), 246–252 (2015)
3. Rossignoli, C., Ricciardi, F.: Electronic marketplaces. In: Rossignoli, C., Ricciardi, F. (eds.) Inter-Organizational Relationships. Contributions to Management Science, pp. 97–115. Springer International Publishing, Heidelberg (2015)
4. El Kholy, W., Bentahar, J., El Menshawy, M., et al.: Modeling and verifying choreographed multi-agent-based web service compositions regulated by commitment protocols. Expert Syst. Appl. **41**(16), 7478–7494 (2014)
5. Özer, A.H., Özturan, C.: Multi-unit differential auction-barter model for electronic marketplaces. Electron. Commer. Res. Appl. **10**(2), 132–143 (2011)
6. Lin, C.C., Chen, S.C., Chu, Y.M.: Automatic price negotiation on the web: an agent-based web application using fuzzy expert system. Expert Syst. Appl. **38**(5), 5090–5100 (2011)
7. Chow, Y.L., Ooi, J.T.L.: First-price sealed-bid tender versus English open auction: evidence from land auctions. Real Estate Econ. **42**(42), 253–278 (2014)

8. Varian, H.R., Harris, C.: VCG auction in theory, practice. Am. Econ. Rev. **104**(5), 442–445 (2014)
9. Ding, L.L., Kang, W.L., Liu, X.M.: Model and bidding strategies of multi-attribute auction based on buyer's preferences revealed. Syst. Eng. **2**, 013 (2015)
10. Gothelf, N., De, Y., Havelange, G., et al.: About the choice between a reversed multi-attribute auction and a reversed auction with a quality threshold. In: Proceedings of MCDA (2015)
11. He, D., Kumar, N., Shen, H., Lee, J.-H.: One-to-many authentication for access control in mobile pay-TV systems. Sci. China Inf. Sci. **59**, 052108 (2015). doi:10. 1007/s11432-015-5469-5
12. Xia, Z., Wang, X., Sun, X., Wang, Q.: A secure and dynamic multi-keyword ranked search scheme over encrypted cloud data. IEEE Trans. Parallel Distrib. Syst. **27**(2), 340–352 (2015)
13. Shen, J., Moh, S., Chung, I.: Enhanced secure sensor association and key management in wireless body area networks. J. Commun. Netw. **17**(5), 453–462 (2015)
14. Ma, T., Zhou, J., Tang, M., Tian, Y., Al-Dhelaan, A., Al-Rodhaan, M., Lee, S.: Social network and tag sources based augmenting collaborative recommender system. IEICE Trans. Inf. Syst. **E98-D**(4), 902–910 (2015)
15. Fu, Z., Sun, X., Liu, Q., Zhou, L., Shu, J.: Achieving efficient cloud search services: multi-keyword ranked search over encrypted cloud data supporting parallel computing. IEICE Trans. Commun. **E98-B**(1), 190–200 (2015)
16. Srinath, T.R., Singh, M.P., Pais, A.R.: Anonymity and verifiability in multi-attribute reverse auction. arXiv preprint arXiv:1109.0359 (2011)
17. Schartner, P., Schaffer, M.: Unique user-generated digital pseudonyms. In: Gorodetsky, V., Kotenko, I., Skormin, V.A. (eds.) MMM-ACNS 2005. LNCS, vol. 3685, pp. 194–205. Springer, Heidelberg (2005)
18. Srinath, T.R., Kella, S., Jenamani, M.: A new secure protocol for multi-attribute multi-round e-reverse auction using online trusted third party. In: 2011 Second International Conference on Emerging Applications of Information Technology (EAIT), pp. 149–152. IEEE (2011)
19. Parkes, D.C., Rabin, M.O., Shieber, S.M., et al.: Practical secrecy-preserving, verifiably correct, trustworthy auctions. Electron. Commer. Res. Appl. **7**(3), 294–312 (2008)
20. Zhu, X., Liu, J., Jiang, S., et al.: Efficient weight-based private matching for proximity-based mobile social networks. In: 2014 IEEE International Conference on Communications (ICC), pp. 4114–4119. IEEE (2014)
21. Goldreich, O.: Foundations of Cryptography: Volume II (Basic Applications). Cambridge University Press (2004)
22. Cramer, R., Shoup, V.: Signature schemes based on the strong RSA assumption. ACM Trans. Inf. Syst. Secur. (TISSEC) **3**(3), 161–185 (2000)

TransPro: Mandatory Sensitive Information Protection Based on Virtualization and Encryption

Xue-Zhi Xie, Hu-Qiu Liu, and Yu-Ping Wang(✉)

Tsinghua National Laboratory for Information Science and Technology,
Computer Science and Technology, Tsinghua University, Beijing 100084, China
xiexuezhi@aliyun.com, liuhq11@mails.tsinghua.edu.cn,
wyp@mail.tsinghua.edu.cn

Abstract. With the growing population of networked devices, the potential risk of leaking sensitive data has been seriously increased. This paper proposes a novel approach named TransPro based on virtualization technology, which can provide mandatory protected transmission between different network hosts. Through TransPro, all output sensitive data is encrypted before sent to network, and all input network data is decrypted before handled by the sensitive application. TransPro works in the host OS and VMM, and it does not need to manually modify application code. We have evaluated TransPro using security analysis and attack tests. The results show that TransPro can offer a safe information transmission with a little overhead.

Keywords: Sensitive information protection · Virtualization · Encryption · Mandatory transmission

1 Introduction

With development of information and network technology, increasing numbers of people tend to handle daily affairs on the internet [1]. However, the sensitive information like address books, passwords and financial information, also suffers from serious security threats during data transmission.

In most cases, we assume that the operating system is trustable [2]. However, lots of security problems (such as "black screen" and "Snowden incident") have indicated that the operating system security is not satisfactory enough. Many empirical studies also show that many commercial operating systems (such as Windows XP) is not trustable enough, and they can be attacked easily. According to the study in [3], more than 1/3 of vulnerabilities are related to buffer overflow, integer overflow and missing permission check etc., and attackers can easily use these vulnerabilities to get the privilege of the operating system for sensitive-information interception. Specifically, many applications open the internet ports without enough low-level security protection, so they can easily be the back doors of the system without effective control [4].

© Springer International Publishing AG 2016
X. Sun et al. (Eds.): ICCCS 2016, Part I, LNCS 10039, pp. 443–455, 2016.
DOI: 10.1007/978-3-319-48671-0_39

To protect sensitive information in network communication, many applications encrypt the data in their code. However, this method requires the application to rewrite the file operation interface and manage encryption keys, which brings much manual work of program modification and update. Besides, many approaches (such as role access control mode [5], mandatory access control) have been proposed. However, in most cases, they can be easily disabled and bypassed when built on an untrustable operating system [6].

To protect sensitive information in the untrustable operating system, we propose a practical approach named TransPro. It encrypts sensitive information with mandatory protection policy and works in the host OS and VMM (Virtual Machine Monitor). TransPro encrypts all the data from the guest OS based on the rules defined by the user, and it can control the target of the sensitive information and close dangerous internet connections. With TransPro, the following functionalities can be safely achieved:

(1) Malicious applications is allowed to run on the guest OS with the sensitive application together.
(2) The guest OS can be untrustable.
(3) The sensitive application and guest OS do not need manual modification.
(4) Allow the guest OS to offer limited network service.

The remainder of this paper is organized as follows. Section 2 describes the related works. The overview of TransPro is described in Sect. 3. The implementation of TransPro is shown in Sect. 4. The experimental evaluation is introduced in Sects. 5 and 6. Finally, the conclusion is made in Sect. 7.

2   Related Work

Sensitive-information security in network has received much attention for a long time, and many approaches have been proposed to solve similar problem [7–10].

Access Control. Access control [5] has been widely used for information protection and system security. Mandatory Access Controls (MAC) and Discretionary Access Controls (DAC) are two common models in access control, which can offer standard security services using authentication and authorization. However, they can not resist malicious attacks when the system is hijacked or in an untrustable state.

Attack and Rootkit. Sensitive information can be easily leaked when the attacker successfully get the operating system privilege. Many attackers try to hack the operating system through the backdoor, rootkit [11], swarm, Trojan virus, etc. When the operating system is hacked, it will be untrustable and unreliable. Most approaches of resisting rootkit try to enhance the reliability of the operating system and defend the attack of virus. However, these approaches can actually work well when the operating system is trustable, but they can be easily disabled or bypassed when the operating system is untrustable.

Leaks and Vulnerabilities. Privacy is a kind of special sensitive information, especially in the Android operating system [12,13]. A framework for the detection of privacy-violating information flow [12] is presented to analyze the bytecode of applications, and it has been used to analyze privacy related Android APIs to detect privacy leaks. Teasurephone [13] is another approach of protecting privacy data on mobile phone, and it limits the application's permission to access sensitive information based on program context.

Virtualization. Virtualization is a promising way to protect sensitive information in untrustable system. Terra [14] provides a virtual machine platform to perform trusting computing, and sensitive applications are separated into different VMs (Virtual Machines) based on a trusted VMM. The approaches of [15,16] provide a novel framework to tolerate buggy and malicious drivers based on hardware virtualization. Inspired by these approaches, Our approach TransPro is also based on virtualization technology and encryption, and it provides a security mandatory protective transmission environment for network data.

3   Design of TransPro

3.1   Model Hypothesis and Analysis

In virtual machines, the guest OS in a VM connects to the outside network through VMM. Taking Vmware VMM as shown in Fig. 1 for example, it has four ways to share the network: (1) Bridged, (2) NAT, (3) Host-Only, (4) Internal. Even though VMM provides network isolation between guest OSs, VMM must works under the mode of "Bridged" or "NAT" when the guest OS needs to connect to internet directly, and the malicious applications can send out sensitive data to malicious server easily when the guest OS is untrustable.

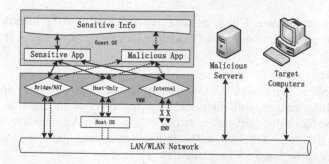

Fig. 1. Transfer environment analysis.

Before introducing the protective sensitive information transmission method, the model hypothesis is based on the following conditions:

(1) The user is trustable and reliable, the owner and receiver of the sensitive information are also trustable.
(2) The information leakage caused by covert channel is out of our research.
(3) The hardware of system is trustable, and there is no back door and Trojan horse on the hardware level. The attackers cannot directly expose to the computer and get the hardware, and they also cannot change the physical connections to monitor the board bus.
(4) The BIOS system and the virtual machine monitor (VMM) are also secure. The whole procession between booting and host OS can be protected by the trust chain.

As result, if VMM works under the mode of "Host-Only", the guest OS cannot send any sensitive information to the outside network directly, and VMM offers a useful network isolation. Thus a sensitive information protective transmission approach (TransPro) can check and encrypt sensitive data flow before sending out to the target servers, and no plain data can be sent out to outside network directly without TransPro.

3.2   Theory Model

Referring to the model of sandbox, TransPro consists of the following key components: sensitive application set, sensitive information flow set, guest OS set, VMM host set, host OS set, rule policy set, transfer module, encrypt module and decrypt module.

Sensitive Application Set: P is a set of sensitive applications, and it will produce sensitive data or consume it. TransPro protects the sensitive data of network connection which transmits from the sensitive application A to sensitive application B with mandatory and enhancement encrypt policy. Applications run on the one endpoint A of the connection is denoted as P_A, and the other one is denoted as P_B.

Sensitive Information Flow Set: I is a set of sensitive information flow, and all network connections among I will be enforcement checking in VMM and guest OS.

Guest OS Set: The system G is sensitive as the application P produces lots of sensitive information, and the operating system G is untrustable. The guest OS would not block or reject any network connections. All sensitive applications can run on the guest OS well without limitations on guest OS, and original applications can be handled by TransPro.

VMM Host Set: M is used to denote the VMM, and it should be modified by TransPro. VMM will call encrypt module interfaces to encrypt sensitive information and reject or block the illegal connections. It is the most important part of TransPro.

Host OS Set: H is the host OS, and it is a lightweight Linux OS. As the system does not install any incredible user program, the safety can be guaranteed.

Rule Policy Set: The rule policy is denoted as R. They are defined by the user, and can be stored in abstract structure.

Transfer Module: T_m is used to denote the transfer module, and all data must be checked by T_m before sending out. According to the policy defined by users, T_m decides to call the encrypt module to encrypt sensitive data or decrypt the cipher text data. Sensitive data packet will be appended ahead to denote the data which is encrypted by T_m.

Encrypt Module and Decrypt Module: The encrypt module E_m and decrypt module D_m will be called by T_m. To simplify the implementation, TransPro uses symmetric encryption algorithm to encrypt and decrypt sensitive data.

All sensitive data can be transmitted by the following model with Eq. 1. More details about the module T_m will be introduced in the following subsections.

$$(I_i, P_A) \otimes G \vee M \xrightarrow{\quad T_m(R), E_m/D_m \quad} M \vee G \otimes (I_i, P_B) \qquad (1)$$

In the formula, sensitive information I_i in the sensitive application P_A, which runs in the guest OS, with the help of VMM, TransPro calls the transfer module T_m to encrypt the sensitive information with the rules policy R. The operation $\otimes$ means data exchanging within the guest OS, and the operation $\vee$ means that TransPro transfers data with the help of VMM host. When the encrypted sensitive information arrived at the receiver, TransPro calls the transfer module to decrypt the sensitive information. By the help of VMM, sensitive information I_i will be received by the sensitive application P_B. The process of sensitive information transmission from P_B to P_A is same to the above description.

3.3   Data Transfer and Rules Policy

Transfer module works on the host OS and acquires the extra information of VMM. VMM gets the current process ID and process name to transmit data to Transfer module. Transfer module selects a basic policy to protect sensitive information with rules defined by the user.

Transfer module has defined the following basic policies:

(1) User can change the transfer module state into running state with full encryption policy at any time.
(2) Transfer module upgrades the protection level when sensitive data needs high level protection.
(3) Only user can lower the protection level, otherwise the whole system starts with the low level protection.

(4) User can set the whitelist and blacklist on internet address for sensitive application, which means the internet package from the whitelist can be transmitted into guest OS directly.

When the guest OS runs high level sensitive application, the sensitive information will be inactive. With rule 3, transfer modules can protect residual data in memory. To lower the protection level for transfer module, TransPro must restart the guest OS and host OS.

4   Implementation

The implementation of prototype system is shown in this section. Subsection 4.1 gives the framework of TransPro. Details about the design of mandatory protective transmission of transfer module is shown in Subsect. 4.2, and the cipher text management and key classification policies are shown in Subsect. 4.3.

4.1   Framework

The main process for a network connection is shown in Fig. 2. In the normal protection model, the sensitive information is active when the sensitive application is running.

(1) When the sensitive application P_A sends information to the network actively, and TransPro will check with the following steps: (I) VMM host actives the transfer module T_m to check whether P_A is in the white list, and it will be allowed to send out directly when the internet target address is in the white list. (II) T_m checks whether the target address is in the blacklist, and the connection will be blocked when the connection is forbidden. (III) Otherwise, all sensitive information will be encrypted by the E_m and then send out.

(2) When the outside network hosts try to connect the sensitive guest OS, TransPro will check with the following steps: (I) VMM host actives the transfer module T_m to check whether P_B is in the blacklist, and it will be denied directly. (II) T_m checks whether the target address is in the white list, and the connection will be submitted the guest OS directly. (III) Otherwise, all sensitive information will be decrypted by the decrypt module D_m and then submit to the guest OS.

4.2   Design of Mandatory Protective Transmission

For the sensitive application in the guest OS, TransPro does not need the user to modify the code. Transpro can offer a whole system mandatory protective transmission with mandatory encryption policies. To simplify the implementation of TransPro, all data will be encrypted by the host OS and then sent out. As the guest OS can not use the physical network card to send data directly, the guest OS can not connect other network hosts except the host OS.

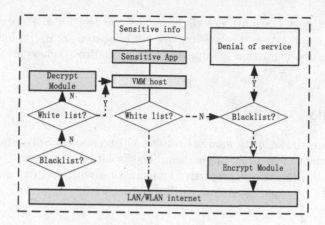

Fig. 2. Main process of TransPro.

There are three methods to implement the encrypt and decrypt policies. (1) TransPro encrypts all connections and denies illegal connections. Under this occasion, the guest OS will fail to connect the outside network when TransPro enters the protection mode. (2) VMM offers the methods to get the sensitive application name and process ID. TransPro allows or disconnects the network connections when sensitive application starts to offer service. With this occasion, TransPro can offer partial encryption and decryption service. (3) Develop a network agent to implement the similar function of Transfer module. The guest OS only can connect to the host OS directly and connect to the outside network with the help of TransPro module.

Associated with the steps in Subsect. 4.1, TransPro will execute the reverse operation to decrypt the sensitive information. In the following implementations, TransPro uses the whole system encryption and decryption policy. It will encrypt all the outflow of network and try to decrypt all the inflow.

4.3   Cipher Text Label Management and Key Classification

To enhance the security of TransPro, all sensitive applications holds special ciper text labels and encryption keys should be regularly updated and allocated. TransPro produces encryption key based on the certification, which is acquired and allocated manually originally[1]. Based on this certification, TransPro generates a temporary key for each network session, and the communication process is similar to HTTPS protocol.

Of course, TransPro also allows the user to input special session key for special network session which is marked by the destination port number and address. Under this situation, the connection between two sensitive applications

---

[1] It also can be allocated by the existing certification network. To simplify the implementation, the certification is manually allocated with self protocol, and TransPro can work in the LAN network for this design.

from different gust OS must use the same session key for the decryption and encryption. In this paper, the session key are allocated by users, and the symmetric encryption algorithm is imported into TransPro to encrypt and decrypt sensitive data.

5   Security Analysis

In this section, the security analysis results will be shown. Subsection 5.1 gives the enhancement of security mechanism. The isolation of system is introduced in Subsect. 5.2. Mandatory protective transmission with security enhancement and the trusted computing is described in Subsect. 5.3.

5.1   Enhancement of Security Mechanism

This system uses a mandatory protective method, the sensitive network data flow is transmitted through the mandatory protective encryption and decryption. Any data that is out of the trusted domain must be encrypted by the encryption module. For an untrusted applications within Trojans and spyware software, TransPro will disconnect the network connection when the host tries to connect the unknown network address.

In fact, even if the malicious application in guest OS can send out data without permission, the malicious receiver can not get the sensitive plain data directly as the data has been mandatory encrypted and protected by TransPro. Because the host OS only executes TransPro and VMM, so no sensitive information is stored in the host OS.

5.2   Isolation for System

Another property of security is isolation, the encryption module E_m and decryption module D_m is under the domain of host OS, and the sensitive application works in the guest OS. As the VMM offers strong isolation, the encryption module E_m and decryption module D_m are not controlled by the guest OS. Thus, malicious applications can not bypass or disable TransPro.

5.3   Trusted Transmission Path

The encryption and decryption operations are in the VMM, and the host OS only installs the key module and keeps itself small enough. Untrusted applications are allowed to install in the host OS, and all user applications are installed in the guest OS. To simplify the host OS, TransPro tries to build a trusted transmission path from the host OS to sensitive application running in the guest OS. As the physical hardware attacking is unavailable in our threaten model, and the path from physical hardware to host OS can be trusted. All TransPro systems obtain the same key management policies, and session keys are allocated based on their private certification for symmetric encryption algorithm.

6   Evaluation

6.1   Environment

The CPU of host OS A and host OS B is "Pentium(R) Dual-Core CPU E5400 2.7 GHZ" and "Pentium(R) Dual-Core CPU E5500 2.8 GHZ", and network card of theirs is "Marvell 88E8056 Gigabit Ethernet Card" and "Marvell 88E8057 Gigabit Ethernet Card". To evaluation the basic mechanism of TransPro and simplify the theory model, we use the VMware software to run guest OS. Both host OS A and B only installs the tool TransPro and Vmware software, and the detail version of VMM is "Vmware 11.0.0 Linux X86_X64". More details about the evaluation environment is shown as Table 1, and VMM works under the network mode of "Host-Only".

Table 1. Environment for evaluation.

	Guest OS	Host OS A	Guest OS B	Host OS B
OS	Ubuntu 3.11.0	Ubuntu 3.11.0	Ubuntu 3.11.0	Ubuntu 3.11.0
Cache	2048 KB	2048 KB	2048 KB	2048 KB
Memory	512 MB DDR2	4G DDR2	512 MB DDR2	2G DDR2
Hardware	40G	200G	40G	200G

TransPro runs on the host OS. Figure 3 shows evaluation environment of the connection between two computers between host OS.

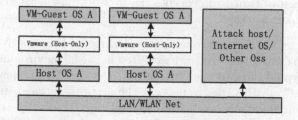

Fig. 3. Test architecture of TransPro.

6.2   Attack and Malicious Application Test

To verify the security of TransPro, two attacking test methods are imported to evaluate as shown in Fig. 4.

(1) The malicious application is already installed in the guest OS, and it try to send out sensitive information with the network service.
  • The transfer module rejects the connecting when the target address is in the black list.

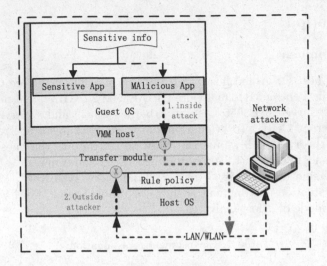

Fig. 4. Two attack test cases.

- The transfer module encrypts the network flow and sends out to the outside network.

(2) An attacking host in the internet tries to attack the target guest OS, as the guest OS is protected by the transfer module and guest OS does not expose port to the internet directly. TransPro works under the following steps to handle the attack: (1) TransPro denies the illegal connection when the guest OS does not opening the service or the source address is in the black list. (2) TransPro sets the address into blacklist when it always tries to scan ports of guest OS. (3) TransPro decrypts the network flow package and discards the invalid data package.

As no plain text is sent out to the network directly, the sensitive information is protected. The two attack tests are executed in the lab environment, TransPro sends out encrypted data to the outside net host for the preview situation as shown in Fig. 5. TransPro tries to decrypt the network package, and the output of the decryption module is invalid and useless.

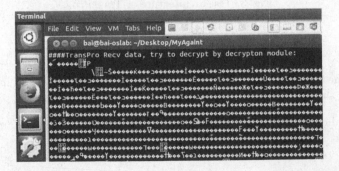

Fig. 5. Cipher text from the network which is encrypted by TransPro.

6.3 Performance Comparison Between Host and Guest OS

To evaluate the overhead of TransPro, we have developed a network tool with the file transfer function, and three situations are taken into consideration as shown in Table 2.

(1) We run the test tool on the Linux OS which runs on the physical machine directly. It is denoted as *Linux(Ave)* in the 1st column.
(2) The tool runs in the guest OS, and TransPro is disabled. It is denoted as *Guest-Linux(Ave)* in the 2nd column.
(3) TransPro works in the whole system encryption mode. It is denoted as *TransPro(Ave)* in the 3rd column.

Table 2. Performance comparison evaluation.

	Linux(Ave)	Guest-Linux(Ave)	TransPro(Ave)
NET+File(12M)	11.8 MB/s	11.34 MB/s	10.68 MB/s
NET+File(65M)	11.7 MB/s	11.51 MB/s	11.50 MB/s
NET+File(135M)	11.8 MB/s	11.58 MB/s	11.49 MB/s
NET+File(750M)	11.7 MB/s	11.70 MB/s	11.53 MB/s

Compared with the 2nd column and the 3rd column in Table 2, TransPro only brings little runtime overhead to the original system. Original overhead between Linux and Guest-Linux is nearly same with each other, and the main limitation of transferring speed is hardware speed. TransPro holds tight relationship with the network, and to evaluate the network overhead of CPU, the additional overhead of CPU utilization between Guest-Linux and TransPro system is about 5 %.

6.4 Comparison with Previous Approaches

To validate the effectiveness of TransPro, we make comparisons with previous approaches. The results are shown in Table 3.

Table 3. Comparison with other methods.

	Health system	Rootkit(leak)	Vul(attack)
DAC	Y	N	N
MAC	Y	N	N
XEN/iKernel	Y	N	*
TransPro	Y	Y	Y

In Table 3, the *vul(attack)* means the network attacking with the vulnerabilities. The virtualization methods can defense partial attacking as the inside network port does not open to the outside network directly when VMM network works under the NAT model. TransPro offers safe network connections and protects sensitive information even runs on a untrustable guest OS.

7   Conclusion

In this paper, we propose a practical and effective approach named TransPro, which can provide a mandatory transmission protection to run sensitive applications. TransPro works in the host OS and VMM, and encrypts sensitive information before sending to the internet, and decrypts the cipher text before being analyzed by the sensitive application. It does not require the user to modify the code of the sensitive application. We have evaluated the ability of TransPro with the security analysis and attack tests. The results show that TransPro can offer a safety information transmission with a little overhead.

References

1. Zhou, M., Zhang, R., Xie, W., Qian, W., Zhou, A.: Security and privacy in cloud computing: a survey. In: 2010 Sixth International Conference on Semantics Knowledge and Grid, pp. 105–112 (2010)
2. Pang, D.Q., Zhang, A., Xie, C.: Realization proposal and security model of operating system based on credible computation. J. Liuzhou Vocat. Tech. Coll. **11**(4), 51–54 (2011)
3. Chen, H., Mao, Y., Wang, X., Zhou, D., Zeldovich, N., Kaashoek, M.F.: Linux kernel vulnerabilities: state-of-the-art defenses and open problems. Second Asia-Pac. Workshop Syst. **5**, 1–5 (2011)
4. Barrantes, G., Ackley, D.H., Palmer, T.S., Zovi, D.D., Forrest, S., Stefanovi, D.: Randomized instruction set emulation to disrupt binary code injection attacks. ACM Trans. Inf. Syst. Secur. **8**(1), 3–40 (2005)
5. Sandhu, R.S., Edward, J.C., Hal, L.F., Charles, E.Y.: Role-based access control models. IEEE Comput. **2**, 38–47 (1996)
6. Kyle, D., Brustoloni, J.C.: UCLinux: a linux security module for trusted-computing-based usage controls enforcement. In: ACM Workshop on Scalable Trusted Computing, pp. 63–70 (2007)
7. Yongjun, R., Jian, S., Jin, W., Jin, H., Sungyoung, L.: Mutual verifiable provable data auditing in public cloud storage. J. Internet Technol. **16**(2), 317–323 (2015)
8. Jian, S., Sangman, M., Ilyong, C.: Enhanced secure sensor association and key management in wireless body area networks. J. Commun. Netw. **17**(5), 453–462 (2015)
9. Ma, T., Zhou, J., Tang, M., Tian, Y., Al-Dhelaan, A., Al-Rodhaan, M., Lee, S.: Social network and tag sources based augmenting collaborative recommender system. IEICE Trans. Inf. Syst. **E98–D**(4), 902–910 (2015)
10. Fu, Z., Sun, X., Liu, Q., Zhou, L., Shu, J.: Achieving efficient cloud search services: multi-keyword ranked search over encrypted cloud data supporting parallel computing. IEICE Trans. Commun. **E98–B**(1), 190–200 (2015)

11. Embleton, S., Sparks, S., Zou, C.C.: SMM rootkit: a new breed of OS independent malware. Secur. Commun. Netw. **6**(12), 1590–1605 (2013)
12. Mann, C., Starostin, A.: A framework for static detection of privacy leaks in android applications. In: The 27th Annual ACM Symposium on Applied Computing, pp. 1457–1462 (2012)
13. Seifert, J., De Luca, A., Conradi, B., Hussmann, H.: TreasurePhone: context-sensitive user data protection on mobile phones. In: Floréen, P., Krüger, A., Spasojevic, M. (eds.) Pervasive 2010. LNCS, vol. 6030, pp. 130–137. Springer, Heidelberg (2010)
14. Garfinkel, T., Pfaff, B., Chow, J., Rosenblum, M., Boneh, D.: Terra: a virtual machine-based platform for trusted computing. ACM SIGOPS Oper. Syst. Rev. **37**(5), 193–206 (2003)
15. Tan, L., Chan, E.M., Farivar, R., Mallick, N.: iKernel: isolating buggy and malicious device drivers using hardware virtualization support. In: The 3rd IEEE International Symposium on Dependable, Autonomic and Secure Computing, pp. 134–144 (2007)
16. Perez, R., van Doorn, L., Sailer, R.: Virtualization and hardware-based security. IEEE Secur. Priv. **6**(5), 24–31 (2008)

Key Recovery in Public Clouds: A Survey on Cross-VM Side Channel Attacks

Stelvio Cimato[1]([✉]), Ernesto Damiani[1,2], Silvia Mella[1], and Ching-Nung Yang[3]

[1] Dipartimento di Informatica, Università Degli Studi di Milano, Crema, Italy
{stelvio.cimato,ernesto.damiani,silvia.mella}@unimi.it
[2] Department of Electrical and Computer Engineering,
Khalifah University, Abu Dhabi, United Arab Emirates
[3] Department of Computer Science and Information Engineering,
National Dong Hwa University, Hualien, Taiwan
cnyang@mail.ndhu.edu.tw

Abstract. Isolation across virtual machines is one of the pillars on which the cloud computing paradigm relies on, allowing efficient use of shared resources among users who experience dedicated services. However side channel attacks have been recently demonstrated possible, showing how an adversary is enabled to recover sensible information by observing the behavior of a VM co-located on the same physical machine. In this paper we survey the current attacks, focusing on the ones targeted to extract private RSA keys, and discuss some possible countermeasures, offering a picture of the security challenges cloud providers need to address in order to provide strong guarantees to their customers.

1 Introduction

The possibility of provisioning on demand scalable and configurable computing resources offered by cloud computing, has made this paradigm the mainstream model for the deployment of IT solutions. In the Infrastructure as a Service scenario (IaaS) cloud providers sell computing infrastructures to clients who rent the computing resources and pay for their usage only when effectively needed. This business model has been implemented by many companies such as Google, Microsoft or Amazon that are offering their services and have changed the landscape of the IT market.

A founding principle in cloud computing is the sharing of physical infrastructures among multiple customers, who are given the illusion of infinite number of available dedicated computing resources. Multi-tenancy allow several Virtual Machines (VMs) belonging to different customers to be run on the same physical server, ensuring optimal utilization and drastic reduction of costs.

Data security, however, is one of the main concerns that are generally adversing the widespread usage of cloud computing. A lot of security challenges arise since customers are called to move their sensible data and computation in an untrusted environment managed by a third-party cloud provider. In the IaaS model, the situation is more challenging, since the computations of different

© Springer International Publishing AG 2016
X. Sun et al. (Eds.): ICCCS 2016, Part I, LNCS 10039, pp. 456–467, 2016.
DOI: 10.1007/978-3-319-48671-0_40

users must be carried out on the same physical machines, relying on isolation mechanisms offered by the hypervisors or by the original operating systems running on the VMs in the virtualized environment.

A new class of attacks is emerging as a serious threat to the virtualized infrastructures: recently the existence of side channels has been shown to be the cause of data leakage across co-resident VM instances [31]. These attacks re-elaborate older ideas that have been introduced in non virtualized scenario and are based on the analysis of physical implementations of cryptographic algorithms to retrieve information on the secret used during the computation [23]. The observation of physical features such as power consumption, electromagnetic emission, acoustic emission, and so on, has been used to execute side-channel attacks to the computation. Even when some countermeasures are used to thwart these attacks, such as blinding techniques in the case of RSA computations [9], researchers showed how knowledge on some of the bits composing the secret key can still be used to recover the whole secret [4,6,7,22]

In the IaaS model, side channel attacks exploit shared micro-architectural components to break the isolation of VMs and threaten the privacy of customers sharing the physical servers. Most of the recently proposed attacks rely on the observation of accesses to the shared memory, which can return information on the data used during the computation, leading, for example, to the recovery of a cryptographic key. Cache based attacks introduced in [3,29] for single machines and targeted to the recovery of symmetric keys, have been successfully translated to the cloud scenario and applied to implement side channel attacks across VMs. The research line started by Ristenpart et al. in [31] have demonstrated how fine-grained information can be extracted by observing the behavior of shared memory components, due in part to vulnerabilities caused by features introduced by the hyper-visors [33], memory management procedures [34], or weak implementation of cryptographic libraries [36].

These attacks have a deep impact on the community and also on the cloud computing platforms, since after recognizing the potential of those security vulnerabilities, cloud providers have adapted their platforms and have disabled some of the features exploited by the attackers (such as memory deduplication in VMWare platforms). The same occurred also for software providers, who are continuously updating their library to prevent some of the side channel attacks (like done for the OpenSSL and libgcrypt versions). On the other side, researchers are exploring novel and refined ways for side channel attacks [35], showing how the extracted information can be used not only to get information on other customers' data, but also on the virtualized environment and on the exploited hardware [27]. In turn, this amounts to the development of new techniques and new countermeasures based on a deep and updated analysis of the current situation in the virtualized scenario [10].

Contribution. In this paper we survey the most common and recently introduced cross-VM side channel attacks, presenting the basic notions needed to understand the hardware and software requirements they are based on in Sect. 2. We focus on the attacks targeted to the extraction of RSA keys and in general of public key cryptosystems: for this reason we show the techniques available to prevent some of these attacks by modifying the standard computations in Sect. 3. Finally we describe the attacks in Sect. 4 and discuss some of their characteristics and some possible countermeasures in Sect. 5.

2   Background

2.1   Memory Management in VM

Different technologies have been adopted with the aim of improving memory utilization and reducing access time to recovery the fetched data. Some of these techniques have been found during the time affecting the security of the cloud infrastructure and some side channel attacks have been discovered.

One of the feature that has been utilized to attack is memory deduplication, at first introduced to optimize the running time of several virtual machines hosted on the same physical machine, and included as standard feature in Linux kernels (starting with v2.6.32). This technique is referred also as Kernel SamePage Merging (KSM in short) and allows merging duplicated memory contents into a single page entry to save resources. The baseline is that several large applications that are commonly run on different machines share a lot of common parts (that is the case of portions of the operating systems) and for this reason there is no need to allocate different memory spaces.

Memory deduplication, however, may be used to carry a side channel attack, disclosing the memory content of a victim VM. By tracing the differences in write access times on deduplicated memory pages, it is possible to check the loading of an application or file on the target VM. The attacker loads the tested content belonging to a process or a file in the memory of the attacker's VM and waits for these pages to be deduplicated. After that, the attacker tries to get write access to the pages, and register longer write access time in the case of deduplicated content, revealing that those pages are shared with the victim VM. KSM has been used by Suzaki et al. [32] to detect the existence of some demons on Linux OS, and a browser and its downloaded files on WindowsXP. De-duplication has been implemented in different hypervisors such as VMware ESX and PowerVM, and different OS including Linux and Windows versions.

2.2   Cache Hierarchy

Processes running on the same CPU can share cache memory, which are small banks of fast memory used by the processor to store recently accessed data. Under the locality principle, recently used values tend to be re-used and having them stored in the cache saves time and reduces main memory accesses. Modern CPUs usually have three cache levels, called L1, L2 and L3, being the first two levels private to each core. The L3 cache, also called Last Level Cache (LLC) is split into slices, is shared between the cores, and contains usually several megabytes.

When the CPU needs to read or write data in main memory, the CPU checks the cache levels starting from L1 to L3, accessing immediately the data if the address is found (*cache hit*) or searching in the next level if the data is missing (*cache miss*). When data is transfered between the cache and the memory, a block of bytes (usually 64) called a *line* is moved into a given location inside the cache. Caches are n-way associative, meaning that sets of n lines are loaded into the cache. Each line is loaded in a specific set according to its address, and when a cache set is full, another line needs to be removed before storing the accessed line. When a line is evicted from L1 it is stored back to L2, which can lead to the eviction of a new line to LLC, etc. The replacement policy decides the victim line to be evicted.

2.3 RSA

RSA is a public key system for encryption and signature. To generate a key pair, two large distinct primes p and q are chosen and the modulus $N = p \cdot q$ is computed. In common settings, N is 1024, 2048 or 3072-bit long, with p and q of the same size. Then a public exponent e is chosen such that $1 < e < \phi(N)$ and $\gcd(e, \phi(N)) = 1$ where $\phi(N) = (p-1)(q-1)$ is the Euler's totient function. The most common values for the public exponent e are 3, 17 and $2^{16} + 1$ (this is also the default value for the public exponent in the OpenSSL library). Finally the private exponent d is computed as the multiplicative inverse of e modulo $\phi(N)$. The encryption scheme is defined by the public key (N, e), the private key (p, q, d), the encryption function $Enc(m) = m^e \pmod{N}$, and the decryption function $Dec(c) = c^d \pmod{N}$. In the signature scheme based on RSA, the message is signed by using the private key and verified by using the public key. CRT-RSA is a common optimization to speed up decryption [30]. The private key is split into $d_p = d \bmod (p-1)$ and $d_q = d \bmod (q-1)$. These two exponents are then used to compute $m_1 = c^{d_p} \bmod p$ and $m_2 = c^{d_q} \bmod q$. The original message is obtained using Garner's formula [13]: $h = q^{-1}(m_1 - m_2) \bmod p$ and $m = m_2 + hq$.

3 Exponentiation and Countermeasures Against Side Channel Attacks

In this section we will recap the most common techniques used to implement modular exponentiation and discuss how they leak information on the secret data. We will also describe the most common countermeasures used to prevent SCA, usually based on uniformity of operations and blinding techniques. Uniformity of operations means that the sequence and the execution time of the operations do not depend on the value of secret data. An example of such approach is given in Sect. 3.1. Blinding means replacing an intermediate value by a randomized value. In particular, the exponent, the base and the modulus may be blinded. These techniques will be described in Sect. 3.2.

3.1 Square and Multiply

A common technique to implement exponentiation is the square-and-multiply algorithm [15]. Given the binary representation of e as $e_{n-1}2^{n-1} + e_{n-2}2^{n-2} + \cdots e_1 2^1 + e_0$, the square-and-multiply algorithm computes $x = b^e \bmod N$ as described in Algorithm 1.

Algorithm 1. Square and Multiply

1: $x \leftarrow 1$
2: **for** $i = n - 1$ to 0 **do**
3:      $x \leftarrow x \cdot x \bmod N$
4:      **if** $d_i = 1$ **then**
5:          $x \leftarrow x \cdot b \bmod N$
6:      **end if**
7: **end for**
8: **return** x

Thus exponentiation consists of a sequence of modular Square and Multiply operations. A sequence of squaring and multiplication corresponds to a bit of the exponent equal to 1, while a single squaring corresponds to a bit equal to 0. Thus, the implementation leaks information on whether only the square is computed or both square and multiply operations are performed. If the attacker is able to trace the execution of the square-and-multiply algorithm (e.g. by observing the execution time at each step) he is able to retrieve the private exponent.

To prevent this kind of leakage, Square-and-Multiply-Always should be implemented. In this algorithm, a fake multiplication is computed when the bit of the exponent is 0 and the result is accumulated in a temporary variable that will not be used to compute the final result. Thus, the execution time at each step does not depend on the corresponding value of the exponent's bit. A pseudo-code for Square-and-Multiply-Always is given in Algorithm 2.

Algorithm 2. Square and Multiply always

1: $x \leftarrow 1$
2: $y \leftarrow 1$
3: **for** $i = n - 1$ to 0 **do**
4:      $x \leftarrow x \cdot x \bmod N$
5:      **if** $d_i = 1$ **then**
6:          $x \leftarrow x \cdot b \bmod N$
7:      **else**
8:          $y \leftarrow y \cdot b \bmod N$
9:      **end if**
10: **end for**
11: **return** x

3.2 Blinding

Blinding techniques are based on the randomization of intermediate variables. Thus, the target value is different for all traces, so that they cannot be aligned and processed together to reduce the noise, making recovering of secret data infeasible. An emerging methodology, called horizontal attack [8], allows recovering the secret data by analyzing single traces making the blinding techniques not effective any more. In [4,11,22] the authors show which is the amount of information that should be extracted from a single trace to recover the entire secret key. However, most horizontal attacks require advanced trace pre-processing and characterization. The main problem is that the information extraction is limited by noise and unlabeled information. *Exponent blinding*, introduced by Kocher [23], consists in adding a random multiple of $\phi(N)$ to the private exponent d. In particular, exponentiation is computed by using the exponent $d^* = d + \ell\phi(N)$, for some $\ell > 0$ randomly chosen at each execution. The dimension of ℓ is a tradeoff between security and efficiency. If it is too small, it allows some combination of brute-forcing and side-channel as in [12]. On the other hand, if it is too big, then it would make the decryption process less efficient. Thus, it is a safer choice to use ℓ with bit-size 64. The correctness of RSA is still valid, since $m^{ed^*} \equiv m^{ed+e\ell\phi(N)} \equiv m^{1+(k+e\ell)\phi(N)} \equiv m \left(m^{\phi(N)}\right)^{k+e\ell} \equiv m(1)^{k+e\ell} \equiv m \bmod N$. In CRT-RSA exponentiation is computed by using $d_p^* = d_p + \ell_1(p-1)$ and $d_q^* = d_q + \ell_2(q - 1)$, for some $\ell_1, \ell_2 > 0$ randomly chosen.

Modulus blinding was presented by Giraud in [5]. It consists in multiplying the modulus by a random integer r, obtaining $N' = r \cdot N$. All modular multiplication are computed using the randomized modulus except for the last one that is performed with the original modulus N. Giraud suggested to use a random integer of 32 bits. *Base blinding*, consists in multiplying the message by a blinding factor r^e, where r is a random integer and e is the public exponent. Thus, decryption is performed over $c^* = c \cdot r^e$. Finally, the correct message is recovered with a multiplication by r^{-1}. Giraud suggested to use a random integer of 32 bits.

4 Side Channel Attacks Based on Last Level Cache

Most interesting and recent cross-VM attacks take advantage of the possibility to extract information by observing or actively modifying the behavior of the LLC. In general the LLC is shared across all cores in most modern CPUs and isolation mechanisms implemented by the hyper-visors should ensure that the VMs running on the same physical machine cannot access each other's data. However sophisticated techniques have been proposed to profile and monitor the LLC, and use the extracted information to investigate on the co-located VM or to directly recover a secret key used in some running cryptographic operation.

To improve on the efficiency of the attack, a more detailed knowledge on the structure and the usage of the LLC is needed, often acquiring more details on the hardware platform that is being used. For this reason many studies addressed the problem of recovering the slice selection algorithms used for different processors as done in [26] for the Intel CPUs, or in [19] where the authors reverse engineered the slice selection algorithms for the Intel Xeon E5-2670 chipset (that are commonly used in the Amazon EC2 cloud). The attack scenarios generally taken into account, include usually some techniques to detect co-location across the attacker and the victim's VM, and some knowledge on the software used, that can be exploited to extract the secret information. The most common strategies adopted to recover secret information are PRIME + PROBE and FLUSH + RELOAD and will be described below.

4.1   Co-location Detection

Cloud infrastructures introduce novel threats coming from other customers due to the transparent sharing of physical resources among different virtual machines (VMs). An adversary can then be assigned the same physical server as the target customer and try to break the isolation between VMs, usually exploiting some vulnerabilities of the hypervisor or via side-channels. In 2009, Ristenpart et al. [31] showed how an adversary can co-locate and detect co-resident VMs in public clouds, taking as use case Amazon EC2' platform. In detail, the authors showed that it is possible to build a map of the internal cloud infrastructure with the aim to identify where a particular target VM is likely to be placed and use that knowledge to start new VMs until one is placed on the same physical machine like that of the target. Co-location of VMs is detected by running a number of co-residence checks based on the observation of round-trip times for small packets sent around and on the inspection of the IP assigned to the VMs. Since then cloud providers adopted some countermeasures, and the analysis reported in [19] shows how most of the past techniques are no more effective. Still a test based on the LLC profile has been shown valid and capable to detect co-location of non-cooperating victims on public clouds (such as Amazon EC2, Google Cloud Engine, and Microsoft Azure) in [27].

4.2   Prime + Probe

PRIME + PROBE is a general access-driven attack technique that enables an attacker to learn which cache set is accessed by the victim's VM. Measuring the access time to the shared cache sets, the attacker can detect memory access patterns, that in turn can be used to crypt-analyze the used cryptographic function. More in detail, the attack is composed of three steps. In the first step the attacker *primes* the cache sets with its own data, filling the shared cache. In the second step, the attacker waits for the victim to access the cache, forcing the eviction of some of the code previously loaded. Finally, in the *probing* phase, the attacker tries to access the same data, recording the needed time. In case the victim used some of the cache sets, probe time is higher than when the accessed data are still stored in the cache lines. Monitoring the access time to the shared cache set gives the attacker info on which cache set has been accessed by the victim, that can be used to recover the current state of execution of the victim's code.

4.3   Flush + Reload

FLUSH + RELOAD is a variation of the PRIME + PROBE technique, relying on the fact that memory pages can be shared between the attacker and the victim processes. The attacker will monitor the access time to cache lines that have been flushed away: lower access time means that the victim has already reloaded the code into the cache. Also in this case, the attack is executed in three steps. Firstly, the attacker will evict specific data from the cache hierarchy. Then, in the second phase, she will wait for the victim to reload come cache sets. Finally, the attacker tries to red the data again, determining which data has been accessed by the victim on the base on the registered access time, since accessing the sets reloaded by the victim will be faster than accessing the evicted data in the first step. The FLUSH + RELOAD attack relies also on the possibility for the attacker to share common libraries with the victim and to modify the content of the cache, usually exploiting the `clflush` instruction whose effect is to evict a cache line from all the cache hierarchy. Introduced by Gullasch et al. [18] on a single time-shared core, the FLUSH + RELOAD technique has been extended to cross VMs attacks in virtualized environments in [34]. In [28], a FLUSH + RELOAD attack is launched from a web page using Javascript code, and enabling an attacker to recover information on victim's behavior such as network traffic and mouse movements. An extension of the attack, called FLUSH + FLUSH has been recently presented in [16], where the execution time of just the `clflush` instruction is monitored and used to detect the state of the cache, obtaining an improvement of the performance and making more difficult the attack detection.

5   Discussion

Practical applications of side channel attacks based on the techniques previously presented have been shown possible, allowing an adversary to recover information belonging to other users executing processes on the same physical machines.

As regards RSA keys, a FLUSH + RELOAD based attack has been presented in [34], where the private key is extracted from a victim program using the GnuPG library v1.4.13. The novel versions of the GnuPG library (v.1.4.14) and v.1.5.3 of libgcrypt specifically adopt a countermeasure against this attack implementing the Algorithm 1. The FLUSH + RELOAD technique has been applied by Benger et al. to recover ECDSA keys [2] and by Irazoqui et al. to recover AES keys [21] when VMware VMs are used. Cache Template Attacks have been introduced by Gruss et al. [17] to attack cryptographic implementations, but also any other event which might be of interest to an attacker, such as keyboard stokes. An attack targeting Paas has been reported by Zang et al. [37] showing how it is possible to exploit the FLUSH + RELOAD technique to collect potentially sensitive application data, to break user accounts and SAML single sign-on. The FLUSH + RELOAD technique requires however the deduplication feature to be active in the exploited VMs, feature that has been recently disactivated by default in VMWare and in Amazon AWS servers as reported in [20].

The category of attacks extending the PRIME + PROBE technique, however, has been proved still threatening the private keys from cloud services using cryptographic libraries [19,20,24]. Indeed these attacks rely on the sharing of cache memory among cores of the same processor and on the usage of large pages for mapping guest physical memory in virtualized environments, both features generally used to improve the performances. Other than recovering the RSA keys [19], the technique has been used against square-and-multiply and sliding-window exponentiation algorithms, recovering an El-Gamal key in the GnuPG library, and the AES key in an OpenSSL implementation (v 1.0.1f). In general the approach can be used to attack the implementation of public key crypto-systems as done in the past, even when the deduplication mechanism has been disactivated (and the FLUSH + RELOAD technique is not applicable). As a result, GnuPG updated the library `libgcrypt` to version 1.6.3 adopting the exponent blinding technique to prevent information leakage.

Recently, the *CacheBleed* attack has been disclosed, enabling the attacker to recover 60 % of the private RSA exponent after observing 16.000 decryption operations [35]. The attack relies on the scatter-gather implementation used for modular exponentiation in OpenSSL (v 1.0.2f) and recommended by Intel, to prevent cache-based timing attacks to the secret exponent. The attack can be executed only on a particular micro-architecture where cache is divided into banks and conflicts may occur when concurrent accesses are requested at the same time.

5.1   Countermeasures and Research Challenges

Strategies to prevent access-driven side channel attacks are based on different approaches that can involve hardware resources, the hyper-visor layer, or the software libraries. Some of the attacks indeed, affect only particular platforms, and changes to the mechanisms regulating the fetching of cache lines from the central memory have been proposed. Other countermeasures directly suggest the dis-activation of some feature usually exploited by the hyper-visor such as deduplication, huge pages mapping, LLC isolation, or avoid co-location of VMs. While memory deduplication is no more implemented, in the other cases the adoption of those countermeasures could affect the performance of the offered services. Other approaches exploit directly some characteristic of the platform and change the partitioning mechanism of the cache: The Intel cache allocation technology introduced to optimize memory usage has been used also to obtain secure cache partitions that cannot be shared [25]. At software layer, basic algorithm for the execution of cryptographic primitives have been modified to prevent side channel attacks, adopting for example constant time implementation versions. Some software based mechanisms have been recently proposed in [38], where a memory management subsystem has been implemented to prevent both FLUSH + RELOAD and PRIME + PROBE attacks via the modification of the mechanisms for page sharing and cache line replacement. Protecting the cryptographic key using a scatter/gather technique to avoid unwanted disclosure has been proposed in [1].

An interesting research direction is reported in [10], where authors describe an approach based on static analysis for the analysis of several countermeasures against cache side channel attacks implemented in modular exponentiation algorithms. Another interesting aspect is to investigate the algorithmic countermeasures available to contrast side channel attacks, usually based on modifications to the standard computation of cryptographic procedures [14], generalizing the approaches presented in Sect. 3.2 and proving their effectiveness. How these techniques can be applied without affecting too much the efficiency of the computation and included in the commonly used cryptographic libraries remains a challenge.

6   Conclusions

The trend towards the massive use of virtualized infrastructure is confirmed by the expansion in the offer and in the business of the companies that are offering those kind of services. Using IaaS platforms allows economies of scale and improved efficiency. On the other side, the risks coming from breaking the isolation among co-resident VMs is clearly reported by many attacks described in the literature recently. To have a clear picture of what is the current state of the art of the vulnerabilities and the attacks is important in order to adopt the right countermeasures. A more rigorous classification of the requirements and the goals of the attacks, as regards both hardware and software resources, is needed, in order to increase the knowledge of all the actors – the cloud providers and the customers – to prevent unwanted access to sensible data, and to drive the selection of the services, platforms and software libraries.

References

1. AlBelooshi, B., Salah, K., Martin, T., Damiani, E.: Securing cryptographic keys in the IAAS cloud model. In: Raicu, I., Rana, O.F., Buyya, R. (eds.) 8th IEEE/ACM International Conference on Utility and Cloud Computing, UCC 2015, Limassol, Cyprus, 7–10 December 2015, pp. 397–401. IEEE (2015)
2. Benger, N., van de Pol, J., Smart, N.P., Yarom, Y.: "Ooh Aah... Just a Little Bit": a small amount of side channel can go a long way. In: Batina, L., Robshaw, M. (eds.) CHES 2014. LNCS, vol. 8731, pp. 75–92. Springer, Heidelberg (2014)
3. Bernstein, D.J.: Cache-timing attacks on AES (2005)
4. Boneh, D., Durfee, G., Frankel, Y.: An attack on RSA given a small fraction of the private key bits. In: Ohta, K., Pei, D. (eds.) ASIACRYPT 1998. LNCS, vol. 1514, pp. 25–34. Springer, Heidelberg (1998)
5. Giraud, C.: An RSA implementation resistant to fault attacks and to simple power analysis. IEEE Trans. Comput. 55, 1116–1120 (2006)
6. Cimato, S., Mella, S., Susella, R.: New results for partial key exposure on RSA with exponent blinding. In: SECRYPT 2015 - Proceedings of 12th International Conference on Security and Cryptography, Colmar, Alsace, France, 20–22 July 2015, pp. 136–147 (2015)

7. Cimato, S., Mella, S., Susella, R.: Partial key exposure attacks on RSA with exponent blinding. In: International Conference on E-Business and Telecommunications, pp. 364–385. Springer (2015)
8. Clavier, C., Feix, B., Gagnerot, G., Roussellet, M., Verneuil, V.: Horizontal correlation analysis on exponentiation. In: Soriano, M., Qing, S., López, J. (eds.) ICICS 2010. LNCS, vol. 6476, pp. 46–61. Springer, Heidelberg (2010)
9. Coron, J.-S.: Resistance against differential power analysis for elliptic curve cryptosystems. In: Koç, Ç.K., Paar, C. (eds.) CHES 1999. LNCS, vol. 1717, pp. 292–302. Springer, Heidelberg (1999)
10. Doychev, G., Köpf, B.: Rigorous analysis of software countermeasures against cache attacks. arXiv e-prints, March 2016
11. Ernst, M., Jochemsz, E., May, A., de Weger, B.: Partial key exposure attacks on RSA up to full size exponents. In: Cramer, R. (ed.) EUROCRYPT 2005. LNCS, vol. 3494, pp. 371–386. Springer, Heidelberg (2005)
12. Fouque, P.-A., Kunz-Jacques, S., Martinet, G., Muller, F., Valette, F.: Power attack on small RSA public exponent. In: Goubin, L., Matsui, M. (eds.) CHES 2006. LNCS, vol. 4249, pp. 339–353. Springer, Heidelberg (2006)
13. Garner, H.L.: The residue number system. Papers presented at 3–5 March 1959, Western Joint Computer Conference, IRE-AIEE-ACM 1959 (Western), pp. 146–153. ACM, New York (1959)
14. Kiss, Á., Krämer, J., Rauzy, P., Seifert, J.-P.: Algorithmic countermeasures against fault attacks and power analysis for RSA-CRT. In: Standaert, F.-X., Oswald, E. (eds.) COSADE 2016. LNCS, vol. 9689, pp. 111–129. Springer, Heidelberg (2016)
15. Gordon, D.M.: A survey of fast exponentiation methods. J. Algorithms **27**, 129–146 (1998)
16. Gruss, D., Maurice, C., Wagner, K.: Flush+flush: a stealthier last-level cache attack. In: 13th International Conference on Detection of Intrusions and Malware, and Vulnerability Assessment, DIMVA 2016, Proceedings (2016)
17. Gruss, D., Spreitzer, R., Mangard, S.: Cache template attacks: automating attacks on inclusive last-level caches. In: 24th USENIX Security Symposium (USENIX Security 15), pp. 897–912 (2015)
18. Gullasch, D., Bangerter, E., Krenn, S.: Cache games-bringing access-based cache attacks on AES to practice. In: 2011 IEEE Symposium on Security and Privacy (SP), pp. 490–505. IEEE (2011)
19. Inci, M.S., Gulmezoglu, B., Irazoqui, G., Eisenbarth, T., Sunar, B.: Seriously, get off my cloud! Cross-VM RSA key recovery in a public cloud. Technical report, IACR Cryptology ePrint Archive (2015)
20. Irazoqui, G., Eisenbarth, T., Sunar, B.: S$a: a shared cache attack that works across cores and defies VM sandboxing - and its application to AES. In: 2015 IEEE Symposium on Security and Privacy, pp. 591–604, May 2015
21. Irazoqui, G., Inci, M.S., Eisenbarth, T., Sunar, B.: Wait a minute! A fast, cross-VM attack on AES. In: Stavrou, A., Bos, H., Portokalidis, G. (eds.) RAID 2014. LNCS, vol. 8688, pp. 299–319. Springer, Heidelberg (2014)
22. Joye, M., Lepoint, T.: Partial key exposure on RSA with private exponents larger than N. In: Ryan, M.D., Smyth, B., Wang, G. (eds.) ISPEC 2012. LNCS, vol. 7232, pp. 369–380. Springer, Heidelberg (2012)
23. Kocher, P.C.: Timing attacks on implementations of Diffie-Hellman, RSA, DSS, and other systems. In: Koblitz, N. (ed.) CRYPTO 1996. LNCS, vol. 1109, pp. 104–113. Springer, Heidelberg (1996)

24. Liu, F., Yarom, Y., Ge, Q., Heiser, G., Lee, R.B.: Last-level cache side-channel attacks are practical. In: 2015 IEEE Symposium on Security and Privacy, pp. 605–622, May 2015
25. Liu, F., Ge, Q., Yarom, Y., McKeen, F., Rozas, C.V., Heiser, G., Lee, R.B.: Catalyst: defeating last-level cache side channel attacks in cloud computing. In: HPCA (2016)
26. Maurice, C., Le Scouarnec, N., Neumann, C., Heen, O., Francillon, A.: Reverse engineering Intel last-level cache complex addressing using performance counters. In: 18th International Symposium on Research in Attacks, Intrusions and Defenses (RAID) (2015)
27. Inci, M.S., Gulmezoglu, B., Eisenbarth, T., Sunar, B.: Co-location detection on the cloud. In: Standaert, F.-X., Oswald, E. (eds.) COSADE 2016. LNCS, vol. 9689, pp. 19–34. Springer, Heidelberg (2016)
28. Oren, Y., Kemerlis, V.P., Sethumadhavan, S., Keromytis, A.D.: The spy in the sandbox-practical cache attacks in Javascript (2015). arXiv preprint arXiv: 1502.07373
29. Osvik, D.A., Shamir, A., Tromer, E.: Cache attacks and countermeasures: the case of AES. In: Pointcheval, D. (ed.) CT-RSA 2006. LNCS, vol. 3860, pp. 1–20. Springer, Heidelberg (2006)
30. Quisquater, J.-J., Couvreur, C.: Fast decipherment algorithm for RSA Public-key cryptosystem. Electron. Lett. **18**, 905–907 (1982)
31. Ristenpart, T., Tromer, E., Shacham, H., Savage, S.: Hey, you, get off of my cloud: exploring information leakage in third-party compute clouds. In: Proceedings of 16th ACM Conference on Computer and Communications Security, pp. 199–212. ACM (2009)
32. Suzaki, K., Iijima, K., Yagi, T., Artho, C.: Memory deduplication as a threat to the guest os. In: Proceedings of 4th European Workshop on System Security, EUROSEC 2011, pp. 1:1–1:6. ACM, New York (2011)
33. Suzaki, K., Iijima, K., Yagi, T., Artho, C.: Software side channel attack on memory deduplication. In: SOSP POSTER (2011)
34. Yarom, Y., Falkner, K.: Flush+reload: a high resolution, low noise, l3 cache side-channel attack. In: 23rd USENIX Security Symposium (USENIX Security 14), pp. 719–732 (2014)
35. Yarom, Y., Genkin, D., Heninger, N.: Cachebleed: a timing attack on OpenSSL constant time RSA. Technical report, Cryptology ePrint Archive, Report 2016/224 (2016)
36. Zhang, Y., Juels, A., Reiter, M.K., Ristenpart, T.: Cross-VM side channels and their use to extract private keys. In: Proceedings of 2012 ACM Conference on Computer and Communications Security, CCS 2012, pp. 305–316. ACM, New York (2012)
37. Zhang, Y., Juels, A., Reiter, M.K., Ristenpart, T.: Cross-tenant side-channel attacks in paas clouds. In: Proceedings of 2014 ACM SIGSAC Conference on Computer and Communications Security, pp. 990–1003. ACM (2014)
38. Zhou, Z., Reiter, M.K., Zhang, Y.: A Software approach to defeating side channels in last-level caches (2016). arXiv preprint arXiv: 1603.05615

An Outsourcing Data Storage Scheme Supporting Privacy Preserving and Data Hiding Based on Digital Watermarking

Zhangjie Fu[✉] and Xinyue Cao

Jiangsu Engineering Center of Network Monitoring,
College of Computer and Software, Nanjing University of Information Science
and Technology, Nanjing, China
wwwfzj@126.com, cao2013xinyue@163.com

Abstract. Outsourcing data storage systems reduce storage costs of IT Enterprises and maintenance for users, which have attracted much attention. It is an acceptable way to use cryptography technologies to ensure privacy preserving and access control in secure outsourcing data storage scheme. In this paper, we propose an outsourcing data storage scheme which combines digital watermarking and cryptography technology to support privacy preserving and data hiding. We use the multi-granularity encryption algorithm to preserve the privacy of outsourcing data. The RSA-based proxy re-encryption (PRE) algorithm is used to make the key transportation safe. And the decrypted data containing hiding data is approximate to the original data. Experiments show that our scheme is secure and feasible.

Keywords: Digital watermarking · Outsourcing data storage · Data hiding · Privacy preserving

1 Introduction

In the environment of cloud computing, the data can be stored and distributed easily and quickly. Because vast amounts of data floods in people's lives, outsourcing data to a cloud can be a cost-saving method for storage and maintenance. But cloud data is stored in one or more cloud service providers (CSPs), which are often distributed geographically in different locations. So the data is out of users' control when uploaded to the cloud.

To improve the security of the outsourcing data, encryption and digital signature technologies are used in many schemes. However, encryption can only protect the data during transmission from the sender to the recipient. Once the data is decrypted, the data will be the same as ordinary data and will not be protected. The posterior [1] of the data is a critical issue in outsourcing data storage schemes. The digital signature technology is a common method for identity authentication and copyright protection, which appends signature information to the original data. However, digital watermarking is a more effective identification technology to give a fair and just settlement

© Springer International Publishing AG 2016
X. Sun et al. (Eds.): ICCCS 2016, Part I, LNCS 10039, pp. 468–474, 2016.
DOI: 10.1007/978-3-319-48671-0_41

when dealing with copyright dispute cases. It directly hides authentication information in the digital media without affecting data utilization.

Many existing schemes only research on cryptography technologies, whereas applying digital watermarking to the outsourcing data storage scheme is still in initial stage. Boopathy and Sundaresan [2] proposed a model of data storage and access process with digital watermarking technology in the cloud. In this paper, we further explore the use of digital watermarking in the outsourcing data storage and design an outsourcing data storage scheme supporting privacy preserving and data hiding. Here we focus on image data in the cloud.

We design an outsourcing data storage scheme supporting privacy preserving and data hiding, which combines encryption technologies and digital watermark technology. In this scheme, encryption algorithm can use either simple exclusive-OR operation by a stream cipher [3] or other symmetric encryption algorithms. Here we use the multi-granularity encryption algorithm [4] and the RSA-based proxy re-encryption PRE algorithm to enhance the security of key transportation.

The rest of this paper is organized as follows. Section 2 summarizes the related work. Section 3 introduces the proposed scheme including the detailed methods. Experiment results are given in Sect. 4. Section 5 concludes the paper and shows the future work.

2 Related Work

Many secure outsourcing data storage schemes are proposed in recent years. Many researches on healthcare information systems (HISs) [5] and searchable encryption [6–8] are proposed. And they mainly concern about the security issues on data transmission and utilization. Here we do not research the Internet transmission and search. We focus on data confidentiality, key management and access control in the cloud data storage schemes.

In this paper, encryption must be used in plain image. The keys are managed by an assigned organization DWVS, not by the ownership. In the transmission of encryption keys, the encryption algorithm is based on RSA which reduces the computational complexity. And we introduce digital watermarking into the outsourcing data storage scheme to hide data.

Digital watermarking can be divided into spatial domain watermarking and frequency domain watermarking [9]. Spatial domain digital watermarking technology directly embeds watermark information into the image pixels. Frequency domain [10] algorithm embeds watermark information into coefficients of transform domain. LSB watermark algorithm makes little impact on the image, which cannot make the human visual perception system perceived.

Here we use a simple multi-blind watermark algorithm based on modified LSB substitution to hide data. The position of embedding only depends on the embedding key. The extraction of the watermark does not need the original image and original watermark.

3 Proposed Scheme

We first descript the notations used in the paper in Table 1.

Table 1. Notations used in our scheme

Notation	Description
DWAS	digital watermarking allocation server
DWVS	digital watermarking verification server
CSP	cloud server provider
DO	data owner
DU	data user
Kc	encryption key of DO/decryption key of DU
Kw	data hiding key of DWAS/data extracting key of DWVS
APK/ASK	public key/secret key of DWAS
VPK/VSK	public key/secret key of DWVS
OPK/OSK	public key/secret key of DO
UPK/USK	public key/secret key of DU

In this paper, we propose an outsourcing data storage scheme supporting privacy preserving and data hiding based on digital watermarking. The sketch of the proposed scheme is shown in Fig. 1. There are five parties in the scheme: DO, DU, DWAS, DWVS and CSP. RSA asymmetric encryption algorithm is used during the transmission of keys, and the security problem turns into the difficulty of calculating the private keys.

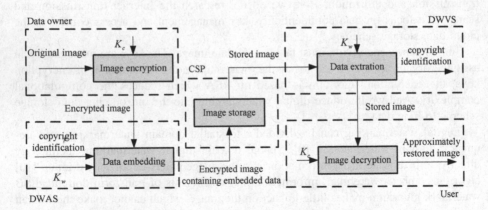

Fig. 1. Sketch of the proposed Scheme

In this scheme, DO assigns DWVS as a proxy. DWVS is given a re-encryption key $r_{o \to u}$, which can transform K_c under DO's public key OPK into K_c under DU's public key UPK. Here we give a formal description of a PRE scheme [11].

During the transmission of keys, the RSA encryption algorithm is used. It makes the security problem into a problem of calculating the private key. Unless knowing the decryption key K_c, you will not decrypt the data. When DO forwards the encryption key K_c, proxy re-encryption based on RSA algorithm is used. This ensures that the proxy DWVS transmits K_c to DU, but he does not know K_c. From above, the key transmission is secure and no one can obtain the original data. Therefore, we focus on the image encryption and data hiding in the encryption domain.

Then four modules including of image encryption, watermarking embedding, watermarking extraction and image decryption will be detailed.

3.1 Image Encryption

DO creates an original image I. Assume I is a gray image sized $M \times M$ pixels in uncompressed format. DO encrypts the original image I with the encryption key K_c. Multi-granularity encryption algorithm [4] is introduced as follows.

- Divide the original image I into h equal-sized non-overlapping blocks $\{B_i\}_{i=1}^n$. Each block B_i is composed of $m \times m$ pixels.
- Random permutation with multi-granularity encryption: pixels random permutation in each block with the seed of s_1 and blocks random permutation with the seed of s_2.
- The encrypted image E is generated. The encryption key K_c includes the parameter m, the seed of random permutation s_1 and s_2.

This algorithm is simple and has good performance. The algorithm keeps the histogram statistical properties of the local image. And from the key transmission part above, K_c cannot be obtained except for legal DU.

3.2 Watermarking Embedding

DWAS embeds the secret watermarking W into the encrypted image E. W should be unpredictable and random. Zhang [3] embeds watermark information by flipping the 3 LSBs of each encrypted pixel. But only embedding to the LSBs can easily be filtered out by deleting the LSBs plane of image. So we choose random bit plane of the pixels between the 3rd and the 6th to embed watermark bit. The embedding position only depends on the data hiding key K_w.

Assume the secret watermarking image W is sized $N \times N$. W can be converted into a binary sequence set S. When embeds W into the encrypted image E, the steps are as follows. Assume the secret watermarking image W is sized $N \times N$. W can be converted into a binary sequence set S. When DWAS embeds S into the encrypted image E, the steps are as follows.

- Select $N \times N$ pixels in the encrypted image E with the seed of random permutation s_3.
- From these chosen pixels, the certain bit plane is selected with the seed s_4 and is replaced by the bit $s \in \{0, 1\}$ from the binary sequence set S.

- The encrypted image $\hat{E}$ with secret watermarking is obtained. The data hiding key K_w consists of the parameter N, the seed s_3 and s_4.

Then DWVS sends the encrypted image $\hat{E}$ with secret watermarking to CSP and only DWVS can obtain the data hiding key K_w.

3.3 Watermarking Extraction

DWVS extracts the secret watermarking W' from the encryption domain with the data extracting key K_w when the copyright dispute cases occur. That means the appealer must encrypt the pirate plain image with K_c before uploading it to DWVS. Then DWVS can extract the secret watermarking from the appealer's encrypted image $\hat{E}$. This extracting algorithm is similar with the watermarking embedding process.

3.4 Image Decryption

DU can decrypt the encrypted image $\hat{E}$ with secret watermarking using the decryption key K_c. And DU can obtain an image I' approximating to the original image I if DU has the privilege of access. The detailed multi-granularity decryption algorithm is similar with the image encryption process.

4 Experiment and Analysis

To study the performance of the proposed scheme, MATLAB software 7 is used. The test image Lena of 8-bit gray level sized 512×512 pixels is selected as an original image and shown in Fig. 2(a). We use multi-granularity encryption algorithm [4] to generate the encrypted image shown in Fig. 2(b). The encrypted image with embedded data is shown in Fig. 2(c). Figure 2(d) is the decrypted image.

(a)　　　　　　　(b)　　　　　　　(c)　　　　　　　(d)

Fig. 2. (a) Original Image (b) Encrypted image by DO (c) Encrypted image embedded with secret watermarking (d) Decrypted image with secret watermarking

The quality of the decrypted image with secret watermarking can be evaluated by Peak Signal-to-Noise Ratio (PSNR).

$$PSNR = 10 \times log_{10}\left(\frac{255^2}{\frac{1}{M \times M}\sum_{i=1}^{M}\sum_{j=1}^{M}(I(i,j) - I'(i,j))^2}\right), \quad (1)$$

where I is the original image, I' is the decrypted image with secret watermarking. $M \times M$ is the size of image I in pixels. In this scheme, image Lena, airfield, aerial, bridge sized 512×512 are used and parameter PSNR is obtained in Table 2.

Table 2. PSNR value

Image	PSNR(dB)
Lena	57.25
Airfield	57.01
Aerial	57.11
Bridge	57.05

From Table 2, the PSNR value is greater than 57 dB, which means the decrypted image with secret watermarking has high quality.

5 Conclusion and Future Work

In this paper, we propose a scheme which combines digital watermark and cryptography technology in outsourcing data storage. We use the multi-granularity encryption algorithm to preserve the privacy of outsourcing data. The RSA-based proxy re-encryption (PRE) algorithm is used to make the key transportation safe.

In the future, we will take the key updating into account and use attribute-based PRE. With such PRE algorithm, data owner can assign several users with the same set of attributes at a time. We also can add fragile watermark to verify the integrity of images.

Acknowledgments. This work is supported by the NSFC (U1536206, 61232016, U1405254, 61373133, 61502242), BK20150925, and PAPD fund.

References

1. Drel-Khameesy, N., Rahman, H.A.: A Proposed model for enhancing data storage security in cloud computing systems. Emerg. Trends Comput. Inf. Sci. **3**(6), 970–974 (2012)
2. Boopathy, D., Sundaresan, M.: Data encryption frame-work model with watermarking security for data storage in public cloud model. In: IEEE International Conference on Computing for Sustainable Global Development (INDIACom), pp. 903–907 (2014)
3. Zhang, X.: Reversible data hiding in encrypted image. IEEE. Sig. Process. Lett. **18**(4), 255–258 (2011)
4. Yin, Z., Luo, B., Hong, W.: Separable and error-free reversible data hiding in encrypted image with high payload. Sci. World J. 2014(2014), 1–8 (2014). doi:10.1155/2014/604876

5. Xiong, N., Vasilakos, A.V., Yang, L.T., Song, L., Pan, Y., Kannan, R., Li, Y.: Comparative analysis of quality of service and memory usage for adaptive failure detectors in healthcare systems. IEEE J. Sel. Areas Commun. **27**(4), 495–509 (2009)
6. Fu, Z., Wu, X., Guan, C., Sun, X., Ren, K.: Towards efficient multi-keyword fuzzy search over encrypted outsourced data with accuracy improvement. IEEE Trans. Inf. Forensics Secur. **11**, 2706–2716 (2016)
7. Fu, Z., Ren, K., Shu, J., Sun, X., Huang, F.: Enabling personalized search over encrypted outsourced data with efficiency improvement. IEEE Trans. Parallel Distrib. Syst. (TPDS) **27**, 2546–2559 (2016). doi:10.1109/TPDS.2015.2506573
8. Fu, Z., Sun, X., Liu, Q., Zhou, L., Shu, J.: Achieving efficient cloud search services: multi-keyword ranked search over encrypted cloud data supporting parallel computing. IEICE Trans. Commun. **E98-B**(1), 190–200 (2015)
9. Cheung, W.N.: Digital image watermarking in spatial and transform domains. In: 2000 Proceedings of TENCON, pp. 374–378. IEEE (2000)
10. Wang, S.H., Lin, Y.P.: Wavelet tree quantization for copyright protection watermarking. IEEE Trans. Image Process. **13**(2), 154–165 (2004)
11. Chen, Y.R., Tygar, J.D., Tzeng, W.G.: Secure group key management using unidirectional proxy re-encryption schemes. In: Proceedings of IEEE International Conference on Computer Communications (INFOCOM), pp. 1952–1960, 1975–1980 (2011)

Distributed Quantum Computation Assisted by Remote Toffoli Gate

Ming-Xing Luo[✉] and Hui-Ran Li

Information Security and National Computing Grid Laboratory,
Southwest Jiaotong University, Chengdu 610031, China
luomxgg@163.com

Abstract. Distributed quantum computation requires quantum operations to act on logical qubits over a distance. We will develop a formal model for the telegate-based distributive quantum computation. We show that a controlled-controlled-NOT (Toffoli) gate as an elementary gate of the universal quantum computation may be remotely implemented by exploring a high-level quantum system. These remote Toffoli gates cost at most two Einstein-Podolsky-Rosen (EPR) pairs, whereas four or six EPR pairs are required from the teleportation-based quantum computation or the remote CNOT gate, respectively. Thus, the previous Toffoli gate-based circuit synthesis may be used as an elementary subroutine of this distributed quantum computation.

1 Introduction

Quantum computations have been designed as physical processes that directly incorporate the laws of quantum mechanics [1,2]. Unlike the classical computer based on data encoding using bits 0 and 1, quantum computer directly uses the superposition of basic physic states $|0\rangle$ and $|1\rangle$-qubits, i.e., $\alpha|0\rangle + \beta|1\rangle$. In physics, these encoded states may be obtained using one degree of freedom (DoF) of photons, atoms, ions, or electrons [3], or different DoFs of photons [4–6].

A large-scale quantum computer may solve problems faster than classical computers with the best known algorithms. As a theoretical trial, Deutsch and Jozsa extended the earlier black box problem with a probabilistic scheme [7] to one with a deterministic scheme. Although their problem is easily solved on a probabilistic classical computer, it has inspired new schemes, such as Simon's exponential speedup scheme [8] over classical probabilistic algorithms, and Grover's quadratic speedup scheme for database searching [9]. In particular, Shor provided the first nontrivial sub-exponential speedup algorithm [10] for integer factorization over the best number field sieve algorithms [11,12]. Farhi et al. [13] tested the quantum adiabatic algorithm with polynomial complexity for the small examples of the 3-SAT problem. Recently, Lloyd et al. [14] show that the quantum algorithm, which reveals the eigenvectors that correspond to the large eigenvalues of the unknown state. This algorithm may be used to speed up solving machine-learning problems such as clustering and pattern recognition [15,16]. These results have inspired many studies on quantum computations

© Springer International Publishing AG 2016
X. Sun et al. (Eds.): ICCCS 2016, Part I, LNCS 10039, pp. 475–485, 2016.
DOI: 10.1007/978-3-319-48671-0_42

[17–24]. Some algorithms have been experimentally implemented at small scales [25–30].

In experiment, quantum memories may be formed out of matter such as atoms with localized spins at quantum dots [31–34]. When these quantum systems are prepared, they may be geographically distributed or collocated with other distributed systems to overcome the inherent limitations on size of a single quantum computer. Thus, similar to the classical cases [35], distributed quantum computation is defined and should be built using two or more quantum computers to solve a single problem [36–48]. To setup a distributed quantum computation, the quantum channel should be defined to transfer quantum information at different quantum computers. One time-consuming method is to directly transfer particles. This method may be inefficient for information interchange, unstable for physical correlation and insecure for confidential information processing. Quantum entanglement provides another opportunity to indirectly transfer quantum information. The so-called quantum teleportation [49] is not only a typical application different from classical information transmission, but also a primitive structure for previous distributed quantum computations [36–43]. In these applications, quantum systems may be teleported to complete a joint system evolution among distributive systems for a common goal. As an alternative to teleporting information (teledata), elementary logic gates such as the controlled-NOT gate may be directly implemented in the distributed system, which is referred as telegate [44–47].

In this paper, motivated by the telegate [44–48] and cost analysis of distributed quantum computation [36,45], we propose a new telegate-based quantum computation model with balanced resource requirements. The Toffoli gate as an elementary gate may be used to synthesize the quantum circuit. These universal gates are also convenient for multiple-controlling logic gates that are derived from natural decomposition of the joint system evolution [3,21]. Thus, a remote Toffoli gate-based quantum computation may be naturally followed. The new telegate-based quantum model results in a natural distributive quantum computer (QDC) architecture. Each party holds only a few logical qubits and is connected to other neighbors. The quantum information transmission is assumed to be completed with an entangled channel, probably using a strong probe laser beam as an example. The one-sided or double-sided optical cavities are candidates to bridge remote qubits. Unlike previous telegate schemes of the remote CNOT gate with one EPR pair [44,45,47], a nontrivial three-qubit gate, i.e., controlled controlled-NOT gate or Toffoli gate [48,50], may be remotely implemented with no more than two EPR pairs using an auxiliary four-dimensional (ququart) state. If the teleportation-based quantum model [36–43] or teleporting CNOT gate [44,45,47] is considered, our schemes will save one half or two thirds of entanglement resources, respectively. This reduction presents obvious advantage for large-scale quantum applications. Of course, except an elementary gate to synthesize the quantum circuit, a Toffoli gate may be used for quantum fault-tolerant computation or quantum error correction [51–56].

This article is organized as follows. In Sect. 2, we present distributive Toffoli gate vias bipartite or tripartite system. Subsequently, the hybrid decomposition of general unitary gate is shown in Sect. 3. The last section presents conclusions of our proposals.

2   Distributive Toffoli Gate

2.1   Toffoli Gate on a Bipartite System

Previous results show that the CNOT gate may be implemented in remote systems with only one EPR pair [44,45,47,48]. A similar result for the Toffoli gate may be obtained with higher efficiency. This three-qubit gate is described as $|A\rangle|B\rangle|C\rangle \mapsto |A\rangle|B\rangle|AB \oplus C\rangle$ in the computation basis, as shown in Fig. 1. A Toffoli gate generally costs six CNOT gates [3,21,57]. If an auxiliary high-level system is applied, a Toffoli gate will cost only three general controlled NOT gates [57–59]. In the following part, remote Toffoli gates will be directly implemented with quantum entanglements using an auxiliary high-level system.

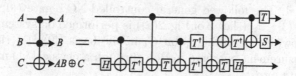

Fig. 1. Toffoli gate and its decomposition circuit [3,21]. T and S are special qubit rotation operations, and H is Hadamard operation.

Assume that two separated parties Alice and Bob have to implement a Toffoli gate on their qubits A_i in the state $|\phi\rangle_{A_1 A_2 A_3} = \sum_{i_1,i_2,i_3=0}^{1} \alpha_{i_1 i_2 i_3}|i_1 i_2 i_3\rangle$. Here, $|\phi\rangle_{A_1 A_2 A_3}$ may be an entanglement or a product state. Alice has two qubits A_1 and A_2, and Bob has qubit A_3. A shared EPR pair $|\Phi\rangle_{C_1 C_2} = \frac{1}{\sqrt{2}}(|00\rangle + |11\rangle)_{C_1 C_2}$ is used to complete this task. The schematic circuit is shown in Fig. 2(a) using an auxiliary 4-dimensional quantum system D (under the normal basis $\{|0\rangle, |1\rangle, |2\rangle, |3\rangle\}$, which is encoded by multiple energy levels of an atom or two degrees of freedom of a photon [4–6,57,58]) in the state $|0\rangle$. Here, an elevation E on system D is defined as

$$E = |1\rangle\langle 0| + |2\rangle\langle 1| + |3\rangle\langle 2| + |0\rangle\langle 3| \tag{1}$$

The detailed evolution of the joint system is shown as follows. First, three controlled elevation CEs are performed by Alice to change the joint system in the state $|\phi|0\rangle_D$ into

$$|\Psi_1\rangle = \sum_{i_1,i_2,i_3=0}^{1} \alpha_{i_1 i_2 i_3}|i_1 i_2 i_3\rangle_{A_1 A_2 A_3}|2i_1 + i_2\rangle_D \tag{2}$$

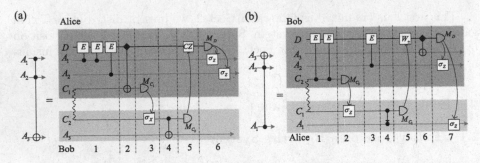

Fig. 2. Remote Toffoli gate on a bipartite system (red lines). (a) Remote target qubit. (b) Hybrid remote control qubits. σ_z is Pauli phase flip operation. D is an auxiliary four-dimensional quantum system in the state $|0\rangle$ (black line). C_1C_2 is an EPR pair $|\Phi\rangle_{C_1C_2}$ (blue lines). E and $W_\pm$ denote proper quantum operations. M_Y denotes the quantum measurement in system Y in a proper basis. (Color figure online)

where the controlled elevation gate is defined by $CE = |0\rangle\langle0| \otimes I_4 + |1\rangle\langle1| \otimes E$ and performed on the joint system of A_1 and D or A_2 and D. I_4 is an identity matrix of rank 4. The followed general controlled-NOT gate $(|0\rangle\langle0| + |1\rangle\langle1| + |2\rangle\langle2|) \otimes I_2 + |3\rangle\langle3| \otimes \sigma_x$ (slice 2 of Fig. 2(a)) is performed on system D and qubit C_1 by Alice. Now, by measuring qubit C_1 in the basis $\{|0\rangle, |1\rangle\}$ (in slice 3) and sending its measurement outcome to Bob through a classical channel, Alice will collapse the state into

$$|\Psi_2\rangle = \sum_{i_1+i_2\neq2} \alpha_{i_1i_2i_3}|i_1i_2i_3\rangle_{A_1A_2A_3}|2i_1+i_2\rangle_D|0\rangle_{C_2}$$
$$+ \sum_{i_3=0}^{1} \alpha_{11i_3}|11i_3\rangle_{A_1A_2A_3}|3\rangle_D|1\rangle_{C_2} \tag{3}$$

where σ_x is performed on qubit C_2 by Bob for measurement outcome $|1\rangle_{C_1}$.

In slice 4, Bob performs a CNOT gate on their qubits C_2 and A_3, and then collapses its into

$$|\Psi_3\rangle = \sum_{i_1+i_2\neq2} \alpha_{i_1i_2i_3}|i_1i_2i_3\rangle_{A_1A_2A_3}|2i_1+i_2\rangle_D + \sum_{i_3=0}^{1} \alpha_{11i_3}\sigma_x^{A_3}|11i_3\rangle_{A_1A_2A_3}|3\rangle_D \tag{4}$$

after Bob measures qubit C_2 in the basis $\{|\pm\rangle := \frac{1}{\sqrt{2}}(|0\rangle \pm |1\rangle)\}$ and sends his measurement outcomes to Alice through a classical channel (in slice 5). Here, a phase flip CZ which is defined by

$$CZ = |0\rangle\langle0| + |1\rangle\langle1| + |2\rangle\langle2| - |3\rangle\langle3| \tag{5}$$

is performed on quantum system D by Alice for the measurement outcome $|-\rangle_{C_2}$.

Finally (in slice 6), Alice measures quantum system D in a general basis $\{|D_i\rangle, i = 0, 1, 2, 3\}$, which is defined by

$$\{|D_0\rangle = \frac{1}{2}(|0\rangle + |1\rangle + |2\rangle + |3\rangle), |D_1\rangle = \frac{1}{2}(|0\rangle - |1\rangle + |2\rangle - |3\rangle),$$

$$|D_2\rangle = \frac{1}{2}(|0\rangle + |1\rangle - |2\rangle - |3\rangle), |D_3\rangle = \frac{1}{2}(|0\rangle - |1\rangle - |2\rangle + |3\rangle)\} \tag{6}$$

The state in Eq. (4) will collapse into

$$|\Psi_4\rangle = [\sum_{i_1+i_2\neq 2} \alpha_{i_1 i_2 i_3}|i_1 i_2 i_3\rangle + \sum_{i_3=0}^{1} \alpha_{11i_3}(\sigma_x^{A_3}|11i_3\rangle)]_{A_1 A_2 A_3} \tag{7}$$

The recovery operations are shown in Table 1. Thus, Alice and Bob have implemented a Toffoli gate on their remote qubits A_1, A_2 and A_3 with only one EPR pair.

Table 1. The relations between measurement outcomes of quantum system D and feed-forward operations for implementing a Toffoli gate on remote three qubits.

Measurement outcome	Feed-forward correction	
	Qubit A_1	Qubit A_2
$|D_0\rangle$	I	I
$|D_1\rangle$	σ_z	I
$|D_2\rangle$	I	σ_z
$|D_3\rangle$	σ_z	σ_z

Similarly, if Alice has qubit A_1 and Bob has qubits A_2 and A_3, they can implement a Toffoli gate on their remote qubits with an EPR pair $|\Phi\rangle_{C_1 C_2}$ and an auxiliary four-dimensional quantum system D. The schematic circuit is shown in Fig. 2(b).

2.2 Toffoli Gate on a Tripartite System

Unlike the Toffoli gate in a bipartite system in Fig. 2, assume that three parties Alice, Bob and Charlie jointly implement a Toffoli gate on three qubits A_i in this subsection. The schematic circuit is shown in Fig. 3 using an auxiliary four-dimensional quantum system D in the state $|0\rangle$ and two EPR pairs $|\Phi\rangle_{C_1 C_2}$ and $|\Phi\rangle_{C_3 C_4}$.

First, because two controlling qubits A_1 and A_2 belong to Alice and Bob, respectively, they can locally get the joint system using the subcircuit defined by slices 1–5 in Fig. 2(b). Then, Bob performs a general controlled-NOT gate $(|0\rangle\langle 0| + |1\rangle\langle 1| + |2\rangle\langle 2|) \otimes I_2 + |3\rangle\langle 3| \otimes \sigma_x$ on system D and qubit C_3 (in slice 6).

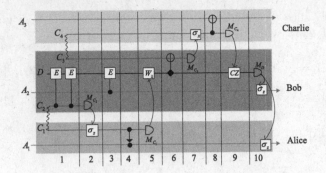

Fig. 3. Remote Toffoli gate on a tripartite system (red lines). A_1 and A_2 are two controlling qubits, whereas A_3 is the target qubit. CZ, E, and $W_\pm$ are the same as these defined in Fig. 2. M_Y denotes the measurement on system Y in a proper basis. D is an auxiliary four-dimensional system in the state $|0\rangle$. $|\Phi\rangle_{C_1 C_2}$ and $|\Phi\rangle_{C_3 C_4}$ are two EPR pairs, which are shared by Alice and Bob, and Bob and Charlie, respectively. (Color figure online)

The joint system will be changed into

$$|\Psi_1'\rangle = \sum_{i_1+i_2 \neq 2} \alpha_{i_1 i_2 i_3} |i_1 i_2 i_3\rangle_{A_1 A_2 A_3} |2i_1 + i_2\rangle_D |\Phi\rangle_{C_3 C_4}$$

$$+ \sum_{i_3=0}^{1} \alpha_{11 i_3} |11 i_3\rangle_{A_1 A_2 A_3} |3\rangle_D (\sigma_x^{C_3} |\Phi\rangle_{C_3 C_4}), \qquad \bullet \ (8)$$

which may collapse into (after slice 7)

$$|\Psi_7'\rangle = [\sum_{i_1+i_2 \neq 2} \alpha_{i_1 i_2 i_3} |i_1 i_2 i_3\rangle |2i_1 + i_2\rangle |0\rangle + \sum_{i_3=0}^{1} \alpha_{11 i_3} |11 i_3\rangle |3\rangle |1\rangle]_{A_1 A_2 A_3, D, C_4} (9)$$

after Bob measures qubit C_3 in the basis $\{|0\rangle, |1\rangle\}$. Here, a Pauli flip σ_x is performed on qubit C_4 by Charlie for the measurement outcome $|1\rangle_{C_3}$.

Now, Charlie performs a CNOT gate on her qubits C_4 and A_3 (in slice 8). In slice 9, Charlie measures qubit C_4 in the basis $\{|\pm\rangle\}$ and sends the measurement outcomes to Bob through a classical channel. $|\Psi_1'\rangle$ may collapse into

$$|\Psi_2'\rangle = [\sum_{i_1+i_2 \neq 2} \alpha_{i_1 i_2 i_3} |i_1 i_2 i_3\rangle |2i_1 + i_2\rangle + \sum_{i_3=0}^{1} \alpha_{11 i_3} (\sigma_x^{A_3} |11 i_3\rangle) |3\rangle]_{A_1 A_2 A_3, D} (10)$$

where a phase gate CZ is performed on quantum system D for the measurement outcome $|-\rangle_{C_4}$.

Finally, Bob measures auxiliary quantum state D in a proper basis, and $|\Psi_2'\rangle$ will collapse into $|\Psi_4\rangle$ in Eq. (7). Thus, a Toffoli gate may be implemented on three remote qubits with two EPR pairs. The total costs of entanglement are shown in

Table 2. Entanglement (EPR pair) cost of telegate vs teleporting qubits (telequbit for short) to implement CNOT gate or Toffoli gate. Here, Toffoli$_{CNOT}$ denotes implementation of Toffoli gate using its detailed decomposition with CNOT gates shown in Fig. 1.

Elementary gate	Using telegate		Using telequbit	
	Bipartite	Tripartite	Bipartite	Tripartite
CNOT	1	-	2	-
Toffoli$_{CNOT}$	4	6	2	4
Toffoli	1	2	2	4

Table 2, where our remote implementation of a Toffoli gate is more efficient than that with a remote CNOT gate [44–48] or teleportation [36]. Furthermore, the cost of remotely implementing a multi-controlling qubit gate [21] with multi-partite is shown in Table 3, where the multi-controlling qubit operations are more efficient with a remote Toffoli gate than with a remote CNOT gate.

3   Hybrid Decomposition of General Quantum Operations

Consider a general quantum application involving n qubits, whose evolution may be described by a general $2^n \times 2^n$ unitary matrix U. One simple simulation is realized using the Cosine-Sine (CS) decomposition of U [3], which states

$$U = (L_1 \oplus L_2)e^{i\sigma_y \otimes \Theta_{2^{n-1}}}(R_1 \oplus R_2) \tag{11}$$

where $X \oplus Y = \mathrm{diag}(X, Y)$ and $\Theta_{2^{n-1}} = \mathrm{diag}(\theta_0, \theta_1, \cdots, \theta_{2^{n-1}-1})$ for proper angles θ_j, and σ_y is Pauli matrix defined by $(0 \quad i; -i \quad 0)$. By recursively applying this decomposition for $L_1 \oplus L_2$ and $R_1 \oplus R_2$, a diagonal decomposition of U may be obtained with various exponential operations $e^{i\sigma_y \otimes \Theta}$.

In the follow, these exponential operations should be decomposed. In fact, define

$$\Lambda^n(X) = I_{2^n-2} \oplus X \tag{12}$$

for any qubit operation X and an identity operation of rank $2^n - 2$. A general rotation $e^{i\sigma_y \otimes \Theta_{2^{n-1}}}$ may be rewritten as

$$e^{i\sigma_y \otimes \Theta_{2^{n-1}}} = \prod_{j=0}^{2^{n-1}} \Lambda_j^n(\theta_j) \tag{13}$$

where $\Lambda_j^n(\theta_j)$ denote multi-controlling rotations with qubit rotations

$$R(\theta_j) = \begin{pmatrix} \cos(\theta_j) & \sin(\theta_j) \\ -\sin(\theta_j) & \cos(\theta_j) \end{pmatrix}, \tag{14}$$

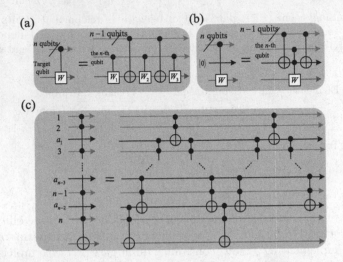

Fig. 4. General decomposition of multi-controlling gates of (a) without auxiliary qubit, (b) with one auxiliary qubit, and (c) with $n-2$ auxiliary qubits. Red lines denote controlling qubits while blue line denotes target qubit. W is an arbitrary qubit operation and may be decomposed into $W_3\sigma_x W_2 \sigma_x W_1 = W$. (Color figure online)

and all of their target qubits are the first qubit while their controlling terms are the last $n-1$ qubits. The followed simulation of multi-controlling gates is completed with combinations of CNOT gate and Toffoli gate, as shown in Fig. 4.

Table 3. The entanglement cost of the telegate based on Toffoli vs CNOT decomposition to implement $n+1$-qubit $\Lambda^n(W)$ gate with $n+1$-partite.

Used elementary gate	Gate's number	Telegate's cost
Toffoli gate	$16n - 44$	$32n - 88$
CNOT gate	$96n - 264$	$96n - 264$

Specially, the multi-controlling NOT gate $\Lambda^n(\sigma_x)$ may be synthesized using circuit shown in Fig. 4(c). Here, red lines denote controlling qubits, black lines denote auxiliary garbage qubits while blue line denotes target qubit. From this circuit, $\Lambda^n(\sigma_x)$ costs $4(n-2)$ $\Lambda^2(\sigma_x)$ (Toffoli gate). Hence, combining with circuit in Fig. 4(b), $\Lambda^n(\sigma_x)$ costs $2 \times 4(n-1-2) + 2 = 8n - 22$ $\Lambda^3(\sigma_x)$ (Toffoli gate), and $\Lambda^n(W)$ requires $96n - 264$ CNOT gates. Required EPR pairs are shown in Table 3, if distributed quantum systems are considered. It shows that remote implementations of multi-controlling qubit operations are more efficient with remote Toffoli gate than these using remote CNOT gate.

4   Conclusions

This paper has presented a general model for the telegate-based quantum computation. This quantum computation model is completed with hybrid telegates, i.e., remote CNOT gate and remote Toffoli gate. Compared with the previous remote CNOT gate [44, 45, 47], the remote Toffoli gate may be implemented with one EPR pair for a bipartite system or two EPR pairs for a tripartite system using a high-level quantum system [58, 59]. These entanglement costs are only one quarter or one third of these costs with a remote CNOT gate, and one half of the cost of remote implementation using teleportation [49]. Unlike the recent hybrid system of remote Toffoli gate [48], our motivation in this paper is to propose a general theoretical model for telegate-based quantum computation by combining the remote CNOT gate and remote Toffoli gate.

Acknowledgements. This work is supported by the National Natural Science Foundation of China (No. 61303039), Chuying Fellowship, CSC Fund, and Open Foundation of China-USA Computer Science Research Center (Nanjing University of Information Science and Technology) (No. KJR16132).

References

1. Feynman, R.: Simulating physics with computers. Int. J. Theoret. Phys. **21**(6), 467–488 (1982)
2. Deutsch, D.: Quantum theory, the Church-Turing principle and the universal quantum computer. Proc. R. Soc. A **400**(1818), 97–117 (1985)
3. Nielsen, M.A., Chuang, I.L.: Quantum Computation and Quantum Information. Cambridge University Press, Cambridge (2000). pp. 216–271
4. Barreiro, J.T., Langford, N.K., Peters, N.A., Kwiat, P.G.: Generation of hyperentangled photon pairs. Phys. Rev. Lett. **95**, 260501 (2005)
5. Wang, X.L., et al.: Quantum teleportation of multiple degrees of freedom of a single photon. Nature **518**(7540), 516–519 (2015)
6. Luo, M.X., Wang, X.: Parallel photonic quantum computation assisted by quantum dots in one-side optical microcavities. Sci. Rep. **4**, 5732 (2014)
7. Deutsch, D., Jozsa, R.: Rapid solution of problems by quantum computation. Proc. R. Soc. A **439**(1907), 553–558 (1992)
8. Simon, D.R.: On the power of quantum computation. SIAM J. Comput. **26**(5), 116–123 (1997)
9. Grover, L.: Quantum mechanics helps in searching for a needle in a haystack. Phys. Rev. Lett. **79**(2), 325–328 (1997)
10. Shor, P.W.: Polynomial-time algorithms for prime factorization and discrete logarithms on a quantum computer. SIAM J. Comput. **26**(5), 1484–1509 (1997)
11. Murphy, B., Brent, R.P.: On quadratic polynomials for the number field sieve. Aust. Comput. Sci. Commun. **20**, 199–213 (1998)
12. Rivest, R., Shamir, A., Adleman, L.: A method for obtaining digital signatures and public-key cryptosystems. Commun. ACM **21**(6), 120–126 (1978)
13. Farhi, E., et al.: A quantum adiabatic evolution algorithm applied to random instances of an NP-complete problem. Science **292**(5516), 472–475 (2001)
14. Lloyd, S., Mohseni, M., Rebentrost, P.: Quantum principal component analysis. Nat. Phys. **10**, 631–633 (2014)
15. Bishop, C.M.: Pattern Recognition and Machine Learning. Springer, Berlin (2006). pp. 130–211
16. Gu, B., Sheng, V.S., Wang, Z., Ho, D., Osman, S., Li, S.: Incremental learning for v-support vector regression. Neural Netw. **67**, 140–150 (2015)

17. Chen, B., Shu, H., Coatrieux, G., Chen, G., Sun, X., Coatrieux, J.-L.: Color image analysis by quaternion-type moments. J. Math. Imaging Vis. **51**(1), 124–144 (2015)
18. Xia, Z., Wang, X., Sun, X., Wang, B.: Steganalysis of least significant bit matching using multi-order differences. Sec. Commun. Netw. **7**(8), 1283–1291 (2014)
19. Regev, O.: Quantum computation and lattice problems. SIAM J. Comput. **33**(3), 738–760 (2004)
20. Kuperberg, G.: A subexponential-time quantum algorithm for the dihedral hidden subgroup problem. SIAM J. Comput. **35**(1), 170–188 (2005)
21. Barenco, A., et al.: Elementary gates for quantum computation. Phys. Rev. A **52**, 34–57 (1995)
22. Nielsen, M.A., Dowling, M.R., Gu, M., Doherty, A.C.: Quantum computation as geometry. Science **311**, 1133–1135 (2006)
23. Radhakrishnan, J., Rotteler, M., Sen, P.: Random measurement bases, quantum state distinction and applications to the hidden subgroup problem. Algorithmica **55**, 490–516 (2006)
24. Kawachi, A., Koshiba, T., Nishimura, H., Yamakami, T.: Computational indistinguishability between quantum states and its cryptographic application. J. Cryptol. **25**, 528–555 (2009)
25. Chuang, I.L., Vandersypen, L.M.K., Zhou, X., Leung, D.W., Lloyd, S.: Experimental realization of a quantum algorithm. Nature **393**, 143–146 (1998)
26. Jones, J.A., Mosca, M., Hansen, R.H.: Implementation of a quantum search algorithm on a quantum computer. Nature **393**, 344–346 (1998)
27. Vandersypen, L.M.K., et al.: Experimental realization of Shor's quantum factoring algorithm using nuclear magnetic resonance. Nature **414**, 883–887 (2001)
28. Lucero, E., et al.: Computing prime factors with a Josephson phase qubit quantum processor. Nat. Phys. **8**, 719–723 (2012)
29. Feng, G., Xu, G., Long, G.: Experimental realization of nonadiabatic holonomic quantum computation. Phys. Rev. Lett. **110**, 190501 (2013)
30. Tame, M.S., Bell, B.A., Di Franco, C., Wadsworth, W.J., Rarity, J.G.: Experimental realization of a one-way quantum computer algorithm solving Simon's problem. Phys. Rev. Lett. **113**, 200501 (2014)
31. Sun, C.P., Li, Y., Liu, X.F.: Quasi-spin-wave quantum memories with a dynamical symmetry. Phys. Rev. Lett. **91**, 147903 (2003)
32. Simon, J., Haruka, T., Ghosh, S., Vuleti, V.: Single-photon bus connecting spin-wave quantum memories. Nat. Phys. **3**, 765–769 (2007)
33. Reim, K.F., et al.: Towards high-speed optical quantum memories. Nat. Photon. **4**, 218–221 (2010)
34. Diniz, I., et al.: Strongly coupling a cavity to inhomogeneous ensembles of emitters: potential for long-lived solid-state quantum memories. Phys. Rev. A **84**, 063810 (2011)
35. George, C., Dollimore, J., Kindberg, T., Blair, G.: Distributed Systems: Concepts and Design. Addison-Wesley, Reading (2011). pp. 230–312
36. Gottesman, D., Chuang, I.L.: Demonstrating the viability of universal quantum computation using teleportation and single-qubit operations. Nature **402**, 390–393 (1999)
37. Cirac, J.I., Ekert, A., Huelga, S.F., Macchiavello, C.: Distributed quantum computation over noisy channels. Phys. Rev. A **59**, 42–49 (1999)
38. Meter, R.V., Munro, W.J., Nemoto, K., Itoh, K.M.: Arithmetic on a distributed-memory quantum multicomputer. ACM J. Emerg. Tech. Comput. Syst. **3**, 1–23 (2008)

39. Spiller, T.P., et al.: Quantum computation by communication. New J. Phys. **8**, 30 (2006)

40. Danos, V., D'Hondt, E., Kashefi, E., Panangaden, P.: Distributed measurement-based quantum computation. Elect. Notes Theoret. Comput. Sci. **170**, 73–94 (2007)

41. Love, P.J., Boghosian, B.M.: Type II quantum algorithms. Phys. A **362**(1), 210–214 (2006)

42. Yimsiriwattana, A., Lomonaco Jr., S.J.: Distributed quantum computing: a distributed Shor algorithm (2004). arXiv:quant-ph/0403146

43. Huang, Y.F., Ren, X.F., Zhang, Y.S., Duan, L.M., Guo, G.C.: Experimental teleportation of a quantum controlled-NOT gate. Phys. Rev. Lett. **93**, 240501 (2004)

44. Meter, R.V., Nemoto, K., Munro, W.: Communication links for distributed quantum computation. IEEE Trans. Comput. **56**(12), 1643–1653 (2007)

45. Ying, M., Feng, Y.: An algebraic language for distributed quantum computing. IEEE Trans. Comput. **58**(6), 728–743 (2009)

46. Wang, H.F., Zhu, A.D., Zhang, S., Yeon, K.H.: Optically controlled phase gate and teleportation of a controlled-NOT gate for spin qubits in quantum dot-microcavity coupled system. Phys. Rev. A **87**, 062337 (2013)

47. Luo, M.X., Li, H.R., Wang, X.: Teleportation of a controlled-Not gate for photon and electron-spin qubits assisted by the nitrogen-vacancy center. Quantum Inf. Comput. **15**(15), 1397–1419 (2015)

48. Luo, M.X., Wang, X.: Universal remote quantum computation assisted by the cavity input-output process. Proc. R. Soc. A **471**(2184), 20150274 (2015)

49. Bennett, C.H., et al.: Teleporting an unknown quantum state via dual classical and Einstein-Podolsky-Rosen channels. Phys. Rev. Lett. **70**, 1895 (1993)

50. Toffoli, T.: Reversible computing. In: de Bakker, J., van Leeuwen, J. (eds.) Automata, Languages and Programming. LNCS, vol. 85, pp. 632–644. Springer, Berlin (2005)

51. Shor, P.W.: Scheme for reducing decoherence in quantum computer memory. Phys. Rev. A **52**, R2493(R) (1995)

52. Calderbank, A., Rains, E., Shor, P.W., Sloane, N.: Quantum error correction via codes over GF(4). IEEE Trans. Inf. Theor. **44**, 1369–1387 (1998)

53. Calderbank, A.R., Shor, P.W.: Good quantum error-correcting codes exist. Phys. Rev. A **54**, 1098–1105 (1996)

54. Knill, E., Laflamme, R., Martinez, R., Negrevergne, C.: Benchmarking quantum computers: the five-qubit error correcting code. Phys. Rev. Lett. **86**, 5811–5814 (2001)

55. Steane, A.M.: Error correcting codes in quantum theory. Phys. Rev. Lett. **77**, 793–797 (1996)

56. Shi, Y.: Both Toffoli and controlled-NOT need little help to do universal quantum computation. Quantum Inf. Comput. **3**(1), 84–92 (2003)

57. Yu, N., Duan, R., Ying, R.: Five two-qubit gates are necessary for implementing the Toffoli gate. Phys. Rev. A **88**, 010304(R) (2013)

58. Lanyon, B.P., et al.: Simplifying quantum logic using higher-dimensional Hilbert spaces. Nat. Phys. **5**, 134–140 (2008)

59. Luo, M.X., Ma, S.Y., Chen, X.B., Wang, X.: Hybrid Toffoli gate on photons and quantum spins. Sci. Rep. **5**, 16716 (2015)

Author Index

Printed in the United States
By Bookmasters

Printed in the United States
By Bookmasters